8 —
ᴵLT

The One Light

Books by Bede Griffiths

The Golden String: An Autobiography

The Marriage of East and West:
Sequel to The Golden String

Christ in India
Essays Toward a Hindu-Christian Dialogue

Cosmic Revelation
The Hindu Way to God

The New Creation in Christ
Christian Meditation and Community

A New Vision of Reality
Western Science, Eastern Mysticism and Christian Faith

Return to the Center

River of Compassion
A Christian Commentary on the Bhagavad Gita

Modern Spirituality Series: Bede Griffiths

The One Light
Bede Griffiths' Principal Writings

edited by
Bruno Barnhart

Templegate Publishers
Springfield, Illinois

Published by
Templegate Publishers
302 East Adams Street
Post Office Box 5152
Springfield, Illinois
62705-5152
217-522-3353
templegate.com

ISBN 0-87243-254-8

Library of Congress Control Number: 2001093891

This book is dedicated to three spiritual pioneers
who devoted their lives to a rebirth of the Gospel
in the light of India's wisdom.

Jules Monchanin 1895-1957

Henri Le Saux (Abhishiktananda) 1910-1973

Bede Griffiths 1906-1993

Acknowledgements

I am grateful to the community of New Camaldoli for the time, freedom and support that has made it possible to complete this work. Thomas Grady first suggested the project and helped in its early stages of development. Special thanks are due to Lynne Clarkin and to Sr. Pascaline Coff, O.S.B., who read the manuscript and made valuable comments and suggestions. Sr. Pascaline and the community of Osage Monastery provided a context for the presentation and discussion of many of the ideas which have gone into the various introductions. Thanks are due also to the editors of Bede Griffiths' books — particularly of the larger volumes, *River of Compassion* and *A New Vision of Reality* — for their skill and labor. Templegate deserves recognition for having faithfully kept Bede's books available through the years. I am grateful to those who have studied Bede's work and commented on it, furthering the common process of understanding, and especially to Shirley Du Boulay. Her biography, *Beyond the Darkness*, has proven indispensable for an understanding of Bede Griffiths' life and development.

I am grateful as well to these authors, editors and proprietors for having given permission to use extracts from the following books and periodicals: *River of Compassion*, the Bede Griffiths Trust; *Universal Wisdom*, the Bede Griffiths Trust; *The Tablet* (London) and the *National Catholic Reporter* (Kansas City, MO) for letters and articles by Bede Griffiths; *Vedanta and Christian Faith*, The Dawn Horse Publishing Co., Middletown, CA; *A Human Search: Bede Griffiths Reflects on His Life; An Oral History* edited by John Swindells, 1997, Triumph Books, Liguori, MO; *Kurisumala: A Symposium on Ashram Life*, Francis Acharya. 1974, Kurisumala Ashram; *The Other Half of My Soul: Bede Griffiths and the Hindu-Christian Dialogue*, Beatrice Bruteau, Quest Books, Theosophical Publishing House, 1996, Wheaton, IL; *Science Today and the New Creation*, reprinted from *Ancient Wisdom and Modern Science*, Stanislav Grof (Ed.) State University of New York Press, 1984, Albany, NY. All rights reserved; *The Monastic Order and the Ahsram*, the American Benedictine Review, June 1979; *Christianity in the Light of the East*, the Monastic Bulletin of the Alliance for International Monasticism, London, the Hibbert Trust, 1989; *Monastic Studies*, Father Laurence Freeman and the World Community for Christian Meditation

CONTENTS

INTRODUCTION

Bede Griffiths, an English Benedictine monk who lived for many years in India, became a well-known spiritual teacher and author as well as a pioneer in Hindu-Christian dialogue. Since his death in May 1993, interest in Bede Griffiths and his vision of the "marriage of East and West" has continued to grow. Along with such figures as Thomas Merton and Henri Le Saux (Abhishiktananda), he marks the dawn of a new era of spirituality for the West. Bede signals the emergence of a 'second wisdom' in which Christianity, encountering the ancient spiritual traditions of Asia, begins to recover its own simplicity, depth and fullness. It is in a new context that wisdom is reborn today, however: in dialogue with the personal and critical consciousness, the freedom and creative dynamism that have emerged in the modern West. The significance of Bede Griffiths' life and work unfolds in the dramatic interplay of these three worlds: Christian gospel, Asian wisdom and the contemporary West with its desperation and its promise.

THE BACKGROUND

Bede Griffiths' long life (1906-1993) spans the twentieth century. The significance of Griffiths and his work emerges against the background of the dramatic changes in the world and in Christianity which have taken place within these hundred years. It is in the twentieth century that the world has suddenly become one world. It is the century of two world wars, in which technological advances in communication and in transportation have suddenly contracted the globe. Now, despite violent divisions, the world - and humanity within it - begins to pulsate as a single huge organism. At the same time, the horizons of the known world have been immeasureably expanded by breakthroughs in astronomy, physics and the biological sciences.

Within this twentieth century world, at once exploding and contracting, Christianity undergoes a crucial phase of transformation which finds expression in the Second Vatican Council (1962-1965). The church crosses a critical threshold to encounter the world and its religious traditions with a new openness — signified by the appearance of a new word — *dialogue*. Emerging from the defensive confinement of a Postreformation Catholicism, the church seems to step suddenly into adulthood.

Bede Griffiths' life and work reflect these epochal developments within western Christianity — and particularly within Catholicism. Bede entered a Roman Catholic Church which had been confined for centuries within a massive fortified complex of doctrine and institution. During his life this situation began to change dramatically. The Second Vatican Council opened the doors and windows to interaction and interchange not only with the other Christian churches but with contemporary Western culture and — most important for Bede - with the other great religious traditions.

Bede exemplifies in his life and thought this movement from containment to openness, from defensiveness to exposure, from polemic to dialogue. He himself becomes the living model of an expansive Christianity: a faith which moves forward and outward, confidently meeting and integrating everything that it encounters - even the ancient religious traditions which had seemed totally alien to Christian faith.

THE LIFE[1]

Alan Griffiths was born to a middle-class Anglican family at Walton-on-Thames on December 17, 1906. He proved early to be an excellent student, and from 1919-24 he attended the school known as Christ's Hospital in Sussex. At the end of this time, Alan had his first great spiritual experience, which initiated a life-long quest for the sacred. This was an overwhelming perception of the divine presence in nature, recorded at the beginning of his autobiography, *The Golden String*.[2] Alan won a scholarship to Oxford, where C.S. Lewis became his tutor. Their friendship would continue for 40 years. At Oxford he acquired two further lifelong friends, Martyn Skinner and Hugh Waterman.

2

With these two Oxford friends, Griffiths embarked upon an experiment of common life. Together they rented a cottage at Eastington in the Cotswolds, and lived there very simply for the better part of a year (1930). It was during this time that he began a serious reading of the Old and New Testaments which would develop into a conscious movement toward Christianity and the church. Alan was further moved in this direction by reflecting intensely upon Newman's *The Development of Christian Doctrine.*

During the next year, in a time of solitude, Griffiths experienced an interior conflict which culminated with his praying throughout an entire night. He was seized by a powerful experience of conversion which would soon bring him into the Roman Catholic church.[3] Alan formally entered the church on Christmas Eve, 1931. Within a few weeks he joined the Benedictine Priory of Prinknash, where he had been preparing for this formal conversion. He would make his solemn profession in the monastery at the end of 1937 and be ordained to the priesthood a little over two years later. At Prinknash, Dom Bede Griffiths (as he was now called) served as guestmaster, a role for which he was well endowed.

Bede was sent in 1947 to a dependent monastery, St. Michael's Abbey at Farnborough, as prior. His term as superior was not a successful one, and at the end of 1951 he was removed from this office and sent to the monastery of Pluscarden, in Scotland, where he would remain until his departure for India in 1955. It was while serving as novice master at Pluscarden that Bede wrote *The Golden String,* which was published in 1954 and immediately found a warm reception. Soon he became interested in the Asian spiritual traditions and began to study their sacred writings.

In 1955 Bede responded to an invitation to accompany Fr. Benedict Alapatt, O.S.B., to India, with the intention of initiating a monastic community there. (He would continue to live in India until the end of his life.) In August of the same year the two Benedictine monks began their new monastic experiment, which was named Nirmalashram. This project was unsuccessful, and in 1958 Bede joined a Belgian Cistercian monk, Fr. Francis Mahieu, in starting a Christian ashram in nearby Kerala, at Kurisumala[4]. Here the monks followed an Eastern Christian liturgical tradition - the Syriac rite - rather than their accustomed Roman tradition. Bede remained at Kurisumala, serving as novice master and teacher, until 1968, when he was invited by Father Francis to take over the direction of another ashram in the south of India, Shantivanam.

While a student Bede had begun to align himself with the English working class, and his concern for the poor found expression during the early years of his monastic life in India. Strongly influenced by the work of Vinoba Bhave, a disciple of Gandhi, Bede initiated projects to build up the rural village life and its economy around Madurai. These efforts would continue later on behalf of the villagers who lived in the vicinity of Shantivanam.

By the early 1960's, Bede was beginning to be known internationally through his writings. In 1963 he made his first trip to America - a symbolic beginning of his re-integration of that western world upon which he had so firmly turned his back when he went to India eight years earlier. A first collection of Bede's articles, published in 1966 as *Christ in India*, manifested his lively concern not only with the project of an Indian Christian monasticism and the interaction of Hinduism and Catholicism, but also with such public issues as social justice, peace and the nuclear threat.

It was in August 1968 that Bede went to Shantivanam in the southern state of Tamil Nadu, as superior. Shantivanam, or Saccidananda Ashram, had been founded by Jules Monchanin and Henri Le Saux (Abhishiktananda), who had preceded him in the project of an Indian Christian monasticism. Under Bede's direction and in the warm radiance of his personality, the little monastery took on new life and gradually became, for the Indian church, a model Christian ashram. Before long Bede was joined at Shantivanam by two brothers from Kurisumala who would long remain his disciples and companions: Amaldas and Christudas. Bede continued to write, when time permitted. In 1973, *Vedanta and Christian Faith* was published, followed by the enchanting *Return to the Center* in 1976. At the time of the silver jubilee celebration of Shantivanam, in 1975, opposition to Bede's program of inculturation at the ashram (e.g., the liturgical use of Asian sacred texts, of

Hindu ritual gestures and religious symbolism) burst into public controversy. He was not unequal to the challenge, defending with vigor and intelligence this new way which had been authorized by the Second Vatican Council.

Bede travelled to America once again in 1979, this time to stay at Osage Monastery in Oklahoma, a little Shantivanam in North America. The community had been founded by Benedictine Sr. Pascaline Coff after living for a year (in 1976) at Bede's ashram. He would continue to travel to North America and to Europe until the end of his life. In 1985 Bede toured Australia, where he addressed large audiences and left a deep and lasting impression. In 1980 Father Bede became a member of the Camaldolese Benedictine congregation, and in 1982, Shantivanam itself was incorporated into the Camaldolese family - a small, thousand-year old contemplative congregation including not only monasteries but also hermitages. Shantivanam gradually became a spiritual center for western pilgrims. The ashram would become an influential model in the inculturation of Christian monastic and liturgical life in the forms of Indian religious tradition.

In 1982, Bede (as well as Mother Teresa) accepted an invitation to address the conference of the International Transpersonal Association in Bombay; *East and West: Ancient Wisdom and Modern Science*. This event signaled another important turning point in the evolution of Bede's thought, as we shall see: an integration (already begun several years earlier) of the '*new science*' into his vision.

The impression of spiritual freshness that Bede left with others is confirmed by his own words. When almost 70, he said, "I always feel about 21, just beginning to explore life and always finding new things." The most enduring and significant friendships that colored Bede's life were the three that he had begun at Oxford - with Martyn Skinner, Hugh Waterman and C.S. Lewis - and a newer relationship with Russill D'Silva, who came to Shantivanam as a candidate in 1986. While Russill soon left the ashram and married, he and his wife Asha continued to be very close to Bede in his last years. Bede's biography[5] by Shirley Du Boulay admits us to the affective side of his life which does not appear often in his own writings: the joys and emotional tensions that rarely broke through his exterior composure. So strong and coherent was Bede's persona — English as well as monastic — that one would assume without thought that he had transcended these common struggles.

In late January of 1990, Bede experienced his first stroke. This marked a turning point not only in his exterior life (he retired as prior of Shantivanam soon afterwards) but in his spiritual development as well. He described this physical crisis as the occasion of his 'discovery of the feminine.' Together with this came a new realization of a dark side of human life: personal experience of emptiness, of mental and emotional chaos, of a disintegrating body, of an impending return to the earth. On recovery, however, Bede found new energies within himself. During 1991 and 1992 he traveled widely, going to America, Europe and Australia. He spent some months with his friends Russill, Asha and Wayne Teasdale in an experiment of a simple contemplative lifestyle in the United States. In July 1991, Bede led the *John Main Seminar* in Indiana, lecturing on meditation in the world of today.

In December 1992 and January of the next year, Bede experienced further, severe strokes. His left side became paralyzed and he discontinued his daily teachings in the little temple at Shantivanam. During the following months, confined to his cell, Bede endured a long and painful ordeal. He was continually surrounded by devoted friends and disciples, however, and cared for with great tenderness by those at the ashram. He died at Shantivanam on May 13, 1993, at the age of 86. In his later years Bede had become for people all over the world a prophet and icon of the universal spiritual wisdom upon which he had centered his life.

THE WRITINGS

Bede Griffiths has become widely known through his writings, which include ten books and several hundred articles.[6] Beginning with *The Golden String*, his successive books unfolded with grace and clarity a synthetic vision of the wisdom of East and West. Christian revelation was brought into a creative interaction with the Hindu Vedanta, and the spiritual light of the Asian traditions was made accessible to westerners. Nine books were published during Bede's lifetime. *Universal Wisdom* (1993), a selection which he had made of the scriptures of the great religious traditions, was published after his death.

The Golden String (1954) is Bede's account of the 'first half' of his life, from childhood until the time of his departure for India. A beautifully written account of his personal experience, it quickly became a best-seller and is still in print after nearly half a century. We shall present substantial extracts narrating Bede's first spiritual awakening, his conversion to Christianity and entrance into the Catholic church.

Christ in India (1966), a collection of 21 essays, was published just after the conclusion of the Second Vatican Council when Bede had been in India for a decade. Focusing principally on the relation of Christianity and the Asian traditions, it contains Bede's major articles on Christianity and the East from as early as 1953. Included are reflections on an Indian Christian monasticism, on Indian Catholicism, on a non-violent society and on church renewal. Written with Bede's characteristic passion and clarity, these pieces bring forth again and again his developing vision of a new Christianity.

Vedanta and Christian Faith (1973), the least-known of Bede Griffiths' books, is a collection of three lectures in which he presents a Christian theological vision which has developed in the light of Hindu thought. The three critical questions which he confronts are "The Mystery of the Godhead," "Creation and Incarnation," and "The Ultimate State of Man and the Universe." This small book is Bede's first substantial draft of a synthesis of the two worlds of Hinduism and Christianity.

In *Return to the Center* (1976), Bede's vision has been thoroughly permeated by the unitive light of the Vedanta. The book's orientation, as its title suggests, is back toward the primal Mystery and inward to the unitive core of the person. It is consistently profound and sometimes hauntingly beautiful. Interwoven with this series of theological meditations upon the traditions of East and West is a poetry of personal experience. At this time in his life Bede has been caught and held by the gravitation of the unitive 'center,' which absorbs all differences into itself.

The Marriage of East and West (1983) is subtitled 'A Sequel to *The Golden String.*' In fact, Griffiths quickly abandons the mode of autobiography in favor of a further, more systematic exploration of the integration of East and West. An introductory section, 'The Discovery of India' is followed by a development in three successive layers: "The Vedic Revelation,' 'The Judaic Revelation,' and 'The Christian Revelation: The Rebirth of the Myth.' Dominated by the tension between eastern and western epistemologies, the edifice leans strongly toward the East. Here Bede writes at length of the ultimate sapiential principles which he finds in the Vedanta: nonduality (advaita) and the unitive Self (atman).

Beginning with *The Cosmic Revelation: The Hindu Way to God* (1983), Bede Griffiths' books will consist almost entirely of edited transcriptions of his recorded talks. No longer shall we experience the same fusion of intuitive sweep and literary elegance. This book is a revision of six talks given in the United States. As the title indicates, the conferences are a presentation of the teachings of Hinduism - once again, chiefly the Vedanta - and only in the final talk does Bede bring this tradition into confrontation with Christianity. At this point the reader may be surprised to find a sharply critical examination of Hindu religion and theology. Bede concludes by proposing once again the complementarity of the religious traditions of East and West.

In *River of Compassion: A Christian Commentary on the Bhagavad Gita* (1987), a series of talks given at Shantivanam, Bede presents the *Gita* to westerners. The commentary presents the Hindu classic as a series of 'yogas' (integrations or ways of union): principally *karma* yoga, the way of work, *bhakti* yoga, the way of love and devotion and *jnana* yoga, the way of contemplative knowledge. Key verses of the *Gita* are commented at length. There is a frequent confrontation with Christian tradition. *River of Compassion* is probably Bede's most successful demonstration of the affinities and complementarities of Hinduism and Christianity. He is clearly moving toward a broader integration in this book; spirituality

8

returns to the marketplace. We seem to be sitting around him and listening to his living words.

A New Vision of Reality (1989) was edited from a series of talks given at Shantivanam around the beginning of 1983. This is Bede Griffiths' fullest attempt at an overall synthesis, embracing not only the ancient religious traditions of Christianity and the East (still principally Hinduism), but the perspectives of contemporary physics, cosmology and transpersonal psychology. Audacious synoptic views of cosmology, anthropology, spiritual theology and the history of consciousness demonstrate Bede's formidable powers of assimilation and integration. In conclusion, he imagines more concretely a 'New Age' both for humanity as a whole and for the Christian church.

The New Creation in Christ: Christian Meditation and Community (1992) presents Bede Griffiths' five lectures at the 1991 John Main Seminar in Indiana, together with a transcript of listeners' questions and his responses. Here Bede is concerned with meditation - particularly 'Christian meditation' and the use of a mantra - and with the movement of contemplative life and prayer beyond the confines of monasticism, to people in the world.

Universal Wisdom: A Journey through the Sacred Wisdom of the World (1993), published just after Bede Griffiths' death, is a selection of scriptures and spiritual poetry from Hinduism, Buddhism, Taoism, Sikhism, Islam, Judaism and Christianity. The general Introduction (about 36 pages) is a dense synthetic reflection written by Bede, who also supplies a brief introduction to each of the successive parts. The collection itself, idiosyncratic and exclusive, gives us another view of Bede's horizons, at the end of his life.

Two small books, edited and published after Bede's death by his friend Roland Ropers, present Bede's personal selections from the Book of Psalms and from various provinces of the literature of East and West. *Psalms for Christian Prayer* (1995), brings together the 95 biblical Psalms which Bede found relatively free of the anger, hatred and desire for vengeance which he found incompatible with sacred wisdom. *Pathways to the Supreme: The Personal Notebook of Bede Griffiths* (1995), with a longer introduction (11 pages) by Bede, contains a series of selections from his favorite authors, ancient and contemporary. The order in which the texts are presented is significant, corresponding to the successive 'ways' of cosmic revelation (here understood as primitive religion), of poetry, of philosophy (the 'perennial philosophy' in its Greek, Chinese, Buddhist and Hindu expressions), of Christian revelation, and finally the 'way of mysticism.'

Bede Griffiths, one quickly realizes, was a gifted writer. His elegant prose was not the product of labored revision. Of the writing of his early books, he recalls:

> I sat down every day after breakfast for about two hours and began to write. It just came out, just flowed out. I forget how long it took - maybe six months. That [*The Golden String*] was my first experiment in writing a full-length piece.
> When I first came to India, I didn't write, but I did some translations. When I came here to Shantivanam, I began to write *Return to the Centre*. It is very interesting, looking back now, that this book came out absolutely spontaneously. I wrote it in longhand completely, and made no corrections at all. It just came out like that. It's extraordinary. I think *The Marriage of East and West* was probably the same.[7]

Bede's articles appeared in a wide range of journals. Early pieces were published in the English Benedictine *Pax*, then in the progressive American Catholic journal *Commonweal* and the English Dominican *Blackfriars*. Many further articles came out over the years in *The Tablet* and *The Examiner*, and his pungent letters appeared frequently in *The Tablet*. He also contributed to a number of Indian publications and to western monastic journals.[8]

PHASES OF THE VISION

Bede reflected upon his own intellectual development again and again. We find this self- conscious process already taking place in *The Golden String*, and continuing explicitly in *The Marriage of East of West*. The process will reach its synthetic culmination in *A New Vision of Reality*. Often Bede takes a fresh look not only at the 'objective' world of the spirit and its evolution, but also at the successive stages of his own journey. The evolution of Bede Griffiths' vision, in the light of this continual reflection, appears with great clarity. We can distinguish five phases.

I Awakening: the Divine manifest in nature, in poetry; the wisdom of myth and imagination

We have mentioned the experience which was Bede's spiritual awakening and which would remain a central point of reference throughout his long life. This was a revelation of the divine presence in nature. Already, he had embraced the English Romantic poets as kindred spirits. Bede (then Alan) was awakening to wisdom, and thus to his lifelong vocation and search. Wisdom was a knowledge which was more and other than rational: a knowing through intuition, imagination, symbol and myth. He was to find it not only in his beloved poets but in the literature of primitive religions.[9]

Bede rejected a modern West which had abandoned the timeless wisdom of antiquity for an empirical and purely cerebral knowledge. While still at Oxford, Bede proclaimed a 'religion of imagination' which he found emerging in the writings of the English Romantic poets, particularly Wordsworth. Associated with this orientation toward the intuitive or 'feminine' side of consciousness, and with his rejection of the rationalist and industrialized West, were a constellation of other attitudes. From those early years he was concerned with social justice and the rights of working people, espoused socialism, and then attempted an alternative to the western economic system in his quasi-monastic experiment with two friends at Eastington. The orientation which emerges in these early experiences and choices will re-emerge later, characterizing Bede's life and thought until the end.

II Christian conversion: revelation, Christ, the Church

A first major transformation of Bede's perspective came with his dramatic conversion to Christ and the church. Now his consciousness and vision would be centered emphatically in the biblical, historical revelation. His further awakenings would occur along the way of an explicitly religious journey. Bede's perennial criticism of western civilization, following his conversion, became a theological judgment on history. He came to see the violence and confusion of the twentieth century West as the direct result of a general abandonment of Christ and the church in the era of Renaissance, Reformation and Enlightenment. [10]

This conversion was costly for Bede: he found the surrender of his personal autonomy — his 'reason' — extremely painful and difficult. The Christian experience, further, planted deep in Bede's psyche and consciousness an enduring foundation of faith which would assert itself in strong — if usually unspoken — tension with the more characteristic movement of Bede's personality and thought. Jesus Christ and the church — and the historical particularity which is intrinsic to both Christ and church — would stand as a permanent counterpole to the universal and unitive wisdom toward which Bede was so powerfully drawn as he found it expressed in nature, in poetry and in the eastern traditions. Associated with his Christian experience was an awakening to the primacy of love and a discovery of the principle of self-sacrifice. Bede's Christianity, in his writings, often remains implicit. This is true especially when he is looking East, presenting the 'Vedic Revelation.' Bede's attention is most frequently focussed on the new and unexplored country rather than on that which is already known. Sooner or later, however — and almost certainly at the end of the reflection — the invisible matrix of Christian faith will become explicit together with the eastern wisdom, and a theological integration will be attempted.

III Eastern wisdom: Vedanta, nonduality, the Self

When Bede discovered the sacred writings of India, he rediscovered the intuitive, imaginative consciousness which he had found in the English Romantic poets. But now it was as if he were drinking this wisdom in full purity and strength at its source. It is clear that in the discovery of the Vedanta and its unitive wisdom Bede has found a language for the deepest movements of his thought.

During his early years in India, Bede was much concerned with the uniqueness of Christianity, insisting repeatedly on the essential differences between the great religions. He saw the relationship between the traditions of East and West emphatically in terms of the *fulfillment* of Indian religious traditions by Christ. In a dialectical relationship with this position was his conviction that a *common core* exists within all the great religions; in Bede's writings one experiences a frequent shifting between these two views. This mobility is characteristic of the 'alternating current' of Bede's thought, capable of following the logic of each principle through to its implications, without immediate confrontation with other viewpoints. While Bede's position will gradually evolve from fulfillment toward complementarity, both perspectives are there from the start and continue together until the end.

By the 1950s, the *Perennial Philosophy* was emerging at the center of Bede s thought as the common core of all religions. In the following decades this 'universal tradition' would be more and more clearly identified with nonduality, the *advaitan* reality. Alongside this first principle of nonduality, there emerged a second within the 'Vedic Revelation' in which Bede immersed himself: the search for the 'Self,' the *atman*. This personal journey becomes, for Bede, the heart of the eastern wisdom and he will often speak of it as the central axis of spiritual life. Bede's early quest of intuitive wisdom has, at this point, become the journey toward realization of the unitive Self. Bede will make a series of correlations between elements of the Vedanta and elements of Christian faith. '*Sat* (being) — *cit* (knowledge) — *ananda* (bliss) becomes an expression of the Trinity of Father, Word and Holy Spirit[11]. *Purusha* is correlated with Christ, particularly as 'Cosmic Person.'[12] *Atman* is equated with the Holy Spirit. Vedanta has become the interpretive lens through which Bede understands the Christian experience.

Within this 'Hindu' phase, a change in direction takes place. As Bede comments the *Bhagavad Gita* in the conferences which would be published as *River of Compassion*, we can sense an inflection of his own spiritual orientation away from the strict interiority of the *Upanishads* and toward a balance of spirit and world which is closer to that of the Gospel. The exclusive grip of the 'center' and of *atman* upon Bede's psyche, so evident in *Return to the Center* and in *The Marriage of East and West*, loosens. As that period of intense interiority and renunciation of the world comes to an end, a phase

13

of integration begins.

IV   Wisdom and science: cosmology, consciousness and evolution

It was around 1980 that Bede's rediscovery of the West took a pivotal further step: an encounter with the "new science" articulated by such innovators as Fritjof Capra, David Bohm and Rupert Sheldrake. Moving from his earlier categorical rejection of western science and technology, Bede began to incorporate the insights of contemporary physics, biology and transpersonal psychology with the ancient wisdoms, into a new and comprehensive vision of reality. This fresh horizon would call forth Bede's *New Vision of Reality* (1989). Here he brings the ancient religious traditions of Christianity and the East together with conceptions of the contemporary sciences in a new evolutionary perspective. Bede now develops a coherent cosmology, bringing elements of the 'perennial philosophy' together with classical hylomorphism[13] and principles of the holistic new physics. Here matter and consciousness are not distinct entities but two manifestations of a third primary reality which is unitive spirit.

In turning towards the modern West and its culture, Bede begins to assimilate not only the scientific perspective but a dynamic principle of development: *evolution*. He sees the principle of evolution operative first in the physical and biological world and then in the progressive development of human consciousness. This vision of a continuing positive movement beneath the surface of human history is a radical turnabout from his position in *Return to the Center*, where the only meaningful journey was a return to the Source. Bede largely adopts the vision of the evolution of consciousness conceived by Ken Wilber — who, like himself, understands consciousness as essentially unitive, *nondual*.

V   The feminine; descent into darkness and body; unitive experience

Bede Griffiths' consciousness underwent a dramatic change in 1990, after his first stroke.[14] He did not, as after earlier transitions, bring forth a book in which his vision was recast in the light of this new experience, but he often spoke about what had happened to him. Bede declared repeatedly that at the time of this physical trauma,

14

'the feminine' or 'the mother' broke into his consciousness and life in a decisive way. At the same time he was initiated into the nondual experience which he had sought for so long. Woven with these two threads was a third: a new experience of darkness and chaos, of disorientation and a shadow of death which accompanied his illness.[15] In this stage we witness a second 'descent from the mind' parallel to that which Bede experienced in his conversion to Christianity. Once again we have the sense that thought — the continual activity of this vigorous mind — has given way to another, more powerful reality which is invading Bede's person as if from outside. Here there is also a strong recollection of the first phase, with its preferential orientation toward the 'feminine' side of consciousness. The unitive core of the third phase is also realized after the stroke.what in Bede called his *advaitan* experience While the ambitious intellectual construction of the fourth phase is not reflected here at the end, Bede's existential return to the world of the body recalls his late acceptance of natural science. Our final phase, however, is a realization on a level distinctly other than that of conceptual reason.

From beginning to end, Bede Griffiths' life was a quest of *wisdom*, of spiritual *knowledge*, of the knowledge that is experience, love, union. At an early point he realized that this knowledge is essentially *unitive*: that it is a participation in the one, absolute reality which is the source of all things. He followed the track of this unitive knowledge to India, settling in that 'Orient' as the homeland of wisdom, the place of the primal Source. The clarity itself of Bede's reflection upon his spiritual journey and of his distillations of the spiritual literature of India is significant, however. We become aware that, throughout these many years of his dedicated monastic life 'on the ground,' what Bede has been able to share with us of his journey has remained largely on the plane of the mind. It is here at the end, while he is living on the edge of bodily collapse, that the level of Bede's own enlightenment deepens. At this point, the unitive realization accompanies and reflects his personal integration of body, psyche and spirit. Now it is more apparent than ever that what he is able to understand and to put into words for us is the merest trace of what is happening.

These phases of Bede's overall theological development can be resumed briefly as a progressive integration of different *ways of knowing*. Rejecting the rational-empirical mentality which had been dominant in the West since the Enlightenment, Bede begins to develop his personal theory of knowledge. The way of knowing proper to the human person is not abstract and analytical reason, the 'masculine' and 'left-brain' activity of the mind, but rather an intuitive knowing through participation in that which is known. The key terms are *intuition* and imagination, symbolism and myth. In a second phase, explicit *faith* dramatically appears and takes up its central place in Bede's life. In a third phase, as Bede is more and more immersing himself in the tradition of the Vedanta, contemplative knowing (*jnana*, Bede will call it[16]) becomes central in his thinking. This is *unitive* consciousness and insight on the level of spirit or atman, an immediate participation in the divine Absolute. It is experienced especially in meditation, and becomes the light in which a spiritual philosophy is conceived and developed.[17] In a fourth phase, scientific *reason* returns, but now within the intuitive and organic vision of the 'new paradigm.' This level of science is not directly empirical but intuitive and synthetic; it integrates without too much strain into Bede's own intuitive philosophy. In Bede's final theoretical synthesis, the perennial philosophy has been fused with an evolutionary scheme which proceeds from elemental matter — the stuff of positive science — to the heights of unitive consciousness. In his final phase of life, body and unitive spirit are both present to Bede's consciousness in a very simple way, while knowledge and love, too, have become inseparably fused.

THE EVOLVING MYTH

Can we identify a continuum that joins these successive phases? Can one figure be discerned throughout the development of Bede's thought? This ambitious question invites preconceived paradigms and personal interpretations, but the risk is worth taking. It is less hazardous because Bede has been so generous in expressing his personal experience as well as his thoughts.

One vigorous and decisive movement stands out in Bede's early life: he rejects one world and sets out in search of another, more adequate world. This movement, I believe, determines the shape of his life and offers a perspective for interpreting the evolution of his thought. Bede rejects the civilization and culture of the modern West; he turns away from the world into which he had been born. At the same time we find him looking eagerly for an alternative world and beginning to elaborate a vision — a *myth*[18] — of such a world. This double movement -and a third which follows — will define his life. The third movement is a re-integration of that which had been rejected. This further integration, however, originates from a new viewpoint and aspires to comprehend all reality. This is evident as Bede justifies his rejection of the modern western mind. The materialist reductionism of this culture has lost the primordial fullness, exchanging the 'great chain of being' for a flattened consciousness and a flattened world.[19]

Bede himself could seem a godlike stranger in this world. His stature and striking good looks, refined charm and brilliant intellect helped to create a mythic aura around him which grew in his later years and nurtured the privileged atmosphere of Shantivanam. His spiritual-theological myth flowed forth as a natural further expression of this personality. A few perceptive friends pierced through the myth; his many critics had never succumbed to it. Bede, with his soaring, unbroken spirit, *lived* the myth. From time to time, and particularly toward the end of his life, intrusions of a rougher reality would alter the stream's course, but never arrested it.

As Bede rejects one world — the world that is in front of him and then quickly behind him — he creates another world. Already at Oxford we find him developing a *perfect alternative world*, with the help of the English Romantic poets, then attempting to live out the myth a little later with his two friends. This myth-making activity will be a permanent and dominant element in Bede's personality, while its direction moves through a series of successive creations. The essential nature of Bede's perfect alternative world appears very early in his life. It is a unitive world, where all reality is experienced in the one divine ground.[20] This unitive world is Bede's personal myth. Its basic and enduring form is the primordial wisdom or perennial philosophy, which Bede sees as the common core of all of the great religious traditions of the world and which he believes to have prevailed everywhere in human culture prior to the time of the modern West. In addition to this basic expression, the myth assumes a series of more specific forms, corresponding to the successive stages of his life and thought (which we have schematized above).

The first specific form of Bede's unitive myth is found in his 'religion of nature', supported by Wordsworth and the other Romantics. He brings forth some lines from Wordsworth to express his notion of the Unitive in this pre-Indian phase: it is the immanent "spirit of nature."[21] In the second phase, the Roman Catholic Church assumes the mantle of the unitive myth.[22] In the third phase of Bede's thought, as we have outlined it, the unitive myth finds its site and expression in the Vedanta. It is nonduality, the advaitan experience, and is identified with Bede's basic myth of the perennial philosophy. Soon the specific myth is located in the spiritual experience which Bede finds at the heart of the Vedantan tradition: the realization of the atman, or Self. The myth, however, necessarily embraces the whole of reality, the 'three worlds' of Bede's sapiential vision. A further transformation of the unitive myth occurs within this same 'Hindu' period of Bede's thought. The center of gravity of the myth migrates from atman to purusha, from Self to Person. We can see this in the change of perspective between *Return to the Center* and *The Marriage of East and West* on the one hand, and *River of Compassion* and *A New Vision of Reality* on the other hand. In the two earlier books, it is the unitive mystery of brahman and atman — and particularly the interior experience of atman — that is central. In the two later books, purusha, as the Cosmic Person, is emerging as the center of a vision which is no longer oriented so predominantly toward the interior of the human subject but moves outward to embrace the whole of humanity and the cosmos. As the focus of the unitive myth shifts from interior Self to cosmic Person, the continuity of the myth itself persists: we are presented with a perfect alternative world, and with a central point at which all of reality can be grasped as one.

River of Compassion, Bede's commentary on the *Bhagavad Gita*, seems to reveal more precisely the turning point between these two phases, as Bede guides us through the reorientation of Hindu spirituality that takes place from the *Upanishads* to the Gita. We seem to observe, at the same time, this pivotal transition in Bede's own perspective. The actuality of this personal re-orientation is borne out by the further course of Bede's life and thought. Earlier forms of the myth will always remain alongside the later expressions, but without their old centrality and power.

STEPS TOWARD THE MARRIAGE

Bede presents himself with the problem of the 'marriage of East and West' at an early point,[23] and continues to grapple with it until the end of his life. The two words — East and West — themselves have some of the vague comprehensiveness of myth. It is in *The Marriage of East and West* that Bede presents the encounter of Hinduism and Christianity as that of "the two most powerful myths in the world today."[24] 'Myth,' in that book, is his preferred word for the truths of the religious traditions. While myth must be clarified today, he insists that this clarification must come about through the recovery of mystical experience and through experience of the contemporary world, rather than through the work of 'reason,' of learning and scholarship.[25]

The problem of the 'marriage' is confronted on different levels: first, as the confrontation of two modes of consciousness and thought: the rational-analytical and the intuitive-holistic-mythical, or 'masculine' and 'feminine' dimensions of mind that Bede attributes to the West and to the East.[26] On this level, the 'marriage' does not present an enormous challenge. Bede works towards its resolution in his own thought and writing — as have many twentieth century western thinkers.

On a second level, it is a question of bridging the gap between Christianity and the 'perennial philosophy': more concretely, between Christianity and the Vedanta. This is the form in which Bede struggles with the problem from the time of his going to India until the end of his life: what is the relationship between the mystery of Christ and the nonduality of the *Upanishads*? In *The Marriage of East and West*, he finds the two revelations to be complementary manifestations of the one ultimate and ineffable Mystery.

We can distinguish three further stages in Bede's progress towards a resolution of his problem of the 'marriage of East and West,' (now understood as the integration of Hindusm and Christianity) at three successive moments of his life.

I — In *River of Compassion*, Bede examines a development within Hinduism — the movement from *Upanishads* to *Bhagavad Gita* — which brings the Indian tradition very close to Christianity. With the emergence of a divine Person in the supreme position, there is a new centering of spirituality within the human person living in the world. The ways of devotion and of active service develop, and a new balance between interiority and life in the world which resembles that of the New Testament. In Bede's vision, at this point, Hinduism and Christianity are on intimate speaking terms. Person and world are taking their place in the theological picture. Myth and the reality of personal experience in this world are coming into a less unequal balance.

II — In *A New Vision of Reality*, Bede has found a development within western science which brings it into relationship with the East. This is the 'new paradigm' science of Fritjof Capra, with its organic-holistic-romantic model (or myth) of the universe. An evolutionary cosmology enters as mediator into the developing relationship between Hinduism and Christianity, bringing the relationship further into the world. This is a world known also through a 'western' scientific reason which has now been joined with unitive intuition, the 'feminine' dimension of consciousness. Cosmos and evolution join with a Christian conception of salvation history in a picture which is now centered in the 'cosmic Person.' This emergent figure — still 'mythical' but becoming more concrete and historical — not only brings together Christianity and the other religions, but integrates Bede's 'three worlds' within itself. The nondual Absolute of Hinduism has become a supreme Person, incarnate in all of humanity and in the matter of the universe. This grand intellectual synthesis is the final form of Bede's unitive myth.

III — In *Bede's physical crisis* — his first stroke and the changes which follow upon it — the convergent development is in Bede himself. It takes place not, first of all, in Bede's mind, but in his body and psyche. Intellectual synthesis gives way to personal integration. Myth comes to more equitable terms with human reality. At this final point, the elements which have until now been hidden in the shadows seem to come forward to be acknowledged and gathered together in the single light of his consciousness. Bede's powerful rationality falls humbly into place within the flux of feeling and intuition, however, and the ongoing process hardly rises to the level of clear articulation. 'Eastern' nonduality has become less and less myth or idea, and more and more the basic quality of Bede's own consciousness. The mystery of Christ, too, is now primarily something that is taking place in his own flesh and blood.

A fourth development remains to be considered: that is, the evolution of Christianity itself which is taking place throughout Bede's labor of mediation between his own tradition and the wisdom of Hinduism.

THE GIFTS FROM THE EAST

Let us single out some of Bede Griffiths' main contributions to the rebirth of a Christian wisdom in our time. First of all is wisdom itself: his quest of the 'golden string.' It is his conviction — and his ability to communicate that conviction — that there is another way of knowing, which is deeper than the ordinary way that we think in the contemporary West. There is a fuller spectrum of consciousness and you recognize its music in his voice as he speaks or writes. It is this fullness of voice which is to be recovered in Christianity.

Bede's second contribution, intrinsic to his conception of wisdom, is the principle of nonduality, or *advaita*, and of a unitive absolute, the One. When Bede immerses himself in the world of the Indian scriptures — particularly in the *Upanishads* — he discovers a perspective in which everything is one rather than multiple, in which all things are embraced within a single, ultimate reality. When Bede speaks of the *perennial philosophy* or the *primordial wisdom* or the *universal wisdom*, he can include within each of these expressions several levels of meaning — or several concentric spheres of meaning. The core meaning, however, is that unitive reality, or unitive absolute. Generally, when Bede speaks of the perennial wisdom in his later years, he means the principle of *advaita*, or a single nondual reality, *brahman-atman*. That absolute Reality, or unitive principle — which lies at the core not only of Hinduism but of Buddhism and Taoism — becomes the heart of Bede's vision. Identified with 'God' or 'Father,' the first divine Person, it becomes a key to a new Christian vision. There remains the further work of re-interpreting the mystery of Christ from this perspective of nonduality.

His third contribution is the unitive self, or atman. As soon as Bede has written about the nondual Absolute, he usually moves to the atman, because it is through the Self that the unitive ground of all reality is experienced. The search for the Self, Bede writes repeatedly, is the heart of the Vedantan way. In this focus upon the Self, Bede joins Thomas Merton and Abhishiktananda. The critical further step that is needed here from the Christian theological perspective is the correlation of this nondual self with baptismal initiation.

Bede Griffiths' fourth step towards a recovery of wisdom is his recognition of the divine dimension of the feminine. Repeatedly he identifies the Holy Spirit with the 'feminine side' of God. This is a very important point. This 'feminine' Spirit is the divine energy which is the mother of creation, which brings forth all life, which moves the process of evolution. It is also is "that divine life latent in the universe from the beginning, latent in nature, and becoming conscious in us....The Spirit is this energy of love in us, the power of the divine. It is the Source of our real being, by which we become conscious of the divine life in us and know ourselves as sons [and daughters] of God..."[27] This concept of a unitive 'divine feminine,' however, requires further differentiation from the archetype of the Mother.

Bede's fifth gift is something we observed early in our study: the vision of total integration which Bede conceives in terms of the three levels of being: spirit, soul (or mind) and matter (or body) — or, roughly speaking, God, humanity and the universe. Here too we can look toward a further differentiation: a differentiation of the 'masculine' and 'feminine' poles of this intermediate human level of mind-soul. The tripartite vision of cosmos and human person may thus open laterally into a further fullness which corresponds to the cruciform mystery of Christ as it is found in the New Testament.[28] Corresponding to what we have called Bede Griffiths' basic myth, we can see his contribution towards a new wisdom in terms of the realization of a *Christian advaita*. Bede brings together Hinduism and Christianity within the vital energy field of his own spirit. Within this creative matrix there gradually occurs a quasi-fusion of unitive Absolute and Christ-event, giving birth to a vision of Christian non-duality in two stages. Firstly, Bede tells us that participation in God, the nondual Absolute, is realized in the *communion of love* which is Christian life and relationship. Secondly, the One is known in the great event of incarnation which is the *Cosmic Person*, gradually emerging as the center of Bede's synthesis.

With Abhishiktananda, we may imagine a further — or rather prior — moment of Christian advaita which is rooted in *baptismal initiation* as the moment of identity, a pure unitive participation in the One, as if before differentiation into Word and Spirit, knowledge and love. This simple and primordial unitive participation, the moment of identity, may be understood in Jesus' self-identification in John's gospel, "I AM." In his last years, Abhishiktananda came to see the baptism of Jesus as the realization of the divine "I AM" in the human person at the very outset of the gospel. From this point, 'Christian wisdom' may be regenerated today.

Abhishiktananda apparently lost himself into this moment of identity, this pure 'East' of the beginning. Bede, on the other hand,[29] followed the way of relationship and synthesis rather than that of primal identity, and returned westward to integrate that which he had earlier left behind — and indeed the whole of reality — into an expansive cosmic vision. The eastern keys which Bede and Abhishiktananda have put in our hands have now to be brought to bear upon the New Testament and upon the experience and thought of the Christian tradition.

BETWEEN THE OLD AND THE NEW WISDOM:
GOSPEL AND PERSON

The western world into which Bede was born and in which he was
educated had been travelling through a spiritual desert — a sapiential parenthesis — for centuries. Apparently we had to lose one wisdom, the 'old wisdom,' in order to discover another wisdom — the
new wisdom of which Bede is a prophet. During this eclipse of the
sacred and of contemplative consciousness, a process has been
moving swiftly forward. Something has been emerging — the *human
person*. We can see the waves of this emergence moving through
Bede's developing vision. It is not only the collective or cosmic person that is emerging, however, but also the individual person: the
personal 'subject' as conscious, free and differentiated — differentiated even from the matrix of the old wisdom. Here emerges the tension between Vedanta and Gospel, between Beginning and End,
between atman and the human person as 'new creation,' free and
creative in this world and its history.

The old wisdom — whether in the East or in the Christian West
— tended invariably to enclose itself once again within the structures of the old cosmic order, to return to a containment within the
static, non-historical architecture of archaic religion and classical
thought. The human person returned to its condition of prisoner
within the iron order of the 'great chain of being.' But Paul pro-
claims that something has happened to this old order, to ' the poor
elements of this world,'[30] in the light and energy of the Christ-event.
According to the New Testament, when Jesus came into the world
the old structures of the cosmic order surrendered their sovereignty to the Son of Man — and thus to the human person. The Incarnation generates a new creation according to its own intrinsic principle.

Something new is happening: the birth of the human person.
That can be observed in the history of the western world, perverse
as it may often seem. With the coming of the Gospel and the gift of
Pentecost the person is freed at its center. This human person then

becomes a luminous, creative center within the world. The world is being recreated out of the human person. This is the wisdom of the West, of which the West is only superficially aware. A new Christian wisdom must incorporate this dynamic with its expansive and creative energy.

We become aware that it is no longer possible to put on the old clothing of a venerable tradition — even a Christian tradition. The human person cannot be adequately held within a static container, Jesus teaches, and the inexpressible lightning flash of the Gospel and of our own inner being verifies it. Bede wrestled with this problem throughout his life. Once again, at the time of his commentary on the *Bhagavad Gita*, as he begins to turn back toward the West, we can feel the newness stirring within him. The awareness of the new thing that is the human person moved beneath the surface of his mind like a child within the womb, swimming toward birth. The tensions that we find in his life and thought — between East and West, old and new — may be centered in this progressive birth of the person, which was only gradually emerging into his awareness.

BEDE'S DUALITIES

Bede Griffiths is a man of many contrasts and polarities, held within a deep and powerful unifying energy. Let us note some of the dualities that the reader will find in Bede and in his work, and that he works to integrate in his thought. First and most obvious is that between East and West. This leads us to a second dialectic between Christianity — a particular revelation at a concrete point in time and space — and the 'cosmic revelation' represented by Hinduism and Buddhism. Sometimes Bede will write in the language and logic of the biblical Word, and sometimes he will follow the logic of nonduality, of *advaita* and the *atman*. We shall find two contrasting expressions of unitive mind in Bede's writing, one more interior and spiritual, the other more imaginative and intellectual. If on the one hand he writes again and again of the interiorizing journey to the 'center' which is the realization of the Self in pure nondual consciousness, on the other hand he will more and more turn outward toward an all-comprehending *gnosis*, an intellectual vision which integrates the three worlds of cosmos, humanity and absolute Spirit.

A further polarity, closely related to the East-West polarity, is between past and future, between a backward and a forward perspective. We may be astonished to find Bede looking in both directions at once: toward a new Christianity and toward a recovery of the pre-Christian spiritual traditions. For him the two are inseparable; they are one thing. To look ahead is to look back. Bede's thinking is bold and creative, intuitively synthetic — yet its intuitions remain visibly circumscribed. His innovations are often new combinations of traditional ideas. Sometimes Bede's work has a patchlike or mosaic structure in which distinct blocks of thought — old and new — are placed side by side. This is particularly true of *A New Vision of Reality*.

Still further polarities will be found between reason and intuition, conscious and unconscious, masculine and feminine consciousness. These dualities are all related for Bede, as if aligned in two parallel columns. There is obviously some approximation in global conceptualizations of this kind. An additional polarity in Bede's thought is between a spirituality which ascends into unitive spirit and a descending or incarnational way. Here too there is a development in his thought. Finally, there is the underlying struggle between an unchanging cosmic *order* (exemplified in the various schemes of spiritual development which Bede brings forward from Hinduism — and implicit in his conception of the perennial philosophy itself) and the *person*, as it emerges in the New Testament and in the history of the West.

In Bede we find, coexisting, nonviolence and aggressiveness, contemplative detachment and protest, obedience and fierce criticism of authority. Bede's personality exhibits a paradoxical co-existence of naivete and critical acuity. Bede does not see the shadow of people that are close to him and he often does not see the shadow of his own ideas, nor the other side of the argument. On the other hand, he is acutely conscious of the shadow of western civilization and of the church. He moves by passionate intuition rather than by the detached and even-handed survey of alternatives which we observe in a Thomas Aquinas. Yet, in *River of Compassion*, we find him patiently and judiciously weighing different spiritual paths and different interpretations of the *Gita*.

SUGGESTIONS FOR THE READER

These observations about Bede's thought and writing suggest a few general principles of orientation for those who are encountering his work for the first time. The points that follow are closely related, one flowing from another. First of all, one needs to allow for the theological-literary, or mythic factor. We must distinguish between Bede the spiritual pilgrim and subject of experience, and Bede the interpreter, theologian and writer. Often the human, experiential reality with its irregularities and obscurities is not accurately reflected in the seamless and limpid theological discourse. It is important to keep in mind the continual gap between reality and ideal, experience and thought, existential fact and literary expression. Bede's clarity itself can be deceptive when he is writing of mysteries, and he is writing of mysteries most of the time.

Secondly, when reading Bede's earlier writings, it is helpful to recall the general lines of development of his thought which we have reviewed. Often the early enthusiasm was later replaced by a more critical attitude or simply tempered by his subsequent experience. Elements of the Vedanta (the interior path to the Self, for example) which he wrote about with an unconditioned admiration in *The Marriage of East and West* were realized only to a modest degree in his own spiritual journey.[31] While he never completely abandoned the personal myth of a past age of universal wisdom, Bede came to look more hopefully toward the future and even to find many expressions of the Spirit around him in the once unacceptable modern world.

Thirdly, an iceberg principle should temper our judgment of Bede's passionate affirmations and negations. We have seen some of the polar opposites which co-inhabit his consciousness. There is always much more of him than is visible at a given moment. The mystery of Bede, the indeterminate and dynamic fullness that is just beneath his surface, is always greater, more alive and more intelligent than any particular affirmation. Moreover his affirmations are often impulsive, occasional and enthusiastic — and consequently one-sided. The essential point that he is completely ignoring will probably appear at another moment, duly underlined.

Finally, therefore, one will need a generous tolerance for mystery and for the unresolved. It is better not to demand the wrong kind of consistency from Bede. One needs to allow plenty of space for that which has not yet emerged into clarity — or which is essentially beyond rational comprehension. If in reading Bede we are frequently dealing with a dynamic paradox, this derives from the unitive wisdom underlying his thought — and from the boldness with which he grasps both horns of a colossal problem. He could pursue the logic of one principle at one moment and follow the logic of another principle at another moment, with no anxiety about the compatibility of the two principles and their implications. He trusts in a unity which is deeper than the explicit correlations and deeper than the contradictions.

One will do well therefore, in reading through Bede Griffiths' life work, to cultivate a continual awareness both of the single mystery at the heart of all of his writings and, correspondingly, of the unitive *center* beneath the level of one's own consciousness. It is from that luminous core that Bede's thought has come, and he would probably feel well rewarded for his labors in having awakened us to it. To dwell there calls not only for reflection but for silent meditation. From that invisible point of rest where the opposites are balanced, we can accompany him with delight on these adventures beyond the familiar boundary marks.

This collection is intended both as an introduction to Bede's work and as a permanent resource for reference. One need not read the texts in the order in which they are arranged here. Sooner or later, however, it is advisable to follow the line of development of Bede's life and thought and to become acquainted with each aspect of his intellectual world. It is our hope that the present volume will both draw the reader to his books themselves and suggest a perspective from which they can be read more fruitfully.

THE STRUCTURE OF THIS BOOK

The seven sections of this collection are arranged both topically and chronologically. The order parallels in a general way the phases of Bede Griffiths' life and work, but often an early piece has been placed in the midst of later material, or vice versa, to maintain consistency of subject. Because of the nature of these writings, it has been impossible to avoid some overlapping and repetition. Bede's thought often circles around the same center in different essays, and he moves over the same ground again and again, with new accents. The orderly structure of this book is deceptive, therefore. The writings characteristically refuse to conform to a linear arrangement, so there is some arbitrariness in the division of the material and there are loops in the continuity.

Section One begins with Bede Griffiths' narrative of his personal awakening, and continues with the various dimensions of the sapiential world which unfolded from that moment: the scope of his epistemology and of his universe is exposed to view. In sections Two and Three, "West, Part One" and "West, Part Two", after a look at the western civilization which Bede has rejected, we follow his process of conversion to Christianity and share his insightful synthetic views of the Christian mysteries and the church. In sections Four and Five, "East, Part One" and "East, Part Two", we accompany Bede in his discovery of India and his personal appropriation of the eastern wisdom, first on the level of theoretical and then of practical teaching. Included by association in section Five is Bede's account of his (Christian) method of personal prayer. Section Six brings together these two great currents of East and West as we share Bede's thought on the relationship between Christianity and the Asian religions — and on the 'universal wisdom' which he finds at the core of all religion. In section Seven we encounter the dynamic processes — both in Bede's evolving view of history and in his personal experience — which characterized the final years of his life. This seventh section concludes with Bede's final theological synthesis in *A New Vision of Reality*.

Most of the material which follows is from Bede Griffiths' books, where he has set out his vision with continuity and fullness.

Journal articles are included especially when they exhibit an exceptional passion, clarity and force, when they relate to a concrete situation or event of special significance, or when they present a fresh synthetic view. Articles and letters are included, for example, which express Bede's views on aspects of the church and its renewal around the pivotal moment of the Second Vatican Council. Bede's articles and his letters to journals — e.g. *The Tablet* — are often masterful: concise, pungent and powerful.

Bede's words have been printed in their original form, without alteration for the sake of inclusive language. A concern for fidelity to Bede's precise thought, especially because of his frequent theological use of 'man,' has governed this decision. Bede was very sensitive to such issues, and this would certainly be reflected in his language, were he writing and speaking today. One of his favorite themes was the systemic 'masculine' imbalance of the modern West and its culture, in which feminine values and feminine voices are ignored.

If one seeks a single consistent theme running through the whole collection and holding it together, this will most likely be Bede's developing vision of a *unitive wisdom*, which initiates us to a deeper consciousness and a world both larger and more simple than the world we had known. His charism as a 'wisdom' thinker appears early in his life, continues through his conversion to Christianity, unfolds its dimension of unitive depth in his appropriation of the Vedanta and finally broadens into a synthesis of cosmic proportions.

I

MIND, WORLD AND SPIRIT

In *The Golden String*, Bede Griffiths recalls, step by step, the awakening of his mind and heart. The pattern of his life, indeed, will seem to Bede and to his readers to unfold as a never-ending succession of discoveries. Bede's personal awakening is the discovery of a new way of *knowing*. He seems to experience all reality at once in this epiphany: a moment of enlightened consciousness which will continue to guide his journey. He embarks upon the path of 'wisdom.'[1]

Bede will take pains to describe this way of knowing through intuition, imagination and myth. Through his passionate writing we feel the expansive force of a mind and spirit which refuse to remain imprisoned within the boundaries imposed by a particular culture. He will be satisfied with nothing less than final realities: God, the universe, and the inner Self which is one with both universe and God.

1. Awakening: Nature and Spirit

Bede's autobiography, The Golden String, *begins with the story of his spiritual awakening.[2] It happened in 1924, when Bede was eighteen years old and about to leave his school, Christ's Hospital, for Oxford. This experience of the Divine in nature and in his inner self would continue ever afterwards to be the touchstone of his sense of spiritual reality. We can imagine Bede's subsequent life and quest unfolding from the grace of this moment.*

The enchantment of this experience comes through to us in Bede's evocative writing. It is a transfiguration of the world around him: singing birds, hawthorn trees in blossom are suddenly filled with the divine glory. He describes the scene in a biblical language of Paradise and of angels, but there is no distinct manifestation of God, no divine vision or word. The epiphany takes place outside the enclosure of formal 'religion,' and does not immediately lead him to the Scriptures or to church. In Bede's spiritual awakening we may already sense the direction of his life's work: a re-connecting, an opening of faith and religion once again to the breadth of all creation and to the depth of the interior self. Bede's own reflection upon this first experience of a transfigured world reveals the realities which are hidden but implicit in his account of it: To discover God is...to discover oneself.

This initiation — a kind of baptism in nature — is, for Bede, the beginning of Blake's 'golden string' which leads one into the ultimate secret of life.

> I give you the end of a golden string;
> Only wind it into a ball,
> It will lead you in at heaven's gate,
> Built in Jerusalem's wall.
> *William Blake*

One day during my last term at school I walked out alone in the evening and heard the birds singing in that full chorus of song, which can only be heard at that time of the year at dawn or at sunset. I remember now the shock of surprise with which the sound broke on my ears. It seemed to me that I had never heard the birds singing before and I wondered whether they sang like this all the year round and I had never noticed it. As I walked on I came upon some hawthorn trees in full bloom and again I thought that I had never seen such a sight or experienced such sweetness before. If I had been brought suddenly among the trees of the Garden of Paradise and heard a choir of angels singing I could not have been more surprised. I came then to where the sun was setting over the playing fields. A lark rose suddenly from the ground beside the tree where I was standing and poured out its song above my head, and then sank still singing to rest. Everything then grew still as the sunset faded and the veil of dusk began to cover the earth. I remember now the feeling of awe which came over me. I felt inclined to kneel on the ground, as though I had been standing in the presence of an angel; and I hardly dared to look on the face of the sky, because it seemed as though it was but a veil before the face of God.

These are the words with which I tried many years later to express what I had experienced that evening, but no words can do more than suggest what it meant to me. It came to me quite suddenly, as it were out of the blue, and now that I look back on it, it seems to me that it was one of the decisive events of my life. Up to that time I had lived the life of a normal schoolboy, quite content with the world as I found it. Now I was suddenly made aware of another world of beauty and mystery such as I had never imagined to exist, except in poetry. It was as though I had begun to see and smell and hear for the first time. The world appeared to me as Wordsworth describes it with "the glory and the freshness of a dream". The sight of a wild rose growing on a hedge, the scent of lime tree blossoms caught suddenly as I rode down a hill on a bicycle, came to me like visitations from another world. But it was not only that my senses were awakened. I experienced an overwhelming emotion in the presence of nature, especially at evening. It began to wear a kind of sacramental character for me. I approached it with a sense of almost religious awe, and in the hush which comes before sunset, I felt again the presence of an unfathomable mystery. The song of the birds, the shapes of the trees, the colours of the sunset, were so many signs of this presence, which seemed to be drawing me to itself.

As time went on this kind of worship of nature began to take the place of any other religion. I would get up before dawn to hear the birds singing and stay out late at night to watch the stars appear, and my days were spent, whenever I was free, in long walks in the country. No religious service could compare with the effect which nature had upon me, and I had no religious faith which could influence me so deeply. I had begun to read the romantic poets, Wordsworth, Shelley and Keats, and I found in them the record of an experience like my own. They became my teachers and my guides, and I gradually gave up my adherence to any form of Christianity. The religion in which I had been brought up seemed to be empty and meaningless in comparison with that which I had found, and all my reading led me to believe that Christianity was a thing of the past.

An experience of this kind is probably not at all uncommon, especially in early youth. Something breaks suddenly into our lives and upsets their normal pattern, and we have to begin to adjust ourselves to a new kind of existence. This experience may come, as it came to me, through nature and poetry, or through art or music; or it may come through the adventure of flying or mountaineering, or of war; or it may come simply through falling in love, or through some apparent accident, an illness, the death of a friend, a sudden loss of fortune. Anything which breaks through the routine of daily life may be the bearer of this message to the soul. But however it may be, it is as though a veil has been lifted and we see for the first time behind the facade which the world has built round us. Suddenly we know that we belong to another world, that there is another dimension to existence. It is impossible to put what we have seen into words; it is something beyond all words which has been revealed.

There can be few people to whom such an experience does not come at some time, but it is easy to let it pass, and to lose its significance. The old habits of thought reassert themselves; our world returns to its normal appearance and the vision which we have seen fades away. But these are the moments when we really come face to face with reality; in the language of theology they are moments of grace. We see our life for a moment in its true perspective in relation to eternity. We are freed from the flux of time and see something of the eternal order which underlies it. We are no longer isolated individuals in conflict with our surroundings; we are parts of a whole, elements in a universal harmony.

This, as I understand it, is the "golden string" of Blake's poem. It is the grace which is given to every soul, hidden under the circumstances of our daily life, and easily lost if we choose not to attend to it. To follow up the vision which we have seen, to keep it in mind when we are thrown back again on the world, to live in its light and to shape our lives by its law, is to wind the string into a ball, and to find our way out of the labyrinth of life.

But this is no easy matter. It involves a readjustment to reality which is often a long and painful process. The first effect of such an experience is often to lead to the abandonment of all religion. Wordsworth himself was to spend many years in the struggle to bring his mystical experience in relation with orthodox Christianity and it may be doubted whether he was ever quite successful. But the experience is a challenge at the same time to work out one's religion for oneself. For most people today this has become almost a necessity. For many people the very idea of God has ceased to have any meaning. It is like the survival from a half-forgotten mythology. Before it can begin to have any meaning for them they have to experience his reality in their lives. They will not be converted by words or arguments, for God is not merely an idea or a concept in philosophy; he is the very ground of existence. We have to encounter him as a fact of our existence before we can really be persuaded to believe in him. To discover God is not to discover an idea but to discover oneself. It is to awake to that part of one's existence which has been hidden from sight and which one has refused to recognize. The discovery may be very painful; it is like going through a kind of death. But it is the one thing which makes life worth living.

I was led to make this discovery myself by the experience which I have recorded at school. This was the beginning for me of a long adventure which ended in a way for which nothing in my previous life had prepared me. If anyone had told me when I was at school or at Oxford that I should end my life as a monk, I should have doubted his sanity. I had no idea that any such thing as a monastery existed in the modern world, and the idea of it would have been without meaning to me. I have tried to show, however, that the steps which led to this revolution in my life, though they were in some ways exceptional, nevertheless followed a logical course, and I hope therefore that they may be found to have more than a personal interest.

I was one of those who came of age in the period after the first world war, and I shared its sense of disillusionment at the apparent failure of our civilization. In an effort to escape from the situation in which we found ourselves I was led, with two Oxford friends, to make an attempt to "return to nature", and to get behind the industrial revolution. The attempt was, of course, in one sense, a failure, but it led to the unexpected result that I made the discovery of Christianity. I read the Bible seriously for the first time, and found that the facts were quite different from what I had supposed and that Christianity was just as much a living power now as it had ever been. I then had to find a church in which I could learn to practise my newfound faith, and after a long struggle, which cost me more than anything else in my life, I found my way to the Catholic Church. From that it was but a short step to the monastic life, and so by successive stages a radical change in my life was effected. In recording these stages I have tried to show how each step was accompanied by a long course of reading, in which all the reasons for the change were worked out.

2. Intuitive Wisdom[3]

Bede's 'golden string' of wisdom had begun with an experience which opened both the world around him and the world within him to a new magnitude, depth and luminosity. The experience would be interpreted against the background of a growing aversion to the culture of the modern West, which he saw dominated by the cold rationality of empirical science. In opposition to this merely 'logical' mind, Bede begins to develop a theory of intuition. This is a knowing through contact, through participation, through union. Its organ is not merely the brain but the whole person: body, mind, soul, spirit. Philosophy, poetry and religion, for Bede, converge upon a single point, which is the transcendent and unitive Mystery.

Poetry and mysticism both derive from a common source, the ground or depth of the soul, where the Mystery of Being is experienced. But the poet is always driven to 'symbolize' his experience, to express it in words or in paint or in music. The mystic seeks the experience in itself, beyond words or sounds or images.[4]

The poet's way is that of word and image, the 'kataphatic' or positive way. The mystic's way toward the same Mystery is the 'apophatic' or negative way of pure union. Bede himself, his intellect drawn both to the pure contemplative fullness and to the immanence of the divine in nature, would journey between the two paths.

In The Marriage of East and West, *Bede Griffiths presents in succession the Vedic Revelation, the Judaic Revelation and The Christian Revelation. Significantly, this latter is subtitled 'The Rebirth of the Myth'. Further, Bede begins this part not with a presentation of the Christian reve-*

lation but with a long discourse on the 'Way of Intuitive Wisdom.' It is primarily through the perspective of intuitive truth and myth that Christian truth is meaningful for him at this time. Once again the epistemology[5] is primary. Bede is attempting to bring to life once again a Christian wisdom which had been virtually absent from the western world for centuries. It is through intuition and imagination that this wisdom is to be newly appropriated. Bede writes at length of a subject which is obviously of central importance to him. Never quite systematic, he presents his view with depth and thoroughness. He writes first of the rationalistic one-sidedness of western culture since the time of the Renaissance, when the harmony of medieval Christianity was lost. Encountering more fully the wisdom of the Vedanta, Bede felt that he had rediscovered the truth of imagination at its source.[6] Western rational consciousness, at this point, appears to surrender its primacy completely before this fuller way of knowing that has belonged to the human person from earliest times.

Intuition, approaching its greatest purity, becomes self-reflection. We recall Bede's interpretation of his initiatory experience as a self-discovery; he will come to see the central axis of the spiritual life as the realization of the atman, or unitive self.

As Bede writes beautifully of the mind in terms of a polarity of 'masculine' and 'feminine' dimensions, we feel the strong preferential inclination toward the feminine side which pervades The Marriage of East and West. *'Feeling intellect,' the organ of intuitive knowing through which we are able to know the divine Absolute, appears on the feminine side of the balance rather than as the marriage of 'feminine' feeling with 'masculine' intellect. Bede will employ the profound symbolism of male and female to express the inner structures of the human person, of the cosmos, and even of God. This perspective has strong foundations in the biblical writings.[7]*

The balance can only be restored when a meeting takes place between East and West. This meeting must take place at the deepest level of the human consciousness. It is an encounter ultimately between the two fundamental dimensions of human nature: the male and the female the masculine, rational, active, dominating power of the mind, and the feminine, intuitive, passive and receptive power. Of course, these two dimensions exist in every human being and in every people and race. But for the past two thousand years, coming to a climax in the present century, the masculine, rational mind has gradually come to dominate Western Europe and has now spread its influence all over the world.

The western world — and with it the rest of the world which has succumbed to its influence — has now to discover the power of the feminine intuitive mind, which has largely shaped the cultures of Asia and Africa and of tribal people everywhere. This is a problem not only of the world as a whole, but also of religion. The Christian churches, Catholic, Orthodox, and Protestant, have all been shaped by the western mind. They have built up structures of doctrine and discipline, of law and morality, which all bear the impress of the western genius. The eastern churches have retained something of an oriental character but are still dominated by the Greek mind. Even the original Semitic tradition which gave birth to Christianity, though deeply intuitive, has still a dominantly masculine character. All the Christian churches, eastern and western, have to turn to the religions of the East, to Hinduism, Buddhism, Taoism and the subtle blend of all these in Oriental culture, and to the deep intuitions of tribal religion in Africa and elsewhere, if they are to recover their balance and evolve an authentic form of religion which will answer to the needs of the modern world.

What then do I mean by intuition as distinct from reason, by this feminine power of the mind? This is a question which has been with me from the time when I began to think at all for myself. I tried to answer it when I first began to study philosophy, in two essays on "The Power of the Imagination" and "The Power of Intuition." Both these essays, it may be remarked, were rejected by Catholic periodicals at the time because they were not sufficiently 'Thomistic.' And indeed, I felt at the time that this is the great weakness of the philosophy of St Thomas Aquinas, magnificent as it is in its own way, that it has no place for the power of intuition. It is true that St Thomas allows in a roundabout way for a power of knowledge by 'connaturality' or 'sympathy', an 'affective' knowledge, but it has very little place in his strictly rational system. For him, as for the Greeks and for modern Western man, knowledge is to be found in concepts and judgements, in logic and reason, in systematic thought. Western science, for all its concern with observation and experiment, remains firmly attached to this mode of thought and as such is an inheritance from Greek and scholastic philosophy.

What then is intuition? Intuition is a knowledge which derives not from observation and experiment or from concepts and reason but from the mind's reflection on itself. What distinguishes the human mind above everything else is not its powers of observation and experiment, which animals also possess in some degree, nor its power of logical and mathematical reasoning, which a computer can imitate quite successfully, but its power of self-reflection. The human mind is so structured that it is always present to itself. When I eat or even when I sleep, when I feel joy or sorrow, when I love or hate, I do not merely undergo a certain physical or psychological process. I am present to myself, and in a certain sense aware of myself, eating and sleeping, experiencing joy or sorrow, loving or hating. When I know something I know that I know, in other words, I know not only what I know, but also myself as knowing. Every human action or suffering is accompanied by a self-awareness, a reflection on the self. The difficulty is that this self-awareness, this self-reflection, is not conscious in the ordinary sense. It is often referred to as 'unconscious.' Jung has made us familiar with this concept of the knowledge of the unconscious underlying all conscious knowledge. But this is an unsatisfactory term, since there is a kind of consciousness in this state. It can be called 'subconscious,' but this again suggests that it is not really a state of consciousness. It may be called 'subliminal,' that is, beneath the threshold (limen) of consciousness. Maritain in his *Creative Intuition in Art and Poetry* speaks of it as 'beneath the sunlit surface' of the mind. This comes nearer to the truth. Intuition belongs not to the sunlit surface of the mind, but to the night and the darkness, to the moonlit world of dreams and images, before they emerge into rational consciousness.

Let us try to grasp this. When I am eating or sleeping, when I simply experience my physical being, there is a dim, obscure awareness of myself eating and sleeping. The baby who has just learned to suck its mother's breast or remains blissfully asleep, has already an obscure awareness of itself, which will ultimately grow into full self-consciousness. Even before birth the child in the womb is beginning to experience itself. The proof of this is that all these experiences remain indelibly impressed on the mind, that is the memory. Years afterwards a person may discover that the trauma of birth or the experience of neglect in infancy have permanently affected the psyche and can be brought back to mind. I have said that even in sleep there is an obscure self-awareness. This is obvious in dreams, but even in deep sleep which Hindus call *sushupti*, it is held that there is a self-awareness. The mind sinks back into its source and the memory of it remains. One can understand the difficulty of what we are attempting to do. We are trying to bring up into rational consciousness and to express in rational concepts what is beyond rational consciousness but which nevertheless leaves its mark on the rational mind.

Perhaps we could speak of the 'passive intellect.' There is an active intellect, the *intellectus agens*, which abstracts rational concepts from our sense experience and develops scientific theories. But there is also a passive intellect. Before the intellect begins to act, it receives the impressions of the experience of the body, the senses, the feelings, the imagination. This is the source of intuition. All my experiences of my physical being, of my own body and of the world around me, of my emotional reactions and the images which they arouse in me, are impressed on the passive intellect. There is no such thing as a mere sensation, a mere feeling, a mere thought. Every sensation, every feeling, every imagination affects my mind, modifies my being. I live and act as a whole. However obscure this self-awareness may be, it is there in every action and in every sensation, in every thought and feeling. I am present to myself in every moment of my being. This is the very structure of my mind, of my consciousness. If I probe my consciousness sufficiently, I can become aware of this subliminal consciousness. I can go beneath the surface of my mind and explore its depths.

This is what has been taught in the West as a method of psychoanalysis, but the western psychologist rarely goes beyond the level of the dream consciousness and that of repressed emotions, whereas in the East, in Hindu and Buddhist and Taoist yoga, they have penetrated to the depths of the psyche and discovered its original ground. This is what western man has to learn to do. He has to find the path of self-realization which has been followed for centuries in the East.

The self is not the little conscious ego, constructing its logical systems and building its rational world. The self plunges deep into the past of humanity and of the whole creation. I bear within my mind, my memory in the deep sense, the whole world. The movement of atoms and molecules, which make up the cells of my body, are all registered in the passive intellect. The formation of my body in the womb of my mother in all its stages is all stored in my memory. Every impulse of love or hate, of fear or anger, of pleasure or pain, has left its mark on my mind. Nor am I limited to the experience of my own body and feelings. I am physically and psychologically linked with all the world around me. My body is the focus of electro-magnetic phenomena, of forces of gravitation and of all kinds of chemical changes. My feelings are reactions to a whole world of feelings both past and present in which I am involved. All this has left its impression on my mind. Well did Hamlet remark: 'What a piece of work is man!' My mind is an unfathomable mystery, reflecting the whole world, and making a me a center of consciousness among innumerable other such centers, each reflecting all.

Intuition, then, is the knowledge of the passive intellect, the self-awareness, which accompanies all action and all conscious, deliberate reflection. It is passive: it comes from the world around me, from the sensations of my body, from my feelings and spontaneous reactions. This is why intuition cannot be produced. It has to be allowed to happen. But that is just what the rational mind cannot endure. It wants to control everything. It is not prepared to be silent, to be still, to allow things to happen. Of course, there is a passivity of inertia, but this is an 'active passivity.' It is what the Chinese call wu wei, action in inaction. It is a state of receptivity. 'Let us open our leaves like a flower,' said Keats, 'and be passive and receptive.' These words inspired me at the very beginning of my journey, but it is only now that I realize their full significance. There is an activity of the mind which is grasping, achieving, dominating, but there is also an activity which is receptive, attentive, open to others. This is what we have to learn. The classical expression of this intuitive wisdom is to be found in the Tao Te Ching, which speaks of the Spirit of the Valley and the Mystic Female. 'The door of the Mystic Female,' it says, 'is the root of heaven and earth.' 'In opening and closing the Gates of Heaven can you play the part of the female? In comprehending all knowledge can you renounce the mind?' 'Attain to the utmost emptiness, hold firm the basis of Quietude.' 'To return to the root is repose.'[8] These are the principles which underlie the wisdom of the East, which the West has to discover and which China and the East have to recover if the world is to find its balance.

The passive intellect is the 'feeling intellect' of Wordsworth. It is the intellect united with feeling, with the emotions. It was thus that Wordsworth described poetry as 'emotion recollected in tranquillity.' It rises in the emotions and ascends to the level of the intellect, where it is 'recollected', gathered into unity and given meaning. Wordsworth described the whole process beautifully, when in the 'Lines written above Tintern Abbey' he spoke of sensations

> felt in the blood and felt along the heart
> and passing even into the purer mind
> with tranquil restoration.

This describes the whole process of intuitive knowledge. It is an integral knowledge embracing the whole man, starting from the 'blood,' the physical being, passing through the heart, the seat of the affections, the psychic being, and finally reaching the 'purer mind,' not the reason but the intellect, the intuitive mind.

Thus intuition exists at every level of our being. It starts with the 'blood,' with bodily awareness. Even at this level the intellect, the self, is present. The idea of 'thinking with the blood' is not an illusion. There is a very profound self-awareness at this deepest level of our being. Tribal people, especially in Africa, always tend to think with the blood, expressing themselves in the beat of drums and the movements of the dance. This is an authentic mode of knowledge, of self-discovery and self-affirmation. All simple people tend to live more from their bodies than from their minds, that is, from the intuitive knowledge of the body rather than from the rational knowledge of the mind.

D.H. Lawrence, who was the prophet of this kind of knowledge, has expressed it well: 'We have lost almost entirely the great intrinsically developed sensual awareness or sense-awareness and sense-knowledge of the ancients. It was a great depth of knowledge, arrived at direct by instinct and intuition as we say, not by reason. It was a knowledge based not on words but on images. The abstraction was not into generalizations or into qualities but into symbols, and the connection was not logical but emotional.'[9] It must be emphasized that this is real knowledge: it is not merely sensual or emotional experience. It is sense awareness, emotional experience reflected in the mind, not in the rational mind, the abstract intelligence, but in the intuitive mind, the passive intellect. It finds expression not in abstract concepts but in concrete gestures, in images and symbols, in dance and song, in ritual sacrifice, in prayer and ecstasy.

It is the great illusion of the western world that knowledge consists in abstract thought and that an illiterate person is ignorant. In reality, many illiterate people possess a wisdom which is totally beyond the reach of western man. Ramakrishna, the Hindu saint, who more than anyone else was responsible for the renewal of Hinduism in the last century, was an illiterate Brahmin, who spoke from the depths of an intuitive wisdom.

Intuition, then, can exist at the level of bodily instinct. People who habitually go barefoot and expose their bodies to the sun, as they do in many parts of Asia and Africa, have an intuitive awareness of the power, the sakti in Hindu terms, in the earth, in the air, in the water and in the fire of the sun. They experience these forces of nature acting upon them and have an instinctive knowledge of the hidden powers of nature. A farmer often has an instinctive knowledge, a knowledge by sympathy, of the productive powers of the earth, of the effects of the seasons of the year, and the changes of the moon, and of the weather reflected in the sky. Rational scientific knowledge can increase the precision of this kind of knowledge and make it systematic, but it alienates man from nature and creates an artificial world.

People who live in a world of concrete roads and buildings, of steel structures and plastic instruments, lose touch with the world of spontaneous feeling and imaginative thought. This is because the rational, scientific mind separates itself from the 'feeling intellect,' the source of intuitive wisdom. It is not that science and reason are wrong in themselves, but that they are divorced from sense and feeling. What we have to seek is the 'marriage' of reason and intuition, of the male and the female, then only shall we discover a human technology corresponding with man's deepest needs.

3. Sexual Wisdom[10]

In the course of this long treatise on intuitive wisdom in The Marriage of East and West, *Bede Griffiths pauses to consider 'sexual knowledge.' This perspective on sexuality is congruent with his basic sapiential approach. Earlier, Bede had been influenced by D.H. Lawrence with his 'knowledge of the blood.' Sexual relationship is, in Bede's view, a spiritual way which is finally to be consummated in unitive experience on the level of spirit. He departs from much earlier spirituality of both East and West by vigorously affirming the positive value of human sexual life and relationship. At the same time he orients sexuality firmly toward spiritual realization. Bede has understood the centrality and the complex influence of the sexual element in human life. As he approaches sexuality in different ways, we feel the convergence of the spiritual and the intellectual with the affective and bodily dimensions of the person.*

The first level of intuition, then, is on the physical level. This includes, of course, the sphere of sex. Sex itself is a means of knowledge. It is significant that the Hebrew speaks of a man 'knowing' a woman in marriage: 'Adam knew his wife, Eve, and she conceived.' Let us remember in passing that by a reverse process knowledge is spoken of in terms of sex. A 'concept' is something 'conceived'[11] by the mind, a fruit of the union between the mind and nature, between *purusha* and *prakriti* in Hindu terms.

Again, we must remember that sex in a human being is never a merely physical process. It involves the body, the feelings, the affections. It is 'felt in the blood and felt along the heart,' to apply the

44

language of Wordsworth, and 'passes even into the purer mind.' It touches the depths of human consciousness awakening the intuitive powers of the mind and transforming the self. A man knows a woman in sexual union with a knowledge deeper than any science or philosophy. This is the wisdom by which most people live, a wisdom of human intimacy and affection, engaging the whole person. But this union takes place at three levels. There is first the level of the physical senses, of the blood and the nerves and the resulting orgasm, and this is already a kind of knowledge. The self is present in this experience; it is already a specifically human experience. But deeper than the physical intimacy is the emotional union. There is a craving for warmth, for closeness, for intimacy in every human being. The first impulse of the baby is for the warmth and intimacy of the mother's breast. But behind this desire for warmth and intimacy there is a desire for love, for emotional satisfaction. The intimacy desired is not merely physical but psychological. In sexual union also it is not merely the physical intimacy which is sought but a sharing of love, a self-giving, a communion, in which each enriches the being of the other[12]. This again is a form of knowledge, a knowledge of love, of communion, in which each discovers the other.

In this union of love the man learns to know the woman and the woman learns to know the man, they mutually discover their own masculinity and femininity. This goes far beyond a merely emotional state. It is an awakening to the self. Each discovers a new aspect of his and her self. In every sexual union this self-knowledge is present, but when the emotional union is superficial, self-knowledge remains latent. It is only when the emotional union is deep and lasting that self-knowledge can grow. When this takes place a new level of knowledge is reached. It is no longer a merely physical or emotional intuition, it is a growth in personal knowledge, an awakening to the inner self. Like every intuition it is a reflection of the self on the self, a self-presence, but here the self discovers a new dimension of its being. The passive intellect, the inner vision is awakened to a new level of understanding. In a really profound union of love this may pass into a state of ecstasy. The self goes beyond itself and awakens to the ground of its being in self-transcendence. Then man and woman go beyond the duality of sex and discover their oneness in a love which is total fulfilment.

It is important to realize that all sexual love tends towards this transcendent state. No man or woman can be finally satisfied with a physical or emotional union. Love goes beyond the body and the feelings and reaches to the depth of the human being, where the division of male and female no longer exists. The man and the woman find the totality of their being; in each the male and the female are united, and the division of human nature is overcome. This is the supreme intuition of the self, which is found in the great mystics. It is no accident that the mystical experience is so often described in terms of sexual union. This is not a 'sublimation' in the Freudian sense. It is an opening of human nature to the full dimension of its being. It is of the very nature of human love that it cannot be satisfied with physical contact or emotional sympathy. It seeks a radical fulfilment in total self-giving. For some, sexual union may be the way to this total self-giving and self-discovery; others may awaken to this ecstasy of love in the presence of nature like Wordsworth; others may find it in loving service and self-sacrifice. But whatever the way, this ecstasy of love leads to the supreme wisdom, to the discovery of the depth of the self, no longer in isolation, but in the communion of love, for which it was created. . .

4. Imaginative Wisdom and Knowledge of the Self[13]
Bede's exploration of the world of intuitive experience in The Marriage of East and West *continues, ascending to imagination and finally to the pure reflexive knowledge of the self which he finds at the heart of the Hindu Vedanta.*

There is, then, a sphere of physical, biological intuition and of emotional, affective intuition. But beyond these there is the sphere of imaginative intuition. It is here that the intuitive power of the mind is most clearly manifest. The experiences of the body with its sensations and emotions are all reflected in the imagination. The imagination is primarily a passive power — it reflects the images of the world around us and of our own internal experiences. It is the sphere of what Jung called the archetypes. Human experience is

46

structured round certain primordial images — the father, the mother, the child, the bride, the bridegroom, the water and the fire, the shadow and the darkness   these are all archetypal images in what Jung called the 'unconscious,' but which I would call the subliminal depths of consciousness. For these archetypes are all forms of intuition; they are images reflecting the self, rising in the depth of self-consciousness. In most people these archetypes are hidden, they have not come up into the light of reflective consciousness. But in the poet and artist, the archetypes emerge into the light of consciousness. The passive intellect receives these images from the depths of its physical and emotional experience and sheds on them the light of intelligence. This is when the intuition beings to emerge from the darkness of physical and emotional experience into the clear light of knowledge.

But this knowledge is not a rational, abstract, conceptual knowledge. The mind does not 'abstract' (draw out) from the experience of the body to form a concept and to reason from it. The intellect illumines the actual concrete experience, penetrates into the physical and emotional world and fills it with light. Not only poets but most people in a normal society live from the imagination rather than from abstract reason. It is only the artificial world of Western man that seeks to educate everyone in habits of abstract thought and creates logical systems, expressed in the jargon of the scientific mind.

In a normal human society, such as still exists in a large part of Asia and Africa, man lives by the imagination and expresses himself in the language of the imagination, in gestures and rituals, in speech consisting of symbols, which reflect the self and the world in concrete images often accompanied by music and dance. But, of course, it is in great poets and artists that we can see the full development of the human imagination. They bring to perfection what in most people is obscure and inchoate, but it is because they draw on a basic human faculty common to all men, that the great poets speak to all men. Homer and the Greek tragedians, Virgil and Dante, Shakespeare and Goethe all speak this universal human language and it is to them that we go for the deepest understanding of human nature. In the same way, it is to the great novelists like Tolstoy and

Dostoyevsky, with their imaginative insight, that we look for the deepest understanding of our human condition today.

What therefore is the poetic imagination? Maritain[14] has defined it as 'the intercommunion between the inner being of things and the inner being of the human self.' There is, as we have seen, a presence of the self in every human experience, but in most people this presence is only half realized, or not at all. In the poet this self-presence becomes conscious, the latent self-awareness grows into a conscious awareness through his experience of the world around him. He is more than usually sensitive to the world of the senses, to sight and sound and touch and taste and smell, and these sensations with their accompanying images enter deep into his consciousness. They are reflected in the depth of his being, in the passive intellect, and become intuitive. That is, the intellect penetrates into the depth of his self-consciousness and draws forth the images in it, which focus his experience. The world is reflected in his imagination in all its concrete richness, where feeling and thought are fused together.

The abstract rational mind creates a world of concepts, separated from concrete reality, but the imaginative mind recreates the concrete world, reflecting it in symbols, whether of words of rhythmical movements or of painted signs or of architectural forms. All genuine art springs from this profound experience of the self in the world and the world in the self. It is a primordial human experience, from which language itself and every form of self-expression emerges. It is the neglect of this world of the imagination, of 'art' in the deepest and widest sense, in favour of a world of reason dominated by 'science,' that has caused the imbalance of Western civilization. This does not mean that science and reason are wrong in themselves. They are essential elements in human nature, and the development of these faculties in the West from the time of the Greeks is an essential element in human progress. But the domination of science and reason, and the practical suppression of art and imagination in normal education, has caused a fundamental imbalance in Western culture.

This is but one aspect of the domination of man over woman, of the aggressive male intellect over the feminine, intuitive imagination, which has affected all Western culture. It is typical of this outlook that it thinks that man and woman only differ physically and that the different races only differ in their colour. It does not recognize the profound, psychological difference between man and woman and between Asian, African and European man. This is due to blindness to the feminine aspect in human nature. Every man and woman is both male and female, and in every person the marriage of the male and the female has to take place. When man refuses to recognize the feminine aspect in himself, he despises or exploits woman and exalts reason over intuition, science over art, man over nature, the white races with their dominant reason over the colored peoples with their intuitive feeling and imagination. This has been the course of Western civilization over the past centuries. Now we are awakening to the place of woman in society, to the meaning of sex and marriage, to the value of art and intuition and to the place of the colored peoples in the civilization of the world. What has to take place is a 'marriage' of East and West, of the intuitive mind with the scientific reason. The values of the scientific mind with the scientific reason. The values of the scientific mind must not be lost, but they need to be integrated in the wider vision of the intuitive mind.

Both reason and intuition by themselves are defective, just as man is defective without woman, woman without man. Intuition by itself is blind. It is an obscure awareness of the self in the experience of the world. The intuition easily becomes swamped by emotions. This is the negative aspect of woman, the source of fickleness and instability, the *femina mutabile semper* of Virgil. It creates the image of the wanton, the temptress, the scarlet woman. It is the source of credulity and superstition, of witchcraft and sorcery, of vagueness and confusion of thought. The growth of science and reason in the West was largely a reaction against this unbalanced intuition, seen in the superstitions of the medieval church, the cult of witchcraft and sorcery, and religious fanaticism. Yet the answer to this was not the rejection of the intuitive mind, but its marriage with the rational mind. Intuition begins in the darkness of the child in the womb. It grows through the awakening of emotional and imaginative experience, but it eventually has to be drawn up through the passive intellect, on which all this experience of the senses and the emotions is impressed, into the clear light of the mind. It is then that the marriage of imagination and reason, of the active and passive intellect, takes place. It is this that we see in the great poets. In them the deep experience of physical being and the riches of emotional and imaginative life are informed by reason.

Reason itself, the active intellect, is taken up into the intuitive mind, that is, into the reflective knowledge of the self, and reason itself becomes intuitive. It is this that we find in Dante. He draws on the depth of human passion and sensitivity, goes through all the emotions of love and hate, of hope and despair, of joy and sorrow, and embodies all this profound experience in a vast imaginative vision. All this comes out in the sound and melody, the rhyme and rhythm, the verbal richness and concrete imagery of his verse. But with all this there is a skeleton of hard reason, of subtle philosophy and theology, of doctrine and argument. Yet this skeleton of abstract thought is integrated in the imaginative vision of the whole. Philosophy and theology have been made into poetry, and the intuitive power of the mind has assimilated all these diverse elements into itself.

But even with Dante we have not yet reached the culmination of the intuitive mind. The poet synthesizes all these elements of human experience into a unitive vision, but he remains dependent on images and concepts. There is a further vision which goes beyond images and concepts, as Dante himself experienced when in the culminating vision of the *Paradiso* he said:

> Henceforth my vision mounted to a height
> Where speech is vanquished and must lag behind.[15]

There is a point where intuition, having passed through the realms of darkness and of twilight into the sun, now passes beyond. It carries with it all the deep experience of the body and the blood, and all that the emotions and the imagination have impressed upon it, and now passing beyond images and thoughts, it 'returns upon itself' in a pure act of self-reflection, of self-knowledge. This is the

50

experience of the mystic, who, set free from all the limitations both of body and of soul, enters into the pure joy of the spirit. The spirit is the culminating point of body and of soul, where the individual person transcends himself and awakens to the eternal ground of his being. The obscure intuition of physical being, the broadening intuition of emotional and imaginative experience, the light of reason discovering the laws and principles of nature and of man, all these are reflections of the pure light of intuition, in which the soul knows itself, not merely in its living relation with the world around or with other human beings, but in its eternal ground, the source of its being. At this point of the spirit the soul becomes self-luminous, or rather it discovers that it is itself but the reflection of a light which shines forever beyond the darkness, a light which is ever the same, pure, transparent, penetrating the whole creation, enlightening every human being, yet remaining ever itself, tranquil and unchanged, receiving everything into itself and converting all into the substance of its own infinite being.

It is the discovery of this infinite, eternal, unchanging being, beyond the flux of time and change, beyond birth and death, beyond thought and feeling, yet answering to the deepest need of every human being, which is the goal of all religion and of all humanity. Here there is no longer a division between man and woman, for male and female are one. Here there is no longer a division between man and nature, for nature and man have found their unity in their source. Here there is no longer a division between classes and races and religions for here all have found the truth and the life for which they were seeking.

Yet this Being is not remote from any one or any thing. It is in each person and each thing as the ground of its own unique and individual being. The whole creation is grounded in this one Being; every atom and electron, every living cell and organism, every plant and animal, every human being, exists for ever in this eternal being. Time and change, body and soul, life and death veil this one reality, yet they themselves are its manifestations and exist in it. As an ancient saying has it: 'Everything that is there is here, everything that is here is there.' The world of time and space is a reflection of this eternal world; as Plato said: 'Time is a moving image of eternity.' All that takes place in time is seen and known in that eternal being. We are conditioned by time so that we see one thing after another and can never grasp the whole. But the intuitive vision is a vision of the whole. The rational mind goes from point to point and comes to a conclusion: the intuitive mind grasps the whole in all its parts. It is of this intuitive power of the mind that Eckhart said: 'This power has nothing in common with anything else, it knows no yesterday or day before, no morrow or day after (for in eternity there is no yesterday or morrow); there is only a present now; the happenings of a thousand years ago, a thousand years to come, are there in the present and the antipodes the same as here.'[16]

It is difficult for us with our time-bound minds and space-bound bodies to understand this eternal reality, or rather it is impossible, but that there exists in each one of us something that corresponds to that eternal being, a little spark, a ray of light, which touches our minds and awakens us to this transcendent mystery. The little spark is present in every human being, but for many it is totally hidden, for others it is kindled only occasionally, so that they get glimpses of that other world. It is only the mystic who penetrates beyond and sees the light, and even for him it is rarely that he can remain for long in such a state. It is only after death that we shall finally pass beyond the shadows and the darkness and see all things and all persons as they really are, in their eternal truth and their infinite reality.

It is the purpose of every genuine religion to reveal this transcendent mystery and to teach the way to its attainment. But this revelation is given not to the rational but to the intuitive mind, and the way to discover it is not by argument but by self-surrender, the opening of the self to its eternal ground. 'Not by the scriptures, not by the intellect, not by much study is this Self to be known. He whom the Self chooses by him the Self is attained.'[17] When we penetrate beyond the rational mind, we come upon a deeper self, a self that takes hold of our whole being, body and soul, and draws us into its infinite being.

5. *The Wisdom of Myth*[18]

Bede continues: myth is the language of intuitive knowledge, from its first stir-rings on the bodily level of human existence. It is the matrix of human under-standing, in which world, person and spirit are known in their primal unity.

But words here are inadequate, they stumble and fall. I am using abstract nouns like being, truth, reality, infinity, eternity. Each in its way points beyond our present mode of existence and directs the mind to that which is beyond the mind. But the words are of value only in so far as they awaken the little spark of intuition, and enable us to 'see into' the truth. That is why this knowledge cannot be attained by learning, it cannot be produced. We have to allow our-selves to be transformed, to become 'passive,' but with a passivity that is infinitely receptive. There is a parallel between the original darkness of the mind, the state of 'deep sleep,' what the Chinese call 'the uncarved block,' where everything is potential waiting to receive the light, and this final state of total receptivity. The difference is that the potentiality of matter is conditioned; it has to go through various stages of evolution before it can be capable of life; and again life has to go through many phases of development before it can become conscious; so finally consciousness has to develop through sense, through feeling, through the imagination, through reason before it can become fully conscious of that being which is the source of matter, of life and of consciousness. But the hidden germ of intuition, of receptivity was present from the beginning, and the ultimate mystical experience is only the flower of that intu-ition which was hidden in the root of matter.

It is here that we can see the place of myth in human evolution. A myth is an expression of the intuitive mind. At first the mind may be almost totally absorbed in matter, in the body. The expression will be in bodily movements, in ritual and dance and the beating of drums. But this will be accompanied by deep feelings, an emotional involvement in the rhythm of nature, of earth and plants and ani-mals, of sun and moon and sky, and this may be symbolized in some concrete object, a stone, a tree, an animal totem. But already there is a stirring of the imagination, of archetypal images from the depths of the unconscious, structuring the universe and giving it meaning.

And behind all this the intuition is at work, a self-awareness, inchoate at first but growing with every contact with the external world, and building up the myth as the expression of this totality of experience, structuring the universe around the self. This self-awareness will at first not be so much individual as social, and not merely social but cosmic, an awareness of the self in the interdependence and intercommunion with the cosmic mystery. One can understand, therefore, how the myth embraces the totality of existence, giving man a place in the universe and organizing every aspect of his life.

Now myth is the source of all religion. One can see it at work in the most advanced as in the most primitive religions. In Greek religion one can see the evolution of the myth in the clearest way. Homer still lives in a mythological world, and the marvel of his poetry is that of the rational mind awakening to the world of myth and giving it an imperishable expression in a language which is rich and concrete, drawing on the depths of human experience, and structuring it in the light of a pure intelligence and giving it an ineffable beauty and grace. In Aeschylus the myth acquires a deep religious and moral meaning and the drama remains essentially that of a mythological world. In Sophocles the myth is still meaningful but it is the human drama which holds the center of the stage. In Euripides, the 'rationalist,' as Gilbert Murray called him, the myth has begun to lose its power and scepticism is taking its place.

From the time of Socrates myth gives way to reason and survives only as a background to poetry, while science and reason gradually take its place. This was a long process and it is only in the last hundred years that science and reason have come to dominate the world and the myth has died. Yet this is exactly our problem. Man cannot live without myth; reason cannot live without the imagination. It creates a desert, without and within. It becomes the sword of destruction, bringing death wherever it goes, dividing man from nature, the individual from society, woman from man, and man and woman from God. This is what the triumph of reason has done, and now we have to go back and recover the myth, return to the source, rediscover our roots, restore the wholeness to man and creation. The myth has to be reborn.

6. Threefold Universe, Threefold Person[19]

In his initiation as a young man, Griffiths experienced the opening of visible nature to the world of spirit, and found this epiphany expressed in the language of the poetic imagination which wedded thought and feeling. Already there at the beginning we can perceive the three interlinked worlds of body, soul and spirit which he would find articulated in the 'perennial philosophy' — and particularly in the Vedanta. At the center stands the human person as a metaphysical tree of life, bringing together within himself/herself divine fullness and material cosmos. As intuitive knowing joins these three worlds, in Bede's view, so does human sexual experience.

Bede is prone to threefold patterns; he will often interpret the vedantic 'sat-cit-ananda' in terms of the Christian Trinity of divine persons. If the history of thought abounds in triadic schemes, this is particularly true of Christianity, for which the divine Trinity is the basic theological principle. A tripartite view of the human person appeared already in Aristotle — parting from a Platonic dualism which consistently ignored body and matter — and it was developed by early Christian writers such as Irenaeus, Origen, Gregory of Nazianzen and Cassian. William of St. Thierry, in the twelfth century, gave this anthropology its clearest and simplest medieval expression as he applied it to the spiritual journey.

... there are beginners, those who are making progress, and the perfect. The state of beginners may be called 'animal,' the stage of those who are making progress 'rational,' and the state of the perfect 'spiritual'.[20]

Once again the symbolism of male and female is central for Bede. He sees this duality running through the universe as the duality of form and matter (or 'passive energy,' pure potentiality). It pervades the human soul as the polarity of conscious, active, ordering mind and unconscious, passive receptivity. In the Christian Trinity, the same polarity exists in its archetypal form as that of Word and Holy Spirit.

Bede tends to confine the masculine principle — the 'pure light of reason' — to the power of forming concepts. At the same time, he tends to see the feminine principle as unbounded, so that at one moment it is identical with matter and at another moment it is a pure intuitive power which knows the divine One by participation. Pneuma, or Holy Spirit, is equated with atman, unitive Self, by Bede, and both of these tend to be identified with the feminine principle. But the feminine principle is also matter, pure potentiality.

Bede's brief account of the history of humanity rises to a peak at the time of the Upanishads, when human reason breaks through to 'a pure intuition of reality,' when 'reason and imagination meet in a marvellous marriage and the masculine and the feminine unite to form the complete man.' As the Incarnation appears, in The Marriage of East and West, *simply as the final capstone to this 'supreme period in human history,' we may sense the need for a further theological development in which the dynamic principle within the Christ-event will be differentiated and emerge into the light.* [21]

The Vedic seers had reached an understanding of the threefold nature of the world, at once physical, psychological and spiritual. These three worlds were seen to be interdependent, every physical reality having a psychological aspect, and both aspects, physical and psychological, being integrated in a spiritual vision. The cows and horses of the Vedas were not merely physical cows and horses, they were also the cows and horses of the mind, that is psychological forces, and beyond that they were symbols of the cosmic powers, manifestations of the Supreme Spirit.

This understanding of the threefold nature of the world underlies not only the Vedas but all ancient thought. In the primitive mind (which is also the natural mind) there is no such thing as a merely physical object. Every material thing has a psychological aspect, a relation to human consciousness, and this in turn is related to the supreme spirit which pervades both the physical world and human consciousness. It is interesting to observe that western science is now slowly coming round to the oriental view of the universe, which is, in fact, the view of the 'perennial philosophy', the cosmic vision, which is common to all religious tradition from the most primitive tribal religions to the great world religions, Hinduism, Buddhism, Islam and Christianity.

The view of the universe on which western science has been built, that of matter as a solid substance extended in space and time, and of the human mind as a detached observer capable of examining and describing the universe and so gaining control over it, has now been demolished by science itself. The Newtonian model of a world of solid bodies moving in space and time has been replaced by the model of relativity and quantum physics, in which matter is seen as a form of energy and the universe as a field of energies, organized in space-time, so as to form a unified and interdependent whole.

This comes very close to the Buddhist view of the 'insubstantiality' (*anatman*) of the universe and of the dynamic character of the elements (*dharmas*) as constantly changing parts of an organized whole. But western science has been compelled to go even beyond this and to recognize that the human mind as observer is already involved in that which it observes. What we observe is not reality itself, but reality as conditioned by the human mind and senses and the various instruments which it uses to extend the senses. What we observe, as Heisenberg said, is not nature itself but nature exposed to our method of questioning.[22] The old understanding of science is gradually giving way to the view that 'consciousness and physical reality (or empirical reality) should be considered as complementary aspects of reality.'[23]

Thus a revolution is quietly taking place in western science and it is slowly beginning to rediscover the ancient tradition of wisdom, according to which mind and matter are interdependent and complementary aspects of one reality. The same process can be observed in western medicine where it is gradually coming to be realized that all disease is psychosomatic and that the human body cannot be properly treated apart from the soul.

We are slowly recovering, therefore, the knowledge which was universal in the ancient world, that there is no such thing as matter apart from mind or consciousness. Consciousness is latent in every particle of matter and the mathematical order which science discovers in the universe is due to the working of this universal consciousness in it. In human nature this latent consciousness begins to come into actual consciousness, as a human consciousness develops it grows more and more conscious of the universal consciousness in which it is grounded. Thus we begin to discover the threefold nature of the Vedic universe. There is the physical aspect of matter (*prakriti*), the feminine principle, from which everything evolves, and consciousness (*purusha*) the masculine principle of reason and order in the universe. These correspond to the Yin and Yang of Chinese tradition and the matter and form of Aristotle. Beyond both the Yin and the Yang, beyond both matter and form, is the supreme principle, the ground of Being, the Great Tao, from which everything comes and which pervades all things. In the Vedic tradition the two principles were conceived as heaven and earth, and the whole creation came into being through their marriage.

These two principles, which are to be found in all ancient philosophy, are no less fundamental in Christian doctrine. St Thomas Aquinas, who built up his system of philosophy on the basis of Aristotle, regarded the 'form' and 'matter' of Aristotle as the basic principles of nature. Matter according to this philosophy is pure 'potentiality,' form is the principle of actuality. Pure matter, or 'prime matter' as Aristotle calls it, does not actually exist. It is a metaphysical principle which is basic to all physical being. Matter, as we know it, is a combination of form and matter, or of act and potency. In every physical object there is a form, a structure, an organizing power or active energy, and a material principle, a passive energy, a potentiality of being which is actualized by the form.

It is difficult to grasp this principle of potentiality precisely because it has no actuality and is not intelligible in itself; for form is the principle of intelligibility as well as of actuality. It can only be grasped in relation to the form which actualizes it. It can be compared to a womb, a darkness, a capacity of being, to which form brings life and light and actuality. It is the chaos, the 'tohu' and 'bohu' of the book of Genesis. It is the source of flux, of change, of that indeterminacy which science discovers even in the atom. This is what in Hindu tradition is called *maya*, which Sankara described as 'neither being nor not-being.'[24] It is the irrational element in existence, the meaningless, the absurd. Yet this principle is not evil in itself. In itself it is a pure potency, a pure capacity of being, and as such has a kind of purity, an innocence, a simplicity which exists at the heart of creation.

This principle is, of course, not merely a physical but also a psychological principle, since the physical and psychological are but two aspects of one reality. It is the ground of the unconscious in man. Beyond all levels of human consciousness, mental and imaginative and emotional and physical, there is a ground of unconsciousness, a primeval source, a womb of darkness, from which all life and consciousness springs. It is the world into which we enter in deep sleep, what in Hindu doctrine is called sushupti, the state of being beyond the waking and the dreaming state. It is the source of irrationality, of those violent contradictions in human nature, of the insanity which plagues us. And yet it is not insane or irrational in itself; it is only in association with sanity and reason that it develops these characteristics. In itself, as has been said, it has a certain purity and innocence. It is pure receptivity, which is the feminine aspect of the human soul. The masculine aspect is active and communicative, the feminine aspect is passive and receptive. The feminine has its roots in the unconscious, the darkness of the womb, and is the source of instability and change like the waxing and waning of the moon; the masculine is the source of stability and order and has its source in the light of the sun. Yet both are necessary for existence   without the feminine principle the infinite variety of nature would not exist; the white light of the sun would never be broken up into the multiple colours of the rainbow.

Moreover, these two principles have their source in the Supreme Spirit itself. The one who is beyond all change and multiplicity manifests itself in these two principles eternally. Purusha is the active principle in the Godhead manifesting itself as light and life and intelligence; Prakriti is the feminine principle, which in the Godhead is the Sakti, the divine power or energy. In the Christian tradition there has been very little recognition of this feminine aspect of God. Yet God is both Father and Mother, and in Oriental tradition this has always been recognized.

It is a fact, however, that in the Bible the name for the spirit (*ruah*) is feminine and in the later Syriac tradition, which preserved the same name, the Holy Spirit was spoken of as Mother. There is also in the Old Testament the tradition of a feminine Wisdom (Hebrew hochmah, Greek *Sophia*, Latin *Sapientia*) which reveals a feminine aspect in God. It may be possible therefore to see in the Holy Spirit the feminine aspect of God in the Trinity. The source of the Trinity is both Father and Mother, the Son or Word is the active principle of intelligibility, the source of order in the Universe; the

Holy Spirit is the feminine principle of receptivity, an infinite capacity for love, which receives perpetually the outflowing of Love through the Son and returns it to its source in the Father. . .

Bede briefly develops the Vedic myths of the sun, of light and darkness, and then returns to his overall theme.[25]

. . . Everything has at once a physical and a psychological, including a social, meaning and behind all the symbols is the one supreme Reality which is manifesting itself at every level of existence.

It is this vision of the universe which we need to recover. The western mind has split the world into two halves, conscious and unconscious, mind and matter, soul and body, and western philosophy swings between the two extremes of materialism and idealism. This is due to a disease of the mind, a schizophrenia, which has developed in western man since the Renaissance, when the unitive vision of the Middle Ages was lost. This medieval vision is in other respects no longer adequate, and western man has to recover his equilibrium by rediscovering the vision of the ancient world, the perennial philosophy, which is fully developed in the Vedanta and Mahayana Buddhism, but is implicit in all ancient religion. In this vision of the world the three principles matter, mind and spirit are seen to interpenetrate one another. It is a disease of the merely rational mind that causes us to see them as separate from one another, to imagine a world extended outside us in space and time, and the mind as something separate from the external world. In reality the world we see is a world which has been penetrated by our consciousness; it is the world as mirrored in the human mind. But beyond both mind and matter there is a still further principle of Spirit which interpenetrates both mind and matter, and is the source of both energy and consciousness.

The understanding of man as body, soul and spirit is found in St Paul[26] and in the early fathers of the church, though later it was unfortunately displaced by the body-soul conception of Aristotle. But in India this threefold character has always been accepted. Man has a body, a physical organism, a structure of energies, forming part of the physical universe. He has a psychological organism, consisting of appetites, senses, feelings, imagination, reason, and will, which forms his personality and is integrated with the physical organism. But beyond both body and soul, yet integrated with them, is the spirit, the pneuma of St Paul, the atman of Hindu thought. This spirit in man is the point of his communion with the universal spirit which rules and penetrates the whole universe. This is the point of human self-transcendence, the point at which the finite and the infinite, the temporal and the eternal, the many and the One, meet and touch. It is to this point of the spirit that we are led by meditation, when going beyond both physical and psychological consciousness we experience the depths of our own inner being and discover our affinity with the spirit of God. 'The spirit of God,' as St Paul says, 'bears witness with our spirit that we are children of God.'[27]

Man was created in this state of communion with God, and all ancient religion bears witness to the memory of this blissful state of consciousness. The fall of Man was a fall from this spiritual consciousness with its center in God to the plane of psychic consciousness with its center on the ego, the separated human soul bound by the laws of the physical organism. This is the state in which we find ourselves today and for many people even the memory of that higher state of consciousness has been lost. The psychic consciousness dominated by the rational mind is taken to be the norm of human life and as a consequence man finds himself dominated by the powers of the physical world, the 'elemental spirits' of St Paul, or in Indian terms the darkness of ignorance (avidya) and the illusion of maya which is the world separated from God. In India from the earliest times man has sought to be liberated from this bondage to matter (or maya) and to attain to enlightenment, the state of the Buddha, the enlightened one, and so to discover his true self, his spirit or atman, in which he knows himself as one with God, the universal spirit and source of all.

II

WEST: PART ONE
CIVILIZATION AND CHRISTIANITY

The obverse of Griffiths' personal awakening to the light of wisdom was his turning away from the European consciousness of his time. This passionate combination of attraction and repulsion is an intrinsic feature of his personality, and will motivate his development of an alternative world vision. Our next series of texts begins with Bede's judgment of the culture and civilization of the modern West and continues with his conversion to Christianity followed by his (later) theological vision of the Christian mysteries.

At first, Christianity was part of that stale 'West' from which Alan (Bede) turned away in his awakening to the divine presence in nature, in poetry and in the self. Then, through his reading of the Bible and his subsequent study of Christian tradition, a change began to take place within him. Dramatically, in the course of a severe internal conflict, he yielded to an 'irrational' but irresistible force within him, and surrendered to the God who had grasped him. Alan turned to Christ and the church. Despite the seeming irrationality of this driving force, there dawned upon his mind a new and luminous coherence, a light which projected a new intelligibility everywhere he looked. Alan was now committed to a lifelong relationship with this Mystery which would gradually reveal to him its scope and beauty. His wisdom quest was now permanently anchored to the fact which is at once Christ and church.

The ever-reflective Griffiths will meditate again and again upon the mysteries of this faith to which he has committed himself, expressing the central core of meaning as it glows within him at each stage in his life. We shall find a great simplicity and coherence in his articulations of the mystery of Jesus Christ and of the Holy Spirit, of the essential Christian experience, of the recreation of humanity in Christ. This unity of vision originates in the contemplative light of

Bede's consciousness. Later, in this same light,   broader and more complex syntheses will take shape.

7. *Background: A world without spirit*[1]

Bede Griffiths' thought develops against the dark background of the modern, industrialized English civilization into which he was born. Rationalist, materialist and one-sidededly 'masculine,' this western world, upon which he had turned his back, seemed to provide him with an unfailing confirmation of his own chosen path. In one writing after another throughout his life, he would recount the 'decline of the West.' In The Golden String, *Bede recalls how he and his two Oxford friends, appalled by the drabness of industrialized England, attributed this modern estrangement from beauty to the 'scientific mind':*

It was when the human mind became separated from its roots in feeling and instinct that it became diseased, and the infallible mark of the disease was the ugliness of its productions. This was how we explained the ugliness of the modern city in comparison with the beauty of the Cotswold towns and villages which we visited. When the mind was in harmony with nature, as it had been in the past, then its products had a spontaneous beauty, which flowed from men's hands with the same certainty as ugliness passed from the machine into its products.[2]

Bede's condemnation of the modern West , later in this same autobiography,[3] *rests upon a simple theological judgment: the western world, in abandoning the orthodox Catholic tradition, has abandoned its principle of truth and life. The disaster is not only aesthetic; after briefly recounting the positive achievements of modern western civilization in* The Marriage of East and West, *Bede continues:*

But the limitations of Western science and democracy have become more and more evident. The disastrous effects of western industrialism, physical, social and psychological, polluting the world and threatening to destroy it, are only too evident. But this is not an 'accident' due to the misuse of science and technology; it is due to a fundamental defect in western man.[3]

During the Middle Ages "the genius of Greece and Rome blended with the oriental Semitic culture of the Christian religion to create a balanced and harmonious way of life," and a rich culture was achieved.

But at the Renaissance this harmony was lost, and the dominant, aggressive, masculine rationalist mind of the West took charge, so that Europe remains today in a permanent state of imbalance. The balance can only be restored when a meeting takes place between East and West.[4]

Bede's diagnosis has apparently shifted during these thirty years: central here in The Marriage of East and West *is the East-West polarity. Later, as in the following text from* A New Vision of Reality, *the negative verdict will be more nuanced but no less categorical. Bede's matured judgment of the contemporary Western mind, in* A New Vision of Reality *centers upon its reductionism. The West, during the last three centuries, has abandoned that 'universal wisdom' which recognized the three interrelated spheres of matter, soul and spirit. Everything has been reduced, in this rationalist culture, to matter and its permutations. With elegant clarity, he demonstrates the effects of this destructive principle of reductionism in each sector of life. But with this clarity comes hope. Bede discerns, in recent decades, the beginnings of a reversal of this direction and a recovery of the perennial philosophy with its threefold vision. Paradoxically, the signs of this recovery appear within science itself - a new science in which the mechanistic view of nature gives way to an organic vision. While he continues to look back toward a golden age of unitive wisdom, of human and social wholeness, a vision of the future begins to come together in Bede's mind.*

There is a general feeling today that we are at the end of an age, an age which began three centuries ago with the discoveries of Galileo and Newton and resulted in the gradual development of a materialist philosophy and a mechanical model of the universe. This has in the course of time affected our whole society. The present industrial system and modern technology are the direct result of this mechanistic concept of the universe. The whole social, political and economic system of the West is governed by it, and even art, morality and religion are affected by it. So we live in a world which came into being in the last three centuries, and has come to a head only in the last century.

The basic principle of this world is its materialistic philosophy. This materialism is explicit in Marxism but it is implicit practically everywhere and it governs people's attitudes of mind and behaviour. Its basic principle is reductionism; it is the reduction of everything to certain material principles and to its material base. To take a simple example, all music can be reduced to vibrations on strings or in a pipe, mere vibrations in the air, and those vibrations may then be treated as being what music is, without concern for any other value which belongs to it. Fritjof Capra has shown convincingly in *The Turning Point*⁵ how this mechanistic system has come to dominate every aspect of science and of practical life today. He shows how modern physics was at first an attempt to explain everything in terms of atoms, where everything was reduced to material particles which obeyed mechanical laws and could be known by mathematical calculations. So the whole physical world came to be reduced to a machine. In biology the attempt still continues to explain all life in terms of physics and chemistry, and to believe that living beings are simply more complicated machines. More seriously for practical purposes, in medicine the human body is conceived from a biological point of view as a mechanical system obeying physical and chemical laws, and to be treated simply as a physical entity and manipulated by genetic engineering, without relation to the psyche or to the whole human person.

Psychology is obviously less amenable to reductionism than medicine. Nevertheless many of its methods are conspicuously reductionistic. Behaviorism, for instance, is a serious attempt to reduce the human psyche to the status of a machine by analysing it only in terms of external behaviour. Another example is the psychoanalysis of Freud and the tremendously influential method based on his work, where the attempt is made to explain the whole human personality in the light of the unconscious, which is seen in terms of repressed appetites, instincts and desires. In Freudian psychology all the higher levels of consciousness, the motives of the heart, morality and religion are explained in terms of the unconscious. This is typical of the whole method. It is an attempt to explain the higher in terms of the lower and to reduce the higher to the level of the lower, so that, to take a glaring example, religion is regarded as repressed sex.

In sociology the attempt is made to reduce society to individual persons who are either left free to seek their own advantage or have to be organised by the state. From this arises capitalism and communism, in both of which systems society is reduced to a multitude of individuals. Finally, in economics this principle is most obvious where the whole aim is to conceive society simply in terms of production and distribution. In Marxism society is deliberately reduced to the economic base, which is conceived as determining the whole. In capitalism society is judged in terms of monetary value so that the prosperity of a nation is evaluated in terms of its gross national product, by the money which is being circulated in it and the way it is being used.

This is a drastic system by which everything is reduced to the material level, and it has had extraordinary success. Scientifically it has led to great discoveries being made and it has undoubtedly produced an impressive system of technology. On a social scale it has produced states with tremendous power building up influence all over the world. But at the same time it is gradually producing inevitable evil effects, rapidly exhausting material resources, polluting the environment and leading to the build-up of armaments which threatens to lead to a nuclear war capable of destroying our entire civilisation and the whole planet. All this is the result of three centuries of materialism building up to its height in the first part of this century.

In the second part of this century we have begun to discover what has been taking place and in what we are involved, and a new movement has begun which is the opposite of all this. We are beginning now to be able to replace the mechanistic system and mechanistic model of the universe with an organic model. This is the beginning of a return to the traditional wisdom, the wisdom by which human beings have lived over thousands and thousands of years and with which the great societies of the past have been built up. In this ancient traditional wisdom the order of the universe is seen always to be three-fold, consisting not only of a physical dimension but also of a psychological and a spiritual world. The three worlds were always seen as interrelated and interdependent. This understanding of the three orders of being and of their interdependence is what is known as the perennial philosophy.

Materialism is correct in so far as it recognises the material basis of reality, and science has explored this basis further than has ever been done before. This is a positive achievement. The rational, logical mind has been used in the analysis of matter, and this has led to the organization of matter to such an extent that it is hoped that by this means all human needs can be satisfied. This is why many people think that this age is in advance of any previous age. But it is only in this respect that the present age is in advance of others. In all other respects it is to be judged as being far below. A little exaggeratedly perhaps, Coomaraswami once made the remark, "From the stone age to the twentieth century, what a descent!" There is something in this. The perennial philosophy was present in the stone age and human beings lived by that. In this view, as has been said, there was the order of nature, the physical world, then the psychological, social world and, highest of all, the divine spiritual world, and all three were seen as interdependent and integrated. If we want to see the decline of the modern world we cannot do better than to compare stages in the development of art.

Looking back on the history of art from the stone age onwards, you see how the ancient wisdom was embodied in every form of art. In the early stages art in whatever form was the expression of the religious instinct, the sense of the sacred. Everything in nature was held to be sacred, because it was pervaded by the universal Spirit. Art, whether in the form of stone implements, or burial places, or roughly carved figures, or paintings as in the paleolithic caves, or pottery or clothing, was a way of expressing the sense of the sacred, of enacting the sacred mystery which pervaded human life. When the great civilizations arose in Egypt and Babylon, the temple became the centre of civilized life and all the arts were used to adorn the temple and to provide for human needs. Agriculture and pottery and weaving were no less sacred than the service of the temple. All alike were ways of expressing and manifesting the all pervading mystery.

When the great awakening took place in the first millennium to the transcendence of the mystery with the Upanishads, the Buddha, the Hebrew prophets, art was less conspicuous. The Israelites were forbidden to make an image of their God and the early Buddhists made no image of the Buddha. The Hindu temple also had not yet come into being. But as these religions became established and as Christianity with its doctrine of incarnation emerged from Judaism, there was a flowering of art in every form over all the ancient world, in China, India, Persia, Greece and Rome. In Greece Athens was leading the way already in the fifth century before Christ and Greek influence seems to have been responsible for the development of Buddhist sculpture. Gradually throughout all these regions a marvellous synthesis of art and poetry and philosophy was achieved, which gave rise to Hindu sculpture and architecture, Buddhist painting and sculpture, the Chinese art of every kind and the cathedrals of Europe with their sculpture and stained glass and the painting of the icons in eastern orthodoxy. Everywhere art expressed the mystery of religion, the sacred mystery revealed in the Scriptures and embodied in every form of art and poetry, music and dancing, and even the simple articles of daily use. Even Islam, which had rejected all images, developed a style of architecture of the utmost refinement.

It was this period then, between AD 500 and 1500, that saw the great flowering of art and culture which took place all over the civilised world. After that the hold of the perennial philosophy with its holistic vision began to loosen. Individual geniuses arose but the sense of a cosmic vision and a cosmic whole was gradually lost and art and culture became more and more fragmented. Today we inherit this fragmented universe and we are as far as possible from the sacred universe of earlier times. The present system of industrialization which emerged in the nineteenth century marked the death knell of traditional art.

8. Christianity: The beginning of Faith[6]

It was in 1930, during the experiment in common life with his two Oxford friends in the Cotswolds, that Bede began his serious reading of the Bible. The Old Testament wisdom literature made a deep and lasting impression on him. But it was his reading of the four Gospels that confronted him with the challenge of Christ. As he read these different narratives of Jesus' life, passion and resurrection, he looked for signs of factuality and authenticity, and found them to be undeniably and abundantly present. The facts, moreover, were inseparable from the one great assertion: here was the decisive Truth in which the meaning of human life was to be found.

I began the New Testament with St Mark's Gospel, because I thought that this was the most primitive and that there if anywhere was to be found the authentic portrait of Christ. I expected to find there the figure of the human Christ, free from all the accretion of later legend, which had been familiar to me from my boyhood, but as soon as I began to read for myself I found that it was very different from what I had been led to suppose. The human figure was there certainly as real and living as the figure of Socrates in the Apology and the early dialogues of Plato. There was no mistaking its actuality; it had all the roughness and unexpectedness which one finds in a character from life as opposed to the smoothness and conventionality of legend and the ideal portrait. But with this element of realism and of living humanity there was another element, that of the supernatural, which was no less evident than the first, nor was this something which could be easily detached, leaving the human figure unimpaired. The two elements were woven together into the substance of the Gospel, so that they could not be separated without doing violence to it. The miracles were described with the same graphic realism as the other events, and clearly belonged to the same structure. In the same way the human teaching which I had always loved was implicated, I found, with supernatural claims of an astonishing kind, which had the same quality of authentic utterance. It was this character of authenticity which impressed me above everything. I approached the Gospels in the same frame of mind as I had approached the Apology of Socrates, the Meditations of Marcus Aurelius or the Confessions of St Augustine, and I judged them by the same standard. I could no more doubt the quality of the character and personality revealed in them than I could doubt that of Socrates or Marcus Aurelius. It was clearly the authentic voice of truth, and if there were elements in the teaching which I could not properly understand, I was prepared to accept them as I accepted them in Plato or St Augustine. I could wait until further light was given.

This authentic speech was intimately related to the facts which were recorded, so that the one could not be separated from the other. The climax of the whole story, for instance, turned on the answer of Christ to the question of the High Priest: "Art thou the Christ, the Son of the Blessed?": when he replied unequivocally: "I am." It was clearly impossible to dismiss this as an accretion; so it was the keystone in the structure of the whole. So when I came to consider the question of the miracles, especially the Resurrection, I had to ask myself: "Could they be abstracted from the whole without destroying the structure?" and it was clear that they could not. The evidence for the Resurrection in St Mark was more of the same factual character as the rest, and was all the more striking for its extreme brevity. The problem of reconciling the three accounts of the Resurrection, which had disturbed me so long ago, now appeared in quite a new light.

When I turned to St Matthew and St Luke, I found in them the same kind of actuality as in St Mark, though there was not quite the same realism. Yet in certain ways it appeared that St Matthew was nearer to the original speech of Christ, particularly in the Sermon on the Mount. Here if anywhere was the authentic voice of the teacher, and yet once again could it be detached from the whole? The structure of St Matthew was different; there was a considerable difference in tone: but there was the same inner coherence, the same sense of an organic whole. Again St Luke was different from St Matthew; he was a Greek writing for Greeks, while St Matthew was a Jew writing for Jews; he was perhaps further removed from the source: but there were elements in his Gospel like the parables of the Good Samaritan and the Prodigal Son, which were clearly as authentic as anything in St Matthew or St Mark.

So when I came to compare the different accounts of the Resurrection I was not troubled by the apparent discrepancies. Here were three distinct accounts of the same event, all with the same quality of actuality, depending on the evidence of eye-witnesses, differing in detail and in point of view, and yet all clearly bearing witness to the same fact. There was no harmonization, or smoothing out of the differences; the stories were left to speak for themselves by their candour and originality. Always I came back to this overwhelming impression of truthfulness, that quality of truth which I sought in all literature, and which I had learned to recognise by the beauty, the rightness, of its expression. Judged simply as literature, the essential truth of the Gospels could not be doubted, but this truth was a truth not merely of idea but of fact, of history; the two were so interwoven that they could not be separated. I could not, of course, pass a final judgment on them at this stage, and it was many years before my mind became clear on the subject; but the first impression was that there was a solid objective truth in the Gospels which had to be faced. When I read the accounts of the Virgin Birth in St Matthew and St Luke, my impression was the same. They both had an extremely primitive character; one had only to compare them to with the stories of the Golden Legend to see the difference between pious fancy and recorded fact. Perhaps the conditions of life in which I was living helped me to see this also. It was difficult to imagine the Annunciation taking place in London or Birmingham any more than in any of the great cities of the Roman Empire. It had taken place in a remote village among the hills of Galilee, and I found no difficulty in believing that it might have taken place in one of our Cotswold villages. Here in the country men's minds were open to the wonder of the natural and the supernatural world, which the civilization of the towns hid from them.

What, after all, was my objection to the supernatural? Was it not one of those prejudices of the scientific mind, which I believed to be the cause of the impoverishment and the degradation of human life? The scientific mind could never get beyond the phenomena of the external world, and by mistaking its mathematical abstractions for the ultimate reality was depriving human life of all meaning. I had learned that behind the phenomena of nature there is a power which is not only the source of their existence but also the cause of all their acts; and I had come to believe that this power was not only a rational power but also a moral power, which revealed itself as a personal will. Was it not possible that this will could not only reveal itself to the mind of the prophet but could also act through him on the phenomenal world? What difficulty was there in believing that that wisdom, which I had learned from the Wisdom of Solomon penetrates all things by reason of its pureness, could not only work through the ordinary laws of nature, but could also transcend them? I do not think that my mind was at all clear about this for some time, but I realized certainly that I had been a victim of prejudice about the supernatural, and that this must now be discarded along with all the other prejudices of the modern mind.

When I turned to St John's Gospel I was confronted with a graver problem. It was clear that it differed completely not only in its point of view, but still more in its whole style and character. And yet I could not but be impressed again with its factual nature. It was as close to the actuality of history in certain respects as St Mark, and once more the discourses however different their tone and bearing, were no less closely interwoven with the facts. I did not attempt to reconcile their differences, but again I judged the impression of St John's Gospel as a whole. It was clear that this was one of the most significant works of human genius. Whatever its precise import might be, it was the record of an experience of unfathomable depth. Both the person and the doctrine portrayed were of a beauty beyond all human imagination; there was nothing in Plato which could be compared with them. I realized that to reject this would be to reject the greatest thing in all human experience; on the other hand, to accept it would be to change one's whole point of view. It would be to pass from reason and philosophy to faith.

9. Conversion[7]

Bede's conversion to Christianity, in his middle twenties, stands out boldly from the other transitional events in his life. Although Bede describes the experience, in his autobiography, with his usual lucidity, it is something that clearly cuts across the grain of his personality and moves counter to the normal flow of his mind and heart. The beginnings of this reversal of direction which brought him into the church, as he describes them in The Golden String, *appear as rational stages of reflection upon the Christian tradition. Then something else takes over; what seems at times to be an alien force invades Alan's life and brings him to his knees. He is very conscious of a 'power' which is present and which is impelling him to go where he would never have gone by himself.*

We can imagine this meteoric event remaining within him like a buried seed, often invisible as he continues on his way in quest of wisdom. From beneath the bright surface of his mind the Christ-reality will exert a steady influence, appearing more visibly from time to time, illumining, correcting, ultimately asserting its sovereignty.

The inner conflict of Bede's conversion, as he recounts it, centered upon the surrender of his 'reason,' or rational ego. This strong rationality is, indeed, central to his personality, and is evident everywhere in his writings - no less when he is writing of the mystery. It is manifested in the luminous clarity of his writing, in his continual drive toward coherence and an all-embracing synthesis. This rationality is one with his insatiable demand for meaning, with his

Up to this time my religion had been to some extent external. It had engaged my mind and imagination, my feelings and my will, but it had never really touched my heart. Behind all my fervour and enthusiasm there had been an intense egoism. I acknowledged no real authority over myself. My religion was based on my own reason and my own will, and though I had come theoretically to accept the authority of the church, it had no real effect on me.

Now for the first time I felt an overwhelming need to repent. I did not clearly understand what repentance was, nor was I aware of any particular sin of which I had to repent. It was simply that the unrest in my soul had turned from discontent with the world to a feeling of discontent with myself. There was nothing conscious or deliberate about it; it came to me as a command, and I kept saying to myself, scarcely knowing the meaning of what I said: "I must repent, I must repent." I went up in this state of mind to a small chapel at the top of the house one evening, and there, as I prayed, a resolution formed itself in my mind that I would not go to bed that night but would spend the whole night in prayer. Again the resolution seemed not to come from my own volition; it was an instinct with the force of a command.

I went, therefore, to my room and began to pray kneeling on the floor beside the bed, and immediately a furious conflict started in my mind. Reason and common sense told me that it was absurd to behave in this way. Beneath my unconventional behaviour, in many ways I was still deeply conventional, and I dreaded what people might think of me. Although I affected to despise the world, I was in fact still governed by its standards, and the idea of staying up all night in prayer appeared to me utterly absurd. I was also frightened of the isolation into which I felt that I was being driven. I had no real contact with anyone in London, and the people with whom I was staying, though good and kind, would have had no understanding of the conflict in my mind. I felt myself to be utterly alone in this vast city and I could find no human justification for what I was doing.

However, these were comparatively external considerations; what really terrified me was the conflict with my own reason. Until this time my reason and instinct had always gone hand in hand. My first experience of the beauty and mystery of nature had been confirmed by my reading of the poets and then of the philosophers. My discovery of Christianity had also gone on rational lines; at each stage I had seemed to find the book which I needed to satisfy both my reason and my instinct for beauty and holiness. Even my prayer had been perfectly rational and had been satisfied by the ordered beauty of the Book of Common Prayer, but now something irrational seemed to be coming into my life. There had been the desire for fasting which, though I might justify it by reason to some extent, came upon me as an irrational impulse; and now this call to repentance had come, as an apparently irrational urge, and my reason rose up against it. Which was I to obey, this obscure instinct, this apparently irrational urge, or my reason and common sense? The conflict was the most intense that I had ever endured, and it was part of the terms of the conflict, that it could not be answered by reason, because it was precisely the place of reason in my life which was in question.

The conflict went deeper than I could possibly understand. I had lived up till now by my own will. I had worked out my own philosophy and religion for myself and without knowing it I had made a God of my own reason. I had made myself the judge of everything in heaven and earth, and I acknowledged no power or authority over me. Even if theoretically I now acknowledged the authority of God and the church, in practice I was still the ruler and the judge. I was the center of my own existence, and my isolation from the rest of the world was due to the fact that I had deliberately shut myself up within the barriers of my own will and reason. Now I was being summoned to surrender this independence. Something had arisen in the depths of my own nature which my reason was powerless to control. I was being called to surrender the very citadel of my self. I was completely in the dark. I did not really know what repentance was or what I was required to repent of. It was this darkness which really made me afraid. Is not this the one thing of which we are all afraid? The darkness which is outside the sphere of our consciousness, the abyss where all known landmarks fail? This was what I was really facing and it was this which filled me with such unspeakable horror. I do not wish to exaggerate the nature of this ordeal, but it was indeed the turning point of my life. The struggle went on for many hours, but I realised at length that it was my reason which I had to renounce. My reason was the serpent which was threatening to devour my life. It was not merely the reason of convention and common sense, but the very autonomy of my reason which I was required to sacrifice. I had to surrender myself into the hands of a power which was above my reason, which would not allow me to argue, but commanded me to obey. Yet this power presented itself as nothing but darkness, as an utter blank.

In this state of mind I had but one resource. I had never been in the habit of meditating on the passion of Christ, but the scene in the Garden of Gethsemane had impressed itself on my imagination. I had always felt that in those hours Christ had faced the utter darkness of death and dereliction, the full tide of the power of evil sweeping over the world. Now I felt that this hour had come upon me, and I could only place myself beside him in the Garden of Gethsemane and wait for the night to pass. Once I had made up my mind not to listen to reason, the conflict ceased. It was only a matter of enduring to the end. So I set myself to remain kneeling on the floor, fighting against sleep and keeping my mind fixed on the figure of Christ. Somehow I managed to endure until it was morning. When I rose, I felt worn out and hopeless; I did not know what was to become of me. I did not feel that I could stay where I was and nothing else offered itself to me.

But as I was leaving my room, I suddenly heard a voice say: "You must go to a retreat." When I say that I heard a voice, I do not mean that I heard any sound. It was simply that this was signified to me interiorly, but in such a way that it did not appear to come from myself. I believe that I had heard the word "retreat" used once, but I am certain that I did not know what it meant. I associated it, I think, with some kind of clerical conference which I had heard of taking place in the country. The message came to me as a direct inspiration, though I did not know what it signified. I went, therefore, to an Anglo-Catholic church nearby and asked the priest if there was such a thing as a retreat to which I could go. He thought for a minute and then said: "Yes, there is one beginning this morning at Westminster House." The retreat was for a group of ordinands, but he thought that it would be possible for me to attend it. I went round to Westminster House which I found to be a house of the Cowley Fathers.

It is difficult to describe what happened when I reached there. The retreat conferences were given by an old priest called Father Tovey. They were very simple in character and dealt with the fundamental doctrines of Original Sin and Redemption, of the Incarnation and the Holy Trinity. This was the first time that I had ever heard these doctrines expounded in a way which had any meaning to me. He based himself on St Thomas, which I recognised with pleasure, but he gave them a living personal application which touched my heart. I had studied philosophy and theology, and I knew the elements of church history and church doctrine, but the simple truth of the faith had never before been set before me. Now it penetrated my soul in such a way that I was appalled to think that I had never understood it before. I had rejected the church and gone my own way, working out my religion for myself, and here all the time the truth had been among the people I had despised. My whole life seemed to have been one gigantic mistake. I had turned my back on the truth, and sought it blindly in the opposite direction, and now I had been forced back to the point from which I started.

The repentance for which I had blindly asked the night before now came over me like a flood. I went to confession for the first time in my life and tears poured from my eyes, tears of a kind which I had never known before. My whole being seemed to be renewed. When I went into the church and heard the chanting of the Psalms, it seemed that the words were being spoken in the depths of my own soul and were the utterances of my own prayer. They were chanting the 119th Psalm; it must have been in plainchant, though I did not know it, and no doubt this must have stirred my soul, for there is no music on earth like it; but it was the words which engraved themselves on my mind:

Blessed are those that are undefiled in the way: and walk in the
    law of the Lord.
Blessed are they that keep his testimonies and seek him with

their whole heart....
With my whole heart have I sought thee: O let me not go
    wrong out of thy commandments....
Open thou my eyes that I may see the wondrous things of thy
    law.

I had come through the darkness into a world of light. That eternal truth and beauty which the sights and sounds of London threatened to banish from my sight was here the universal law. I heard its voice sounding in my ears. The very stones of the house seemed to be the living stones of a temple in which this song ascended. It was as though I had been given a new power of vision. Everything seemed to lose its hardness and rigidity and to become alive. When I looked at the crucifix on the wall, the figure on it seemed to be a living person; I felt that I was in the house of God. When I went outside I found that the world about me no longer oppressed me as it had done. The hard casing of exterior reality seemed to have been broken through, and everything disclosed its inner being. The buses in the street seemed to have lost their solidity and to be glowing with light. I hardly felt the ground as I trod, and I think that I must have been in some danger of being run over. I was like a bird which has broken the shell of its egg and finds itself in a new world; like a child who has forced its way out of the womb and sees the light of day for the first time.

When I returned to the house I went to my room and took up the New Testament. There I read the words of St John: "Not that we loved God, but that He loved us," and suddenly the meaning of what had happened dawned on my mind. Through all these years I had thought that I had been seeking God. The presence which had appeared to me beneath the forms of nature that day at school; the beauty which I had found in the poets; the truth which philosophy had opened to me; and finally the revelation of Christianity; all these had seemed to be steps on my way of ascent towards God. Now I suddenly saw that all the time it was not I who had been seeking God, but God who had been seeking me. I had made myself the center of my own existence and had my back turned to God. All the beauty and truth which I had discovered had come to me as a reflection of his beauty, but I had kept my eyes fixed on the reflection and was always looking at myself. But God had brought me to the point at which I was compelled to turn away from the reflection, both of myself and of the world which could only mirror my own image. During that night the mirror had been broken, and I had felt abandoned because I could no longer gaze upon the image of my own reason and the finite world which it knew. God had brought me to my knees and made me acknowledge my own nothingness, and out of that knowledge I had been reborn. I was no longer the center of my life and therefore I could see God in everything.

That night before I went to bed I opened a book by St John of the Cross and read in it the words: "I will lead thee by a way thou knowest not to the secret chamber of love." The words struck home to me as though they had been spoken to me. Though I had never been without affection for my family and had had many friends, yet I had never till this moment really known the meaning of love. My strongest feelings had gone into my love for nature and for poetry. Yet always I had had the feeling that in love the secret of life was to be found. And now I felt that love take possession of my soul. It was as though a wave of love flowed over me, a love as real and personal as any human love could be, and yet infinitely transcending all human limitations. It invaded my being and seemed to fill not only my soul but also my body. My body seemed to dissolve, as things about me had done, and felt light and buoyant. When I lay down I felt as though I might float on the bed, and I experienced such rapture that I could imagine no ecstasy of love beyond it.

During the retreat Father Tovey had compared the action of grace to a small child standing over an open trapdoor into a cellar where his father is standing. The cellar is in darkness and the child can see nothing. But he knows that his father is there, and his father tells him to jump. That is what had happened to me; I had jumped into the darkness, and I had been caught in the arms of love.

10. Jesus Christ: The Incarnation[8]

Bede Griffiths' contribution to contemporary christology is a reassertion of the Christ-mystery in unitive perspective. He opens Christian theology to a new sapiential vision in the larger world of today's cosmology, anthropology and of the meeting of religions. Bede's presentation of Christ is far from the image which had been dominant in a dogmatic and devotional postreformation Catholicism. In contrast to that over-externalized, isolated, often opaque and hard-edged image, Bede's Christ-figure is without edges, transparent, referential, a Christ more of meaning than of power. This Jesus, not confronting but integrating, is readily universalized. Bede's ambivalence toward the 'personal' is manifested in his tendency to go quickly beyond Christ himself, either toward God or toward the cosmic pleroma. If his Christ seems constantly to be receding from us, perhaps this is finally to be connected with Bede's tendency to reject the present world, the present life, in favor of an alternative reality. Jesus tends to become the doorway to one or another of these alternative realities: either unitive fullness in the divine Absolute, or the unitive fullness of a cosmic synthesis.

Theologians have distinguished three dimensions in Bede's christology[9]: the historical, the psychological-mystical and the cosmic. Firstly, Bede sees Jesus Christ, in contrast to the mythological deities of Hinduism, as a concrete historical person - and indeed as the center of history. Secondly, Jesus brings to humanity a new relationship to God: a personal relationship of communion with God which goes beyond the advaitan 'identity' with God which is disclosed in the Upanishads and developed in the Vedanta tradition. Thirdly, Jesus is the Cosmic Person in whom cosmos and history are brought together, in whom the world and all humanity are brought together in God. In this cosmic Christ the 'three worlds' of the universal wisdom are finally reconciled.

Jesus Christ is the center and, ultimately, the whole of Christian theology. Bede affirms again and again the centrality of Jesus Christ and of the mystery of Christ. This mystery is also a center of tensions: between spirit and matter, between past and future, masculine and feminine, between duality and non-duality, confrontation and integration. Bede's Christ is subject to these tensions. His affirmations about Christ are best understood as complementary rather than consistent in a linear way. They represent different aspects of the one mystery of Christ which are not easily built into a single coherent theological system.

Bede's thought develops around two epicenters: the Christ-mystery and the unitive realization of atman/brahman. As the years pass, his focus moves from the mystery of Christ and the church inward to the unitive Self, and then outward again to the Cosmic Person in whom all creation is gathered into the divine Unity. The tension between the two centers, however — Christ-mystery and unitive Absolute or atman — is never quite resolved in Bede's thinking; rather, there is an alternation between the two perspectives. Bede's christology develops within the powerful field of force of the unitive Absolute, which mod-

ifies it both directly and through Bede's need to see all religious traditions - including Christianity - as embodiments of this one supreme reality. Thus the profile of Christ in his theology is softened and reduced. In the end, however, Christ as the Cosmic Person (or Christ-purusha) emerges more and more as the reconciling center in which the unitive Absolute, humanity and the cosmos are brought together. The unitive Reality, in the Christ-purusha, has become incarnated in humanity and in the material universe, bringing the three worlds together in himself. If Bede seems to have returned from the Upanishads and Sankara to Paul, however, he will frequently reassert the primacy of the transcendent mystery - as in a lecture a year before his death:

So Jesus is taking us beyond the personal form of God. He is the personal form of God, but we have to go beyond the personal form to the Father who is the transcendent mystery beyond. And all our mystical tradition teaches us that we have to go beyond all images and concepts to this mystery. The great authority is Dionysius the Areopagite.[10]

Besides this movement toward transcendence, a second force exerts a strong influence on Bede's vision of Christ: that is his drive towards universality and the reconciliation of the world's religious traditions. We can feel this drive in his words during an interview about six months later. He has been speaking of his early attraction to the Cosmic Christ.

Everything we can say about God and the Infinite is limited, is symbolic, is a type of analogy, and points to something that cannot be expressed. Every religion points towards this inexpressible mystery. That's the only way we can get beyond our conflicts. If we remain in our own religious conditions, with different languages, different modes of thought, expression, and so on, we are all in conflict. We kill one another in defending our particular beliefs. When we go beyond the images, the concepts, the sacramental aspect, the signs, to the reality, then we discover unity that embraces the whole creation, all humanity, and all religion. So that's what we are really seeking today, I think. And it's coming, but slowly and in spite of all the conflicts that arise.[11]

For Bede, Christ is the creative Word from which the universe comes and the Cosmic Person in whom the universe returns to God. And it is in Jesus Christ that we enter into the communion of love which is God. From the narrative style of Bede's account of his conversion, we move to the second of the three theological essays in Vedanta and Christian Faith *(1973). This is Bede's early 'christology from above.' He succinctly presents the mystery of Christ in its mystical and cosmic dimensions.*

How then are we to understand the incarnation? The Christian doctrine is expressed by saying that in Christ the divine and the human nature were united in one person. In his Person, that is in his Self, in the ultimate ground of his being, he was God. He knew himself as the Word of God, the expression of the mind of the Father. But at the same time he was conscious of himself as man, having a human soul and a human body, sharing the limitations of human nature. If we compare this with the experience of a Hindu seer, a Ramakrishna or a Ramana Maharshi to take examples from modern times, we find an essential difference. For the Hindu seer the experience of God is an experience of "identity" of pure being in conscious bliss. This is certainly a profound experience, a genuine experience of God, but it is not the same as the experience of Christ. His was an experience of identity in relationship. He does not say, I am the Father — that he could never say - but "I and the Father are one."[12] It is a unity in duality, by which he can say, "I am in the Father and the Father in me,"[13] which is yet based on an identity of being, by which he can say, "He who sees me, sees the Father."[14] It is the experience of the Absolute in personal relationship, and that would seem to be the distinctive character of the Christian experience of God. For Christ communicates this experience of Sonship to his disciples — "to as many as believed in him, he gave the power to become sons of God"[15] — and this comes about through the gift of the Spirit, by which man is raised to share in the life and consciousness of God.

The significance of the incarnation is, then, that through it mankind is raised to a participation in the divine consciousness. Christ experienced himself as the Logos, the Word of God, expressing the mind of the Father, and communicating the divine spirit to the world. Christ as Logos is the Self of the universe. "In him," as St Paul says, "all things were created."[16] Every created thing from an atom to a man is a "word" of God, and in the Logos, the Word of God, all these "words" are held in the unity of the divine consciousness. When, through sin, this unity was disrupted and man fell from the divine life, then the "Word became flesh,"[17] the Logos assumed the life of the universe and the nature of man to himself and restored it to the unity of the divine life and the divine consciousness. Yet we must not suppose that this "descent" of God implies any change in God. To speak of a "descent" of God or God "becoming" man is to use the language of mythology - though there is no harm in doing so, as long as one understands what one is doing. But strictly speaking by the incarnation God does not descend to man but man is raised to God: a human nature is raised to participation in the nature of God, and in so doing raises up mankind with him. But all this takes place in man; God himself does not change. The whole process of creation, sin, redemption, incarnation and final restoration takes place in man and introduces no change into the being of God, to whom the whole process of time remains always present in its totality.

We may look upon the whole creation, therefore, as a process, by which the universe is being led by a gradual evolution through life in nature and consciousness in man to a participation in the divine life and consciousness. This conception of an evolution of the universe towards an "omega point," an ultimate state, in which life and consciousness converge on the plenitude of life and consciousness in God, has been put before us in recent times in the Christian tradition by Teilhard de Chardin and in the Hindu tradition by Sri Aurobindo. These would seem to represent the most powerful insights of modern man, working within the tradition of orthodox religion, to penetrate into the ultimate meaning of life. In the Christian view we find in Christ the point at which human consciousness, evolved over an immense period of time from matter and life, enters finally into the divine consciousness. In the resurrection of Christ matter itself is transformed and becomes the vehicle of the divine life. In him the universe thus finds its ultimate meaning as an expression of the mind of God. In him human history finds its culmination and man realizes his destiny as Son of God.

11. The Cosmic Christ[18]

In A New Vision of Reality *(1989), Bede has raised the question of the relationship between Jesus' expression for himself in the Gospels, 'the Son of*

Man' and the primordial, representative Man of the biblical tradition. Toward the end of this book, Jesus as Cosmic Person will emerge as the center of Bede's final cosmic and evolutionary synthesis

It is this theme that I particularly want to develop, because this primordial man or cosmic person appears also in the Iranian, Chaldean and Egyptian traditions. In other words, these countries surrounding Israel, Persia, Babylon and Egypt all had this idea of a primordial Man, an archetypal Man, from whom creation comes. The idea of the cosmic Person is also developed in Hinduism, Buddhism and in Islam. It is very much a universal concept. It seems clear that if we see Jesus in that context we have an image which relates him much more meaningfully to the history of the world and to humanity's understanding of God. It is very doubtful whether Jesus himself had any knowledge of these traditions, but I think it is very probable that in his mind he understood himself as that primordial Man. Significant here are the passages in St John's Gospel where Jesus uses the phrase "I am". "I am" is, of course, the name by which Yahweh revealed himself to Moses and it has become customary to think that by using this phrase Jesus is identifying himself with God. The phrase "before Abraham was I am"[19], has certainly been taken to indicate the he must be God. This, I suggest, is not necessarily so. The primordial man was before Abraham and before all men, and I think it is very probable that Jesus is identifying himself there with this primordial or heavenly man, who is prior to all creation.

The evidence from Jewish tradition is very interesting. In that tradition, it is true, there is very little evidence of this primordial man until the Book of Enoch which was written a little before the time of Christ. It was certainly circulating during his time and could therefore have been known to Jesus. In the Book of Enoch the figure of the Son of Man appears and is identified with the Ancient of Days, who is the primordial ancient one who existed before creation. This supports the understanding that when Jesus said, "Before Abraham was, I am," he was identifying himself with that Son of Man, before creation. The text of Enoch also goes on to say that this Son of Man was hidden until his manifestation at the end. He was hidden from the world and would be manifested at the end, and that links him with the

Son of Man in Daniel. Here then there is a Son of Man who existed from the beginning but who would come at the eschaton, the end, and is present now in the world today as the incarnate one. Another point here is that the Son of Man in the Book of Enoch is also identified with the Messiah, and that goes further in corroborating the idea that Jesus would have seen himself in those terms. Although Jesus was reluctant to accept the title of Messiah because it was open to being understood in a purely political sense, yet he could accept it in a transcendent sense.

There was a serious problem for the Jews concerning the Son of Man and Adam. Adam was a fallen man and they therefore found it very difficult to identify the original, primordial Son of Man with Adam, the first man. They did reach a stage, however, when this identification was made. Philo, the great Jewish philosopher who wrote in the first century AD, had an interesting, although quite unacceptable, theory that there were two Adams. The first chapter of Genesis speaks of the Adam who is made in the image of God and Philo says that that Adam was the heavenly, primordial man. On the other hand, the second chapter of Genesis speaks of a man, Adam, made from the dust of the earth and it was this Adam who fell and brought sin into the world. This theory of Philo's is artificial but it does show the problem presented for the Jew by this concept of the heavenly man, and it provides a clue as to why the theme of the heavenly Man was not much developed.

In contrast to the Jews the Gnostics generally took up the concept of the heavenly man and gave it their own interpretation. They held that Adam, the first man, was perfect. He was the archetypal man. The world had fallen away from him and redemption consisted in restoring everything as it had been in the beginning. The end, in other words, was the restoration of the original state. That is typically Gnostic. In the Judaeo-Christian tradition, however, there is always a movement of ascent towards an end. The world is understood as moving forward in an evolutionary ascent towards its ultimate fulfilment and there is no question of simply going back to the beginning.

The archetypal man is said to have been made in the image of God. In the New Testament Jesus is conceived as the *eikon tou theou*, the image of God. He is the one who, as primordial man, comes from heaven. Thus Jesus says in St John's Gospel, "No one has ascended into heaven but he who descended from heaven, the Son of Man."[20]

There is a very interesting passage in St Paul's letter to the Philippians where he speaks of Jesus being in the form of God, the *morphe tou theou*.[21] Most exegetes take this to mean that he was God, but I prefer to follow Oscar Cullman who, in his *Christology of the New Testament* (1967), presents most clearly and convincingly another point of view. The Greek word *morphe*, form, is the same as *murti* in Sanskrit. God has no morphe in Himself. Jesus being in the form or the image of God means not that he was God but that he was this primordial man who was precisely and by definition the image of God. He was the form in which God was revealing himself, the manifestation, that is, or the *morphe* of God. What happened was that he emptied himself of that *morphe*, that heavenly state, and took the form of a man. The universal man became a man and took the form of a slave and, as the suffering servant, accepted death, even death on the cross. So the heavenly man becomes a man and that man accepts suffering and death, and therefore God raised him up. God raised him up from death and gave him a name which was above every name in heaven and on earth. In other words, he was exalted to the supreme state as Lord and as Christ, but not precisely as God.

St Paul developed this further, not using the title Son of Man, but referring to Christ as the second Adam. In the first letter to the Corinthians for instance he wrote, "The first man (Adam) was from the earth, a man of dust; the second man is from heaven."[22] Here Paul is using the same image but he sees the "heavenly man" coming at the end, not at the beginning. Again, he wrote in the letter to the Romans about this first Adam "who was a type (*typos*), of the one who was to come."[23] So in Paul's view Adam is the man who fell, and he is a type of the new man in Christ who is to come and fulfill all things. Paul speaks constantly of the new man in relation to the old, a good example being his exhortation to put off the old man with his evil works and put on the new man created in the likeness of God.[24] And also in the letter to the Ephesians there is the beautiful text to which we referred above, which says that he has "broken down the dividing wall of hostility (between the Jew and the Gentile), that he might create in himself one new man in place of the two, so making peace."[25] This is the idea of Christ as the new man who re-unites broken humanity in himself, and in this sense is the new Adam.

The letter to the Colossians goes further than this when it speaks of Christ as "the image of the invisible God."[26] Christ is the image, the icon, of God who is invisible, and an image in the deepest sense is that which reflects, so the text is saying that Christ reflects, or manifests, the invisible God. It goes on in the same verse to refer to him as "the firstborn of creation", which is to say that Christ is not only the man who comes at the end, but the man who was in the beginning. This is the ancient idea that the spiritual world comes first and the heavenly man is the archetypal man, the man who was in the beginning, who is the exemplar from whom all humanity derives. The original man is precisely the archetype, or the firstborn, of creation. And "in him all things were created. . . all things were created through him and for him,"[27] but, as we saw previously, not by him. God creates all things in Christ, through Christ and for Christ, for this archetypal man. The text of Colossians goes on to say that "in him all things consist."[28] In him all things come together and hold together. He becomes that center which gathers the whole creation in unity. Finally it is said that "in him dwells the fullness of the Godhead bodily." We can see now precisely how it can come to be said that Jesus is God. He receives the fullness of the Godhead "bodily"[29], that is, in his human being. He is the Cosmic Man in whom the fullness of the Godhead is revealed.

This conception of Jesus as the Cosmic Person or Cosmic Lord, who is God's self-manifestation to the world, gives us the key to the New Testament understanding of the relation of Jesus to God. This is shown in the use of the term Son of God, as used both by Jesus himself and by his disciples after him. Whether Jesus himself actually used this language has been debated, but, as Oscar Cullman has shown, it is difficult to avoid the conclusion that it goes back to him, though he used it with great discretion. There is no doubt that Jesus experienced himself in relation to God as a son to a Father. He uses the term *Abba*, "Father," in addressing God, and it has been shown that this was a term of extreme intimacy. This "Abba experience" was fundamental in the life of Jesus. He knew himself in this relation of profound intimacy with God as his Father, and the statement in both St Matthew's and St Luke's Gospels, "No one knows the Son but the Father and no one knows the Father but the Son and he to whom the Son chooses to reveal him,"[30] certainly expresses the mind of Jesus himself. He knew himself in this unique mode of consciousness, which could only be expressed by speaking of himself as the Son in a unique sense. This, of course, becomes the main theme of the Gospel of St John, who was no doubt building on the knowledge of Jesus' own intimate experience.

This is borne out in an interesting way in the letter to the Hebrews, where it is said, "God who in various ways spoke of old to our fathers by the prophets, in these last days has spoken to us by a Son, whom he appointed heir of all things and through whom he made the world."[31] Here Jesus is seen, as in St Paul, as the "heir of all things," that is, as the One who "brings all things to a head" and is the end of all evolution, but also as the Cosmic Person through whom the world was made. But it is most interesting that while the writer of the Letter to the Hebrews has this exalted understanding of the nature of Jesus Christ, he at the same time has the most profound sense of his humanity.

Nowhere in the New Testament is the human frailty of Jesus brought out so profoundly as in this same letter, where it is said, "In the days of his flesh Jesus offered up prayers and supplications with loud cries and tears to him who was able to save him from death and was heard for his godly fear." Again the figure of the heavenly man and the suffering servant are brought together, and it is said, "though he was a Son he learned obedience from the things which he suffered."[32] Once again we see the rich complexity of the New Testament concept of Christ. To this we have only to add the cry of Jesus on the cross, "My God, my God, why have you forsaken me?" to realise the depth of the mystery of Christ, who though he was "in the form of God," yet emptied himself and experienced that sense of separation from God, which is the burden of fallen humanity.

In the Letter to the Hebrews Jesus is also said to be the reflection, the *apaugasma*, and the character, the stamp or impress, the expression of the Godhead.[33] The term *apaugasma* comes from the Book of Wisdom, the last book of the Old Testament, probably written in Alexandria under Platonic influence like the letter to the Hebrews itself. This again expresses the exact relation of Jesus to God as an image, a reflection, a mirror held up to the Godhead.[33] It is this that underlies the conception of the Word, the Logos, of God in St John's Gospel. This Word is conceived primarily as the Word of God which came to the prophets in the Old Testament and has now been fully revealed in Jesus. But it also has a wider significance. The concept of the Logos was widely known in the Greek world in which the Gospel of St John was written, and there can be little doubt that the author of the Gospel was aware of it. The Logos was first conceived by Heraclitus as the Reason by which the universe is governed. In speaking of Jesus as the Logos the Gospel is clearly relating Jesus to that Primordial Word which Philo the Jew had already related to the God of the Old Testament. We come back therefore to that primordial self-manifestation of the Godhead, the Word which expresses the mind of God, which manifests his Person. But St John goes on to say that "all things were made through him and without him was not anything made that was made."[34]

This opens up a new horizon. The Word of God is the expression of the Mind of God, and in the Mind of God are contained the ideas of all created things. The Greek fathers spoke of the logoi or the "energies" (*dunameis*) in creation, which all reflect the Logos, the Primordial Word and the Primordial Energy. In that Word of God the whole creation comes forth eternally. All things come forth from God eternally in his Word and through that Word are brought forth in time and space. Again we see how this Word is none other than the Cosmic Person, the Archetypal Man, through whom everything comes into existence and in whom all things "hold together." All things come forth through the Word in time and in space and are given form by the Word which is the exemplar of all creation. And all things derive their energy from that Uncreated Energy, which is the source of all created energy. At the same time all things are being drawn back to the source of their being by the same power of the Word. As St Paul says, "It was his plan in the fullness of time to bring all things to a head in him, things in heaven and things on earth."[35]

This then is the place of Christ in the perspective of the New Testament. He is not precisely God but the Word of God, the Image of God, the Self-revelation, the Self-manifestation of God, who is reflected in the whole creation and who brings the whole creation back to God. The nearest the New Testament can come to saying that Jesus is God is to say in the Prologue to St John's Gospel that the Word who "became flesh" in Jesus was God (*theos*) with, or in relation to, God (*pros ton theon*). This places Jesus immediately "with God", or better perhaps "in relation to" God, and it is from this that all the later theology of the Trinity derives. It is, therefore, perfectly correct to say that Jesus is God, but always with the qualification that he is "God from God," that is, he receives the Godhead from the Father, which is what characterises him as the Son; and furthermore he is not simply God, but God in man and man in God. He is the "Word made flesh." In this view the Son comes forth eternally from the Father. And this process is not merely a temporal process but an eternal reality. The Son comes forth eternally from the Father as his Self-manifestation, his Self-expression, and manifests God in the whole creation, drawing everything in time and space into the fullness of the divine being. Seen in this perspective Jesus does not appear as an isolated phenomenon, a sudden appearance of God on earth. He is the fulfilment of the whole plan of creation, drawing the manifold of creation back to unity, drawing all humanity back to God, to that fullness of being for which it was created. In this perspective also Jesus can be seen in relation to those other forms of the Primordial Person, the Universal Man, which are found in the traditions of Hinduism, Buddhism and Islam.

12. The World Transformed in Christ[36]
In another chapter of A New Vision of Reality, *Bede develops the cosmic dimension of the Christ-mystery. In this further step toward his final synthesis, the newness which entered the world in the Christ-event is exerting its transformative power upon the elements of the material creation.*

In the Bible itself this incomprehensible Godhead, which is one with the mystical vision of India and of Islam, is revealed in Jesus of

Nazareth. That is the essential Christian faith. The ineffable Godhead, the one absolute reality, was revealed in the historic person of Jesus of Nazareth at a particular time and at a particular place. It has to be emphasized that, in the biblical faith, it is a matter of the infinite being manifest in the finite, the eternal in the temporal, in a specific historical time and place. This is a key point by which the Christian revelation is distinguished from the Hindu and the Buddhist view. For the Hindu the *avatara* is first of all not historical. Many *avataras* are purely mythological, the tortoise, the fish, the boar and the lion, for instance. Even Krishna and Rama, the supreme *avataras*, are not fully historical. They are legendary figures, probably with some historical background, but in their case the historicity is not important. Any Hindu will say that whether Krishna lived or not he is a symbol of the divine, a symbol of the Godhead. As such he is of infinite value, whereas his historicity, or otherwise, is not significant.

It is the same with the Buddha. Buddha was a historical person, no doubt, but for the Buddhist this is not important. There were hundreds of buddhas and *bodhisattvas*, all symbols of the great *sunyata*. But in the Christian tradition the infinite reveals itself in a historic time and place and this gives value to history and time. In the Eastern traditions time is cyclic. In Hindusim everything comes out from the *brahman*, as the *Bhagavad Gita* says, and it returns and comes forth again in endless cycles. But in the Judaeo-Christian tradition all time is moving towards an end, the *eschaton*, which is the final fulfilment of all things. This is why Jesus is said to be not an *avatara* who can come again and again, nor a buddha who has many other buddhas before and after him, but rather the one who brings the whole purpose and meaning of the entire universe to a head. It was the divine plan, "in the fullness of time, to bring all things to a head in him, things in heaven and things on earth."[37] That is one of the central affirmations of the gospel.

The infinite, then, is manifest in Jesus, in this historic person coming within the historical context of Israel. He was the prophet who was expected to initiate the Kingdom of God, the priest who was to reconcile man with God, and also the king, the ruler, the messiah, who was to rule as God, in the place of God. Jesus was born in that historic context and was recognized to be the fulfilment of all these roles as God's revelation on earth. That is the understanding of Jesus within the Hebrew context. Further, Jesus' earthly life ended at the crucifixion and the crucifixion is an historic event. "He was crucified under Pontius Pilate," as the Creed says. It is really an extraordinary thing that it should be of the essence of Christian faith that Jesus was crucified under Pontius Pilate at a particular time in history and under a particular Roman governor. This kind of thing is absolutely alien to Hinduism or Buddhism. When Krishna or Rama, or Buddha in the Mahayana, lived is of no account whatsoever; they are manifestations of the eternal, not confined to any time or place.

Jesus, on the other hand, manifests the infinite God in historic time and place and in his historic death, dying on the cross. There are many ancient myths of the god who dies and rises again but these are symbolic figures and their meaning is deep but different. Jesus' death, on the other hand, is not simply symbolic. He was an historic person, and the descriptions we have of his suffering and death, in the four different accounts in the Gospels, are given in minute detail. On that historic death and on the resurrection the whole Christian faith centres. The experience of the disciples after the death of Jesus, that the body was not to be found in the tomb and Jesus' appearances to them, convinced them that he was risen from the dead. They understood that, unlike Lazarus who was raised from the dead but simply carried on with his limited life in this world, Jesus was alive for evermore, transcending this world. What this means is that in the death and resurrection of Jesus the matter of this world was transformed. In other doctrines, in other great faiths, matter is often conceived simply as an appearance and the appearance disappears when we have reached the one reality. But in the Christian understanding the matter of the universe is transformed. The atoms, the molecules, the cells of Jesus' body, which are part of this cosmic energy, were changed. Matter is a temporary condensation of energy and that structure of energy which made up the body of Jesus on the cross was transformed into a new structure. It may be suggested that in the resurrection that structure of energy became a psychic body, which is a more subtle body. His body was first of all what is called a gross body which anyone could recognize, and then it became a subtle body, which could not always be recognized. This subtle body could appear and disappear, as we know from the Gospel narratives. Finally he becomes a spiritual body at the Ascension. He transcends matter at both the gross and the subtle levels and enters the spiritual level and, with that transformation, the matter of this universe is taken up into the Godhead. That is the Christian mystery. It is amazing when we begin to grasp it, that the matter which exploded in the so-called Big Bang fifteen or even twenty billion years ago at that point was finally transfigured. In fact the transfiguration has been going on all through history and we ourselves are involved in this transformation of matter, as consciousness is working on matter. The Christian understanding is that in Jesus consciousness finally took possession of matter, and this means that matter was spiritualized. In him the matter of the universe was, in other words, made totally conscious and became one with God, in the Godhead.

It is also important to emphasize that the soul of Jesus did not disappear. In the view of Shankara and so many others the *jivatman* disappears at death. You simply realize yourself in the total reality and there is no jiva, no individual, any more. But the soul of Jesus, the unique Jew of the first century with all his personal characteristics, is eternal in the Godhead. It is not that he disappears into the Godhead. Rather, both the body (*soma*) and the soul (*psyche*) are taken up into the spirit (*pneuma*) in the transcendent one and are totally transfigured in the One. This is beyond our comprehension but we can perhaps try to conceive how it takes place.

We see that in Christ the world of space and time is not annihilated; it does not disappear but it is transfigured, and that is precisely what St Paul means by the New Creation. The New Creation is this present creation transformed into the spiritual creation, matter no longer obeying the present laws which, as we know, are related only to this particular stage in evolution. All material laws are simply stages in evolution. At the inorganic level there are certain laws operating, and then new laws come into being as the earliest living creatures emerge. Later, new laws develop pertaining to the animal level and, later still, other new laws develop pertaining to human persons. The next stage is the transcendence of finite being, as we enter into the divine consciousness and into the divine mode of being. That is the New Man of St Paul, which is also the heavenly Man and can be related, as we saw, to the perfect Man of the Muslim tradition and the *purusha* of the Hindu. But there is this great difference here in Christianity, that the individual human being of Jesus does not disappear in the Ultimate but rather is fully realized. As with Kashmir Shaivism and Mahayana Buddhism, the Christian tradition recognizes interrelationship in the Absolute. Shankara denied any relationship or differentiation in the Absolute. For him the Absolute is *saccidananda*, pure being, pure consciousness and pure bliss, with no differentiation whatever. Kashmir Shaivism, on the other hand, maintains the differentiation into Shiva and Shakti which we have discussed , and the *spanda*, the pulse or stirring of will between them which is self-conscious within the One. The One is totally one without duality, yet there is also differentiation. This is expressed in the gospel when Jesus says, "I am in the Father and the Father is in me."[38] If Jesus had been an advaitin he would have said, "I am the Father" or "I am God." Jesus never says that. In saying, "I am in the Father and the Father in me", "I know the Father and the Father knows me," "I love the Father, the Father loves me," Jesus is affirming total interpersonal relationship.

It is very significant indeed that physics now sees the whole universe as a web of dynamic interrelationships. When we come to the human person, our lives are also a network of interrelationships. At the human level the child is related to the mother and then to the father, brothers and sisters, friends and so on, in a web of relationships. The question is, do these relationships disappear in the ultimate? In this Christian understanding there are relationships in the ultimate and Jesus himself expresses this by saying, "I am in the Father and the Father in me," and also when he prays "that they may be one as thou in me and I in thee, that they may be one in us."[39] Jesus' prayer is that as he is in the Father in his personal relationship, so we may also be in him and he in us, which means that we also enter into that interpersonal relationship within the Godhead.

There is a very important concept here. As in Kashmir Shaivism and in Buddhism there is the principle of differentiation in the

Ultimate, so in the Christian view the logos, the Word of God, is the principle of differentiation in the Godhead. The Father is the source, the one, the origin, from which everything comes, and the Father knows himself in the Son. He expresses himself and differentiates himself in the Son. So there is interpersonal relationship there in the ultimate, in eternity. But also, at the very moment that he differentiates himself in the Son he unites himself with the Son in the Spirit, just as in the other doctrines there are the two movements, the going out and coming in, which are identical in the Godhead. We speak of this as being in time, of course, but time is the category of the created universe, not of God. So in the Trinity the Father eternally knows himself, differentiates himself, in the Son, and is eternally united with himself, in the Holy Spirit. So here is the same principle of differentiation in unity that we saw in the other spiritual traditions.

Putting this in another way may perhaps make it more intelligible. The Father expresses himself in the Son, totally and perfectly, but in the Son and in the Word all the potentialities of creation are present and therefore in expressing himself in the Son, the Father expresses the possibilities latent in himself in his Word. St Thomas Aquinas, and the Christian tradition generally, calls these possibilities "ideas" in God. This is based on Plato, where the notion of ideas meant that everything in this world exists first as an eternal idea. Every plant and tree and animal and person has its eternal idea, its archetype, in God. These ideas in God are identical with God. There is no differentiation at that stage. God knows himself in all these. He knows himself in you and in me, eternally. Eckhart says, "God only spoke one word, and in that word the whole creation came into being." Then by an act of the creative will, like the will that stirs between Shiva and Shakti in Kashmir Shaivism, these possibilities of being, these finite possibilities, appear in space and time in the universe as we know it and reflect their archetypes in the One. And as they emerge from the eternal into time they are being drawn back from time and space into the eternal. We are all in that movement of *pravritti* and *nivritti.* So everything comes forth from the Father in the Word and everything is being drawn back to the Father in the Spirit.

13. The Christian Experience of God[40]

For Bede Griffiths, dogma, ritual and religious institution are empty and life-less unless they open the person to spiritual experience. In his sapiential per-spective, doctrine opens to experience, and experience is the manifestation of identity: that is, of a transformation of the self. Thus reuniting theology and spirituality in the totality of the person, he moves beyond the individualized, analytical and 'psychologized' western spirituality of recent centuries. In examining Bede's view of Jesus Christ, we have quickly been led inward to the experience of God in Christ which belongs to those who have become children of God in him.

When Bede sets out, in A New Vision of Reality, *to give an account of the Christian experience of God, he moves quickly to John's Gospel. There, once again, he finds the relationship of Jesus with his Father to be the para-digm for our own experience. If, like John, Bede rarely mentions baptism, he is — again like John — continually unfolding the meaning of baptismal initi-ation: the new union with God in a reciprocal indwelling or interiority, the new communion of love. Two dimensions assert themselves: the realization of a new self in God, and the new relationship of loving communion with God. This communion, in turn, opens into a new relationship of koinonia between human persons, which constitutes the church, or the body of Christ.*

Repeatedly, Bede contrasts the Christian mystical experience with the Hindu experience. He accents the consistent transcendence of God for the Christian; the new union with God is a 'unity in distinction,' a 'communion of love, of personal relationship,' but never the 'identity with God' which the Hindu mystic experiences. The Christian experience is 'always in terms of community,' while the Hindu mystical experience is 'essentially individual.' Bede finds in the sharing of goods among the early Christians an expression of the incarnational dynamic which is distinctive of Christianity: 'the descent of God into the whole context of human life.'

For the Hindu, the unitive experience is a realization of the inner divine Self, or atman; for a Christian, the inner self is not divine but a capacity for grace, for union with God in the gift of the Holy Spirit. Bede's scrupulous the-ological orthodoxy here commands respect, but one may wonder whether Abhishiktananda — like Eckhart and John's Gospel itself — may not, through apparently excessive affirmations of a divine 'identity' conferred upon the human person in faith, have more faithfully expressed the blinding core of the mystery of divinization.

As Bede turns from John to Paul, he traces Paul's expression of the mys-tery in terms of the gift of the Spirit, of incorporation in the body of Christ, and in the final transformation of the earthly body into a spiritual body. If this transformation takes place definitively in the resurrection, Bede — with some spiritual writers of the Christian East — sees it beginning in this present life: sexuality, the 'divine energy in us,' is transformed from a predominantly physical into a spiritual energy.

It is into this [Jewish] tradition, then, with all its expectations, that Jesus comes. It must always be remembered that the God of Jesus is Yahweh, the God of the Old Testament. But of course Jesus brings a new understanding of the nature of God and his relation to humanity. In the later stages of the Old Testament the utter holiness of God was seen as making him utterly separate, totally transcendent. The danger of an utterly transcendent God is that he becomes too remote. He is so much above you that the only way in which you can properly relate to him is in awe and worship and in humble obedience. Jesus brought God down to earth, as it were, in his experience of God as Father. It is generally agreed that his Abba experience was unique. Jesus experienced God in utter closeness to himself and addressed him as "Abba," which is a term of great intimacy. So what happens with Jesus is that this transcendent God of infinite holiness and infinite righteousness, but also of infinite mercy, becomes present to man. He was present in some way in the Temple, no doubt in the king, and had been experienced in his closeness to the people of Israel. But now in the New Testament there is this bringing God down to earth, and making him present in a human being.

Jesus comes to reveal God's presence in himself. He reveals this first of all in terms of the Kingdom or rule of God which he declares is present in himself, but he also reveals God's presence in terms of sonship. He expresses his relationship to God in this way, "No one knows the Son except the Father, and no ones knows the Father except the Son . . . " This is a unique *gnosis*, a unique knowledge. Only the Son knows the Father and only the Father knows the Son. So it is quite clear that he experienced God in a unique way. It is important that we put Jesus into the context of history. Just as we tried to see the Hindu revelation in the context of its history, so we try to see Jesus in the context of his history, and he comes as a man who experiences God as his Father in this absolutely unique way, and sees himself as the Son. But it must not be forgotten that, as we saw before, in the Son he also includes his brethren, all humankind, so that in him and through him this new relationship to God is opened up to all. So he says, "No one knows the Son except the Father, and no one knows the Father except the Son and anyone to whom the Son chooses to reveal him."[41] Jesus makes known this relationship of intimacy, of relationship to God, so that we also can share in that relationship and can know ourselves as children of God.

In St John's Gospel this relationship of the Father and the Son is expressed in the terms, "I am in the Father and the Father in me." That is a relationship of total interiority. But Jesus goes on to pray for his disciples, "that they all may be one; even as thou, Father, art in me, and I in thee, that they also may be in us . . . "[42] So here we have this revelation of total intimacy such that he is *in* the Father and the Father *in* him, and that he wants to share that relationship with his disciples so that they also are in the Father as he is. This is the center of the Christian revelation. The God of Israel, the transcendent holy One manifesting himself in Jesus, reveals this relationship of Father to Son, of Son to Father, and communicates that relationship to his disciples in the Spirit. That is the central Christian revelation and the central Christian experience. It must always be remembered that what is revelation from one point of view is experience from the other. There is no revelation coming down from above without any relation to human experience. It always has to be experienced in order to be revealed. It is only through our experience that we know God.

Jesus can say then, "I and the Father are one."[43] He knows himself as one with the Father, and yet, as we saw, in distinction from the Father. He does not say, "I am the Father" but "I and the Father are one." This is unity in distinction. This mutual interpenetration combining unity and distinction developed, as we shall see in the next chapter, in the whole course of Christian mysticism, as one of its fundamental elements. This is what distinguishes the Christian experience of God from that of the Hindu. The Hindu in his deepest experience of *advaita* knows God in an identity of being. "I am brahman," "Thou art that." The Christian experiences God in a communion of being, a relationship of love, in which there is none the less perfect unity of being.

When Jesus reveals himself as one with his disciples he uses the striking image of the vine. "I am the vine. You are the branches. Abide in me, and I in you."[44] We cannot hope for a more intimate relation that this, the vine and the branches. He is the vine and we are the branches of the vine. We share in his life, not separate from him but as truly part of him as branches of the vine. So Jesus comes to reveal that life in God and to communicate that life to us so that we also, in and through him, become sons of God and experience the Spirit as he does. And so later on St John in his letter can say, "Our *koinonia*, our common life, is with the Father and with his Son Jesus Christ."[45] We as a community share in the knowledge and love of the Father and the Son. We share in their life.

Jesus communicates to his disciples the mystical experience he has of his relation to the Father and they form a community, a koinonia, with him. *Koinos* means "common" and *koinonia* is "common life," "community." The Christian mystical experience is always in terms of community. The Hindu experience is essentially individual and has no positive relationship to the community whereas the Christian experience, although certainly personal and individual, is always also implicitly or explicitly a community experience. This is very important. It comes out clearly in the Acts of the Apostles when, after Pentecost, the Spirit descends on the disciples. Jesus had promised them that when he departed he would send the Spirit and that the Spirit would abide with them. So the Spirit descends and then it is said that the disciples were all "of one heart and soul." The experience unites the people together in one. Then another dimension of the experience is revealed. "They sold their possessions and goods and distributed them to all, as any had need."[46] So the descent of the Spirit forms the community and the community is such that in it everything is shared, even at the economic level. This is a particularly Christian understanding. It is the descent of God into the whole context of human life. That is the primary importance of the historic dimension, that God is always seen in relation to the human world, to human history and to human relationships. As St John brings out very strongly in his letter, anyone who does not love his brother whom he has seen, cannot love God whom he has not seen.[47] So this love of God is totally expressed in the love of our neighbor. Love of God and love of neighbor can never be separated. Comparing this with *bhakti* in Hinduism, *bhakti* is always a personal relationship to God, a self-transcendence, going beyond and being one with God, but, although the relation to the neighbour is certainly there, it is not normally expressed. It is an experience of identity, not of relationship. The relationship to the neighbour is implicit but not explicit, whereas in the Christian context the relation to the neighbour is always explicit and fundamental. And so it is an experience of God in the Spirit which brings this experience of being of one heart and one soul with others, and this then spreads out into daily life in the sharing of the goods of the world. These three aspects characterise the Christian mystical experience in the New Testament.

In St Paul we find these three aspects very clearly brought out. First of all St Paul develops the doctrine of the Spirit. In the Synoptics and even in the Fourth Gospel it is very little developed, whereas in St Paul it is basic. In the first letter to the Corinthians he makes very clear the relationship between the human spirit and the divine Spirit. He says that God is "revealed to us through the Spirit. For the Spirit searches everything, even the depths of God." Through Jesus, particularly through his death and resurrection, the Spirit has been communicated and now this Spirit encounters our spirit. The text continues, "For what person knows a man's thoughts except the spirit of the man which is in him? So also no one comprehends the thoughts of God except the Spirit of God."[48] So in us there is a spirit by which we know ourselves and by which also we can know God. At that point of the spirit we are open to the Spirit of God. There is a very important distinction between the Hindu and the Christian understanding here. In the Hindu tradition there is *jivatman*, the individual self, and there is *paramatman*, the supreme Self. But in the normal understanding, as seen in the advaitic school, the individual self is identified with the supreme Self. "I am brahman." "Thou art that." It is an identity with the Absolute. That is a genuine and profound mystical experience without a doubt. By contrast, in the Christian understanding the human spirit is never identified with the Spirit of God.

The spirit in man is rather the capacity for God, the capacity to receive, and always the experience of God comes as a gift, as a grace from above. So the spirit of man receives the Spirit of God. This St Paul brings out in the letter to the Galatians where he says, "God had sent the Spirit of his Son into our hearts crying Abba! Father!".[49] That is an exact description of the Christian mystical experience. God had sent the Spirit of his Son into our heart or into our spirit. In the Spirit we are united with Christ the Son. We become sons in the Son and we are able to say, "Abba, Father." We share in Jesus' experience of the Father. We enter into the dynamic of the trinitarian experience. In the Spirit we become one with the Son and in the Son we are able to know the Father. The whole Christian tradition is based on the experience of the Trinity. The Trinity is not a dogma revealed from on high but an experience, an experience first of all of Jesus in his relation to the Father, and then of the disciples of Jesus who share his experience in the Spirit.

In the letter to the Romans Paul clarifies this by saying, "When we cry Abba, Father, it is the Spirit himself bearing witness with our spirit that we are children of God."[50] The Spirit of God enters into our spirit and actually transforms it, and our spirit is revealed as a capacity for the Spirit of God. Through that we realise ourselves as children of God. This is very close to the Hindu experience of the atman, but in the Christian understanding the spirit in man is a capacity, a receptive power; it is not identical with the Spirit of God. We receive the Spirit and in that Spirit we know ourselves as sons. Experiencing this sonship, in relation to the Father, we return to the source in the Father. But this experience of God in the Spirit can only take place when we have died to ourselves. "You have died and your life is hidden with Christ in God," says St Paul. We are dead. We died to ourselves in baptism and this dying goes on in the whole Christian life which is a continual process of dying to ourselves, to the ego, and identifying with our real Self which is hidden with Christ in God. In other words, it is a continual going beyond creaturely existence to experience the true Self in Christ in its ultimate transcendence, hidden in God. It is a going beyond, into the Ultimate. The way St Paul[51] expresses this is authentic mystical doctrine.

If we now finally compare the Hindu and the Christian mystical experience we see in the Hindu the profound exploration of the Spirit, the *atman*, the Spirit within, and we see how this implies the transcendence of the lower self, the ego, and the experience of the ultimate Self. Furthermore, that ultimate Self is conceived in the form of a person, *purusha*, to whom we give our love, our *bhakti*, and we realize that that person loves us. As Krishna says in the *Bhagavad Gita*, "You are dear to me."[52] God loves us. So there is in Hinduism a profound experience of self-transcendence, opening the divine, experiencing the divine as the very inner Self but at the same time as one who is the object of love and who gives love. Then there is the stage of going beyond that, as we saw, to the ultimate oneness, to ultimate unity. The Christian experience is distinctive in that identity with God is not claimed. In the Hindu experience the immanence of God is dominant and there is more concern with realizing God as within one and oneself as within God, whereas for the Christian, coming out of the Hebrew background, God is always transcendent and one never identifies oneself with God. There is always a distinction between God and the human person. The point is, however, that in Jesus, although that distinction is always present, total unity in distinction takes place. Jesus as man is one with God, with the Father. He knows himself as the Son in a unique way and calls us also through the Spirit to become sons, to experience the ultimate oneness with the Father. However all this is a gift of God, a grace, transforming us. It is essentially a communion of love. It is a communion so profound that we know ourselves as one with God as Jesus is one with the Father, but at the same time it is a communion of love, of personal relationship, of being "all in each and each in all."

Thus we experience God in unity and distinction in the mystery of the Trinity, but we also experience ourselves as living in one another as members of the body of Christ. St Paul particularly develops the striking image that we are members of the body of which Christ is the head. Just as Jesus spoke of the vine and its branches, St Paul speaks of the head and its members. Each of us experiences through the Holy Spirit, through the power of love, this unity in the body where we are distinct members of the one body. We share the one life, members of the one Person, but each distinct in his or her place. We are, as St Augustine put it, persons within the Person, a communion of persons in love.

This mystical community experience also penetrates into the physical world. It is the whole creation that, as we saw, has been restored to unity with God through Christ, and our whole person, including the physical body, is not discarded but is rather transfigured. That the body itself is holy is a fundamental aspect of Christian experience. St Paul speaks of the body as the "temple of the Holy Spirit" and declares that "the body was not made for immorality but for the Lord."[53] This is deeply significant. It means that sexuality is itself holy. It is a divine energy within us. It can be used for immorality but it can also be consecrated to God, whether in marriage or in virginity. In both cases it is the same energy which is being used, either externally in a physical relationship or internally in a spiritual relationship. The ultimate aim of life is, in fact, to convert this physical energy into a spiritual energy, so that the body itself becomes what St Paul calls a "spiritual body," that is, a body which has been wholly penetrated by the divine Spirit. This is the meaning of resurrection. Every human body is created for the resurrection, which means for the gradual transformation of the physical energy of the body into a spiritual energy which is no longer subject to the ordinary laws of matter. Matter, as we know it, is conditioned by space and time, but the body in the resurrection is beyond space and time. This was revealed in the body of Christ at the resurrection. He appeared to his disciples in a "subtle" body, a body which is already not determined by ordinary space and time, but could appear and disappear at will. Then at the ascension he passed beyond space and time altogether and entered into the eternal order of being, transcending this world.

14. The mystery of the Holy Spirit[54]
Christian experience is the actualization of the mystery of Christ in the Holy Spirit. Bede Griffiths was a man of the Spirit and when, in Return to the Center, *he turns to write about the Holy Spirit, the expansive movement of his thought overflows all the distinctions of theological science. The Spirit is divine energy, life and love. It is 'the feminine principle in the Godhead,' the dynamic principle of evolution and of consciousness and of human transfor-*

mation. We feel here the presence of the divine Sophia,[55] *the mysterious woman who is the divine Wisdom, who labored with God to bring forth the creation and who is present everywhere and "though she is but one,... can do all things."*[56]

Perhaps the proper language of the Spirit is poetry rather than prose, and perhaps with graceful necessity she resists and exceeds definition as does springtime, music or love. Bede, once again attentive to theological precision, offers some cautious distinctions along with his inclusive equations. The word 'Spirit' is ambiguous, however, also in Bede. It represents the highest of the three spheres of reality which we have considered. It is the divine Spirit, within the trinity of divine Persons. This Spirit is poured out upon believers, but already present in the hearts of all people — and indeed within every creature. There is some tension here between Spirit as divine gift and Spirit as an intrinsic principle within the human person.

Bede also equates the Holy Spirit with the atman, the divine Self which is present in every person — and indeed in every created being. One perceives a strain here as well, for Bede has already identified the Spirit as the divine feminine principle. Is the Self, then, feminine? A further problem is involved in his conception of the Spirit as the active principle in creation, evolution and human development, since he had characterized the feminine principle in creation and in the human person as the passive, receptive and maternal principle. Corresponding to the creative 'Form' which is the divine Word, the Spirit is described here as the divine Energy which generates, enlivens, guides, transforms and consummates creation.

Bede's intuitions about the Holy Spirit are infinitely suggestive; each affirmation opens further questions. How does the newness that comes into the world with Christ relate to the universal immanence of the Spirit in creation and in humanity? What is the interaction between Word and Spirit in history and within the individual person? How is this related to the masculine-feminine polarity within humanity which Bede has frequently affirmed? What particular lines of manifestation of the Spirit characterize East and West? What is the relation of the Holy Spirit to human creativity in its various forms? Bede's understanding of the 'Third Person' of Christian tradition is evocative, dynamic and profound — and may leave us with the conviction that in trying to gain an understanding of the Spirit we are always at the beginning.

We come forth from the Father in the Son and we return to the Father in the Spirit. The Spirit is the *Sakti* — the power — of the Godhead, the breath by which the Word is uttered, the energy which flows from the Father into the Word and overflows in the creation. It is by the Spirit that the 'ideas' in the Word are given form and substance and the creation comes into being. "The Spirit of God was moving over the face of the waters."[57] The Spirit is the feminine principle in the Godhead, the Mother of all creation. It is in her that the seeds of the Word are planted and she nurtures them and brings them forth in creation. The Spirit is the source of energy in the stars and atoms, of life in plants and animals. It is the source of evolution in the universe. It is the Spirit in man which first gives us life "the Lord God 'breathed into his nostrils the breath of life; and man became a living being"[58] and then awakens consciousness in us. It is the Spirit which is continually drawing us into the divine life. For the Spirit is that divine life latent in the universe from the beginning, latent in nature and becoming conscious in us. By the Spirit we know that we are not merely flesh and blood, formed from the matter of the universe, not merely the subject of sensations, feelings, imaginations and thoughts, but an energy of love which seeks always to transcend the barriers of space and time and to discover the divine life. The Spirit is this energy of love in us, this power of the divine. It is the Source of our real being, by which we become conscious of the divine life in us and know ourselves as sons of God.

The Spirit is the atman, the Self, which dwells in the heart of every creature. It is this Spirit of which it is said: "It is not born, it does not die; it sprang from nothing, nothing sprang from it. It is the ancient, unborn, eternal, everlasting. It is not killed though the body is killed. It is smaller than the small, greater than the great. Though sitting still, he walks far; though lying down, he goes everywhere. He is bodiless within bodies, unchanging among things that change."[59] "It is inside all this and it is outside all this."[60] The Spirit is one in everyone and in everything. It is ever the same, yet it appears different. Just as the light of the sun is ever the same but appears in different colors according to the nature of the thing in which it shines. So the Spirit manifests in each thing according to its capacity to receive it. It is energy, light and heat in the sun and the stars, life in plants and animals, consciousness in man. It adapts itself to the capacity of every man. It is the speed of the athlete, the skill of the artist, the imagination of the poet, the intelligence of the philosopher, the wisdom of the seer. Or rather it is the Source of all these things, containing all power in itself and remaining for ever unchanged. The life of the body, the thoughts and feelings of the soul, are alike the effects of the Spirit in man. It is the source of our very individuality, what makes us capable of judgement and choice and decision, the principle of freedom and responsibility. In every man the same Spirit is present, adapting itself to his capacities. Of this Spirit it is said: '[She] is more mobile than any motion; because of her pureness she pervades and penetrates all things."[61]

We must be careful to distinguish between the soul and the Spirit. The soul is the jivatman, the source of our separate existence, of our individual being. It is what Aristotle calls the 'form' of the body, that which gives life to the body and determines us to a bodily existence. But the soul is also the source of reason and free will, by which it is open to the Spirit, the Paramatman. The Spirit is the source of unity and universality, the soul of diversity and individuality. If the soul identifies itself with the body, it becomes enclosed in its separate existence, but if it opens itself to the Spirit, it can transcend its separate individuality and realize its identity with the Spirit. When the soul identifies itself with the body, man becomes the natural or 'psychic' man of St Paul,[62] who lives "according to the flesh;"[63] when the soul identifies itself with the Spirit, it becomes the spiritual man, who lives "according to the Spirit."[64]

This identification takes place through the activity of the mind and the will, either accepting the 'law of the flesh' and submitting to the appetites and desires, or accepting the 'law of the Spirit' and allowing itself to be transformed. When the soul submits to the law of the flesh, though it appears to be acting freely, it is really subjecting itself to the law of nature — to *prakriti*, to the law of *karma* — so that it becomes bound by its actions. When it submits to the law of Spirit, it becomes passive to the action of the Spirit. The mind and the will become instruments of the Spirit. But it is not a forced submission imposed from without; it is a free and loving submission, the Spirit working from within, confirming the judgement of the mind and establishing the freedom of the will. In fact, the Spirit is the source of all the action, both of the body and of the soul, but when the soul refuses to acknowledge this and asserts its own independence, it blocks the free movement of the Spirit and blinds its own judgement. When the veil of egoism is taken away, it opens itself to the light of the Spirit and allows it to act freely.

But what is the exact relation of the soul to the Spirit? The *Upanishads* speak of two birds on one tree, of which one eats the fruit, while the other looks on without eating.[65] The first is the *jivatman*, the individual soul, which eats the fruit of this world and becomes subject to the law of nature, of birth and death. The second is the *Paramatman*, the supreme Spirit, which is ever one and the same, the silent witness of the activity of the soul. When the soul looks up and beholds the Spirit, the eternal Ground of its being, who is also the Lord, the Creator, it is released from the bondage to nature and becomes one with the Spirit. As St Paul says: "He who is united to the Lord becomes one spirit with him."[66] But does the soul then become God? It depends what one means by 'becoming God'. Obviously, the relation between God and the soul, or between *jivatman* and *Paramatman*, cannot properly be expressed, because one of the terms is the absolute Transcendence which is beyond our comprehension. Sankara[67] evades the difficulty by saying that the jivatman has no real existence. It is a mere appearance of the one, eternal Spirit, with no more reality than the form of a snake which is mistakenly imposed on a piece of rope. The rope — the *Paramatman* — is the one reality; the snake — the appearance of the *jivatman* — is the product of *maya*. The soul in reality is the Spirit and there is no essential difference between them. Ramanuja says that the soul in *moksha*, that is, in its final state of liberation, is joined to the Lord without ceasing to be different from him, and enjoys an intuitive vision of the supreme Spirit.[68] Madhva will only say that the soul, which is eternally different from God, comes to dwell with him and has continual sight of him.[69] Saiva Siddhanta comes, perhaps, nearest to a Christian view when it says that the soul by grace shares in the very nature of Siva, the supreme God, and becomes one with him in love without losing its individuality.[70]

What, then, is the Christian view of this relationship? We have to say that originally the soul exists in God in an absolute identity of being beyond all distinctions.[71] When the soul comes into being in the

Word, as an eternal idea in the mind of God, it still has no separate being. As Aquinas says, the 'ideas' in God by which he knows all possible and existent beings are identical with the divine being.[72] They are distinct not in reality (*in re*) but only in conception (*ratione*). It is only when the Spirit of God, his eternal will and energy, gives existence to the soul, that it begins to have a separate being. Even so, all that the soul has of being comes wholly from the Spirit, it has nothing of itself at all. All that the soul has of itself is its limitation of being, which is determined by the body which it informs. The one Spirit, therefore, which is ever one and the same the *Paramatman* is present to every soul, giving it existence, sustaining it in existence and drawing it into union with itself. In other words, in each one of us there is a soul which gives 'form' to the matter of the body, which determines us to a bodily existence and which is subject to all the passions of the body. But in each of us there is also a presence of the Spirit, which gives existence to the soul as well as to the body for the Spirit is present in every particle of matter, giving it existence and form and substance which watches over the soul, inspires and directs its mind and will, and enables it to awaken to its source of being in the Spirit and to be transformed by its power. But what is this transformation? The soul discovers its source of being in the Spirit, the mind is opened to this inner light, the will is energized by this inner power. The very substance of the soul is changed; it is made a "partaker of the divine nature."[73] And this transformation affects not only the soul but also the body. The matter of the body its actual particles is transformed by the divine power and transfigured by the divine light like the body of Christ at the resurrection. This is the 'divinization' of man, which will be manifested in the resurrection of all men. "We shall all be changed, in a moment, in the twinkling of an eye, at the last trumpet. For the trumpet will sound, and the dead will be raised imperishable, and we shall be changed. For this perishable nature must put on the imperishable, and this mortal nature must put on immortality."[74]

This is *moksha*, this is final release, but it is not a release from the body or the soul, but the taking up of body and soul into the life of the Spirit. Both body and soul here realize all their potentialities. Matter, according to Aristotle, is potentiality. It has no being in itself, only an infinite capacity for being. It is Spirit which gives being and actuality to matter, building up the stellar universe and the innumerable forms of life, drawing out the infinite potentiality of matter into ever new forms of being. In the human being matter transcends itself, it emerges into consciousness. The Spirit working within matter draws this new mode of being from the potentiality of matter. But our present mode of consciousness determined by the present state of our bodily existence is only a transition phase in the evolution of matter. The presence of psychic powers in human nature which transcend our normal consciousness is already evidence of this. Extra-sensory perception, telepathy, thought-reading, foreseeing the future, appearing at a distance, spiritual healing in various ways, are all now well attested. In the science of Yoga there are various powers, or *siddhis*, by which the control of the mind over the body and the expansion of the powers of the mind can be developed.[75] But all this is only a foretaste of that radical transformation of the matter of the body which will take place in the resurrection.

15. Spirit as Mother[76]

This vigorous piece appeared in The Tablet *as a meditation for Trinity Sunday. Bede Griffiths has long been aware of the 'masculine' imbalance of historical Christianity, and he proposes that the feminine is to be found - somehow - within the theological heart of Christian tradition, that is in the divine Trinity. Bede marshals all the biblical suggestions that he can find which would support a feminine understanding of the Holy Spirit. The strongest of these indications is the Sophia, or feminine divine Wisdom of the late Old Testament tradition. This feminine figure disappears in early Christianity, as the divine Wisdom is understood to find its definitive expression in the man who is Jesus Christ. Bede is aware that she continues to question Christianity and especially today when the patriarchal structures of thought and institution begin to lose their exclusive grip upon us. Sophia had begun to emerge for Bede from the pages of the Old Testament many years earlier, when he was first discovering the Bible.[77] This feminine voice of wisdom seemed to be whispering within his heart when he turned his back on the West to seek the other half of his soul in India.*

Now, however, it is in the context of the contemporary church and its glaring needs that Bede passionately argues for the introduction of this feminine principle of understanding into the theology and spirituality of the Christian

West. Our tradition has not yet integrated the realities of sexuality and marriage, and has not yet allowed women to find their place or their voice in the church. Does the vitality of Christianity itself depend upon the recognition of this feminine principle as a divine Energy, and its emergence into an unfettered interaction with the Word?

Bede's forceful presentation of the Holy Spirit as 'divine Feminine' refers us to images of receptivity and maternity. Other visions of the feminine are finding expression in our time. Is not the Holy Spirit — or divine Feminine, Sophia — the very principle of newness and creativity, continually springing forth and never grasped, bringing forth that which has not yet been conceived by the human mind?

One of the greatest defects of the Christian religion, whether Protestant, Orthodox or Catholic, is that it has no concept of God as Mother. The Holy Trinity in Christian tradition consists of the Father, the Son and the Holy Spirit. The Father and the Son are both masculine by definition and even the Holy Spirit, though it appears as a dove or as tongues of fire, is usually referred to as "he." This is surely very strange, since the Supreme Being is by nature neither masculine nor feminine, and there is no reason why it should be represented as masculine rather than feminine. The reasons why it is so represented in the Hebrew tradition are clearly sociological. The Jews were a patriarchal people, and man alone was held to have supreme authority in the home and in public affairs. St Paul even suggests a theological reason for this, saying that "man is the image and glory of God, but woman is the the glory of man" and "man was not made from woman but woman from man, neither was man created for woman but woman for man."[78] But this is a view which would hardly be accepted today. It is clearly based on a peculiar Jewish understanding of man. For the Hindu there is no such problem. Even in the Vedas God is addressed as both Father and Mother, and the Hindu devotee calls on God as "my Father, my Mother." The name of Siva, the figure of the Supreme God, can be masculine, feminine or neuter, and Siva is often represented as male and female.

Is it possible to discover a feminine aspect of God in the Christian tradition? I believe that it is. Though Yahweh in the Old Testament is generally represented as a very masculine figure, yet there is another side to him, and Isaiah puts into the mouth of

Yahweh the touching words: "Can a woman forget her sucking child, that she should not have compassion on the son of her womb? Yes, these may forget, yet will I not forget thee."[79] In the New Testament we have also the beautiful saying of Jesus: "O Jerusalem, Jerusalem, killing the prophets and stoning those who are sent to you. How often would I have gathered your children together, as a hen gathers her brood under her wings, but you would not."[80] These are clear indications of a feminine aspect in God, but they do not take us very far. But there are two aspects of Old Testament thought, which would seem to give a solid basis for a conception of God as Mother. The first is that the Hebrew word for Spirit — *ruach* — is feminine. The significance of this is not developed in the Old Testament, but in the Syriac tradition, which is akin to the Hebrew, the word *ruha* or *ruho* remains feminine, and this led to the actual conception of the Holy Spirit as Mother. The expression "our Mother the Holy Spirit" is found in the *Odes of Solomon* at the beginning of the 2nd century, in the *Gospel of Thomas* at the beginning of the 3rd century; and in Aphraates in the 4th century. Here then one can say that there was a tradition in the church which recognised the Holy Spirit as feminine and could speak of her as Mother. But unfortunately, the word for Spirit in Latin is masculine and in Greek neuter, so that this development did not take place in the Greek or Latin church.

There is, however, another concept in the Old Testament, that of Wisdom, which also has a feminine form, the word *hochmah*. Fortunately in this case both the Greek and the Latin had feminine nouns for wisdom — *sophia* and *sapientia* — so that the concept of a feminine figure of Wisdom was preserved in all three traditions. In the Greek tradition this led to the dedication of the famous church of Constantinople to *Hagia Sophia* or Holy Wisdom, and to the development of a form of sophiology by Russian writers like Soloviev in the last century, in which this aspect was given great importance. In the Latin church these passages from the books of Wisdom, which referred to a feminine Wisdom, were applied to the Virgin Mary, but in the original Hebrew tradition, wisdom is quite clearly an attribute of God himself. In the book of Proverbs we read: "The Lord possessed me in the beginning of his way, before his works of old. I was set up from everlasting, from the beginning, ere ever the earth was...I was daily his delight, rejoicing ever before him."[81] Again in the book of Sirach we read: "Wisdom shall praise herself and glory in the midst of her people. In the congregation of the Most High shall she open her mouth and glory in the presence of his power. I came forth from th mouth of the Most High."[82] Finally, in the book of Wisdom, we have the clearest testimony: "Wisdom is more mobile than any motion, yes, she pervades and penetrates all things by reason of her pureness. For she is a breath of the power of God and a clear effluence of the glory of the Almighty. Therefore can nothing defiled find entrance into her. For she is an effulgence from everlasting light and an unspotted mirror of the working of God and an image of his goodness."[83]

It is obvious that we have in these texts a clear affirmation of a feminine aspect in God. In the early church these texts were applied sometimes to the Son and sometimes to the Spirit, but as the Latin church could find no place for a feminine aspect in God, they were eventually applied to the Virgin Mary, where the application is, to say the least, very remote. Would it not be possible for the church today to apply these texts to the Holy Spirit, thus recognizing a feminine aspect in God? In his brief period of office, Pope John Paul I spoke once of God as Mother. This is, I believe, the first time that a Pope or any authority in the western church has spoken of God as Mother. Could this not be a precedent for a further development of the doctrine of the Holy Spirit as Mother? This does not mean, of course, that the Holy Spirit is properly feminine, but that just as there is a father figure in Christian life and worship, as well as the figure of the Son, so also there should be a mother figure to represent the feminine aspect of God. It is permissible to speak of God as both Father and Mother, and Julian of Norwich even speaks of Christ as our Mother. But it seems most appropriate to use the feminine gender of the Holy Spirit, both because of the tradition of the Old Testament, which we have mentioned, and because of the characteristic of the feminine is *receptivity*, and this would seem to be also the characteristic of the Holy Spirit. In the first chapter of Genesis the Spirit is described as "brooding" over the waters. She is the mothering spirit, who receives the seed of the Word and nourishes it and brings forth the created world. In the same way when Mary is about to conceive, it is said that the Holy Spirit "overshadowed" her. The Spirit prepares the womb in which the son of God is to be received. Can we not think of the Holy Spirit as the Mothering Spirit, who lies deep in the heart of all creation, nourishing the seeds of the Word and "groaning in travail," as St Paul puts it, to bring the whole creation to fulfilment? Even in the Holy Trinity itself, could we not say that the Holy Spirit is the "receptive" power of God, the womb, in which the Father places the seed of the Word?

These are speculations and I put them forward for what they are worth. But the need to study the feminine aspect of God and to give it a place in our theology is surely evident. The practical consequences of this are also only too clear. When God is conceived as wholly masculine in character, it is almost inevitable that the church should be dominated by the male sex. The place of woman in the church and the very nature of sex and marriage would all be affected by a proper understanding of the place of the feminine in God. Perhaps it will only be when we have learned to recognise God as Mother that woman will find her rightful place in the church.

16. Fullness: The Christian Mystery[84]

When Bede Griffiths steps back, in Return to the Center, *to look at Christianity as a whole, it is as 'Mystery' that he sees it. This is the perspective that corresponds to his basic orientation towards wisdom and a wisdom theology. Turning aside from the rationalized conceptions of the Christian theology of his time, he goes to the heart of the matter: the mystery of Christianity is 'a participation in the inner life of the Godhead.' It is known solely by a participation in the experience of Jesus. Here is the core of the vision both of the New Testament and of patristic Christianity, which has remained accessible in the theology of Eastern Christianity. Only with the movements of biblical, patristic and liturgical recovery which prepared the way for Vatican II did this vision begin to re-emerge within Catholicism. At this time it became possible once again to understand the life of Christian faith as participation in a single all-comprehending reality, radically simple and impervious to rational analysis. Bede, already thoroughly at home on this unitive level of understanding, unfolds the central Mystery with a lucidity which prob-*

112

ably owes much to his years of immersion in the Vedanta.

Bede writes successively of Trinity, Incarnation, eucharist, church, and returns to the simplicity of his starting point — but now as a mystery of divine love, manifesting itself in the world and communicating itself to humanity. It is in the light of this vision, he proposes, that we are to evaluate the doctrines, the ritual and the institutional organization of the church. Everything is to be judged — and recreated — in the light of this interior Mystery and its realization in the life and experience of human persons in this world.

Every religious doctrine always ends in mystery. According to Christian faith the mystery of the Godhead is revealed as a Trinity. But what is this Trinity? It has been put into conceptual terms in the formal 'three persons in one nature or essence'. But 'persons', 'nature' and 'essence' are simply terms of Greek philosophy which have been used to make this mystery intelligible to the rational mind. The mystery itself derives from the experience of Jesus. Jesus experienced himself in relation to God as a son to his father,[85] but this sonship was not merely temporal but eternal. He knew himself as coming from the Father not only in time but in eternity.[86] He knew himself as eternally one with the Father, as dwelling in the Father and the Father in him.[87] Again, he knew himself as communicating in the Spirit, which comes from God and is communicated to the world, and this also not only in time but in eternity.[88] To understand the mystery of the Trinity it is necessary to participate in the experience of Jesus. It is necessary to receive the Spirit of God, to share in the divine life and so to become the son of God, to be one with Jesus as he is one with the Father.[89] This is the mystery of Christianity, this participation in the inner life of the Godhead, a mystery which cannot be expressed in words, but which is indicated by analogy by the words 'Father', 'Son' and 'Spirit'. If we stop at the words or the concepts signified by them, we shall always remain outside, unenlightened. But if we pass beyond the words and the concepts to the reality signified by them, then we know the Truth, then we are one with God.

It is the same with the incarnation. Jesus knew himself as a man, a man like us in all things except for sin.[90] He is man as God intended him to be, as every man aspires to be. He is the perfect man, the model of human nature. But he also knew himself in the depths of his being, in the eternal ground of his soul, as God, as the Word of God expressing the mind of God, as the Son manifesting the Father.[91] This mystery has been expressed by saying that in the person of Jesus there are two natures, a divine and a human nature. He is perfect God and perfect man. But again, 'person' and 'nature' are terms of Greek philosophy: they translate the mystery of Christ into rational terms. But if we would know the mystery, we must share in the experience of Jesus. We must know ourselves as sons of God, eternally coming forth from the Father, as words of God expressing his mind. We have to know ourselves as God, God by participation in the divinity of Christ, as we participate in his humanity.

This mystery of the kingdom of God, of the divine life among men, is revealed, then, in the doctrine of the Trinity and the Incarnation, of the Father sending his Son into the world and communicating his Spirit, of the Word becoming flesh, the eternal Wisdom manifesting itself, in a human life. But every religion needs not only a doctrine but also a ritual. The divine Mystery has to be expressed not only in words but also in actions. A ritual action is an action by means of which the divine Mystery is symbolized; the exterior rite reveals and communicates the interior reality. Such is the ritual of the Eucharist. The day before he surrendered his life on the cross Jesus took bread and wine and blessed them and gave them to his disciples in a ritual action which he told them to repeat in memory of him.[92] By this ritual action the mystery of his death and resurrection, of the divine life communicated to men, was symbolized and made present. Here, under the symbols of bread and wine, the divine life is present among men, the eternal Wisdom gives itself to be the food of men, the unutterable mystery of the divine love offering itself in sacrifice to the world is shared in a ritual meal. This in turn is a symbol of the fact that this divine Mystery is present everywhere, present in the earth and its produce, present wherever human beings meet and share together, present in every gesture of unselfish love.

The church as a visible institution is constituted by the Eucharist. For the church in this sense is simply the community of those who have recognized the presence of the divine life, of the kingdom of God, in Jesus, and who meet together to share this divine life in the ritual meal which he instituted. But, of course, the divine life is not confined to the Eucharist. It is present everywhere and in everything, in every religion and in every human heart. The Eucharist is the 'sacrament' of the divine life the outward and visible sign of this divine mystery instituted by Christ and the church itself is the 'sacrament' of the kingdom of God, the sign of God's presence on earth. It has the value of a sign, of something which makes known the hidden mystery. The doctrine, the ritual and the organization of the church all belong to the world of signs, to the sacramental order, which manifests the divine Mystery, the one eternal Truth, by means of human words and actions and a human organization. The danger is that the signs may be taken for the reality, the human may overshadow the divine, the organization stifle the Spirit which it is intended to serve.

What, then, is the essential Truth which is signified by the doctrine, the ritual and the organization of the church? If we attempt to put it into words we can say that it is the presence of the divine life among men, of the infinite, eternal, transcendent mystery of being, which is the Ground of all religion and of all existence, manifesting itself in the person of Jesus Christ. In this revelation the mystery of being reveals itself as a mystery of love, of an eternal love ever rising from the depths of being in the Godhead and manifesting itself in the total self-giving of Jesus on the cross and in the communication of that love to men in the Spirit. The organization of the church, with its doctrine of Trinity and Incarnation and its eucharistic ritual, has no other purpose than to communicate this love, to create a community of love, to unite all men in the eternal Ground of being, which is present in the heart of every man. This is the criterion by which the church is to be judged, not by the forms of its doctrine or ritual, but by the reality of the love which it manifests. Yet though this love must be manifested, it remains in itself a hidden mystery. It cannot be judged by any external standards; it can be known only by those who experience it in themselves. The divine Mystery will always remain hidden from those who set up to judge it by rational standards. It always transcends reason and reveals itself in the depths of the heart. "Blessed are the pure in heart, for they shall see God."[93]

115

The essential nature of the church, therefore, is to be this mystery of love, of the divine love revealing itself and communicating itself to men. All the sign-language of doctrine and ritual has no purpose but to reveal and communicate this love. This is the light in which the doctrine, the ritual and the organization of the church are to be judged. When the dogmas of the church, instead of opening the heart and the mind to this mystery of love, become obstacles to the knowledge of the Truth, and people are prepared to imprison and torture and kill one another for the sake of these dogmas, it is obvious that they have ceased to serve their purpose. When the ritual of the church, instead of being a center of unity by which people are gathered together in the love of the Spirit, becomes a barrier dividing the different churches from one another and from the rest of mankind, it has lost its meaning. When the organization of the church, established in pomp and wealth and power, no longer serves to unite humanity in love, it has ceased to fulfil the purpose for which it was instituted.

What is the answer to this problem? Is it to abolish the church, to get rid of dogmas, rituals and organization? This is a common temptation, but it never works. It only ends in the substitution of another church, another dogma, another ritual and another organization. The kingdom of God, the reign of the Spirit, has to take shape in this world. Wherever people share a common ideal, they inevitably form a society, and that society needs some doctrine or ideology to express its purpose, some outward sign to identify it, some organization to hold it together. It is true of the State, of any political party, of a cultural or friendly society, no less than of the church. No, the organization is necessary, but it has to be continually changed and adapted to changing circumstances in order to serve its original purpose. This is what is required of every religion. It has continually to renew itself. Its dogmas become fixed, its rituals stereotyped, its organization rigid. It has to find new ways of expressing its doctrine to make it meaningful, new forms of ritual which will embody the inner experience of the Spirit, new structures of organization which will respond to the needs of humanity. Every religion today is in the process of renewal. It has to discover again its original message, to define it in the light of the present day, to manifest its power to transform men's lives.

The original message, the essential truth, of every religion is the sacred Mystery, the presence in this world of a hidden Wisdom, which cannot be expressed in words, which cannot be known by sense or reason, but is hidden in the heart — the Ground or Center or Substance of the soul, of which the mystics speak — and reveals itself to those who seek it in the silence beyond word and thought. All myth and ritual, all doctrine and sacrament, is but a means to awaken the soul to this hidden Mystery, to allow the divine Presence to make itself known. Myth and ritual, word and sacrament, are necessary to make known the Mystery, and therefore every religion has its sacred tradition, its scriptures and its rites, by which the Mystery is revealed. But all these rites and doctrines are liable to become superstitions. The words and the actions remain but the inner meaning is lost or distorted. Every religion has, therefore, to renew itself continually, to rediscover the hidden Mystery to which it is intended to bear witness. The danger in every religion is, on the one hand, a slavish literalism, which clings to the letter or the outward form and loses the inner spirit, and, on the other hand, a crude rationalism, which empties the words and actions of all deeper meaning. The Bible and the Eucharist have both been subjected to this process continually.

17. The New Humanity[94]

In A New Vision of Reality, *Bede looks at the Christian Mystery from a universal and an evolutionary perspective. Jesus came to bring the Holy Spirit, which would create a 'new humanity,' and immediately with his death and resurrection the boundaries of Israel, which had circumscribed the biblical 'history of salvation,' are burst and the Spirit is poured forth into all peoples. As the barriers of the Jewish Law are swiftly dismantled, the utter simplicity, luminosity and power of the Mystery are manifest in the world. It is in the light of this simple, all-embracing Mystery that the narrowness, rigidity and fragmentation which have plagued historical Christianity are clearly revealed.*

If, in the last text,[95] we felt primarily the interior gravitation of the Mystery, here it is the expansive power of the Spirit that is evident, reaching out to embrace all creation. This is the breadth of the vision[96] which has emerged from the Pauline letters, especially those to the Colossians and Ephesians. Its length stretches from the first moment of creation over the whole span of evolution, as all reality is gathered into the one 'Cosmic Person' who is Christ. We shall look at this synthesis in more detail later.[97]

If we look for the basic inspiration which underlies Christianity, it is to be found in the life and teaching of Jesus of Nazareth. Jesus came to set Israel free from its bondage to the Law, that is, to its religious tradition, and to take it back to the source of all religion. It is clear that Jesus left behind no definite structure of religion. He chose twelve disciples, whom he called "apostles," and by all accounts gave Peter a position of leadership among them. He also left behind a "memorial" of his death and resurrection, the central "mystery" of his life, but beyond that it is difficult to discern with certainty any other formal structure. What he communicated to his disciples was the gift of his Spirit, which was to lead them into all truth. The essential mystery of the Gospel is this gift of the Spirit, that is, the opening of humanity to the life of the Spirit, which had been lost at the Fall, and its return to the communion with God in which the meaning and purpose of human existence is to be found. It was this which was to lead his disciples to discern the significance of his life and teaching and to enable them to become the nucleus of a new humanity.

It was St Paul who had the deepest insight into this matter of religion and law. He himself had been brought up as a Jew "educated according to the strict manner of the Law,"[98] but his conversion brought about a radical change in his understanding of the place of law in religion. He was able to discern that the whole law of Israel, though holy in itself and given by God, yet had only a relative value. All the sacred rites of Israel, circumcision, the worship of the temple, even the institution of the Sabbath were all seen as of relative importance and could be dispensed with. So he was able to say, "neither circumcision nor uncircumcision count for anything, but a new creation."[99] In this way he broke through all the restrictions of Judaism and opened the way of salvation to all humanity. As he said, "There is neither Jew nor Greek, neither slave nor free, there is neither male nor female, but you are all one in Christ Jesus."[100] Thus all the barriers, economic, social, political, even the division between the sexes, were overcome and the fundamental unity of mankind was proclaimed.

But this principle of freedom from the Law has now to be applied to all religion. Christianity in the course of time has built up its own structure of law and religion, of ritual and dogma and organization, which have now become a barrier, separating the Christian churches from the rest of humanity. So also Islam, Hinduism and Buddhism have developed their own structures of law and ritual and are divided from one another. We have to learn to go beyond all these differences in the external forms of religion and discover the hidden mystery which lies at the heart of all religion. In Christianity it was the mystery of the resurrection which gave this insight into the ultimate meaning of religion. The resurrection of Jesus was seen as the passage beyond time and space to the eternal transcendent Reality. This was accomplished, not merely for Jesus himself, but for all humanity. The resurrection marks the beginning of a new humanity and, as St Paul says, a "new creation."[101] Just as Israel closed in on itself and saw salvation in terms of its own limited existence, so the Christian churches have closed in on themselves and separated themselves from humanity as a whole. But in the wider perspective which we can discern today, Jesus died for all humanity and the salvation which he achieved was won for all humanity. We must never forget that in its deepest reality all humanity is one being, just as the whole creation is one being. As St Gregory of Nyssa, one of the greatest of the Greek Fathers, proclaimed, "All men from the first man to the last are one image of Him Who Is." Adam in the book of Genesis represents humanity as a whole, and when this Adam falls all humanity falls with him. So also Christ is the new Adam, the new representative of redeemed humanity, and with his resurrection humanity as a whole is redeemed from sin and death.

It is of great significance that Jesus left his disciples with the understanding that he would return again at any time and bring the world to an end. In a real sense it can be said that the resurrection itself brings the world to an end. It is the passage of human nature beyond time and space, and reveals the whole of this spatial temporal world as a passing phenomenon. We see the one Reality reflected through the changing forms of space and time, but we know that these forms are conditioned by our present mode of consciousness.

When we pass beyond this limited mode of time-space consciousness, we shall see the eternal Reality as it is. As St Paul says, "now we see in a glass darkly but then face to face."[102] The whole of human history is a passage from our present mode of existence and consciousness into the eternal world where all the diversities of this world are seen in their essential unity. Our present mode of consciousness is dualistic, but as the mystics of all religions have discerned the ultimate reality is non-dual. This new mode of being and consciousness is the *nirvana* of the Buddha, the *brahman-atman* of the *Upanishads*, the *al haqq* of the Muslim mystics and the kingdom of heaven of the Christian Gospel. It is here and here alone that we can find the meeting place of all religion.

As we saw earlier, the sin of humanity had been their separation from the Spirit, their falling back into the separate self, and thereby coming into conflict with nature, with their fellows, and with God. Jesus comes as the man who offers himself in sacrifice in total surrender, to God, to the Supreme, and in doing this he reverses the sin of Adam. Adam, the primal Man, had fallen by disobedience, by following his mind and will rather than surrendering to the Spirit. Jesus, the new Adam, the Son of Man, the representative Man, makes a total surrender to the Spirit, to God, to the Father, and by that he overcomes humanity's separation from the Father, from God, reuniting humanity as one body in himself. He breaks down all the barriers that have been set up and finally he reconciles creation with himself, as a new creation.

This then is the birth of a new humanity and it can be regarded as a new stage in evolution. Humanity had developed through various levels of complexity, through the hunting, the pastoral and the agricultural stages to the great civilisations. Now with Christ a new stage is taking place and a new humanity is being born. The new humanity is born "not of blood, nor of the flesh, nor of the will of man, but of God," Jesus is the new Man who is born of God, who is the Son of God.

At Pentecost the Spirit returns to man. Whereas in the Fall of man the Spirit had departed and humanity had centred on itself, now the Spirit returns. Adam, the first man, as St Paul says, was a living soul whereas Jesus, the second Adam, is a life-giving spirit.[103] Jesus had transformed the disobedience of Adam into this new man who is now the *anthropos pneumatikos*, the man of the Spirit, and he continues to communicate the Spirit to mankind. At Pentecost, it is said, there were people present from all nations on the earth. This is an exaggeration of course, but it means that people representing the entire Roman Empire, which were all the nations Israel knew, were gathered together in Jerusalem for this festival. It was symbolic of the fact that the Spirit was to be given to all nations.

Through the receiving of the Spirit this new humanity became what St Paul calls the dwelling-place of God in the Spirit.[104] In other words, we are made into the temple of God in which the Spirit can dwell. St Paul describes this in writing to the Ephesians where he speaks of the "immeasurable greatness of his power in us who believe, according to the working of his great might which he accomplished in Christ when he raised him from the dead."[105] It was God who raised Christ from the dead. Christ made that sacrifice of himself, the total sacrifice, and thereby he overcame death which was the consequence of sin. The disintegration of man was healed by this surrender on the cross which is also the reintegration of man. St Paul continues, "And made him to sit at his right hand in the heavenly places, far above all rule and authority and power and dominion, and every name that is named, not only in this world but also in that which is to come."[106] This is a reference to the cosmic powers of which we have spoken. Jesus, through the resurrection, is raised above humanity and also above the whole cosmic order, above all the cosmic powers, and, as St Paul puts it, he is made "to sit at God's right hand in the heavenly places." That refers to the transcendent order of consciousness. It is appropriate to translate these biblical images into the framework we have been using so far. We have spoken of the three worlds where the earth is the physical order, the air is the psychic or psychological order, and the sky, or heaven, the spiritual order. God dwells in heaven, in the spiritual order, whereas, significantly, the spirits are said to dwell in the air. St Paul speaks of the "prince of the power of the air."[107] The spirits of the air, along with angels and other beings, represent an intermediate state, the psychic or psychological realm. Man, of course, dwells on the earth. So Jesus goes beyond the physical and beyond the psychic world, beyond the angels and the gods, to the transcendent world, the transcendent reality itself. "He has put all things in subjection under this feet," which means, as we have seen, that the whole material creation becomes subordinate to him.

The passage continues, "and has made him the head over all things for the church, which is his body, the fullness of him who fills all in all."[108] The church is this body of humanity which has been rescued from sin and restored to life in the Spirit and now it becomes "the fullness of him who fills all in all." The word "fullness" in Greek is *pleroma* and it corresponds to the Sanskrit *purnam*. In principle, the whole creation has been restored to that fullness. Whereas sin is disintegration and falling apart, redemption is reintegration. It is the gathering of everything into a whole, bringing it into the fullness of God. The whole of humanity is gathered into the fullness of the divine life. And further, all things, the whole creation, as well as the whole of humanity, now become the body of Christ. Christ is, as it were, the soul of the body and he reunites it in the Spirit, with God. "The fullness of him who fills all in all" means that the whole creation is now filled with this power of the Spirit, through Christ who is himself that fullness, in whom "the fullness of the godhead dwelt bodily."[109] That is the understanding of the new humanity which emerges in the New Testament.

When the church is seen in this way it is being understood in the highest sense. We need to recover this insight and emphasize it today. The church as it is known today may seem to bear little resemblance to it, but this is the vision of the church in the New Testament and in the early church Fathers. For instance, in the Shepherd of Hermas there is a beautiful passage where the church appears as an old woman. The Shepherd asks why she appears like an old woman and the text says it is because "she was from the beginning and for her all things were created."[110] So the church is the new humanity, the body of humanity, which God planned from the beginning. It falls into sin and is divided and disintegrated but now it is reunited. Its previous separations are healed, it is reintegrated and becomes the body of

Christ, the body filled with the Holy Spirit. In this sense it is from the beginning and for this all things were created. The whole creation and humanity is created precisely for this unity in God through Christ. That is the plan of salvation as seen in the New Testament.

All this makes it evident that this work of the Spirit has been going on in all humanity from the beginning. Certainly at Pentecost a fullness of the Spirit was revealed, but the Spirit was present from the time that man fell from Eden. The redemptive work of the Spirit was already taking place from the very beginning. In all primitive peoples and in the hunting, agricultural and pastoral peoples there was a presence of the Spirit. The Holy Spirit is present in all creation, in all humanity, drawing humanity back to God, back to Christ, back to the Truth.

Looking back at myth and ritual, which we discussed earlier, we can see that through myth God revealed Himself to the ancient world. At that point there was no *logos* since people were at the pre-rational stage. The *mythos* comes before the *logos*, for the *mythos* is the symbolic story appropriate at the imaginative level of development, whereas the *logos* requires for its understanding the reason and the intellect. Before the development of reason human beings had to learn through myth, and myth was expressed in ritual. So all ancient myth and ritual was the way in which the Spirit was made present and through which the Word was revealing himself. So the Word of God "which enlightens every man coming into the world" [111] was revealing himself through the myths and rituals of the ancient peoples. When it comes to understanding this, there are two possibilities. The myth and the ritual can be accepted as a means or sacrament, through which God is revealing himself, and this is the way of true religion, or the myth and the ritual can be idolized, which means that they are made an end in themselves. We are always either open to the Spirit and take part in the work of redemption, or we close in on ourselves and settle for substitutes for the Spirit in which case we isolate ourselves from God, from the truth. So that is how the Word and the Spirit are present from the beginning, building up humanity into the new body, the new humanity.

The final point here is that this rebuilding of each person, the creation and humanity into one is conceived as coming to fulfillment in a person, the person of Christ. For many people this is a great difficulty for they cannot see the stellar universe or the universe of the atom in terms of a person. But it is in fact a very profound insight. As St Thomas Aquinas said, the person is the highest being in the universe. We understand that matter is the lowest level of organization, it is comparatively unstructured. The atomic level, the living cell and the plant mark stages in organisation, in the development of a more complex structure. The level of animal intelligence is a further stage and finally the level of the human being is reached. Each human person has the capacity for knowledge and love, that is, a capacity to structure the universe around them and to further its organization. A person is essentially a being capable of knowledge and love, which means being capable of receiving the universe into oneself by knowledge, that is, by symbol and language, and capable of acting on the universe by art and science. And so "person" is really the supreme reality in the universe, the point at which the universe enters into consciousness. It is significant that nearly all ancient people saw the ultimate Reality in terms of a person. In Hinduism we have the *purusha*, the cosmic person, in whom the whole universe comes together. In Buddhism we have the *tathagata*, the one who has reached Reality and who is the supreme Person. In Islam there is the "universal man", *al-insan al Kamil* and in Christianity we have Christ as the cosmic Person, the one in whom all things were created. "All things were created through him and for him...and in him all things hold together."[112] He is the person who personalizes the universe and the universe comes to a head as it were, in him. In this way the whole of humanity is seen as growing, as St Paul put it, to mature manhood, to "the measure of the stature of the fullness of Christ."[113] The whole of humanity is growing to the full stature of the man, Jesus Christ, who is none other than the primordial Man who was there in the beginning and who has now been revealed as the Lord, uniting all humanity with God. That is the vision of St Paul and of the New Testament as a whole.

III

WEST: PART TWO
MYSTERY AND DRAMA OF THE
CHURCH

It was with passionate conviction and a firm stride that Alan Griffiths entered the Catholic Church. The story of his conversion, as narrated in *The Golden String*, moves forward with the irresistible necessity that marks Augustine's *Confessions* or Merton's *Seven Storey Mountain*. The light of wisdom shone for him with blinding power from within this 'Body of Christ.' Very soon, however, the tensions and contrasts between his mystical vision of the church and its concrete reality would begin to disturb him. This conflict would intensify as Bede attempted to realize his prophetic vision at Shantivanam, in the context of the Catholic Church of India during the tumultuous years following the Second Vatican Council. The struggle would continue until the end of his life. With the New Testament and early Christian tradition, Bede envisioned the church as an earthly embodiment of divine Wisdom, within which all of humanity and the universe itself are recreated in God. This sapiential conception of the church bore little resemblance to the institutional reality of the Roman Catholic Church, as he experienced it.

Bede's attitude toward this ecclesial institution was often not a tolerant one. He responded to any inordinate exercise of authority with sharp criticism, and he vigorously resisted efforts of the local bishop to move the ashram of Shantivanam from its path of Indian inculturation back onto unquestionably safe ground. Bede was never censured by Rome. His way of 'indianization' gradually found more and more acceptance among the hierarchy both in India and abroad, as a faithful expression of the principles of the Second Vatican Council.

The passion with which Bede Griffiths pursued the roots of contemplative wisdom that he found in the Vedanta is matched by the radicality and uncompromising clarity with which he set forth his view of the church of the future. This was to be a church on the scale of all humanity, unburdened of the cultural accretions of twenty centuries, vibrant with the freedom and pluriform vitality that were born on Pentecost morning.

18. Discovery of the Church[1]

We return to Bede's autobiography. After the dramatic crisis of his initial conversion to Christianity,[2] young Griffiths became confused and restless once again. He decided to take up a life of solitary prayer and meditation and rented a cottage at a lonely farm in the Cotswolds. Still restless and uncertain, he gave himself resolutely to prayer until, arriving at what he felt once again was a point of complete self-surrender, he suddenly realized that he should begin to live a life of work on the remote farm.

He met a young woman who lived in the nearby town, and they became friends. "I think that this was the only time that the idea of marriage ever entered my mind; but it was really a relation of friendship, not of love, and our ways soon divided."[3] In a short time he would be led to his next step: entry into the Roman Catholic Church.

My own way lay in a different direction. I began to read again without much definite purpose, and I bought three books, *The Journal of George Fox*, the *Autobiography of Richard Baxter* and the *Diary of John Woolman*, the Quaker. I discovered then a new aspect of that seventeenth century which I had always loved, the tradition of non-conformity. I felt again the wonderful strength of the religious spirit in seventeenth-century England and this new aspect appealed to me in its own way no less than the Anglicanism of Hooker and Jeremy Taylor. I do not know exactly what conception of the church I had at this time, but I think that I would have regarded the Quakers and Congregationalists, no less than the Anglicans and Orthodox and Catholics, as all alike members of the one mystical Body of Christ, though differing in their forms of worship and belief.

It happened that shortly after this I saw an advertisement in a catalogue of Newman's *Development of Christian Doctrine*, which I proceeded to buy. I do not think that my mind had ever seriously returned to the thought of the Roman Church, and I bought the book simply out of general interest, but its effect on me was to prove decisive. I had always felt a deep sympathy with Newman. His approach to the church by way of the Bible and the Fathers and the High Church party had been that which I had followed. Now I found Newman turning all his learning and all his powers of exegesis to showing that the church of the Scriptures and the Fathers was none other than the church of Rome. Newman's method also appealed to me; I had always been interested in the historical approach. I believed that the church which Christ had founded was a historical reality, that it had had a continuous history from the time of the apostles to the present day. I had thought that this continuity might be found in the Church of England, but now the overwhelming weight of evidence for the continuity of the Roman Church was presented to my mind.

The problem was, how could one reconcile all the developments which have taken place in the church of Rome with the primitive simplicity of the Gospel? What was the connection between the religion of the Gospels and the complete structure of Catholicism as seen, for instance, in Dante or St Thomas or a Gothic cathedral? That the religion of Dante and St Thomas was a corruption of the Gospel I could not believe. The polemic of the Reformation had ceased to have any meaning for me. I knew that it was the modern world which was corrupt and decadent, and that Dante and St Thomas marked one of the pinnacles of human greatness.

How then could one reconcile the vast elaboration of dogma and ritual and what looked like mythology in the Middle Ages with the original Gospel? Newman gave me the answer, an answer which accorded with everything which I knew from other sources. He saw the church as a living organism, beginning like a seed in the New Testament and gradually developing according to specific laws until it reached its full stature. Now this view accorded perfectly with that view of the church as the Mystical Body of Christ which had impressed itself on my imagination when I first read St Paul. St Paul had compared the church to a human body composed of many organs, but all subject to one head and animated by one spirit. Thus the idea of the church as a living organism was clearly part of the teaching of the New Testament. Again Christ himself had spoken of his Kingdom as a grain of mustard seed, which beginning very small gradually grows to be a great tree so that the birds of heaven come to rest among its branches. Here then was the authority of the Gospel itself for this gradual organic development of the church from small beginnings to a great stature.

This principle accorded also with all that was known of the processes of nature and history. Newman's book had been written a few years before Darwin's *Origin of Species*, when the conception of organic development was first applied on a large scale to the structure of living beings. Every species in nature was seen to develop gradually from small beginnings, adapting itself to new conditions and assimilating elements from outside, and yet preserving its essential type. These developments could only be explained on the assumption that there was an inner principle of growth in an organism which enabled it to select those elements which were favourable to it and to reject those which were hostile, and so to perfect its species. It was evident also that there were false developments, failures in adaptation, which resulted in the corruption of a species and its gradual extinction.

I had also been familiar, ever since I had read Spengler, with the application of this principle to human history. I had seen how human civilisations have their rise and fall, and how this can be seen to depend on the development of certain principles of growth and corruption inherent in them. Thus, everything disposed me in favour of Newman's view of the growth of the church. But it was the particular application of this theory to individual doctrines which really convinced me. Newman showed how every Christian doctrine had undergone this process of development. It was not a matter of certain doctrines which were peculiar to the church of Rome: the most fundamental doctrines of the Trinity and the Incarnation had undergone a similar development. I had often been disturbed by the Athanasian Creed with its apparent imposition of the most complex theological dogma on the simple doctrine of the New Testament, but now I could see the reason for it. Newman supported me in my belief that the New Testament was addressed to the Imagination. It was first of all a record of facts, which were presented to the mind in the most vivid, imaginative way. It was a poetic history, and, in addition, the doctrine of the New Testament was presented entirely in imaginative terms. There were no abstract philosophical concepts; all was

128

expressed in the richly symbolic terms of poetry and imagination. Christ spoke of himself in terms of the Messiah and his Kingdom, two concepts of infinite imaginative significance. He compared himself to a Bridegroom, to a Shepherd, to a Vine. Even the terms in which he spoke of his relation to God were profoundly symbolic; he spoke of God as his Father, of himself as the Son, of the Spirit which he would send. Now these terms set forth the Object of faith, as Newman showed, in the way which makes the deepest impression on the mind and nourishes love and devotion, but they are lacking in precision. It was inevitable that as the minds of men began to reflect on them and to draw out their meaning, they should be given a more exact expression. In Newman's own words, "what was an impression on the imagination became a system or creed in the reason."

Thus the development of theology was like the development of any other science. It was simply the application of an exact philosophic reason to the evidence of the New Testament. The whole weight of Greek philosophy was gradually brought to bear on the revelation of the New Testament, and the Summa of St Thomas was the organized structure of human thought working on the material provided by the original revelation. But what was to show that this was a genuine development and not a corruption of the Gospel? Here Newman showed that as the church was the Body of which Christ was the Head, so it was necessarily guided and directed in the course of its evolution by his Spirit. The church as an organ of divine revelation, founded by Christ and inspired by his Spirit, was necessarily infallible in its teaching. It was simply the organism through which the divine message was communicated to men, and therefore it was always preserved in truth. The idea that the church was infallible had long been familiar to me. I saw clearly that it could have no authority to teach in Christ's name if this was not so.

Where did this infallible authority reside in the church? I knew that in the early church it was held to reside in the Bishops. Some time ago I had bought Archbishop Wake's translation of the works of the Apostolic Fathers, and this had created a great impression on me. I had often wondered what was the link between the church of the Apostles, as it is seen in the New Testament, and the church of later times, and these letters of the Apostolic Fathers had provided the answer to my question. They were the immediate successors of the Apostles, and they showed what the church was like at the end of the first and the beginning of the second century. St Ignatius of Antioch in particular revealed that the Bishop at this time had taken the place of the Apostles. The bishop was the representative of Christ in each individual church. Each church formed as it were a cell in the Mystical Body of Christ. It was an organic unit, modelled on the pattern of the whole, and the bishop as the head occupied the position of Christ. It was through him that the teaching of Christ was given to the people; "the bishops were sent by the Apostles, the Apostles by Christ, Christ by God," as an early writer had put it.

It was clear, then, that the infallible guidance in the teaching of the church came through the bishops, and this I knew was the universal belief of the early church. Among these bishops the Bishop of Rome was held to have a unique position because he was the successor of St Peter. I do not think that I had ever studied this question before, but Newman was able to show me that this doctrine was no less universal in the early church. Christ had founded his church on St Peter and given him the supreme authority over it, symbolised by the "keys," like the power of a steward over a house. I saw now that in the organization of the church, as it spread throughout the Roman Empire, the Bishop of Rome as the successor of St Peter was held to have the same authority among the other bishops as St Peter held among the Apostles. As the bishop represented Christ in his own diocese and was head of the body of the church there, so the Bishop of Rome represented Christ as head of the whole body of the church throughout the world.

Newman showed how this doctrine could be seen developing step by step from the first words spoken by Christ to St Peter through the Fathers of the second and third centuries to the great Fathers of the fourth and fifth century, St Athanasius, St Ambrose, St Jerome, St Augustine. It was true that the doctrine had not always been clear from the beginning, but neither had the doctrine of the Trinity and the Incarnation, of Original Sin and Grace. The authority for holding each doctrine was precisely the same; it was the witness of the universal church. In each case there had been a development, in the one case a theoretical development by the simple application of reason to the doctrine of the New Testament, in the other, a practical development also, as circumstances called for the exercise of the power of the popes.

It was especially striking how the early popes, far from resting their authority on any worldly power, regarded themselves as mystically identified with St Peter. Thus an early pope could say: "We bear the burden of all who are laden; yea rather the blessed Peter beareth them in us, who as we trust in all things protects us and defends us the heirs of his government." And again, St Leo could say: "Blessed Peter has not deserted the helm of the church, which he had assumed...his power lives and his authority is preeminent in his See." It was clear that the sense of the church as a living organism was so strong that St Peter was considered to continue to exercise his authority through the pope, just as Christ himself continued to live and act in the church in all its members.

What Newman showed of the papal authority he showed also of all the other doctrines which were in dispute, of Purgatory and Indulgences, of the *cultus* of the Saints and their relics; all alike could be seen to be organic developments of the original doctrine of the Gospel, evolving by the same law as an oak tree develops from an acorn, or an embryo into a complete animal. Newman enumerated seven principles by which the genuineness of the development could be tested and distinguished from a corruption. They were the preservation of its type, the continuity of its principles, its power of assimilation, its logical sequence, its power to anticipate the future and to conserve the past, and finally its chronic vigor. Each of these tests was then scientifically applied to the doctrine of the Roman church and it was shown how it had answered to the test. It would scarcely be possible to find a more rigorously scientific demonstration, but at the same time it was the work of a man who was not originally inclined to the view which he was expounding and whose life depended on the result of his investigations. When Newman began to write the *Development of Christian Doctrine*, he was an Anglican; when he finished, he was a Catholic.

The effect of this argument on my mind was immense. It corresponded in all its main principles with the lines on which my mind had been previously working, while it extended their range. It filled in all the gaps in my knowledge and gave a coherent meaning to everything I knew. I had recognized the greatness of the medieval church long ago. I had seen how our civilization had declined as it had departed from those principles on which the medieval world had been built. I had discovered in the Bible the source of those principles and in the church the society in which they were to be found embodied. I knew that there was no basis for life to be found in the world today apart from the church, and I had sought to find in the Church of England the living representative of the church which Christ had founded. Now I saw that the living church, which could show a continuous evolution from the day of Pentecost and whose doctrine had been built up through successive centuries through the guidance of the indwelling Spirit, was none other than the church of Rome.

Here at last was the society which I had been seeking which had stood out uncompromisingly against the illusions of the modern world and preserved the tradition of the past; here at last I could find a genuine basis for my life. I began to realize now something of the significance of that act of prayer which had changed my life. I had renounced the world then with all the strength of my will, without seeing any alternative and trusting myself blindly to the hands of God. Now God had answered my prayer in a way which had been utterly beyond me. He had shown me the only alternative to the world, to that civilization which I knew to the founded on false principles. He had shown me the living church, the Pillar and Ground of truth, the source of life and salvation.

I thought all this out while I was working on the farm during the day, and returned each evening to my cottage to read more of Newman. I remember that we were topping turnips at the time, and as I went up and down the rows with the men I thought to myself that if ever my life had been sane and my mind calm it was now. I was free from all the distractions of the outside world. I was living a simple life in harmony with nature and among kindly practical people, unaffected by the sophistication of town life. There were no ties of emotion now to hold me back. I knew that I should give pain to my mother, but I repeated to myself again and again the text of the Gospel: "Unless a man will hate his father and his mother and his wife and his children, and his own life also, he cannot be my disciple." I knew that true love will never hesitate to give pain to those it loves when truth demands it and that my mother would not ask for anything else.

It only remained for me to make contact with the Catholic Church. It will give some idea of the isolation in which I had lived, when I say that I did not know the name of a single Catholic to whom I could turn. My only resource was to go to my bookseller in Winchcombe and ask him if he knew whether there was such a thing as a Catholic church in the neighbourhood. He replied that there was one round the corner, and there I went. This time no obstacle presented itself. The priest was a Father Palmer, the son of an old English Catholic family, who told me proudly that he had nearly been sent to Christ's Hospital to school, but when his mother heard that it would be necessary for him to attend a Protestant service, she had replied that she would rather go to the workhouse with her eleven children than submit to that.

He understood my need and lent me two books by R.H. Benson, which exactly suited me. The first was *Christ in the Church*, which showed that the doctrine of the Mystical Body of Christ was indeed the doctrine of the Catholic Church: that as Christ had acted through his human nature while he was on earth, so now he acted through the organism of his church, exercizing his authority through her ministers, teaching the truth about her doctrine, saving souls through her sacraments. The other book was *The Friendship of Christ* which showed me how, while Christ continues to live and act through the social organism of the church, he is none the less present to each individual soul, revealing himself as its friend and lover.

Thus all that I had come to believe was confirmed, but I still held back. I had been through so many phases of thought, that I felt that I could no longer trust my mind alone. I needed some further assurance that the church was in fact the Body of Christ, and I remember that I wrote to my mother and told her that I would do nothing until I received this assurance that the church was still today inhabited by the Spirit of Christ. I would wait until I received a positive assurance of the presence of Christ in the church.

19. The Christian Community[4]

Following the path which had been personally traced by J.H. Newman in his Development of Christian Doctrine, *Griffiths had arrived at the rational conclusion that the Roman Catholic Church was the place of Christ's truth and life in this world. But he still needed the positive evidence of a living Catholic community. This he would soon find in the Benedictine monastery of Prinknash.*

At Prinknash, Alan Griffiths found an actual community and a way of life which corresponded to the desire that had been burning within him. Here was a simple life, centered in the gospel and the great commandment of love. It was a life that integrated prayer, work and study and seemed to offer the personal unity for which he longed — corresponding to that larger unity which he had discovered in the church. The final stage of Griffiths' movement into the Catholic Church nearly coincided with his choice of monastic life.

I did not receive any formal instruction, and I think that Father Palmer was rather shocked when he came over later, to find that I had not even been through the Catechism. But I absorbed the faith at a deeper level than any provided by the Catechism. I attended the Offices in church every day, and I found there the full extent of that prayer which I had begun to discover in the Book of Common Prayer in the Church of England. It began at four o'clock in the morning and extended throughout the day and gave me exactly what I had been looking for. The intervals I spent mostly in reading in the library, where I found all the books that I could possibly desire. In a very little time every lingering doubt was removed; here was the fullness of truth for which I had been seeking. I had found in the faith the key to all truth, and I realised that only now could I really begin to assimilate it.

But it was not only intellectual certainty which I desired; I wanted to find a life which would satisfy my whole being, my heart and soul and body as well as my mind. It was some time before I felt a complete conviction in regard to this. I saw that the life was based not only on prayer but also on work, and I got the impression that the work was taken seriously. All the work of the house was done by the monks, and there were a garden and a farm and a carpenter's shop with many other kinds of workshops. Above all, I found a spirit of kindness and charity in the place such as I had never experienced before. I had been used to ordinary kindness and family affection, but I had never known a kindness which was based on principle and pervaded the most ordinary acts of life. Here was that kind of courtesy and grace in the ordinary acts of life which had first attracted me in the life of St Francis of Assisi, and I soon found that it had its source in the Rule of St Benedict. "Let all guests who come," it was said, "be treated like Christ himself, for he will say, I was a stranger and you took me in." This was the sign for which I had been seeking. I saw now visibly present in the church the spirit of Christ, which is the spirit of Charity, and I hesitated no longer.

I was received into the church on Christmas Eve 1931 and made my first communion at the midnight mass in the little church at Winchcombe. It was a still moonlit night, and as I made my way past the great perpendicular parish church, where I had previously gone to communion, to the little Catholic church in a by-street, I knew that a new epoch had begun for me. I had found the hidden source of life which had once created the Cotswold world which I had loved and the civilization of England, and which was now relegated to the by-streets of modern England. When I read the office of Matins for Christmas Day with its great Sermon on the Incarnation by St Leo, I knew that I had found the authentic voice of Christianity, and that in the mass of that little church I was in communion with the Catholic Church throughout the world and throughout the ages.

It was less than a month after my reception into the church that I entered the monastery to try my vocation as a monk.

20. Heaven's Gate[5]

At the end of The Golden String, *Bede Griffiths has found 'heaven's gate / built in Jerusalem's wall.' His Epilogue to this autobiography sings with the satisfaction which he finds in this fullness which is the church. The Second Act of his story comes to a triumphant conclusion. A new phase will begin very soon, as he travels to India. And as he is confronted more and more through the years with the earthly realities of the church and its institutional aspects, the gap between ideal and actuality will draw forth a series of impassioned pleas for renewal.*

Where is the clue to the center? Where is the Golden String to be found? The Golden String is Christ; he is the clue to the center. The sacrifice of Christ is the central event of human history; it is the event which alone gives meaning to life. It was in the Resurrection of Christ that the illusion of this world was shattered and mankind was set free from the bondage of space and time. If we have lost the way and become enslaved again by the appearance of this world, it is because we have deliberately turned our backs on the truth. We have denied the validity of sacrifice and therefore we have become haunted by a sense of guilt.

The human imagination has always been haunted by the feeling that we must die in order that we may live; that we have to be born again. To be a Christian is to accept this mystery of death and resurrection in one's own life; it is to pass through the world of appearances into the realm of Being. It is to commit oneself to the view that the world as we know it is not the world for which we are created. It is to confess that we are "strangers and exiles on earth," that we have here "no abiding city." Already science has begun to recognize that the outward forms of matter, the molecules and atoms, the protons and electrons with which it deals, are only a kind of algebra, a symbolic representation of certain elemental powers whose real nature we do not know. We know that we ourselves, and the whole universe of which we are a part, are in a state of evolution, passing continually from one state of being to another. Everything is subject to the same law of transformation.

But what is the end of this process? Of this science can tell us nothing, but divine revelation comes to our aid. It tells us that the whole of this world of space and time is destined to pass away; there is to be "a new heaven and a new earth," where "time will be no more." Mankind is to be reunited in a new order of Being, a society transcending the limitations of this world, in which man will participate in the life of God. We are to enter into the vision of God, that vision of all things in their essential truth, which is the object of all our quest on earth.

And yet when we have said this, we have to confess that the mystery remains. Nothing which we can conceive of God or of eternal life can have more than a remote resemblance to the reality. Christianity does not explain the mystery; it only opens up the way of approach to the mystery. God himself remains the unfathomable mystery, the incomprehensible Being. Nothing which we say of him can ever be more than a remote analogy of the truth. The very name of "God" is only a convenience of speech. Even if we say that God "exists," we have to admit that his existence is of a different kind from anything that we know. If we say that he is wisdom, truth, goodness, beauty, love, we have to acknowledge that though he is all that we can conceive of these things, yet he is infinitely beyond our conception. Even the dogmas of the church, of the Trinity, the Incarnation, the Eucharist, do not define the mystery properly speaking. They only express in human terms what he has chosen to reveal concerning himself. They are, like the sacraments themselves, signs of a mystery which cannot be expressed. And yet we need these signs if we are to approach the mystery. They are in the language of Blake's poem, "Jerusalem's wall"; they are the ramparts which defend the City of God. It has been the tragedy of the modern world that we have thought that by breaking down the walls we could open the City to all men. But we have only succeeded in profaning the truth and emptying life of its meaning. For the divine mystery can only be approached by faith, and the dogmas and sacraments of the church are the walls in which the gate of faith, which is "heaven's gate," is to be found. The moment we attempt to enter of ourselves, to do without the church, we shut ourselves out of the City. But when we learn to accept the dogmas and sacraments of the church, then we can enter by faith into the heart of the mystery; we can pass through the sign to the thing signified, through the image to the reality.

Thus the church herself is the great sacramental mystery. Her hierarchy, her sacraments, her dogmas, are nothing but signs and instruments by which the divine mystery is manifested to mankind. If we stop short at the sign, then it becomes a wall which separates us from the truth; but if we enter by the gate of faith through the wall, then we discover the City of God. We shall never rebuild our civilization until we begin to build up again the walls which have been pulled down, and accept the church as the guardian of the divine mystery.

Then science and philosophy and art will once again recover their significance by being related to the true end of human life. Without the recognition of an end which totally transcends this world, science can only become a system of idolatry, philosophy can only contemplate the meaninglessness of human existence, and art can only disintegrate into fragments. But once we place the church at the center of existence as the guardian of divine truth and divine love, then the whole world recovers its meaning.

Then we realize that the whole universe is a sacrament, which mirrors the divine reality; that each created thing, though nothing in itself, is of infinite value and significance because it is the sign of a mystery, which is enshrined in the depths of its being. Then every human being is known to be not merely an isolated individual carried along on the flux of time and doomed to extinction, but a member of a divine society, working out its destiny in space and time and subject to all the tragic consequences of subservience to the material world, but destined to transcend the limitations of time and space and mortality and to enter into that fullness of life where there shall be "neither mourning nor weeping nor pain any more." The suffering of this world can have no meaning as long as we attempt to judge it in the light of this present time. We are like people who hear snatches of music, which they have no means of relating to the symphony as a whole. But when we have passed beyond the conditions of this present life we shall then have that integral knowledge in which the whole is known in every part and every part is seen to mirror the whole.

21. The Myth of the Church[6]

Already in The Marriage of East and West, *Bede Griffiths sees the church in a cosmic and evolutionary perspective: humanity develops in the creative interaction of Word and Spirit, awakening to the inner divine Presence. The church, then, is as large as humanity itself, embracing within itself all the religions. Larger still, the church comprehends all creation, the whole universe. Here the resurrection of Jesus Christ is the pivot of history and evolution, the point at which the creative divine energy of the Spirit begins the re-creation of the world.*

Everyday Christian experience and the very human, historical reality of the church do not obviously correspond with this splendid Myth of the church.

Bede Griffiths' view of the church is characterized by an extreme polarity; it is important to understand the relationship between the two sides. Behind the critical radicality with which he will speak of institutional Catholicism lies the mystical idealism of his sapiential vision of the church. She is essentially cosmic before she is institutional, eternal before she is temporal; she is 'the created aspect of the uncreated Spirit', the world awakened to consciousness and bringing forth a new creation from within itself. The church far exceeds the bounds of any church institution. Bede Griffiths would break open the container of western culture and of over-rational consciousness in which he sees the church confined. It is particularly in religious traditions of the East that he finds the inner wisdom — the simple intuitive light — in which the mystery of Christ can once again be discovered in its simplicity and power. This mystery, however, belongs to all humanity; it is as Christians learn it from outside the boundaries of their churches — and of Christianity itself — that the church itself will come into her fullness. We hear more and more insistently, as Bede concludes his presentation of the church, his characteristic 'beyond': beyond concept and institution to the Myth; beyond myth itself to the Mystery.

In Christian tradition the figure of the Mother is found in the church. In an early Christian writing, *The Shepherd of Hermas*, the church appears in the form of an old woman. When it is asked why she appears as an old woman, the answer is given: 'Because she was created first of all. On this account is she old, and for her sake was the world made.'[7] It is necessary to see the church in this cosmic aspect. The church as a historical institution has a very recent origin and occupies a very small part of the world. But the church in herself is the eternal Mother; she is the created aspect of the uncreated Spirit. 'For her sake the world was made.' The world in a real sense is the 'becoming' of God. He, who is infinite, unchanging being in himself, reveals himself, expresses himself, in the finite, changing nature of the world. The eternal Word, in whom the 'archetypes' of all created beings exist eternally, manifests himself in time. The whole creation, from the smallest atom to the furthest star, is a manifestation in space and time, in multiplicity and change, of that unchanging One. The Spirit, immanent in nature from the beginning, receives these 'seeds of the word' into her womb and brings them forth in creation. From the first beginning of matter, through all the stages of evolution, of organic growth and consciousness, the Spirit is structuring these forms, moulding them by her inherent power.

In man this Spirit is at work organizing the chemicals which make up his body, building up the cells, developing the nerves and the muscles and the glands, structuring the organs of touch and taste, of smells and sight and hearing, finally bringing all this complex organism, through the elaborate structure of the brain, into consciousness. With consciousness, Nature, the Mother, awakens to a new mode of being, and begins to discover, to become conscious of, her meaning and destiny. Over millions of years the Spirit is working through Nature, responding to the action of the Word, the Cosmic Person, the *purusha*, who unites himself with his bride, his Sakti, to bring forth this world. As consciousness grows in man, Nature becomes conscious of the immanent power within her and the church is born.

The church is Man become conscious of his destiny as a son of God. In the biblical perspective Adam is Man, created in the image and likeness of God, and called to be a son of God. When Adam sins, he fails in his calling; he fails to respond to the Spirit, and falls back on his limited time-bound nature. The upward movement of evolution from matter through life and consciousness to eternal life in the Spirit is checked. But at the same time the mystery of redemption begins. A new power of the Spirit, the *Sakti*, enters the creation and begins to draw man back into the life of the Spirit. This is the beginning of the church, humanity drawn out of sin by the power of the Spirit and responding to the Word of God. In this sense, the church is present in humanity from the beginning of history. Wherever man wakes to consciousness and knows himself in his basic intuitive consciousness as open to the transcendent mystery of existence, the power of the Spirit is in him, drawing him to eternal life. The presence of the Spirit in this sense can be traced in all the religions of mankind. Everywhere, in ritual and sacrifice, in doctrine and sacrament, in prayer and worship, there is a presence of the Spirit drawing man to God, a response to the Word of God seeking to unite mankind with himself: in other words, a presence of the church. We need to recover this understanding of the Universal church, the church which was 'created first of all...for whose sake was the world made.'

It is not only the whole of humanity but the whole creation which constitutes the body of the church. Matter was created from the beginning with an innate tendency towards life and consciousness. Human consciousness was created from the beginning with an innate tendency towards the final and perfect consciousness of the Spirit. The same Spirit was present in matter, in life and in man, from the beginning drawing him towards itself. In Jesus this movement of matter and consciousness towards the life of the Spirit reached its culmination. In him the divine consciousness took possession of human consciousness, and both body and soul, matter and consciousness, were transformed. In him the marriage of God and Man, of Nature and Spirit, of *purusha* and *prakriti*, was consummated.

But this consummation of the union of God with man in Jesus necessarily affects the whole creation. This was the consummation for which the whole creation had been 'groaning in travail,' as St Paul says, from the beginning. The whole creation is an organic unity just as Man himself is an organic unity. At the Resurrection Jesus becomes the 'head' of this Cosmic whole, and the whole creation becomes his Body, and this Body of creation, redeemed from the forces of sin and division, is what constitutes the church. 'He has put all things under his feet,' says St Paul, 'and made him the head over all things for the church, which is his body, the fullness of him who fills all in all.'[8] The church is the Pleroma, the fullness, the consummation of all things, the term of the whole evolutionary process. The divine *purusha* has taken possession of *Prakriti*, Nature, and filled her with his presence. In other words Nature has been wholly penetrated with consciousness, and Man and Nature have become one with the eternal Spirit. The Resurrection thus reveals the plan of the whole creation. What was accomplished in Jesus through his sacrificial death and his rebirth to eternal life, is what is destined to happen in all men and in all creation. We are all members of this fallen and redeemed humanity, each of us bearing in himself the marks of the Fall, of sin and suffering and death, and each of us is called to pass beyond sin and suffering and death into the new life of the Resurrection. 'The first Adam,' it is said, 'was a living soul, the second Adam became a life-giving spirit.'[9] The 'Word became flesh,'[10] the divine Spirit entered into the depths of matter, of life and of consciousness, into the midst of human sin and suffering, and raised up this fallen world to new life and new consciousness in himself. Thus the church is present in all creation and in all humanity; it is the 'becoming' of God, the manifestation of the infinite, eternal Being in the course of time and change and history, not simply as a static presence, but as a dynamic power, changing the course of history and transforming the world.

For while the church has this cosmic dimension, this universal character, it is also a historical institution. This is in accordance with the biblical tradition, which while it looks towards the final consummation of creation and man, at the same time sees this great Myth rooted in historic time and place. Jesus, who is the cosmic Lord and Universal Savior, is also the man who was 'crucified under Pontius Pilate.' So also the church, which is the consummation of the world and of history, has its beginning in time. While the Bible sees the plan of God extending to all humanity, from the first to the second Adam, it also sees it working out in the history of a particular people and coming to a head at a particular time. Jesus comes announcing the coming of the kingdom of God: 'The Kingdom of God is at hand,'[11] and he prepares a group of disciples to whom this 'mystery' of the kingdom of God is entrusted. They are to be the nucleus of the 'people of God,' the new humanity, which comes to birth through his death and resurrection. At Pentecost this new humanity comes into being; the Spirit descends and transforms the disciples by his power and presence. A new age begins in which this power of the Spirit is to spread through the world and humanity is to be gathered into the kingdom of God. Such is the mission of the earthly church, to be the witness, or rather the embodiment, of the power of the Spirit, acting as a leaven in creation and bringing it to fulfillment in the kingdom of God.

But once the church enters into the world, it becomes subject to all the vicissitudes of time and change. This is the hazard which faces every religion. The spirit which inspired the religion, which is the presence of God himself, becomes overshadowed by human sins and infirmity. When we look at the Christian churches today and recall their history, it often seems more like a record of human sin than of divine grace. If we look deep enough, we shall see that the Spirit of God is always present, changing people's lives, moving them to love and service, often effecting radical changes in society, inspiring people with ideals of sacrifice, with visions of truth, with the fire of mystical experience. But the other side, not only of sin, but of human limitations, of cultural blindness, above all of narrowness of mind and fanaticism, is only too evident. If the myth of the church is to be revived today, it must find new forms of expression. Its universal meaning has to be discovered, its relationship to all the religious traditions of mankind, its relevance to the world in which we live. Such a rebirth of the myth of the church is already taking place, but it still has a long way to go. Above all, we have to discover the source of those deformations which have afflicted all the churches and have led to their present state.

We have first of all to consider the cultural limitations of Christianity. It was the product of a Semitic culture which had a very narrow horizon. Israel grew up in the small world of the Middle East, bounded by Egypt on one side and Babylonia on the other. Influences from Persia and from Greece later came to enrich it, but its vision, though profound, remained very limited. It had no knowledge of the cultures of India or China or the rest of the world, and imagined that all those who were outside Israel were without knowledge of God, just as the Greeks imagined that all who were not Greeks were 'barbarians.' Also, its vision was temporally very limited, so that it did not extend beyond the year 5000 BC and imagined that it was living in the 'last age' of the world.

It was from this milieu and with these limitations that the Christian church came out into the Graeco-Roman world. The Greeks brought with them their genius for philosophy, and the Romans their genius for law, and the theology and organization of the church were built up by these means. This certainly gave the church a profound theology and powerful organization but it also brought grave limitations. Greek philosophy was essentially a rational philosophy, and though Plato brought to it the insights of intuitive wisdom, its influence was more and more felt in the development of logical rational thought and scientific system which are characteristic of western man. The church thus became dominated by that system of rational thought, which is the cause of the imbalance of the western world, though the imaginative insight and intuitive wisdom of the biblical tradition was never wholly lost. The result of this was that the church became obsessed with the need to construct logical formulas and rational systems by which to express its faith. When these formals or 'dogmas' came to be reinforced by the legal system of Rome, the Inquisition came into being, and the attempt was made to impose this doctrinal system by force. The Reformation was a revolt against this rational legal system and sought to set the church free by a return to the Bible, but again the western mind introduced its logical formulas and legal systems and each church set itself up as alone professing the true faith. The result is that the church today consists of innumerable sects, each claiming to represent the true faith and denouncing the others as 'heretical.' The ecumenical movement has come to seek to overcome these divisions and to return to the unity of the church, but unless it abandons the search for doctrinal formulas and legal systems, and recovers the intuitive wisdom of the Bible and of ancient man, there is little hope of success.

It is here that the encounter with eastern thought, with its intuitive basis, is crucial. Christianity cannot grow as a religion today, unless it abandons its western culture with its rational masculine bias and learns again the feminine intuitive understanding of the East. The suppression of women in the church is but one of the many signs of this masculine domination. This does not mean, of course, that the real values of science and reason, of logical and systematic thought have to be abandoned. Reason has to be 'married' to intuition; it has to learn to surrender itself to the deeper intuitions of the Spirit. These intuitions come, as we have seen, from the presence of the Spirit in the depths of the soul. They are an expression of a growing self-awareness, of an integral knowledge not of the mind or reason alone, but of the whole man, body, soul and spirit. Faith itself is a function not of the rational but of the intuitive mind. It does not consist, as western man has often thought, in an assent to logical propositions, but in a grasp of the 'mystery' of truth as a whole. The intuitive mind, it will be remembered, does not analyze but grasps the whole, or rather opens itself to the whole, allows it to take possession. So faith opens itself to the mystery of God, to the unfathomable truth and allows it to take possession of the soul. So for a Christian faith is an openness to the mystery of God in Christ mediated through the myth of Christ. The myth appeals to the imagination, to the heart, and transforms the person. Later, reason may come to distinguish different aspects of the myth and relate them to one another, but always a return must be made to the 'mystery,' to the reality, which both myth and reason seek to express.

The reunion of the Christian churches can only come, therefore, through a rediscovery of the 'mystery of Christ' in all its dimensions, and this means that it must be related to the whole history of humanity and of the creation. This will only come when we have learned to discover the presence of this mystery, that is, of the church, in all the religions of mankind. Every genuine religion bears witness to some aspect of the divine mystery, embodied in its myths and rituals, its customs and traditions, its prayer and mystical experience, and each has something to give to the universal church. The narrow-mindedness which has divided the Christian churches from one another, has also divided the Christian religion from other religions. Today we have to open ourselves to the truth in all religions. Each religion must learn to discern its essential truth and to reject its cultural and historical limitations. This may be a painful experience, a rejection of innumerable elements in religion which have grown up with the cultural and historical development of a religion and have often been identified with the religion itself. Yet this seems to be the only path open to humanity today. What stands in the way is the dominant mentality of the western world. This is the hour of trial for western man. Will he continue to build up his scientific world with nuclear power leading to the devastation of the earth, or will he learn to repent, to turn back, to rediscover the source of life, the wisdom of Mother Earth, which is also the wisdom of the East?

The church also has to learn the secret of this intuitive wisdom. Though the Mystery of Christ is always present in the church, and is the secret presence by which she lives, yet the doctrinal and sacramental structures of the church are all the product of the western mind, whether it is Roman Catholicism or Greek Orthodoxy, or Anglicanism, Lutheranism or Calvinism, or the various Protestant churches in Britain and America. All alike are developments of the Mystery of Christ produced by the Western mind. Neither papacy nor episcopacy or any other system of church government is found in the New Testament. They are the work of the Greek and Roman genius, building on the foundation of the New Testament. Jesus himself gave no system of government to the church. He founded it on twelve disciples to represent the new Israel, the new people of God, and according to the earliest tradition, gave Peter, as the Rock (*Cephas*), a position of leadership in it; he also gave it by all accounts the sacramental rites of baptism and the eucharist. But beyond this he left everything to the guidance of the Holy Spirit, who was to lead his disciples into all truth. All that has been erected on this foundation, all doctrinal and sacramental and legal systems, are the work of the western mind, guided no doubt by the Holy Spirit in varying degrees, but all alike conditioned by historical circumstances.

The fact that Rome became the center of Christendom is an accident of history and the Bishop of Rome only acquired his present position after many centuries. One may hold that this development was providential, but there is no reason to believe that the present structure of the papacy is permanent, or that the church may not acquire a new structure in the context of future history.

In the same way, episcopacy as a system of government was only gradually established and there is no reason to hold that the present structure, whether in its Roman or Greek or Anglican or Lutheran form, should always remain. All church structures are subject to the law of historical growth.

In the same way the doctrinal structures, built up by the Western mind on the foundations of the faith of the apostles, are all historically conditioned and bear the mark of the limitations of the western mind. It is certain that the people of Asia will never accept Christianity in its present form. Five centuries and more of missionary activity have shown the futility of the attempt. Christianity remains for the people of the East a foreign religion, moulded by the western mind.

We have to go beyond all these historical structures and recover the original Myth of Christianity, the living truth which was revealed in the New Testament. But this cannot be done by the western mind alone. We have to open ourselves to the revelation of the divine mystery, which took place in Asia, in Hinduism and Buddhism, in Taoism, Confucianism and Shintoism. Nor can we neglect the intuitive wisdom of more primitive people, the Australian Aborigines, the Polynesian Islanders, the African Bushmen, the American Indians, the Eskimoes. All over the world the supreme Spirit has left signs of his presence. The Christian mystery is the mystery of God's presence in Man, and we cannot neglect any sign of that presence. Even the atheist and the agnostic can bear witness to this mystery. Atheism and agnosticism signify the rejection of certain images and concepts of God or of Truth, which are historically conditioned and therefore inadequate. Atheism is a challenge to religion to purify its images and concepts and come nearer to the truth of the divine mystery.

We have always to bear in mind that the divine Mystery, the ultimate Truth, always lies beyond conception. The great myths of the world reveal different aspects of this mystery according to the imaginative insight of the different peoples of the world. In Jesus the Myth took a particular historical form which is recorded in the New Testament and preserved in the church. But the Myth is capable of ever new understanding as the human mind reflects upon it. It has been given a particular rational and legal structure by the Western mind, but the eastern mind and the primitive intuitive mind throughout the world is capable of discovering new depths of meaning in it, and the modern western mind, freed from the shackles of a mechanistic model of the universe, is capable of rediscovering the meaning of the Myth. The building of the church as the manifestation in history of the presence of God in man, is therefore the work of all mankind. The Hindu, the Buddhist, the Muslim, the humanist, the philosopher, the scientist, have all something to give and something to receive. The Christian, to whatever church he may belong, cannot claim to have the monopoly of the Truth. We are all pilgrims in search of truth, of reality, of final fulfilment. But we have to recognize that this Truth will always remain beyond our understanding. No science or philosophy or theology can ever encompass the Truth. No poetry or art or human institution can ever embody it. The great myths are only reflections in the human imagination of that transcendent Mystery. Even the Myth of Christ belongs still to a world of signs, and we have to go beyond the Myth to the Mystery itself, beyond word and thought, beyond life and death. For the ultimate Mystery can only be known through the passage of death. 'You have died,' wrote St Paul, 'and your life is hidden with Christ in God; when Christ who is our life appears, you also will appear with him in glory.'[12]

Jesus left his disciples with the expectation that he would appear again and bring this world to an end. This is the condition under which we all live. At no time in history has the world been nearer to destruction than it is at the present moment. There are forces present in the world which are capable of destroying all life on this planet and those who control these forces are themselves beyond control. It may be that the Western world will change, or at least a sufficient number will be there to initiative a change, to undergo a *metanoia*, a change of heart, and set the world on another course, bringing about this marriage of East and West. But there can be no finality even in this. Our destiny is not in this world, and we have to be prepared to go beyond death. We have to die to this world and everything in it, that is, everything that changes and passes in this world, to find the reality which does not change or pass. Above all, we have to go beyond words and images and concepts. No imaginative vision or conceptual framework is adequate to the great reality. When Christ will appear in glory, it will not be in any earthly form or in any manner we can conceive. 'For now we see in a mirror dimly, but then face to face;'[13] and we shall only 'appear in glory,' when we have died to ourselves and become a 'new creation.'[14] Then alone shall we encounter the fullness of truth and reality which is also the fullness of wisdom and knowledge and the fullness of bliss and love. Then only will the final marriage take place, of East and West, of man and woman, of matter and mind, of time and eternity.

22. A Church Divided by Sin[15]
As he completed The Golden String *(The book appeared in 1954), Bede*

Griffiths already saw the church as coextensive with the whole of humanity. In this light, the divided Christianity of the twentieth century stood out with stark clarity. It was natural for him to see the history of western civilization and culture since the Renaissance and Reformation as an almost unmitigated decline. While Bede recognized the dark shadow of historical Christianity — corruption, violence and oppression — he found the cause of these evils within Christendom in the sin of individuals rather than in any systemic shortcomings. The church stands radiant and inviolate in the world, above these personal failings. If the Gospel of Christ had so far failed to transform this world, it is 'we' who must assume the blame. It is due simply to the infidelity of believers that the church has been divided and that humanity has not yet been drawn together around its center, Jesus Christ.

The divisions which at present exist among Christians are but one aspect of that deeper conflict which divides mankind and dismembers the Body of Christ. For we must always remember that the bounds of the church are coextensive with mankind. When the Word of God, who is that Wisdom by which and through which and for which all things exist, assumed a human nature, he came to unite all mankind in one Body in himself. There is no man from the beginning to the end of the world, who does not receive grace from Christ and who is not called to eternal life in him. He is the true light which enlightens every man coming into the world. It is the same Spirit which from the beginning of history has been leading all men by his grace; it is the same Word, which enlightens them through their reason and conscience and prepares them for the revelation of himself. All men, therefore, who are guided by their reason and conscience and follow the light which has been given them, are truly by their implicit faith and desire disciples of Christ vitally related to his church. And yet while we hold to the absolute universality of grace and believe that no one is deprived of it save by his own deliberate choice, we must hold with equal certainty that God chose to reveal himself to one particular people and establish among them the unique way of salvation. All religious traditions contain some elements of the truth, but there is only one absolutely true religion; all religions have taught something of the way of salvation, but there is only one absolute Way. Christ is the Way, the Truth and the Life, and without him no man comes to the Father.

149

In the same way we must believe that there is one church, which was founded by Christ upon the Rock of Peter, to be the way of salvation for all mankind. In this church all those elements of truth which have been dispersed among the different peoples of the earth are gathered into unity; it is the center from which they derive their value and significance. The church with her hierarchy and sacraments is the sole basis of unity for mankind, for it is this visible, hierarchical church which constitutes the mystical Body of Christ on earth. Her ministers and her sacraments are simply the chosen instruments of divine grace, the means by which men are incorporated into the Body of Christ and made to participate in the light of his truth. It is the building up of this Body of Christ, this City of God, which is the real purpose of human life. Material civilizations and social cultures have their rise and fall, but their value lies simply in their capacity to assist mankind in its progress towards this City of God. This is the standard by which they are to be judged. Our own civilization will pass, as those of the past have done; there is no need either to fear or to regret it. For the "schema", the "outward form" of this world, as St Paul called it, is passing away; but beneath the outward form there is being built up continuously the Body of Christ, which is the unity of mankind in Truth and Charity. It is a hidden and mysterious process, which will only be realized in its fullness when this world of space and time has passed away altogether. Then we shall see the church as it really is, as the fulfilment of the whole creation, the achievement of man's destiny by his participation in the life of God.

But what, it may be said, of all the scandals of church history, the evil within the church, the corruption of popes and bishops, of clergy and people, the atrocities of the Crusades, of the Inquisition and the wars of religion? There can be but one answer to this question. This was the mystery of the Crucifixion of the Body of Christ. Christ was crucified once in his natural body, but he is crucified daily in his mystical body, the church. This is what all Christians experience daily in their lives. Christ is crucified in us when that truth and charity, which constitute the essence of the church, are betrayed by us. The church remains essentially holy, but we who make up the members of the church betray her by our sins.

Not long ago Mr. Middleton Murry wrote a book in which he spoke of "the betrayal of Christ by the churches." To this Father Gerald Vann wrote a reply in which he spoke of "the betrayal of the church by the Christians." Both were concerned with the same facts, but Mr. Murry spoke as a Protestant, Father Vann as a Catholic. It is impossible for Christ to be betrayed by the church, because the church is his Body and lives by his life, which is essentially holy. But the members of that Body may sin and so betray both Christ and the church, and this is the situation in which we find ourselves. We are all more or less guilty, and the responsibility for the world's misery lies with the Christian people as much as with anybody.

All the great errors of our civilisation from the Reformation to the Russian revolution have arisen because of the failure of Christians to embody the truth of Christ in their lives. If Communism presents itself now as the great enemy of our civilization, it is because it embodies, in however distorted a manner, that thirst for social justice which Christianity failed to satisfy. When Marx declared that the aim of Communism was to "realise the essence of man" in the classless society, he was proclaiming what is the real aim of Christianity itself. For Christ is truly the Perfect Man, in whom all the potentialities of human nature are realised, and it is by membership of his Body, that we become part of a social organism in which all the conflicts of class and race and religion are transcended, and man realizes his true nature as a son of God.

Such is the vision of the church which Catholicism presents to us. It corresponds with all the deepest needs of mankind at the present day. While remaining true to that tradition of faith and doctrine which has been handed down from the beginning, it seeks to embrace all that is true in modern science and ancient philosophy. It envisages mankind in the whole length and breadth of its history as part of a divine plan, through which the destiny of man is to be fulfilled in a new order of being transcending this world of space and time. It faces the full tragedy of the situation in which we find ourselves, and finds the source of conflict in human life in the free choice of the will by which man becomes subject to sin.

To be a Christian is to accept the responsibility for sin not only in oneself but in others also. It is to recognize that we all bear the responsibility for one another.

23. *The Arrested Gospel*[16]
In a letter from Bede's South Indian ashram of Shantivanam to The Tablet *thirty years after* The Golden String, *we hear a very different voice. For many years now, Bede has been confronted again and again by the dissatisfaction and alienation of Europeans and North Americans who have left western Christianity behind to come to India in search of spiritual wisdom. He takes up their cause against a 'formal, dogmatic, moralistic' Christianity which they have found to be 'a positive obstacle to their interior growth.'*

Hinduism, Buddhism and Sufism have attracted these seekers with a promise and an experience of meaning and fulfillment which they had not found in their own religious tradition. Many of these spiritual pilgrims, on the other hand, found in Bede Griffiths and the life of his ashram a Christianity that spoke to their hearts as well as to their minds. Bede argues that 'biblical Christianity,' as it has developed so far through a western consciousness, is no longer enough. It is in opening itself to the traditions of the East that Christianity will discover itself once again as "an interior religion, a religion of the heart and not of the head," a religion of personal experience which gives meaning and direction to human life.

Sir: May I add a further comment to the notes from an ashram which you published in *The Tablet* of 24 March? We have had the same experience here in our ashram in South India of people coming from the West in "search of God." They are of all ages from 20 and even under to over 70, of both sexes and from many countries. They are almost all sincere seekers of a deeper meaning in life than the West seems to give them. They go to Hindu ashrams and Buddhist monasteries and to any Guru who will teach them a method of Yoga or meditation which will enable them to find the truth and the life which they are seeking. Those who come to our ashram are nearly all Christians, mostly Catholic, though some are Jewish and some have no particular religion. What is disconcerting is that so many Christians, especially Catholics, seem to find their religion an obstacle to their search for truth and reality. For most of them, Christianity is deemed to be identified with a formal, dogmatic, moralistic religion, which is a positive obstacle to their interior growth.

What is the reason for this? I suggest that it may be that in the past, when western society was nominally Christian, a formal religion was normally sufficient to give one a sense of direction in life. But now that this is no longer so, a formal religion simply breaks down in contact with the realities of life. What people today are seeking is an interior religion, a religion of the heart and not of the head, which at the same time gives a sense of meaning and direction in life. This is what Hinduism, Buddhism, Sufism and other forms of eastern doctrine give and Christianity in the way in which it is now presented seems unable to give to many people. May this not be a sign that Christianity today needs to come to terms with oriental religion? Is biblical Christianity, as interpreted in the West, any longer an adequate religion for the world today? The Bible belongs to the history of humanity as a whole and needs to be interpreted in the light of eastern experience no less than western.

It is perhaps significant that Donald Nicholl is at present conducting a seminar at the Ecumenical Institute in Jerusalem on "The People of the Book in the light of Asia." May it not be that the "people of the Book" — Jews, Christians and Muslims — cannot solve the problems of the world today, unless they are willing to learn from the religions of India and the Far East? God did not only reveal himself to Israel, but has revealed himself in other ways to other people and we need the witness of all people to the truth of Christianity.

24. Defending the Emerging New Church[17]
Cardinal Joseph Ratzinger, as head of the Congregation for the Doctrine of the Faith under Pope John Paul II, firmly and diligently exercised his office as custodian of Roman Catholic orthodoxy. His name came to signify doctrinal caution; for many, it connoted an over-frequent, rigid and repressive use of authority in the church. In August 1984, Cardinal Ratzinger was interviewed at length by the Italian journalist Vittorio Messori. Extracts from the interview soon appeared in the Italian magazine Jesus, *and the next year a more extended edition of it was published as a book.[18]*

The Cardinal's largely negative assessment of developments within the church since Vatican II prompted a vigorous response from four English theologians, in the Dominican journal New Blackfriars.[19] *Further indignant responses soon appeared in* The Tablet. *Bede joined in to affirm his own faith*

153

in the continuing movement of the Spirit in a church which was suddenly, in this new openness, discovering itself. For Bede, the meaning of the Council and its turbulent aftermath was clear: the collapse of an obsolete institutional model, the 'old Roman system,' and a rebirth of the living church, a community anointed and empowered by the Holy Spirit.

In this and other communications to The Tablet, *we find Bede Griffiths passionately involved with current issues of the church and its life. Here is a corrective to the impression which we might draw from some of his books, that Bede's attention was exclusively directed to the interior life and the realization of the 'Self,' that he was out of touch with the pivotal events of the time of the Council or, worse still, that he had had turned away from the life of the church in his movement to the East. When, in his writings, Bede is expounding the Vedanta or the 'universal wisdom,' Christ and the living church have not been left behind. We shall find them reappearing swiftly from within, particularly in a situation of challenge.*

Sir: Perhaps the "scandalous optimism" which Cardinal Ratzinger finds in the church today can be reconciled with what others call the "scandalous pessimism" of Cardinal Ratzinger, if one considers that what is collapsing today is the old system of Roman Catholicism and what is taking its place is a new understanding of the Catholic Church.

Consider the following facts:

1) in the years since the Second Vatican Council, tens of thousands of priests and religious have left the priesthood and the religious life, and seminaries and novitiates have been closed down, so that in many parts in a few years there will not be a sufficient number of priests to maintain the system.

2) The attendance of Catholics at Mass has dropped in most countries to between 10 and 20 percent and in some countries even below this. At the same time regular formal confession has in many places almost disappeared.

3) Since the publication of the encyclical *Humanae Vitae*, the directives of the Holy See have come to be considered as irrelevant by many Catholics and are simply ignored.

4) The whole clerical system in which the church is ruled by a male priesthood, so that women and married people are denied any share in the government of the church, is coming to be questioned.

On the other hand, there are the following facts:

1) The biblical movement has spread throughout the church and Catholics are learning to find in the Gospel itself the guide and inspiration for their lives.

2) The church is seen as the People of God, in which each and all receive the same gift of the Holy Spirit and share as members of the Body of Christ in the authority of Christ, the Head.

3) The offices of bishops and priests are seen as "ministries" in the church, to which some are called for the service of the people, but there are many other ministries mentioned in the New Testament to which both men and women, whether married or single, may be called, so that all alike can share in the government of the church.

4) The church is seen today not as a closed system of dogma and morality controlled by a clerical hierarchy, but as a charismatic community, empowered by the Holy Spirit to proclaim a message of liberation to all humanity.

This may seem to some an example of that "scandalous optimism" of which Cardinal Ratzinger complains and they would wish to restore the old Roman system, brought up to date along the lines of the new Code of Canon Law. But is that possible, or even desirable? Perhaps that is one of the questions which the Synod of Bishops will be called to answer.

25. The Claims of the Papacy[20]

If Bede Griffiths found Cardinal Ratzinger, chief of the prepotent Roman congregation, hardly aware of the power of the Holy Spirit working within the People of God, he was himself painfully conscious of the progressive concentration of institutional power in the Bishop of Rome. Two very different visions of the Catholic Church were encountering one another in these decades after the Council. Bede vigorously opposed the conception, which had developed during the middle ages and prevailed until the present in Roman Catholicism, of church authority as residing ultimately — and sometimes almost exclusively — in the pope.

Sir: Michael Penty[21] has shown that the claim to political power on the part of the popes has been "laid to rest" by the declaration on religious freedom of the Second Vatican Council. But the much more serious claims of the power of the pope over the other bishops and over the church as a whole have never been repudiated. It is true, as Martin Brett says,[22] that these claims were never formally adopted but they were implicitly accepted by the popes of the Middle Ages and have never been repudiated. Yet every one of these claims is questioned today by Catholic scholars and theologians as well as by all the Christian churches.

It is the whole medieval conception of the papacy which is questioned today and which appears to be fatally flawed. It is this that has been responsible for such tragic divisions among Christians and which remains as an insuperable obstacle to Christian unity. We have to go beyond the medieval papacy to the ancient understanding of the pope in the church before the division between East and West, if we are to have any hope of Christian unity.

26. The True Magisterium[23]

We may be surprised at this crisp lesson in ecclesiology from Bede Griffiths, less than three years before the end of his life. Bede re-envisions the distribution of teaching authority within the Roman Catholic Church so that it becomes a property of the whole body rather than being concentrated at the apex of a hierarchical pyramid. If India is a long way from Rome, Bede's conception of the charism of truth in the church is even farther from the institutional 'received version.' Once again, he clearly affirms the primacy of the magisterium of the Holy Spirit speaking through the people who are, themselves, the church. If this doctrine is revolutionary, so are Jesus' words, "But you are not to be called rabbi, for you have one teacher, and you are all brethren. And call no man your father on earth...Neither be called masters..."[24]

We hear a great deal today about the magisterium of the church, and those who have a position of authority in the church are even required to take an oath of loyalty and make a solemn profession of faith in the teachings of the magisterium. It is important, therefore, to understand exactly what is meant by this word magisterium.

Many people today think that the magisterium consists of the pope and the Roman Curia, but this is mistaken. "Magisterium" comes from the Latin *magister*, a master, and signifies authority to teach. Strictly speaking there is only one such authority in the church and that is the Holy Spirit whom Jesus promised to his disciples to

156

"lead them into all truth." The apostles, as St Paul says, were commissioned by the Holy Spirit to preach the gospel in the name of Christ, and it is generally believed that the apostles commissioned others named presbyters (elders) and bishops (overseers) to succeed them. Thus it is generally recognised today that the bishops who derive this authority from Christ through the apostles constitute the magisterium of the church.

But there are in fact four organs of the magisterium. The first is that of the pope and the Roman Curia, which is concerned with the day-to-day administration of the church. But that is subordinate to the authority of the bishops in communion with the pope who constitute the magisterium properly speaking. This was made clear at the Second Vatican Council.

But it is here that a third organ of the magisterium came into play. The bishops were accompanied by *periti*, or expert theologians, who advised the bishops and were actually responsible for developing the understanding of the church which emerged at the Council. In a sense it is to the theologians that the word magisterium properly applies, since a theologian is a *magister sacrae doctrinae*, a master of sacred doctrine, who has been commissioned to teach theology in the name of the church. The theologian, of course, does not speak or act on his own, but as a member of the church in cooperation with his fellow theologians.

There is still another organ of the magisterium, perhaps the most important of all, and that is the laity. The laity consists of the people (*laos*) of God. Each of them receives in his or her baptism the gift of the Holy Spirit and is given authority to teach, to govern and to offer sacrifice in the name of the church, sharing in the authority of Christ, the supreme master, as prophet, priest and king. The laity, therefore, through the gift of the Spirit in baptism and its confirmation in the sacrament of confirmation, all alike share in the magisterium, or the teaching authority of the Church.

Strictly speaking, it is the laity, the people of God, who constitute the church, while popes, bishops and priests are "ministers" chosen from among the laity and commissioned by the Holy Spirit to act in the name of the church.

In the course of the centuries the Roman Church has developed a structure by which all authority is seen to come from above, from the pope and the bishops, but this is not the ideal of the church as found in the New Testament. It is of the whole church that it is said, "You are a holy nation, a royal priesthood," and all members of the church share equally in the gift of the Holy Spirit.

In an authoritarian structure of society — what in the Soviet Union is called a "command structure" — all authority is seen to belong to the rulers who have the right of command, while the rest of the people are required to obey. It is this system which has been overthrown in the Soviet Union and in Eastern Europe, and the right of the people to share in the government of the country has been admitted. The Catholic Church today still retains what is basically a command structure but the place of the laity as the people of God with authority to share in the government of the church is coming to be recognized.

The authority of popes and bishops need not be denied, but it has to be recognized that they are responsible to the laity, the people of God, for their teaching and their actions. Just as the pope has no authority apart from the bishops, so the pope and the bishops have no authority apart from the people from whom they are chosen and whom they represent.

The church forms the body of Christ and all alike share in the gift of the Spirit and in the authority of Christ the head. One may hope that as the secular world more and more discovers the value of freedom and democracy, the Roman Church also may come to recognise the unity of the church, including all baptized Christians, as the body of Christ, and the right of the layman and laywoman to speak and act under the guidance of the Holy Spirit in the name of the church as a whole.

27. Ecumenism and Renewal[25]
Coming to Catholicism from outside, Bede Griffiths had brought with him an awareness of the values and prophetic voices which were present among other Christians. His vision widened further, however. It soon proved impossible for Bede to conceive of the reunion of the Christian churches without the opening of Christianity to a respectful encounter with the other religions. By virtue of

a cosmic revelation or cosmic covenant, Hindus, Buddhists and Muslims participate in the economy of grace and already experience an implicit presence of Christ and of the church. Church renewal must open Catholicism to a 'renewal of the Christian spirit' and break down the 'monolithic unity' which makes the church unapproachable to non-Catholics. The essential principle of diversity, rooted in a deeper unity, will open the church to its true universality. Ecclesial renewal, ecumenism and the birth of a true 'world church' are inseparable. Bede's view, expressed with breathtaking sweep of thought in a 1963 Examiner article (reprinted in Christ in India), *would not essentially change through the years. In the lucid simplicity and sublime confidence of this vision, the agonized conflicts of twenty centuries seem things of the past, hardly more than troubled dreams of the night.*

When Pope John first summoned the Vatican Council he put before it three objectives. The first was the renewal of the Catholic Church from within; the second was the reunion of Christendom through the development of an ecumenical spirit in relation to the separated churches; the third was the manifestation of the mission of the church to the world.

These three objectives cannot, of course, be taken altogether separately; each is implied in the other. The renewal of the church has been shown to be intimately related to the ecumenical attitude towards separated Christians, and the mission of the church to the world is in turn largely dependent on the development of a renewed and reunited Christianity. Yet we can see that there is a difference of emphasis and the emphasis of the first sessions of the council was clearly on the interior renewal of the church.

The adoption of the schema on the liturgy, especially that part of it which concerns the use of the vernacular, has opened the way to a renewal of the Christian spirit, which has been sought ever since Pius X published his encyclical on the liturgy, in which he said that the full participation of the laity in the liturgy of the church was the indispensable source of the Christian spirit. But it is only now that the reforms have been made which make this participation possible. As long as the language and a great many of the ceremonies of the liturgy are unintelligible to the majority of Christians it is idle to expect any serious renewal of the Christian spirit. But now that the principles of a complete renewal of the liturgy have been drafted and approved, there is nothing which stands in the way, unless it should be the failure on the part of the different hierarchies to put these principles into practice.

The debate on the place of the bishop in the church in relation to the pope, which occupied so much time in the second session of the council, is also an important element in the renewal of the church. Nothing stands so much in the way of creating an image of the church as truly catholic and universal as the impression which is given of the church as a vast monolith with the pope at its head and the bishops occupying a position of inferiority, totally subordinate to him. This was, of course, never wholly true, but it cannot be denied that the place of the bishop in the church has not been fully realized since the Council of Trent, or even since Hildebrand. It may be said that already one of the principal effects of the Vatican Council in having brought so many bishops to Rome is that it has awakened this consciousness among the bishops, and however the place of the bishop may eventually be defined, it is impossible that this consciousness should be lost.

It need hardly be said how much this will affect the attitude of the Eastern churches to the Catholic Church. The one really serious obstacle to the reunion of East and West is the position of the pope. The Orthodox feel with some justice that the papacy had undergone a long evolution in the West, which has taken it very far in many respects from the position which it occupied in the early centuries. But once the principle of the collegiality of the bishops as successors of the apostles is finally established and the supreme authority of the church is seen to reside alike in the bishops with the pope at their head and in the pope as the head of the college of bishops, but in neither apart from the other, then the possibility of the acceptance of such a position by the Orthodox churches becomes very real.

In any case, the acceptance of the principle of diversity in the church, not only in liturgy, but also in theology, in spirituality and in discipline, which was brought out so strongly in the Council, opens the way to breaking down the image of a monolithic unity and to giving the eastern churches the position which belongs to them by right. As long as the idea remains that the Latin church, with its liturgy and theology and canon law, is the norm for the whole Catholic Church there can be no hope of any serious rapprochment with the East. We have to realize that the traditions of the eastern churches are just as ancient and venerable as those of the Roman Church and that for the most part they are quite independent of it. Greek and Russian theology and spirituality, its customs of a married clergy and the use of icons, and so many other diversities, which belong to the eastern churches, set them apart from the Latin church, not in any position of inferiority but as sister churches, expressing differences of culture which are absolutely necessary if the church is to realize her true catholicity.

Thus the renewal of the church from within has already begun to open the way to the reunion of Christendom, at least in regard to the great world of Orthodoxy. But this conception of cultural differences in the church has also a definite bearing on the third objective of the council, the mission of the church to the world. The problems of the church in the face of the modern world in regard to poverty, race, war and such matters of burning importance came up for discussion in the fourth session under the famous 'Schema 13.'

But the question of the relation of the church to other religions is perhaps the most fundamental problem of all, because it concerns the very nature of the church and divine revelation. The church is confronted today with at least three other religions, Hinduism, Buddhism and Islam, each claiming to be universal and each numbering several hundred million followers. So far the attitude of the church to such religions has been mainly negative. They have been regarded as 'false' religions and no attempt has been made to come to terms with them. But it is clear now, as a result of the council, that such an attitude cannot be maintained. It is a hopeful sign that the present pope should have established the Secretariat for non-Christian Religions, whose work runs parallel with that for Christian Unity. Now that this has come into existence, the whole problem of the relation of the church to these other religions, that is of the mission of the church in the strict sense, will have to be faced.

It seems clear that what is required is an extension of the principle of the ecumenical movement among Christians to the sphere of our relations with other religions. It is not possible in the modern world to go out to 'convert' Muslims, Buddhists or Hindus. Such an attitude only produces resentment and often a violent reaction. We have to learn to approach the Muslim, the Buddhist and the Hindu as we have learned to approach our separated brethren among Christians. We have first of all to learn to meet them with love and respect, recognizing that each one is our brother, sons of a common Father and called like us to eternal life. It is only on this basis that any real encounter between the church and other religions can take place.

We have then to learn to understand these other religions and to see them in their true relation to the church. This may involve a certain development in our theology, but the principles of such a development seem to be clear. It cannot be doubted that the way of salvation is open to all men. Christ assumed the nature of all men, died for all men and redeemed all mankind. There is therefore no man from the first to the last man who is outside this saving economy of grace. When we ask ourselves how this saving grace of Christ reaches those who are outside the visible sphere of the church, the principles of an answer are given by tradition. Aquinas himself, asking the question how men could be saved before the coming of Christ, replies that though they could not have an explicit faith in Christ, they could have an implicit faith, in as much as they had faith in divine providence, since 'belief in his providence includes all those things which God dispenses in time for man's salvation.'[26]

There is therefore the possibility of an implicit faith in Christ, through which a man can be saved, wherever there is a genuine faith in divine providence. This is what is sometimes called the Covenant of the Natural Law, or the Cosmic Covenant. It extends to all men without exception and it is to this 'cosmic' covenant that such religions as Hinduism, Buddhism and Islam belong, though in Islam we have to recognize also positive influences from both Judaism and Christianity. Thus we cannot look upon the Hindu, the Buddhist or the Muslim as outside the covenant of grace. Through the elements of truth in their religion, which derive from this cosmic revelation, by which God makes himself known through nature and conscience, they belong to the economy of grace. There is already a 'presence' of

Christ and therefore of the church in all genuine religion, however hidden it may be.

It is our task, therefore, to meet this presence of Christ in our brothers in other religions, as we have learned to meet it in our separated christian brothers. Just as we recognize a common faith and baptism and a common bible with other Christians, we have to recognize an implicit faith and desire for baptism (in so far as they believe in and desire God's will for their salvation) and the elements of a common revelation in every religion. It is obvious that this involves a considerable rethinking of our conception of the mission of the church. We have to acknowledge that the church has not only to teach but also to learn from other religions. We have to seek for those elements of truth which exist in each religion and try to present the Gospel not simply in opposition to such religion but as its fulfilment.

The reform of the liturgy already suggests the way in which the church could divest herself of western forms in the liturgy by adopting the language and soon one may hope the music and art and architecture of the different peoples of the world, instead of clinging to the outmoded forms of Gothic and Baroque. But a more serious problem arises in regard to theology. Must we continue to present our Catholic doctrine in terms borrowed from Greek philosophy? It is now coming to be recognized that just as unity in sacramental worship can be expressed in diverse forms of liturgy, so unity in faith can find expression in various forms of theology. We have already a Greek and a Latin theology which differ not only in their expression but also in their mode of thought. Can we not conceive a theology which would make use of the modes of thought and expression of the Vedanta or of Confucian philosophy, just as the Fathers and Aquinas made use of Greek philosophy?

Such a diversity both in liturgy and theology would be in harmony with the new understanding of the government of the church which is coming into light as a result of the Vatican Council. The movement now is towards a decentralization of the church, which would allow much greater freedom for the bishops' conferences in the different parts of the world. In this way one could envisage a return to something like the old patriarchal system, by which the great partriarchates, Antioch, Alexandria, Constantinople and Rome each constituted a separate 'province' of the church with its own distinct liturgy and school of theology and system of church government.

It is not difficult to conceive on these lines how we might eventually see new churches rising in India, China and Japan and in different parts of Africa, each having its own distinctive cultural forms, adapted to the traditions of the different people, with its own liturgy, its own forms of theology and its own system of church government. At the same time the speed of communication today makes it easy for all churches to keep in touch with the centre, so that the unity of the church, with its one faith and sacramental order and its hierarchy acknowledging the pope as the successor of St Peter and the head of the whole church, would not be endangered.

Such a development would open the way to a genuine ecumenical spirit towards the different religions of the world, by which the church would be able to meet each of them at the deepest level of its doctrine and spiritual life. On the part of the church there would be a profound assimilation of the cultural forms of these religions, particularly their philosophy and their spiritual discipline. On the part of the other religions there would be the possibility of a real confrontation with the mystery of Christ, not presented under alien cultural forms but in a manner which would bring out the deep affinities existing in all the great religious traditions. In this meeting every kind of syncretism, of course, has to be avoided, which might impoverish the truth of the Christian message. But this is exactly what the Greek and Latin Fathers accomplished in regard to Greek philosophy and Roman Law. To undertake this synthesis with the Vedanta, and Mahayana Buddhism, with Chinese and Islamic philosophy is surely the task of the church of the future.

28. The Church of the Future[27]
How then, given his ready and far-reaching criticism of the existing Roman Catholic institution, would Bede Griffiths envision the church of his ideal? In a 1982 Tablet *article, Bede steps forward to offer what he calls a 'blue-print of an ecumenical church.' Wiping the drawing-board clear of fifteen centuries' accretions, he imagines an open and pluralistic church on the model of that which had prevailed before the separation of Eastern and Western*

Christianity. The church of the future might be, says Bede, a constellation of bishops' conferences analogous to the five patriarchates of the fifth century.

The model, as Bede develops it, is characterized by a decentralization of power and maximal space for pluralism of every kind. Ministry is broadened by a reconception of the papal office as well as by elimination of the obligation to priestly celibacy, of the restriction of the priesthood to men — and (with a hardly perceptible smile) of the College of Cardinals. Bede is clearly enjoying this exercise. Requirements for membership and communion are minimal: 'simply baptism in the name of the Father, the Son and the Holy Spirit, and faith in Jesus Christ as Lord and Savior.' This radical reconception of the church is an immediate corollary of Bede's unitive and sapiential perspective: Christianity is essentially something simple and inexpressible, a personal participation in the mystery of Christ. Everything else is accessory. Baptismal initiation, rarely mentioned by Bede in his writings, is given its central theological place in this sketch of the church. With compact clarity, this article shows us Bede's fundamental unitive principle at work on the communal and institutional reality of Christianity, right down to the point of concrete implications. The plan has not yet been adopted.

In view of the Pope's projected visit to Britain in the near future, the question of the relation of the Anglican Church and the other churches to the Roman Catholic Church acquires a new urgency. We should surely be thinking seriously about the kind of church which we envisage, when we think of the reunion of the Christian churches, and especially of the changes required in the Roman Church. Most people would probably agree that the greatest obstacle to the reunion of the churches is the present system of the papacy. It is this that has been the source of conflict ever since the time of the Reformation and it remains a problem for most other churches today. But the present system of the papacy is not something that belongs to the permanent constitution of the church. It grew up in the Middle Ages in the West after the separation of the eastern churches from Rome, and its structure was determined by historical circumstances, which no longer have validity today. The concentration of all power and authority in the church in the Pope and the Roman Curia was a gradual process, which culminated in the first Vatican Council and the decree on papal infallibility. But the Second Vatican Council began to reverse this process and we are now in a position to see more clearly what should be the basic structure of the Catholic Church and how the present structure of the Roman Church could be adapted to it.

We cannot do better than to take as a model for the church the structure of the church in the fifth century, before the division of the Greek Orthodox Church and the other eastern churches from Rome. In the fifth century under Pope St Leo the primacy of the church of Rome was recognized by all the eastern churches. At the Council of Chalcedon, when St Leo presented his Tome on the Incarnation, this was accepted by all the eastern bishops present, who cried out with one voice: "Peter has spoken by the voice of Leo." But while the primacy of the Bishop of Rome as the successor of Peter was generally acknowledged, there were four other "patriarchates," which were held in no less honour. There was that of Jerusalem, which was held in honour as the seat of the original church, though it now had little power. There was then the patriarchate of Antioch, representing the churches of the Syrian East; the Patriarchate of Alexandria, representing the Egyptian or Coptic Church and that of Ethiopia; there was the Patriarchate of Constantinople, representing the Greek churches, and finally there was the Patriarchate of Rome, representing the West. This, which is the most ancient model of the church, when it had reached its full expansion over the Roman Empire, is surely as good a model as we could wish for the church today. Since the Second Vatican Council the various bishops' conferences have gradually begun to assume an authority over their respective churches and it would not be difficult to envisage a development of the bishops' conferences into something like the ancient patriarchates. There could be a conference of European bishops' churches, of which the Pope would be head; a conference of North American churches, of African churches and finally of Asian churches together with the Australian church. Each of these conferences, like the ancient patriarchates, would be responsible for their churches in every way. In the ancient church each patriarchate had its own liturgy, its own system of theology and its own ecclesiastical organisation. The pope normally never interfered in any of the affairs of the other patriarchates. Only when a dispute arose which could not be settled within the patriarchate would recourse be had to the Roman See. This is surely how we should look forward to the development of the church today.

The bishops' conferences would be responsible for the appointment of bishops within their own conference, for the development of the liturgy, for doctrinal development in the context of their own culture and for the organization of their churches. If the Orthodox or the Anglican churches were to be reunited, they would each form a separate bishops' conference, managing their own affairs in all things, only acknowledging a center of unity in the church of Rome, and a right of recourse in matters of dispute. Other Christian churches, which were prepared to recognise this ministry in the service of unity in the Bishop of Rome, would also be able to form lesser conferences in communion with the larger ones. This would demand a recognition of other forms of ministry in the church beside the traditional ones of bishop, priest and deacon. In the early church there was a diversity of ministries; St Paul in his letter to the Corinthians mentions "apostles, prophets, teachers and administrators" and the letter to the Ephesians adds "pastors and evangelists." It would not be difficult to recognise the different Protestant ministries on this basis. The recognition of diverse ministries would, of course, demand the acceptance of a married clergy, which would be necessary with the Anglican and Orthodox churches also. It would also allow for the ordination of women to the ministry on an equality with men.

The structure of the Roman Church itself would, of course, have to be gradually changed. One would think that the recognition of the Vatican as a secular state with papal diplomats would no longer be required. The College of Cardinals, which is a product of the Middle Ages and has no place in the original constitution of the church, could be allowed to lapse, and the election of the pope given to a Bishops' Synod, which would be a permanent body, chosen from all the bishops' conferences. Other Christian churches having no bishops could also be represented in the Synod, which would thus include women as well as men. The doctrine of papal infallibility, which is at present such an insuperable stumbling block, could then be given a new interpretation. This doctrine was proclaimed at the first Vatican Council, when the position of the pope as head of the whole church reached its climax and supreme authority was held to reside in him alone. But the second Vatican Council has enabled us to see that the pope has no authority apart from the bishops, just as the bishops have no authority apart from the laity, the people of God. The gift of infallibility was given by Jesus to the whole church, when he communicated to the church the gift of the Holy Spirit, which was to guide his disciples into all truth. This gift of the Spirit is given to all Christians at their baptism and every Christian shares in the teaching authority of the church. The bishops and the pope have a special ministry of service to the church in preserving the truth of the apostolic teaching, but this authority can only be exercised in so far as they share in the communion of all the faithful. The charism of infallibility, or more simply of adherence to the truth of the Gospel, therefore, belongs to the whole church, though it may be exercised on occasion by the pope or the bishops, in the name of the church.

How would this pattern of the church work out at the parish level? Could not one envisage the different churches retaining their own autonomy? In any given area there might be a Roman Catholic, an Anglican, a Methodist and a Baptist church and others, each preserving its own traditional way of worship and organization. But these churches would all be in communion with one another. Anyone would be free to go to communion at another church, while respecting the distinctive way of worship of the other church. The representatives of the different churches would meet regularly and share their work as far as possible in common. The boundaries of the different churches would be fluid and crossing over from one to another would not be a problem. Each church would seek to witness to its own tradition while respecting the values of the other churches. In the same way the Christian churches in a given area would be in contact with Hindus, Buddhists, Muslims and people of other religions in their neighborhood and would share in prayer and meditation and in discussion with them. The Christian community would be an open community, ready to enter into dialogue with other communities both religious and secular, recognizing both religious and secular values, wherever they may be found, and ready to cooperate with them.

Finally, what would be the requirement of faith for communion in this "ecumenical" church? Could it not be simply baptism in the name of the Father, the Son and the Holy Spirit, and faith in Jesus Christ as Lord and Savior? All other developments of the apostolic faith would be considered as the witness of a particular church, which the other churches would respect, but would not be required to accept for themselves. In regard to communion in the eucharist, the same principle would be accepted. The eucharist would be recognized as the sacrament ordained by Christ, in which the Christian people meet together to enter into personal communion with Jesus Christ and with one another by partaking of the bread and the wine, as Jesus asked them to do, in memory of him. The exact significance of the rite could be left for theological discussion and a variety of formulations could be recognized. All that would be required would be that all should seek to do what the Lord had commanded them.

Is such theological pluralism permissible? The theory behind it would be that the object of Christian faith is not any particular set of doctrines, but a divine "mystery," what St Paul called the "mystery of Christ," which cannot properly be expressed in words. The language of the Bible and of the creeds and councils of the church are attempts to express this mystery in human terms, but all are historically and culturally conditioned. None of these expressions can be taken as absolute. The nearest we can come to a simple affirmation of the mystery is the statement "Jesus is the Lord," or in its more extended form: "This Jesus, who was crucified, God has made Lord and Christ." These are the basic affirmations of Christian faith, which every Christian can make. This is the foundation of Christian faith. All doctrinal statements which bring out the implications of this fundamental faith are secondary. In the same way the Christian or Catholic Church is the communion of those who share this basic faith and are united with one another in a common baptism. Baptism itself is an initiation into the mystery of Christ, and the eucharist is a participation in the same mystery, as are the other sacraments. But the sacramental order and the doctrine concerned with it can take many different forms. Finally, the different ministries in the church, from popes and bishops to pastors and evangelists are "charisms" or manifestations of the working of the Spirit in the church, whose actual

169

forms and structures will vary according to historical and cultural conditions.

This "blue-print" of an ecumenical church is a projection into the future, which may seem rather remote from our present situation, but it is surely worthwhile to reflect on what may be the possibilities for the future. It is offered as a rough sketch to be changed and emended perhaps out of recognition.

29. The Church in the New Age[28]

As, toward the end of A New Vision of Reality, *Bede Griffiths imagines a coming 'New Age,' he turns once again to re-envision the church. While his mind soars as swiftly and cleanly as a hawk over the clutter of the centuries, we become aware once more how uncommon is this fusion of sovereign intellectual freedom with a profound Christian faith. Again, it is a question of finding a viewpoint prior to the divisions and the particularizations of our divided Christianity. The trait of 'exclusivism' which Bede finds already in the Semitic beginnings of Christianity and which has endured through these two millennia must be overcome so that the 'unique revelation of God in Jesus Christ' may be opened to the whole world.*

Once again, Bede is concerned with the role of the church of Rome and its bishop and he refers us once more to the fifth-century model of autonomous patriarchates. This time he goes still further back, to the ecclesial vision of St. Irenaeus in the second century and finally to the New Testament. Rome must become, as in those early days, a center of communion rather than a center of power. The structure of ministries in the church is a second key to renewal: the ministries should be re-constituted on the basis of the New Testament itself, before the institution of pope, bishops or priests as we know them. As the church fathers integrated Greek thought with scriptural revelation, a new Christian theology would draw upon the traditions of Hinduism, Buddhism, Taoism and Confucianism. Liturgy would undergo a parallel inculturation in the context of the music and dance of Asian and African peoples. Bede returns to the beginning — to the still incandescent plasma of New Testament Christianity — to recover the simplicity and freedom that are needed if the Gospel and the church are to be opened to all the peoples of the earth.

. . . we are learning, and we shall continue to learn, that all the different religious traditions, from the most primitive to the most advanced, are interrelated and interdependent, and that each has its own particular insights. For the Semitic religions in particular, Judaism,

Christianity and Islam, it is important that they give up the exclusive claims which characterize them. This would free them to recognise the action of God in all humanity from the beginnings of history. For the Semitic religions this is a particularly difficult problem. All three tend to extreme exclusivism and on that account have brought so much conflict into the world.

For Christianity this enlargement of its horizons would involve a recognition of the limited character of its original revelation, coming as it did from within a Semitic culture in the limited world and thought-forms of the Ancient Near East. Emerging from that world it spread through the Roman Empire from Palestine through Greece to Rome. For centuries the whole sphere of Christianity was simply the Roman Empire centered around the Mediterranean and completely without contact with the greater part of Asia, Africa, America and Australia. Yet we have seen that Christianity is a unique revelation of God in Jesus Christ and that, although it was conditioned by the circumstances of its origin, this revelation has a unique message for the whole world. The Christian Church began as a Jewish sect and only gradually realised its vocation as a universal religion. It developed its structures from the second century onwards entirely in the context of Graeco-Roman culture, with an extension which must not be overlooked in the Syrian East, in Egypt and Ethiopia. The doctrine of the church remains essentially based on a Semitic foundation developed by the Greek genius in terms of Greek philosophy, while the organisation of the church remains a Roman structure built on the foundation of the original Jewish community.

In the course of the centuries these structures within Christianity have expanded and a whole system of theology, philosophy and morality, a sacramental order and an ecclesiastical hierarchy, have developed. Though it derives from Jesus and the apostles in the first century, the Christian Church as such received its definitive structure in the second century, its evolution in the Roman Empire being determined by the circumstances of the time. All these structures which we have inherited are western structures built on the foundation of the original Semitic revelation. These structures of doctrine, discipline and sacrament are thus historically conditioned. They are integral ele-

171

ments in a historical development which has taken place gradually over many centuries. In the course of its history and this is the great tragedy the Asian and African churches were separated from the main body. In Asia, where St Paul conducted his missions, the churches which were centered on Antioch were separated in the fifth century, while the churches of Africa, based on Egypt and Alexandria, were also separated. The result was that by the fifth century Asia and Africa were lost to the church. Then in the eleventh century Eastern Europe, centred on Byzantium, separated from Rome which was the center of the western church. Finally, at the Reformation the churches of Northern Europe were separated from Rome. It is this tragically divided church that we have inherited. The separations which have accumulated over the centuries are all still present today. It will be one of the tasks of the new age to see the reconciliation of these divided churches as each recognises the other as a particular expression of Christian faith and worship, and as each seeks to reconcile the differences. There are valid elements in every Christian church. Each is a way of expressing Christian faith and worship. There are obvious limitations and obvious differences in each but today we seek to discern the differences and overcome the divisions, in contrast to previous times when we were engaged in dividing from one another and in asserting our own values at the expense of those of others.

Reconciliation within the Christian Church will involve recognition of different ministries. The present ministries of the different churches all derive from the second century or later. In the New Testament there is neither papacy, episcopacy nor priesthood. The only priesthood, properly speaking, in the New Testament is that of Christ himself and of the people, which St Peter describes as a "holy priesthood". It would be necessary to reconsider the different ministries in this light.

The present system of the papacy dates from the Gregorian reform of the twelfth century. It is important to recognise that this movement had its value at the time. One must consider that the Holy Spirit was present in each development of the church but each was limited to its particular historic horizon. It was only when the Eastern Church separated from the Western that the papacy began to develop its present structure. It would be necessary to go behind the present structure of the papacy to the fifth century if a reconciliation is to be found with the Eastern churches. The Eastern Church will never be reconciled with the present system of the papacy which is an evolution of the last ten centuries. In the fifth century there were five patriarchates: Jerusalem, Antioch, Alexandria, Constantinople and Rome. Already in the fifth century the primacy of the Pope, St Leo, was fully recognised but he was *primus inter pares*, the first among equals, and he normally never interfered in the affairs of the eastern churches. There was a right of appeal to Rome and the right of intervention in grave necessity was recognized, but the patriarchs were responsible for the liturgy, theology and the whole conduct of their churches just as the pope, as patriarch of the West, was responsible for the Western churches. At that time the pope only appointed bishops in his own patriarchate. So this was a very different structure of the church from that of later centuries, and yet it was a unified church which recognised the primacy of the pope. So we could go back to that point as a model for the reorganisation of the church today, particularly in the light of the eastern churches.

With regard to the other churches apart from the Eastern Church, it will be necessary to go even further back for a model. The person to go to is St Irenaeus, that great theologian and churchman of the second century. He was the most representative figure in the Catholic Church at the time, being a bishop in Gaul, coming originally from Asia and being in close touch with Rome. He shows the Roman Church at that time as the center of Christendom. He speaks of it as being founded by the chief of the apostles, Peter and Paul, not Peter alone, notice, and he uses a very important phrase, *potiorem principalitatem*. This may mean "more powerful presidency" or perhaps "more powerful origin". The original was written in Greek and we only have the Latin translation so we cannot be quite sure of the meaning. But because the Roman Church was founded by Peter and Paul it has a kind of primacy without a doubt. Then Irenaeus says in a very important sentence, "With this church it is necessary that every church should agree, or come together (*convenire* in Latin), every church, that is, the faithful from all parts (*eos qui sunt undeque fideles*)." This is an excellent model of the Roman Church as a center of unity to which people come from all parts. It seems to me that we have a model, there in the second century, of Rome seen as the seat of Peter and Paul, as a center of unity to which people come from all parts and where the true faith is always preserved. That was St Irenaeus' point. It is to be noticed that the emphasis is on the church itself, rather than on the bishop. The bishop became more important in the course of time but at this point it was the church that was important. This brings out further the function of Rome which is that it should be a center of unity rather than a center of power. Today many people in all churches see the possibility of a papacy which would be a centre of unity, of the pope as exercising a ministry of unity on behalf of the whole church. This would mean that Rome would no longer be the center of power and domination which it had become in the Middle Ages.

This character of the Roman Church is brought out further by St Ignatius writing in the second century to the Roman Church, again not to the bishop but to the church. He speaks of the church as "presiding over the charity" (*prothestos tes agapes*) or, perhaps, "presiding in charity." Again it is a difficult phrase to translate, let alone know the exact meaning of, but it looks as though the church herself is considered as a charity, a school of love. The pope has this function of "presiding over the charity" or "presiding in charity." The point is that it is a presidence of love rather than of power. That takes us back to the second century. But now we have to go further back still, because Irenaeus speaks always in terms of episcopacy which was fully developed by this time in the second century. But when we go back to the New Testament there is neither episcopacy nor priesthood in the usual sense. On the other hand we find a great many other different ministries. St Paul speaks of apostles and prophets but also of evangelists, pastors and teachers, helpers and administrators. So that was the structure of the church in the New Testament and it seems that we have to go back to the New Testament itself to restructure the ministries of the church. In that light the ministries of other churches which have no bishops could be reconciled with the church as a whole. We should also be aware that in the New Testament women played a very considerable part in the ministry of the church, and any attempt at renewing the structures of the ministry of the church would involve women having ministries in equality with men. That would be the normal development that we would expect. So this is how the development of the ministries in the church could be envisaged, while remembering, of course, that in the New Testament the position of Peter among the apostles still remains a valid and unquestionable fact which has meaning for the church today just as it had then.

When the church has been opened in this way to a more universal structure of ministry it would be much more possible for her to open herself to the cultures of Asia and Africa and to answer the needs of the people in the Third World. So far the church has had a European structure. In its liturgy, theology, canon law and organization it is a totally western structure. We are only today beginning to discover the possibilities of structuring the church, not in the light of Europe, but in the light of Asia, Africa and South America. That is clearly where the future lies.

It may be that the basic communities in South America, particularly in Brazil, could provide a model for the church in the Third World. In these communities lay people, men and women, meet regularly to study the Scriptures, to celebrate the eucharist, and to reflect on their life and experience in the light of the Bible and the eucharist. They also relate their political and socio-economic problems to their experience of the Bible and the eucharist and try to develop these aspects of their lives within this context. These basic communities, in Brazil in particular where there are tens of thousands of them, are all in communion with the bishops and the clergy, but they are lay communities. This kind of involved and committed community may well be the model for a renewed Christian church. Such communities could be compared to the monastic communities at the break-up of the Roman Empire. In many respects we seem to be entering a period not unlike that of the Roman Empire in the fifth century when the entire structure began to collapse. It was monastic communities, integrated communities with a physical, social base and a religious character, which were the sources from which the new civilisation emerged. As economic, social and political tensions increase in the present world there will be an ever stronger need for small communities, based on the new vision of life, which could in time form the basis of a new civilization, like the monasteries in the Middle Ages. These communities would be communities of men and women, married and single, basically Christian but also open to people of other religious traditions and of other understandings also, where a new culture would gradually be formed.

Along with this a new theology would be developed, particularly as the church comes into contact with the religious cultures of Asia and Africa. Again we must remember that our present theology was first built up entirely in contact with Greek philosophy. The whole system was based on divine revelation in the Scriptures interpreted in the light of Greek philosophy. Today theology has drawn on modern philosophy, especially existentialism, but nowhere until the present time has the church succeeded in evolving a theology based on the experience and the wisdom of Asia and of Africa. Our present theology was evolved in Europe and we have to look forward to a theology which would evolve in contact with Hindu, Buddhist, Taoist and Confucian thought and at the same time a liturgy which would develop from contact with the art, music and dance of Asian and African peoples. It would be an assimilation of the cultures of Asia and Africa into the life of the church, just as in the early centuries there was an assimilation of first of the culture of the Greeks and the Romans and then of all the "barbarian" peoples of Europe. That was how the church emerged in the Middle Ages. It brought its original Semitic wisdom, religion and faith and interpreted it in the light of the Greek and the Roman world. Then later it assimilated the "barbarian" peoples with their wonderful gifts, creating that great church of the Middle Ages which we have inherited.

IV

EAST: PART ONE
THE WISDOM OF INDIA

Much of Bede's writing is a presentation of the spiritual teaching of the Vedanta to the contemporary West. Often he is simply condensing this thought, diffused through the stories and aphorisms of the Hindu scriptures, into a compact and integral form. The doctrine, as it comes to us clarified in the limpid waters of Bede's mind, is most simple and coherent. Its basic principle is a single all-embracing reality to which correspond a unitive Self, a spiritual path, an experience and a way of knowing.

The way of the *Upanishads* which Bede transmits is a pure distillate, a particular stream selected out of the immense complexity of Hindu thought. Bede will point out other streams as well, as he traces the historical development of Indian spirituality from Vedas and *Upanishads* through *Bhagavad Gita* and the tantric traditions. Very often we find him tracing the shining stream with a contagious enthusiasm. Occasionally he pauses for a critical reflection in the light of Christian revelation, and we may realize once again that we have underestimated the depth and complexity of his understanding. Deep beneath the surface of Bede's thought and writing lies a central conviction and affirmation of the ultimate unity of all reality and therefore of all religious traditions. This gravitational center continually gives his writing a tone and a pattern of convergence, which should not mislead us. From time to time, Bede will turn to a critical confrontation of Christianity and the Asian traditions, and the major distinctions will be clearly articulated. For most of this journey, however, we shall be carried along in the precritical mode by his spiritual energy and the power of his eloquent prose. Hindu scholars have pointed out, however, that this eastern wisdom is coming to us through Bede's Christian consciousness.

30. Bede's Discovery of India[1]

Bede Griffiths had always felt himself a stranger in the world of the modern West. When in 1955, at the age of forty-nine, he set foot on the soil of India, Bede felt that he had come home. His words here at the beginning of The Marriage of East and West *curiously recall the final chapters of* The Golden String, *in which he described his entering the Roman Catholic Church as a similar homecoming. These two experiences will continue to question one another throughout Bede's life. Within both of them we can also sense something of his personal need, of the specifically human and emotional dimension of his quest.*

'The Marriage' was intended, in fact, to be a continuation of his autobiography. Quickly, however, it becomes something different: an exploration of the riches of Indian wisdom and a re-conceiving of the Christian tradition in the light of that eastern wisdom. Here in the opening pages, still in the mode of personal narrative, we share Bede's first impressions of India. Once again, we are admitted to an experience of coming alive, this time in the kind of world that Bede had earlier dreamed of — where nature, humanity and Divinity live still in communion. His ever-youthful eyes and passionate heart imbue the scene with the colors of paradise and the luminous depths of a world still transparent to the Divine. We find ourselves in the midst of a living myth. Bede is not merely dreaming; many other westerners have encountered the old India with a similar wondering delight.

The story moves between sensuous description and philosophical reflection as he immerses himself in this world of the East where body, soul and spirit still freely walk together. It is good to let ourselves feel the enchantment of Bede's discovery, to awaken within ourselves to this primal country.

When I wrote *The Golden String*[2], telling the story of my search for God, which led me to the Catholic Church and to a Benedictine monastery, I thought that I had reached the end of my journey, at least as far as this world was concerned. But in fact, even while I was writing *The Golden String*, a new era was about to begin in my life, which was to bring about changes, as profound as any that had gone before. I had been led to the discovery first of God, then of Christ, and finally of the church. But now I have been led in a strange way to retrace the path I had taken and to make new discoveries about God, about Christ and about the Catholic Church. It was as though I had been climbing a mountain, and having reached the peak, discovered further ranges beyond with new peaks, opening up a new horizon.

All this came about through my meeting with an Indian Benedictine monk, who was planning to make a monastic foundation in India. For years I had been studying the Vedanta and had begun to realize its significance for the church and the world. Now I was given the opportunity to go the source of this tradition, to live in India and discover the secret of the wisdom of India. It was not merely the desire for new ideas which drew me to India, but the desire for a new way of life. I remember writing to a friend at the time: 'I want to discover the other half of my soul.' I had begun to find that there was something lacking not only in the western world but in the western church. We were living from one half of our soul, from the conscious, rational level and we needed to discover the other half, the unconscious, intuitive dimension. I wanted to experience in my life the marriage of these two dimensions of human existence, the rational and intuitive, the conscious and unconscious, the masculine and feminine. I wanted to find the way to the marriage of East and West.

My discovery began even before I reached India. I travelled by boat and I remember how at my first encounter with the East, at Port Said and Aden, I was fascinated with the spectacle of this world of immeasurable beauty and vitality. It was not the beauty of nature which struck me now, but the beauty of human nature, of what Blake called the 'human form divine.' It was the same when I reached Bombay. It was not the poverty and the misery which struck me so much as the sheer beauty and vitality of the people. On all sides was a swarming mass of humanity, children running about quite naked, women in saris, men with turbans, everywhere displaying the beauty of the human form. Whether sitting or standing or walking there was grace in all their movements and I felt that I was in the presence of a hidden power of nature. I explained it to myself by saying that these people were living from the 'unconscious'. People in the West are dominated by the conscious mind; they go about their business each shut up in his own ego. There is a kind of fixed determination in their minds, which makes their movements and gestures stiff and awkward, and they all tend to wear the same drab clothes. But in the East people live not from the conscious mind but from the unconscious, from the body not from the mind. As a result they have the natural spontaneous beauty of flowers and animals, and their dress is as varied and colourful as that of a flower-garden.

Often, looking down on the scene at a railway platform, I have thought that it looked like a flower-garden, the women with the brightly-coloured saris sitting in circles here and there, the children running about with movements and gestures of spontaneous joy. After all these years in India this remains my deepest impression. There is poverty and misery enough in India, but above all in the villages and among the poorest there is an abundance of life and joy.

But, of course, this is not a merely animal life and beauty, it has the grace of human intelligence. They live from the unconscious, but it is the human unconscious, what Jung has called the anima as opposed to the animus. Every human being is both masculine and feminine. In the man the masculine aspect, the animus, is normally dominant, and in the woman the feminine or anima. In every person a certain balance or harmony has to be achieved, but in the West today the masculine aspect, the rational, active, aggressive power of the mind, is dominant, while in the East the feminine aspect, the intuitive, passive, sympathetic power of the mind is dominant. The future of the world depends on the 'marriage' of these two minds, the conscious and the unconscious, the rational and the intuitive, the active and the passive. In India and all over the world today these two minds are meeting, but often the impact of the West on the East is that of a violent aggression, whether by armed power as in the past, or by the much more subtle aggression of science and technology exploiting man and nature, as at present.

The present system of industrialism in the West is the product of the violent, aggressive, rational mind of the West — whether organized in a capitalist or a socialist system makes no difference, except that the latter tends to be more oppressive and inhuman which can only lead to the destruction of the ancient cultures of the East. Yet it still remains possible to conceive of a development of science and technology which would seek not to dominate nature in the style of the West but to work with nature, building up from the basis of the village economy, as Mahatma Gandhi sought to do, and so create a new culture, in which man and nature, reason and intuition, the Yang and the Yin in Chinese terms, would be brought into harmony.

But there is something more in Indian culture than a search for harmony between man and nature, conscious and unconscious; there is a profound awareness of a power beyond both man and nature which penetrates everything and is the real source of the beauty and vitality of Indian life. I realized this most clearly when I visited the Cave of Elephanta outside Bombay. The cave has a forest of pillars inside it, not uncommon in Hindu temples, which creates an atmosphere of mystery and immensity, and as you approach, the great figure of Siva Maheswara — the Great God — with his three faces, representing his benign and terrible and contemplative aspects, looms out of the darkness from a recess in the wall. It is colossal and overwhelming at first, but when you look into the front face you see that it is in deep contemplation. There is absolute peace there, infinitely distant yet infinitely near, solemn, benign, gentle and majestic. Here carved in stone is the very genius of India and the East. This is what I had come to India to find, this contemplative dimension of human existence, which the West has almost lost and the East is losing. Here engraved in stone one could encounter that hidden depth of existence, springing from the depth of nature and the unconscious, penetrating all human existence and going beyond into the mystery of the infinite and eternal, not as something remote and inaccessible, but as something almost tangible engraved in this stone. Here was the secret I had come to discover. The mind of the East is open not only to man and nature in an intuitive understanding, but also to that hidden Power which pervades both man and nature and reveals to those who are attuned to it the real meaning of human existence.

If the West as a whole has lost this intuitive awareness of the presence of God in man and nature, the church in the West is faced with the same problem. Christianity was originally an eastern religion (like practically all religions), but its movement from the beginning has been predominantly westwards. It passed with St Paul through Asia Minor to Greece and Rome, and then in the course of time to Europe and America. As a result, though always retaining its eastern basis it has become a western religion. Its theology is Greek, its organization Roman, its cultural expression European.

This was immediately evident in Bombay. The churches are either Gothic or Baroque; the statues and pictures are from European models; altars and candlesticks and stained glass are often imported from abroad. Everything is done to make the church appear foreign to India. Yet the Indian people somehow manage to transform even these artificial buildings. They swarm everywhere, pressing up against the altar rails and through the doors and windows, overwhelming the Victorian propriety of the churches with their spontaneous vitality.

Yet this, of course, is on a superficial level. The Indian Church has to undergo a radical transformation, if it is ever to respond to the needs of the Indian people. It has to rethink its theology in Indian instead of Greek terms, and to adapt its organization to Indian instead of Roman models. Even its Semitic base cannot go untouched. Christianity shares with Judaism and Islam a Semitic structure of language and thought. It has to learn to see this Semitic tradition with all its unique values in the light of the Oriental tradition, to learn what Hinduism, Buddhism, Taoism and Confucianism have to teach it. Then only will the 'marriage' take place in the church as in the world between East and West.

It was only gradually that this realization came to me. When we arrived in Bangalore, we bought a property some miles outside Bangalore in a village called Kengeri and there we began our monastic life. At this time, though I wanted to continue the study of Indian thought, I had no idea of changing our style of life. We wore the traditional Benedictine habit. We built a chapel in the western style, with chairs and reading desks. We had our meals sitting at table with spoons, knives and forks. Our cells were simply furnished with wooden beds and straw mattresses, a table, a chair and a shelf for clothes and books. This is what I then considered a model of simplicity. It was only gradually that I discovered that nearly all these things were unheard-of luxuries in the neighbouring village. A few rich people might have tables and chairs and even a radio or a gramophone, but most of the villagers normally sat on the floor, ate with their hands from a plantain leaf, and slept on a mat on the floor.

Thus I gradually became aware of a standard of poverty and simplicity which was far beyond anything which I had imagined in

Europe. At the same time I realized that this poverty and simplicity did not mean that the people were any less cultured. There was an old man in the village who was a Sanskrit scholar, and from him I learned much of the traditional Hindu wisdom. There were also several students studying at the university, well acquainted with Western ways, one of whom became one of my closest friends. He was western-minded in many ways and admired western culture, but he had no difficulty in sitting on the floor for his meals and eating with his hand, and every week without fail he would visit the little temple of the monkey god Hanuman near our monastery and conduct the worship there. So I began to realize how a primeval religion and culture could exist side by side with Western ways.

At this time I was studying Sanskrit with Raimundo Panikkar, who embodies in a unique way this meeting of East and West. His mother was a Spanish Catholic and his father came from a well-known Hindu family. He had been brought up in Europe, had taken degrees in science, philosophy and theology, and had now come to India to discover his Indian heritage. Together we explored this Indian culture which was now beginning to unfold before my eyes. We spent some weeks together visiting the temples in the old Mysore State.[3]

At the very beginning there was an unforgettable experience, when we were invited by a man whom we met on the way to visit his home. He took us to a tiny two-roomed cottage, where we sat crossed-legged on the floor, and two little boys gave us a concert of Indian classical music. There was no furniture in the house. One little boy was lying ill on a mat on the floor and the others sat beside us, one playing a stringed instrument and both singing together, beating the time with their hands and completely absorbed in the music. The mother prepared tea in the kitchen, which we drank from small brass vessels, but later she too came and played and sang herself. The father explained to us the meaning of the songs, which were either in Sanskrit or one of the south Indian languages, and were all, of course, religious. So there we were sitting on the floor in this little cottage with no modern conveniences, brought face to face with one of the most profound religious cultures of the world.

Our visits to the temples only confirmed this impression. At

Belur, Halebid and Somnathpur we found architecture and sculpture of a beauty and refinement equal to the finest Gothic art, but beyond the outward form of beauty there was the deep inner meaning of the temples.

Halebid in particular was a most enchanting place, and old temple set in a lovely valley with a broad river flowing by, reminding one of Tintern or Fountains. Round the outside of the temple there are sculpted friezes in ascending order, representing first the animal world elephants, horses, birds then the human world with stories from the Hindu epics, the *Ramayana* and *Mahabharata*, and finally the divine world, the world of the gods and goddesses. It was a manifestation of the cosmic mystery in stone, the divine life manifesting itself in the three worlds, the animal, the human and the divine.

Another impression of lasting significance was the figure of a naked man standing upright to be found in many of the Jain temples here, above all the colossal figure in the temple at Sravan Belgola. This, I believe, is the figure of purusha, the Primeval Man, the Archetypal Man, who appears in the Rig Veda, of whom it is said that he contains the whole creation in himself. 'Three quarters of him is above in heaven, one quarter is here on earth.' This is akin to the Adam Kadmon, the first Adam, of Jewish tradition and the Universal Man of Muslim tradition. When Jesus called himself the Son of Man he was relating himself to this primeval tradition and revealing the underlying unity of religions. Thus the temples in Mysore revealed Hinduism as the Cosmic religion, the religion of God's revelation in the Cosmos and in Man.

But perhaps no less significant was the impression made when we sat down by the river beside a little shrine, in which there was nothing but a roughly-carved lingam and yoni — the male and female organs. A European would be inclined to regard this as 'obscene' but for a Hindu it has no such significance. For the Hindu sex is essentially 'holy.' It is a manifestation of the divine life and is to be worshipped like any other form of the divinity. God manifests himself in all the works of nature, in earth and fire and air and water, in plant and animal and man. Sex is one of the manifestations of the divine power the *Sakti* which sustains the universe and has the character of a sacrament.

It is this vision of a cosmic unity, in which man and nature are sustained by an all-pervading spirit, which the West needs to learn from the East. It is this that explains the extraordinary sacredness which attaches to every created thing in India. The earth is sacred, and no ploughing or sowing or reaping can take place without some religious rite. Eating is a sacred action and every meal is conceived as a sacrifice to God. Water is sacred and no religious Hindu will take a bath without invoking the sacred power of the water, which descends from heaven and, caught on the head of Siva, is distributed in the fertilizing streams of the Ganges and other rivers. Air is sacred, the breath of life which comes from God and sustains all living creatures. Fire is sacred, especially in its source in the sun, which brings light and life to all creatures. So also with plants and trees, especially certain plants like the tulsi plant and certain trees like the banyan. Animals are sacred, especially the cow, which gives her milk as a mother, but also the elephant, the monkey and the snake. Finally man is sacred; every man is a manifestation of God but especially a holy man, in whom the divine presence can be more clearly seen.

This is the sacred universe, in which man has lived as far as we know from the beginning of history and which has been completely demolished by the western scientific world. Every trace of sacredness has been removed from life so that western man finds himself in a universe in which both man and nature have been deprived of any ultimate meaning.

31. The Vedic Revelation

Bede had been acquainted with the Hindu spiritual literature, as well as Buddhist and Taoist texts, since 1930[4]. Nearly twenty five years later, while at Pluscarden, he was once again reading the Vedas and the Tao Te Ching and seeking correlations with Christian texts.[5] Soon after Bede's arrival in India in 1955, he took up the study of Sanskrit, the language of the Indian spiritual classics, with Raimon Panikkar.[6] He plunged enthusiastically into the Vedic tradition. As Bede introduces his presentation of the wisdom of Hinduism in The Marriage of East and West *with a historical overview of the Vedic literature, it is evident where his interest lies. The account moves swiftly to the* Upanishads, *'often known as Vedanta'; it is from the* Upanishads *and then from the* Bhagavad Gita *that Bede will bring forth his distillation of Indian wisdom. He sees the turn from exterior ritual to an interior spirituality, just preceding the period of the* Upanishads, *as "the great turning point in the development of the Hindu religion, in fact in the development of Indian history, or I would even say the history of the world."*[7]

In presenting this Indian wisdom as 'The Vedic Revelation,' Bede is deliberately placing it in confrontation with the biblical revelation of the Judaeo-Christian tradition. This, he explains, is an explicit affirmation of the universality of God's communication with humanity. A little later in the same introductory conference,[8] *Bede deals with two problems which confront Christians in encountering the Indian sacred scriptures: an inadequate grounding in their own Christian faith and a crude misconception of Hindu religion as polytheistic. Our two selections are from the same chapter of* The Cosmic Revelation.

I[9]

We are going to reflect on what I call the Vedic Revelation; and I use the word revelation intentionally because I think we have to recognize today that God has revealed himself in other ways than through the Bible. God has been speaking to man, "in many and various ways," as it says in the letter to the Hebrews, from the beginning of time.

Today we are aware of the presence in other religions of a wisdom and experience of God which challenges the church. I feel that we are really entering a new epoch. For almost two thousand years the Christian Church grew up with the understanding that it alone was the true religion; that there was no religion outside Christianity which was not fundamentally false, or at best no more than a natural religion. Only today, in these last few years, have Christians begun to discover the riches which God has lavished on other nations. I like to recall an inter-religious meeting that we held in our ashram, at Shantivanam, some years ago where a representative of the Secretariat for Non-Christians in Rome, said: "We come to share one another's spiritual riches."

I believe that this expresses the mind of the church today. We have come to share one another's spiritual riches. We have the immeasurable riches of Christ to share with others. But today we recognize that God has also lavished his riches on other people. It is a great challenge to our faith and to our religion to relate ourselves now to these other religions.

So when we study the Vedic revelation, the Vedic scriptures, we must approach them as something which God has given to man. There are defects, no doubt, in every scripture where God and man work together, but there is something of the "word" of God in the Vedas. They speak of *vac*, the Sanskrit for 'word,' in the Vedas as the mediator between God and man. Therefore I would like to approach this subject in a spirit of reverence and of humility and with a great desire for truth. And where there is anything challenging, let it be tested by whether it is true to Christ and to what God has revealed in Christ, and let us try to see other religions in their relation to him.

In India we often begin talks with the Gayatri mantra, a short chant. It is the most sacred mantra of the Vedas, and is used again and again as the most sacred utterance. It may not seem much at first, but the more one reflects on it, the more meaning it has.

> Om bhur bhuvah svha
> tat savitur varenyam
> bhargo devasya dhimahi
> dhiyoyonah pracodayat
> om shanti shanti shanti

The translation is: 'Let us meditate on the glorious splendour of the divine light. May he illuminate our meditation.' The chant is preceded by the word *Om* which is repeated three times. It is a sacred word; like *Amen* from the Hebrew. And we end with *shanti, shanti, shanti,* 'peace, peace, peace.' This is the peace of God which we invoke on ourselves and on the whole world.

In this spirit of reverence we approach these Vedic scriptures. The word veda means 'knowledge,' the same as the Latin root *video* to know, to see. The Vedas are the sacred scriptures of India and the consensus is that they date in their present form from about 1500 B.C. In this form, ancient as it is, they already show a long history of development. The Vedas were written in Sanskrit; and Sanskrit is perhaps the most beautiful and elaborate language in the world. They were brought to India, as far as we know, during the Aryan invasions of the second millenium BC, which brought the Sanskrit language and the Vedic religion with them.

Veda means 'knowledge,' not simply human knowledge but knowledge that is given by God. The Vedas are called sruti from the root sr, which means 'to hear.' So the Vedas are what has been heard not what has been made up, but what has been heard.

The authors of the Vedas are called *rishis*, which some think comes from the root *drs*, 'to see;' they are 'see-ers.' There is no doubt in the mind of the Hindu that these scriptures are a revelation, something which has been heard and seen. They use two other words in describing them. The first is *nitya*, that is, 'eternal.' Most ancient religious traditions will say that their scriptures are eternal — the Torah of the Jews, for instance. The Jews always say that the Torah is eternal and that God revealed it to Moses. So also the Koran is said to have been written on tablets in heaven and dictated to Mohammed by the archangel Gabriel. Thus the Vedas also are eternal. Secondly, they are called *apauruseya*, 'without human authorship.' So they are what has been heard, what is eternal and has no human authorship. We are in the presence of what we must surely call a revelation. It is not the same as the Christian revelation; it is in fact different in many ways. I hope that in the course of these talks we will come to understand the differences between the Vedic revelation and the Christian revelation, but I think we have established that it is legitimate to use this word 'revelation' of the Vedas.

The Vedas are a little complex and it is not necessary to remember all the details, but for those who are interested there are actually four Vedas. The first is the *Rig–Veda*. *Ric* means 'hymn' and this forms the main part of the Vedas. They are hymns addressed to the gods. The Rig-Veda is the most ancient and dominant part of the Vedas. Then comes the *Sama–Veda*, the musical setting for these hymns, which were chanted at the sacrifice. The center of the whole Vedic religion was the fire sacrifice, of which we will speak later.

Thirdly, there is the *Yajur–Veda*, which is the Veda of the ritual formulas of sacrifice. They were written both in prose and verse to be used at the offering of the sacrifice. Finally there is the Atharva-Veda, which belongs to a different strata. The Rig, the Sama and the Yajur are the original Vedas. The Atharva–Veda comes largely from the indigenous people, it is supposed, and consists to a very large extent of oracles and charms and magic spells. But it has also some wonderful philosophical and theological doctrine showing a more developed stage of religion.

The Vedas proper are not of great practical importance today. They are very little read except by scholars. After the four Vedas there are three stages of development of Vedic revelation: the first is the brahmanas. The Brahmanas are the commentaries on the sacrifice. Very early the sacrifice was thought to be the centre of the whole religion. The sacrifice had a mystical meaning, often a magical meaning. The Brahmanas revealed this mystical meaning of the sacrifice and also all the details of it. They are rather boring to read but they have gems within them.

The Brahmanas were followed by the *Aranyakas*, the 'forest books' *aranya* is 'forest.' This marks the great turning point in the development of the Hindu religion, in fact in the development of Indian history, or I would even say the history of the world. It was at this point that the seers retired into the forest to meditate. Thus, from being a comparatively external religion, centered on the fire sacrifice, it became an interior religion. They sought to build the fire in the heart. The word *tapas* means 'asceticism, self-control, discipline' — there is no exact translation — but its original meaning was 'heat.' The belief was that when one practiced this self-discipline, this self-control, one generated an inner heat, an inner fire, and so instead of building the fire outside and making offerings to God on it, one built the fire within and offered one's thoughts, one's sins, one's whole being in this interior fire. This is the turning point: interior religion manifests itself, and all the depth of Hindu religion stems from that movement.

The third and final stage is that of the *Upanishads*, which are the discussions of the seers, the *rishis*, with their disciples. Today very few people read the Vedas, the Brahmanas or the Aranyakas, but the Upanishads are the central teaching of Hinduism. They are the actual inspiration of all that is most authentic in Hinduism, and they are what we ourselves have to study. The word *upanishad* literally means 'to sit near to' and it is supposed to indicate the disciples sitting at the feet of the master. The Upanishads are the discourses of the master to the disciple. They are intended to create and develop a mystical experience. This must be clearly understood, because so many European scholars have been led astray. They approach the Upanishads as if they were the dialogs of Plato, or some philosophical treatise. They miss the mystical meaning and consequently misinterpret the main message of the Upanishads. So we have to be cautious of the scholars when we are studying the Upanishads. The Upanishads are often known as Vedanta the end of the Vedas, the final stage of the Vedas, the quintessence, one could call it, of the Vedas.

II[10]

Now we come to the doctrine, if I may call it that, of the Vedas. Again, when we use a word like doctrine we have to be very careful. In the West we have developed everything along the lines of doctrine and we consider Christian faith in the light of belief in certain doctrines. But in Hinduism everything turns to experience. It is the aim of the Upanishads to awaken this experience, and it is the aim of every devout Hindu to have this experience of God. What we have to discover is that experience of God which has its roots in the Vedas, which comes to light in the Upanishads and is given its fullest, most perfect expression in the Bhagavad-Gita. I hope in these six talks to cover that ground. It's a great deal, but I want to concentrate on this experience of God as something meaningful and valid for the Christian and for the whole of the world.

I believe that God has given this experience of the Upanishads, the Gita, and the Hindu tradition to the world. We are being called to encounter it and to relate it to the Christian experience of God. In our ashram we have had many people coming to share this experience with us and we have found that those who come with a mature Christian faith find that their faith is enriched and deepened by this experience of the Hindu scriptures. I may say that immature people can be thrown off their balance very easily if they have no deep understanding of their own faith. One must really understand one's Christian faith and live one's Christian faith, and only then can one understand and live out the Hindu experience in the light of Christ.

That is the real challenge. It is a particular challenge to the monastic order because one's aim in life is to seek God. We have other works which we do, but the call of a Benedictine monk or nun is essentially to seek God. What the Hindus have been doing from the time of the Vedas to our time is a constant search for God, a search to find out the ultimate truth and ultimate reality, and to experience it in the depth of the heart. That is what we seek.

Now we come to the Vedas themselves and immediately we come up against great problems. Many will say that the Hindu religion is polytheistic and from that point of view dismiss it altogether. The Bible is very emphatically monotheistic, but in the Vedas there are hymns to different gods.

A deeper knowledge makes us realize that the Hindu understood this relationship of the one and the many in a way different from the Hebrew. The Hebrew tradition began with many gods. As you may know one of the words of God in the Hebrew, *Elohim*, is plural. It must have been 'the gods' originally, but in the course of their history the Hebrews learned that this *Elohim* was not many, but one; and his name, as revealed to Moses, is Yahweh. They were forbidden to worship any other god. They recognized other gods at first: as the psalm says, "The Lord, the God of gods, has spoken." In many of the early parts of the Bible they speak of these other gods. But Yahweh was supreme above all the gods. And then, in the Prophets, Yahweh was seen to be everything and the gods of the nations were nothing in comparison. The last stage is that the gods of the nations become demons. So first of all they are 'gods,' as in the book of Job: when the sons of God appear before God, Satan is among them. Then they become nothing. Finally they become anti-gods; they become demons. This is the tradition which we have inherited and this is why Christian missionaries on the whole have simply rejected Hinduism as polytheism and therefore against God.

The Hindu approach was the exact opposite. We find it defined very clearly in the Rig-Veda itself. In the first book of the Veda, (not first in time; the first in the collection), it says: *"Ekam sat vipra bahuda vadanti"* — "the one being the wise call by many names." The Hindu view is that the gods and goddesses are the names and forms of the

One Being who has no name and no form.

This is a very profound doctrine. The ultimate worship of the educated and instructed Hindu is always to that 'one being,' the *ekam sat*. The gods are names and forms under which the one God manifests himself. It is interesting to find, as the result of certain surveys recently made show, that even the villager today has the same understanding. They will say quite spontaneously that there is only one God and that the gods are *nama rupa*, names and forms of that one God.

Now that is quite a coherent view. There is one absolute, infinite, transcendent Being who is beyond all the gods and all that can be named in heaven and on earth. The gods are devas in Sanskrit, 'the shining ones.' They are much more like the angels, though that distinction was never made clear as in the Hebrew tradition. They are perhaps nearest of all to the "cosmic powers" of St Paul. The gods of the Vedas are the powers of nature, powers of the sky, powers of the earth, powers of the sea, powers of the fire, and our own powers the power of sight, for example: we look out on this world around us, and that is a divine power. There is a god who is enabling us to see and to hear, to speak and to act. All these are powers of the One Being. That is the basic Hindu understanding. And that is why we must be very careful when we hear words like polytheism being used about Hinduism. It's not really polytheistic. Polytheism is the worship of the many apart from the One, and many Protestants would say on the same grounds that Catholics are polytheists, that they worship the saints. There is probably some truth in that. An ignorant person is always in danger of making an absolute of a particular personal form and worshipping not God in the saint but the saint in himself. But the traditional doctrine is that there is one infinite Being, and all the gods and goddesses and all angels and saints are forms and manifestations of that One. That is our first and fundamental point.

32. Vedanta: The Upanishads[11]

It is in the final texts of the Vedas, the Upanishads, that Bede finds the heart of the wisdom of India. This wisdom is condensed, for him, in the 'knowledge of the Self', and it emerged in the 'axial period' about five centuries before Christ. At this time, he sees a critical step in the evolution of human consciousness occurring around the world. Out of the background of imaginative and intuitive knowing, of mythical consciousness, the rational intellect emerges. In the 'marriage' of reason and imagination, a new reflexive self-consciousness emerges, and a new experience of pure spirit occurs. At this moment is born 'intuitive thought.' " This is the time when reason and imagination meet in a marvelous marriage, and the masculine and the feminine unite to form the complete man." From the moonlit and starlit night, the human person comes into the daylight of the spiritual intellect, of the sun at the center of the person.

In this axial moment the human person awakens to the light of pure consciousness, to itself as spiritual person. From this pivotal awakening, Bede asserts, will flow both the contemplative realization of the Self in the East and the scientific comprehension of the external world in the West. A shaft of unitive light joins the three worlds of the divine, the human and the cosmic as, at their center-point, the human person awakens to self-possession.

In the unitive experience which takes place among the Indian rishis now as the Vedic period gives birth to the Upanishads, *Bede finds the essential revelation of Hinduism. From this point will unfold his exposition of the Vedanta. It is also for Bede the central point in human history, and this will prove a point of tension both with the Christ-centered perspective of his own tradition and with his later evolutionary perspective.*

The revelation of the Vedas, which was given in the rich poetic language of myth and symbol, was developed in the Upanishads in a more philosophical form. The Upanishads come at the end of the Vedic period (500 BC) and form the basis of the Vedanta — the end (*anta*) of the Vedas. In them is to be found the quintessence of Hindu doctrine, the supreme wisdom, which is one of the great inheritances of mankind. They belong to that period in the middle of the first millennium before Christ, which saw also the rise of Jainism and Buddhism in India, of Taoism and Confucianism in China, of Zoroastrianism in Persia, of philosophy in Greece and of prophecy in Israel. It has been called by Karl Jaspers the 'axial period' in human history. It marked the emergence of rational understanding out of the mythical imagination of the ancient world. From the beginning of history, or more accurately from the time of the first emergence of human speech, man had lived in the world of the imagination, of intuitive wisdom in which sense and feeling, desire and thought and will had all been focused on symbols of words and gestures, of dance and song, of images and paintings, of rituals and sacrifices, in which the world of the gods, of the cosmic and psychic powers, was seen reflected in the human imagination. This was the world of the Vedas. Now in this period of the Upanishads, the rational mind breaks through the image and the symbol and emerges into the light of pure thought. The concept begins to take the place of the image.

Yet we must be clear that this is not a case of reason replacing imagination. It is rather that the 'truth of the imagination,' as Keats had called it, emerges into a clearer light. At this period precisely we find the perfect marriage of imagination and reason in intuitive thought. Intuition, as we have said, is at first blind; it is a confused and obscure grasp of reality, in which the seeds of all future knowledge are contained. It is the embryonic thought, in which the future structure of thought is contained, as the structure of the mature human being is contained in the embryo. As the power of reason develops, this dark embryonic knowledge, which is the knowledge of childhood, begins to be illumined by reason, and the language of images and symbols is formed, creating the vast, rich world of myth in which man lived for thousands of years. Then in this 'axial' period reason pierced through the veil of the symbol to discover the truth contained in it.

It is impossible to exaggerate the importance of this moment in human history. It is the point at which man reaches the knowledge of himself, the atman, the Self, of the Vedic seer, the 'know thyself' of the Delphic Oracle. From the night of the moon and the stars with all their brilliance, he emerges into the light of the sun and the day.

But there is no break in continuity at this point. The power of reason which was already at work in the imagination, creating the myth and the symbol, now breaks through into a pure intuition of reality. The first intuition of the soul had been dark and confused, it had grown with the rich symbolic intuition of imagination; now it passes beyond images and symbols into the pure light of thought. Yet human understanding can never dispense with images and symbols. Even when it passes beyond into pure intuition, it still needs images and symbols to clothe its thought. That is why at this period we come upon the great flowering period of poetry, the epic of Homer and the Greek tragedians, the imaginative genius of the Hebrew prophets, the

Book of Poetry in China, the Ramayana and the Mahabharata in India. This is the time when reason and imagination meet in a marvellous marriage, and the masculine and the feminine unite to form the complete man. It is no accident that at the end of this period we meet the figure of the perfect man, in the form of Rama and Krishna in India, the Bodhisattva in Buddhism, and Jesus, the Christ, the Messiah, who brings to fulfilment the promises made to Israel and the prophecies concerning the Messianic Priest and King.

It is to this supreme period in human history, therefore, that the *Upanishads* belong. They spring from the soil of the rich imaginative tradition of the Vedas, and they bring to it the pure light of the intelligence. At this point we can watch the human spirit emerging into self-consciousness, human reason beginning to form clear concepts and the physical world becoming the object of scientific knowledge. The wisdom of the Upanishads is inexhaustible. It arises from a profound intuition of ultimate reality, a passing beyond all the outward forms of nature and the inner experience of man to the pure intuition of the spirit.

33. *The Mystery of Brahman*[12]

In Return to the Center, *Bede writes in a single chapter of 'The Mystery of Nirvana and Brahman.' His approach to the brahman of Hinduism is by way of Buddhist apophatism, the 'negative way', and the concept of nirvana.*[13] *Nirvana, he informs us, is a term also found in the* Bhagavad Gita. *It is as ineffable yet ever-present Mystery that Bede introduces us to the 'essential truth of Hinduism' which is brahman.*

The unitive drive of Bede Griffiths' intellect has found here in the Vedanta a point beyond which it is not possible to go. Brahman is the invisible and ineffable ground and fullness of reality, the "one, unutterable Mystery of Being." Not only Bede's intellectual hunger but his insatiable spiritual thirst glimpses its final fulfillment here. For several pages we circle in the rarified air of this region while he brings to our attention the many lines which find here their central point of convergence.

We may reasonably expect that brahman can be inferred within every religious tradition. Bede points out correlatives not only in Buddhist nirvana but in the divine persons of Christianity: the Father is nirguna brahman, the 'naked Godhead,' while the Son is saguna brahman, manifestation of the Father who has become a human person in Jesus Christ. Bede will then corre-

late the Holy Spirit with the atman which is one with brahman. He will find another trinitarian analogy in the Sat-Cit-Ananda which is, again, identical with brahman. The unitive reality denoted by the name brahman will reappear everywhere in Bede's exposition of the Vedanta, but more often under the terms atman, advaita, nonduality and purusha. Again and again we shall seem to re-experience this arrival which is so characteristic of Bede Griffiths.

These profound conceptions of the Indian spiritual philosophers would be encountered with less surprise by Christians of another time than ours, especially within one of the spiritual traditions drawing from Neoplatonism. Since the thirteenth century in the West, almost entirely cut off from the 'way of unknowing,'[14] we have confined our conceptions of Divinity almost exclusively within rational categories and relational images.

The essential truth of Hinduism is the doctrine of the brahman. The brahman is the Mystery of Being, the ultimate Truth, the one Reality. Yet it also can only be described by negatives. It is *neti, neti,* not this, not this.[15] It is unseen, unrelated, inconceivable, uninferable, unimaginable, indescribable.[16] Yet though beyond sense and thought, it is experienced in the depth of the soul as the very ground of its being. It is the atman, the Self, the real being of man as of the universe. 'I am the brahman,"[17] 'Thou art that,'[18] 'All this [world] is brahman.'[19] These are the *mahavakyas*, the 'great sayings', of the *Upanishads*, in which the Mystery of Being is revealed. When experienced in this way, it is known as Saccidananda, as Being, Knowledge, Bliss.[20] It is experienced as absolute Being (*sat*), the fullness of reality, the one, infinite, Transcendence. But it is known not by intellect, or by reason, or by learning; it is known in pure consciousness (*cit*), a pure intuition in which the knower, the thing known, and the act of knowing are one. There is here no duality, all differences have been transcended, there is only the One 'without a second'. And this is an experience of infinite bliss (*ananda*). All desires are here fulfilled, the soul has entered into its rest, it attains to peace shanti the peace that passes understanding. This is the supreme goal, the ultimate state, which like the *Bhagavad Gita* calls 'the nirvana of brahman'.[21]

But one may ask, is this nirvana of brahman, like the nirvana of the Buddha, an impersonal state? It depends what one means by 'person'. If by 'person' one means the self which is shut up in the body, enclosed in this world, occupied with its own thoughts and feelings and appetites and desires, then certainly this self cannot enter nirvana; it is this self which must die. But if by 'person' one means the Self which is open to the Infinite, to the Eternal, to Truth, to Love, then nirvana is the realization of this Self, the fulfilment of its being. To enter nirvana is to become one's self, to become what one really is. It is to behold the Self in all things and all things in the Self.[22] In this sense nirvana is the most personal of all experiences. That is why at the heart of Buddhism, in spite of its negative doctrine, there is found a person of infinite compassion, the person of the Buddha. That is why Krishna can say, 'He who sees all things in the Self and the Self in all things, sees me in all things and all things in me.'[23] The ultimate Mystery of Being, the brahman, is revealed not only as the Self of all men, but as the Lord dwelling in the hearts of all men, as an object of worship and of love. The *Bhagavad-Gita* revealed the Supreme Being as a God of love. 'The Lord dwells in the heart of all beings, O Arjuna. . . . In him seek refuge with thy whole soul: by his grace thou shalt win the peace supreme, the everlasting realm.'[24] There is, therefore, no conflict between the personal and the impersonal in the ultimate state. The brahman, the ultimate Ground of Being, is one with the atman, the ultimate Ground of the Self, and this in turn is one with the Lord, the personal God. The Person in its ultimate Ground is the eternal Saccidananda, Being in the plenitude of self-knowledge and the perfection of blissful love — what in Christianity was to be revealed as Father, Son and Holy Spirit; the Father, the source of being; the Son, the Word, the wisdom, the manifestation of the Father; and the Spirit, the blissful love of the Godhead which is everlasting joy and peace, flowing from the Father to the Son, and from the Son to the whole creation.

Of course, all these terms are used in a transcendent sense. We have to use the method of affirmation, negation and transcendence. If we say that brahman is Saccidananda Being, Knowledge, Bliss we first of all affirm that brahman is Being, absolute Being, Reality itself. We then go on to deny that brahman is being in the same sense as any other being, so that we have to say that brahman in a sense is not-being. But finally we say that brahman is Being in a transcendent sense, he is Being in a manner which transcends every mode of being which we can conceive. It is the same with every other attribute. Brahman is consciousness — *cit* — but it is consciousness which transcends any mode of consciousness which we can conceive. Brahman is bliss — *ananda* — but it is a bliss which transcends any mode of bliss which we can conceive. In this sense brahman is called *nirguna* 'without attributes'. But this does not mean that brahman lacks these attributes of being, consciousness, bliss, truth, love but that these attributes exist in him in a manner that transcends all conceptions. In saguna brahman — brahman 'with attributes' — these attributes are manifested, they become known. In this sense we can say that *nirguna* brahman corresponds with the Father in Christian theology — the ultimate ground of the Godhead — while *saguna* brahman corresponds with the Son, the Word of God, the manifestation of the hidden Godhead.

Saguna brahman is manifested in the *trimurti* — the three forms of Brahma, the Creator, Vishnu, the Preserver, the Siva, the Destroyer, but also the Regenerator of the universe. These are the basic forms under which God is worshipped in India, but in practice Brahma is scarcely worshipped at all he has but one temple in India today — and Vishnu and Siva both alike assume the functions of the Supreme Being. Both alike are worshipped as the one, eternal, infinite transcendent Being manifesting himself to the world. In a sense this is true of all the Hindu gods. Each is a particular manifestation of the one, infinite Transcendence, each is a particular aspect of brahman. In Hebrew monotheism Yahweh was elevated to the position of the one Supreme God and all other gods were considered first of all as inferior to him, and then as nothing in comparison with him, and finally as demons, that is, powers opposed to him. But Hinduism followed another path. Each of the gods was considered to be a manifestation of the one supreme Reality, the absolute Transcendence, which is 'without a second'. The danger of this is that each particular god may come to be worshipped for himself without reference to the One, and this is properly polytheism. But in Hinduism the tendency has been the opposite. Each god tends to assume all the attributes of the one God, and becomes no more than a name for the one Supreme Being. This is particularly true of Vishnu and Siva, who are simply names of

God. It is also true of the Mother-Goddess — the *devi* — who becomes the Sakti of brahman, the power of the Supreme, and is eventually indistinguishable from the absolute brahman.

Just as the gods are manifestations of the brahman, so the whole universe, with everything in it, is a manifestation of brahman, the one, unutterable Mystery of Being. The brahman, as Vishnu, pervades the whole world; every atom, every grain of sand, every blade of grass, is a form of brahman. As the Upanishad says, 'All this is brahman.[25] But is this pantheism? If by pantheism we mean that God is identical with the world and the world with God, then no Hindu system is pantheism. Though brahman is immanent in all things, it also transcends all things. As the Rig-Veda puts it: 'All creatures are one fourth of him, three fourths are eternal in heaven.'[26] This is putting it crudely, but the meaning is clear. Another way of putting it is to say: 'As the one fire after it has entered the world, though one, becomes different according to whatever it burns, thus the one Self in all things becomes different according to what it enters, and exists also without.'[27] Or again: 'As the one air after it has entered the world, though one, becomes different according to whatever it enters, thus the one Self within all things becomes different according to whatever it enters, and exists also without.'[28] Or again: 'As the sun, the eye of the world, is not contaminated by the external purities seen by the eyes, thus the one Self within all things is not contaminated by the misery of the world, being himself without.'[29] This comes nearer to the truth, but it comes nearest of all when the brahman, the Self, is compared to a person: There is one ruler, the Self, within all things, who makes the one form manifold. The wise who perceive him within their self, to them belongs happiness, not to others.[30] It is when the Self is recognized intuitively within that the real relation of brahman to the universe is known, and that cannot properly be expressed in words.

Everything, and every person, exists eternally in brahman in its uncreated Ground, beyond words and thoughts. This is the ultimate Mystery of Being, which can only be known when sense and reason are transcended and the Self is known in its eternal ground. When things and persons come forth into space and time, then they begin to have a separate existence and receive name and form. Then they begin to be objects of sense and thought. But even so, they are wholly pervaded by brahman. They have their being in him and are only properly known in him. The knowledge of things and persons in their state of separation apart from brahman is *maya*, illusion. This is the ignorance — *avidya* — which goes by the name of science today. It is not altogether false. It is a partial, incomplete knowledge of appearances which is true as far as it goes. But when it is mistaken for real knowledge, for the knowledge of things as they are, it is an illusion. To know things as they are, one must know one's self; one must go beyond sense and reason and know the Self in all things and all things in the Self. This is wisdom, this is enlightenment, this is to know the Truth.

Every human being is a manifestation of the brahman, the one, eternal Self. In so far as he imagines himself to be a separate being, existing apart from the One, he is a product of *maya*, a mere illusion. When he comes to know his true self in the brahman, then he attains enlightenment. As the Upanishad says: 'Two birds, inseparable friends, cling to the same tree. One of these eats the fruit, the other looks on without eating.'[31] The two birds are the individual soul — the *jivatman* and the supreme Self — the *Paramatman*. The individual soul eats the fruit of this world and gets entangled in maya, thinking itself a separate being. But when it recognizes the other, the true Self, who is also the Lord, then it is set free. This beautiful parable shows the true nature of the soul. It is a temporal manifestation of the one, eternal Self. When it forgets its true nature and gets immersed in this world, it is full of misery, but when it recognizes its true Self, in the Lord, dwelling in the heart, then it attains to peace. In Christian terms we can say that when the soul turns to God and is united with him, it finds its true self, its real being, and is freed from the illusion of sin. Or going deeper, we can say that the Spirit of God dwells in the heart of every man. When we recognize this Spirit as our true Self, the life our soul, the breath of our being, then we are united with the Lord, with Christ the Saviour, and through him attain to the peace of the Father.

The Father is *nirguna* brahman, the naked Godhead, the abyss of Being, the divine darkness, without form and void, the silence where no word is spoken, where no thought comes, the absolute nothing-ness from which everything comes, the not-being from which all being comes, the One without a second, which is utterly empty yet immeasurably full, wayless and fathomless,[32] beyond the reach of thought. He cannot be named, cannot be expressed, cannot be con-ceived. The Son is *saguna* brahman, the Word, through whom the Father receives a name, by which he is expressed, by which he is con-ceived. The Son is the manifestation of the Father, his Image and Likeness, making known the hidden depths of the Godhead. In the Son the whole creation comes forth eternally from the Father. Everything that is hidden in the abyss of the Godhead comes to light in him. He is the light in which everything is known and receives name and form. He is God 'with attributes,' revealing the power, the wis-dom, the glory, the life, the light, the truth, the love, which is hidden in the Father. He is the consciousness (*cit*) of the Father, expressing his being, the Self in which he eternally reflects himself and makes himself known. Each of us comes forth eternally from the hidden depths of the Father into being in the Word. There we receive name and form. There we are known from all eternity. In the Father we exist from all eternity in an unfathomable unity of being without distinc-tion. In the Son we exist eternally in distinction of being, and yet without distinction, because in God all creatures are God.[33] This is our eternal uncreated being in the Word. But when we come into being in time, then we become distinct and separate. Then we come to exist not simply in God but in ourselves. Yet even so, the grace of God is always drawing us back to himself. We come forth from God in order that we may exist in ourselves and know ourselves as distinct and separate, each a distinct and unique reflection of God, with a capacity of freedom, a power to choose and to will our own being. It is then that we can choose to separate ourselves from God, to refuse to recognize our dependence on God, to create an illusory independ-ence and become subject to *maya*. Or we can choose to return to God, to find our real being in him, to know ourselves as expressions of his being, as manifestations of his Word. This is the drama of sin and redemption.

Each of us has in the ultimate ground of his being an eternal being in the Father, beyond word and thought, hidden in the darkness, in the uncreated Source of being, where no creature appears, no distinction is known. And each of us has an eternal being in the Son, where we come into being from the Father, each a unique manifestation of the one Word of God, each a unique image and reflection of his being, distinct from all others as a living idea in the mind of God, yet inseparably one with God, sharing the divine nature. Again, each of us has a separate, finite existence, in which we are separated from God, fallen from the divine life, shut up in this world of matter, divided by space and time and imprisoned in ourselves. But finally, each of us has an existence in which we are being called to return to God, to awaken to the divine life within us, to respond to the movement of the Spirit, to listen to the voice of the Word, to recover our divine nature and finally to return to the Father, to lose ourselves in that abyss of Being from which we came. For in that abyss of Being, in that nirvana of brahman, everything that has come forth not only in time but in eternity, the divine Saccidananda, Father, Son and Holy Spirit, is found in the absolute plenitude of Being, which is yet so far beyond thought that it appears to us as a darkness, a void, an abyss of nothingness.

34. Atman: Discovery of the Self[34]

Central to the new human consciousness which emerged in the axial period was an awakening to a new interiority. While the journey within characterizes human spirituality almost universally, and is found throughout the Christian mystical and contemplative traditions, in the Vedanta it seems to reach an unsurpassable purity and depth in the realization of the Self. Bede presents the unitive wisdom of the Vedanta as a way of pure introversion in which one journeys beyond words, forms, images and feelings to an experience of pure spirit, of the atman. Here, Bede insists, is an unquestionably genuine experiential reality which challenges Christianity to develop a new and more comprehensive understanding of mysticism. In this essay from Christ in India *Bede, committed to a 'theology of fulfillment,' finds a further consummation of the Hindu experience of the Self in a personal union with God through knowledge and love. We shall find that this is not just an abstract theological conviction; it corresponds to Bede's personal experience. Ultimately, his own path is not that of pure interiority and the realization of the Self.[35] Further writings of Bede Griffiths on the realization of the Self will be found below in*

Part V.[36]

What then is the nature of the Hindu mystical experience? It has been analyzed by Maritain and other Catholic philosophers and its essential structure seems to be clear. It is an experience of the Self, that is the substantial being of the soul in its ultimate depth beyond sense and reason by an act of pure reflection on itself. We can catch the actual movement of the Hindu mind in this act of introversion in the words of the Katha Upanishad: 'The Self-existent pierced the opening of the senses so that they turned outward; therefore man looks outwards not within himself. *Some wise man, desiring immortality, turned his eyes inwards and saw the Self.*' In these words one can discern the direction which the Hindu mind was to take for the whole course of history. Everywhere we see a movement of introversion, a deliberate turning from the external world, from the senses and the imagination and all that they have to offer, even from the world of reason in so far as it is based on the evidence of the senses, to discover the hidden source of Being, the root of the Self. The whole science of Yoga which is one of the six *darshanas* or systems of Hindu philosophy, is nothing but a scientific method of breaking through the world of the senses and separating the soul from its subjection to the body. In the ultimate stage of Yoga, that of 'seedless' *samadhi*, the soul is found in its isolation, separated from the physical universe and enjoying the experience of its own pure spiritual being.

It might be thought, and it has sometimes been said, that such an experience is unnatural and that it only leads to the soul's absorption in itself, but all the evidence of Hindu history contradicts such a view. It is clear that in this experience of the Self in the ground of its being the Hindu soul was brought into contact with God. Without images or concepts, but in the actual experience of its own spiritual substance the soul experiences the presence of God, the one, infinite, eternal, absolute Being, 'without a second' and this experience is one of absolute bliss. Such is the testimony of all Indian history. From the earliest texts of the Upanishads where we read of one who says: 'Friend, your face shines like one who has seen the brahman,' to the recorded evidence of those who have known the great seers of modern times like Ramakrishna and Ramana Maharshi, one can sense the reality of a mystical experience in which there is a pure consciousness of transcendent being in absolute bliss. I think that we have to take this experience with the utmost seriousness. There is something in it which is final and absolute. To the Hindu today no less than in the past this is the one, supreme reality for which everything in the world is to be sacrificed and compared with which everything else is of little worth. This is the secret wisdom of India, which sets her apart in the world and makes her the spiritual leader of mankind.

35. The Three Meanings of Atman[37]
In River of Compassion, *Bede offers this clarification while commenting on chapter six of the* Bhagavad Gita.

Ultimately there is only one Self, the supreme Self, which is manifested at different levels of reality. First of all, the Paramatman, the Supreme Self, can be conceived as beyond all word and all thought. It is the ultimate transcendent mystery. Secondly, the atman can be conceived as the source of all reality, the source of all creation, of consciousness and of human existence. Thirdly, the same atman can be conceived as indwelling in each person, each thing. In each one of us the One, the Supreme Spirit, is dwelling. That Supreme Spirit dwelling in me is my higher Self. These three senses are fundamental. The absolute Supreme, beyond everything, the *Parabrahman* or *Paramatman*, then the brahman or atman as the source of everything, the creator Spirit, and then the atman or brahman manifested in every person in every thing, the indwelling Self. That is my higher Self and it is ultimately one with the Supreme.

36. Eastern Religious Experience
In an article written for the North American journal, Monastic Studies *(1972), Bede finds essentially the same experience of the unitive Absolute emerging at the axial time in Hinduism, in Buddhism and in Taoism. Swiftly he sketches a spiritual map of the world, contrasting these three great 'oriental' traditions with the three 'Semitic' traditions of Israel, Christianity and Islam. Here he develops only the Hindu experience of brahman/atman, as typifying the Asian family of religions. This is a direct experience, an interior realization of the Self as one with the ground of all being, as 'immanent in nature and the soul.' The various practices of Yoga open the human person to an intervention of the Transcendent which is equivalent, in Christian terms,*

204

to the visitation of the Holy Spirit.

I38

About five centuries before the birth of Christ, the eastern world awoke to a profound experience of God, or rather of an absolute, infinite, transcendent Reality, which was known variously as brahman or atman or nirvana or Tao, which was destined to shape the religious life of the East for all succeeding centuries. In its depth and intensity this experience can only be compared to the experience of God in Israel, which took place at about the same time, and was destined to shape the religious life not only of Israel but also of Christianity and Islam. These two religious traditions, the oriental and the Semitic, have often appeared to be in violent opposition with one another, but a deeper study reveals that they are essentially complementary, and it is one of the principal tasks of the church at the present time to come to an understanding of this oriental tradition and to integrate its religious insights into its own tradition.

In order to deal adequately with this subject it would be necessary to study the experience of God, or the Absolute, not only in Hinduism but also in Buddhism and Taoism, but as there is a basic similarity in this experience and the time at our disposal is strictly limited, we will confine our attention to Hinduism, and within Hinduism to the classical system of Yoga, in which the nature of this experience and the method by which it can be realized has been reduced to a fine art. It may be added that this system of Yoga is basically the same in Buddhism and in Taoism, so that what is said of Hinduism will have its bearing on the whole oriental tradition.

The Hindu experience of God which took shape in the *Upanishads* was essentially the discovery that beneath all the external forms of nature there is one, absolute, infinite, transcendent Reality, which was known as the brahman. At the same time it was discovered that beneath all the phenomena of human consciousness, beyond not only sense but also thought, there is the one, absolute, transcendent Self, the atman; and this Self, the ground of all consciousness, it was declared, is one with the brahman, the ground of Being. This is expressed in the great saying of the Upanishads: Thou art That - Thou, the Self in its transcendent ground, art one with That, the transcendent ground of the universe. Now this affirmation is not a matter of philsophical speculation, but of religious experience. The Self is known not by abstraction or by any philosophical method but by direct experience beyond sense or reason in the ground or center of the soul. The soul knows itself by direct intuition in its own ground as one with the ground of all being, and this experience of Being in pure consciousness is one of absolute bliss.

Such in its barest outline is the original Hindu experience of God as *Saccidananda*, Being-Knowledge-Bliss, which underlies all subsequent Hindu religion. It is, one may say, an experience of God, the one transcendent Reality, in his immanence in nature and the soul.

II[39]

... However, it is not in the sphere of physical or psychological analysis and control that the greatest value of oriental spirituality is to be found. It is in the penetration of the mind beyond the physical and psychological level to the ground of the Spirit, to the ultimate encounter with God, that the East has most to teach us. We have in the West a wonderful tradition of contemplative and mystical prayer, but it has been reached almost entirely by reliance on divine grace, and no precise method has been elaborated to enable the soul to reach this state. In the East every effort has been made from the earliest times to pass beyond the level of the sense and the reason and to reach the center or ground of the soul, where it is in direct contact with the ultimate source of Being. This is done by learning to still the mind, to allow all movements of the discursive mind to cease by concentrating the mind on a single point, so that it becomes totally recollected in itself. A great assistance in this is the use of japa, the repetition of the divine name, as in the prayer of Jesus, which has the effect both of quieting the discursive mind and focusing it on the transcendent Reality. When this stage is reached the soul is gathered into itself without distraction and is freed from all the impediments of the mind and the senses.

It is in this state of total recollection, both mind and body being in harmony and the spirit at rest in itself, that the soul is perfectly open to the action of God. At this point there is a transition from the natural to the supernatural order. Something intervenes which is not of this world. Whether it is the Chinese Tao, the Buddhist nirvana, or the Hindu atman, there is an experience of absolute transcendence, so much so that no words can express what then takes place. This is the point at which in Christian prayer the action of the Holy Spirit intervenes. All these techniques of yoga, physical, psychological and spiritual, should be seen as a means of preparation for the free action of the Holy Spirit which has to take possession of the soul. According to the teaching of St Thomas, in the state of contemplation it is the gifts of the Holy Spirit which take control. The soul is passive to the action of the Spirit, *patiens divina*, as he says. This is the state for which all oriental methods of prayer and meditation are a preparation. The soul has to become completely passive to the divine action, so that we can say: "I live no longer, it is Christ who lives in me."

Now this state of contemplation, understood in the sense that body and soul are brought under the control of the Holy Spirit, so that we act not of ourselves but by the action of the Spirit of Christ in us, is the end or goal of all monastic life, and in fact of all Christian life.

37. *The Mystical Tradition in Indian Theology*[40]

Writing of Hindu mysticism in another Monastic Studies *essay ten years later, Bede describes the same experience once again. Here he focuses upon the meaning of the language of nonduality or identity used for this unitive realization in the Upanishadic literature. The experience of the Absolute through the Self by the way of interiorization is an experience beyond every duality. How can this undoubtedly genuine experience be rendered in terms acceptable to a Christian, for whom the ontological distinctness of God and the creature cannot be violated? Bede finds a solution in the biblical conception of the human person as created in the image of God: a conception which remained central to Christian mystical theologians from early centuries through the middle ages. Meister Eckhart or Abhishiktananda would probably have taken the riskier path, asserting the union in bold language, accenting the magnificent paradox.*

207

The Hindu approach to this mystery is by way of the exploration of consciousness. The brahman, which is the source of all, the beginning and end of creation, is present in the heart of man as the source of consciousness. It is "the great Being, infinite, limitless, consisting of nothing but knowledge (*vijnana-ghana*)," or in a still more striking phrase, "the Person of light, consisting of knowledge (*vijnana-maya*) within the heart."[41] But this presence cannot be known by the senses or by the rational mind. "It is unseen but seeing; unheard but hearing; unperceived but perceiving, unknown but knowing." The disciple has to be taught to go beyond the outer senses and the inner mind, the physical and psychic worlds, in order to know the true self within. As the Mandukya Upanishad puts it, it is beyond the waking state and the dream state, beyond even the state of deep sleep, where both sense and mind are at rest. It is the "fourth" state, turiya, the state beyond our present mode of consciousness.[42] In the Katha Upanishad it is shown how the disciple must go through death and be instructed by Yama, the god of death, if he is to know that which lies beyond. Only then can he awake to the supreme reality and "recognize the Ancient, who is difficult to be seen, who has entered into the dark, who is hidden in the cave, who dwells in the abyss as God."[43] This is the supreme knowledge, which cannot be attained by argument, or by learning, or by the Scriptures, but which is given to him whom the Self chooses.[44] This conception of the supreme knowledge as a gift of grace is found both in the Katha and in the Mundaka Upanishad and is undoubtedly an authentic part of the Upanishadic tradition, though Sankara was unable to accept it.

This knowledge of the Supreme is expressed in the Upanishads by the great *mahavakyas* — "I am brahman" — "Thou art That." How are we to understand these expressions? It is clear that they are the expression of a mystical experience which cannot be properly expressed. Sankara, at least as he is generally understood, interprets them in terms of identity. But it seems that even in Sankara it is possible that his understanding was deeper than it appears, and the words are certainly capable of a more profound interpretation. In the Katha Upanishad we have the image of the "two who have entered into the cave, the seat of the Supreme."[45] In the Svetasvatara Upanishad this is elaborated in the following terms: "Two birds, inseparable friends, cling to the same tree. One eats the sweet fruit, the other looks on without eating." This is then interpreted: "On the same tree man sits grieving, immersed, bewildered by his impotence. But when he sees the Other, the Lord (Isa), and knows his glory, his grief passes away."[46] The two birds are, of course, the *jivatman* and the *paramatman*, the individual and the supreme self. What is the relation between them? It seems possible to interpret this relation in terms of an image in a mirror. The image in the mirror is not different from the original in that it is one and the same reality which is present in the reflection and in the original. But the image in the mirror has not the same kind of reality as the original. It has a wholly relative reality. In this sense the image and the original are "not two." Sankara himself uses the image of the sun reflected in different pools of water. It is one and the same sun which is reflected in each pool; there is only one being, but it is reflected in a multitude of different forms. In each pool it is one and the same sun which is reflected and yet each is different. It would seem that this conception would come as near as possible to a true interpretation of the intuition of the *Upanishads*. In the Upanishads it is not suggested that the world is unreal. In the Svetasvatara Upanishad, where the word *maya* is used, it signifies no more than that which is "made," while the maker is the mayin.[47]

If this explanation is accepted, then the sayings, "I am brahman," "Thou art That," can be interpreted in the sense that there is one reality, one being, which when conceived as the source or ground of creation is called brahman, and when conceived as the source or ground of consciousness is called atman. Each created thing and each individual soul is an image or reflection as in a mirror of this one reality. The image has its own relative reality. It is not unreal, but neither is it wholly real, since its whole being is from another. In our present mode of consciousness we see this one reality reflected in the mirror of this created world. But when we wake to the *paravidya*, to the supreme knowledge, then we see that one reality alone, in which all the images are contained. When this awakening takes place then there is no more duality.[48] Then the person knows himself not as reflected through his senses or his mental consciousness but in his original

209

state, in the ground of his eternal being and consciousness, and in this knowledge he experiences absolute bliss. This is the supreme knowledge; the soul comes to know its self in its original being (*sat*), and this knowledge (*cit*) brings absolute bliss (*ananda*). Thus as far as it can be named this state of being is called Saccidananda. But the word is only a pointer to a reality which has to be experienced. The Jnani (knower) is one who has experienced this state of being and is able to communicate his knowledge to another, when he is ready to receive it. In other words this is a mystical experience in which the soul knows itself in its original ground of being, beyond sense and reason, where all differences as conceived by the mind disappear and the one reality is experienced without duality in a unitive vision, which communicates absolute bliss.

It cannot be doubted that this mystical experience to which the Upanishads bear witness is one of the most profound experiences of God, or of absolute Truth, in human history, and any theology in India which is worthy of the name has to take account of this experience and integrate it in the total experience of Christian faith. It is clear that if we accept the view that the created world is an image or reflection of the uncreated being or brahman, and that the human soul by a free gift of grace - "he whom the atman chooses, he knows the atman " - is able to know brahman by an intuitive knowledge of its inner self, and that even this knowledge cannot be attained, as the Katha Upanishad again says, "unless evil ways are abandoned, and there is rest in the senses, concentration in the mind, and peace in the heart,"[49] it is then clear that there is nothing contrary to Christian faith in such a conception. Translating it into Christian terms we can say that the Spirit illumines the mind by its own free action and the soul comes to know itself as the image of God made in the likeness of Christ, in whom the Father, the original source of being, reveals himself.

38. Realization of the Self, Union with All[50]
Bede is commenting verse 28 of the same sixth chapter of the Gita, in River of Compassion. *We shall find that this rediscovery of the world within the Self is followed, still within the Gita, by a new development within the Hindu tradition: spiritual energies are redirected toward service to humanity and the*

world.[51]

Once we reach this inner point where we seem to be isolated, we suddenly discover ourselves to be in communion with everyone and everything. Zaehner goes on, "This is brahman's saving touch which brings unbounded infinite joy. It is the touch of which the Buddhists know nothing. Yet it is the most real of all, the 'union of opposites' — that of the point without magnitude, the human self, and of the utterly unmeasured and unmeasurable, the inconceivably great." It is the paradox of the Self, which is more minute than the minute, and yet greater than the great, vaster than the vast. It is that point where one expands into infinity. So Zaehner says, "by the maximum concentration of all that is in us into the infinitely small, the timeless Self, one finds that this nothing is, nevertheless, conformed to infinity." Although Zaehner doubts that this is a Buddhist experience, this emptiness which is total fulfillment is, as I understand it, very much the Buddhist experience of nirvana in the Mahayana tradition. Zaehner continues, "It can almost be said that when this process of integration reaches its goal, there is an explosion. The self bursts asunder and finds itself utterly available to brahman's saving touch. One seems to be concentrating one's self, separating from everybody and getting more and more isolated, and then on reaching that point, one suddenly explodes and realizes: 'I am at one with the whole of creation, with all humanity.' " This interconnection and interpenetration of all things, which is now revealed, is not what the classical Sankhya had conceived. This is something new, although it was already present in the *Upanishads*. There is a beautiful passage in the *Chandogya Upanishad*, which speaks of this experience of brahman, how "He is myself within the heart, smaller than the grain of rice, a barley-corn or a mustard seed or a grain of millet or the kernel of a grain of millet." Likewise in the Gospel, the Kingdom of Heaven is compared to a grain of mustard seed. It is the tiniest thing in the world. It has no dimension at all. Yet it is "greater than the earth, greater than the air, greater than the sky, greater than all these worlds." Then the Upanishad concludes: 'All works, all desires, all sense, all tastes belong to it. It encompasses all the universe, does not speak and has no care. This my Self within the heart, is that brahman. When I

211

depart from hence I shall merge into it. He who believes this will never doubt." When one goes beyond the senses and the mind, at that point the whole world is rediscovered but in a new dimension. One is no longer subject to the senses; one is completely free but can use and enjoy them to the full. So all senses, all tastes, all desires, all works, are found there but in a totally new way.

Commenting the following verse 6.29 of the Gita:

. . . That is this final vision — on finding the Self, one finds all things, all creation in that Self. Again it is a kind of circumcession, or mutual interpenetration. The fullest reality of all is realized within. Some people imagine that when one is meditating, one is getting more and more isolated and separated from the world, and that in a sense is true. There is separation on the level of sense and even on a psychological level. But if one reaches the depth of reality then one rediscovers the whole creation in its depth, in its center, in its unity. Then one finds all things in one's Self. This is a very common idea in the *Upanishads*.

39. Advaita: Nonduality[52]

Advaita or nonduality is the state of the Absolute, which is participated through enlightenment, contemplative experience. Advaita Vedanta, one of the three philosophical systems in Vedanta, teaches that there is only one reality: cosmos, the soul and God are identical. Its best known exponent is Sankara. Bede rejects this extreme statement of advaita, but sees nonduality as a central teaching of the Vedanta. If, in following Bede through these successive facets of the Upanishadic wisdom we come to feel that we are always learning the same thing, that there is only one truth here, our impression is correct. Held by the gravitational force of this one mystery, we circle around the unitive Absolute.[53] This 'supreme idea,' as we have already seen, is a key which unlocks the great traditions of the East. More surprisingly, this key opens the New Testament and Christian theology as well. Western exegetes and theologians — with a few exceptions like Meister Eckhart — have hardly begun to use it. Abhishiktananda, less attentive to theological balance than Bede, committed himself to a total experiential realization of advaita.[54]

From the beginning of history, as far as one can tell, man has recognized behind all the phenomena of nature and consciousness a hidden power. Or rather, the phenomena of nature and his own consciousness were all seen to be 'enveloped' in a cosmic whole. As his power of discrimination developed, he was able to distinguish the powers of nature, of earth and sky, of water and fire, the powers of the 'gods', from his own powers of speech and action, of thinking and feeling, and to know himself as a conscious being. But the sense of the whole remained, the consciousness that the gods of earth anc sky were also in his heart and mind, and that in myth and ritual, in prayer and sacrifice, he could experience his oneness with the whole creation.

It is this sense of a cosmic unity which lies behind the Vedic tradition, and in the *Upanishads* the source of this cosmic unity receives a name. It is called brahman and atman, and gradually through deep meditation the nature of this brahman and this atman was revealed. It is known not by argument or reasoning, not by any activity of the sense or the rational mind, but by an immediate experience of the spirit, the atman, in man. It is this experience of the spirit which the Upanishads seek to communicate and to interpret in words, as far as it can be expressed in words. It is known as *Saccidananda*, Being or Reality, experienced in pure consciousness, communicating perfect bliss. But such a state of conscious being is a state of personal consciousness. It is misleading to speak of brahman or atman as 'impersonal'. A person is a conscious being, a being possessing itself in conscious awareness, and brahman is therefore the supreme Person, the Purushottaman. Every human being is a person just in so far as he participates in this supreme consciousness.

Each of us is conscious in so far as we share in this universal consciousness. The new-born child has a spark of this consciousness in it, which grows as it learns to share through language and gesture in the consciousness of its mother and father, its family and environment. Growth in consciousness is growth in this shared experience of the family, the tribe, the nation, the race. But this consciousness can grow beyond the boundaries of time and space, and enter into a transcendent consciousness, a consciousness transcending the limits of matter and mind, of the categories of sense and reason, and become aware of the universal consciousness which embraces the whole creation. This is the sole source of consciousness in man and the uni-

213

verse. 'There is no other seer but he,' says the Upanishad, 'no other hearer but he, no other perceiver but he, no other knower but he, this Self, the Ruler within, the immortal.'[55] All our seeing, and hearing and perceiving and knowing, is an effect of and a participation in the consciousness of that one, universal Being.

What characterizes this consciousness in the Vedic tradition is its non-duality. Of this it is said: 'Where there is duality, one smells another, one sees another, one hears another, one speaks to another, one perceives another, one knows another, but when everything has become the Self, by what and whom should one smell and see and hear and speak to and perceive and know another? By what should one know that by which all this is known? How should one know the knower?'[56] This is the classical statement of the doctrine of non-duality (advaita) and it takes us to the heart of the problem. How should one know the knower? The rational mind can only work through the senses and discover an 'object' of thought. Even the most abstract thought is conditioned by this distinction between subject and object. But how can we know the subject, the I, without turning it into an object? The moment I speak of myself, of an I, I have turned it into an object. This is the limitation of the rational mind. It remains imprisoned in the categories of an objective world. How to escape from the prison of the rational mind?

In all religious traditions, Hindu, Buddhist, Muslim, and Christian, it has been recognized that there is a knowledge above reason, a knowledge which is not derived from the senses and is not determined by the categories of rational thought. It is a knowledge not of an object but of the subject, the I which knows, not the I which is known. In Hindu tradition this has always been regarded as the ultimate form of knowledge, the knowledge of Self. It must be recognized that this is not a theory which would be a product of the rational mind, but an experience. The mind, turning back on itself, knows itself intuitively. It is an experience in which being and knowing are one that is why it is called saccidananda, because being (sat) is experienced in a pure act of knowing (cit) in the bliss (ananda) of oneness, of non-duality. The knower, the known and the act of knowing are all one. Yet when we have said this, we have already begun to interpret

214

the experience by means of rational categories, while the experience itself is beyond reason. Yet the attempt has to be made, because this experience has often been misinterpreted. It has often been interpreted to mean that the knowledge derived from sense and reason is an illusion (*maya*), and that the world of ordinary experience is therefore unreal. But this is not so. The knowledge of sense and reason itself derives from this universal consciousness. It is the one being who sees and hears and knows in us. Every particular form of human consciousness is a reflection of the one consciousness.

How, then, shall we describe this knowledge of non-duality, this knowledge of the Self? We must say that the one Self, the universal consciousness, is present in all our experience, but its action is limited by the faculties of sense and reason. What we experience is the one reality, reflected through the senses and the rational mind. But when in meditation we transcend the categories of space and time and of the rational mind, we experience this one reality in itself. The finite, changing temporal world of our experience is known in its infinite, changeless ground. All the multiplicity of creation is known in the simple unity of its origin.

But we must not suppose that the multiplicity and variety of the world is lost in this vision of the unity, as though it had no ultimate reality. On the contrary, as has been said: 'Everything that is here is there, and everything that is there is here.' There is not a particle of matter in the universe, not a grain of sand, a leaf, a flower, not a single animal or human being, which has not its eternal being in that One, and which is not known in the unitive vision of the One. What we see is the reflection of all the beauty of creation through the mirror of our senses and our imagination, extended in space and time. But there in the vision of the One all the multiplicity of creation is contained, not in the imperfection of its becoming but in the unity of its being. Of this the great Sankaracharya, the doctor of advaita Vedanta, has said: 'The knower of brahman enjoys all desires, all delights procurable by delightful objects without exception. Does he enjoy all desirable things alternately as we do? No, he enjoys all desirable things simultaneously, as amassed together in a single moment, through a single perception, which is eternal...which is non-different from the essence of brahman, which we have described as truth, knowledge, infinity (*satyam, jnanam, anantam*).'[57] It is a defect of our minds that we have to go from point to point, from one thing to another, in an ever-changing world. If we had perfect knowledge, we should know the whole in all its parts and all the changing phenomena of nature in an unchanging vision of perfect unity.

But the question remains, What becomes of the individual self in the knowledge of the one Self? Does it simply disappear? Here again it is easy to misinterpret the experience of non-duality. There is no doubt that the individual loses all sense of separation from the One and experiences a total unity, but that does not mean that the individual no longer exists. Just as every element in nature is a unique reflection of the one Reality, so every human being is a unique center of consciousness in the universal consciousness. Just as no element in nature is lost in the ultimate reality, so no individual centre of consciousness loses its unique character. It participates in the universal consciousness; it knows itself in the unity of the one Being; it discovers itself as a person in the one Person. A person is not a closed but an open center of consciousness. It is relationship. Every person grows as he opens himself to the totality of personal being, which is found in the supreme Person, the *Purushottaman*. This is what is found in the Christian doctrine of the mystical Body of Christ. This Body embraces all humanity in the unity of the One Person of Christ, and in the final state, as St Augustine says, there is only 'one Christ, loving himself.'[58]

This opening of the individual consciousness on the universal consciousness is a movement of self-transcendence. Every growth in human consciousness is a movement of self-transcendence.[59] The individual self grows by contact with other selves, transcending the limits of its own consciousness by contact with another form of consciousness. Human nature, it has been said, is constituted by its capacity for self-transcendence.[60] The final stage in human growth is reached when the human consciousness goes beyond its natural limits, beyond the categories of time and space, and encounters the supreme consciousness, the consciousness of the One. This is what is described in religious language as 'grace.' As it was said in the Katha

216

Upanishad: 'He whom the atman chooses, he knows the atman.'[60] The atman is the Supreme consciousness, the one Self which is the source of all consciousness in man and in animals. In the human consciousness there is an innate capacity for freedom, the power to choose according to the dictates of reason. When the human consciousness, working through sense and reason, reaches the limit of its capacity, it is drawn by 'grace', by the power of the Spirit, the supreme consciousness working in it, to transcend its personal limitations and to participate in the divine consciousness, the consciousness of the supreme Self. This is what in Hindu tradition is called the 'fourth' state, the state beyond the physical, the vital and the mental, the passing beyond into the state of *ananda*, of bliss consciousness.[61]

40. Nonduality in Bede's Experience[62]
In an interview about five months before his death, Bede Griffiths attempts to express the awareness of advaita, or nondual consciousness, into which he had come after his stroke of January 1990.[63] This is a nonduality in which - as Bede had always insisted - the distinctions, the individual differences, remain.

Advaita does not mean "one" in the sense of eliminating all differences. The differences are present in the one in a mysterious way. They are not separated anymore, and yet they are there. To me, this is extremely important. When we go to a deeper level of consciousness, we should not lose the diversity of things and their individuality. On the contrary, the diversity, the multiplicity, is taken up into the unity. It cannot be put into words properly, and it cannot be explained rationally. It is simply an experience of *advaita*. The more one reads from the Hindu or the Buddhist or the Taoist or the Christian mystics, the more one realizes that this nonduality has been the great discovery beyond the rational mind with all its dualities of good and evil, light and darkness, black and white, conscious and unconscious, male and female. All these divisions are there, but they are contained in a unity. That is the important thing.

The Tibetan *Dzogchen*, which I came across fairly recently, I think puts it more profoundly than anywhere else: We all have a deep sense that the whole multiplicity of being is contained in the unity of the one, in this nondual relationship not one, and not two. Personally, I have taken this (and it came gradually) to be a sign of the Trinity. The God, in the Christian sense, is not a person. We tend to project an image of the Father, or of Christ, or something, but these are projections. Beyond all the projections, the Father is simply the ground, the source, the origin. He is the one beyond name, beyond form. From the one comes the self-expression, the self-revelation, the self-manifestation of the one. That is the Word the Word that expresses the Father as the source.

This idea comes through very much in the work of Meister Eckhart. In that Word is contained the whole universe. When the Father expresses himself in his Word, the whole of creation is present in the universe — you and I, the trees and the earth, the sun and the stars. Everything is contained in that one Word, in its nondual reality. It's not simply one; the Father and the Son are not a monad. If they were simply one, that would not be an identity. Rather, it is union in relationship.

The Trinity comes to me now as a key to the understanding of life. From the Father — the source, the origin, the *sunyata*, the abyss of being, the void, the emptiness, the darkness — comes forth the Word the wisdom, the light, the sun. It is a nondual relationship. The Son is not the Father, and the Father is not the Son. They are not separate, either; it's neither one nor two. It is what is called a *subsistent* relationship. This is a key to life, because today we see the whole universe in terms of this interdependent relationship.

In the physical universe and the psychological universe, we are all members of this whole, in which each is an integral element; all interwoven, interdependent, distinct, and yet one. So the Son reveals the Father, the abyss, and manifests all that is latent in the godhead. All the seeds of creation are present there. And in the Son those seeds come to life. The whole of creation is mirrored in the Son, and all time and space, and you and I, and every detail of human existence is already present in that one reality. That is why Saint Paul could say he [Christ] knew us in him before the foundation of the world. We all come from this depth of the abyss beyond. Then comes this Word the "ideas," as Plato would say — and the whole of creation is present in the Word. The "ideas" come into manifestation through the Spirit. The Spirit is the *Shakti*, the energy of the divine power, and it is what propels the whole universe. When we speak of the great "Big Bang," the beginning of creation, it is simply the "ideas" and the Word being manifested through this power of the Spirit. The *Shakti* manifests the whole of creation, and then it comes out into space and time. I really see the Trinity as a key to understanding this profoundly.

Interestingly, the founder of Saccidananda Ashram, Father Monchanin, once said that our aim is *advaita* and the Trinity: nonduality and the Trinity. They are often opposed, of course. Many think of *advaita* as monism, in that it sort of removes all differences; and then the Trinity becomes three solid persons, all separated. But really it is a nondual mystery.[64]

All this experience and insight have really only emerged since my stroke. From that time I have gone on reflecting over it, and the experience continues. In a way, I never feel separated from the earth or the trees or people or whatever. It is all one, and yet the differences remain. This is so important.

The danger of *advaita* is that it tends to minimize the universe, and even to deny it. It is *maya*, an illusion, or it is just a play, not taken seriously. In this true *advaita* everybody and everything has its own unique reality; but the divine reality is present in every plant, every animal, every atom, every proton. The divine is totally present in each one. And, of course, it is mirrored interestingly in the human body. Many today are interested in reflexology. The whole system of the organism, the body, is reflected in the sole of the foot and in the palm of the hand, and also in the eyes (iridology). Nature's method is everywhere, putting the whole into all the parts. Each part represents makes present the whole. That leads us to the understanding of the human being as a microcosm, a little world. The whole universe is present in each one of us. We are a little world in ourselves, and the whole world is mirrored in each particular part. This is the view which is gradually coming through to me. It is so wonderful . . .

219

41. Buddhism: The Mystery of Nirvana[65]

Unlike Thomas Merton, Bede Griffiths was inclined — through his own experience and his personality — more toward Hinduism than toward Buddhism. Hinduism responded to his attraction to the warmth and fullness of a maternal beginning, to the 'feminine' side of spirituality, to a synthesis of the apophatic and cataphatic (negative and positive) ways. Buddhism, the pre-eminent religion of paradox which one might call a contemplative Asian protestantism, essentially represents a differentiation of the apophatic or negative way. This is an orientation straight into the eye of the mystery, beyond the mediation of names, forms and modes of experience. Here the unitive is found in the purity of an ineffable realization at the core of the individual self (a self which is denied ultimate reality), rather than in a conclusive affirmation like that of Bede - a synthetic consummation in which cosmos and humanity are reassumed into the divine One.

Starting with the quintessential Buddhist concept of nirvana, Bede gives us a fine brief summary of the doctrine and development of Buddhism. It is his identification with the one inner realization at the heart of the traditions that gives him the empathetic understanding to write with sensitivity and grace of a path that is, temperamentally, not his own. Bede's sense of the 'universal wisdom' and its unitive core recognizes with delight the authenticity of the Buddha's austere way.

The essential truth of Buddhism is the doctrine of nirvana. Nirvana is the holy Mystery, the unutterable Truth, the ultimate State. It can only be described by negatives: it is not born, not become, not made, not compounded.[66] It is the cessation of becoming, the cessation of craving, the blowing out of the lamp. It is deathlessness, peace, the unchanging state. All these are but words which point to the inexpressible Truth. But, though it cannot be known, it can be realized. The Buddha is one who has realized this state; he is the enlightened one who has attained the goal, and he teaches the way to the goal. The way is the Dhamma, the noble eightfold path, the way of right view, right thought, right speech, right action, right living, right endeavour, right mindfulness and right contemplation. And the society in which this way is to be found, this goal is to be realized, is the Sangha. By having recourse to the Buddha, the *Dhamma* and the Sangha, one can attain nirvana, one can realize the ultimate Truth. This is the essential teaching of Buddhism, and though it may appear altogether negative, empty and void, yet because it is essentially a mystical doctrine, it has infinite depth. Because of this the Buddha appears as a being of infinite compassion. Though the story of the *Bodhisattva* who takes a vow not to enter nirvana until every soul has been saved comes from a later age, it is a true expression of the original message of the Buddha. Indeed, the whole Mahayana doctrine, with its vast mythology, its complex philosophy and its elaborate techniques of meditation, is an authentic development of the original intuition of the Buddha, just as the elaborate theology and liturgy and mystical doctrine of the Middle Ages is an authentic development of the teaching of Christ. The teaching of the Buddha and the teaching of Christ both have this infinite depth, because they derive from the one source, the ultimate Truth, the Ground of being itself.

42. *The Challenge of Buddhism*[67]

In his introduction to Universal Wisdom, *Bede presents Buddhism in a dramatic light. It is 'the greatest challenge to all religions,' 'the most radical philosophy ever propounded.' It 'strikes at the root of existence as we know it.' It is as the purely negative or apophatic way, and the apophatic vision of reality, that Buddhism brings forth these admiring exclamations. Buddhism is the way of renunciation not only on the level of bodily asceticism but on the level of the mind itself: of thoughts, feelings and desires. It is by renouncing all attachment to world and senses and even to particular thoughts and experiences, that the mind comes to know itself, and in this experience of pure consciousness it knows the nondual, absolute reality and unlimited fulfillment. This sounds hardly different from the way of the Hindu sannyasi, the advaitan way or quest of the nondual Self pursued by Abhishiktananda - except for the further renunciation of a positive language for such spiritual realities as the Self. Bede does not mention here the apophatic spirituality which is at the heart of the spiritual theology of Eastern Christianity and which appears in such western spiritual teachers as Meister Eckhart and St. John of the Cross. For Christianity, however, the apophatic way alone is not sufficient, as Bede will point out at the appropriate moment.*

Buddhism presents the greatest challenge to all religions, especially to those which believe in a personal, creator God. Gautama Buddha coming at the end of the Vedic period (563-483 BC) rejected all the traditional beliefs and practices of religion. The Vedic gods, the ritual sacrifices, the Brahmin priesthood and the whole caste system, which has provided the religious basis of Hindu society ever since, were all rejected in favor of a negative philosophy, which might be considered a sort of nihilism. The great insight of Buddha was into the transitoriness of the world. "All is passing (*anitta*), all is sorrow (*dukka*), all is unreal (*anatta*)." This was the basis of Buddha's teaching. The end of all things is nirvana, the "blowing out", the extinction of all being, the eradication of all desire. It might be said that this was the most radical philosophy ever propounded. It strikes at the root of existence as we know it. Yet behind this negative philosophy there is a profound insight. Nirvana is the end of all becoming, of all desire, of all that makes life worth living for most people. Yet when all change and becoming has ceased, when all desires, all "clinging" to life, has come to an end, there is an experience of absolute bliss. This was the experience of Buddha, as he sat beneath the Bo tree. He entered into deep meditation. He allowed all movement of the senses to cease, put an end to all desire, and then in the silence and solitude of the mind he experienced the bliss of pure consciousness. He entered into the depth of the soul, the ground of consciousness, and there found the peace, the joy, the fulfillment for which he had been seeking. This is the message of Buddhism today. As long as we remain engrossed in the world of the senses, ever seeking the fulfilment of our desires, we can never find peace. All over the world today, as in all Asia in the past, this message of "enlightenment," of inner peace, is being heard. The teaching of Buddha was handed on by his disciples by word of mouth and only came to be put into writing after several centuries, but the essential teaching has come down to us particularly in the Dhammapada, the path of the Law.

The teaching of the Dhammapada is clear. It is not the body or the senses but the mind which is the cause of all human problems and it is the mind which is also their cure. As long as the mind attaches itself to thoughts and feelings and desires, it is carried away into a world of illusion and becomes subject to passion and desire. But when the mind withdraws from the impressions of the senses and realizes its own inherent nature, it experiences inner joy and peace and fulfilment. The note of joy sounds all through the Dhammapada, the joy of those who have renounced passion and desire and all attachment to the material world, and have found inner peace and freedom, and who know the truth. The western mind has concentrated its attention on the material world, to understand its working by science, to control it by technology and to make life in this world as attractive as possible. It has succeeded beyond all its dreams in analyzing matter down to its minutest particles, in exploring the furthest limits of time and space, in unifying the human world and creating a standard of life which has never been known before. But all this has been done at the cost of polluting the earth, the water and the air, of destroying innumerable species of plants and animals, and of using up the resources on which human life depends. All this is the result of following a philosophy which made the knowledge and control of the material world its goal. The western world has now to undergo a *metanoia*, a change of mind, which will enable it to recover the ancient wisdom, the perennial philosophy, on which human nature actually depends.

Buddhism, first in the Hinayana tradition and then in the Mahayana, is one of the sources of this eternal wisdom. Buddha broke through the bondage of the human mind to the senses and the material world and set it free on the path of truth and peace. Buddhism may seem to be a religion without God or creation or a soul, but Buddha set the human mind free from its attachment to the body and the material world and opened it to truth and life. There is no God in Buddhism and no Creator, but there is in the peace of nirvana infinite wisdom and infinite compassion, and what else do we mean by "God"? This is the challenge which Buddhism presents both to the religion and to the science of the west. Buddha saw that all the images and concepts of "God" and all the rituals and practices of religion have no value, unless they are sustained by the mind, which goes beyond all images and concepts, and realizes its true nature, not as dependent on the body and senses but as the source of the life of the body and the intelligence of the brain. Western science has grown up under the illusion that there is a material world "outside" the mind. It is now slowly learning, what the perennial philosophy has known all along, that the world, which appears to be outside us, is inconceivable apart from the mind which observes it. It was the experience of physicists in the present century working with quantum physics, which finally made it clear that the world which the scientist observes is not reality in itself but reality exposed to human consciousness, to the mind and the brain of the scientist.

It was this discovery of the independence of the mind from the senses for which Buddha was responsible. In the early Hinayana tradition the emphasis was on the practical aspect of this discovery. Buddha saw humanity imprisoned in the world of the senses like people trapped in a burning house, and his aim was to set them free, to teach them by the "eightfold noble path" how to be free from the pain, the sorrow of this world. His was a message of salvation for suffering humanity. Everything depends on the Knowledge of the "four noble truths," of suffering, the cause of suffering, the end of suffering and the way to the end of suffering. This way depended essentially on knowing the nature of the mind, and it was the exploration of the nature of the mind which led to the great development of Mahayana doctrine. This development took place many years after the passing of Buddha, but one may hold that it was implicit from the beginning. There is a vast literature of Mahayana doctrine, not only in Sanskrit but also in Tibetan and Chinese, but beneath all its complications there is an essential truth proclaimed in it and it is this that we need to understand. We have chosen the treatise on the Awakening of Faith by Ashvaghosa as an example of it, but perhaps this quotation from the Lankavatara Sutra can indicate its essential message.

> When all appearances and names are set aside and all discrimination ceases, then that which remains is the true and essential nature of things, and as nothing can be predicated of the nature of essence, it is called Suchness (*tathata*) of Reality. This Universal, undifferentiated, inscrutable Suchness is the only Reality, but it is variously called Reality (*dharma*), Body of Reality (*dharmakaya*), Noble Knowledge (*arya jnana*), Noble wisdom (*arya prajna*). This Dharma of the imagelessness of the Body of Reality is the Dharma which has been proclaimed by all the Buddhas, and when all things are understood in full agreement with it, one is in possession of perfect knowledge (*prajna*) and is on the way to the attainment of the noble knowledge (*arya jnana*) of the Tathagatas[68]

(that is, the Buddhas, who have "attained to that" or reached the goal of Reality). This is the essential teaching of the Mahayana, which, as we shall see, is found alike in Hindu, Chinese and Greek philosophy, that when we pass beyond the "discriminating" or analytical knowledge of science and philosophy, we come to the knowledge of reality itself in pure consciousness.

43. Purusha: The Personal God

If the way of the Upanishads, as Bede had introduced us to it, seemed to lead away from the world of person and personal relationship, into the nondual depths of the Self — to the frontier of Buddhism — this is not its only expression. Bede returns again and again to the threefold manifestation of the Absolute in the Vedanta: brahman, atman, and purusha: the personal God or Lord. In two short texts from River of Compassion, *he first provides us with an overview of the historical emergence of purusha and of parallel conceptions in the world's religious traditions, and then relates purusha, the personal God, to the other two principal concepts of the divine Absolute in the Vedanta: brahman and atman.*

I⁶⁹

The *Gita* is bringing the whole doctrine of yoga and samkhya, of discipline and doctrine into relationship with a personal God. It opens the way to a new understanding. The same process is also found in the *Upanishads.* They begin with brahman, the mystery of being and realize more and more that this mystery of being is the atman, the inner Self. They reveal that the human self is one with the Supreme Self, the Being of the whole creation, and than, as it develops in the Upanishads, this atman, this brahman is seen to be *Purusha,* the personal God, the Lord, who is an object of worship.

Finally in the *Gita* the personal God becomes an object of love so the whole process gradually unfolds. I think we can properly speak of this process as revelation. R. de Smet, an authority on Indian philosophy, spoke of the "holy history of India." It is really remarkable how one can see this new understanding, this conception of a personal God coming to light a little before the time of Christ. I think that it is a movement that took place in many parts of the world, not simply in Israel. There was an advance both in Buddhism with its idea of the

225

bodhisattva and in Hinduism with the idea of a personal God as the embodiment of love and compassion, these developments taking place at about the same time. We realize that God is revealing himself in many ways, not only to Israel, but to India, to China, and to primitive people also. The question arises as to how Christ is related to all this. We can say that Christ is the Word, the Self-revelation of God, and as such is present in all genuine religion. This Word is present in Hinduism and Buddhism, gradually revealing his personal character. In Jesus this process reaches a climax and the personal character of God is finally revealed.

II[70]

What we are discovering is that these three concepts, brahman, atman and purusha, or the personal God, are all ultimately identical. They are the one reality realized in different ways. When that one reality is seen manifested in the whole creation behind all the phenomena of the senses, we call that reality brahman. When that one reality is seen in ourselves as the root and ground of our own being, the principle of our own life and consciousness, we call that reality atman. And when we see that one reality, that one Self as an object of worship, as the Lord, Isha, then we know it as a person, as *purusha*, in the relationship of love. So there can be an awareness of the universal cosmic being, the brahman; an awareness of the Self, the atman, the ground of our own being and consciousness; and there can be at the same time an awareness that this brahman, this atman, is the Lord who is worshipped, the *purusha*, the Cosmic Person, with whom there is a relationship of love. And that is what the *Gita* is concerned to bring out, the ultimate reality of love. So we not only enter into this new universe of communion with the creation and communion with humanity, but we discover the Person of God at the heart of the universe. "He sees me in all and he sees all in me, then I never leave him and he never leaves me." The Gita is here giving the same message as the Gospel. For the Christian, Christ is the personal aspect of God, the person in whom the universe finds its ultimate meaning and who reveals himself as love.

44. A Myth Evolves: Purusha, The Supreme Person[71]

In The Marriage of East and West, *Bede develops at length the emergence of a personal Divinity, first in the Svetasvatara Upanishad and then in the Bhagavad Gita.*

The supreme 'trinity' of Hinduism is brought together with his trinity of interfused worlds. The supreme Reality is known as brahman, pervading the cosmos, as atman, the immanent ground of human consciousness, and as purusha, the trancendent - and personal - God and Lord. Bede's lucid mind struggles to cut a clear path through the profuse foliage of Indian mythology and over the uncertain terrain of this long history. Now he poses a second historical turning point, in addition to the axial emergence of unitive consciousness in the earlier Upanishads: it is this emergence of the consciousness of a personal Deity who is one with the immanent Absolute: the realization of purusha. He calls upon Thomist philosophy for a language, acceptable to western Christians, in which to express the Vedanta's view of the relationship between divine transcendence and immanence and of the unitive inner relation of created beings with God. Once more he recurs to the metaphors of image and mirror. No such translation is required for the Hindu concept of purusha; here we find an immediate consonance with the Judaeo-Christian revelation and with a western consciousness which has been formed in the matrix of personal and interpersonal reality. Bede will return to purusha when he proposes, as the core of his final synthesis, the Cosmic Person.[72]

In the early Upanishads, the center of interest is the brahman and the atman, the eternal spirit immanent in nature and in man. Yet this spirit is recognized as also transcendent. It exists in all things, but it also exists without. In the later *Upanishads*, such as Svetasvatara (c.300 BC) the transcendent aspect of the one reality comes into evidence. Even in the earliest Upanishad, the Brihadranyaka, we find evidence of this, when it is said, 'If a man clearly beholds this Self as God and as the Lord of what is and what will be, then he is more afraid.'[73] Again in the Isa Upanishad, it is said 'all this, whatsoever moves on earth, is enveloped by the Lord.'[74]

But it is in the Svetasvatara Upanishad that the concept of the personal God is fully developed. There it is said that in the supreme brahman there is a triad. This triad consists of first of all the *pradhana*, the perishable, that is, the material world: then there are the souls, the *jivatmas*, and finally there is Hara, the Lord, the

Imperishable who rules both matter and souls. When a man finds out these three, it is said, that is brahman.[75] How are we to understand this? What is the relation between God and nature and man, and how are they related to brahman? There are different schools of Hindu thought in regard to this — *advaita*, *visistadvaita* and *dvaita* [76] — and the debate continues to the present day. In a sense, of course, there can be no answer to this question. The ultimate reality, whether we call it brahman or atman or God, is beyond conception. These are words taken from common speech which reflect the reality but can never express it. This applies to all human speech. Language reflects the world, reality itself, through the medium of the human senses and imagination and the concepts of the rational mind. But the reality itself is always beyond our images and concepts. It can only be known when we transcend both body and soul and experience the one reality in the depths of our being where we are one with that which we contemplate, when being and knowing are one. Yet in the light of this inner experience words can be used to indicate the nature of this reality, words which reflect it, however remotely, and point towards it. This is what we find in the *Upanishads*.

Let us return to the analogy of the three worlds. There is the material world, including the human body, which is experienced through the senses. But this world, as we have seen, is not independent of the senses. The material world is present to us in and through our senses. This material world, as modern physics describes it, is a field of energies, and our own bodies with their senses and their appetites and their mental images and concepts are part of this field of energies. The energies, which make up the world as we experience it, are both physical and psychological. Together they form an interdependent whole. This is what in Hindu terms is called *prakriti* or nature. But beyond *prakriti* there is *purusha*, the principle of consciousness. Human consciousness is normally reflected through the senses and the imagination, but there is a sphere of consciousness beyond the senses and the imagination, which can be experienced in meditation, in which, as we have seen, the soul attains to self-knowledge by a pure reflection on itself. This sphere of consciousness is *purusha*, the spirit, the self, which is the source of all consciousness, the principle of all real knowledge, the ground of personal being. In this ground of truth and reality, the source of personal being, all souls find their center of unity.

Just as the physical and psychological worlds are recognized as an interdependent whole, so in this world of the spirit all consciousness is seen to have its source in one consciousness, an all-pervading spirit, which penetrates and embraces the whole field of physical and psychic energies and unites them in one. This sphere of consciousness can be experienced as the 'ground' of all being, pervading the whole creation, when it is known as brahman. Or it can be experienced as the ground of human consciousness, the inner spirit, when it is known as atman, the self, that is the immanent principle of both being and knowing. But it can also be experienced as transcendent being, as 'God' the 'Lord', and then it is known as *purusha*. This is how the concept of the personal god arises.

Reality is experienced as one, infinite, eternal being, at once immanent and transcendent, pervading everything and enveloping everything. But this same reality is also experienced as consciousness (*cit*), as a pure intelligence, as totally transparent to itself. But a being possessed by conscious intelligence is what is meant by a person (*purusha*) and so the infinite, eternal spirit, the 'one without a second', is recognized as a person. This is what we find in the Svetasvatara Upanishad. This is a comparatively late Upanishad which marks the awakening of devotion to a personal God. The gods of the Vedas, it is true, were personal, but there each God — Agni, Mitra, Surya — is seen as an aspect of the 'one being' (*ekam sat*), and the ultimate reality itself is not conceived as a personal god. But now in the Svetasvatara Upanishad that step is taken. The ultimate reality, the brahman, is conceived as a personal being, the object of worship and adoration. So it is said, 'those who know beyond this (world) the Supreme Brahman, the great, hidden in all creatures and alone enveloping everything as the Lord (*Isa*), they become immortal.'[77] This Lord who is one with the Supreme Brahman is said to be the person (purusha) who fills the whole universe. He is called Bhagavan, the name which is universally used of the personal God in India today, and is named Siva.[78]

This name of Siva is of great interest. In this Upanishad, he is identified with Rudra, the God of storm and thunder of the Vedas, who dwells in the mountains. But it seems that he really goes back beyond the Vedas and was originally a Dravidian God. There is a figure found at Mahanjadaro, the ancient Indian city destroyed by the Aryan invaders, which is seated in lotus posture and seems to represent Siva as Pasupati, the Lord of creatures. Siva would then have been one of the gods of the indigenous people, an enemy of the Aryans. He is represented as an outcast, dwelling in the graveyard, covered with ashes, as the destroyer, wearing snakes about him and accompanied by demons. He is also the God of fertility, having as his emblem the *lingam*, the male organ, which is represented in the inner sanctuary (the garbha-griha or 'womb house', the source of life) in temples of Siva all over India today.

But Siva is also the great ascetic, dwelling on Mount Kailas, absorbed in meditation, and as destroyer he is conceived as the destroyer of sin who renews the world by his grace. Finally, he comes to be revered as the God of love, his name Siva meaning the 'kindly,' the 'gracious,' and in a famous Tamil Poem, the *Tirumandiram*, it is said: 'the ignorant think that Siva and Love (*anbu*) are two; they do not know that Siva is love.'[79]

This is a marvellous example of the evolution of a myth. A myth is a symbolic story in which many elements may combine, elements derived from the world of nature and of human psychology, from history and social and economic conditions. In the course of time these different and often conflicting elements are re-interpreted and given new meanings, until eventually a coherent symbol of spiritual reality is evolved. Thus the God Siva for a Hindu devotee today is a name for the ultimate reality beyond name and form, who is one with the brahman, the absolute truth and the final good, revealing himself to his devotees as a God of infinite grace and love, and the *lingam* is the sign of the formless deity, God beyond name and form.

In the Svetasvatara Upanishad, we can watch this process of the transformation of an ancient myth into a profound philosophical symbol, still retaining its 'numinous' character but developed into a theological figure as the personal god. The God of the Svetasvatara

Upanishad is the great brahman, who is immanent in all creation, but he is also the transcendent Lord (*Isa*) who creates and rules the world by his power. He is said to have his hands and feet, his eyes and ears and head in every place, but at the same time, 'he grasps without hands, hastens without feet, sees without eyes, hears without ears.'[80] He is the *purusha*, the cosmic person with a thousand heads, a thousand eyes, a thousand feet, but he also dwells within the heart of every creature and encompasses the world on every side. He 'possesses the purest power of reaching everywhere and is the imperishable light.'[81] He is smaller than the smallest, 'the person not larger than a thumb.' [82] Yet he is the creator of all, the great Self, always dwelling in the heart of man, the lord of immortality. Finally, he is the 'lord of lords, the god of gods, the master of masters,'[83] the one God of whom there is no place for a second. It would be difficult to find a more impressive expression of the one supreme creator God.

Yet this transcendent God, who creates and rules and encompasses everything, is also said to be immanent in everything, and to 'assume all forms.'[84] He can even be said in a sense to 'become' all things. He is the *dehi*, the dweller in body (*deha*), the 'incarnate self,' who assumes various forms in various places. Yet at the same time he has 'no beginning and no end,' he has many forms yet he envelops everything. How are we to understand this? We must go back to the concept of the spirit, the atman, who is pure being and pure consciousness. It is he who pervades the whole creation, as the active power of energy, life and consciousness in nature and in man. It is he who gives 'form' to every created thing. But he does not merely 'give' form. He is the active principle of matter. St Thomas Aquinas asks in what sense can God be said to be 'in' all things — and he replies that he is 'in' all things by his power, his presence and his essence.[85] By his power, because it is his power alone which gives existence to each thing and preserves it in existence. By his presence, because this power is not exercised at a distance since there is no distance in God, so that he is actually present in every created being. By his essence, because he is not present in part, since there is no part in God, but the very essence of God, in Christian terms, the Holy Trinity, is present in every particle of matter. The divine being, which is also intelligence and consciousness, is therefore present totally in every created thing. It is in this sense that St Paul can say: "in him we live and move and have our being."[86]

Can we now see how God, the Supreme Spirit, which is *sacci-dananda*-being, consciousness and bliss, can be said to 'become' the whole creation? The whole creation exists eternally in God; when God, the infinite being, expresses himself, manifests himself, speaks his word, the whole creation comes into being in that one word. God does not create in time. Creation is an eternal act in God; it is the act by which God himself exists. As Eckhart says, God only speaks one Word, and in that word the whole creation is contained. In God the whole Creation exists eternally in identity with him. As St Thomas again says, the 'ideas' in God, the archetypal forms, which are the principles of all created beings, exist eternally in God and are identical with the divine essence itself[87]. In God you and I and everyone and everything exist eternally in identity with him. This is our eternal archetypal being. When creation comes into being in time, then each of us assumes his own particular created form, his separate identity, but the divine archetype is present still in each one of us. In this sense the world can be said to be a 'manifestation' of God. It is like a mirror which is held up to the face of God. The created world is a 'reflection' of the uncreated archetypal world. Like an image in a mirror, it has only a relative existence. Its existence is constituted by this relation to God. It is in this sense that we can say with the Hindu school of Advaita, that God and the world are 'not two' (*adwaita*). The created world adds nothing to God and takes nothing from him. Creation makes no change in him; change is in the creature.

This conception of the world as a reflection, an image, of God is entirely acceptable from a Christian point of view. According to the biblical tradition, man is an image of God, and the Greek fathers interpreted this in the sense that man (and with him the whole creation) is like a mirror held up to the light of God. Each human soul is a reflection of that uncreated light. This is the point of the 'spirit' in man; the point where the human being receives the imprint of the Spirit of God. This again is a dynamic point, a point of receptivity, by which we can either open ourselves to the divine light and grow as persons in truth, or turn upon ourselves and become self-centered, obscured by ignorance and sin. The spirit in man is the point of meeting between God and man, of created being with the uncreated light. In every man the uncreated light is always present this is his eternal, archetypal being but whether he receives that light into his soul and is transformed by it, or whether he turns away from the light and becomes darkened and obscured, depends on the inner dynamism of the intellect and will, the created spirit in man. In this sense, therefore, we can speak of God taking the 'form' of man.

The uncreated being, which is pure consciousness and bliss, dwells in the heart of every man, shaping both his body and his soul. While remaining ever the same in his pure consciousness and bliss, he enters into the consciousness of man, into the life of plants, into the energies of matter. He is present everywhere in everything, shaping the forms of matter and life and mind, but remaining in himself ever the same.

This concept of a personal God was further developed in the *Bhagavad Gita*, which was probably composed at about the same time as the Svetasvatara Upanishad. The *Bhagavad Gita* forms part of the great epic of the Mahabharata, in which Vishnu rather than Siva is represented as the figure of the supreme God, especially in his 'incarnation' as Krishna. Krishna, along with Siva, is a beautiful example of the evolution of a symbol of God. Unlike Siva, who is essentially a cosmic figure, Krishna seems to have had a basis in history. The Mahabharata itself is the story of a great war, which, like the Trojan War of Homer, must have had a historical origin. But the historical character of Krishna was soon enriched by legend and gradually the figure of a Supreme God emerged, who was like Siva a God of love, and in the *Bhagavad Gita* is represented as the one Supreme Lord, the creator of all. Nowhere is the utter transcendence of the creator God so clearly expressed as when Krishna says, 'By me whose form is unmanifest, all this world is pervaded; all beings abide in me, but I do not rest in them.' And then lest it should appear that he depends in some way on the world, he continues: 'Yet they do not abide in me; behold my sovereign power! I am the support of all beings but I abide not in them, myself being their cause.'[88]

It would be a mistake to say, as is done in some schools of Hindu thought, that this personal creator God is inferior to the Supreme. Again and again it is shown that Krishna as God is identical with brahman and atman. Thus it is said that 'he who knows brahman (Brahmavid) abides in brahman (or 'is established in brahman' — *brahmani sthita*), his reason (*buddhi*) steady, his delusion gone.'[89] And again: 'He whose spirit (*atman*) is unattached to things without and who finds joy in the spirit having his spirit joined by Yoga to brahman, enjoys imperishable happiness.'[90] And a little later, Krishna identifies himself with this brahman, this atman. 'He who knows me, who accept sacrifice, and self-discipline, the great Lord of all worlds, and the friend of all beings, attains peace.'[91] Surely it is clear that brahman, atman and the 'Great Lord' *(Mahesvara)* are one and the same. They are three names for the same one reality looked at from a different point of view. What the Gita establishes beyond doubt is that that which is known in the Upanishads as brahman and atman is also purusha, the personal God. This is made very clear when it is said: 'There are two spirits *(purushas)* in this universe, the perishable, and the imperishable' that is, the world of matter and the world of mind. 'But there is another Supreme spirit *(purusha)* who is the highest self *(Paramatman)*, the changeless Lord, who enters and supports the three worlds.'[92] Here we can see clearly once again the structure of the three worlds — the world of matter, the perishable; the world of mind, or consciousness, the imperishable; and above them both the world of Spirit which pervades the three worlds and manifests himself in all, and hence the words *brahman, atman* and *purusha* can all be used on occasion of each of the three worlds. But the spirit himself is beyond both mind and matter, beyond the perishable and the imperishable, and is therefore known as *Parabrahman, Paramatman, Purushottman* the supreme brahman, the Supreme Self, the Supreme Person.

45. Beyond the Stillness: The Person[93]
Commenting chapter 15 (verses 16,17,18,19) of the Gita in River of Compassion, Bede makes an assertion which is very significant — and which is suprising in the light of his earlier writings about the experience of ultimate Reality according to the Vedanta. The Supreme Person is beyond the samadhi, or unitive stillness which many have identified with final realization of atman, or the unitive Absolute. We seem to be observing more than the theo-

logical progression from Upanishads *to* Bhagavad Gita *within the Hindu tradition. It is likely that a seismic shift is taking place between nonduality and person in Bede's own experience and in his vision. We shall see a corresponding shift from a focus on pure interiority — the realization of the Self — to the development of a comprehensive 'gnosis': a vision of the evolution of the world and humanity centered in the Cosmic Person.*

The Gita says that there are two purushas in the universe, the perishable, the *kshara*, and the imperishable, the *akshara.* "The perishable is all things in creation. The imperishable is that which moves not." But beyond these two persons is the *Purushottaman*, the supreme Person, who manifests himself in these different levels. In himself he is the imperishable Supreme, beyond all. When the mind withdraws in meditation beyond all movements of the manas and, concentrating in the buddhi, is fixed and still, then it becomes aware of the cosmic unity. Now this is the point which Zaehner brings out, and I think it is very important. In the earlier stage of the Upanishads no distinction was made between the three levels of manifestation. There was only the perishable and then the imperishable. So in the Shvetashvatara Upanishad there are two birds on the tree. One eats the fruit and the other looks on. The first is the jivatman, the other, uninvolved, is the paramatman. But here a further distinction is made. There are three levels, not two. The self manifests first on the level of the body, then in the soul, and the mahat, the cosmic order, the angelic order, the order of light. The Gita is saying that there are two purushas, persons, the perishable, which is the world of nature, of becoming, and the imperishable, which is the world of spirit, the unchanging, the intelligible world. But beyond those the Gita recognizes another, the highest Spirit, beyond the imperishable. It is the Purushottaman, the Supreme Person, the highest Self who pervades and sustains all, the changeless Lord.

People often confuse the state of stillness, of quiet, the state of oneness with the final state of the Absolute. Samadhi may be no more than this cosmic consciousness. One has gone beyond the mental consciousness, and realized the unity of the whole creation; one is at one with the whole, one realizes the One pervading all, one is standing above everything in a pure state of bliss and it seems that is all;

235

and very often people stop there. But now the Gita says that beyond that is the Lord himself. The Lord is beyond the kutastho, the 'still-point." He is beyond this cosmic order altogether. He pervades all and sustains but he is beyond all.

If we stop at the imperishable we get the idea that we leave the sense world behind and go into the state of samadhi, the state of pure intelligence and pure bliss, and we have forgotten about the world altogether. But in the understanding of the Gita we go beyond that stage and we realize the Supreme Person. We realize that he is active in the whole creation, in every person and everything. That is also the Christian vision. One has to go beyond both the sensible and the intelligible world, beyond even the 'still state' of brahman, and discover the personal God, who is 'known by love,' who reveals himself to those who open themselves to his love. When one comes to the Lord beyond, one is open to all humanity. And then one is free! But when one reaches Purushottoma, the supreme Person, then one is at his disposal and one can do anything, including work in the world. That is the Christian view of sannyasa. We go through samadhi, the experience of oneness, to the total surrender to the Lord, and then, because he is a personal God and because he is love, he takes us to himself and sets us free to do whatever he wills us to do in the world. So that is the true sannyasi who has attained the state of pure love and also pure abandonment and availability for everyone and everything.

There is the same distinction in Buddhism between the pratyeka Buddha who seeks enlightenment for himself alone and enters nirvana and the boddhisattva who refuses to enter nirvana until all souls have been saved. So also the Christian goes beyond the passive state of contemplation to the experience of the Trinity, when he knows himself in Christ as Son of the Father and experiences the power of the Spirit which moves him to the service of love . . .

. . . Vedantic philosophers often talk as though when one reaches the supreme state there is no longer a Lord to adore, there is no worship, there is no love left. One simply is that One and this is considered to be the supreme state. But that is only a particular level of consciousness. If we go beyond that level, there is activity, there is love, there is adoration. We come back to the origin, in a sense. We become like a little child, but with the wisdom which comes from total fulfill-ment.

This has to be understood in the light of the Christian tradition of contemplative life. Those who reject the contemplative tradition remain at the lower level of faith and activity, which is very good in its way, but is far from perfect. The division is often made between the active life and the state of those who have reached this higher state of samadhi, of contemplation. But there is a higher state still, which goes beyond both and fulfills both. One can be a contempla-tive, in perfect stillness, and at the same time fully active. Jesus was the perfect example of that. Many Christians interpret Jesus in the New Testament simply as a man going about doing good, helping people and always busy and active, and they do not realize that he had gone beyond. In his six weeks in the desert and in the depths of his being he was enjoying pure samadhi. He was a pure contemplative, always abiding with the Father as the source of his being, and always seeing what the Father does as the source of his action. He is in that state of transcendent awareness in which he is one with the Father, and at the same time perfectly natural and human. That is why, in the case of the Gospels, the three Synoptic Gospels have to be corrected by the Fourth Gospel. St John profoundly grasped the depth of the inner life of Christ, and was able to see his whole life and work in the light of this inner experience.

This state is known in Hinduism as *sahaja samadhi*, the state in which the yogi has gone beyond all forms of asceticism, of sadhana, and is able to live and act with perfect naturalness. Of this Ramana Maharshi in our day is the supreme example.

46. The Divine Poet[94]

In River of Compassion, *Bede is commenting Gita 8.9, which speaks of "the Poet, the Creator, who rules all things from all time, smaller than the smallest atom, but upholding this vast universe, who shines like the sun beyond darkness, far far beyond human thought." As the Supreme Person continues to emerge more fully at the center of Bede's vision, East and West draw clos-er and closer to one another.*

This is a beautiful passage. This *kavim puranam*, the ancient poet, comes in the *Upanishads*. He is the seer or *rishi*. The Indian had a much finer idea of the poet than the Greeks. Plato, though he regarded the poet as inspired, rejected him from the Republic because he told immoral stories of the gods. But in the Vedic tradition, the poet was the one who had vision; he was the one who saw and had knowledge. The *Vedas* are the poetic expression of this divine knowledge. So the creator himself is a poet. He is also "smaller than the smallest atom," and is the ordainer or dhataram, which signifies firmness and can be translated supporter, establisher, creator. He is of unthinkable form, *acintya-rupam*, literally 'whose form cannot be conceived.' Then there comes a reference to the *Svetasvatara Upanishad*, "I know that great Person of the color of the sun beyond the darkness; only by knowing Him, one goes beyond death. There is no other way to go." This is one of the most beautiful expressions of faith in the personal God by which one goes beyond death. For a Christian, Christ is that supreme Person who has passed beyond death, and who, in the Resurrection, shines like the sun beyond the darkness.

47. The Eastern View of the Universe[95]

Reading through this third chapter of A New Vision of Reality, *one will wait in vain for Bede to bring forth an analytical view of the material world such as he has briefly sketched, from the perspective of western science, in his first chapter. Here one will not find the familiar satisfactions of a clear boundary, a firm conceptual foothold, a meshing of hard-edged ideas. Hindu cosmology is taken as representative of all the Asian traditions, and from beginning to end, the discussion moves forward fluidly, on a mythological- theological rather than an analytical-empirical plane. If Bede's central indictment of western science is its reduction of all reality to matter, the Hindu cosmology which he outlines for us exemplifies the opposite tendency: to spiritualize the material world. Here is the antithesis of a self-contained physical science: the world of matter and body becomes little more than the external context or vessel for the development of human consciousness. Consciousness, in turn, quickly rises beyond itself into the divine Absolute. In this vision of three inter-fused worlds, an invisible, ascending current seems to carry each of the two lower worlds swiftly above itself into the next world.*

Bede's treatment of the Upanishadic view of the universe remains on a metaphysical plane; our attention is continually directed upward. Once again a hierarchy of being unfolds, culminating in the unitive Absolute - which is also brahman, the ground of being. Our inquiry into the Hindu vision of the universe leads us through a progressive series of conceptions of Divinity. The Absolute is conceived as relating to the world as transcendent Source, as Preserver, as immanent and all-embracing Plenitude. Always implicit in these conceptions of the universe is the central concern: a spiritual ascent in which one progressively transcends the universe to attain spiritual realization. The universe, it becomes unmistakably clear, can only be understood in terms of the two higher worlds of human consciousness and of Divinity. The 'turn toward the world' that we had found in Bede's commentary on the Gita (in River of Compassion*) has not, it seemed, brought forth a corresponding cosmology - except that the world is brought into a context of personal Divinity.*

As Bede turns to the Tantric tradition, the universe continues to be contemplated in view of the human person's spiritual realization. The sannyasi's ascending path of renunciation, however, gives way, under the influence of an 'ancient matriarchal religion,' to a very different paradigm, a way of integration. Now the energies of body and soul become engaged in a positive way and the feminine divine Shakti, immanent within universe and person, emerges as the active principle of transformation and realization. While the path is still an ascent, it is now the ascent of psychic energy, or kundalini, through the seven chakras.

What role will the eastern cosmology play in Bede's final synthesis?[96] *What will remain of this vision of the universe when it has been integrated with the new western cosmology and its evolutionary perspective? Specifically, we shall find little more than the overall framework of the three interpenetrating worlds, which Bede has already identified with the perennial philosophy. Yet there remains something further, reminiscent of the feminine divine energy which he has found in the tradition of Tantra. The spirit of this Hindu vision, like a subtle all-embracing field of energy, will continue to permeate his thought.*

Brahman, then is the ground in which the whole creation is woven. Everything comes out from brahman, emerging as from a source. The text says, "As the spider comes out with its thread or as small sparks come forth from fire, thus do all the senses, all the world, all gods and all being come forth from that Spirit." It is the source. The text goes on to say, "That atman is the *satyasya satya*", which means "the truth of the truth", "the real of the real."[97] The world of the senses is real, but the atman is the reality behind the senses. It is the source behind the sense world. In this context the terms brahman and atman are

239

interchangeable.

So brahman is the source, brahman is the ground in which everything is woven, but brahman is also the end towards which everything is moving. This truth appears again in connection with Yajnavalkya, who had another wife called Maitreyi. This is interesting because Yajnavalkya was going into the forest to become a vanaprastha. After an appropriate time of married life the practice was to retire to the forest to meditate. Yajnavalkya wants to make a settlement with Maitreyi so he says to her, "I am going away into the forest, therefore let me make a settlement with thee." And she said, "My Lord, if this whole earth full of wealth belonged to me, should I be immortal by it"? "No," replied Yajnavalkya, "like the life of rich people will be thy life." In other words, there is no hope of gaining immortality by wealth. Maitreyi responded, "What should I do with that by which I do not become immortal? What my Lord knows, tell me that." Here they have gone beyond the desire for wealth, awakening to the desire for immortality. So he accepts her, and this is what he says, "Verily a husband is not dear that you should love the husband but that you may love the atman, the Spirit, the Self; therefore a husband is dear. Not for the sake of the wife is the wife dear but for the sake of the Spirit, the Self; therefore a wife is dear. Not for the sake of sons are sons dear, but for the sake of the Self."[98] This means that everything that is loved in this world has to be loved not for itself alone but for the sake of that eternal Spirit which is manifesting in it. Brahman, or atman, is the source, the ground and the end of all human endeavour. It is the Supreme Reality, which embraces everything. The whole creation is pervaded by brahman and contained within it.

The Brihadaranyaka Upanishad goes on to say that it is impossible to speak properly of this brahman, this atman, this purusha, for it is beyond words. This brahman or atman is neti neti, "not this, not this." No created thing can express brahman. It, or he, is always beyond words and beyond thought: it is the one reality. So this is the breakthrough beyond the physical and beyond the psychological, to the transcendent reality which embraces both the physical and the psychological and which fills the whole creation. That is the concept of the brahman in the *Upanishads*.

In the Chandogya Upanishad there is a description of the city of brahman, conceived as the human body. The brahman, and in a sense the whole creation, is present in everybody and everything. So, "Within the city of brahman, the human body, there is a small shrine. And in that shrine there is a lotus and in that lotus there is a small space. What exists in that small space in the heart of the lotus, that is to be understood." It goes on to say, "As large as is the space which contains the whole universe, so large is that space within the heart. Both heaven and earth are contained within it, fire and air, sun and moon, and lightning and stars; whatever there is here in the world, and whatever is not, all that is contained within it."[99] So the whole universe is within each of us, as we saw in the last chapter. The whole universe is contained within consciousness. When one goes beyond the outer world of the senses where one is just part of the external universe, one discovers the inner reality and experiences that the whole universe is within. That is the profound insight which was reached in India at this period.

In a later Upanishad, the Katha Upanishad, dated at about 500 BC there is a further understanding of this hierarchy of being. The text reads, "Beyond the senses there are the objects, beyond the objects there is the mind, beyond the mind there is the intellect, beyond the intellect is the great self, beyond the great self is the Unmanifest, beyond the Unmanifest there is purusha, the Person."[100] This maps out the structure of the universe as it was conceived at this time. First of all there are the objects of the senses, then the senses themselves which observe the world around. Beyond the senses there is the *manas*, the mind, which works through the senses. When anything is observed, the senses register the impressions, the sense data, but the mind interprets what the senses register. Beyond the manas is the *buddhi*, which is the intellect as distinguished from the reason. Thomas Aquinas speaks of the *intellectus* and the ratio, and in Greek thinking there is a similar distinction between *nous*, the intellect, and *dianoia*, the reason. In Sanskrit there is the buddhi, the intellect or intelligence, and the manas, the active reason. The buddhi is the pure intelligence which opens us to the source of reality. The manas works through the senses and is the logical, scientific mind, but the buddhi is the higher aspect of the mind which goes not only beyond the senses but beyond the ordinary functioning of the mind and is open to transcendence.

Beyond the buddhi is the *mahat*, or great world, the world of the gods and the cosmic powers. Going beyond the higher self we become aware of the world of spirits, the psychic world, to which we belong. Beyond the physical is the psychic and each of us is a member of that vast world, the great world or the Great Self.

Beyond the *mahat* is the *avyakta*, the unmanifest. The gods, angels and powers are all manifestations of an unmanifest which is the source from which they come. And again, beyond the unmanifest is *purusha*, the Person, the Supreme, and from him everything comes. The text says, "Beyond the unmanifest there is purusha; beyond purusha there is nothing. That is the goal. That is the highest road." At that stage we have reached the Ultimate.

There is a progression from the senses, through the mind, through the intellect, and through the cosmic mind or cosmic order, to the Unmanifest. Before anything comes to be manifest, whether physically or psychologically, it has an unmanifest source which is rooted in the Person, the supreme cosmic Being, from whom the whole creation comes. That is the structure of the universe as it emerged in the Upanishads in the fifth century before Christ.

Now we take a step further to the Svetasvatara Upanishad, about 300 BC, where we see the figure of purusha emerging more clearly. In the early Upanishads the interest was primarily in brahman, the reality behind everything, and in the atman, the Spirit within everything. Now the interest moves to the personal God and their understanding of the universe was expressed in terms of the *purusha*, the cosmic person, who embraces the universe and yet goes beyond it; three parts are in heaven and one part is here on earth. The text says, "What is praised in the Upanishad is the highest brahman and in it there is a triad."[101] The highest brahman is the sole support, the imperishable, but within that brahman there is first of all the isha, the Lord. This shows how the personal God comes to be related to brahman. Brahman is the ultimate Reality and the Lord, the ishvara, the personal God, is a manifestation of brahman. Beneath isha, or Hara, which is

242

another name for him, is jivatman, the individual soul. Beneath that is the pradhana, the material universe. So here are the three worlds again, the pradhana, the material universe, the jivatman, the psychological world of the soul, and beyond that, Hara, or ishvara, the Lord, and all are embraced in brahman. brahman embraces the whole, the material, the psychological and the spiritual. All are contained in him. This is an insight of great profundity.

The Svetasvatara Upanishad is also important because in it for the first time the god Shiva comes to be recognised as the Supreme Reality. Shiva was a god from outside the Aryan culture and only here is he being brought into the main tradition of the Vedas and the Upanishads, and recognised as the Supreme. The word Shiva means the Blessed, the Kindly One. Having originally been considered as very fierce, he was given this beautiful name and gradually a most beautiful character was built up around him. Eventually he was considered as the God of love and recognised more and more to be the source of all.

The Svetasvatara Upanishad describes the work of purusha when it refers to him as the creator and supporter of the gods. The Supreme is above the gods. The gods are on the level of the angels and are the cosmic powers but he, the Lord, is beyond them all. Earlier he had been known as Rudra, the great seer, the maharishi, but now he comes to be understood as the Lord of all, the sovereign of the gods, the one in whom all the worlds rest, who rules over all beings. The text goes on to speak of him "who is more subtle than the subtle, in the midst of chaos creating all things." Matter is chaos, as we saw in chapter one. It is potentiality of being, indeterminate, unpredictable, the base from which everything comes. The idea here is that Shiva, the Lord, is creating continuously in the midst of chaos. "In the midst of chaos, creating all things, having many forms and alone enveloping everything."[102] Creating the worlds from chaos, he takes the form of all the universe. He is in the earth and in the plants and in the trees, and in animals and in men. He is manifesting in the earth and the sky and the stars and the sun and the moon, manifesting in all creation. Enveloping all things, he is within all things. Embracing all things, he transcends all things. That is the cosmic

Lord, Shiva.

We come now to a very important development. The Vedic period, the time of the Vedas, the Brahmanas, the Aranyakas and the *Upanishads* came to an end about 500 BC, although many of the *Upanishads* like the Svetasvatara Upanishad, to which we have just alluded, date from later times. Contemporary with the Svetasvatara Upanishad is the Bhagavad Gita. Whereas in the Svetasvatara Upanishad Shiva is the form of the Supreme God, the Supreme Reality, in the *Bhagavad Gita* the Supreme Reality is Vishnu. The majority of Hindus are either Shaivites or Vaishnavites. Vishnu belongs more to the Aryan world. He is the god of heaven, a gracious god, the pervader of all things. Vishnu manifests himself through a series of incarnations, avataras, and the great avatara of Vishnu was Krishna. The *Bhagavad Gita* was written to celebrate the avatara of Vishnu as Krishna. In the Bhagavad Gita Krishna is revealed as the supreme Lord of creation, the creator of God. This is a development along the same lines as the Svetasvatara Upanishad.

The *Bhagavad Gita* marks an advance even on the Svetasvatara Upanishad in that Krishna is revealed as both totally transcendent and totally immanent. In the *Bhagavad Gita* Krishna says, "All this visible universe comes from my invisible being. All beings have their rest in me but I have not my rest in them." [103] The whole creation comes from him; all rest in him and depend on him, but he does not depend on them. Then he says, "In truth they rest not in me. Consider my sacred mystery, my *maya*. I am the source of all beings, I support them all but I rest not in them." [104] There is here the concept of a totally transcendent God. Krishna transcends the whole universe. It comes forth from him and he supports it, but he does not rest in it and in a real sense it does not rest in him. He is transcendent over it all. This is a profound insight which was reached at that point.

Later, in the tenth book of the *Bhagavad Gita*, Krishna speaks of the whole universe as being in himself. "I shall reveal to thee some manifestations of my divine glory. For there is no end to my infinite greatness. I am the beginning, the middle and end of all that lives." [105] Krishna is the source, the middle and the goal to which all is tending, the all-pervading Lord. He then gives various mythological accounts of all these forms which are in him. Then in the eleventh book, the book of the great theophany, Krishna reveals himself to Arjuna as the Lord in whom the whole creation exists. The text says, "Then Krishna appeared to Arjuna in his supreme divine form . . . and Arjuna saw in that form countless visions of wonder. He saw in that radiance the whole universe, in all its variety, standing in a vast unity, in the body of the God of Gods."[106] The whole creation in all its variety and yet in its unity was revealed within the body of the Lord, the Lord who sustains the whole universe and carries it in himself. But he has made it clear that, while he is immanent and sustains all, he is also transcendent and beyond all. The vision of Krishna as the Lord is a wonderful theophany. Arjuna bows in adoration before him and says, "I have seen what no man has seen before. I rejoice in exaltation and yet my heart trembles with fear."[107]

A further stage in the development of the idea of God is found in the Tantras. This was a very important movement. So far we have been considering the Vedic religion in its original form, but now it seems quite clear that as the Aryans came down through India from the North to the South more and more of the indigenous people, basically Dravidians, were drawn in to this religion. The history of Hinduism is the history of the gradual assimilation of the different peoples of India into the Vedic world. It seems clear that Shaivism as a whole derives from the indigenous Dravidian religion. Shiva is still the great God in the South, while Vishnu is more popular in the North. There has been mixing, but it is clear that the former derives from the ancient matriarchal religion.

The earliest Tantric texts date from the third century AD but Tantrism goes back beyond that. At first Tantra was an undercurrent and is not documented among the Dravidian peoples much earlier than the third century. It belongs essentially to the world of magic and of myth. At this stage the Tantra begins to enter the main stream of Hinduism and a new development takes place. So far the aim had always been to go beyond the physical and beyond the psychological to the Supreme Reality, and to see everything in that light. In practice that entailed a strong tendency towards asceticism, which prevailed in Hinduism as a whole. Leaving behind the body, the soul, the mind and all its activities, the aim was to unite oneself with the supreme *brahman*, the supreme *atman*. That is the basic movement of *sannyasa*, renunciation. The Tantra arose in opposition to that, to assert the values of nature and of the body, of the senses and of sex. All that world which tended to be suppressed in the other tradition now comes to life. This is why Tantra is particularly important today. There is a great revival of Tantrism taking place at the moment. The late Swami Muktananda of Ganeshpuri in Maharashtra, for instance, was one of the great exponents of it. People are discovering this other side of nature, the side represented by the mother, and are coming to appreciate the Great Mother, the earth mother, who nourishes us all, from whom we all come and from whom we all receive our bodily existence and the power of the senses.

A key doctrine of the Tantras is, "that by which we fall is that by which we rise." In other words, as we fall through the attraction of the senses, through sex, passion and desire, so we have to rise through them, using them as the means of going beyond. The Tantra has the marvellous vision of the whole cosmos in terms of *shakti*. Shakti is energy. This is where the link with the contemporary world is so fascinating because, in the tradition of the Tantra, Shakti is the source of the universe and she is the mother, she is feminine. Whereas the other religions are patriarchal, Shaivism stems from the matriarchal religion where the mother is the source of all. The mother goddess (*devi*), is shakti, energy. In Shaivism Shiva is normally considered to be consciousness or spirit, and Shakti is his energy, his power. The world comes into being through shakti, through energy. Iconographically Shiva is portrayed in deep contemplation, surveying the creation, while Shakti, his consort, moves the whole universe. With this there is the beginning of a new understanding of the universe as a form of energy. Tantra was explored deeply and its teaching brought to light by Sir John Woodruffe, a British judge in Calcutta in the last century.

Of particular interest is the tantric conception of *bindu*. Bindu is a point, but a point in which all the energy of the universe is concentrated. Bindu is said to be the origin of the universe, the whole energy of the universe is concentrated in a single point. From that highly concentrated point energy expands outwards. That is very near to how we today conceive the origin of the universe. All the energy seems to have come out from a point, from nothing, in a sense. It is interesting that in the Tantra the energy is understood to come out of the bindu in mathematical form, in triangles and squares, for instance. Galileo also had this idea that the geometrical forms come out from the original matter. So there is this concept of original matter exploding, as it were, into the forms of the universe. The universe was considered to be in the form of a yantra. A yantra is a structure, a kind of diagram or picture, composed of triangles and squares. In that yantra all the powers of the universe are concentrated. Again the practice associated with this comes very near to magic at times. If one constructs a yantra it is accorded tremendous power. Still today in a Hindu temple, in the inner sanctuary there is often a yantra which is held to have this magical power in it. There can be real power in those yantras because they are designs in which, as it were, the power of the universe is concentrated.

In Tantra it is understood that everything comes forth from the bindu and it structures itself in the physical universe in a mathematical form. The yantra, is a representation of the structure of the universe. By meditating on the yantra one unites oneself with the whole universe.

The universe is composed of centers of energy known as *chakras*. Out of the bindu come all the chakras, each of which is a center of energy — we would speak in terms of atoms, molecules, cells, organisms. The whole universe comes forth in these centers of energy, culminating in the highest human center of energy, the human consciousness. The important point here is that, as the universe comes forth from the bindu and structures itself around the person, so the same power is present in one's own body. One's own body is a microcosm: the whole universe is within.

This idea is particularly worked out in Kundalini yoga, where the understanding is that Kundalini is the serpent power. The serpent was always the symbol of this earth power. That power is supposed to be coiled up like a serpent at the base of the spine and is understood to be the source of all psychic energy. That energy, kundalini, rises up through seven chakras, or energy centers, from the base of the spine to the crown of the head. As the Kundalini, which is really the goddess Shakti herself, rises up through the body the whole being is gradually transformed, from the physical, through the psychological, until finally spiritual evolution is attained. It all takes place within, and what takes place within is reflecting and resonating with what is taking place in the universe outside. The whole process is conceived as the marriage of Shiva (consciousness) with Shakti (energy).

That is the vision of the universe in the Hindu tradition, in which there are many similarities with the vision of the Western scientist and philosopher today. Western science, having lost itself in materialism, is discovering its mistake and is opening itself now to the ancient wisdom, and East and West are beginning to come together.

V

EAST: PART TWO
THE WAY:
LIFE AND SPIRITUAL PRACTICE

From the time of his youthful spiritual awakening, Bede Griffiths' quest for wisdom reached toward a knowledge which was integral rather than abstract, an immediate embrace of reality rather than a merely objective knowing. On one hand this integral knowledge grows toward a full participation in the unitive Mystery. On the other hand it moves toward incarnation; this knowledge demands embodiment in living. Griffiths' early experiment in sharing a simple life with his two friends at Eastington appears, in this light, as a first sowing of the seed of faith in the earth.

Bede's monastic commitment, following swiftly upon his Christian conversion, is a further expression of this integrity which compelled him to express his faith in lived reality. India opened before him new possibilities and new exigencies in this living out of his vocation. Here was a level of poverty and simplicity unlike anything he had seen in the West. Here he found a monastic tradition twenty five centuries old centered in an utter renunciation of possessions and the other human securities. This 'blessed simplicity' attracted him as the natural correlative of the unitive wisdom, the 'nonduality' which he sought. Upon this way of self-emptying he pursued his quest of unity and universality.

Yoga has become the comprehensive name for the varied spiritual paths and practices of Hinduism. Corresponding to the renunciation and simplicity of the sannyasi is this 'way of union' (yoga) in which the person becomes freed in body, soul and spirit to realize within himself or herself the Absolute, the One.

As in early Christian monasticism, the personal path of simplicity expressed itself in a characteristic way of relating to other persons, a social behavior which stood in sharp contrast to the egocentric ways of the world. Today, following Gandhi, this way is called 'nonviolence.' Bede, in India, quickly appropriated this position in opposition to the massive organized violence - of both the active and the structural varieties - that has marked the twentieth century.

Bede's commentary on the Bhagavad Gita (*River of Compassion*) will bring a new perspective to many of these elements of the Indian spiritual life which he had already presented from the tradition of the Upanishads. The emergence of a personal God will be accompanied by a change in the orientation of spiritual practice. The ways of devotion and of service will broaden the path of spirituality beyond the limits of traditional sannyasa, opening it to ordinary people in the world. We seem to accompany Bede himself into a 'Mahayana' phase.

India offered Bede Griffiths an integral vision within which all these different dimensions of consciousness and activity could be understood and lived as one just as, in this eastern light, he had found the three worlds of matter, consciousness and spirit to be one. The integral quality of Bede's own life witnesses to the validity of his vision.

48. *Hindu Monasticism: The Sannyasi*[1]

The sannyasi, or renunciant, is the essential expression of Indian monasticism and its engagement with the Absolute. This model of an 'absolute life' immediately engaged the radical idealism of Bede Griffiths. Much like the early Christian desert monks of Egypt and Syria, the sannyasi strives through a life of solitary asceticism to break free of every attachment - and finally of the basic attachment to the self, or ego - and thus to attain realization of the Self. As Bede opens Return to the Center *with a chapter on the life of a sannyasi, he first recalls the moment of his youthful spiritual awakening. This way of life, we infer, is the natural - perhaps for him inevitable - unfolding of that first experience. He describes his own way of life at Shantivanam and then, like a present-day Cassian or Benedict, points toward the absolute simplicity which is the ideal of the sannyasi. Listening to Bede, one may feel the inviting touch of that Spirit which* "blows where it wills, and you hear the sound of it, but you do not know whence it comes or whither it goes."[2]

I sit here on the veranda of my cell, watching the sun set behind the trees, and recall the day, nearly fifty years ago, when I watched the same sun setting over the playing-fields at school. My cell is a thatched hut surrounded by trees. I can listen to the birds singing, as I did then, and watch the trees making dark patterns against the sky as the light fades, but I have travelled a long way both in space and in time since then. There are tall palmyra palms around me, and young coconut trees growing up between them, and the bananas are spreading their broad leaves like green sails. I can hear a robin singing, but it is a black Indian robin, and the voice of the cuckoo which comes from the distant woods is that of the Indian cuckoo. I have made my home here in India, in the Tamil Nadu, by the banks of the river Cavery, but my mind has also travelled no less far than my body. For sixteen years now I have lived as an Indian among Indians, following Indian ways of life, studying Indian thought, and immersing myself in the living traditions of the Indian spirit. Let me now try to reflect on what India has done to me, on how my mind has developed over these years, on the changes which have taken place in my way of life and in the depths of my soul.

The first thing that I have learned is a simplicity of life which before I would have not thought possible. India has a way of reducing human needs to a minimum. One full meal a day of rice and vegetables — at best with some curds and ghee (clarified butter) — is considered sufficient. Tea or coffee with some rice preparation and some pickle is enough for breakfast and supper. Nor are tables and chairs, spoons and forks and knives and plates considered necessary. One sits on the floor on a mat and eats with one's hands — or rather with the right hand, as the left hand is kept for cleansing one's self. For plate there is a banana leaf. There is thus no need of any furniture in an Indian home. The richer people who have adopted Western ways make use of tables and chairs and beds and other conveniences, but the poor man — and that is the vast majority — is still content to sit and sleep on the floor. Nor are elaborate bathrooms and lavatories considered necessary. In the villages the majority of people will take their bath at a pump or a well or in a neighbouring tank or stream, and most people still go out into the fields or by the roadside or by a stream to relieve themselves. There is a beautiful simplicity in all this, which makes one realize something of the original simplicity of human nature. Even clothes are hardly necessary. Most men today, it is true, wear a shirt and a 'dhoti' — a piece of cloth wound round the waist and falling to the feet — and women wear a sari and a blouse to cover the breast, but this is comparatively recent. Even now clothes are still felt to be things which are put on for the occasion, and are easily discarded. A man will take his shirt off when he wants to relax, and a laborer will wear no more than a 'langothi' — a piece of cloth wound round the middle and between the legs.

All this makes the life of a *sannyasi* — one who has 'renounced' the world — immensely simple. He needs no house or furniture. He may live in a cave or take shelter beside a temple or on the veranda of a house. For clothing he needs only two pieces of cloth which should not be stitched one to wear round the waist and the other for a shawl to cover the shoulders or the head. There are even some sannyasis who renounce all clothing and are said to be 'clothed with the sky.' For food he needs only one meal a day, which he gets by begging or, more often, which a householder will offer him unasked. He can thus reduce his life to an absolute simplicity. He is totally detached from the world, depending on divine providence for his bare needs of food, shelter and clothing. Does this not bring him very near to the first disciples of Christ, who were told to take 'no gold, nor silver, nor copper in your belts, no bag for your journey, nor two tunics, nor sandals, nor a staff,' and to the Son of man himself, who had nowhere to lay his head?[3] What a challenge this presents to a world which takes pleasure in continually increasing human needs and so makes itself more and more dependent on the material world.

I have not been able to reach this extreme degree of detachment. I have my little hut, which is simple enough, just one small room with a thatched roof, but it is solidly built of brick with a concrete floor. I have also a table, a chair and a bed, which are luxuries for a sannyasi, but I have not been able to learn to sit and sleep always on the floor. I have also my books and my typewriter, but these are not really 'mine,' any more than the hut and the furniture — they are, as we say, 'allowed for my use.' A *sannyasi* is one who does not possess anything, not even the clothes on his back. He has renounced all 'property.' This is the real renunciation which is demanded, the renunciation of 'I' and 'mine.' A sannyasi is one who is totally detached from the world and from himself. It is detachment which is the key-word. It does not matter so much what material possessions you have, so long as you are not attached to them. You must be ready to give up everything, not only material attachments but also human attachments — father, mother, wife, children — everything that you have. But the one thing which you have to abandon unconditionally is your 'self.' If you can give up your self, your 'ego,' you can have anything you like, wife and family, houses and lands — but who is able to give up his self?

49. The Call of the Absolute[4]

As Bede Griffiths is concluding the account of his personal "Discovery of India" with which he has begun The Marriage of East and West, *he describes the way of life to which he has now been guided. "At every stage I have been conscious that it was not I who was leading, but that something was leading me. Now it has led me to the point where I have become a 'sannyasi.'" Then he proceeds to unfold the spiritual meaning of the life of the sannyasi, bringing us to the edge of human possibility. We may wonder whether we are not going beyond the limits of a Christian anthropology and onto the uneasy soft shoulder of credibility. Can a human being made of flesh and blood renounce 'the whole world of 'signs', of 'appearances' and truly live? Can a faithful child of God 'go beyond all religion, beyond every human institution, beyond every scripture and creed' and there, more truly, encounter Divinity?*

That is the far country from which the fragmentary, excited reports of Abhishiktananda have come back to us. There it becomes vitally important to discern spiritual ideal from spiritual reality. There the explorer may fall captive more fatally than ever to 'ego,' as it merges with that most captivating archetype, the Absolute. Bede was more humble and realistic in his practical pursuit of sannyasa and in his teaching on the subject than might be suggested by his theoretical development of the idea here. Unlike his uncompromising French fellow-monk, he was prepared to adapt the ideal of the sannyasi to a more or less ordinary life within the church and the world.

A sannyasi is one who renounces the world to seek for God, but his renunciation goes far beyond what is ordinarily understood by the 'world.' A sannyasi is one who renounces not only the world in the biblical sense of the world of sin, the world which today is so clearly set on the path of destruction. A sannyasi renounces the whole world of 'signs', of appearances.

The world which is studied by science, the world of politics and economics, the world of social and cultural life, which most people take for reality, is a world of appearances with no ultimate reality. It is all passing away at every moment and everybody is passing with it. The church also belongs to this world of 'signs.' The doctrines and sacraments of the church are human expressions or signs of the divine reality, which are likewise destined to pass away. So also Christ himself is the 'sacrament' of God; he is the sign of God's grace and salvation, of God's presence among men, and this sign also will pass, when the Reality, the thing signified, is revealed. Finally God himself, in so far as he can be named, whether Yahweh or Allah or simply God, is a sign, a name for the ultimate Truth, which cannot be named. Thus the sannyasi is called to go beyond all religion, beyond every human institution, beyond every scripture and creed, till he comes to that which every religion and scripture and ritual signifies but can never name. In every religion, whether Christian or Hindu or Buddhist or Muslim, it has been recognized that the ultimate Reality cannot be named and the sannyasi is one who is called to go beyond all religion and seek that ultimate goal.

Yet when we say that the sannyasi goes beyond religion this does not mean that he rejects any religion. I have not felt called to reject anything that I have learned of God or of Christ or of the church. To go beyond the sign is not to reject the sign, but to reach the thing signified. In the language of St Thomas Aquinas, it is to pass from the *sacramentum* to the *res*. As long as we remain in this world we need these signs, and the world today cannot survive unless it rediscovers the 'signs' of faith, the 'Myth,' the 'Symbol,' in which the knowledge of reality is enshrined. But equally fatal is to stop at the sign, to mistake the sign for the ultimate reality. It is this that sets one religion against another and divides Christians from one another, from people of other religions and from the rest of the world. This is essentially idolatry. Whether it is the Bible or the church or any dogma or creed, when it is forgotten that they belong to the world of signs and appearances, to the world which is passing away, they become idols far more deadly than any graven image. The sannyasi is one who is called to witness to this Truth of the Reality beyond the signs, to be a sign of that which is beyond signs.

But when we have said this, we have admitted that the sannyasi, though he may witness to the world beyond signs, yet himself still belongs to this world. To be true to his vocation he also must disappear, as Jesus himself, the great Sannyasi, disappeared after the Resurrection. He showed himself to his disciples after his Resurrection speaking of the kingdom of God,[5] and then he disappeared. Only when he had gone could the Spirit come. As he himself said: 'It is for your advantage that I go from you, for if I do not go the Spirit will not come.'[6] Like the Master, the disciple must disappear. 'Unless the grain of wheat die, it cannot bear fruit.'[7] We have to die in order that we may live. An ashram is only a stopping place, in which a sannyasi may live for a time — or for all 'time' — but he is always journeying beyond time to the eternal reality. So also every church, every religion, every human community, is only a stopping place, a tent which is pitched on this earth by pilgrims who are on their way to the City of God.

50. Sannyasa as Interior Detachment

In River of Compassion, *Bede has moved to a different view of the life of the sannyasi. Rather than a literal and total abandonment of the visible world of signs, as he found it described in the Upanishads, Bede finds sannyasa presented in the Bhagavad Gita more clearly as that interior renunciation: the renunciation of one's self. The sannyasi will work, but without attachment to the work or its fruits. It is the surrender of the will that matters.*

I[8]

The sixth chapter [of the *Gita*] continues the previous theme and develops it further, revolving around the question of the relation between contemplation and action, or in the Gita's terms, between Sankhya and yoga. Sankhya is the contemplative discipline and yoga the practical discipline.

Krishna is speaking:

6.1 He who works not for an earthly reward, but does the work to be done, he is a Sannyasi, he is a Yogi: not he who lights not the sacred fire or offers not the holy sacrifice.

The point here is that the essence of *sannyasa*, renunciation, is renunciation of the self. It is not a renouncing of action or external things;

it is a matter of inner renunciation. The man who works without attachment, free from any self love is a true sannyasi and also a yogi. This means that contemplation and action are one. Contemplation is freedom from all attachment, so that one adheres to God, to brahman. In the Gita it gradually becomes clear that this means adhering to, and living in, the personal God. This brings freedom from all attachment and from all desire of reward, and in that freedom one does one's work. That is always the teaching: do not seek the fruit of your actions. This is the true meaning of both sannyasa and yoga.

"Not the man who builds no sacrificial fire and does no work" (Zaehner). The word for "no work" is akriya, which can mean no work in the ordinary sense, but here more probably means no holy work or ritual. That was the ancient idea of the sannyasi and it still remains today. A sannyasi does not build a sacrificial fire for he has given up all ritual. The Hindu sannyasi is not supposed to perform any ritual. He is not a priest. This is important also for Christian monks. It has always been recognized that the priesthood is completely secondary in the monastic ideal, and should never be identified with it. The monk is essentially not a priest. He may undertake a priestly duty for a specific purpose in the monastery or elsewhere, but it is not an essential part of his vocation, because the priesthood is a specific service to the community and the monk as such has no particular ministry or work to do.

In the Hindu tradition, before initiation into sannyasa, the disciple, if he is a Brahmin or of high caste, removes the sacred thread and undergoes a funeral ceremony. This is like the Christian monastic profession where the monk lies prostrate in the sanctuary, as a symbol of his total self-sacrifice. Formerly he used to be covered with a black pall to show that he had died to the world. The sannyasi renounces all worldly attachments, all family bonds, all caste. He is free from all bondage to the social order. This led to the idea, as we have seen, that the sannyasi is beyond work. Work binds and if he continued to work he would be in bondage of *karma*. Therefore he does no work. The Gita, however, teaches that he should do his work, but that he should do it without attachment, not seeking any reward and offering all he does as a sacrifice; then he is a true sannyasi.

256

6.2 Because the Sannyasi of renunciation is also the Yogi of holy work; and no man can be a Yogi who surrenders not his earthly will.

This is the test. The word for earthly will is samkalpa. Zaehner translates this as 'purpose,' but I think Mascaro's version is better. The earthly will is the egoistic will; therefore without renouncing his "earthly will" no one can be a yogi. The essential need is the renunciation of the ego, of the self. The ego, when it is centered on itself, is the root of all evil for it then becomes the principle of self-will. He who renounces all self-will is a true sannyasi. That is the essence of sannyasa.

6.3 When the sage climbs the heights of Yoga, he follows the path of work; but when he reaches the heights of Yoga, he is in the land of peace.

More literally it is, "For a sage who is seeking Yoga, action is called the means; for the same sage when he is enthroned in Yoga, serenity is called the means" (B&D). This is very close to the idea of the early Christian monks: that all action is a preparation for contemplation. That was the common understanding; the active life belongs to beginners and consists in the life of virtue, humility, patience, charity. All this is a preparation for the life of contemplation, when one is no longer in need of such activities. That is one theory and it is very strong in the Hindu tradition also. The sannyasi is beyond action altogether; he is in pure contemplation. But the Gita is suggesting a different view which is much more profound, namely that when the sannyasi has reached this spiritual perfection, he is then free to act in any way that God may call him.

He surrenders himself totally to the divine, to brahman; then he is free to act from the principle of the Spirit within, and not from his own ego, not from any self-will.

6.4 And he reaches the heights of Yoga when he surrenders his earthly will: when he is not bound by the work of his senses, and he is not bound by his earthly works.

So when there is no attachment to sense or to activity, through the earthly will, then he is a true yogi and also a true sannyasi, It is very important to realize that ultimately the yogi and the sannyasi are one and that for both it is a matter of being free from all attachment. The doctrine of the Gita leaves one free to act. That is why Mahatma Gandhi could take the Gita as the guide for his life. Total service of humanity is compatible here with total surrender to God.

So the two ideas are there. The one is that action is preparation for contemplation, and that in contemplation there is no action left and all is quiescence. The other idea which the Gita is putting forward, though it does not always make it clear, is that action leads to contemplation and that contemplation involves perfect detachment which enables one to act freely according to the law of the spirit within.

II[9]

Bede resumes the subject later, commenting on the final chapter of the Gita (at 18.7)[10]

. . . Many used to believe that even religious actions should be abandoned, and even now there is a tradition of the sannyasi who abandons all work altogether. A sannyasi is not supposed to perform any ritual action, and he is not supposed to do any work in an ashram; that should be done by the devotees. He should be simply meditating, uniting with God. That is one way of life but the Gita is opposed to that. The Gita supports the ideal of contemplation and surrender to the Self, in order to act unselfishly. "To leave undone a holy work which ought to be done would be a delusion of darkness."

51. Spirit, Person, and Action in the World[11]

In an illuminating further text from River of Compassion, *commenting Gita 15:16-17, we see the relationship between faith in a personal God and the liberation of the human person in this world. We may recall Jesus' words, "The sabbath was made for man, not man for the sabbath."[12] This development within the Gita is of decisive importance, and here we may sense that a spiritual liberation is taking place within Bede himself. The grip of an ancient archetype is loosening.*

One has to go beyond both the sensible and the intelligible world, beyond even the 'still state' of brahman, and discover the personal God, who is 'known by love,' who reveals himself to those who open themselves to his love. When one comes to the Lord beyond, one is open to all humanity. And then one is free! But when one reaches Purushottoma, the supreme Person, then one is at his disposal and one can do anything, including work in the world. That is the Christian view of sannyasa. We go through samadhi, the experience of oneness, to the total surrender to the Lord, and then, because he is a personal God and because he is love, he takes us to himself and sets us free to do whatever he wills us to do in the world. So that is the true sannyasi who has attained the state of pure love and also pure abandonment and availability for everyone and everything.

52. Hindu Monasticism: The Ashram[13]

In India, an ashram is a place where spiritual seekers gather, usually around a teacher. It is thus a more communal counterpart to the emphatically solitary way of the sannyasi. The ashram, with its lack of formal structure and relative unconcern with 'community' and the mutual relationships of the disciples, presents a sharp contrast to the traditional western monastery which is centered in a Christian conception of koinonia, or communion, and encased within a firm and all-comprehending juridical structure.[14] Bede found the ashram life most congenial to his soul, and worked toward the realization of a Christian ashram for many years in India, at Kurisumala and then at Shantivanam. Saccidananda ashram (Shantivanam), with Bede Griffiths the teacher at its heart, became the image, for many who visited it from the West, of an Indian Christian monastic life. For Bede the ashram, like the sannyasi, is to be understood theologically, as a kind of sacrament: a visible embodiment of the one worthwhile quest, the quest for the One. A Christian ashram must be the place where the experience of God as Trinity - which elsewhere he will call a participation in Jesus' own experience - encounters the Hindu experience of advaita, of the immanent nondual Absolute.

Just as the church today is entering into dialogue with other religions and we can no longer think of Christian life and faith without relation to other forms of religious life and faith, so also the Christian monk everywhere is being called to relate his own monastic tradition to the wider tradition of monastic life throughout the world. In this respect the Hindu ashram offers a very definite challenge to the monastic order. An ashram is not a monastery in the ordinary sense. From the earliest times the Hindu ascetic has normally been a wandering monk. The typical "sannyasi" - one who has renounced the world to seek

God, or "liberation" - is a wandering monk, who goes from village to village, begging his food and never staying more than three days in one place. The ideal sannyasi has no dwelling-place (like the Son of Man who had nowhere to lay his head). He has only the minimum of clothing - just two pieces of cloth (which should not be stitched), a waterpot and a staff. It is interesting to note that when Jesus sent out his disciples, he told them (according to St Mark) to "take nothing for their journey except a staff; no bread, no bag, no money in their belts; but to wear sandals and not to put on two tunics." This is almost exactly the requirement of a sannyasi except that he may dispense with the sandals (as St Matthew's Gospel in fact does). This life of the Hindu sannyasi, therefore, takes us very near to that of the first disciples of Christ.

But though the wandering monk is perhaps the most typical form of monastic life in India, with its total poverty and dependence on divine providence, yet there has been a tradition of settled life among ascetics and monks in India from a very early time. There are traditionally four ashrams, or ways of life in India: that of the student or "brahmachari" (literally one who seeks God, or brahman), who studies the Vedas, the sacred Scriptures, and learns his duty in life; then that of the householder, who marries and brings up a family; then that of the "vanaprastha," or forest-dweller, who retires to the forest to meditate and prepare for death; and finally that of the sannyasi, who renounces the world to live a wandering life, as has been described. It would seem that the ashram, as it is now called, derives from the third form of life, that of the forest-dweller. Even in Vedic times we hear of holy men who retire to the forest, sometimes with a wife, to meditate and discover the indwelling presence of God in the heart. This was, in fact, the decisive moment in the religious history of India, when instead of engaging in external sacrifice in the courtyard of a house, the "rishi," or Seer, retired to the forest to offer the inner sacrifice in the heart. The ashram was therefore from the beginning a place where a holy man retired to meditate and where disciples gathered round him to share his meditation and his experience of God. This remains the essential character of an ashram at the present time.[15]

An ashram normally centers on a guru, or spiritual master, who acts as a guide to others on the path of spiritual life. In this respect he is very much like the spiritual Father of the early Christian monks, such as St Antony. The ashram always remained a very informal community like the communities of hermits or lauras in the Eastern Church. It never developed into a monastery on the lines of those of St Pachomius, St Basil or St Benedict. The relation of the members of the ashram was primarily to their guru, not to one another, and community life, as such, had very little place. The ashram was also always very fluid in its structure. A monk could come or go; he was not bound to remain in the ashram. He might undertake a pilgrimage to the holy places of India, which might take him a year or more. He might settle elsewhere and establish an ashram of his own. It was not the place or the community which was important, or even the guru, except at first. It was the search for God, for "brahman," the ultimate Reality, for final "liberation," which was the one essential thing in his life. Such is the ideal of the ashram today. It is a group of disciples gathered round a master, living usually in a retired place, engaged in prayer and meditation, and often in study as well (but not in manual work), whose one object is to "know brahman" or to know the "Self," the indwelling Spirit. Of course, today there are many types of ashrams, some very large and organized more in the manner of a monastic order, some very small consisting of two or three or just one monk or sannyasi, or it may be a simple layman or "brahmachari," or even a married couple. But always the essential character remains, the search for God, the quest of the Absolute.

The question which we have to ask ourselves is: has the ashram, as described, any place in the monastic life or the church today? Is it possible to adopt the ashram style of life in our Christian search for God? Perhaps the answer can best be given by describing what has been attempted in our ashram of Shantivanam. This ashram was founded in 1950 by two French fathers, Jules Monchanin and Henri Le Saux. Father Le Saux was a Benedictine monk from Kergonan Abbey in Brittany and the ashram was given a Benedictine character from the beginning. In fact, their booklet published on the ideals of the ashram was called *A Benedictine Ashram*.[16] But at the same time they wanted to follow the traditions of the typical Indian ashram, living in Indian style, sitting on the floor both for prayer and for meals, eating with the hand and sleeping on a mat - and so dispensing with practically all furniture and eating utensils. Each of them lived in a small thatched hut, and this custom has also been retained, so that the ashram has a semi-eremitical character. In their time when Latin still prevailed in the liturgy, it was not possible to introduce much change, but since Vatican Council II it has been possible to introduce Sanskrit chanting as well as songs in the local language, Tamil, and other Indian languages. We also have readings from the different Scriptures, the Vedas, the *Upanishads* and the *Bhagavad Gita* in the morning, the Sikh Gura Granth and the Koran at midday, and the "Bhaktas" or devotional poets of India in the evening. We have also a Mass celebrated in Indian style according to the rite approved by the Holy See and we use "arati," the waving of lights before the Blessed Sacrament in the typical gesture of worship in India.

But it was not only in externals that they sought to follow the traditions of an Indian ashram. They began a deep study of Hindu thought and sought to penetrate into the depths of the Hindu experience of God. Father Monchanin's writings were published in French in a book called *Mystique de l'Inde, mystère chrétien* and more recently in English in a book called *In Quest of the Absolute*.[17] Father Le Saux, who took the name of Swami Abhishiktananda, wrote a little book on prayer,[18] which has become famous all over the world, but his most important work, which was published in French under the title *Sagesse Hindoue, Mystique chrétienne* and in English as *Saccidananda* (the name for the Godhead as being 'sat,' *knowledge* 'cit,' and *bliss* 'ananda' in Hinduism) is a most profound study of the Hindu doctrine of advaita, or non-duality, in relation to the Christian doctrine of the Trinity. This was, in fact, the focus of all their endeavor: how to relate the Hindu experience of God, or the Absolute, as "without duality" with the Christian doctrine of Creation, Trinity and Incarnation. Thus, one can say that the ashram centered on this quest for the understanding of God in the light of the Hindu experience of God as "one without a second" and the Christian experience of God as a Trinity of Persons, and of the world as reality distinct from God.

A Christian ashram, therefore, if it is to be worthy of the name, must be a place where a meeting can take place between the Christian experience of God through faith in Jesus Christ and the Hindu experience of "brahman," the One "without a second," the Ground of all creation and the "atman," the Spirit, dwelling in the heart of every man. This meeting has to take place in the depth of a contemplative experience, which is only possible in a life dedicated to the search for God, the quest of the Absolute, that has always been the goal of monastic life.

53. Meditation: The Way Beyond Duality

Bede Griffiths, dedicated to silent meditation throughout his life as a monk, was not a teacher of meditation, and he did not write about it systematically or at length. Meditation, as he uses the word, is neither quite prayer (which implies activity) nor reflection (as the word had traditionally been understood in the West). It is rather, as understood in the East, a practice of stillness through which the consciousness deepens, beyond thought and image, to a unitive level of interiority. Meditation is the practice which corresponds to the experience (or gift) of contemplation. It is the interior practice which most immediately corresponds to the way which Bede has described as the 'discovery of the Self.' In his later years, he would often recommend to newcomers the method of 'Christian Meditation' as taught by Benedictine John Main. In The New Creation in Christ, *his lectures at the 1991 John Main Seminar in Indiana, he spoke at length of the tradition of prayer with a mantra which is exemplified by the Jesus Prayer and by 'Christian Meditation.' In the selections from* The New Creation in Christ *which follow, he presents meditation as the one path which leads directly into the heart of the mystery: into non-duality and into Trinity.*

I[19]

The rational mind based on the experiences of the senses is inherently dualistic. It sees everything in terms of opposites, mind and matter, subject and object, truth and error, right and wrong. But always beyond the dualism of the mind is the unity of the spirit. Meditation takes us beyond the dualities to the unified spirit. Christ came to set us free from this dualism. He is the one who broke through the division in our nature . . .

Christianity came out of a tradition of moral dualism. It then passed into the Greco-Roman culture which was based on a metaphysical dualism. But today it is meeting the religions of Asia, and we are beginning to discover the principle of nonduality. The rational mind demands that everything be one or two, while nonduality, which is beyond the rational, affirms a relationship which is not one and not two. It is only through meditation that we get beyond this duality. We are being called to recover unity beyond duality as our birthright, and it is this alone which can answer the deepest needs of the world today.

. . . Meditation is the only way to go beyond dualism. As long as you think rationally you will have a dualistic attitude. But when you stop the mind, you discover the unifying principle behind everything. I think that in the meditation movement God is leading humanity through this dualism. It is a call that has gone all over the world. Everywhere people are meeting together, discovering this need and responding to it in the different ways of meditation. We are all being called to open our hearts to the nondual mystery which is the mystery of love revealed in the Trinity.

In the doctrine of the Trinity the ultimate Reality is seen as Being in relationship or Being in love. The ultimate reality is not a solitary person nor an impersonal Absolute. It is a communion of persons in love. Every being seeks to express and communicate itself. In the human being the body is one means by which we express ourselves and communicate with others. But the highest expression of our being is the mind. It is through the mind that we find words to express and communicate ourselves. In the Godhead as conceived in the Christian tradition, the Word of God is the expression of the mind of God. It is the self-manifestation of the eternal Wisdom; and the Spirit of God, the Holy Spirit, is the self-communication of the eternal Being, infinite love, which is manifested in the whole creation and comes to a head in the person of Jesus Christ. It is to the experience of the eternal Wisdom communicated in the love of the Holy Spirit that our meditation should lead us.

III[21]

The object of Christian meditation is to encounter Christ in the depths of one's being, not mediated by words and thoughts, but known by his presence in the Spirit. When Jesus was about to leave his disciples, he promised to send them the 'Spirit of Truth' to guide them to all truth. It is this Spirit that we encounter when we enter into the depths of our own spirit. As St Paul says, 'The Spirit of God bears witness with our spirit that we are children of God.'[22] So in meditation we are entering into that depth of the spirit where we encounter the Spirit of God.

Of course, we have to read the Bible. We need words and thoughts. We cannot simply go into the spirit without the help of words, because the mind needs the instruction of faith. We must begin by meditating on Scripture and the teachings of the church, but we also have to go beyond them. And that upsets people who think the Bible is everything and that one must stay with the Bible alone. But the Bible is still words and thoughts, whereas the Word of God is beyond words and thoughts. It is a hidden mystery. Jesus himself is beyond the Bible, He, not the Bible, is the ultimate Reality.

Jesus did not leave us the New Testament. That came later. He left us the Holy Spirit. That was his own Spirit, the Spirit of the Father. In meditation, we try to go beyond the limitation of words and thoughts to open our hearts to the hidden mystery of the Spirit and to be really in the presence of Christ and the Father, to enter into the mystery of the Trinity. This is a tremendous undertaking. We are trying to break through to the ultimate truth of reality. As long as you are in the world of dualities, of churches and doctrines and rituals, there are always conflicts and always will be. It is only when we go beyond all outer expression, all sacraments (outward signs) and enter into the hidden mystery that we can touch the point that unites us all.

As long as we are in the way of ritual and doctrine, we are all fighting one another. But when we get beyond ritual and doctrine, which are signs (and necessary in their own way) to the mystery itself, then we touch the point of human unity, where religions can be reconciled. We are here to reconcile religious conflicts in the world. It is a terrible responsibility. This is our calling: to enter into that depth of the Spirit where we encounter Jesus' own Spirit. Jesus lives in the church through his Spirit. When he departed from his disciples, he ascended and returned in the Spirit to dwell in every disciple, in every human being, because no one is outside his grace. There is a presence within us. When we enter into the silence of meditation, we encounter the real presence of Christ.

IV[23]

. . . The Godhead is a communion of knowledge and love. And we are being drawn into it. That is our calling. That is why meditation is so important. Sacramental rites are wonderful and necessary; the Mass is central. But we are still using external signs: churches, candles, crucifixes, vestments, bread and wine. All these things are external. The mystery is coming *through* these signs. Sometimes the signs can be an embarrassment. There are often so many distractions in a church. But when we get beyond all the outer appearances and enter into the silence, we can encounter the Spirit of God, the Spirit of Jesus, and be in total communion in the heart. That is what we seek: a communion with God, in Christ, which is non-dual. We are no longer two. We are one, but not simply one without any distinction: one in relationship. The Persons of the Trinity are subsistent relationships. Love is a dynamism. It is not a solitary thing. The two commune with each other, penetrate into each other, become one with each other; and that is a nondual relationship, a mystery we cannot express in words. That is where the Gospel is leading us. It is a communion of love where each is in the other and knows no other, in a mystery of self-transcendence since in love the two become united, and one is not lost in the other. That is the mystery of love. The two become more themselves when fulfilled in love.

This is the ultimate Christian experience of God, and it is to this that our Christian meditation must lead us. That is why I say that I feel God is calling us. We are not doing it of ourselves. God is calling us to this way of meditation, to this experience of God in the hidden mystery of the heart. People are being drawn into this all over the world, some as Hindus, some as Buddhists. Often the Christian mystery is not given to them in a meaningful way. They think Christianity is an external religion for 'ordinary' people, but not sufficient for those who are really searching for God. We have to witness to the fact that there is a Christian mystery that can be experienced in the depth of the soul and answers the deepest need of our human nature. That is the challenge: to witness to this gift in meditation, in contemplative prayer through the mantra. John Main found the way for us all.

54. Meditation: Into the Absolute[24]

At the end of his sketch of a final synthesis in A New Vision of Reality, *Bede proposes meditation as a way of ascending through the levels of being (conceived according to the Vedanta) into transcendent consciousness, the Absolute.*

Thus in meditation we seek to go beyond our personal consciousness into the sphere of the transcendent consciousness. Normally, though not always, that means going through the psychic world and problems can arise because of the presence of evil forces as well as good. On account of this one needs a guide, and a Christian needs the guidance of Christ, to take him through that psychic world. It is important not to stop in the psychic world but to pass on through it. It is good to remember that in that psychic world there are not only evil spirits and demons of all kinds, but there are also all the saints and angels. As we go beyond our limited human consciousness we become aware of the whole world of the saints and angels and other holy beings. Today we are generally much less aware of this than people were in the past. In the eucharist we say, "Now with all the angels and archangels and with all the company of heaven we praise and magnify your holy name." This is a conscious relating for ourselves to the whole world of the saints and angels, which is always present although hidden from our normal mental consciousness. We need always to try to keep in mind that not only is the physical world around us, and the ordinary psychological world of our human experience, but also the psychic world of the saints and angels and the cosmic powers. This subtle world is more real than either the physical or the psychological world and enfolds both in itself. When the New Testament speaks of casting out demons or evil spirits it is speaking of realities.

In meditation then we go into that *mahat,* the cosmic order or cosmic consciousness, and then we go beyond that to where everything is gathered into the unity of the one Person, the cosmic Lord. Then in and through the cosmic Lord everything returns to the transcendent unity beyond conception. The ultimate is beyond conception altogether. It is totally ineffable. That is why we constantly have to remember that all the words we use to speak of this are only pointers to that which is totally beyond. The Absolute itself is beyond all human comprehension and we use words, images and concepts taken from everyday finite experience in order to direct our mind, our will and our heart towards the Infinite and to allow that Infinite to enter into our lives and transform them.

55. Christian Contemplation as Unitive Experience

In late 1989, The Vatican Congregation for the Doctrine of the Faith (headed by Cardinal Joseph Ratzinger[25]) stepped into the realm of spirituality with a letter[26] cautioning Catholics against the potential dangers in the use of Asian methods of meditation. The letter is a compact theological treatise on Christian prayer, furnishing in its endnotes a wealth of citations from the tradition and official documents of the church. Criteria are offered for the adoption of practical methods of meditation and for the discernment of spiritual experiences. The document seems a timely and useful resource for bishops and for Catholics drawn to a life of prayer at a confusing moment in history. It would be difficult to point to an untrue assertion in the text. What fault could one possibly find in it?

Once again we are spectators at the collision of two theological worlds. To Bede Griffiths, the sober rational and doctrinal perspective and institutional caution of the letter are offensive; this complacent didactic precision is inadequate to the subject of meditation and contemplation. With his own kind of intuitive precision, he pounces upon the document's weak point. The letter expressed virtually no awareness of the Christian apophatic tradition or of the reality of unitive contemplation, and no recognition of the spiritual vitality which many Christians had experienced in using the eastern methods. Bede's essential point, forcefully affirmed, is the unitive or nondual experience at the heart of Christianity itself, as found in the New Testament revelation and witnessed by orthodox Christian writers. St. Gregory of Nyssa and Dionysius were not too cautious to integrate the unitive wisdom of Neoplatonism (expressed by Plotinus and Porphyry) into their mystical theology. Hindu and Buddhist mysticism offer a similar gift to Christianity today. Bede's response appeared in a letter to the National Catholic Reporter.27

As a response to the challenge presented by Hindu and Buddhist spirituality today, I find the document on Christian prayer and meditation extremely disappointing. There is no hint of the tremendous depth of this spirituality or of its profound wisdom. Eastern meditation is treated as if it were a matter of superficial techniques, of "bits and pieces" a Christian can use if he wishes, but of whose dangers and abuses he must be made aware. What is still more disappointing is that the conception of Christian prayer it presents is most inadequate, ignoring as it does what is deepest and most significant in the Gospel and in Catholic tradition.

The document insists on the "distance" that must always exist between man and God as creature and creator and warns against any attempt to "try and overcome the distance," as if God in Christ had not already overcome that distance and united us with him in the closest bonds. St Paul says, "You who were far off, he has brought near - not kept distant - in the blood of Christ." Jesus himself totally denies any such distance. "I am the vine," he says, "you are the branches." How can the branches be "distant" from the vine?

Later, the document insists that we must "never in any way seek to place ourselves on the same level as the object of our contemplation." Of course, we don't seek to place ourselves on the same level. It is God who has already placed us there. Jesus says, "I have not called you servants, but friends." And to show what such friendship means, he prays for his disciples, "that they may be one, as thou, Father, in me and I in thee, that they may be one in us." The union between Jesus and the Father in the mystery of the Trinity is the closest it is possible to conceive, or rather it is beyond all conception. Yet, it is for this very union that Jesus prays for his disciples.

One of the great teachers of Christian meditation today, Father John Main, has said that Christian meditation is a "participation in the consciousness of Christ. Or rather it is to share in that stream of love which flows between Jesus and the Father and is the Holy Spirit." It is to this depth of contemplative wisdom that Christian meditation should lead us, and it is toward this depth of unitive prayer that many Christians have found that the Hindu and Buddhist and Sufi mystics can lead us.

This reminds us that, centuries ago, the church was challenged by a similar movement of mystical prayer in the fourth century Platonism of Plotinus and Porphyry. But the church in the fourth century did not meet this challenge by a cautious retreat into the past. It boldly accepted the challenge and incorporated into Christian doctrine the profound insights of the Neoplatonists. Jean Danielou in his *Platonisme et Theologie Mystique* has shown how St Gregory of Nyssa steeped himself in the philosophy of Plotinus and by subtle changes adapted it to orthodox Christian doctrine.

Another crisis in Christian mysticism was encountered in the sixth century with Dionysius the Areopagite, now generally thought to have been a Syrian monk of that period who had absorbed the teaching of Porphyry, a later fifth-century Platonist. He boldly went beyond this dualistic, conceptual model of prayer to which the Roman document clings and declared that in contemplative prayer we must go beyond all words and concepts and enter into "divine darkness" so that we come to "know by unknowing."

Anyone familiar with Hindu and Buddhist mysticism will know that it is to this "supraconceptual" knowledge, this experience of a transcendent mystery, transcending word and thought, that they also can lead. This is not to say that Hindu, Buddhist and Christian mystics all have the same experience. But it is to recognize an analogy between them and to look upon the Hindu and Buddhist experience as something of supreme significance, not to be lightly dismissed by a Christian as of no importance.

There is a crisis in the church today. Many Christians are looking to the church for guidance in contemplative prayer and failing to find it. They then turn to Hindu and Buddhist masters for guidance and often through them come to understand something of the depth of Christian mysticism. But for such people, this document offers no assistance whatever. It is, rather, calculated to put them off and make them confirmed in their belief that the Christian Church has nothing to offer those who are seeking God in the dark, often on a lonely path and desperately in need of the guidance the church so often fails to give.

56. Bede's Prayer[28]

At the threshold of his last year, Bede Griffiths was asked by the editors of The Tablet *for an account of his own way of prayer. He responded humbly, simply — and entirely from within the Christian tradition. This will surprise one who has read Bede's extensive writings on the mystical experience at the heart of Hinduism and his letter — not so long before — defending the unitive mysticism of the Asian traditions. While he is doubtless influenced by a pastoral sensitivity, this is not just an accommodation to his English Catholic readers. It is the candor of his final years, when the shining waters subside to expose the rock of his Christian faith. Bede's basic practice of prayer is the Jesus prayer, which he understands as a means of maintaining the presence of God in all circumstances. From the medieval monastic tradition he recalls the four stages of progression to union with God: reading, reflection, prayer and contemplation. Here, uncharacteristically again, he uses 'meditation' in the western sense, as reflection upon a scriptural text. It is at the final stage of 'contemplation' that a convergence with Asian spirituality is implicit, but he does not bring it out. Bede's accent even here is on a loving participation in the mystery of Christ.*

If anyone asks me how I pray, my simple answer is that I pray the Jesus prayer. Anyone familiar with the story of a Russian pilgrim will know what I mean. It consists simply in repeating the words: "Lord Jesus Christ, Son of God, have mercy on me, a sinner." I have used this prayer now for over 40 years and it has become so familiar that it simply repeats itself. Whenever I am not otherwise occupied or thinking of something else, the prayer goes quietly on. Sometimes it is almost mechanical, just quietly repeating itself, and other times it gathers strength and can become extremely powerful.

I give it my own interpretation. When I say, "Lord Jesus Christ, Son of God," I think of Jesus as the Word of God, embracing heaven and earth and revealing himself in different ways and under different names and forms to all humanity. I consider that this Word "enlightens everyone coming into the world," and though they may not recognize it, it is present to every human being in the depths of their soul. Beyond word and thought, beyond all signs and symbols, this Word is being secretly spoken in every heart in every place and at every time. People may be utterly ignorant of it or may choose to ignore it, but whenever or wherever anyone responds to truth or love or kindness, to the demand for justice, concern for others, care of those in need, they are responding to the voice of the Word. So also when anyone seeks truth or beauty in science, philosophy, poetry or art, they are responding to the invitation of the Word.

I believe that that Word took flesh in Jesus of Nazareth and in him we can find a personal form of the Word to whom we can pray and to whom we can relate in terms of love and intimacy, but I think that he makes himself known to others under different names and forms. What counts is not so much the name and the form as the response in the heart to the hidden mystery, which is present to each one of us in one way or another and awaits our response in faith and hope and love.

When I say, "have mercy on me, a sinner," I unite myself with all human beings from the beginning of the world, who have experienced separation from God, or from the eternal truth. I realise that, as human beings, we are all separated from God, from the source of our being. We are wandering in a world of shadows, mistaking the outward appearance of people and things for reality. But at all times something is pressing us to reach out beyond the shadows, to face the reality, the truth, the inner meaning of our lives, and so to find God, or whatever name we give to the mystery which enfolds us.

So I say the Jesus prayer, asking to be set free from the illusions of this world, from the innumerable vanities and deceits with which I am surrounded. And I find in the name of Jesus the name which opens my heart and mind to reality. I believe that each one of us has an inner light, an inner guide, which will lead us through the shadows and illusions by which we are surrounded, and open our minds to the truth. It may come through poetry or art, or philosophy or science, or more commonly through the encounter with people and events, day by day. Personally I find that meditation, morning and evening, every day, is the best and most direct method of getting in touch with reality. In meditation I try to let go of everything of the outer world of the senses, of the inner world of thoughts, and listen to the inner voice, the voice of the Word, which comes in the silence, in the stillness when all activity of mind and body ceases. Then in the silence I become aware of the presence of God, and I try to keep that awareness during the day. In bus or train or travelling by air, in work or study or talking and relating to others, I try to be aware of this presence in everyone and in everything. And the Jesus prayer is what keeps me aware of the presence.

So prayer for me is the practice of the presence of God in all situations, in the midst of noise and distractions of all sorts, of pain and suffering and death, as in times of peace and quiet, of joy and friendship, of prayer and silence, the presence is always there. For me the Jesus prayer is just a way of keeping in the presence of God.

I find it convenient to keep in mind the four stages of prayer in the medieval tradition — *lectio, meditatio, oratio, contemplatio. Lectio* is reading. Most people need to prepare themselves for prayer by reading of some sort. Reading the Bible is the traditional way, but this reading is not just reading for information. It is an attentive reading, savoring the words as in reading poetry. For this reason I prefer the Authorized or Revised Versions of the Bible, which preserve the rich, poetic tradition of the English language.

Lectio is followed by *meditatio*. This means reflecting on one's reading, drawing out the deeper sense and preserving it in the "heart." It is said that Mary "pondered all these things in her heart." This is meditation in the traditional sense, bringing out the moral and symbolic meaning of the text and applying it to one's own life. The symbolic meaning goes beyond the literal, and shows all its implications for one's own life and for the life of the church and the world. It is a great loss when the literal meaning, of which today, of course, we have a far greater knowledge, leaves no place for the deeper, richer symbolic meaning which points to the ultimate truth to which the Scripture bears witness.

Meditation is naturally followed by prayer — *oratio*. Our understanding of the deeper meaning of the text depends on our spiritual insight and this comes from prayer. Prayer is opening the heart and mind to God; that is, it is going beyond all the limited processes of the rational mind and opening the mind to the transcendent reality to which all words and thoughts are pointing. This demands devotion - that is, self-surrender. As long as we remain on the level of the rational mind, we are governed by our ego, our independent, rational self.

273

We can make use of all kinds of assistance, of commentaries and spiritual guides, but as long as the individual self remains in command, we are imprisoned in the rational mind with its concepts and judgments. Only when we surrender the ego, the separate self, and turn to God, the supreme Spirit, can we receive the light which we need to understand the deeper meaning of the Scriptures. This is passing from *ratio* to *intellectus*, from discursive thought to intuitive insight.

So we pass to *contemplatio*. Contemplation is the goal of all Christian life. It is knowledge by love. St Paul often prays for his disciples that they may have knowledge (*gnosis*) and understanding (*epignosis*) in the mystery of Christ. The mystery of Christ is the ultimate truth, the reality towards which all human life aspires. And this mystery is known by love. Love is going out of oneself, surrendering the self, letting the reality, the truth take over. It is not limited to any earthly object or person. It reaches out to the infinite and the eternal. This is contemplation. It is not something which we achieve for ourselves. It is something that comes when we let go. We have to abandon everything — all words, thoughts, hopes, fears all attachment to ourselves or to any earthly thing, and let the divine mystery take possession of our lives. It feels like death and is a sort of dying. It is encountering the darkness, the abyss, the void. It is facing nothingness — or as Augustine Baker, the English Benedictine mystic said, it is the "union of the nothing with the Nothing."

This is the negative aspect of contemplation. The positive aspect is, of course, the opposite. It is total fulfilment, total wisdom, total bliss, the answer to all problems, the peace which surpasses understanding, the joy which is the fullness of love. St Paul has summed it up in the letter to the Ephesians — or whoever wrote that letter which is the supreme example of Christian gnosis: "I bow my knees before the Father, from whom every family in heaven and on earth is named, that according to the riches of his glory, he may strengthen you with his spirit in the inner man; that Christ may dwell in your hearts by faith, that being rooted and grounded in love, you may have power to comprehend with all the saints what is the length and breadth and height and depth, and may know the love of Christ which surpasses knowledge, that you may be filled with all the fulness of

274

God."

57. Yoga: The Way of Union[29]

Yoga can be understood in a general sense as the way of Hindu spiritual practice, comprehending diverse paths with their multiple stages. Bede thought of himself as a Christian yogi and wrote about yoga particularly in the first decades of his life in India. He defines yoga, characteristically, in terms of union: a realization of 'nonduality' in which the three worlds of God, human self and universe are experienced as one. The physical exercises (hatha yoga) which are usually identified with yoga in the West play little part in this view

Bede contrasts the classical raja yoga of Patanjali, which aims at a separation of consciousness from nature through an exacting series of exercises of asceticism and meditation, with the 'Integral Yoga' of the twentieth-century master Sri Aurobindo which embraces both this ascending way and the descent of Spirit into matter to transform it into the 'medium of a spiritual consciousness.' It is in this latter vision that Bede finds the promise of a Christian Yoga. The transformation of matter which has already happened in the resurrection of Christ must take place in each of us as well, in the power of the indwelling divine Spirit. The practices of yoga are to open the person to this transforming energy of the Spirit. 'Spirit,' as Bede uses the word here, signifies both the atman of Hinduism and the Holy Spirit of Christian tradition.

Bede outlines the eight stages of the classical raja yoga of Patanjali, and then briefly explains the three other principal ways. Karma yoga is the way of selfless action. Bhakti yoga is the path of personal devotion. He defines jnana yoga as the way of wisdom which, through conversion, surrender and meditation, leads to the 'knowledge of the Self, the atman, the true Being.' and 'the light of the Word, shining in the heart. By this light all is enlightened, by this everything is known.' It is this light that seems to be reflected to us from the pages of Return to the Center.

The transformation of body and soul by the Spirit is the work of yoga. In the classical system of Patanjali there are two principles which govern not only human life but the whole creation. One is the masculine principle, *purusha*, who is pure consciousness, the other is the feminine principle, *prakriti*, who is the source of all the activity of nature. The cause of all suffering in this world is that purusha, consciousness, has become entangled with prakriti and become subject to the passions of nature. The art of yoga is to separate purusha from prakriti, consciousness from the actions and passions of nature, so that the consciousness becomes free from every movement of nature and enjoys the bliss of pure contemplation, untouched by any taint of mortality. This ideal of *kaivalya*, of total separation from the world, has been present in Hinduism from early times, and for Sankara this remains the goal of life. All the activity of nature is maya; it is an illusion due to ignorance. Wisdom consists of the knowledge of being in pure consciousness without any modification, and this brings lasting bliss — *saccidananda* — the bliss of the pure consciousness of being. There is certainly profound truth in this doctrine. There is an experience of being in pure consciousness which gives lasting peace to the soul. It is an experience of the Ground or Depth of being in the Center of the soul, an awareness of the mystery of being beyond sense and thought, which gives a sense of fulfillment, of finality, of absolute truth. And indeed there is a sense in which this experience is ultimate. It is an experience of the undifferentiated Ground of being, the Abyss of being beyond thought, the One without a second. But does this mean that all other modes of consciousness are illusory, that nature has no reality, that the experience of God is also an illusion?

Though Sankara has many followers among Hindus today, his doctrine has never gained universal acceptance. It has been opposed from the beginning by the Vaishnava philosophers, who were devoted to a personal God, Ramanuja, Madhva, Nimbarka, Vallabha and Caitanya, who have constructed rival systems of Vedanta in opposition to Sankara, and it is rejected by Saiva Siddhanta. Moreover, in modern times it has met with opposition from those philosophers who under the influence of the West have recognized the values of matter and life, of history and personality, of whom Sri Aurobindo is the greatest. In his philosophy[30] there is a wonderful synthesis, based on the Vedanta, of ancient and modern thought. In him the values of being and becoming, of spirit and matter, of the One and the many, of the eternal and the temporal, of the universal and the individual, of the personal God and the absolute Godhead, are integrated in a vision of the whole, which has never been surpassed in depth and comprehensiveness. In the integral yoga of Sri Aurobindo the values of matter and life and human consciousness and the experience of a personal God are not lost in the ultimate Reality, the divine Saccidananda. Matter and life and consciousness in man are seen to be evolving towards the divine life and the divine consciousness, in which they are not annihilated but fulfilled.

This is the goal of a Christian yoga. Body and soul are to be transfigured by the divine life and to participate in the divine consciousness. There is a descent of the Spirit into matter and a corresponding ascent, by which matter is transformed by the indwelling power of the Spirit and the body is transfigured. In kundalini yoga this is represented as the union of *Siva* and *Shakti* in the human body. The divine power is represented as coiled up like a serpent at the base of the spine. This divine energy has to be led through the seven *chakras*, or centers of psychic energy, until it reaches the thousand-petalled lotus at the crown of the head. Then Siva, who is pure consciousness, unites with Shakti, the divine energy in nature, and body and soul are transformed. This is very different from the yoga of Patanjali, where consciousness (purusha) is separated from nature (prakriti) and enjoys the bliss of isolation (*kaivalya*). Yet both these yogas have their place. There must be a movement of ascent to pure consciousness, a detachment from all the moods of nature, a realization of the Self in its eternal Ground beyond space and time. But then there must also be a movement of descent, by which the Spirit enters into the depths of matter and raises it to a new mode of existence, in which it becomes the medium of a spiritual consciousness.

For a Christian this has already taken place in the resurrection of Christ. In his body matter has already been transformed, so as to become a spiritual body, which is the medium of the divine life. The human body by contact with this body of Christ, which is no longer limited by space and time, has within it the seed of the divine life. As St Paul says: "We ourselves, who have the first fruits of the Spirit, groan inwardly as we wait for...the redemption of our bodies."[31] And this 'groaning' is part of the travail of all nature, which waits to be delivered "from its bondage to decay and obtain the glorious liberty of the children of God."[32] This is the cosmic drama, this transformation of nature, of matter and the body, as to become the outward form of the divine Spirit, the body of the Lord. And this transformation is taking place in our own bodies. In every human being matter is being transformed daily into Spirit. We take in matter through our bodies as food, and that matter goes to feed the brain, and the brain produces thought. Thought itself is matter become Spirit. But for most of us this process remains incomplete. Matter is never fully assimilated by Spirit, and at death the matter unassimilated by the Spirit returns to the earth. But in the body of Christ we can see that transformation of matter by Spirit taking place, which is the destiny of us all at the end of time. The body of the Virgin Mary is said to have been transformed in the same way, and doubtless there are other saints and yogis of whom this is true.

The real end of yoga, then, is the transformation of body and soul by the power of the indwelling Spirit, the atman. In the classical system of Patanjali there are eight stages in this process of transformation. The first two stages — *yama and niyama* — give the moral basis without which any yoga is useless. They consist of obedience to the commandments — not to kill, not to steal, to adhere to the truth, to preserve chastity, not to covet. After these come the counsels — cleanliness or purity of mind and body, contentment, in the sense of equanimity in the face of the opposites, good and evil, pleasure and pain, joy and sorrow. Then asceticism or self-control, meditation on the scriptures and devotion to God. This is the basic pattern of moral and spiritual life, which is common to all religions. The next two stages — *asana and pranayama* — are the practice of bodily posture and control of the breath, which are particularly associated with yoga. These are, in fact, the methods of hatha yoga, which aims at the transformation of body and soul by bodily exercise, and the acquisition of *siddhis* — that is, the yogic powers which result from complete control over the body. The next four stages are the stages of meditation, first recollection (*pratyahara*), then concentration (*dharana*), then meditation itself or 'the unbroken flow of thought towards the object of concentration', and finally *samadhi* — the absorption of the mind in the object of its contemplation, when all sense of the distinction of subject and object disappears. But all these are only techniques by which soul and body are brought into subjection to the Spirit and the soul awakens to the divine life within.

Apart from the classical system of Yoga, or raja yoga, there are three ways of yoga, the way of action (*karma*), the way of devotion (*bhakti*) and the way of knowledge (*jnana*). There are not many who can follow the way of body-control and mind-control of the classical system. For most people the way to self-discovery, to union with God, is by action. This was the great discovery of the Bhagavad Gita. At first it was thought that the way to union with God, the path of salvation, was to be found in the practice of asceticism, in silence and solitude, in prolonged meditation. But the Bhagavad Gita declared that the householder doing the ordinary duties of his life could attain salvation no less than the ascetic in the forest. Man could be saved by work: all that was required was that the work should be done with detachment.[33] It is work which is done with attachment, that is, with selfish motives, that binds the soul. We must not seek the 'fruit' of work. We have to make the offering of the work to God, then it is no longer we who act but God who acts in us. The lower self, the ego, must be sacrificed; the action must come from the higher Self, the Spirit in us, then it becomes a holy action. This is the way in which we awake to the presence of the Spirit in us. It does not matter what the work may be, whether it is manual or intellectual, work of organization, of management, of service or of prayer. It has to be done with detachment, it has to be offered to God. Every poet knows this. The poem cannot be manufactured, it has to come from the Self within. In this sense all work is poetry, and should have the seal of beauty, which is the seal of the Spirit, on it.

The second way is the way of devotion, of love for a personal God. This is the second great principle of the *Bhagavad Gita*. In the *Upanishads* the Godhead was conceived as the brahman, the one, absolute, transcendent Being, beyond word and thought. But this brahman was also the atman, the Self, the Ground of human consciousness. It was not only Being but Knowledge and Bliss. But to speak of a being who is knowledge and bliss is to imply a personal being, for a person is simply a conscious being, a being possessed of intelligence and will. Very soon this becomes explicit and the Self was described as God, the Lord, in directly personal terms.[34] Of course, the word 'person' is used by analogy, like all terms which are applied to the Godhead. A human person is the finite being possessing a finite intellect and a finite will. When applied to the infinite being of the Godhead, it can only mean that in the Godhead there is an infinite capacity for knowledge and love, analogous to our human capacity but infinitely transcending it. And this is not only speculation. In the experience of the *bhakti*, in the total surrender of the intellect and the will to the infinite Transcendence, there is an experience of personal relationship; the intellect is illuminated by the eternal light and the will transfigured by the infinite love. This is the experience of the mystics of all religions. Of course, human language fails here, because we are passing beyond the barriers of human nature. The God who is experienced in mystical ecstasy is more than personal and can be described in impersonal terms, as Light, Life, Truth, Beauty, Being itself. But this transcendent Being is more, not less, than personal, and therefore it is misleading to describe it as impersonal. In the Christian doctrine of the Trinity, the Godhead is the one, absolute, infinite, transcendent Mystery of Being beyond word and thought, but within this being there is revealed the plentitude of personal being, of wisdom and love, transcending all human conception, but realized in the fullness of personal relationship, more meaningful than any human knowledge and more real than any human love. To realize this relationship of knowledge and love in one's self by total surrender to the divine love is the way of bhakti. "If a man loves me, he will keep my word, and my Father will love him, and we will come to him and make our home with him."[35]

Finally, there is the way of knowledge *(jnana)*, of wisdom. This is the knowledge of the Self, the atman, the true Being. It is not a knowledge which can be acquired by reason, or by learning, or even through the scriptures.[36] It is a knowledge which comes from above. The path to it is by *metanoia*, by repentance, by turning back, by a return to the source. There must be a radical detachment from the self, that is, from all selfish attachment to the world, the flesh and the ego. This self, the *jivatman*, must be surrendered. It must become completely empty, void, dead to itself. This is the difficult crossing, the passage to the other shore, the passing away. Unless the grain of wheat die, it cannot bear fruit.[37] He who will lose his life shall save it.[38]

This is the great paradox behind all life. All methods of meditation are intended to lead to this point. The mind must die to itself, to its concepts, its reason. The surface mind must cease its activity, all thought must cease. Then in the silence, in the stillness, beyond thought, a deeper mind becomes known, the true Self begins to emerge. This is the *Paramatman*, the supreme Self, the light of the Word, shining in the heart. By this light all is enlightened,[39] by this everything is known.[40] This is the end of the journey; beyond this it is impossible to go. For here the human passes into the divine, the temporal into the eternal, the finite into the infinite. What words can describe this state, what thought penetrate it? It is the ultimate mystery.

58. Stages on the Yogic Path[41]

Commenting the sixth chapter of the Gita (6.25) in River of Compassion, Bede sets forth the successive phases of the yogi's ascent to the unitive Absolute through meditation.

More literally it is, "Little by little let him gain tranquillity by means of reason controlled by steadiness." (B&D translation[42]). The aim is to bring the mind to the point of the *buddhi* where it is steady, stilled and controlled, instead of wandering about through the senses. The whole problem of yoga is that the mind naturally goes from one thing to another; it is always wandering. The question is how to bring it to one point - the single point where it becomes steady and controlled. "By the soul held fast in steadfastness, he must make the mind subsist in the self" (Zaehner[43]). The manas, the lower mind, must be brought under the control of the Self. In the Katha Upanishad the faculties are described as the senses, (*indriyas*), the mind (*manas*), and the intellect (*buddhi*). And so it goes on to say that the yogi must bring speech under the control of the mind. Speech, by which one goes out of oneself and communicates with others, must be brought under the control of the mind. The manas, the mind, must be brought under the control of the intellect, the buddhi. Finally, the buddhi must be brought under the control of the Spirit, the atman. It is a gradual bringing of all the faculties back to their center and bringing them under control at their center. Here the Gita is describing exactly the same process. The buddhi is made firm and strong and controls the manas and the manas and the buddhi together are standing firm in the atman, the true Self. Coming to rest in the Self "he must think of nothing at all" (Z). On reaching that point, thinking stops. We have said that the purpose of yoga is *citta vritti nirodha*, cessation of the movements of the mind. But when one is not thinking, it does not mean that one is not intelligent. Pure intelligence is very active in pure awareness, but there is no movement of thought.

59. The Yoga of Faith and Love[44]

Bede, in River of Compassion, *is commenting the* Bhagavad Gita 6.47: *"And the greatest of all Yogis is he who with all his soul has faith, and he who with all his soul loves me." Here in the Gita — with its concept of a personal God who is worshiped in faith and love — we find the closest point of convergence between Hinduism and Christianity. Bede distinguishes the common way of faith and love from the traditional yogic way of integration of the personality in its center, the Self, through meditation. Best of all is the joining of these two ways: an inner integration which opens itself to love.*

Here the highest yoga is described as the yoga of faith and love. One can see here how the Gita has brought all these elements together: the Buddhist idea of transcending the world of the senses and the passions and reaching that still state of *nirvana*; the yogic idea of becoming brahman, of becoming one with the inner Self, in perfect integration, in the still point of one's being; and then going beyond that to the faith and love which unites us with the Personal God beyond.

That is a view of yoga which is also totally Christian. It integrates the whole person and it culminates in faith and love. All the great religious traditions are trying to help one to reach this inner center of one's being and to discover this inner peace, this perfect joy. How that is discovered depends on one's faith and on one's love. If one simply has a philosophical understanding, a very deep experience may be attained but it is not the same as if one has faith and becomes integrated in the love of God. Different experiences lead to different ways in which the experience is described. The Buddhist *nirvana* and the Hindu *moksha* are not the same, nor are they the same as the Christian vision of God. So the Buddhist, the Hindu, the Muslim and the Christian are all experiencing the ultimate Reality but experiencing it in different ways through their own love and through their own traditions of faith and knowledge. There are obviously various degrees as well. There is a tendency to say that when one reaches the supreme state everything is the same and that there are no differences any more, but I do not think that is true. In a sense, the experience of the ultimate truth is different for each person, since each person is a unique image of God, a unique reflection of the one eternal light and love.

The whole argument of this chapter culminates in this conception of faith and love as the ultimate means of realization. Everything depends on whether one is motivated by faith and love. Many simple people in every religion have faith and love and reach final realization by the grace of God, but they have not learned to meditate. They have not learned to integrate the personality in its inner center. Having faith and love, they stop short of achieving inner integration. Others, on the other hand, have a deep integration but if it is without faith and love, it remains an imperfect state. With some yogis, there is a deeply concentrated state above pain and pleasure, but there may be very little love in their nature. The perfect man is the one who has both integrated his personality in its inner center, in the Self, and who, in that inner center of his being, opens himself to the 'touch of brahman,' to the action of divine grace, allowing himself to be transformed by love.

60. Devotion and Service: Bhakti Yoga and Karma Yoga

It is in the Bhagavad Gita *that two further paths of yoga are developed (we have already encountered them in* Return to the Center, n. 57 *above): ways which are accessible to ordinary people living in the world. Bhakti yoga is the way of devotion to a personal God. Karma yoga is the way of active service. Commenting the Gita in* River of Compassion, *Bede describes this crucial shift from an exclusive tradition of the narrow way of renunciation (in the* Upanishads*) to a broader teaching which embraces a plurality of paths corresponding to the different dimensions of the human person.*

145

The question was, how to reach the knowledge of brahman, of atman. In the *Upanishads*, it is simply by way of jnana, by way of

283

renunciation and self-realization. That was generally understood to mean that one should not do any work, any *karma. Karma* binds one. Whatever work one does, good or bad, one is bound to the consequences. Therefore to reach true knowledge which is free from all limitation, one should renounce work. The *Bhagavad Gita* introduces another understanding which is that ordinary work, selfish work, binds one, whereas unselfish work, that is, work done without any attachment at all, so far from being binding, is a way of reaching God. So karma yoga is the way of work, in total detachment, total surrender and total sacrifice. Making a sacrifice of one's work by offering it to the Supreme is the means by which one attains to the Supreme. The *Gita* maintains that the householder, doing his duty in the spirit of love, detachment and surrender, can reach God, the Supreme, just as effectively, if not more so, than can the sannyasi who abstains from all work whatever.

Ramakrishna advocated the way of bhakti. He said that because this is the Kali Yuga, when people cannot easily attain jnana, they must follow the way of bhakti, devotion. So karma, unselfish action, is a way of reaching the Supreme; and bhakti, devotion to the personal God, is another. That is the position of the *Gita* up to now. [up to chapter 9]

II[46]

Bede is commenting Gita 12.10: 'If thou art not able to practice concentration, consecrate all thy work to me. By merely doing actions in my service thou shalt attain perfection.'

This is *karma* yoga. "By doing actions in my service you shall obtain perfection"; that is the other great way of the *Gita*. All the first six books of the *Gita* were concerned with karma yoga. Again there are differing views. In the strict advaitic view, one should not do any work, any karma, any ritualistic work or any practical work, the only way to attain God is by knowledge. But in the view of the *Gita*, the householder doing his *dharma*, his duty, working in God's service and offering his work to God, is able to be united in God, no less than the yogi or the ascetic.

So that is the other way, the way of devoted service and of course, today, that is what most people are drawn to. Some people are drawn to yoga, but almost everybody feels the call to service of some sort. Unselfish, devoted service is the most practical way to God that exists. It can also be the most effective. One can take the example of Mother Teresa or any of those innumerable people working in religious orders. Theirs is a practical way of finding God, though it has its limitations as we saw and can become an obstacle if one simply gives oneself to work. But work done out of love for God, in the service of one's neighbor, is always effective. That was the way of Mahatma Gandhi. He once said, "My one object in life is to obtain moksha, liberation, and if I thought I could attain it by going to a cave in the Himalayas, I would go there straight away, but I believe that I can find God in my neighbor, particularly in my suffering fellow countrymen, therefore I devote my life to them in order that I may find God." That is the way of karma yoga.

61. Turning Inward to the Self[47]

According to the Vedanta, it is through the realization of the Self, or atman, that one is united with the nondual Absolute. We have already encountered this theme more than once; it comes forth whenever Bede is called upon to describe the Hindu spiritual experience, to express the heart of the Upanishads or the central teaching of the Vedanta. Here in Return to the Center *he calls it 'the great discovery of Indian thought.' As Bede conceives the biblical Fall as a failure of interiority, a lapse from the 'true Self' and from unitive contemplation into captivity to the world of the body and senses, we come very close to the tradition of Christian Platonism as it appears in Origen and Evagrius Ponticus. Redemption, from this perspective, is experienced through a 'return to the center.' Later - as we have seen in texts from* River of Compassion *- he will come to see the goal of the spiritual life differently.*

The whole question is, what is the true Self? What is the true center of man's being? Is it the ego, making itself independent, seeking to be master of the world, or is there an 'I' beyond this, a deeper center of personal being, which is grounded in the Truth, which is one with the universal Self, the law of the universe? This is the great discovery of Indian thought, the discovery of the Self, the atman, the Ground of personal being, which is one with the brahman, the Ground of universal being. It is not reached by thought; on the contrary, it is only reached by transcending thought. Reason, like the self of which it is the faculty, has to transcend itself. As long as it remains turned towards the senses, to the material world, it will always remain defective, unable to discover the Truth. But the moment it turns inwards to its Source[48] and knows itself in its Ground by a pure intuition, then it knows the truth of its own being and the being of the world, and then it becomes really free. "You will know the truth, and the truth will make you free."[49] This is redemption, to be set free from the senses and the material world and to discover their Ground and Source in the Self, which is the Word of God within. The Fall of Man is the fall from this Ground, this center of freedom and immortality, into subjection to the senses and this material world, and reason is the serpent. Reason can either be subject to the eternal Law, the universal reason, and then it becomes wisdom, it knows the Self, or it can seek to be master of the world, and then it becomes demonic. It is the demon of the modern world. In every generation the Fall of Man is repeated, but never, perhaps, on a wider scale than today.

62. The Way of Self-Realization[50]

In The Marriage of East and West, *we find Bede's most highly developed exposition of the 'discovery of the Self.' He describes this way of interiority - which is also the ascent to pure spirit - from several different perspectives within the Hindu tradition. For him, however, the experience of the Self is universal, present in every religious tradition and basic to all human experience. It is "The inner secret of the Gospel." Indeed, some Christian contemplative traditions have followed a very similar route of progressive interiorization.[51] While this narrow way - renunciation of the world and loss of self to gain the self - is reminiscent of the Gospel, the exclusive pursuit of the Self is very different from the way taught by Jesus.*

An evolutionary pattern appears as Bede sets forth the successive stages of preconscious and conscious life. Once again the Upanishads mark the pivotal moment in history when human consciousness was opened to an awareness of self which was at the same time "a pure awareness of being," or absolute consciousness. Bede mentions Christian baptism as a participation in the paschal death of Christ but, unlike Abhishiktananda, does not develop further the promising connection between baptism and the birth of the Self.

As we follow Bede on his path through the stages of consciousness, his

Upanishadic texts provoke digressions on the purusha, or cosmic person, on cosmology and the cosmic powers or spirits. Bede ponders once again the relation between the human spirit and the divine Spirit in both the Hindu and the Christian traditions. For Bede, atman is synonymous not only with Self but with spirit and, in some other texts, with the Holy Spirit of Christian revelation. Here, however, he is careful to preserve the distinction between the transcendent God and the human person. Once again he does this by means of an image of participation: the purified human spirit mirrors within itself the "unborn eternal God."

The *Upanishads* are the record of this human discovery of the self. They seek to answer the questions: Who am I? Am I this body, this physical organism which is part of the physical organism of the universe, or am I this mind, this soul, which thinks and feels and suffers and enjoys? Or is there something beyond both body and soul, in which the real meaning of my existence is to be found? There is the story of how the gods and demons (the powers of nature both positive and negative) came to Prajapati, the creator, and asked him to tell them about the true self.[52] First he told them to look in a pool of water, so they looked in the water and saw themselves "even to the very hairs and nails," and thought that this, that is the body, was their self. But when they realized that this was not what they were seeking and so they returned to Prajapati and he told them, "the self you see in dreams, that is your true self." So they thought that the inner self, the self of thoughts and feelings and desires was their true self. But then they realized that this was not what they were seeking and so they returned to Prajapati and he said "the self which exists in deep sleep, when both body and mind are at rest, that is the true self." So they came to see that the self which is beyond both the body and the mind is the true self, but still they were not content, since that self is unconscious. So they returned to Prajapati again and finally he revealed to them the 'fourth' state (*turiya*), the state beyond waking and dreaming and deep sleep, the state of the awakened self, in which man attains to self-knowledge.

The story is deeply significant. There are three states of consciousness in the Hindu tradition, the waking, the dreaming and the state of deep sleep. Most people think that the real world is to be found in the external world presented to the senses, and that their real self is their bodily existence   the thing which you see in a mirror, the face which you present to the world. When we mature to some extent we begin to realize that the inner self, the self which thinks and feels, with its hopes and fears and joys and anxieties, is the real self. That is what corresponds to the dream state.

But beyond the waking and the dreaming state, there is the state of deep sleep *(sushupti)*. This is somewhat surprising from a western point of view. Most people would feel that the state of deep sleep is simply a state of unconsciousness, and has no significance. But, the Hindu asks, when the body is no longer conscious through its senses, and the mind is no longer conscious through its thoughts, what is that self which remains in deep sleep? It is this self, which is beyond both the body and the soul, beyond all conscious activity, which comes nearest to the real self in the Hindu view. This is the return to the source, to the root, to the ground of being.

But in this state there is no consciousness. It is necessary therefore to go beyond this state to what is called the 'fourth' state *(turiya)*. This is the state beyond body and soul, beyond feeling and thought, in which the person awakes to its true being, in which it discovers its ground, its source, not in unconsciousness but in pure consciousness. This is the goal to be sought, in this is to be found self-realization, self-knowledge. This is the knowledge of the Self, the atman, the Spirit, where the spirit of man reaches and touches the Spirit of God.

We can put it in another way. Human life springs from the darkness of the unconscious, the womb of nature to which we return every night. In that darkness we are one with the earth and the water, the fire and the air. We are in the womb of the Mother. Yet just as all the forms of nature, of sun and moon and stars, of mountains and rivers and seas, are latent in that darkness so all the future forms of life and consciousness are already present in that womb. As the organs of life begin to develop in the child in the womb, so the powers of life begin to develop in nature. The earth brings forth living things, plants and trees and flowers, all these forms were latent in the darkness of the earth, and the light of consciousness, shining in the darkness, brings them forth in the light of day. Life and consciousness are already present in matter from the beginning, but there were no organs through which they could act. In the plant and the tree a dim consciousness is already awakening as recent experiments have proved. They are beginning to emerge from the state of deep sleep, in which the earth is involved, into the dreaming state. The animal lives in the dreaming state. It has appetites, feelings, sensations, imagination, memory and a rudimentary intelligence. The light of consciousness is beginning to dawn, but the animal has no self-consciousness. It remains a apart of nature, determined by an external law, reflecting the world, through its senses and ruled by its appetites. In man, nature awakes to self-consciousness. There is a breakthrough from the dreaming to the waking state. Man becomes conscious of himself, conscious of the world, but this also brings with it a relative freedom. He can detach himself from the world around him, from his appetites and desires, and reflect upon himself. That reason which had been latent in matter from the beginning, organizing the stars and atoms, building up the living cell, giving form to plant and animal, now emerges into consciousness. Yet this light of reason is still very precarious. Man is still largely conditioned by his appetites and desires, he still feels himself to be a part of nature, is scarcely conscious of an individual self. Yet that little spark of reason and self-consciousness is there.

It is now that the drama of human existence begins. Man can allow himself to be ruled by his appetites and senses, to submit to the powers of nature and become their slave. Or he can awake to the 'fourth' state, he can discover the source of reason and consciousness within him, open himself to the power of the spirit and awake to his true self. This is what took place in the Upanishads.

All through the Vedic period consciousness had been growing, but it was still an imaginative consciousness. The world was reflected through the human imagination, a world of gods and demons, in which the divine power was mysteriously hidden. But now the mind breaks through into pure intuition of reality. Man's first intuition had been blind and confused, that obscure intuition of ourselves with which we all begin our lives. As the light of reason grew, this intuition had been filled out with the forms of nature, with the consciousness of the world and the self, of physical and psychic being in which the divine spirit was seen to be reflected in the world of gods. Yet the intuition remained of a whole behind all this diversity, of 'one being' (*ekam sat*) of which all the forms of nature and the self were but 'names and forms' (*namarupa*).[53] Now in the *Upanishads* this intuition issues into the light, into a pure awareness of being, an absolute self-consciousness, an experience of the spirit, the atman, the self, as the ground of being and consciousness, the source of reason itself.

We must try to fathom this intuition of the Upanishads. It is basic to all human experience, it is the ultimate truth; it is 'that which being known everything is known.' It was discovered by the seers of the Upanishads and has been passed down in India from generation to generation; in it is contained the 'wisdom' of India. It has been known in other religions too, in the traditions of Buddhism and Taoism and in the mystical tradition of Islam. It has been present in Christianity from the beginning, and is the inner secret of the Gospel. But it has often been obscured, and today in the West has almost been lost. It is in the Upanishads that this intuition of ultimate reality has been most clearly expressed and where we can see it, springing, as it were, from its source. But to discover it we have to be able to receive it. It will not yield itself to any merely human effort or learning. "Not through much learning is this spirit reached, nor through the intellect, nor through sacred teaching, it is reached by him whom it chooses, to him the spirit reveals himself."[54] This is the great stumbling block. If we think that we can learn the meaning of the *Upanishads* by any methods of modern science, or philosophy or by Vedic scholarship or linguistic analysis, we are doomed to failure. The *Upanishads* demand a *metanoia*, a total change of mind, a passage from rational knowledge to intuitive wisdom for which few today are prepared.

Perhaps we can best approach this inner mystery of the Upanishads by way of the Katha Upanishad. It is a short Upanishad belonging to the middle period (about 500 BC), coming after the early period of the long prose Upanishads (the Brihadaranyaka and the Chandogya), written in verse and forming a real initiation into the secret doctrine of the Upanishads. It begins significantly with the descent of the young man, Nachiketas, to the realm of the dead to receive instructions from Yama, the god of death. In every great religious tradition, it has been recognized that to reach the final truth one must pass through death. It is the meaning behind Aeneas's descent into the underworld in Virgil, and of Dante's descent into hell in the *Divine Comedy*. It is, of course, the meaning of Christian baptism. 'You who were baptized were baptized into the death of Christ.'[55] We have to die to this world and to ourselves, if we are to find the truth. What Nachiketas asks of Yama is 'What lies beyond death?' This is the question which man has asked from the beginning of history and which people are still asking today. But an answer cannot be given on the level of rational discourse. "This doctrine is not to be obtained by argument," says Yama[56]. it can only be learned from one who has had experience of the mystery, who has passed through death into a new life.

This is expressed in the words which take us to the heart of the teaching of the *Upanishads*. "The wise man, who by means of meditation on the self, recognizes the Ancient, who is difficult to be seen, who has entered into the dark, who is seated in the cave, who dwells in the abyss, as God, he indeed leaves both joy and sorrow behind."[57] This is the death we have to undergo, to go beyond the rational understanding, beyond the imagination and the senses, into the primeval darkness, where God, the divine mystery itself, is hidden. It is a return to the womb, to what the Chinese call the 'uncarved Block,' to the original darkness from which we came. But now that darkness is filled with light, it is revealed as God. The senses, the imagination and reason by itself cannot pierce through the darkness, but when we die to ourselves, to the limitation of our mind which casts its shadow on the light, then the darkness is revealed as light, the soul discovers itself in the radiance of a pure intuition; it attains to self knowledge.

This brings us to the third aspect of this supreme reality, that of purusha. purusha is the cosmic man, of whom it is said "one fourth of him is here on earth, three quarters are above in heaven."[58] This is the archetypal man, the pole (*qutb*) or Universal Man, of Muslim tradition, who is akin to the Adam Kadmon, the first man and the son of Man, of Hebrew tradition. This is one of the most profound symbols of the ancient world. It is based on the recognition that man embraces both heaven and earth. Though his body occupies only a little space on a small planet, his mind encompasses the universe. This was beautifully expressed in the Chandogya Upanishad. "There is this city of brahman (the human body) and in it there is a small shrine in the form of a lotus, and within can be found a small space. This little space within the heart is as great as this vast universe. The heavens and the earth are there, and the sun and the moon and the stars; fire and lightning and wind are there, and all that now is and is not yet   all that is contained within it."[59] This is based on the view to which we must constantly return, that the universe is a unity and man is a mirror of the universe. He contains within himself the principle of all material elements and of all psychic consciousness, so that he is a 'microcosm,' a little world. So it was that the macrocosm, the 'great world,' came to be conceived as a Cosmic Man, in whom matter and life of consciousness are gathered into the unity of the spirit.

Purusha is the cosmic person, who contains the whole creation in himself and also transcends it. He is the spiritual principle, which unites body and soul, matter and conscious intelligence in the unity of a transcendent consciousness. The structure of the universe is described in detail (following the Samkhya Philosophy) in the Katha Upanishad. "Beyond the senses," it is said "are their objects, beyond these is the mind (*manas*), beyond the mind is the intellect (*buddhi*), beyond the intellect is the Great Self (*mahat*), beyond the Great Self is the unimanifest (*avyakta*), beyond the unmanifest is purusha. Beyond purusha there is nothing that is the end, that is the supreme goal."[60] This is the basic structure of the universe according to the Vedanta. First there are the senses (*indriyas*) and their objects the bhuta or elements. Then comes the mind, the *manas*, the discursive mind, which works through the senses, what today is called the scientific mind. It is the lowest level of intelligence, since it is wholly dependent on the senses, and is consequently fragmented and dispersed. Above this is the *buddhi*, the intellect or pure *intelligence*, the intuitive mind, from which the principles of reason and morality are derived. It is the 'nous' of Aristotle, the intellectus of St Thomas as compared with the *ratio* or reason. It is the point at which the human mind is open to the divine light. It is also the point of unification of the personality. It is at this point that we become fully human. It is at this

292

point that the drama of human existence takes place. If the *buddhi* turns towards the light, it is illumined by the divine light and transmits the light to the manas and the senses. But if the *buddhi* is turned away from the light then the mind is darkened and the personality is divided.

Beyond the *buddhi* is mahat, the Great Self, that is the cosmic order or cosmic consciousness. This is a concept which is scarcely to be found in western philosophy. Yet it is fundamental to the doctrine of the Vedanta. The *buddhi* is the point where the human being is individualized, where man becomes a person. But the human person is not isolated; it is a dynamic point of communion. Just as every element in the physical world is a dynamic point of relationship with every other element, so every human person is a point of intercommunion and the interdependence with every other person. The mahat is the sphere of consciousness in which the human mind opens upon the universal mind. In Buddhism it is called the 'store-consciousness' (*A laya-vignana*). It corresponds with Plato's world of 'ideas.'

Everything in the physical world has a psychic aspect, a psychological character. The idea which was propagated by Descartes, of a material world extended in space and time outside the mind, is an illusion. It corresponds exactly with what in Vedanta is called *maya*. It is a mental fiction. In reality the physical world is permeated by consciousness; it is one aspect of a complex whole. It is like a reflection in matter of conscious intelligence. In the ancient world it was always understood that every material thing has a spiritual counterpart. These are the 'ideas' of Plato, the intelligences of Aristotle and the Arabian Philosophers, the 'angels' of the Greek fathers and the scholastic theologians. These are the gods, the 'devas' of the Vedas.

For modern western man the gods and angels are relics of a discarded mythology, and of course they are mythological figures, that is symbolic forms; but they are symbols of realities. They are the 'cosmic powers' of St Paul, the powers that rule the universe the powers of earth and water and air and fire, of gravitation, magnetism and electricity. But these powers are not outside the sphere of consciousness. Just as our bodies with all their physical and chemical properties are contained within our human consciousness, so all the powers of nature are contained within the universal consciousness, the Mahat. In our experience these powers operate within the sphere of what has been called the Unconscious, but which is really another level of consciousness. Beneath the level of the reflective, rational consciousness there are other levels of consciousness, imaginative, emotional, vital and physical in which the cosmic powers act upon us. The gods and angels are reflections in the human imagination of the 'archetypes,' the primordial principles of creation, by which the universe is governed.

These powers, of course, are not only good but also evil. Besides the gods, the devas, the 'asuras,' the demons, and beside the good angels are the evil spirits, the *daimones* of the Gospel. It cannot be too strongly affirmed that these are real powers which act on the unconscious, as depth psychology has recognized; that is, on the lower levels of consciousness, bringing man into subjection to the powers of nature. The fact that modern man does not recognize them is one of the many signs that he is under their power; only when they are recognized can they be overcome.

Yet we must not think of these powers as separate beings without connection with one another. They are all parts of the cosmic whole, in which positive and negative forces are both at work, just as they are in the physical world. They form an ordered hierarchy of being representing different levels of consciousness. In the medieval Christian scheme of the universe there were nine orders of angels, beginning with the angels themselves, who are on a level of consciousness just above that of the rational human consciousness. Above them are the arch-angels, the 'thrones, dominations, virtues, princedoms, powers' of Milton's *Paradise Lost*, the powers at work in the destiny of nations, and finally the cherubim and seraphim, the powers of wisdom and love nearest to the Supreme. The evil angels are powers which are in rebellion against the cosmic order, centers of conflict, of violence and disintegration, at work in nature, in the individual human being and in human society. Of these in the Hebrew tradition Satan is said to be the head, the Diabolos, the Deceiver, the source of the Cosmic illusion, the Maya in Hindu terms, the principle of sin and ignorance (Avidya).

But beyond the mahat, the Katha Upanishad tells us, is the *avyak-ta*, the unmanifest. This brings us to the two final principles of the cosmic order, in the Sankhya Philosophy, the earliest system of Hindu philosophy, prakriti and purusha. The avyakta is mula-prakriti, that is nature, considered as the womb, the Mother, the ground of all the creative powers of the world. Prakriti is the principle of 'potentiality,' the first matter of Aristotle, which as we have seen has no being in itself, but is a sheer potency, a *dynamis* in Aristotle's terms, a capacity to be; in this womb of nature the seeds of all future forms of matter and mind lie hid. The gods as well as men all lie hidden in this primal darkness. It is the void, the emptiness which, in Buddhist terms, contains all fullness. It is the ground of human consciousness, the cave, the abyss of which the Katha Upanishad spoke, the unplumbed depth of consciousness, the deep sleep, from which consciousness arises and the world comes into being. But beyond this avyakta, this prakriti, is purusha, the Person, the Supreme, beyond which it is impossible to go.

Purusha is pure consciousness, or rather it is pure being and pure consciousness in one, because at this point all distinction of subject and object disappears. It has been called the 'Person of light consisting of knowledge.'[61] But how do we know this person? It is known by meditation. So the Katha Upanishad continues: 'a wise man should keep speech in mind, and keep that in the self which is knowledge. He should keep knowledge in the self which is the Great (the Mahat) and he should keep that within the self which is Peace.'[62] Here we have set before us the path to the knowledge of the Self. We have first of all to enter into silence, to shut out the world of the senses. Then we have to silence the mind, the busy active mind, in the self of knowledge, that is the *buddhi*, the point of integration of the personality. Now we have to surrender this self, the individual self, to the Great Self, the cosmic consciousness, to those higher spheres of consciousness beyond the rational mind.

Then finally we have to surrender this cosmic consciousness, which still belongs to the created world, to the self of Peace, the Peace which passes understanding. At this point we pass beyond the created world, physical and psychological, the world of men and angels, and we enter into communion with the Supreme, the purusha, the ultimate Reality. Brahman, atman and purusha are now known to be one. Brahman is the one eternal Spirit, infinite and transcendent, pervading the whole creation, one and yet manifold, the ground of all creation, "unseen but seeing, unheard but hearing, unperceived but perceiving, unknown but knowing."[63] In him all this creation, both gods and men and nature, are contained. Atman is that same eternal Spirit, infinite and transcendent, considered as the self of man, the ground of consciousness. When we transcend the limits of the rational mind and open ourselves to the cosmic, universal consciousness, we are carried beyond the limits of this world, both human and divine, and approach the Supreme, the 'one without a second.' This is the leap of faith, which cannot be reached by any human effort. It is the flight to the One of Plotinus. It is of this that the Katha Upanishad says, "He whom the atman chooses, he knows the atman."[64] The lower self cannot reach the higher self, it can only allow itself to be drawn up into its presence, to surrender itself to the self, to the spirit within.

This raises the question, What is the relation of the human spirit — the *jivatman* — to the supreme spirit, the Paramatman? Of this the Katha Upanishad says: "there are the two, drinking their reward in the world of their own works, entered into the secret high place of the heart. Those who know brahman call them light and shade."[65] The Svetasvatara Upanishad draws out this image: "Two birds, inseparable friends cling to the same tree. One of them eats the sweet fruit, the other looks on without eating." Then it explains, "On the same tree man sits grieving, immersed, bewildered by his own impotence (*anisa*), but when he sees the other, the worshipful Lord (*isa*) in his glory, his grief passes away."[66] This shows clearly the state of the human soul. The soul is set between the physical world, the world of the senses and the world of spirit. When it inclines to the material world and becomes attached to it, it becomes confused and powerless, but when it 'looks up and sees the Lord' then its grief passes away. If we would understand this relationship between the soul (the *jivatman*) and the spirit, we can think of the soul as a glass which is held up to the light of the spirit. When the glass is clouded by sin and ignorance, then the light cannot shine through, but when the glass is clean, then the soul is illuminated by the divine light and the whole being, body and soul, is irradiated by the divine presence.

The spirit in man is the 'fine point of the soul', as St Francis of Sales called it, the point of contact between the human and the divine. It is a reflection of the divine light in us. It is a dynamic point, turned to both God and the world. This is the 'pneuma', the 'spirit' of St Paul, as compared with the 'psyche', the soul, of which he says, "we have received not the spirit of the world but the spirit which is from God, that we might understand the gifts bestowed on us by God."[67] The spirit in man is a 'gift' or grace; it is the presence in us of the divine spirit. When body and soul are moved by the spirit, then the whole being of man is transfigured. This was the very purpose of creation from the beginning, that body and soul, matter and mind, man and the universe, might be moved by the spirit and drawn into the divine light and life. Sin is the fall from this state of grace into the state of the 'natural' man, the 'anthropos psychikos' of St Paul as opposed to the 'anthropos pneumatikos', the 'spiritual man.'[68]

There are schools of Hindu thought which consider that when the spirit of man (the *jivatman*) is thus united with the spirit of God (the *paramatman*), the individuality is lost. But this is not necessarily so. It is true that the individual soul ceases to exist as a separate being. It is transfigured by the light and participates in the very being and consciousness of God. This is the state of *saccidananda*, the state of being (*sat*) in pure consciousness (*cit*), in which is found absolute bliss (*ananda*). But the soul that enters into this state of bliss does not lose its individual being. It participates in the state of universal being and consciousness, it enjoys perfect bliss, but that personal being which was conferred on it by creation, that unique mode of participation in the divine being, which constitutes it as a person, is eternal. It may be that in the state of union, as many mystics have testified, the soul no longer experiences any difference between itself and God, but the difference remains. The very purpose of creation was that other beings, both men and angels, and through them the whole creation, should participate each in its own unique way in the one being of God. The state of union is often illustrated by saying that it is like a drop of water merging in the ocean, but it can equally be said that it is like the ocean being present in the drop. In the ultimate reality, the whole is present in every part and every part participates in the being of the whole.

This state of union has been beautifully described in the Svetasvatara Upanishad: "as a metal disk (or mirror) which was tarnished by dust shines brightly when it has been cleaned, so the embodied being (the *dehi* — the dweller in the body) becoming one, attains the goal and is freed from sorrow." Then the final state of the soul is described in unforgettable words: "When by means of the real nature of the self he sees as by a lamp the real nature of brahman, then having known the unborn, eternal God, who is beyond all natures, he is freed from all bondage."[69] This is perhaps the clearest statement in the Upanishads of the nature of ultimate reality. It can be known only by the purified self, the spirit in man, cleansed from all attachment to body or to soul. Then this purified spirit sees the real nature of brahman, the eternal being, mirrored in itself and in the whole creation. Finally this brahman and this atman is recognized as the 'unborn eternal God', the personal God, the purusha, who is the Lord of Creation, beyond all created being.

63. Ascent to the Godhead[70]

In A New Vision of Reality, *Bede Griffiths devotes a long chapter to the journey into the Absolute as it is set forth variously in the traditions of Hinduism. Once again but more quickly this time, he traces the ascending or interiorizing path to the Self as it appears in the Katha Upanishad. Successive stages of consciousness correspond to the ascending levels of the structure of the universe: senses (indriyas), rational mind (manas), contemplative intellect (buddhi), great self or cosmic consciousness (mahat), the unmanifest (avyakta) and finally the purusha, or cosmic Person. Briefly he indicates the praxis - the movement into silence (corresponding to the way of hesychia in the Christian tradition) by which one pursues this journey inward to the Self. Once again, as in* The Marriage of East and West, *Bede shifts to the alternative perspective of the four levels of consciousness — this time according to the Mandukya Upanishad — waking, dreaming, deep sleep and turiya, the state of the awakened atman, of supreme consciousness and of nonduality, advaita. Before moving on to outline the complexities of the yogic and tantric systems, Bede lingers for a moment in the light of this ultimate sunrise.*

In this chapter we are going to explore the ascent to the Godhead. We have seen in chapter three how a breakthrough in consciousness took place in the sixth century before Christ with the Upanishads and the Buddha. This was a breakthrough beyond the senses, beyond the imagination and beyond the mind, to the experience of the absolute, transcendent Reality. From that time there has been in India an exploration of these higher levels of consciousness which has gone further than anywhere else in the world. It is an exploration of inner space which is much more significant than the exploration of outer space. It is the discovery of the levels of consciousness in human existence, leading to the ultimate reality. This is something which has profound meaning for the whole world, and today many people are discovering it in the West as well as in the East. In the West particularly there has recently been the great discovery that there is this inner world to be explored, although knowledge and experience of it was by no means absent before, as we shall see here and particularly in chapter eleven.

We will trace this breakthrough to the transcendent reality in the Hindu tradition. The Buddhist tradition is no less rich, particularly in the Mahayana and in the Vajrayana of Tibet, but to explore that would take us too far afield. So we will concentrate on the Hindu development and see how that tradition has come to explore this reality. It begins with the discovery of *brahman*, the one Reality behind all phenomena. Then comes the realization that this one reality behind all phenomena is one with the Reality behind human consciousness. Whether we move from the outer world to discover the Reality behind it, or from the inner world to discover the reality within, we encounter this one Reality, the *brahman*, or the *atman*, the Self, as it is called.

What is involved then is the search for the Self, the inner Reality of the human being. This is expressed very well in the Isa Upanishad, which, as it were, summarises the doctrine, "He who sees all beings in his self, (*atman*) and his self in all beings, he loses all fear."[71] This is to discover one's self and the whole creation within and this is the goal of this yoga, as it came to be called. So we see at this stage the beginnings of the path of yoga. Here it should be noted that Vedanta is the doctrine and yoga is the practical method of how to explore, how to discover ultimate Reality. We have seen in the previous chapter and elsewhere some aspects of the Vedantic doctrine of the knowledge of that Reality.

The first indication is in the Katha Upanishad, one of the earlier Upanishads dated at about 500 BC, where we see, first of all, the structure of the universe and of human consciousness, as it had come to be understood at this period. There it says, "Beyond the senses *(indriyas)* is the mind, the *manas*. Beyond the mind is the intellect, the *buddhi*. Beyond the intellect is the mahat, the great self. Beyond the *mahat* is the *avyakta*, the unmanifest, and beyond the unmanifest there is *purusha*."[72] This is what Ken Wilber calls the "spectrum of consciousness", the degrees of knowledge, which starts from the senses, the indriyas, through which immediate experience comes. The mind then works on the senses and the aspect of mind working on the senses is the manas, this term being derived from the root *ma*, to measure, so the manas is "the measuring mind." This is the lowest level of mind. Beyond this is the buddhi, the intellect or higher intelligence. This is the mind which knows transcendent reality and the first principles of being and of truth. Aristotle called this the *nous* and St Thomas Aquinas called it the *intellectus*. Whereas the manas is equivalent, in St Thomas's understanding, to the *ratio*, the logical, analytical, discursive aspect of the mind which goes from one thing to another, the intellectus is the pure intelligence.

So far we have gone beyond the senses and the mind to the intellect, but the next stage opens new ground for most in the West. This next stage is that of the *mahat* which is the great Self, the cosmic Self, or cosmic consciousness. Cosmic consciousness arises from the understanding that the world of the senses, the physical world, is a unity in which everything is interconnected. As the science of today says, the whole physical world is a web of interrelated being, and we are part of that web of interrelationships. So also our individual consciousness is part of a larger consciousness in which we all participate. This is the cosmic order, the cosmic consciousness. In that, as we shall see later, are included all the higher realms of being, the angels, the gods and the cosmic powers.

Beyond that world of the mahat is the *avyakta*, the unmanifest. Before anything comes into manifestation to be known by the mind,

300

it is first unmanifest. It is in the seed. That is what is called *mula prakri-ti*, the root nature or the cosmic nature, in which all is gathered up. Using the language of David Bohm we could say that this is the implicate order. The mula prakriti is where all things are implicated in one, like a seed from which the whole creation comes. From the mula prakriti the whole creation comes into manifestation in the world that we see. Then beyond the avyakta is *purusha*, that great cosmic Person whom we have been considering, and he is the end. Beyond purusha there is nothing. He is the goal. So we move from the senses and the mind to the intellect, to the cosmic consciousness, to the unmanifest and finally to the supreme person. Later, as we shall see, further distinctions are made within that ultimate, that person. But at present the purusha is the end.

The Katha Upanishad then shows the path to this supreme goal. The text says, "A wise man should keep down speech in mind." Speech is that by which we go out of ourselves, communicate to others, and when we begin to meditate we have to withdraw from speech into the mind, into the *manas*. Then "he should keep the mind within the self which is knowledge."[73] That is, we should bring the manas into the buddhi. The manas is discursive, it goes from one thing to another, whereas the buddhi is single-pointed, *ekagraha*, one-pointed. It is "the still-point." It is the key point where we open on the transcendent. It must be realised that not only does modern western philosophy not go beyond that but, in fact, it has hardly reached that point. In the West the mind simply stops at the manas. But in the Hindu tradition, beyond the buddhi is the mahat, the great Self, so we open up on the transcendent, cosmic order. It was common knowledge to all ancient people that beyond the human is this cosmic order. The angels in the medieval Christian tradition were part of this, and there were nine orders of angels, nine orders of consciousness, beyond the human. The human is the lowest level of consciousness and beyond are all the other orders. In the Hindu tradition there is this vast cosmic order beyond. It corresponds to a large extent with the world of ideas of Plato, while in Plotinus it is the *nous* which includes all the ideas from which the whole creation comes forth. It is here in Plato and Plotinus that western philosophy comes nearest to the eastern tradition, although these developments tended to be lost later on in the West.

So one goes beyond the buddhi to the mahat, which is cosmic consciousness. Then the Katha Upanishad says he should keep that "in the self which is peace,"[74] the shanta atman. One goes beyond the world of the gods and of the angels which are at the limit of creation to the uncreated, to the source, which is shanta, peace, the peace which passes understanding. One goes beyond understanding, beyond the mind. So that is the path of yoga. One of the first uses of the term yoga itself is found a little later on where the text says, "When the five instruments of knowledge, (that is the five senses) stand still, together with the mind, the manas, (when one's senses are still and the mind is still) "and then the intellect, the buddhi, does not move." When, in other words, one has brought one's whole being to the still point, then "that is called the highest state."[75] When all the external activity ceases, then the interior reality begins to unfold.

We need to notice how this is completely contrary to the western tradition which imagines that when one gets to the intellect one has come to the end. In the eastern tradition the intellect is really only the beginning, when one has gone beyond the gross world and is entering into the subtle world and into the transcendent. The buddhi is the path to that, but the highest state is beyond both the mind and the intellect; it is the transcendent state. Then the Katha Upanishad goes on to say, "This firm holding back of the senses is what is called yoga." So yoga was first the holding back of the senses. Later, in the yoga of Patanjali, yoga is defined as *chitta vritti nirodha*, the cessation of the movements of the mind. When the mind stops moving and centers in itself, then yoga begins. And yoga means union, uniting. "Yoking" is the same word in English. It is the integration of the whole person. All the elements in our nature have to be brought into that unity. At that stage one experiences oneself, one's atman. So that is the path which is mapped out at this stage in the Katha Upanishad.

This development may be traced next in the Mandukya Upanishad, which explains this higher state of consciousness in a remarkable way. The text speaks of four levels of consciousness, the waking state, the dream state, the state of deep sleep and the fourth is *turiya*, the transcendent state. In our waking state, which we imagine to be real, we are in the world of the senses and of the mind, and that is the lowest level of consciousness. In the dream state we go beyond the outer world and begin to experience the inner world. This does not mean ordinary dreaming but the deeper, inner experience of our inner world, the subtle elements. Beyond that is *sushupti*, the state of deep sleep, when one goes beyond one's bodily senses and beyond one's mind, into a deeper center, but of course one is not ordinarily conscious of it. The fourth state, *turiya*, is when one enters into that deep centre in full consciousness. That is the aim of meditation, to go beyond the waking, the dreaming and the deep sleep state into this transcendent consciousness.

The text then has a remarkable description of the fourth state, which is considered the most significant in all the Upanishads and in all Hindu tradition. It says the fourth condition is atman, the Self in its own pure state, the awakened life of supreme consciousness. It is neither outer nor inner consciousness, or semi-consciousness (that is, not the ordinary outer waking consciousness nor the inner consciousness nor something in between the two), nor is it the consciousness of deep sleep. It is neither consciousness nor unconsciousness, for at this stage one has gone beyond the opposites, the dualities, altogether. "It is atman, the Spirit, that cannot be seen or touched, that is above all distinction, beyond thought, and is ineffable."[76] In other words, one goes beyond one's senses, one's imagination, one's mind, and beyond word, until one comes to the Absolute beyond. And union with him is the supreme proof of his reality. This appears totally unreal to the ordinary mind, but when one experiences it one knows the supreme Reality. One knows it by itself. One cannot know it by one's reason or by one's intellect, but only when one enters into it does one know it. The great seers, Ramana Maharshi, for instance, in modern times, are those who experience the inner reality and know the self (*atmavidya*). He, this inner reality, is "the goal of evolution", the end of the whole evolution of consciousness, and "he is non-duality, *advaita*." Dualities are made by reason, and at this stage one has gone beyond one's reason so that there are no more dualities. He is peace and love, *shanta* and *shiva*. Shanta is the ordinary word for peace, while Shiva means "the blessed one," "the kindly one." Shiva, which is here used as an adjective, means "benign" or "kindly." It can be translated "love," although that may be a little strong. So that is the Ultimate as described in the Mandukya Upanishad.

64. The Ultimate State of Consciousness[77]

As Bede concludes this chapter of A New Vision of Reality, *'The Ascent to the Godhead,' he turns once again, with evident pleasure, to the ultimate state of realization of the Self. Quoting Ken Wilber's descriptions again and again, Bede characterizes the final state not as a consummate abstraction from the 'inferior' realities which have been transcended, but as an integration of all reality into the supreme consciousness. This supreme consciousness, moreover, has been fully present from the start! The path brings one, finally, to what one most truly is and has always been. The perfect circle completes itself. In his delight with Wilber's evocation of the ultimate state of consciousness Bede forgets the caution which has often marked his own expressions of nonduality and leaves his Christian correlations and corrections for another chapter. This journey of the development of consciousness, he writes in conclusion, is essentially the same in the different Asian traditions.*

The final stage of the ascent to the Godhead can be summed up in a quotation from Ken Wilber, who has worked deeply in this area. In a very impressive passage he writes of this ultimate transcendence. Wilber is one of the few who have really grasped what is involved here. So many stop at an emptiness, at a void, and leave out the world. Wilber uses the Buddhist term *svabhavikakaya* for this ultimate state of consciousness, while in the Hindu tradition it is called *sahaja samadhi.* It is the state in which we have returned to our own nature. Having found the Ultimate, the person is totally at one with the whole world. One gets the impression that one is going out of this world to the Supreme but now comes the discovery that when one reaches the Supreme, it embraces every level of reality. Every level of reality is included in it. This is how Wilber speaks of it: "As unknowable, unobstructed, unqualified consciousness, it shines forth in completion from moment to moment, like an infinite series of ever newly perfected states, forever changing in its play, forever the same in its fullness." In other words this is perfect rest and perfect activity, the two poles united in one. "It appears to be the end limit of evolution but is actually the prior reality of every stage of evolution from first to last. This was present from the beginning." In other words, whereas one thought one was rising from one level to another, on coming to the end one realizes that one has come back to the beginning. "In just this way it is always and perfectly unattainable, simply because it is always already the case, timeless and eternal. It is just that and all attempts to attain it, even in the casual realm, are finally undone. It is understood to have been fully present from the start." Again and again it is said that one cannot reach liberation; one is free and through all the stages one is trying to get to a state where one already is. It is a matter of discovering who we are and what the universe is. "It is understood to have been fully present from the start, never lost and never regained, never forgotten and never remembered, always already the case prior to any of that. As infinite, all-pervading, all-embracing consciousness, it is both one and many, only and all, source and suchness, cause and condition, such that all things are only a gesture of this one, and all forms a play upon it." Wilber goes on to say that it demands wonder. Wonder is one of the signs of the awakening to brahman. The Kena Upanishad says, "He is seen in nature in the wonder of the flash of lightning; he is seen in the soul in the wonder of the flash of vision."[78] This is that wonder which goes beyond everything, the sudden awakening. So, "As infinity it demands wonder, as God it demands worship, as truth it demands wisdom (*jnana*), as one's true self it calls for identity." In other words, one finds one's self. "In its being it has not instructions and this no-trace continues for ever. Bliss beyond bliss beyond bliss, it cannot be felt. Light beyond light beyond light, it cannot be detected. Only obvious, it is not even suspected. Only present, it shines even now." That is the Ultimate. One has returned to where one was at the beginning, but now in total consciousness. So that is the evolution of consciousness leading to the ultimate state, or ascent to the Godhead, as it has come down to us through the Hindu and the oriental traditions.

65. The Supreme Knowledge
The path of spiritual growth which Bede has been outlining for us can be described in terms of a progressively deeper knowing. While he has been con-

cerned with the issue of knowing from the beginning,[79] only occasionally does he focus upon it - as here, in the course of his commentary on the Bhagavad Gita. *And now it is a question of the supreme knowledge in which everything else is known: the unitive knowledge of the Self.*

I[80]

Commenting Gita 13.11,

It is Vedanta which is intended to lead to the Supreme Knowledge, "the vision of truth which gives liberation." Without the knowledge of the inner self all knowledge is ignorance. It is unrelated to the truth itself. Scientific knowledge by itself is also ignorance because it is simply knowing a part. It is simply an empty knowledge unless it is related to the Supreme. There is a significant movement among scientists today to relate scientific knowledge to the knowledge of the atman, the Reality behind the whole cosmos and all sensory and psychological experience.

Knowledge of science or philosophy will never give one immortality. Wisdom is a knowledge of experience, not a so-called objective knowledge which is really only a partial knowledge. Wisdom is the knowledge which involves our inner being and transforms us. If we know the Self we become the Self. This is wisdom; this is knowledge of brahman.

II[81]

Commenting Gita 13.24,

A better translation is, "Some by meditation, by dhyana, behold the Self in the Self by the Self" (Besant & Das). That is contemplation. When we withdraw beyond the senses, beyond the mind, to our inner person, we discover that indwelling Self. It is by the Self that we know the Self. We cannot know ourselves by the ordinary rational consciousness. We have to go beyond the rational consciousness to the intuitive awareness. It is a unified knowledge: knowing the Self, in the Self, by the Self. It is the difference between intuitive knowledge which is unitive, bringing our whole being into unity, and discursive knowledge which goes from one person to another, from one thing to another. The latter is our ordinary way of knowing; the former is this withdrawing into the buddhi, into the inner center, and uniting all the faculties in one. Then we know the Self by the Self in the Self. And that Self is the Paramatman within, the Supreme Spirit within. At that point we are united with the One. We should keep in mind the illustration of the light shining in the mirror. When the mirror is clouded, we do not see the light. When the mirror is clear, in meditation, then the light shines in and we are simply aware of the light within, we are transparent to the light. Then we know the Self in the Self by the Self. This is what in Christian terminology is called contemplation.

66. The Knowledge which is Love[82]

Bede is commenting Gita 18.55: "By love he knows me in truth, who I am and what I am and when he knows me in truth he enters into my Being." Here, at the end of the Gita, we have arrived in the country of John's Gospel and of the Christian mystical tradition.

"By love he knows me in truth." This love leads to knowledge. In Christian doctrine, true knowledge of God is always 'love-knowledge,' or as St Paul puts it, "the knowledge of the love of God which surpasses knowledge."[83] This is the precise nature of mystical knowledge. When we enter into this depth, this peace, this awareness of brahman, we discover our inmost Self. At the point of the buddhi we encounter the atman, the inner Self. We enter into communion with brahman, with the Reality, the Eternal everywhere, in everything, and within that brahman, at the heart of that brahman, we find the Lord, the personal God. This is the path of self-knowledge, leading to the knowledge of God in all things and finally to the knowledge of the personal being of God. Love, bhakti, is an essential element in this knowledge. That is the ultimate goal. At this stage we become one with the personal God. This is exactly the teaching of St John's gospel. "If a man love me, he will keep my word, and my Father will love him and we will come to him and make our abode with him."[84] And again, "He who abides in me and I in him, he it is who will bear much fruit."[85]

67. Action in Inaction[86]

In River of Compassion *we encounter a distinct shift in values from the teaching of the* Upanishads *which Bede had presented in earlier books* (Return to the Center, The Marriage of East and West). *Together with worship and devotion directed toward a personal God, active work in this world is presented as a valid spiritual path. This work, however, is to have a distinctive quality, which corresponds to the spiritual core of the the earlier ascetical way. It is to be done with detachment - both from the work itself and from its rewards. Ultimately, it is to become an expression of the realized Self. This paradox of inaction-in-action may recall the unknowing-in-knowing which has characterized the journey beyond self to the Self.*

Bede is commenting the Gita 4.18, "He who sees inaction in action and action in inaction, he is wise among men."[87]

The idea of action in inaction is found in the Chinese concept of *wu wei*, or active inactivity. In Taoism, that is the key to all life. The Tao Te Ching says that the power which is the first principle of all creation is eternally inactive, yet it leaves nothing undone. This is paradoxical but the meaning is clear, that every action has to come from an inner center of quiet and peace. We act through the body and the body is controlled through the mind, and the mind is active. But both body and mind are to be controlled from an inner center of reality which is perfectly inactive and still.

It is a state of concentration, of stillness at the center. The inner being is perfectly still, perfectly harmonious, perfectly integrated, united with God; and then from that inner stillness all action flows. Then the action is harmonious according to the law of God, and to the law of nature. That is "action in inaction." It is something that is largely lost today. This is why the world today is so filled with activity, with the 'work ethic,' as it is called in America. It is activity which has no fundamental rest. Once we let action take over, then all that is said about karma is true. We are bound by our actions. This is what happened with the whole industrial system; it cannot be controlled. It has released forces which simply control men, reducing them to slaves of the machine. We have to be rooted in the beyond if we are to have any peace or justice or harmony.

Since the Renaissance the tendency of the West has been to eliminate systematically that beyond, to make science and reason control everything, with the aim of having 'man' in control of the universe. But the result is that he is completely subject to the law of karma. The inevitable forces of nature will drag him down. He cannot escape it. The only escape, as the Gita is teaching us all the time, is to free ourselves from the body, from the mind, above all from the dominion of the scientific mind, and discover the center of peace within. Then we have inactive activity, "action in inaction." The Sanskrit phrase is *karmani akarma. Karma, action; akarma*, inaction. Inaction in action, or worklessness in work.

68. From Self-realization to Service

I[88]

Here Bede develops at some length one aspect of that new development in the spirituality of the Gita[89] which we have already seen. Self-realization no longer appears as the unique and ultimate goal; it is also the condition which enables a person to serve the world with freedom and fullness. Bede is commenting Gita 5.29.

Here is the teaching of the Gita which is also the teaching of the *Upanishads*. When one reaches the true Self, the atman, the very center of one's being, one also reaches brahman, the very center and ground of the whole creation; and that atman, that brahman, is the Lord and is an object of love and worship. So the whole of this yoga finally flowers in worship and love.

This implies also a respect for the creation in which the Lord is present. Ramakrishna gives the impression, which is so common in Hinduism and even in certain forms of Christianity, that the spiritual path is always going beyond this world, until we eventually reach a state of *samadhi* when there is no more activity of any kind. He says that at first we are *bhaktas*, we worship God, we sing songs to God, and we praise the Lord of Creation. But as we go further the soul is lost in God and does not remain in the body for more than twenty-one days. It simply passes beyond.

This attitude also appears in Abhishiktananda's book, *The Further Shore*. The urge to be always going beyond is one aspect of Hinduism. The perfect man is one who has simply gone beyond this world. He has no further concern with the world at all. It is an aspect of the Christian ideal of the monk who, beyond all community life, has gone into solitude and is only engaged in prayer and waiting for death when he finally reaches his consummation. We should not reject that ideal altogether for it is an aspect of life and of *sadhana*. It is one direction in which the spiritual life moves, in the freeing of ourselves from attachment to the world, to the body, the senses, the feelings, the imagination, the mind, and the will; and also the freeing of ourselves from all human contacts and from all human society to become one with God in this ultimate depth of our being.

However the journey does not necessarily stop there, because the God whom we reach at this point is the God of the whole creation, the God who creates and redeems humanity and the cosmos, and who is a God of love. Therefore when we reach that state we enter not merely into pure consciousness, but also into pure love. That love then completely fills our life; it may, and usually does, direct us to some kind of work or service. This ultimate spirit is a dynamic power; it is the Holy Spirit which is love. When we surrender ourselves to it we surrender ourselves to a love which then compels us and may drive us in any direction to whatever work we have to do.

That is the way in which we can escape from the dilemma of simply being taken out of this world. From the Christian point of view it is fundamental that the life of the Spirit is not simply a way of escape from the world. People often say that it is selfish to be simply seeking one's own salvation and then to pass beyond. Each religion, each tradition, has felt this problem. In Buddhism it is noteworthy that the early Hinayana or Theravada tradition was simply intent on reaching nirvana. The *arhat* is the perfect man who has reached nirvana and has passed beyond.

Then at about the time of the Bhagavad Gita, there was the bhakta movement of devotion to a personal God, which later spread all over India. In Buddhism this led to the conception of the *bodhisattva*, who, when he is reaching his goal, makes a vow not to enter into nirvana until all sentient beings have been liberated.

Here the great compassion of the Buddha comes into play. The Buddha himself, instead of passing beyond and entering nirvana after his enlightenment, devoted himself to the liberation of the world. For the rest of his life he preached the Dhamma, the path of liberation. So the bodhisattva is the holy man who is devoted to the salvation of the world. This compassion of the bodhisattva is portrayed in the beautiful figures on the walls of the caves of Ajanta. Buddhism thus has a profound sense of compassion and of service. Similarly in Hinduism there is the path of pure sannyasa, of going beyond, but equally there are the saints of Hinduism, the bhaktas who rejoice in the love of God. Even Shankaracharya, though he was a great advaitin, wrote hymns in praise of God. Having profoundly experienced the One beyond all duality, he spent his life in propagating the doctrine of advaita or nonduality, which led to the renewal of Hinduism. He went all over India and established maths or monastic centers at the four corners of India, so that this doctrine might be spread everywhere.

The two elements are always there and in any spiritual life it is essential to keep this balance of the opposites. On the one hand we are being carried beyond everything to God alone, beyond the whole creation, while on the other hand the very power of God, the Spirit of God moving in us, directs us towards love and towards service. Every Christian and every religious person is called to this pure contemplation, to realize God, but each one has her own gift, her own charism, which calls her to serve the sick or the poor, or to teach, or to preach, or to write books, or whatever it might be; but it should come from this depth of self-realization, God-realization. It should not come from the level of the three lower chakras. There is always the danger that we just work from an ordinary human level; we have some prayer and some spirituality to sustain our work, but without going any deeper. But the deeper one goes in the vertical direction towards God the more one should be able to go out in every horizontal direction towards humanity. Jesus is the perfect example. He lives in communion with the Father and is totally one with the Father; in this bliss of Oneness he is totally open to the whole of humanity. He surrenders his life totally for the world.

A distinction is often made between a lower bhakti and a higher bhakti. The former is simply singing songs and loving God in a rather sentimental way, and that is fine as a beginning, but there is also a higher bhakti. That is the love which engages the ultimate depth of the soul. St John of the Cross describes it as an experience of love which is actually God himself loving in us. It is not our love any longer. The love of God has taken possession and he is living, acting, and moving in us. That is the final fulfillment and that divine love can send us in any direction. We are simply in its hands. It is not for us to decide what we are going to do any longer. That for me is the final answer, and I think the Bhagavad Gita is moving all the time towards that position.

There is a strong tradition of this in Hinduism, but the conflict is never quite resolved as to whether the perfect man is the one who leaves the world, or who is at the service of the world. Perhaps one cannot resolve it.

II[90]

Once again, the highest realization is that state in which one has transcended the opposition of contemplation and action and acts from a contemplative consciousness with perfect freedom. Bede is commenting Gita 15.19

Vedantic philosophers often talk as though when one reaches the supreme state there is no longer a Lord to adore, there is no worship, there is no love left. One simply is that One and this is considered to be the supreme state. But that is only a particular level of consciousness. If we go beyond that level, there is activity, there is love, there is adoration. We come back to the origin, in a sense. We become like a little child, but with the wisdom which comes from total fulfillment.

This has to be understood in the light of the Christian tradition of contemplative life. Those who reject the contemplative tradition remain at the lower level of faith and activity, which is very good in its way, but is far from perfect. The division is often made between the active life and the state of those who have reached this higher state of samadhi, of contemplation. But there is a higher state still, which goes beyond both and fulfills both. One can be a contemplative, in perfect stillness, and at the same time fully active. Jesus was the perfect example of that. Many Christians interpret Jesus in the New Testament simply as a man going about doing good, helping people and always busy and active, and they do not realize that he had gone beyond. In his six weeks in the desert and in the depths of his being he was enjoying pure samadhi. He was a pure contemplative, always abiding with the Father as the source of his being, and always seeing what the Father does as the source of his action. He is in that state of transcendent awareness in which he is one with the Father, and at the same time perfectly natural and human. That is why, in the case of the Gospels, the three Synoptic Gospels have to be corrected by the Fourth Gospel. St John profoundly grasped the depth of the inner life of Christ, and was able to see his whole life and work in the light of this inner experience.

This state is known in Hinduism as *sahaja samadhi*, the state in which the yogi has gone beyond all forms of asceticism, of sadhana, and is able to live and act with perfect naturalness. Of this Ramana Maharshi in our day is the supreme example.

III[91]

This final chapter [of the *Gita*] is again concerned with the question of the relationship between sannyasa, or renunciation, and working for the world. The question is the very practical one of how to relate contemplation and action. That was one of the main themes in the earlier chapters and now it is taken up again. This chapter begins with a distinction which has not been found before, between sannyasa and tyaga. Tyaga is best translated as surrender.

> Gita 18.2 The renunciation of selfish works is called renunciation; but the surrender of the reward of all works is called surrender.

The distinction here is between renunciation of selfish work, that is, all work which is dictated by the ego, the lower self, and surrender of the reward of work, even though its motive may be unselfish.

This can be compared to the ideal of the bodhisattva in Buddhism. In the earlier Buddhism the accent is on the search for nirvana, freedom. One follows the Noble Eightfold Path to reach this final nirvana and then one passes beyond. The bodhisattva of the later Mahayana tradition made a vow not to enter nirvana and receive the reward of his works until all sentient beings had been saved. The ideal here is that after renouncing the world, one returns to the world in service. This is the ideal of the Gita, and that is why Mahatma Gandhi took it as his bible. The aim is to renounce all reward for one's work and to work for the benefit of the world.

18.3 Some say that there should be a renunciation of action -
since action disturbs contemplation; but others say that works
of sacrifice, gift and self-harmony should not be renounced.

This has been a problem both in the Christian and the Hindu tradition. Pure contemplation is very difficult if one is leading an active
life. Therefore, they say, give up the active life for pure contemplation.
But the ideal which the Gita and the Gospels put before us is the
renunciation of the self so as to enter the state of contemplation and
knowledge of God and then to allow one's action to flow forth from
contemplation.

The types of good works are *yajna, dana,* and *tapas.* Yajna is mainly religious sacrifice, but it can be taken in a wider sense. Dana is alms-
giving, and tapas is self-discipline, self-control. . .

69. *The Value of Work in this World*[92]

*What is the relationship between the inner Self and the exterior person? What
is the value of life and activity in this world? Bede weighs four of the Hindu
views on these issues and concludes with a position in the Bhagavad Gita which
is close to that of the balanced theological mainstream of Christian tradition.
God and the human person are seriously engaged with life and history in this
world. Bede is commenting Gita 5.9*

Now here we begin to come upon a problem. The idea is to work
from the center of the person, but what is the relation between the
inner self, which is at peace and in harmony, and the activities of the
senses and the mind? There is one view which suggests that we are
completely detached from our work. This view holds that although
the body, senses and mind are working, we are not working; we
remain totally detached and indifferent. In fact there are three ways in
which this activity can be understood.

One is that all the activity of the world comes from nature, from
prakriti. This was the view of the old Sankhya system. Nature here
includes the mind. The senses, the mind, and even the intelligence, the
buddhi, are all part of nature, and it is these that are working. But
purusha, the person, the inner consciousness, the spirit within, is perfectly inactive and is the witness, not involved at all. This is a sort of
dualism. We encountered the same view in the previous chapter: that
one can keep oneself in that state of inner detachment and let the

314

body function on its own. This is a very common view in Hinduism.

The second view is that of Sankara. According to him all the work of nature, prakriti, is ultimately maya. It has no ultimate reality. If we are involved in it, it is real to us, but if we wake up to supreme wisdom, *paravidya*, and realize brahman, then we realize there is no activity at all. It is pure illusion, it is like a mirage. All activity in the world is ultimately unreal. The only object of life is to get beyond all activity. That is why in that tradition, the pure *sannyasi* does not do any work. He must reach the state where all work ceases except for what is unavoidable; for instance, he has to eat a minimum amount of food to keep the body going. They say of the *jivan mukta*, the one who has realized salvation or liberation while still alive, that he has nothing to do. He simply survives here and looks on, but there is nothing he can do.

Implicit in this view of Sankara is that all the activity of this world is ultimately purposeless. It is a very strong belief in the Hindu tradition that this world ultimately has no meaning. This belief derives from the cyclic view of life. The world comes out from brahman and there is activity, and then it goes back to brahman. There is no meaning or purpose in it. The wise man allows this to go on. He lets the work of nature go on in him, thinking and acting and doing, because his body is still involved in the world. But he is completely detached from, and indifferent to, the whole process.

There is a third view beyond these two which is that the world and all activity is a *lila*, a play of God. This was the view of Ramakrishna. The great mother is playing, and all that goes on in the world is her play. By itself that is hardly satisfactory for it means that all the suffering of the world is ultimately meaningless. The concept of lila, however, can also be interpreted in the way towards which the Gita is working and which the modern Hindu certainly supports, namely that this lila of God has a meaning and a purpose. In this view God is not merely at play but is purposefully active in the world. That seems to be the deeper meaning of the Gita, though it is not held quite constantly.

This is consistent with the Christian understanding of the activity of God. The Crucifixion reveals that suffering is redemptive. The

315

sufferings of this world have a meaning and a purpose and lead to a final fulfillment. God assumes the sin and suffering of the world into his own being, redeeming it and bringing it to fulfillment. On the other hand, many Christians tend to be too involved in history, in work, in service to suffering humanity, and so tend to lose sight of the other side of it. There is a sense in which all this world is passing away and we have to fix our gaze on that which lies beyond. The Hindu, on the other hand, does not realize sufficiently the reality of the human person, of his sufferings, of his destiny, and that this life has an ultimate purpose. It is not just a lila, a play. So what is important is to find an equilibrium, realizing the values of this world, of time and history, but seeing them in the light of eternity. It is always so difficult in one's own life to find this balance. Either we give too much importance to what we are doing, as though everything depends on that, or we give too much importance to prayer, to the world beyond, in New Testament terms, to eschatology.

In the New Testament, the early view was that Jesus was to return at any moment. The *parousia*, the second coming of Christ, was expected at any time so that everything that was done in this world was very relative. St Paul advised, "Those who are married, let them be as though they were not married. Those who buy in the market as though they did not," and so on. The world was a sort of temporary phase which they had to carry on with while they were waiting for the parousia. It was only after some time that the church began to realize that the world was going to last much longer than they had anticipated. Perhaps it is only today that we are realizing the full importance of life in this world. Right through the Middle Ages it was something one had to endure; one had to do one's best, one had to do one's duty, waiting all the time for the world beyond. Now we have gone to the opposite extreme. Many say there is no world beyond. We have got to find everything in this world, we have to find our fulfillment now. So we are always swinging between these two poles. We have to find an equilibrium. There is no simple answer; each person has to find the balance within himself. This is one of the places where Hindu and Christian have to meet together and work together. We must learn from one another. That is the secret.

70. *Changing the World while Looking Beyond*[93]

Bede is commenting Gita 5.11, "The Yogi works for the purification of the soul: he throws off selfish attachment, and thus it is only his body or his senses or his mind or his reason that works." This is a different, apparently regressive position in the Bhagavad Gita, from which Bede moves to an affirmation of the value and importance of work in this world. Again, though, he urges a balance between the two views: we are to work earnestly to change the world, to build for the Kingdom, yet with hearts Godward and free.

Now here another problem comes up. Even if we say that we are to work, to be active, still the idea remains — and this again we find in Christian monasticism — that the work is done for self-purification. It was particularly common in the early monastic tradition. If good works were done, it was for the monks' self-purification. There was little interest in other people. If we serve patients in a hospital, we may not be interested in the patients, but simply in our own purification by means of the work done. That can be a very dangerous standpoint. The *Gita* is saying that one is working for the purification of the Self: the body, the mind, and the senses go on working but the inner self is completely detached from the whole process and is not really concerned. Here then is a problem. The motive Krishna gives for doing the work is really only that it is our *dharma*, duty. Why does Arjuna have to fight? Because he is a warrior and because this is a righteous war. It is the duty of a warrior to fight in a just war. Therefore do your duty, whatever it may be. It is your *swadharma*, your own duty, according to your caste, to do your service in the world. You do it with complete detachment, without feeling the work has any real meaning or purpose in it. You are purifying yourself and you are going to get your own eternal reward, but not in this world. This again is a common view in the Hindu understanding. The world has no ultimate purpose in it. It is all a cyclic movement. It all goes round and round. It was the Hebrews who brought the idea that the world is moving towards a goal and that there is a purpose in it. Even so, it is very difficult to believe that much of the work done in the world is meaningful.

For a person working in a factory, in mass production, for a clerk in business, or for most people in fact, this is the only attitude they feel they can adopt. The attitude is: I have got to earn my living. I do this work for eight hours a day because it is my duty, but I keep my mind completely detached from it. I have no interest in it at all, and in fact I dislike the whole concern, but I keep my mind free, and I try to live a human life outside my work. That is a very common attitude. I think that it is also fairly general in the Christian tradition, along with the idea that we do our work as a duty.

In the past people did their work, whatever it was, for the glory of God and for the salvation of their souls, but were not really interested in changing the human situation. Even today that accusation is made. We build schools and hospitals which keep the present social system going but we do not enquire whether that system itself is not essentially unjust, so that a great deal of work is being put into perpetuating an unjust social system.

There are those who say that we should come out of our institutions and change the structure of society, perhaps joining the Marxists in total revolution. In the Christian context the idea of bringing about change is expressed by saying that in Christ God becomes incarnate, enters time and history, and changes the course of the world. This world has a force in it now which is directing it towards a final fulfillment and in the world we are working for the Kingdom of God. That is a vision common to many modern Hindus and many modern Christians.

Again it is a question of where the emphasis lies. Nowadays the emphasis is more and more on actual change in this world; changing ourselves, changing society and making a more human life. In doing this it is understood that we are working with God. This was the concern of Mahatma Gandhi. He felt that traditional spirituality tended to be too directed toward oneself, its aim being to become completely detached and to live a pure and holy life in devotion to God, while the world was left to go on its own way. For Gandhi it was of crucial importance to change the world.

In this understanding one is working with God for the evolution of the world, for the change of humanity toward a final goal. But there is a danger also in this point of view. If we think too much about changing this world, we can become terribly frustrated because even where a new social order is instituted, as in Soviet Russia, China, or elsewhere, although some improvement may have been made, after a few years the same problems arise in a new form and others present themselves, so that in the end things are a good deal worse. So we begin to ask what is the point of all this? Even though our work is to change the world for the sake of the Kingdom of God, we have also to be always looking beyond. As Jesus said, "My Kingdom is not of this world." So a balance is needed as we endeavor to hold these two opposites together in a living, harmonious tension. Precisely how to do that is one of the main problems of life.

71. The Pure Heart: Surrender and Detachment

In the last texts[94] from River of Compassion, we have seen something new coming forth in Bede Griffiths' presentation of the spirituality of Hinduism. As he moves from the doctrine of the Upanishads to that of the Bhagavad Gita, Bede's own view seems to enter a new and very significant phase of development. We observe an interiorizing, a descent and an opening. The absolute exterior renunciation of the sannyasi[95] gives way to an interior attitude, a disposition of the heart, in a movement which resembles the transition from law to Gospel. The yogi's unwavering ascent to the nondual Self[96] gives way to a descending movement of service to the world: a way of Self-realization which is open to everyone. The following two texts from River of Compassion describe the interior attitude which is at the heart of this new orientation. It is summed up in these two phrases: self-surrender and detachment.

I[97]

Bede is commenting Gita 12.12, "for concentration is better than mere practice, and meditation is better than concentration; but higher than meditation is surrender in love of the fruit of one's actions, for on surrender follows peace."

"Better is concentration than mere practice." I think that this is a good translation, the word simply is *jnana* which means knowledge, primarily, but it seems that it means here that concentration of the mind in knowledge is better than mere yoga practice. Better than simply concentrating the mind is the state of *dhyana*, when the mind dwells on the object of meditation and the mind is filled with that object. It is like an even flow of oil, the mind is in a state of even flow. So that is a better state still, but "higher than meditation is surrender

319

in love of the fruit of one's actions, for from surrender follows peace." The meaning of this seems to be that total self-surrender in love brings one to God more effectively than any other method. So that is the path of the Gita and that is the path which many follow. Such self-surrender to God is the most fundamental way and anybody can practice it. A mother with twelve children trying to earn her living by coolie work can still surrender to God, to the will of God. To accept the will of God in everything that comes, in total self-surrender, is the most perfect way and the most universal. It is not that there is a lower way which everybody can practice and a higher way for a few. The commonest, most universal way is the most profound. The others are special ways. And this is also the difference between the layman and the religious. It is not that the religious has found a better way. For the layman to do the will of God in his state, whatever it is, in total self-surrender, is the perfect way. A religious man adopts certain methods, which can help him to make that surrender but it is not necessarily a better way. The religious who does not achieve his goal of self-surrender is far worse than the layman or the devotee who has made a real surrender.

II[98]

Bede is commenting Gita 12.18, "The man whose love is the same for his enemies or his friends, whose soul is the same in honor or disgrace, who is beyond heat or cold or pleasure or pain, who is free from the chains of attachments..."

"The man whose love is the same for his enemies and his friends." Christians often think of the Gospel teaching, "love your enemies, do good to those who hate you," as something specifically Christian but it is really universal. It is present in Buddhism, and it is equally strong here.

'Attachment' is a key word. Attachment is selfish desire. The soul is at the center in its living relation with God, with the Supreme, and it has the world around it. It can enjoy the world and all the pleasures of the senses and values of human relationship, but without any attachment. The only attachment is to the Lord within. Then one attains the perfect state. But normally we get attached to people, to things, to work, above all to the ego and this is what is fragmenting us. This attachment is sin.

Detachment, therefore, has to apply at every level. It is necessary to be detached, as the Gospel says, from father and mother, from wife and children, from everything we have. Total detachment is the condition of total love. It is not a sort of puritan asceticism; it is total detachment from the self, total surrender to God and therefore a total love for others. It is a total compassion and understanding. That is the aim.

72. Faith[99]

As Bede Griffiths nears the end of his commentary on the Bhagavad Gita in River of Compassion, *we encounter point after point of convergence with Christianity. This is probably the first time that Bede has discussed faith at any length in the course of the several books which he has devoted to Hinduism. He offers a universal conception of faith, however, which would be unacceptable to many Christian theologians who are accustomed to defining faith in terms of a specific revelation through the divine Word. Faith, for Bede, is essentially an interior reality: it is the one divine light shining through the atman, or divine Self, into the mind. Faith, then, is coextensive with human participation in the divine Absolute. Bede is commenting Gita 17.1*

This raises the question of faith. It is more meaningful to look at it in terms of the scheme of first the senses, then the manas, the mind, which works through the senses; next the buddhi, the point where we receive the light from above, and finally the atman, the Supreme, who is shining into the buddhi. The light of the atman shines into the buddhi, the intelligence, and then it is reflected in the manas. Faith is really the reflection of this light of the atman, the Supreme, in the manas, the rational mind. Wisdom or knowledge (jnana) is when we rise above the manas, above all these images and concepts and awaken to truth itself through the buddhi, the intelligence. This makes it easier to grasp what faith is and also helps to see why there can be such tremendous diversities of faith.

Faith is reflected through the manas, which is the mind working through the senses and the feelings, and therefore through the whole cultural environment. This means that the same light of truth can shine in this man and that man, yet each will see it and interpret it and understand it in terms of his own culture. The one light of truth, the

321

one reality, is shining through the whole of creation, through the whole of humanity and through every different culture. Thus the one light of truth is broken up. A good image of this is to think of the one light and the many colors, where each culture is like a color which reflects, as it were, a certain aspect of the one light. This applies to all peoples; to primitive African tribal culture, Australian aborigines, the American Indians, the tribal people in India and Asia. The same light of truth is reflected in different measures, in different degrees, in all these different cultures and cultural complexes with their rituals, sacrifices, prayers, dance, songs, music and worship. With time these complex smaller groups form into the wider religions and then into the world religions: Christianity, Buddhism, Islam, Hinduism. The same one light is shining in each and each one is receiving the truth in its own way. It is very important to see that the one light of truth is shining into every human being through the buddhi and into the manas and the senses. It is broken up at all these different levels. But each is in contact with the truth. There is no human being to whom the truth, or God and grace in religious terms, is not coming in some way. It comes to him through the cultural complex in which he is living, through the images, the modes of thought, the ways of expression, the style of life and so on. Faith is the awakening to the light of truth in our own minds. It is never simply that we believe somebody; that is only the initial stage. Faith proper is always an illumination of the mind from the Supreme.

As he comments the following verses of chapter 17 of the Gita (17.2 and 17.3), Bede extends his conception of faith downwards and outwards, to include every human aspiration and desire. True faith, however, is participation in the divine truth: that is, participation in God.

17.2 The faith of men, born of their nature, is of three kinds: of light, of fire and of darkness. Hear now of these.

17.3 The faith of a man follows his nature, Arjuna. Man is made of faith: as his faith, so he is.

A man is what his faith is because the one light is shining through to each person, and what everybody is seeking, whether they know it or not, is God. One may seek God through drink or through power or through sex or through philosophy or through science, but as a human being one is seeking that truth or that ultimate experience. It is the dynamism of our nature. A man may think that he is an atheist and conceptually he may be an atheist, but the urge to the absolute, to truth itself, to God, is in his nature, and an atheist may be very near to God. He may be seeking the one reality while conceptually he has rejected all images and concepts of God preferring to call himself an atheist. We are what we believe and that applies to any level of existence.

Everybody lives by faith. That is why despair is the worst thing, for to despair is to lose the meaning of life. So Krishna says, "the faith of a man follows his nature, man is made of faith: as his faith is, so he is." And that, of course, applies on every level. If we have a true faith, if we are really illumined from above and receive this true light into our heart, then we are conformed to the truth. Faith is actual participation in the divine truth. That was St Thomas' idea when he said that faith is the *semen gloriae*, the seed of glory. Already the same light which will illumine us in heaven in fullness is present by faith. It may be a tiny spark, but it is a spark from the eternal. So faith links us to the absolute.

73. Nonviolence[100]

As a young man Alan Griffiths was caught up, along with his companions, in the social concerns of the times. Under the influence of a charismatic headmaster at his school he became a socialist.[101] At Oxford he joined the Labour Club and anti-war organizations.[102] But "my faith in socialism and in any form of political action soon declined, as I began to question the whole character of our civilization."[103] This is the voice that is familiar to us in Bede's books, with their reiterated condemnation of western civilization. Even in his writings during the years of monastic life in England, there is little evidence of social concern. His attention and energies had been drawn away from the political and economic world into the alternative world that church and monastery provided. When Bede moved to India, however, through the work and writings of Gandhi he began to develop an integral vision in which contemplative interiority could find its expression in tranformative social action. Bede studied the work of Vinoba Bhave, Gandhi's disciple,[104] seeking a way to contribute to the sarvodaya movement (Bhave's program of renewal of village life in India) as a Christian. At Shantivanam, he initiated a series of projects on behalf of the poor villagers living near the ashram.[105] Gandhi's teaching on non-vio-

lence resonated deeply with Bede's sense of the Gospel and with his vision of reality.

Until now it has been a matter of debate whether it is legitimate for a Christian to refuse to fight, but now the question must be whether it is legitimate for him to fight at all. Even in the last war it was difficult to find a moral justification for the 'area-bombing' of Germany, and still more for the use of the atom bomb on Japan. But now the means of destruction have become so indiscriminate and their effects so far out of proportion to any conceivable 'just' end, that the whole concept of a 'just war' seems to be imperilled.

This, however, is a matter for moral theologians and ultimately for the church herself to decide. But there is another aspect of the problem which should be of more serious concern to the individual Christian. Moral theologians tend to be concerned with finding how far it is possible to go in any particular direction without actually committing sin. But the Gospel of Christ is not concerned merely with the avoidance of sin: that, on the contrary, is what in terms of the gospel comes under the 'law'; it is concerned to show the ideal of life which Christ sets before his disciples. In the Sermon on the Mount we have the Christian ideal set before us in the most absolute terms, and this is the very essence of the Gospel. It is not just a counsel of perfection given to a few chosen disciples; it is the call of the Gospel itself, addressed to all men and summoning them to a new way of life.

At first sight these words strike us as an overwhelming paradox; they seem to be contrary to all normal human values. "Blessed are you poor. . . Blessed are you who are hungry...Blessed are you who weep...Blessed are you when men hate you and cast you off and revile you, when they reject you as something evil for the Son of Man's sake. . . ." These are words which it is difficult even now for us to accept. Is not the whole philanthropic and humanitarian work of the world aimed at relieving poverty, hunger, misery, oppression, and here it seems these very things are praised? It is the same in regard to property, to marriage to courts of law; Christ seems to call on his disciples to renounce all civil institutions. "Unless a man will renounce his father and his wife and his children and everything that he has, he cannot be my disciple."

There is a deliberate force of paradox in these words which warns us not to take them too literally, but at the same time they are meant to present a challenge to all our worldly values. Christ does not deny the value of civil institutions, of property and marriage and law courts; nor does he deny the need to relieve the poor and the hungry and the afflicted. But he wishes to assert that all natural institutions and all human values are of no account in comparison with the kingdom of God. A Christian may accept what this world has to offer; he may marry and possess property and defend himself at law, but he must be prepared to sacrifice all these things at any moment. We cannot exaggerate the radical renunciation which the gospel involves; we can never properly 'belong' to this world again.

It is in this light surely that we must read the words about non-resistance to evil, which strike us still more with the sense of paradox. "But I tell you that you should not offer resistance to injury; if a man strikes you on the one cheek, turn the other cheek also towards him; if he is ready to go to law with you over your coat, let him have your cloak with it; if he compels you to attend him on a mile's journey, go two miles with him of your own accord. . ." Christ does not here deny the right to self-defence; he acknowledges the right, but he calls on his disciples to renounce this right. It is not a command; like the call to renounce marriage and property it is a 'counsel'. But it is a 'counsel' which is offered to all; it is part of the universal challenge of the gospel.

This call, therefore, not to resist evil is embedded in the very heart of the Gospel. Like the call to renounce marriage and property, it is part of the challenge of Christianity. This is the conception which we need to recover in our present situation. It is not a question whether it is 'legitimate' to fight in a war, but whether the world has not reached a point where we may be called upon to renounce this very 'right.' At least we have surely reached the point where we must face this question seriously. We can no longer simply accept war as part of a normal life. It has become something so vast, so inhuman and so destructive that it challenges us to ask whether there is not a way out, a way which is indicated by the Gospel itself.

At present it must be admitted that the command "Resist not him that is evil" has become almost a dead letter in the church. We are sure that it does not take away from us the right to self-defence and from that we go on to accept a whole system of defence by modern weapons of war till the gospel counsel ceases to have any meaning. In the same way we know that we have the right to marriage and property, and so we put all our energies into building up a world, based on these two institutions, which grows more and more complex every day, until we almost forget the meaning of the words, "Unless a man renounce his father and his mother and wife and children and all that he has, he cannot be my disciple." Thus there is the fearful paradox that Christianity, which is based on poverty and non-violence, has come to be identified in the eyes of so many people with capitalism and war.

How has this come about? In the early church there is no doubt that the sense of urgency of the Gospel was overwhelming. The first act recorded of the church after Pentecost was as we have said that "all the faithful held together and shared all that they had, selling their possessions and their means of livelihood, so as to distribute to all as each had need." It is true that we hear no more of this experiment in common living and presumably the need of private ownership soon reasserted itself, but the gesture is significant. It shows the original impulse of the church in regard to private property, and it was destined to endure and to take permanent form in the church in the religious orders, which make the renunciation of private ownership the basis of their way of life.

In the same way we know that in the early church, that is the church of the first three centuries, the command not to resist evil was taken very literally. The Christians believed that they belonged to a new age, an age in which nonviolence was now the law. So they boasted: "We do not draw the sword against any nation, and we no longer learn to fight, because we have become, thanks to Jesus, sons of peace." (Origen). Military service was not forbidden, but it was not encouraged. It was not considered worthy of a Christian. His duty was not to fight but to pray, and it was thus that he could best serve his country. This was, of course, the attitude of a small community of Christians in the midst of a great empire, in which the regular army could be trusted to defend the country. The Peace of Constantine would change all that, and yet it retains its significance for us still.

But the non-violence of the early church was carried further than this; it was carried to the point of death. The goal of life in the early church was found in martyrdom; this was the consummation of the Christian ideal. This is what gives its peculiar character to the early church. The Christians of those days were not afraid to marry and to possess property and to carry on business of all sorts, but they were made to realize that all these things might be taken away from them at any moment. They lived under the constant threat of martyrdom. And this was recognized not as something to be feared but as something to be desired. It was in this way that the Christian could best follow his Master. It was not by fighting but by suffering and death that he would overcome the world and establish the kingdom of God.

It is impossible to exaggerate the strength of this Gospel of non-violence in the early church. It was by this that the Roman Empire was overcome. The whole power of Rome was organized to crush this religion; yet it had to admit defeat and Christianity itself became the religion of the Empire. But this very victory brought with it a change. From this time the ideal of non-violence seemed to lose its power in the church. Gradually the ideal of the 'martial' virtues, first of the Romans, then of the Gothic peoples, was substituted, and the ideal of Christian chivalry was formed. There is no doubt that this ideal had its own beauty, but it belonged to a very limited period of history and was open to grave abuse. It was not an intrinsically Christian ideal but an attempt to 'baptize' pagan virtues. The result has been disastrous; it has simply been the triumph of paganism. The Christian nations have become distinguished above all others for their violence and brutality, and the very ideal of non-violence seems to have faded from men's minds.

There have, of course, been honorable exceptions, like the Quakers, who have preserved the ideal of non-violence down to the present time. But if we would see the force of non-violence in the modern world, we have rather to turn to India and to Mahatma Gandhi. It was he who, partly through the influence of the Gospel and partly through that of ancient Indian thought, recovered the ideal

327

of non-violence for the modern world. This ideal is basic in Indian religion and, one may say, in the Indian character. The Indian has always understood the true strength of character which lies in non-resistance, and it is this which makes an immediate appeal to him in the Gospel. On the other hand, he is all the more shocked to find how little place it has in the life and thought of so many Christians. But it was the genius of Mahatma Gandhi which enabled him to discover in non-violence a means of political and social action which was found to be no less effective against the British Empire than the early Christian action against the Roman Empire.

Maritain, in his *Man and the State*, has written of the importance of Gandhi's example in words which deserve to be quoted. "In my opinion, Gandhi's theory and technique could be related to and clarified by the thomist notion that the principal act of the virtue of fortitude is not attack but endurance; to bear, to suffer with constancy. One has then to recognize that there are two different orders of means of warfare (taken in the widest sense of the word), as there are two kinds of fortitude and courage, the courage that attacks and the courage that endures, the force of coercion or aggression, the force that inflicts suffering on others, and the force that endures suffering inflicted on oneself. There you have two different keyboards that stretch along the two sides of our human nature, opposing evil through attack and coercion, a way which leads at the last extremity if need be to the shedding of the blood of others, and opposing evil through suffering and enduring, a way which in the last extremity leads to the sacrifice of one's own life. To the second keyboard belong the means of spiritual warfare."

This is surely a suggestion of great value to us today. We need to recover this ideal of 'spiritual warfare,' of a form of non-violent resistance, which is specifically Christian and at the same time is the highest form of courage or fortitude that can be found. It is, certainly, no easy form of virtue. As Gandhi himself always insisted, it demands complete self-conquest before it can become effective. In other words, it is essentially a call to sanctity. It cannot be practised without training and leadership. Gandhi spent all his life trying to train his people for this, and in the end he had to admit himself defeated.

Yet it is something to which many people feel themselves drawn. It seems to be the only way of giving oneself wholeheartedly to a cause without seeing it ruined by the use of unworthy means. Maritain has also spoken of the need of a new type of sanctity today. May it not be that we have here the means of such a new type of sanctity?

It is not, of course, a virtue which can be practised in isolation. It has to be closely related to the other virtues which constitute the Christian ideal, especially to poverty, chastity and obedience. In fact, it is among the religious orders that one would like to see this ideal take the deepest root, so that it is seen habitually as an essential element in Christian perfection. But it should not be confined to the religious orders. It needs to be embodied in social and political life and become a force of inspiration there.

Communism, it is generally recognized, cannot be finally overcome by force. Ultimately, it can only be overcome by a spiritual force greater than its own. It has often been said that Mahatma Gandhi was fortunate in having the British to deal with, since they could always be trusted to observe a certain code of honor, however ruthless they might be on occasions. But would his methods have been of any use against communism? In the same way, the early Christians were able to overcome the Roman Empire, but again the Romans, although they were far more ruthless than the British, had not the communists' absolute ruthlessness and determination to eliminate all religion. Can a technique of passive resistance be found which can not only endure all that the communists can inflict but also convert them?

It may be said that communism represents the spirit of absolute violence. Violence belongs to its very essence: it arises from the nature of its creed. Materialism is of its nature a kind of violence to the spirit of man. It is an attempt to subject everything, and above all the human person, to the law of matter, and the law of matter is the law of violence. It seeks to impose itself on every form of spiritual life; it seeks finally to subject everything to the power of this world.

Non-violence on the other hand is essentially an affirmation of the law of the spirit. Gandhi described it as the 'power of truth' and the 'power of love.' It is the power of truth because it is the recognition of the spiritual ground of all reality and the determined effort to bring everything, that is, all matter, into subjection to this spiritual law. It is the power of love because it is the recognition of the spiritual character in every man and the inviolable respect which this demands.

Gandhi saw clearly that one must be absolutely uncompromising in one's attachment to non-violence. You can counter the absolute spirit of violence in communism only by a no less absolute spirit of non-violence. Once you allow any compromise to enter in, however legitimate it may be from another point of view, the whole strength of resistance is lost. One must be committed to the principle of non-violence utterly and completely to the point of death. The secret of the power of non-violence was revealed in the death of Christ. There was then revealed a love which was capable of bearing every insult and torture and, finally, death, without the least resistance, and which thereby raised up a new power of life capable of transforming the world. The secret of this power still remains within the church; it is her secret, her hidden life. The church and the world depend on our power to learn this secret and to show forth this life.

VI

CHRISTIANITY
AND THE EASTERN RELIGIONS

Central to Bede Griffiths' life and work, we have seen, was the problem of the integration of East and West. For him this meant the bringing together of the values of Hinduism and Christianity, Vedanta and Gospel. We find in his works only brief references to the other major Asian traditions, Buddhism, Confucianism and Taoism. This continuing process of dialogue and integration between East and West, between Hinduism and Christianity — these two dualities are not identical — will find expression continually in Bede's thought and writing. It will also be expressed concretely in his life — and in the life of Shantivanam, where Christian faith is embodied in the forms of a Hindu monastic tradition.

Bede Griffiths' Hinduism was first of all the unitive, interior spirituality of the Upanishads. Here the massive complex of Indian religious experience and thought concentrates itself at a single point: the nondual Absolute, which is experienced through the Self, or atman. It is this unitive wisdom which Bede brings to bear upon the Christian revelation and tradition in *The Marriage of East and West*. Sometimes, at this point, it seems that Bede Griffiths is confronting a diminished Christianity with a distillation of the most profound elements of the Hindu tradition. The centrality of the Christ-mystery and the primacy of love will be reasserted, however, and usually in Bede's conclusion. The interaction proceeds by juxtapositions, assertion and counterassertion, by comparison and contrast, never arriving at a final balance or integration. A little later, as Bede comments the Bhagavad Gita in *River of Compassion*, we seem to experience a shift in the balance of his own perspective toward the Christian side: person, faith and love, service and creative action in this world emerge strongly alongside the purely 'contemplative' values of the Upanishadic tradition.

331

In what way can we hope to realize a 'marriage of East and West'? Bede will sometimes characterize East and West as two complementary modes of consciousness, two ways of knowing. On this level there can certainly be an integration: both in the individual person and in a cultural community. Unitive, participative, intuitive consciousness and rational, analytical mind are, after all, complementary aspects of the one human person. On the deeper level of religious experience, the matter may be at once simpler and more complex. The question is simpler because of the universality of participative faith and of its blossoming in unitive or contemplative experience, corresponding to a basic human potential. It is more complex because of the radical uniqueness of each historical religion and of each personal experience and faith-response. We must remember, also, that Christianity is not equivalent to 'West' for Bede. The mystery of Christ transcends the East-West duality and could have been realized with equal or greater fullness in an 'eastern' way. In fact, however, he finds the historical development of Christianity dominated by a 'western' mentality. Bede sees Hinduism and Christianity as distinct and complementary. Through responsible dialogue, both the differentiation and the complementarity become more and more clear. Perhaps here, ultimately, is the meaning of the 'marriage.'

The passionate unitive momentum of Bede's mind makes all of this appear, at times, less difficult than it is. This same unitive passion breaks through the conceptual structures of Christian tradition, opening the way to a liberation and fresh manifestation of the inner form of the Christ-mystery. While this new unfolding must take place in several dimensions, Bede, drawing from the common wellspring of Asian thought, pursues it first along the way of pure interiority. When this interiorizing thrust is later balanced with a more 'incarnational' tendency, Bede's basic drive toward transcendence will retain its primacy. He looks always toward a realization - beyond form and concept - of the pure unitive Absolute, the Mystery which Christians call God and Father.

In Bede Griffiths' early writings he will often present the relationship between East and West explicitly in terms of fulfillment: the intuitions and realizations of Hinduism over thousands of years can only find their complete realization in Christ and the Gospel. At other times, as we have seen, he will speak in terms of complementarity. None of the religious traditions — Christianity included — is sufficient by itself; only in the flowing together of all the streams of spiritual wisdom and experience can the fullness be realized. These two perspectives — themselves complementary — continue to alternate and to interact in Bede's thought until the end of his life without ever coming to a final equilibrium. Given both the limitations of historical Christianity and the ongoing dynamic of the Christ-event, the two terms — complementarity and fulfillment — signify two dimensions of a mystery which will continue to unfold. Without pretending to grasp the overall shape of the development, we can taste in Bede's work the fruits which this encounter with the East offers Christians: at once a new breadth of consciousness and a new depth of self-understanding.

In the context of this encounter between East and West, we include some of Bede's writings on the *universal wisdom*, or *perennial philosophy*. This, as we have seen,[1] is a 'primary myth' for him, expressing his basic unitive conviction: at the center of all the religious traditions of humanity, as at the center of all reality, lives a single Mystery. The perennial philosophy and the Christ-mystery, like 'East' and 'West,' continue to interact within Bede and within his thought throughout his life.

74. The Incarnation and the East[2]

An essay which appeared in The Commonweal *in 1953 clearly expresses Bede Griffiths' view of Christianity and the East before he went to India, and before a new era dawned with the Second Vatican Council. In this confidently christocentric vision, history unfolds as a triumphal expansion of the incarnation through a series of encounters with new peoples and their cultures, until all of humanity has been incorporated into the body of Christ. Effusions of fresh creative energy occur at the moments of encounter of the Gospel with a new people, as a new cultural world is integrated with the revealed Word "in a vital act of creative thought." From his secure rampart of Catholic faith, Bede's mind sweeps over history and over the peoples and cultures of the world with what seems an invincible religious certainty and an effortless intellectual mastery.*

Today, however, he sees Christianity challenged by the encounter with the eastern religious traditions; only by an assimilation of the Asian cultures and wisdom into our theology and spirituality will the door of Asia be opened to the Gospel. If the Gospel has hardly penetrated the Asian peoples, it is largely because it has been presented to them in the language of an alien culture rather than their own. The highly developed spiritual traditions of Hinduism, Buddhism, of Taoism and Confucianism present a challenge to Christianity which may be more profound than the challenge of Greek culture to the early church. The encounter must take place at the deepest point in each tradition; that is, at the point of origin, in the root. This will mean, for Christianity, a more profound self-understanding, a more vigorous spiritual life. The promise of such a new era of encounter and assimilation, Bede writes, is both a further extension of the incarnation to these peoples and a new and deeper discovery of the interior and contemplative dimension of Christianity itself.

To believe in the incarnation is to believe not merely that God became man, but that God became man at a certain time and in a certain place. It is to believe that the divine has entered human history and given it a new meaning and a new direction. It was no accident that Christ was born in Judaea, when Herod was king, and Augustus was emperor. He came in his own words when "the time had been fulfilled," at the moment which St Paul was to call the "fulfilment of history." The whole history of the world had been leading up this point and the whole history since that time is determined by it. For the incarnation does not affect man as an individual alone; it affects the whole of human culture and civilization.

This can be seen in the first great crisis in Christianity, which is reflected in the New Testament. Up till this time the divine revelation had been confined to the Jews. The Jewish culture had remained a thing rigidly apart, strenuously fighting for its own tradition and refusing all but the minimum contact with the Greek and Roman world. With the coming of Christ this barrier was broken down; "He made of the two nations (Jew and Gentile) one," as St Paul said, "breaking down the wall that was between them." Thus with Christianity the Hebrew tradition entered into the inheritance of the Graeco-Roman world, and it is to the fertilizing contact of these two cultures that the church owes her liturgy and theology and canon law.

The next great crisis in the history of the church was that of the barbarian invasions of the fifth and sixth centuries. Having assimilated the culture of Greece and Rome, the church was faced with the hosts of 'barbarians', Goths, Lombards, Franks, Saxons, living outside the borders of the Roman Empire. Again it was the fusion of these two cultures, the Graeco-Roman culture of the church and the primitive but strong and deep culture of the barbarians, which produced the civilization of the Middle Ages.

Thus the incarnation set in motion a development of history by which the Roman Empire became Christian and then, with the conversion of the barbarians, first of the western nations and then of the eastern Slavs, the whole of Europe. The incarnation, we may say, was extended to the whole of Europe; for the church is nothing else, in Bossuet's words, than Jesus Christ extended to mankind.

The next phase in this development of history came with the Renaissance and the discovery of America. Another continent was added to the sphere of the incarnation. At the same time there was the beginning of missionary endeavour, with St Francis Xavier, in the Far East. It is true that there had been Christians in India from an early time and that there were Nestorian Christians in China in the seventh and eighth centuries, but one cannot speak of a real cultural contact of Christianity with China and India at this time. But can we speak of any real cultural fusion of Christianity with the people of the Far East even at the present time? It is a remarkable fact that in spite of Christian missions over a period of four centuries, Christianity has still only touched the fringe of the civilization of the Far East.

What is the reason for this? It is surely the fact that Christianity has been presented to these people in a form of western culture. It has never penetrated the inner life and thought of the East. Thus it is left for us at the present day to face the next great crisis in the history of Christianity, the extension of the incarnation to the East. Christ has become incarnate in Europe and America; He has still to become incarnate in Asia and Africa. Africa, however, does not present such a serious problem; for the native cultures in Africa are not sufficiently strong to demand any great modification of the form in which Christianity is presented to them. But the civilizations of China and

India are not only of the greatest antiquity but also culturally the most profound which the church has encountered since the first days of her mission in the Roman Empire.

It is a remarkable fact, as Karl Jaspers has pointed out in *The Origin and Goal of History*, that in the sixth century before Christ a movement of thought took place which was to shape the destiny of the greater part of mankind for all future time. It was the time of the Hebrew prophets in Palestine and the first Greek philosophers in Europe, of Gautama Buddha and the seers of the Upanishads in India, of Lao-Tzu and Confucius in China. Each of these movements seems to have risen spontaneously without contact with the others and each developed along its own lines so as to form a separate culture. At a certain point, as we have said, the Greek and the Hebrew traditions met and blended, and in the same way with the spread of Buddhism in China and Japan, the Indian and Chinese traditions were fused. But until the present day there has been no comparable fusion of the eastern and western traditions.

This, then, would seem to be the problem with which we are faced today. We realize, as never before, that we belong to 'one world'. Politically and economically, no one nation can stand apart from the rest. At the same time during the last fifty years the wisdom of the East has become known to us, as it had never been known before A book like Aldous Huxley's *Perennial Philosophy*, with its very extensive bibliography, shows how far the fusion of eastern and western thought has already gone on a more or less popular level. Mr Huxley's conception of the relation between eastern and western thought, like that of René, Guénon, Coomaraswamy, and other exponents of eastern tradition, is, of course, not satisfactory from a Christian point of view, but it puts the problem before us in all its urgency.

We are faced with a tradition of philosophy and mysticism, of art and morality, of a richness and depth not excelled, and perhaps not equalled, by the tradition of Greek culture which the church encountered in the Roman Empire. What then is our attitude towards it to be? It is clear that we cannot simply reject it. The attempt to impose an alien culture on the East has proved a failure. There are no doubt elements in this tradition which we may have to reject, just as the

336

church had to reject certain elements in the Greek tradition. But what is required of us is something much more difficult. It is an effort of discrimination, such as the Greek fathers from Clement and Origen to Gregory of Nyssa and Dionysius the Areopagite undertook, not merely rejecting what is wrong but assimilating all that is true in a vital act of creative thought.

It was by this creative energy that the structure of theology was built up by the Greek Fathers, gradually assimilating the principles of Platonic philosophy until they had been incorporated into the very tissue of Christian thought and life. In the same way we know how St Thomas and St Bonaventure in the Middle Ages took up the thought of Aristotle and built that also into the structure of Catholic theology. It is also important to remember how very great was the influence of the Arabian philosophers, Avicenna and Averroes, on the mind of St Thomas, so that a vital contact was made at this point between the Christian and the Islamic traditions.

We have, therefore, in Christian history the evidence of a continuous movement of assimilation, by means of which different forms of culture have been integrated into the Christian tradition, to guide us in our attitude to the cultures of the East. This process of assimilation may extend not only to modes of thought but also to forms of worship. The best example of this is the development of the Slavonic liturgy in the ninth century with St Cyril and St Methodius. It is possible that we may see a corresponding development in China. We know that permission for a Chinese rite was granted in the seventeenth century, though it was afterwards unfortunately withdrawn; and Abbot Lou, the great Chinese convert, who became a monk of St André, in Belgium, was of the opinion that China would never be wholly converted to Catholicism until a Chinese rite was again permitted. What is certain is that there will have to be a contact between Chinese and Christian thought on a deep level, before the Chinese mind will ever become Christian. Abbot Lou suggested the foundation of a Chinese college in Rome, at which both the Chinese could study Catholic theology and Catholics, in turn, could become acquainted with the Chinese classics.

The same process is obviously required in our approach to India.

There is need for a profound study of the doctrine of the Upanishads and of the whole tradition of the Vedanta, and also of Buddhist thought of both the Hinayana and the Mahayana schools. This is a work which will require the greatest discretion. We cannot afford to reject any of our western heritage, as it took shape in the thought of Aquinas, but at the same time we have to open our minds to what will be a genuine development of Thomism, bringing out vast potentialities which are latent in it. There is already much that is common to the western tradition based on Plato and Aristotle and the eastern tradition both of China and India. What is required is a meeting of the two traditions at a deep level of understanding, so that their full potentialities can be realized. This will require on our part a real effort to assimilate the mode of eastern thought, for eastern thought differs from our own most of all in its mode. Whereas western thought tends to be rational and discursive, eastern thought is intuitive and contemplative. The one is the product of the *animus* the other of the *anima*. The difference is therefore primarily psychological.

The meeting of the eastern and western minds will thus be a true marriage of East and West, the masculine mind of the West meeting with the feminine mind of the East in a fertile union. But if the union is to be really fruitful, it will require a generous giving of self on either part. For a long time now the West has taken the path of extroversion. We have concentrated on science and mechanics and all forms of rational philosophy. We stand in desperate need of the opposite process of introversion, of intuitive thought and interior life such as the East can teach us. On the other hand, the East is now turning to our western civilization, whether in its communist or its capitalist form, and is in danger of losing its own roots in tradition. The meeting of East and West which we have in mind, therefore, will be a return of both to what is deepest in their own traditions, the recovery of their roots in the past.

The advantage which we ourselves may hope to gain from this is immense. There are already a great number of people in the West who owe their conversion to Christianity to the discovery of eastern thought. It would seem that the superficial manner in which the Christian faith is often presented has driven many people away from the church, and it has required the contact with the mind of the East to make them realize the deeper aspect of Christianity.

For those who already possess the faith, the deepening of their life of prayer and the enlargement of their insight into the mysteries of the faith can be considerable. But if eastern thought is to have this effect upon us, we have to approach it with great reverence. We must realize that the tradition of the East embodies what is practically a revelation of God to mankind. It is derived from that primitive revelation of God in the order of nature, which was made to man in the beginning, and was renewed in the covenant with Noah. For Noah is the Father not only of the Jews but also of the Gentiles; he is a type with Melchisedech and Job, of that primitive religion which existed all over the world before the election of the Jews and the special revelation made to them. Though this primitive revelation has been obscured and distorted in some respects, it remains nevertheless at the basis of the eastern tradition.

We have, therefore, not merely to impose a western religion on the people of the East, but to show them that their religion finds its true fulfilment in Christ. Clement of Alexandria maintained that what the law was to the Jews, philosophy was to the Greeks — a 'pedagogue' to lead them to Christ. We may say the same of the great philosophical traditions of India and China. The Buddha, Confucius and Lao Tzu were genuine precursors, as Guardini has said, preparing the mind of the East for the coming of Christ. It is through them that the people of the East have up till this time received the light and grace of Christ.

This then is the new light of the incarnation for which we have to look at the present day. Christ has to become incarnate in the East, not as a western teacher come to destroy what they have learned from tradition, but as he came to the Jews, as the fulfillment of all their hopes and desires. Doubtless this will present the same test for the East as it presented to the Jews. There will be the temptation to cling to the old forms and refuse to allow them to grow into the new life which Christ brings. But there must be nothing done on our part, as far as we are able, to alienate Christ from them. We have to remember that Christ belongs neither to the West nor to the East. By divine providence he was born between East and West, and belonged to a people which could mediate between the two. Our religion is not western in its essence, nor is it eastern. It transcends the division of East and West, and offers the one ground on which the two can be united.

Once again we recall the words of Pope Benedict XV: "The Catholic Church is neither Latin nor Greek nor Slav, but universal." There has been a Latin and a Greek and a Slav Catholicism, all differing profoundly in their forms of worship and their mode of thought, and yet essentially one in their faith and communion in the one body of Christ. There is no reason why there should not be a Chinese and an Indian and perhaps also an African Catholicism differing no less profoundly, and yet no less essentially one. For Christ must become incarnate among all men, revealing himself to each people as the fulfilment of its own deepest aspiration and at the same time bringing it into the unity of the whole body of mankind. For in the words of Père de Lubac, "Christ is the 'form' which humanity must put on in order that it may truly be itself."

75. Fulfillment for the East[3]
Bede Griffiths brought with him to India the scholastic theology of his time. He will find himself more and more at home, as he lives there, in the language of an older, more sapiential theology. Meanwhile, he seeks the deepest link between Thomism and the Indian thought in which he has begun to immerse himself. In a Commonweal *article of 1955, Bede presents the theology of St. Thomas Aquinas as a western and Catholic development of the universal wisdom which had flowed from the Asian traditions into Christianity through Plato and Plotinus. What Aquinas brings to this metaphysical vision is the 'western' clarity and precision of Aristotle. East and West encounter each other today, therefore, as two expressions — different but complementary — of the one 'perennial philosophy.' Further, Christianity brings fulfillment to the spiritual tradition of Asia through the mystery the incarnation, "by giving it its center in history and making it a dynamic force in the world."*

St Thomas' conception of God is identical with that of eastern tradition, as we have described it. In the question of the relation between the universe and God, St Thomas introduced an exact conception of creation which clarifies the eastern tradition, but leaves it essentially unchanged. And in the matter of the knowledge of God by contemplation, St Thomas clearly recognizes a mode of knowledge above both reason and faith, admitting man to knowledge of God by experience, an infused wisdom in which the soul becomes passive to the divine action, *patiens divina.*

We have, then, the right to say that this spiritual tradition is an integral part of Catholicism. It is, in fact, nothing but that perennial philosophy, that universal metaphysical tradition, which is the basis of all religion, both eastern and western. To this tradition Catholicism gives a precision which is generally lacking in the East. It firmly upholds the absolute transcendence of God, while admitting his immanence in all creation. It asserts the reality of the material creation while allowing that this reality is wholly relative and dependent on the absolute being of God. Above all, it brings the whole of this tradition into relation with the doctrine of the incarnation, of man's salvation through the redeeming death of Christ and his need of God's grace if he is to enter into a living relation with him.

Catholicism thus acts to confirm and strengthen the tradition of the East by giving it its center in history, and making it a dynamic force in the world. It is here, surely, that the hope of the future lies. If we could recognize the profound affinity which underlies the religions of East and West and explore more and more deeply this metaphysical doctrine which we hold in common, we should open the way to an approach to the East on a deeper level than has yet been made. Then we should perhaps be able to lead the East to see that their own tradition is wonderfully fulfilled in Catholicism, losing nothing of its richness, but receiving strength and confirmation. At the same time we should find our own faith enriched and enlarged.

76. *India and the Christ of History*[4]

Captivated with the India's 'timeless' spiritual tradition, Bede is nevertheless capable of becoming impatient with the massive complex of Hindu mythology and with the static quality which he finds in Indian culture and civilization. We we may be surprised to hear him, for once, identifying with the 'modern mind,' and proposing Christ as the bridge between Indian tradition and the modern mind. The marriage of East and West appears as the meeting of timeless wisdom with the living and transformative power which is Christ in history.

341

In India one continually encounters this paradox of a primeval religion surviving in the same person beside the most up-to-date ideas and customs. Yet there is no doubt that this has set up a conflict in the mind of the Indian today, a conflict which may become critical within the next generation. With all its depth of religious instinct, its sense of the sacred, its fervour of devotion, its ascetic and mystical tradition and its philosophy, which reaches the highest level ever attained by human thought, Hinduism remains bound up with a vast system of mythology which a modern mind must find impossible to accept. It is here, surely, that we must look for the true place of Christ in India.

As long as he is regarded as a symbolic figure like Rama and Krishna, Christ can never have a true birth in the Indian soul. But when it comes to be realized that he is in reality a historical figure, that he suffered under Pontius Pilate, was crucified, died and was buried, that he is the point at which God enters history, not as a symbol but as a person, to change the course of history and to transform it, then the decisive point in the history of India may also be reached. For Christ alone is capable of reconciling the ancient tradition of religion in India with the demands of the modern mind. He is the fulfillment of all that the imagination of the Indian soul sought to find in its gods and heroes, in its temples and sacrifices. But he is also a human being, who enters into history, who remains in his church as a living power capable of transforming its economic and political and social life. His story is, if one may say so, the myth become true. The resurrection of Christ is at once a historical fact, which has changed the course of history, and also a symbol of that ultimate truth in which human life and history can alone find their true meaning.

When the Hindu mind comes to recognize the mystery of Easter, the fact of the resurrection, which sets Christ apart from all avataras, when it acknowledges the uniqueness of the incarnation, only then will Christmas find its proper place in the life of India. Then one may hope also that all the genius of India, its depth of religious insight, which has never been equalled in history, may find its true center in Christ and build up in India a church which will surpass all others in the depth of its understanding of the riches of Christ.

77. Unitive Reality and World, Person, History[5]

In another essay collected in Christ in India, *Bede Griffiths has described the Hindu mystical experience. A progressive movement of introversion along the path of yoga culminates in a realization of the Self which is simultaneously an experience of God. It is this experience of absolute Being which constitutes "the secret wisdom of India, which sets her apart in the world and makes her the spiritual leader of mankind."[6] At this point we may experience an interior wrench, as Bede pulls away from the gravitational force of his own attraction to pure, unitive interiority to set forth more soberly the 'other side' which Hinduism must learn from Christianity. India must receive from the Gospel and the witness of Christians a permanent affirmation of body and soul and world, of personal relationship, an understanding of the significance of time and of history. Within that abyss of divine Being which is experienced in the Self, there is hidden a mystery of interpersonal communion, of knowledge and love, which is only known through Christ. Again and again, this will be Bede's response to the challenge of advaita. There are elements in these early essays which will disappear for awhile from Bede's writings as, in India, he becomes deeply involved with the vision of the Vedanta — to reappear later in a phase of synthesis. Here he cites Teilhard de Chardin, the philosopher of a christo-centric cosmic evolution. A forward-moving principle of development is evident here in* Christ in India, *alongside the movement back toward a unitive origin which will be dominant in* Return to the Center.

The trouble is that for the Hindu mind this experience of God has been so overwhelming that it has made it difficult for it to affirm the reality of this world. The world and the soul are lost in God. It is the paradox of Indian philosophy that whereas Greek philosophy starts from the reality of this world and of man and leads to the knowledge of God, Hindu philosophy starts from the experience of the reality of God and seeks to establish the reality of the world. It is here, it seems to me, that the true meeting of East and West has to take place, and this is where in particular the Hindu mind needs to discover Christ. We have to show the Hindu in the light of our faith, that in this ultimate experience of God, the absolute being, the world and the soul are not lost, nor is the personal being of God absorbed in the impersonal Godhead. It is precisely in this ground of our being, in the real Self, that in our Christian experience we discover the personal relationship which exists between ourselves and God and between one another. In Christian experience there is a mystery of personal relationship even in the ultimate depth of the Godhead. The abyss of the Godhead, as it exists beyond all human conception, is not merely absolute being; it is a mystery of knowledge and love, of personal intercommunion of an incomprehensible kind, of which human communion in knowledge and love is a faint shadow. In the same way, our faith in the incarnation teaches us that the human and the divine nature are united in the person of Christ in such a way that the human is not absorbed in the divine, and in the mystical body of Christ Christians are united to God and to one another in a personal relationship of knowledge and love, in which while sharing in the divine nature, in the divine being, knowledge and bliss, they yet remain distinct in themselves, each a unique reflection of the being of God.

This, it seems to me, is our Christian message to the Hindu. We do not deny in any sense what is ultimate in his experience of religion. On the contrary we strive in all humility to meet him on this very ground, to approach him as a brother who is joined with us in this quest of the ultimate meaning and goal of life. We have to accept his experience of the brahman, of the Self in its ground or substance as an ultimate. But we have to show him that in this ground the world and the soul are not lost. They have to pass through a death and a resurrection, and in that resurrection they are found again, no longer subject to pain and death and corruption but participating, each according to its degree of being, in the very being of God. Thus the world and time, history and progress recover their meaning. There is a real creation, a real fall, a real redemption. Science and history both find their place in a real order of being, in which mankind is progressing, together with the whole created universe, towards a consummation, which will be revealed at the end of time. Thus Christ will appear, as Teilhard de Chardin has suggested, as the term to which the whole creation is moving and all the religions of mankind will be seen as preparing the way for the final manifestation of Christ. In this view Hinduism itself will be seen as a preparatio evangelica, the path by which the people of India have been led through the centuries of their history to their fulfilment in Christ and his church.

78. Fulfillment Again[7]

In his earlier writings, Bede Griffiths presents the relationship of Hinduism and Christianity largely in terms of fulfillment. When a Catholic view credited the other religious traditions with any positive value — and this was not often the case before the Second Vatican Council — this value was as a praeparatio evangelica, a kind of prologue to the Gospel. The aspirations and intimations of the Asian tradition thus would be fulfilled in Christ. We have already seen a number of texts which respond in this way to the problem. In a 1963 Jubilee article, Bede has just described the jnana marga of Sankara, which sees the world as unreality, and the bhakti marga of Ramanuja, which considers world and souls to be parts of God. Between yet beyond these two unacceptable views, the mystery of Christ discloses the true relationship of God and creation and makes possible a personal communion of human persons with God and with one another. While Bede will continue to hold this view, we shall find him more and more drawn into the unitive mystery, less and less prone to swift theological solutions.

Thus, there are these two extremes of what is sometimes called monism, and of pantheism in which all ultimately is divine, is part of God. Christian doctrine stands in between: to my mind it brings the Vedanta and all Indian thought to its fulfilment. It shows that in this center we do not lose the world, we do not lose our fellow men, we do not lose a personal relation to God. On the contrary we find them, because in this center we make a personal contact with Christ, who himself is God in person. Therefore, in the center to which the ecumenical relation with the Hindu should bring us, we should be led to a deeper understanding of our personal relation to Christ in the depths of our souls. From that relation to Christ we reach a personal relationship with God, with the Father, with the Holy Spirit. Our whole Christian experience is an unfolding of relationships of knowledge and of love. That, to my mind, is what the Hindu is really seeking.

A study of their texts would reveal that this is what they have in mind. They are seeking it all the time, but with the material they have and without the light of revelation, they have not been able to reach it. Consequently, I would say we are not simply bringing a new religion to India. We are discovering in the depths of Hinduism its inner dynamism, its inner movement towards fulfillment, which will be found in Christ. That surely is to preach the gospel in the very heart of Hinduism, as it were, in answer to its deepest desires.

Not only do we find this personal relationship to God; we also find it to one another. Instead of losing ourselves in God or the Absolute, which is the tendency in Hinduism and still more in Buddhism, we find ourselves. In that inner depth we reach a personal relationship with one another. We discover the mystery of the person: that we, each of us, are unique manifestations of God; that is what creation means, that God gives to each one of us a being which is unique, which is eternally related to him and which has the purpose of final fulfilment in him. When we reach personal relationships with one another, our whole being is open to the world of creation.

That seems to me to place Christianity in the very center of eastern doctrine, and to be the way the East and West can gradually meet in Christ. Once we begin to see Hinduism, Buddhism and other religions in this light, once we begin to see that they themselves are moving towards Christ, then it gives us a different idea of the place of all these religions in relation to Christianity. I feel that is fundamental. We cannot go on simply taking a negative attitude towards Hinduism, Buddhism or 'pagan heathenism'. We have to take a positive attitude; and here I would like to mention a very remarkable book by R.C. Zaehner called *The Convergent Spirit*; in it he develops the idea of Teilhard de Chardin of the convergence of all creation on Christ.

Teilhard de Chardin's idea is really the idea of Paul, that the whole creation from the beginning all things in heaven and earth converge upon Christ. They come to their fullness, to their head in Christ. Zaehner makes a further point, which seems to me to follow necessarily, that all religions converge on Christ, that there is a movement towards Christ in all religions.

In other words, the mystery of Christ which we find in our religion is present in all religions in an embryonic form from the beginning. When we go to preach the gospel, we are not therefore presenting a new gospel so much as discovering the hidden presence of Christ at work in all different religions and among all different people. Is this not really the essence of the ecumenical approach that we approach our brother in whom Christ is already present, imperfectly,

346

embryonically perhaps but nevertheless there? Always we are going out to Christ in him, and we are ready to learn from him before we begin to teach. This is a new attitude in a sense, but one which flows inevitably from the ecumenical movement and from a consideration of the actual nature of the different religions as they exist today.

79. Complementarity[8]

Bede Griffiths sees the great religions, as time passes, more and more in terms of complementarity. It is evident that the idea had been present in his thinking from the beginning that not only the different cultures and modes of consciousness but the different religious traditions themselves are complementary, as they all express and mediate a single Mystery. While Bede became more sensitive about implying a superiority of Christianity with respect to the Asian religions, his belief in the conclusiveness of the Christ-event would usually find expression toward the end of an article or a book. Here, concluding the final conference in The Cosmic Revelation, *he draws up a kind of balance sheet between East and West, Hinduism and Christianity today. Christians, caught up in "matter and science and history and human progress," need to recover with the help of Hindu tradition a sense of the sacred, of the "eternal dimension of being." Hinduism witnesses to them the sacramentality of the world and all things within it, the divine presence which is everywhere around us, beneath the veil of appearances. What Hinduism is to learn from Christianity is, once again, the mystery of personal communion which is hidden within the mystery of nondual Being.*

We may conclude that both terms — fulfillment and complementarity — describe the relationship between Christianity and the Asian traditions. Neither is adequate by itself, nor are they adequate when combined. The subtle and dynamic complexity of this relationship — like the relationship between two human persons — may not yield to expression in such conceptual formulas. Meanwhile the traditions of East and West challenge one another to a new and deeper life.

Finally, what conclusion can we draw from this? The principle of complementarity. The danger of Christianity today is that it overemphasizes the importance of matter and science and history and human progress in this world striving for a better world. All these things have their value, of course, but the danger is that they absorb all our energies and all our attention. Yet we know that all is going to lead in the end to death. Death is the end of everything, unless there is a resurrection. And so the modern Christian view needs to be complemented with the constant awareness which the Hindu has of the eternal dimension of being.

In the same way, when we look on the external world we have to recognize that it is not just something for science to examine, to manipulate, to change and develop. It is a revelation of God. And that is something we have to recover. The whole creation is a sacrament, a revelation of God.

Then again, as regards human history, there is a process of development. We should be working for a better world. But if we think we are going to reach that goal in this world we will be frustrated and disappointed. We need to look beyond to the resurrection, and only then will that final fulfillment, justice, and truth be discovered.

So the world today needs what the Hindu can give of a sense of the sacramentality of the whole creation and of a transcendent world beyond time, beyond space, beyond this world altogether. This leads us to the point of understanding the sacramental character not only of this world but also of the church. The church also is a sacrament, a sacrament of Christ. And sacraments are signs. In the understanding of theology, a *sacramentum* is a sign, and sometimes that has been lost sight of, and there has been an over-realistic view of a sacrament. But a sacrament always remains a revelation of God under a sign. This was beautifully expressed in that hymn of St Thomas Aquinas Adore te devote latens deitas. The last verse of it goes:

"Jesu quem velatum nunc aspicio
Oro fiat illud quod tam sitio
Ut te revelata cernens facie
Visu sim beatus tuae gloriae."

The translation which really does not do justice to the beauty of the Latin is: "Jesus whom I now see under a veil, grant that that may be which I so much desire, that I may see Thee with face unveiled, and be blessed with the sight of Thy Glory."

We pray that the veil may be taken away, the veil of the sacrament, so that the reality may appear. In the humanity of Christ, God comes to us in a human being who suffers and dies and makes himself

348

known to us as a man, shares our very life with us and yet wants to take us beyond. Jesus, the humanity of Jesus, is a sacrament of God. It is a sign of God's grace, God's love, God's salvation, but we have to go beyond the sign to the reality, to the mystery of the Trinity. That is the last point I want to make.

In the Hindu Revelation, the ultimate reality is *Sat Cit Ananda* — Being, Knowledge, Bliss. The search is for that ultimate Being, that 'ultimate reality' — *sat*, and that ultimate Being and Reality is Conscious; it is cit, 'consciousness,' a conscious awareness of infinite eternal being. And the consciousness of that eternal being is bliss, ananda, 'pure joy.' That is the goal of Hinduism — to reach that sat-cit-ananda, and that *sat-chit-ananda* is pure oneness, one without a second.

In the Gospel there is a further depth revealed. In the ultimate reality there is revealed not merely an identity, but a communion. The final Christian Revelation is that the Godhead itself, the ultimate reality, is a communion of persons, a communion of persons in love, and that gives a further dimension to our understanding of reality. The Hindu believes that God is love in a sense, and that you can love God but not that the Godhead Itself is love. There cannot be love without two. If God is a pure monad as he is in Islam, as he tends to be in Hinduism, he cannot be love in himself. But in the Christian concept the Godhead Itself is love, is a communion of love. There is a distinction within the Godhead Itself, distinction beyond our comprehension which we crudely express in terms of person and relation. These are human terms pointing to the reality. The reality is that God is love, that there is something which corresponds to personal communion in love in the Godhead, and we are called to share in that communion of love.

So also, in the mystical body of Christ which embraces all redeemed humanity, we do not disappear in the Godhead, but we discover a personal relationship of love. Each person is fulfilled and is open to the other person; it is an inter-communion of love in which each embraces the other and all are embraced in God.

In the *Paradiso* in Dante's *Divine Comedy* there is a poetic description which goes as far as human intelligence can towards depicting this mystery of the Trinity as love. And that is what we are called to experience — this communion of love in the mystical body of Christ which embraces the whole creation. All the beauty of the creation is present there for our joy and our thanksgiving. The whole of redeemed humanity is there, and each of us, according to his capacity, is able to go out in love to others and to be embraced in love by others. All creation and all humanity are taken up into this infinite, incomprehensible, inexpressible Being of God, in whom though we can never understand or comprehend him — we know that there is this communion of charity, this communion of love. Jesus expresses it marvellously in the Gospel of St John, when He prays, "That they may be one. As Thou, Father in me and I in Thee, that they may be one in us." That is Christian *advaita*. We are one with one another and one with Christ; we are one in this mystery of the Godhead, and I do not think we can go beyond that. This would be an example of how to relate the Cosmic Revelation to the Christian Revelation. We are all engaged in this task, and it is not something fully accomplished; it is that to which we are moving.

80. Hindu and Christian Mysticism: The Distinctions[9]

In the final section of The Cosmic Revelation *(1983), Bede Griffiths contrasted the mythical and nonhistorical Hindu consciousness with the emphatically historical and world-affirming spirit of the Judaeo-Christian revelation. His conclusion was the complementarity of the two traditions. At the end of his account of Christian mysticism in* A New Vision of Reality *(1989), Bede more concisely and systematically sets forth five features which distinguish the Christian theological vision from other perspectives, and particularly from those of the Eastern traditions. Again, his final word in response to the central Hindu experience of advaita, or nonduality, is that this experience is to find its further and ultimate fulfillment in a participation of that communion of love which is the Trinity.*

To conclude I would like to make some points about Christian mysticism as a whole. First of all it embraces all creation, matter, life, time, history, man, woman. The whole of humanity is taken up in Christ into the life of the Godhead and is restored to unity. The whole creation is gathered into one and in and through Christ the Word, all things and all people return to the Father, in the Spirit. That is the total reintegration of everything, the recapitulation, or gathering into one, of all things. That comes at the end of the world.

Secondly, creation is not a fall and it is not God. Creation is often said to be a fall. Ken Wilber, for instance, in his very remarkable book *Up from Eden*, holds that ultimately creation is a fall from God, but in the Christian view this is not so. The world is created by God as the sphere in which human experience can be worked out, which is essentially God giving himself to the world in love and drawing the world back to himself in love. That is the essence of creation. So rather than a fall, it is an outpouring of love. Sin comes in, of course, and brings disintegration and death but the grace of God comes to restore it and brings us back to God.

Thirdly, the spirit of man is a capacity for God. It is not God. My *atman*, myself, is not God, but rather it is a capacity for God which can be filled by God and can be transformed into God and this is a gift of pure grace.

Fourthly, this capacity is fully realised in Jesus in the resurrection, and so made effective in the church and the sacraments. In Jesus this outpouring of the Spirit of God was complete. In him, as St Paul says, "dwelt the fullness of the Godhead bodily."[10] In him human nature was totally transformed, and in and through him we return to the Father. The resurrection and the ascension release a power in the universe so that now it is working throughout the whole creation and the whole of humanity to bring back creation and humanity into life in God. The church is the sphere in which this divine power is at work, particularly through the sacraments. The sacraments constitute the means by which this power, released at the resurrection, is made present to us, first in baptism, then in confirmation and then renewed each day in the eucharist. In this way, through the church, we are united as members of the mystical body of Christ and in that mystical body of Christ we return to the Father.

Fifthly, the human person is not lost in the divine but enjoys perfect oneness in love. Again and again the tendency is to lose the person in the Ultimate. In both Hinduism and Buddhism this tendency is always at work, so that ultimately there is no individual left and everything dissolves in the pure oneness of being. But in the Christian mystical understanding each person is unique. Each is a unique expression of God, a unique manifestation of the divine, and each is in all and all are in each. There is a total transparency. All are one in God and one in each other. But we are not lost in this oneness; we are found in our total being. "He who will lose his life shall find it."[11] When we lose ourselves totally in that abyss of love, we find ourselves.

Perhaps the fundamental difference is this: that the heart of Christian mysticism is a mystery of love, whereas both in Hinduism and in Buddhism it is primarily a transformation of consciousness. *Brahman* is *saccidananda*, being, consciousness and bliss. It is not specifically love. Love is included, and was marvellously developed as *bhakti*, but this is not so central either in Hinduism or in Buddhism, whereas the essence of the Christian experience is an experience of love, not primarily of consciousness or of knowledge, though these, of course, are included, and love is self-communion. The nature of love is such that we become persons by loving. We have a capacity to transcend ourselves in love, to go out of ourselves and to experience one another in love, and grow as we communicate in love. It is all a matter of interpersonal relationship. In this understanding the basic need of human experience is growth in interpersonal relationships, in love, and that is so basic that we are called into being by love. The love which is given to mother, father, husband, wife, children and friends, all this is simply a created manifestation of a love which created us in the beginning and is drawing us to itself. All created love is a manifestation of the uncreated love from which we come and to which we are moving. In this we do not lose ourselves, just as in a human relationship of love you do not lose yourself. If you love someone you become one with him or her and they become one with you, but you do not cease to be yourself. If that happened it would no longer be love. So it is a communion of love, an experience of oneness in love, and that is the end and meaning of life. This interrelationship in love is the reflection of the life of the Godhead, where the Father and the Son give themselves totally in love and are united in the Spirit in an unfathomable unity. So the interpersonal relationships within the Trinity are the model and exemplar of all interpersonal relationships on earth and ultimately also of all interrelationships in the whole creation. We saw in chapter one how the contemporary physicist describes the universe as a complex web of interdependent relationships. Everything is interdependent and interrelated on the physical level, on the psychological level and finally on the spiritual level; and the Trinity, as far as can be expressed in words, is the exemplar of all interrelationship and the unity of all being in love.

81. Christianity in the Light of the East[12]

Bede Griffiths was invited to present the 1989 Hibbert Lecture, broadcast over the BBC. Rather than simply developing a vision of Christianity under the influence of the 'Eastern light', however, he complements the conceptions of each side with those of the other. From Hinduism and Buddhism he brings to Christianity a sense of the Divine as immanent in the world and in the human person, yet as ultimately beyond name and image. Corresponding to this immanence is a feminine aspect of God. The usual Christian anthropology of body and soul is completed with the dimension of unitive spirit. To the Eastern traditions, on the other hand, Bede brings from Christianity a sense of human community and human solidarity, of progressive history, of human relationship and communion within the ultimate divine Mystery, and this communion as the ultimate state of a redeemed humanity. It is this mystery of love that confers upon life its meaning and fulfillment.

Bede has taken advantage of this opportunity to step back and attempt a fresh synthetic vision of the relationship of Hinduism and Christianity, developing the differences along a continuum from a single starting point. This starting point is the difference between a Semitic and Christian view of "a personal God, a creator, who transcends the world and rules it from above," and an Asian view of Divinity as immanent in the world and in the human soul. This articulation of the Christian view of God, however, is something of a caricature, ignoring the Pauline and Johannine revelation of a new divine indwelling through Christ. And in the end, the remedies that he brings to the one-sidedness of traditional Christianity derive more from the New Testament than from Hinduism. What the East brings to this final picture is the overall perspective of an ultimate nondual mystery; in this unitive light Bede's own Christian faith begins to loose the knots which historical Christianity has tied.

India is a land of mystery. I first encountered this mystery when I visited the cave of Elephanta outside Bombay. It is a cave in which pillars have been carved out of the rock, and at the center is the figure of the great god Maheshwara. He has three faces. One face is gentle and benign, one is fierce and terrible, representing the two aspects of God, and the third is deeply contemplative, somehow uniting those two aspects in a deep contemplation, a deep inner truth and mystery. I felt that there, carved in stone, is the hidden mystery of India, revealing itself to me in that figure of the great god. Ever since then I have been trying to relate my Christian faith to this mystery which is present in India, in all the religions of India.

I have learned to see Christianity from the point of view not of Europe but of Asia. I have come to realize that Christianity, though universal in principle, is in its actual structure a western religion. It had its origin in the Middle East and grew up in a Semitic culture with a specific Jewish character, but it then moved out into the Graeco-Roman world, where it developed a western structure based on Greek philosophy and Roman Law. All the structures of Christianity today, though they have their roots in the original Jewish tradition, are characteristically western in their language, their mode of thought and behaviour. At the Reformation an attempt was made to return to the original Biblical tradition, but again it was the Bible interpreted in the light of western thought. We are now being challenged to re-think our religion in the light not of western but of eastern thought, and to discover another dimension of Christianity. This movement may be as decisive for Christianity today as it was for the early church when it passed from its original Jewish matrix into the Graeco-Roman world.

We have to remind ourselves that two-thirds of humanity today lives in Asia, and for over ninety percent of these people Christianity is a totally alien religion. The Christian faith was carried in the sixteenth century to the European colonies in American and then to those in Asia and Africa, but it always appeared as an extension of the colonial regime. To the average Asian today Christianity remains a foreign religion brought to their country by the colonial powers. They have their own religions and their distinctive cultures, which are often far older than those of Europe, and they have developed over the centuries their own systems of philosophy and spirituality, which have a depth of wisdom and insight which is unsurpassed. In Asia we are confronted with the great tradition of an ancient wisdom, which is part of the inheritance of our common humanity. The question is, how do we relate this traditional wisdom, this perennial philosophy as it has been called, to our own tradition of Christian faith?

In the first place Asian religion challenges us in our very conception of God. Christianity, and with it the other Semitic religions, Judaism and Islam, all believe in a personal God, a creator, who transcends the world and rules it from above. He is said to dwell in heaven and to rule over all things by his power. In the New Testament Jesus speaks of him as the Father in heaven, and it is to this Father figure that Christians look as the origin and end of all things. In the Asian religions, on the other hand, Buddhism does not allow for a creator God at all. Chinese religion speaks rather impersonally of Heaven (tien) and of Tao, the Way. Hinduism, though it allows for a creator God, prefers to speak of brahman, the infinite, eternal reality beyond word and thought, which is the origin and the end of the universe.

Perhaps the essential difference between the two outlooks is that for the Semitic religions God is essentially transcendent, separate from the world, while in the Asian religions, God, or the first principle of being, is essentially immanent. It is the "ground" of being, the inner reality which sustains the whole creation. Thus the Upanishads, the earliest text we have in Hinduism says: "In the beginning this," (meaning the whole universe) "was brahman, one only without a second." This language is often interpreted as a form of pantheism, but in reality it is not pantheism, by which is meant that all is God, but pan-en-theism, which means that God is in all things. This is strictly orthodox Christian doctrine. St Thomas Aquinas, a doctor of the middle ages, asks in what sense God is in all things, and he answers that God is in all things first of all by his power, because he "upholds all things by the word of his power." But then he says he is not in all things at a distance, because there is no distance in God. He is therefore in all things by his presence. He then says that he is not present in all things by a part of himself, as there are no parts in God, therefore he is in all things by his essence. In other words, God our creator is in every particle and sub-particle of matter, in every living thing and in every human being by his very essence. For a Christian this means that the Holy Trinity is in the whole creation, in every part of it. Oriental doctrine helps us therefore to realize an often forgotten aspect of our own Christian faith.

As a result of the separation of God and the creation, the western world has largely lost the sense of the sacred. In India the whole universe is considered as a manifestation of God and consequently everything is felt to be sacred. The earth, the sky, plants, animals, human beings, all alike are manifestations of God and are held to be sacred.

In the western world we have lost this sense of the sacred. We have desacralized nature, and as a result of that we are experiencing today the problems of ecology, where we realize that we may destroy the planet on which we are living. And this is due, in part at least, to this sense that the world of nature is separate from God. It would be unfair to attribute to Christianity all the problems of ecology which face us today, but it can hardly be denied that the concept of a creator God separate from the world is one of the causes of the abuse of the environment which we experience today. The concept of the world as a machine obeying mathematical laws to be controlled by human beings, which we owe to Descartes and Newton, is modelled on the understanding of the creator God who controls the world from above. This brings out the fact also that for the Semitic religions God is always conceived in masculine terms; Yahweh and Allah are both essentially masculine figures. In Christianity both the Father and the Son are masculine, and even the Spirit, which in Greek is neuter, is commonly spoken of as "He." The feminine aspect of God as immanent in creation, "pervading and penetrating all things," though found in the book of Wisdom, has almost been forgotten. Here again the Asian religions with their clear recognition of the feminine aspect of God and of the power of God, the divine *shakti* permeating the universe, may help us to get a more balanced view of the creative process. Today we are beginning to discover that the earth is a living being, a Mother who nourishes us and of whose body we are members.

The same separation between God and creation comes out in the conception of the soul as separate from God and further alienated from God by sin, so that many people speak of a 'gulf' between God and humanity. The Asian religions on the other hand have a very different understanding of the relation between God and the soul. In Hinduism God is conceived as in the soul and the soul in God. This is not far from the saying which St Paul quotes: "in him we live and move and have our being."

It is true that the Hindu uses language which appears to identify the soul with God, when it is said, for instance, "I am brahman" or "Thou art That." These are mystical utterances found in the *Upanishads* which should not be taken literally. What they mean is that in the ultimate depth of my being I am one with that ground of being and consciousness which is the ground of the whole universe. In our Christian tradition we have a corresponding view when we speak of a human being as body, soul and spirit. This is the basic concept of human nature in Christianity as found in St Paul. We have a body, a physical organism, which is part of the physical organism of nature, and we have a soul, a psyche, which is a psychological organism, with its different faculties. But beyond both body and soul we are spirit, *pneuma* in Greek and *atman* in Sanskrit, and this is our point of union with the divine spirit. St Francis of Sales calls this spirit the "fine point" of the soul. It is the point at which the human spirit is in touch with the Spirit of God. This concept of the Spirit has been almost lost today. Most people think of a human being as a body-soul, a psycho-physical organism, and have lost sight of the spirit, the point of human transcendence, which opens us both to God, the eternal Spirit, and to our fellow human beings. For it is at this depth of our being that we are in communion with one another. In our bodies and souls we are all different and divided, but at this point of the spirit we are in communion with God and with one another. Here again the Hindu conception of the *atman*, the Spirit in all creation and in all humanity which is one with the spirit of God, can help us to recover a deeper understanding of our Christian faith.

This can also lead us to a deeper understanding of human community. We tend to think of human beings as isolated individuals, each separate from the other and normally engaged in competition with one another. But a deeper view of humanity enables us to see that beyond all the differences of individuals and nations and races and religions there is a common humanity which binds us together.

It is in the depth of our being, beyond the differences of body and soul, that we discover the root of this common humanity. We have to recover a sense of community, in families and nations, in races and religions, and live not as independent beings but as members of one another. St Paul speaks of the church as the Body of Christ, a body which has many members, all different, yet all necessary to the whole, and all united in one spirit. This is surely a model for a human community today.

We come now to a crucial difference between the Christian and the Asian, especially the Hindu, understanding of religion. For the Christian, just as there is one God, the creator of heaven and earth, so there is one Lord and Saviour, one Incarnation by which God becomes man and enters into human history. But for the Hindu just as there are many "gods," many forms of the manifestation of God in creation, so there are many incarnations, many *avataras*, or "descents" of God as they are called, many appearances of God on earth. Traditionally there are ten *avataras*, but of these several are the mythological figures like the fish, the tortoise, the boar and man-lion. Modern Hindus interpret these in the sense that at each stage of evolution from the time when the earth was covered by the sea to the time when man emerged from the animal, God was present in creation. The supreme forms of the *avataras* were Rama and Krishna, in whom the fullness of the Godhead was revealed. But the number of the *avataras* has always varied, and today most Hindus recognize an *avatara* in every age. As Krishna declared in the Bhagadvad Gita, "When righteousness declines and unrighteousness prevails, then I take birth." Today many Hindus consider Satya Sai Baba the avatara of the present age. He is a holy man in South India who performs miracles every day, producing things out of nothing and healing people, and even on one occasion, it is said, raising somebody from the dead.

What is a Christian to say to all this? I would suggest that the difference of view derives, in part, from a different concept of time. In the oriental tradition, time is always conceived to be cyclical.

Everything moves in cycles. The sun rises and sets, the moon waxes and wanes, Spring is followed by Summer, Autumn by Winter and then returns again. So also the universe comes from God and goes through its cycles of change and then returns again. Human life is part of this cyclic movement; human beings are born and die and are born again. So also the *avatara* comes again and again to renew the world. But in the Christian vision time is not cyclic but linear. The universe has a beginning in time and moves through time to an end, an "*eschaton.*" Jesus Christ is seen as coming at the end of time to bring all things to fulfilment. "It was his plan in the fullness of time," says St Paul, "to bring all things to a head in him, things in heaven and things on earth." In this view there is a fullness and finality in the coming of Christ. Not only humanity but the whole universe is conceived as coming to fulfilment in Christ. This is not to deny that God has manifested himself in "many and various ways," as the Letter to the Hebrews says, in the course of history. But in the plan of God as revealed in the New Testament, Christ comes as the final fulfilment of history, and beyond history of the universe itself.

But there is a serious problem here, in that each of the Semitic religions regards its own religion as a unique revelation of God and refuses to recognize any other. For the Jew, Yahweh is the name of God by which he alone can be worshipped, and to worship God under any other name is a sin. For the Muslim there is no other God but Allah as revealed in the Quran, and Muhammad is his prophet. For the Christian also, except for Jesus there is no other name given as under heaven by which we may be saved. This creates a tremendous problem for the relation between different religions today.

Here again perhaps the Asian religions can help us. The Buddha, because he saw the danger of disputing about the name of God, refused to speak about God at all. He spoke only in negative terms of nirvana, the nameless formless Reality, and his followers spoke of the ultimate reality as sunyata, the Void, the total Emptiness, which is yet absolute fullness. In Hinduism, though there are many names and forms of God, the Godhead itself is said to be without name or form. It is absolute Being (*sat*) in pure consciousness (*cit*) of perfect bliss (*ananda*). So Saccidananda becomes the nearest to a name which can be given to God or the ultimate Reality. But ultimately it has to be said of God that he is "*neti, neti*". . . not this, not this.

Today it would seem that we have to recognize that God himself, the ultimate Reality, whatever name we give to it, has properly no name. It transcends human conception and can only be known by analogy. When we speak of God as the Father Almighty, we are using terms of analogy indicating that there is something in God, the ultimate reality, which corresponds with our experience of fatherhood and of the creative power, as seen in a poet or artist. When we speak of God as a person, we mean that there is something in the ultimate which corresponds with our experience of personal being. But always the Godhead itself, the ultimate reality, transcends all our conceptions. Each religion is a revelation of God given in the context of a particular culture and historical situation, and we have to learn to discern the truth behind the names and forms. Each religion must learn to recognize the values of the other religions, and while affirming the truth of its own revelation learn to recognize the truth in the other, and work together with people of other religions and outside all religion for the good of humanity.

We come now to consider the ultimate destiny, and here we come upon a similar difference in outlook. For the Hindu the ultimate goal of humanity is moksha, or liberation; that is, liberation from our present human condition in which we are limited by space and time, and subject to suffering and death. In the Hindu understanding each person goes through a series of births in this world, in which it gradually gets purified and prepared for the final state of absolute bliss. Many people today are attracted by the theory of rebirth, as it seems to answer the problem as to how most people can be prepared for liberation when they die in such an obviously imperfect state. The Christian answer to this problem is to consider that we are not isolated individuals working out our destiny alone, but that we are all members of a common humanity. The Semitic tradition has a strong sense of the solidarity of mankind. Adam, in Genesis, is not an individual but a representative man, who includes both man and woman in himself. As a result of sin, a falling away from God, this aim is separated from God, and divided in himself, and disintegrated, as we experience ourselves today. But by redemption this Man is restored to unity. Christ is the second Adam, who restores humanity to union with God and to harmony in itself. It is as members of this fallen and redeemed humanity that we journey towards our final destiny, and each member finds itself integrated into the whole from which it has been divided by sin. So St Paul says, "As in Adam all die, so in Christ shall all be made alive."

But the question still remains: Does the individual person survive in the final state? Many Christians today find it difficult to believe in a future life. When the body dies, does the soul survive or does it also disintegrate? We can remind ourselves here of the concept of the human being as body, soul and spirit. That the body does not survive in its present state is obvious, but can the soul, the psyche, in so far as it depends on the body, survive death?

It is difficult to see how our present mode of consciousness, dependent as it is on the senses, can survive bodily death. But the spirit, the *pneuma*, is, as we saw, the point of human transcendence; it is the point where the human is open to the divine, that is, to the infinite and the eternal. It is also the point where human beings communicate. At that point of the spirit we are all open to one another. A person is a being in relationship. I exist as a person through my relation with others. There is no such thing as an isolated person. Scientists today speak of the universe as a complicated web of interdependent relationships. In the same way we can speak of humanity as a web of interpersonal relationships. We are all connected with one another at the deepest center of our being. In our unconscious we are linked with humanity from the beginning of its history. All men, according to St Thomas Aquinas, are one man: "*omnes homines unus homo*," or, as the Greek father St Gregory of Nyssa said, all human beings from the first to the last are but one image of Him who Is. We are all made in the image of God and when we go beyond the limitations of our present mode of being in space and time, we enter into that transcendent consciousness where we are no longer separated from one another, but are integrated into the wholeness, which is present in every part. An illustration of this in the Hindu tradition is the net of Siva, a pearl necklace in which every pearl reflects every other and also reflects the whole. This may give us some indication of the final stage in which each person is totally transparent to every other; as the Greek philosopher Plotinus said, "Each is in all and all is in each." This is as near as we can get to forming an image of our final destiny.

This understanding of personal relationship gives an insight also into the mystery of the Trinity. We must remember that for a Christian God is not properly "a" person. The Godhead is a communion of persons. If we conceive of the person as essentially being-in-relationship, then we are able to see how there can be relations in the Godhead, that is, an ultimate reality.

Human beings relate to one another essentially through knowledge and love. It becomes possible therefore to conceive that in the ultimate state there are relations of knowledge and love. According to Christian revelation the Father, as the Ground and source of the Godhead, knows himself, expresses himself in the Son or Word, and communicates himself in the love of the Holy Spirit. We are, of course, using terms of analogy. As in our human life we learn to know one another and to love one another, so we are able to conceive that in God, the ultimate reality, there is a communion of knowledge and love, a total transparency, which is the exemplar of all relations of knowledge and love which exist among human beings. Even beyond this we can see how the whole universe is conceived as a "complicated web of interdependent relationships," and this is a reflection of the relationships in the Godhead. All our human knowledge and love also is a finite reflection of the infinite knowledge and love which exist eternally in the ultimate reality of which our world of space and time is a reflection.

Finally, Hinduism conceived of the Godhead as *saccidananda*, being in perfect consciousness of itself in absolute bliss. The Christian doctrine of the Trinity adds a further dimension to this by conceiving the Godhead as essentially a communion of love. Being is not only pure consciousness reflecting itself in eternal wisdom, that is, in the Word; it is also pure love communicating itself, flowing out of itself, in the power of the spirit. The Godhead is the fullness of love, that is, of interpersonal relationship. It is not a monad, a pure identity, but a dynamism of love, communicating itself in love to the whole creation. The world, according to this understanding, was created out of love and redeemed by love, and all human love is a reflection of this eternal love. That mystery, which Hinduism, discerns in the universe and in the depths of the human heart, and which the Buddha spoke of as nirvana, is a mystery of love. This love is the ground for human existence, hidden in the depths of the heart.

It is not something remote from our lives, but meets us in every human situation, wherever people suffer and are oppressed, wherever people are imprisoned, tortured and killed, wherever people are dying of cancer or of AIDS, wherever drink and drugs and crime are destroying people's lives. There, if we can learn to discern it, this mystery of love is present. It is the reality which gives meaning to human existence which challenges us in every situation of life. That reality, according to Christian faith, was revealed in its fullness when Jesus was hanging on the cross, rejected, despised, humiliated, exposed to hatred and violence, to pain and death. It was then that the true nature of reality was made known, the truth for which science and philosophy are seeking, which holds the answer to the paradox of our existence. It was then that love itself was revealed, it is that which gives ultimate meaning to our lives.

82. An Indian Christian Monasticism[13]

With incisive clarity, Bede Griffiths sets forth the main issues that confront any project of Christian monasticism in India today. First, any project of a Christian monastic life must integrate itself into the existing context of Indian monasticism, which is the oldest in the world. Secondly, it will be confronted with a choice between identifying with a western (Latin) or an oriental (e.g. Syrian) tradition of Christian monasticism. Finally, the way of life of Christian monks in India must relate to the level of poverty which prevails not only among the sannyasis but among ordinary people.

Bede will go on to describe the efforts which he and the community of Kurisumala Ashram, in Kerala, have made to respond to these challenges. They are challenges which constrain Christian monasticism to rediscover the purity and depth of its own beginnings.

There are three problems which face anyone who wishes to establish any form of the monastic life in India. The first is the problem of adaptation to the pattern of monastic life which already exists in India. India has a good claim to be the original home of ascetic and monastic life and to be the source from which the ascetic ideal spread over the rest of the world.[14] There is evidence for the existence of ascetics in the period of the Vedas, that is at least from the beginning of the first millennium before Christ. But the great movement of the ascetic and monastic life began in the sixth century before Christ with the rise of Buddhism and Jainism and the ascetic movement within Hinduism itself which gave birth to the Upanishads, the mystical treatises which have been the inspiration of Hindu religion and philosophy ever since. This movement is characterized by the renunciation of the world in order to seek for moksha, that is liberation from the wheel of time with its inevitable suffering, and the discovery of the absolute, the state of permanent bliss known as nirvana.

In the early stages, the movement was rather that of solitary ascetics who sought ascetic discipline (*tapas*) and meditation, and this tradition has remained a permanent feature of Hindu asceticism. But Buddhism soon developed a settled form of monastic life, due originally, it appears, to the need to find refuge during the period of the monsoon, when a wandering life was not possible. From this, regular monasteries with permanent buildings soon developed, and this has remained characteristic of Buddhism ever since. Hinduism does not seem to have adopted this type of monasticism until the time of Sankara (ninth century, AD), who established monasteries (*maths*) in the four quarters of India. From that time till the present day, regular monasteries have existed all over India, with the normal conditions of poverty, chastity, and obedience, and a settled rule of life. But alongside these there has always been the looser type of ascetic life in *ashrams*, consisting of groups of devotees gathered around a master and living in community, but not observing strict rules and not bound to poverty, chastity, or obedience. At the present day there are many thousands of monasteries and ashrams all over India, many of which, following the impulse given by Vivekenanda and Mahatma Gandhi, devote themselves to works of charity and to education. Thus there is a regular pattern of monastic life in India, of great antiquity, common to at least three different religions, Hinduism, Buddhism, and Jainism, and showing signs of renewed vigor and vitality at the present day. It is into this pattern that any form of Christian monasticism has to learn to fit itself.

The second problem, which arises from this in part, is what form of Christian monastic tradition should be followed. The Latin church has spread all over India in the last few centuries, but it has shown little capacity to adapt itself to the traditions and customs of the Indian people, and one may question whether, with its western habits of life and thought, it is capable of doing so. On the other hand, the Syrian Church has been in India at least since the fourth century and has shown considerable capacity for adaptation to Indian customs, though it has been, unhappily, very much influenced by the Latin church in modern times. Yet it remains by far the strongest body of Christians in India and the chief source of vocations both to the priesthood and to the religious life throughout the country. It is therefore in this essentially oriental form of Christianity, with its long acclimatization in India, that one may reasonably hope to see the development of an Indian monasticism, based not so much on the western rule of life as on the great eastern tradition of the deserts of Egypt and Syria, which is so much nearer to Hindu and Buddhist tradition and was, in fact, almost certainly influenced by them.

The third problem is the relation of monastic life to the living standards of India. Monastic life in India has always been associated with extreme poverty. In this respect, as in so many others, it is nearer to the tradition of the Fathers of the Desert than to Benedictine monasticism. At the same time the living conditions of the majority of people in India today, in spite of the immense economic development which has taken place in the last fifteen years, remain extremely low, for the most part scarcely above bare subsistence. How is a monastery to relate itself to these conditions? What should be the standard of life of the monk in relation both to the poor of India and to the normal standard of the Hindu *sannyasi*?

These are the questions which have to be answered in any serious effort to establish the monastic life. We do not pretend to have found an adequate answer to any of these problems, but being able to start monastic life from scratch, as it were, without being bound by any particular rule, we have been able to experiment along different lines, and it may be that we are working towards a solution of some of these problems. At least, it may be of interest to readers of *Monastic Studies* to learn how far we have gone in these different directions. (There follows a description of the monastic life as lived at Kurisumala Ashram.)

83. The Future of Christian Monasticism in India[15]

About eight years later, Bede again confronts the prospects for a new Christian monasticism in India. He begins with a brief synthetic look at the two traditions which encounter one another at this point: Indian monasticism and Christian monasticism. It is clear that Bede prefers the simplicity and freedom of the Indian quest for liberation and experience of 'saccidananda' to the "regular disciplined order of liturgical prayer, study and manual work" which is usual in western monasticism — and in which he had once found fulfillment.[16] Then, on the basis of his five years' experience at Shantivanam Ashram in Tamil Nadu, Bede sketches his ideal for an Indian Christian monastic foundation.

The principles of this model are two: commitment to the quest for the experience of God, and a complete openness to the leadings of the Spirit: that is, to the "charismatic and prophetic character of the monk." This means that the community will be open to the world (a spiritual center for visitors of all kinds), and yet dedicated to meditation and personal prayer more than to the liturgy. The monk must avoid commitments to institutional structures, but can undertake any form of service in the freedom of the Spirit. The community, therefore, must remain open to all possibilities: stability and movement, solitude and interaction, contemplative withdrawal and action, celibacy and married life. It will be open to the spiritual riches of all traditions, and a place of theological and liturgical creativity. This vision of a monastic springtime soars both with Bede's invincible optimism and with the powerful current of spiritual energy that animated the church after the Council. At Shantivanam, with Bede at its center, many people did experience this spirit of contemplative freedom. Of the dream of a Christian monastic renaissance in India, however, there have appeared so far only a few modest signs. In the exhilarating air of Bede's company, it could be easy to forget the narrowness of the monastic path.

Indian Christian Monasticism, like the church in India as a whole, is the inheritor of two traditions, Indian and Christian. Indian monastic tradition goes back to the time of the Buddha and the Upanishads, and can claim to be the most ancient tradition of monasticism in the world. There is some ground for holding even that it is the unique source of all monasticism. It is a tradition of 'sannyasa,' of renunciation of the world in order to seek for 'moksha,' or liberation from 'samsara,' the round of birth and death, and to attain to the state of 'saccidananda,' that is the condition of transcendent Being (sat) in pure consciousness (cit) of unending bliss (ananda). This path of renunciation has been followed by an unbroken succession of sadhus and sannyasis from the earliest times to the present day. In the course of time it has been organized into different orders of sannyasis, deriving from some great acharya in the past and centered commonly on a 'math' or monastery, where the tradition of the order is preserved. In modern times new orders have sprung up, of which the Ramakrishna order is the most remarkable, developing to some extent along the lines of Christian religious orders but keeping to the ancient tradition. At the same time a great many yogis and gurus have appeared, each teaching his own method of meditation and ascetic life, each having a large following not only in India but all over the world. Hindu sannyasa like Buddhist monasticism has thus become a world phenomenon, and is attracting today a vast number of young people in the West, who are seeking some experience of God, or of ultimate reality. It is against this background of Indian monastic tradition and of the awakening desire for the experience of God through meditation and asceticism in the West that the future of Indian Christian monasticism must be considered.

Christian monasticism has a similar history of development. Beginning in Syria and Egypt in the 3rd and 4th century after Christ, it was marked by the same tendency towards absolute renunciation and, as has been said, there is some reason to hold that the original inspiration for this monasticism came from India. But from the time of Pachomius in the 4th century Christian monasticism came to be more strongly organized with an emphasis on the importance of manual work and regular discipline. St Basil in the East and St Benedict in the West carried forward this movement and from their time Christian monasticism came to be an established part of the ecclesiastical order, having its clearly defined place in the law of the church.

Nevertheless the freedom of the Spirit was retained, especially in the eastern church and many charismatic saints arose both in the East and the West inspired by the original tradition of total renunciation of the world and total self-giving to God. But for the majority of Christian monks monasticism was a regular disciplined order of liturgical prayer, study and manual work. This is the tradition of monasticism which we have inherited in the West today, but like all other institutions in the church it is now coming to be questioned. The long hours of liturgical prayer have been reduced, sometimes to five, sometimes to three offices in the day. The authority of the abbot like that of other Superiors in the church is coming to be more of a shared authority. Solitary life has once more begun to be cultivated and the possibility of temporary monasticism is coming to be discussed. With this goes a greater emphasis on personal prayer, both in the form of private meditation and also of group prayer and meditation. The monasteries have also felt the attraction of the charismatic movement and at least one monastery in America has become Pentecostal.

The problem has also arisen of a monk's engagement in the world. For a long time monks have been engaged in many parts in school and parish work and of course in giving retreats. But the need is being felt for a more radical engagement and some monks have left their monasteries to engage in work as labourers either in the fields or in factories. Finally the whole concept of renunciation of the world and contemplative life has been challenged and the question of social responsibility and the need for the monk to be integrated in the social and economic life of his time and place has been proclaimed. But against this there is the need to answer the call of modern youth to a deeper life of prayer and meditation, so that the monastery can become a center for the renewal of spiritual life.

Such is the background against which we have to see the question of the future of monastic life in India. In attempting to answer this question I would like to draw largely on my experience of the last five years at Shantivanam, in which we have been compelled to face these various problems. Shantivanam was founded in 1950 by Father Monchanin and Father Le Saux, and was the first attempt in the church in India to establish an authentically Indian Christian monasticism. From the beginning the aim of Shantivanam was to integrate the values of Indian sannyasa with the tradition of Christian monasticism. The essence of Indian sannyasa is the desire to attain to the ultimate experience of God, or the Absolute, of nirvana, or moksha, and this it seems to me, must always be the fundamental aim of Indian Christian monasticism. Other orders are capable of bringing other values to the church and the world, but the monastic order has this one aim to "seek God," to experience the Presence of God in the depth of the soul and to live from the depth of this experience. Certainly in India the monastic order cannot hope to fulfill its function, if it cannot answer to this deepest need of the Indian soul. It is in the light of this that we have to attempt to reconstruct our monastic life.

This means that a monastery should be above all things a place of prayer, a place where people can come to 'realize' God, to discover the inner depth of their own being. For this purpose there must be a certain measure of silence and solitude, in which each can find the freedom to discover himself. But at the same time, it seems to me, a monastery today should be 'open' to the world. The emphasis should not be on enclosure, on keeping the world away, but on becoming a 'center' a place where people of all sorts can come for a short or a long stay according to their needs. It is at this point that some kind of temporary monasticism can be considered; this will mean that greater importance is attached to meditation and personal prayer than to liturgical prayer, including the Mass. The Mass and the Liturgy belong to the world of 'signs.' They are necessary as long as we live in this world, but at the same time they point beyond themselves to an order of being beyond signs, to the transcendent, the absolute, and it is to that the monk's life must always be leading. We need to recover the charismatic and prophetic character of the monk. A monk or sannyasi does not properly belong to the established order of the church. The church itself is a sacrament, a sign, and the monk is one who is dedicated to passing beyond all signs, however holy, to the absolute reality. He stands as it were at the frontier of the church. This was very evident in the Fathers of the Desert, to whose example we must always return, and in St Benedict himself who lived many years without the sacraments at the most critical time of his life.

This charismatic and prophetic character of the monk will mean that there will be much greater freedom in his life. He may wish to lead a solitary life, or to go on pilgrimage from place to place. This will mean that the Christian monk will be much more like the Hindu sannyasi. He may be called to travel, to give lectures and conferences, to undertake some social work, but equally he may be called to a life of absolute solitude in the Himalayas or to a period of prolonged fasting and asceticism. He must never be tied to any institution but have the freedom to follow the call of the Spirit. Of course, there will be a need for discernment of spirits, and here the need of a guru or spiritual father may well be felt. It is to be hoped that the abbot may become, as his name implies, more of spiritual father and less of an administrator. This may well mean that communities will normally become much smaller, consisting of perhaps two or three monks. On the other hand, it may well be that there will be a need for some larger monasteries, of a more traditional type, which can act as co-ordinating centers for the smaller groups or ashrams.

Such are some of the characteristics of monastic life which, it seems to me, we may expect to develop in the church in India. As can be seen it will have a somewhat paradoxical character; a radical renunciation of the world together with a complete openness to the world; a total dedication to the prayer of the heart, sometimes in complete solitude, but also forming a center of prayer. A great freedom, allowing for moving from place to place and yet a fundamental commitment to a guru or spiritual father, and perhaps an attachment to a larger monastery, which will serve to direct him. This it seems to me, will answer the question of the monk's engagement in the life of the world. As long as he is deeply rooted in the prayer of the heart, there is almost nothing which a monk may not do, but his work must never be institutionalized. He must always preserve the freedom of the Spirit. He may undertake social work in the manner of a Gandhian ashram and be deeply involved in the life of the people, like Vinoba Bhave. He make undertake agricultural, or educational or medical work and even assist in building large institutions like Aurobindo or Sivananda Ashram or like the houses of the Ramakrishna Order. But in all this he must have a radical detachment from the work in which he is engaged and be ready to hand it over to others, so as to preserve his own freedom. What we need above all is a renewal in the depths of the Spirit, and nothing can take the place of this. When this is present every work which is undertaken will have a different character from similar institutions elsewhere. Above all a monastery will be tested by its capacity to answer to the need of those who are seeking a deeper life of prayer, whether Christians, Hindus or young people from the West. We are witnessing today one of the great revivals of the spiritual life throughout the world, among Catholics and other Christians, among Hindus, Buddhists and Muslims, and above all among young people without any particular religious faith, or who have positively rejected traditional ways of religion. It is as part of this movement that we must see the growth of monastic life in the church today. We cannot say what particular forms it may take, but there must be an absolute openness to the movement of the Spirit, a readiness to change and experiment, to discover new ways of community life. It may well be that the present rigid division between celibate and married life will no longer prevail. It seems that many are being called to community life in the Spirit from among married people and there is no reason why monastic life should not adapt itself to this need. The Gandhian ashram has always been open to people of both sexes, like many Protestant ashrams, and in the ordinary Hindu ashram, though there is always a center of celibate life, the ashram is always open to all. This should be our model.

Finally, one may expect that monasteries will become centers of ecumenism. This means that, not only like Taize, will they bring Christians of different churches together for prayer and service, but also that they will become centers of inter-faith dialogue where Hindus and Christians and people of other religions may learn to live together. A monastery is a natural center for liturgical development, and one may expect the growth of an Indian liturgy, which is already beginning to take shape, to be fostered in monasteries. The use of the Scriptures of other religions in liturgical prayer is already becoming common, and one may expect that the normal prayer of an Indian monastery will include not only readings from other Scriptures but also songs and chants both in Sanskrit and the different vernaculars. It is from such meditative reading of the Hindu Scripture in a setting of prayer that one may hope that an Indian theology will begin to develop. Already there are moves in this direction and one may hope that the movement will grow in the coming years. The monastery provides a setting for study in a manner of the ancient *gurukul*, which may well be the best setting for the development of an Indian theology. But beyond both liturgy and theology the call of a monastery in India will always be to discover the depth of that mystical experience, from which all Indian religion derives and to integrate it in the life of the church. This will mean the use of all methods of meditation and ascetic life devised in the course of the centuries, which the monk may accept in his life of prayer. A Christian monk must be a Christian yogi. He will follow the paths of karma, bhakti and jnana yoga and will make use of hatha yoga as far as he may find it helpful. But this will not be merely a matter of techniques. It will be essentially an openness of the Spirit in its depths to what the Holy Spirit is asking of the church in India today. He will be ready to draw on the Hindu, the Buddhist, and the Islamic tradition as well as on new movements in the church and the world today, and he will be ready to join with people of all traditions in the search for ultimate reality, for that truth, which is ever ancient and ever new. In all this he will remain faithful to his original calling to 'seek God' by following Christ in that communion of the Spirit, by which all men are being led towards their final fulfilment.

84. The Gita and the Gospel

From time to time in the course of his commentary on the Bhagavad Gita *in* River of Compassion, *Bede points out the ways in which the Hinduism of the Gita has come very close to the Christianity of the New Testament. The foundation of this convergent movement is the emergence of a personal conception of God in the Gita. "The essential teaching of the Gita is that Krishna, the personal, incarnate God, is identified with brahman, the Origin, the One Reality."[17] from this derives a way of faith and love, of grace and self-surrender. This book marks an important turning point in Bede's own spirituality. Less ambitious than A New Vision of Reality, it is probably his most successful demonstration of the deep resonances between Hinduism and*

Christianity. A few short texts from River of Compassion *will illustrate this new orientation that emerges in the* Gita. *With the emergence of the ways of faith and love and service, the classical Hindu tradition of ascetic and contemplative spirituality opens to a human fullness. This mutation is comparable to the emergence of Mahayana Buddhism and of Christianity itself within their respective traditions.*

I[18]

Bede is commenting Gita 12.2, "Those who set their hearts on me and ever in love worship me, and who have unshakable faith, those I hold as the best Yogis."

In a sense the *Gita* was written to balance the view of the *Upanishads* which insists on the realization of brahman as the supreme Absolute and pays less attention to the personal aspect of the Godhead. One purpose of the *Gita* is to show that this personal aspect of brahman is supremely important, and that it is known by faith and love. That is why Christians are particularly attracted to it. Faith, shraddha, and love, bhakti, are the ways by which we come to know God in a personal way.

II[19]

Commenting Gita 12.20, "But even dearer to me are those who have faith and love and who have me as their End Supreme: those who hear my words of Truth, and who have come to the waters of Everlasting Life."

Mascaró's translation, "the waters of Everlasting Life," is too reminiscent of biblical language. Literally it is the amrita or 'nectar of righteousness.' In this passage we have in a nutshell the main teaching of the *Gita*. The method in the *Gita* is to keep going over the same themes, not simply going from one thing to another. It introduces a theme, then takes it up again and develops it much like a musical score, later bringing in another theme and developing that before returning to the first theme again. In the eighteenth chapter it brings the whole to completion by recalling all the basic themes. So again and again one finds that the whole is present in a particular part.

Commenting Gita 12.14,

His mind and his soul are surrendered to me. "Let him worship me with love and then I will love him" (Zaehner). This is an important teaching of the Gita. It is not simply that the soul loves God and is devoted to him, but that God loves the soul. One may get the idea that one is ascending above the mind and the buddhi, reaching beyond and going into a sort of void, but actually as one reaches that point, one meets the descending movement of love which is coming down through the whole universe; at that point one encounters this love, the self-giving love of God.

That is the supreme experience, when the love of the soul for God meets the love of God for the soul. We often think that we are loving God and are trying to reach him, when in fact it is God who is loving us and drawing us towards himself. So this movement of grace and love meets us.

IV[21]

Commenting Gita 18.49-54,

We have here a summary of the basic teaching of the *Gita* on the path of union with God. When we have freed ourselves from the passions, from the senses, from the mind, and all its changes, and from the thought of an 'I' and a 'mine,' then we reach this inner peace, this shanti, then we become brahman, we become one with God. The point where the human meets the divine is the buddhi and when we enter into that point, we enter into the awareness of brahman, of the eternal, everywhere and in everything. It is a part of our own being. That is brahman-vidhya. Brahma-bhuta is the other phase; the individual becomes brahman, becomes God. He is one with brahman, with God; he no longer grieves and no longer feels desire. By desire is meant a passionate desire; it is one of two extremes. We are usually either depressed and grieving over something or passionately desiring, wanting something. When we have freed ourselves from that, we become *sama*, which means sameness. "He is the same to all creatures, to all beings and above all he is *madbhaktim*, devoted to me, the Lord."

"His love is one for all creation, and he has supreme love for me."
That is the goal. So the *Gita* is leading the disciple up step by step.
One frees oneself from all the encumbrances of the body, of the
soul, of the mind and, opening oneself to the divine, to inner peace,
one surrenders oneself to the Lord. This is the final stage, self-surrender.

V²²

Commenting Gita 18.57,
We come now to the climax of the Gita's teaching on the love of
God. This is the way of bhakti; the whole mind is fixed on God all
the time and one surrenders everything to Him and does everything
as an offering to Him. It is a total self-surrender.

85. *Buddha and Christ*[23]

In Return to the Center, *Bede Griffiths had brought out the contrasts and
the complementarity between the figures of the Buddha and of Jesus Christ.
The comparison turns around the place of 'person' in the two religions. Bede,
we recall, has seen the primary change in the movement from* Upanishads *to
the* Bhagavad Gita *in the emergence of a personal God. In Christianity the
personal God encounters the human person in a new and decisive way — in an
absolute way, we might say. Western Christians often forget, consequently, the
'apophatic' principle of divine transcendence. Buddhism challenges us — paradoxically — to recover a sense of the unbounded divine fullness which exceeds
all our ideas, words and images of God. To liberate our conception of God can
be to liberate ourselves as well.*

What of the Buddha — how does he compare with Christ? The
Buddha, unlike Krishna, comes before us as an historical person.
Though legends have grown up round him and it is impossible to
reconstruct his life as a whole, yet the historical basis remains and a
moral character emerges as decisive as that of Jesus or Socrates. He
reveals a type of moral perfection and a compassion which is as real
and universal as the love of Christ. But again there are differences.
The Buddha is not 'God.' He is called *atideva*, 'above the gods.' He is
said to be omniscient. He stands for the ultimate principle of being.
He has his *dharmakaya*, his body of reality, of absolute being, as well
as his *sambhogakaya*, his body of bliss, or spiritual body, and his *nir-*

375

manakaya, his body of incarnation. This brings him very close to Christ. Yet Buddhism will not allow a personal God. True to its basic intuition, the ultimate Reality is conceived in negative terms   it is *sunya*, 'void.' The Buddha himself disappears in this void, because there is no 'self,' no person, in Buddhist thought. This also affects the compassion of the Buddha. His compassion arises from his awareness that all men are deceived and do not know the saving truth of nirvana. When the truth is known, no compassion remains, since no person remains. Buddhist compassion is therefore not the same as Christian love.

These distinctions are necessary but they do not invalidate the revelation of the Buddha or that of Krishna. The Buddha, Krishna, Christ   each is a unique revelation of God, of the divine Mystery, and each has to be understood in its historical context, in its own peculiar mode of thought. To say that God is a person is not necessarily to deny that he is impersonal. It is to affirm that the values of personal being, as we know them, in particular the values of knowledge and love, and therefore of moral responsibility, exist in the Godhead. But they exist in God in a manner beyond our comprehension, to which our concepts are always inadequate, and therefore to say that God is 'impersonal' can also be true. It signifies that the Godhead   or whatever name we give to the ultimate Mystery of being   is so far beyond any concept which we can form of a person, that it is better not to speak of it as a person. And, in fact, we find that the Christian concept of God often becomes so personal that it needs to be corrected by the impersonalism of Buddhism. Again, to say that God is moral perfection signifies that all that we can conceive of moral perfection, of goodness, kindness, gentleness, mercy, pity, grace and love, exists in the Godhead, but again, in a way that transcends our conception. To insist too much on the moral character of God can narrow our conception and lose something of that spontaneous freedom, that ecstasy of joy, which is found in Krishna. Each revelation is therefore complementary to the other, and indeed in each religion we find a tendency to stress first one aspect of the Godhead and then another, always seeking that equilibrium in which the ultimate truth will be found.

86. Trinity and the World Religions[24]

In this late essay, Bede Griffiths reflects on the central Christian mystery of the Trinity in the light of the great world religions. Almost immediately he quotes Raimondo Panikkar, the Indian Christian religious thinker who has been a pioneer in exploring the relation between Trinity and world religions in our time. Bede approves his friend's assertion that the Trinity will be the meeting place of the world religions. He does not, however, adopt Panikkar's precise correlation of the persons of the Trinity with distinct forms of spirituality and with concrete religious traditions. In Panikkar's view the Father relates to the silent, apophatic dimension, which is reflected in Buddhism, while the Son corresponds to the personalistic spirituality which is most evident in Israel and in Christianity, and the Spirit is related to the immanent dimension which is expressed in the Hindu doctrine of advaita as the non-duality of the self and the Absolute.[25]

Bede turns away from the Christian theology which has separated Trinity from creation, and sees the creation coming forth eternally from the Father in the Word (the Son). Pursuing further this unitive movement, he joins Trinity closely with Incarnation. While Bede coordinates Word and Spirit as divine 'Form' and 'Energy' (shakti in Hinduism) active throughout creation, he does not develop the further 'masculine-feminine' polarity of Word and Spirit to which he has referred at other times.[26] He finds reflections of the Christian Logos in Buddhism, in Hinduism and in Islam. Bede finds a trinitarian unfolding in several of the religious traditions; most clearly parallel to the Christian Trinity of Father, Word and Spirit is the sat-cit-ananda or being-knowledge-bliss of Hinduism. Bede offers us an informal, often rambling, sharing of his personal thoughts rather than an orderly lecture. Once we no longer expect from him the satisfaction of a coherent theory of Trinity and world religions, we may find that it is enough to let ourselves be drawn, with Bede, further into this mystery where, somehow, it all comes together.

The Trinity is probably the most difficult subject on which to write within the scope of Christian theology and spirituality, and yet I think it is of vital importance for us to try. This is true because the Trinity is the very heart of the Christian faith and the constant theme of the mystics in our rich contemplative tradition. What follows is not a systematic or scholarly presentation but a reflection on this central mystery. These insights are the fruit of my years in India and indicate my own inner awakening to the reality of the triune identity we call the Holy Trinity. I think it is true to say that this mystery is echoed or mirrored in the other great world religions, especially in their mystical dimension. For this reason, particularly from the vantage of India where so many of the great traditions dwell together within the same all-embracing culture, it is essential to draw attention to what may well be the focus of convergence for the various religions of the planet. As Raimundo Panikkar puts it:

> The Trinity . . . may be considered as a junction where the authentic spiritual dimensions of all religions meet. The Trinity is God's self-revelation in the fullness of time, the consummation both of all that God has already "said" of himself to man and of all that man has been able to attain and know of God in his thought and mystical experience. In the Trinity a true encounter of religions takes place, which results, not in a vague fusion or mutual dilution, but in an authentic enhancement of all the religious and even cultural elements that are contained in each.[27]

What Panikkar has said in the above passage represents in principle what I have come to discover over the years. I think I realized the centrality of the Trinity even before coming out to India, but the depth of the intuition only unfolded in the Indian context. Over the past forty years there has been a continuous development of my ideas on the Trinity. The way in which I would formulate the Trinitarian insight now differs from how I had previously understood it through my western education. Today I am seeing the Trinity in oriental terms and in this I am reacting against Greek theology. The Greeks had an abstract, metaphysical mind, and they divided Christ as it were. They conceived him in terms of a human "nature" and a divine "nature." In his divine nature he is eternally one with the Father and the Holy Spirit, but then in time he becomes man and assumes a human nature. The Greek view leads to the idea of the Trinity as something apart. The Father, Son and Holy Spirit are eternally there, and then apart from that comes the Incarnation, time and history.

But I think a deeper view, which is also the biblical view, is that the Son comes forth from the Father in eternity, and in the coming forth of the Word, the whole creation also comes forth. Christ as man comes forth eternally from the Father. So the whole mystery of creation and redemption is contained in that eternal reality. We still tend to think in terms of the Trinity apart, and then the Incarnation as something separate. I would like to think of the Father as eternally bringing forth the Son in His Word, and in that Word the whole creation from the beginning to the end is contained. In that Word the entire process of Incarnation, life, death and resurrection is contained, because time itself is contained in eternity, or as Plato said: "Time is a moving image of unmoving eternity." This approach makes the Trinity much more real to us, or certainly much more intelligible.

For many it remains a sort of puzzle, Three Persons in One; it becomes a problem rather than a mystery, and then they leave it there. But here in this life we are already involved in the Trinity. The whole creation arises eternally in God. As Maximus the Confessor said, the whole creation comes forth in God in the Word, in the eternal ideas of things. Each one of us exists eternally in God in our eternal idea that He has of us. And St Paul remarks: "He chose us in Him [in the Word] before the foundation of the world."[28] The entire creation is there present from the beginning. We are all present in God in Christ from the beginning. These ideas, the eternal ideas by the eternal will and decree of God, without change in Him, come into being in time and in space. So the creation comes forth in time; matter comes forth; life comes forth; human life comes forth, and as the culmination of the whole process, the Word becomes flesh. This Word which is present in matter, in life, in humanity takes flesh, and in a unique expression of the Divine Word is revealed in Jesus. But the Incarnation is the summit of the whole process of creation.

Karl Rahner describes how there are two movements of God giving himself to the world in man, and man giving himself to God. And when these two movements meet perfectly — God totally giving himself to man and man giving himself totally to God — then that is Incarnation. So the Word is manifesting in the created order, in all of humanity, and in every holy man and woman, in Krishna, the Buddha, Lao-Tzu. These are all manifestations of the Word in time. And Jesus comes as the culmination of that process. As Augustine says, Adam is man. And this man was intended to bring the creation back to God from the beginning. His human consciousness can reintegrate all the movements of creation and bring them back to God. But instead of that man falls away from God and becomes part of this divided universe. So, Augustine says that man/Adam is as it were scattered over the world; his limbs are all scattered. Jesus assumes this man into the Godhead and reunites all these scattered members. Every eucharist is a reuniting of the Body of Christ which has been scattered by sin.

And so, the humanity and creation are reunited in Christ and returned to the Godhead, returned to their being in the Word. As St Maximus said, we all must return to our idea in God; we have fallen away from that idea through sin, suffering and death. But then through redemption and grace we return to our idea in the Word, for we are one with Him. Tauler actually says that every creature in God *is* God.[29]

Of course this statement has to be understood in a deep sense; it has to be understood mystically and not ontologically as pure identity, as is sometimes said in Hindu *advaita*.[30] So there we have this coming forth of the Word from the Father, and the Word comes forth as distinct from the Father. All the distinctions in creation are found in principle in the Word. This is important because in the Hindu view you often hear that all differences disappear in the final state. We would say that those differences are eternally in the Word. There is the distinction between the Father and the Son which is the basis of the distinction of all creation from God, distinction and yet unity. The Son is really the principle of differentiation, and all the distinctions of the created order are contained in the Son as the Word or Logos.

Now, as the Son emerges from the Father eternally and differentiates Himself, and distinguishes the world or creation from the Father, so He returns to the Father in the Spirit. The Spirit is the Love that unites Father and Son. The entire creation comes forth in all its differentiation in the Word, and it returns in the Spirit to the One. The Spirit is the energy in God, the *shakti* or power in Hindu terms, that is the uncreated Energy of Gregory of Palamas. The Word or Son as the *Logos* is the exemplary Form of all creation, the principle of all forms in nature, while the Spirit is the *shakti*, the energy in creation, what makes it to be and to operate. All the energy in matter is a manifestation of the Divine Energy, and all energy in life is a manifestation of this same Divine Energy or shakti. Moreover, all energy in human beings is a manifestation of this same Divine Energy, and when we come to consciousness, that Divine Energy becomes conscious in us. The energy in plants and animals becomes conscious in man. Then we, through the power of the Spirit in us, are able to return to God, to the Word. Thus the Word and the Spirit are revealed in their unity. When the creation arises, the Spirit appears different from the Word. The Energy is different from the Form. But as they develop in man, and above all as we go beyond our limits and open ourselves to grace, then form and matter, Word and Spirit are revealed in their total unity which is eternal, the unity of the Holy Trinity.

It is important to realize that we are all engaged in the life of the Trinity, and all of us come forth from the Father eternally and in time. Equally we all must return to the Father eternally and in time in the Spirit. That is the movement of creation coming forth and returning to God, to the Word in the Spirit. We find something akin to this insight in the great religious traditions of the world. It is a profound intuition that is found alike in the Buddhist, Hindu, Jewish, and Islamic traditions and all the deepest Christian thinkers. I think Maximus the Confessor expresses it the best I have ever found. He says that in moving towards God in knowledge and love, we are simply returning to our idea in Him. Even if we wander from God, our idea, that is the idea He has of each one of us, remains the same. Every person is a part of God, a *moira Theou,* "a part of God" to the extent that by his idea, his essence, he is eternally pre-existent in God. Ecstasy is an anticipation of the life to come when the "divinization of the universe will be achieved by the return of all things to their eternal ideas, essences and causes from which they are now separated." I feel that this view is not only accurate but really expressive of the deepest understanding of the mystery. It should be emphasized that this is not a speculative theory; it is the product of contemplative experience. It is essential for us all to know that the Trinity is not some sort of mathematical problem of how the Three and the One are united, but that it is a mystery that is personally involved with us and in us.

Instead of the abstract scholastic theology, in this understanding we have something concrete, a definitely personal connection. We are in God; we are from God in Christ. This understanding is implicit in the old form of the Gloria. It used to be: "Glory be to the Father, through the Son in the Holy Spirit." We live in the Spirit, and the Spirit comes to us through the Son from the Father. We are living in the Trinity the whole time. And the idea of a gulf between us and God is really an illusion. We are *in* Him. Sin creates the illusion that we are separated beings, but the reality is that we live in Him, and "in Him we live and move and have our being."[31] Furthermore this reveals that God's being is essentially interpersonal relationship. That is what the Trinity signifies. For most people personal relations are the main value in their lives. They experience themselves in relation to their parents, their wives and husbands, to their children, their friends and associates. This is what makes up so much of human life for many people, and to say that the fullness of life, indeed Heaven itself, is the fullness of personal relationship is to describe exactly what the Trinity is. For it is interpersonal relationship, a relationship of knowledge and love, or communion in knowledge and love, personal communion. That is a beautiful insight, and that is where I feel that the Trinity adds something to any other doctrine. All the great traditions have a similar intuition about returning to the idea, but that the ultimate reality of the Godhead is interpersonal relationship, is personal communion in love, I think is a distinctly Christian insight, and reveals the inner depth of the whole mystery.

In each tradition there is a tendency to see ultimate reality in terms of identity, as in strict advaita, but there is also to be found a more profound understanding of unity in difference. Suzuki used to emphasize that the Void, the *sunyata* in the Buddhist conception, is not static but dynamic, and that the whole creation arises from the Void, and then returns to it; it does so without making any change in the Void itself. But that it is a personal dynamism the Buddhist would not hold, and the same is true with the Hindu advaitin. Sankara's doctrine of advaita is much more profound than it often appears. He says something quite similar to St Thomas, that all beings seen apart from brahman are unreal, but when seen in brahman have total reality. This is very similar to St Thomas' view that God is "in" all things by His power, His presence and His essence, so that the Divine essence, the Holy Trinity, is in every particle of matter. Sankara really recognizes that the actual being of all things is their eternal being in brahman. So I think that in each doctrine this original simple notion of identity comes to be modified and is enriched by the added insight that there are relationships in the Godhead, and that relationship characterizes the interaction of God and man.

I think there are historical reasons for the impersonal approach of pure *advaita* and the Buddhist doctrine of the Void. People tend to be so much involved in personal being, in personal relationships involving not only love but hatred and conflict, so that the great need is to get beyond such relationships. The Indian philosophers were trying to get beyond this, to get beyond or transcend all human conflicts and so to move into nirguna brahman, or brahman "without attributes," into nirvana, into the Void. But then we must recognize that in the Void, in nirvana, what is really true and deep in human relationships is not lost but is fulfilled.

The same is true in Sankara's notion of non-duality or *advaita*. His one great concern was to get beyond the multiplicity. Everybody is involved in multiplicity. So many think that that is everything. And he was struggling all the time to transcend the multiplicity so as to reach that One beyond all the multiplicity. He was not concerned much with justifying the world of diversity. But then we have to say that when we reach the One, we find that every detail of multiple being is present in the One eternally in the eternal ideas. Each doctrine has its own perspective. When we see it in its perspective it is valid, but each doctrine also leaves out certain other aspects, and does so because it concentrates on one aspect.

I think, for instance, that Buddhism might well be open to a Trinitarian interpretation. The key to that is the concept of the *Tathagata*.[32] The Buddhists have this interesting understanding that the Buddha himself has three bodies: the *Nirmanakaya*, the earthly body, the Sambhogyakaya, the heavenly body, and the *Dharmakaya*, which is the body of ultimate reality. And the Buddha is one who is "thus gone," or *Tathagata*; he is gone to That, to ultimate reality. And so there is an understanding in Mahayana Buddhism that the Buddha attains to absolute reality and is the one who has indeed attained the reality; he becomes that very reality. That is very like the doctrine of the Incarnation, of the Logos, and suggests an analogy with the Trinity.

Also in Islam there is a profoundly interesting doctrine of the Universal Man. It is fascinating that Mohammed from being a purely human person and the supreme prophet in the Koran becomes in the Sufi doctrine a symbol of the Logos, the Word, the "Pole of the universe" they call it. Thus Mohammed becomes the person who reveals the Ultimate, the Man who is the "eye" of God.

In Hinduism there is the purusha, the Cosmic Person revealed in the Vedas as the divine Man, who has one part on earth and three parts in heaven. So in each tradition there is a definite movement towards this personal manifestation of the One beyond and so also of the possibility of openness to a Trinitarian unfolding. All the traditions converge on the Trinity simply because it is the deepest reality of the Sacred Mystery, and indications are found of its presence in most of the traditions.

One example of this is to be found in the Hindu doctrine of the Absolute as Being-Knowledge-Bliss, what is called *Saccidananda*. Saccidananda comes from the tradition of the *Upanishads*. The upanishadic seers were searching for what is the Reality behind all things, the *sat* or being, and then they came to realize that that being is consciousness (*cit*). Brahman (God) is consciousness, and finally they saw that there was an inner unity between Divine consciousness, the brahman, and the depths of the human consciousness, the atman. This unity is expressed in one of the four *Mahavakyas* or "Great Utterances" or "Sentences" which sum up the mystical wisdom of Hinduism. The fourth mahavakya says: "That art Thou."[33] "That" is brahman and "thou" is the human self, the atman. In the Ultimate Reality that being or *sat* is also *cit* or pure consciousness. And when one enters into that being in consciousness, one experiences *ananda* or pure joy, pure bliss; ananda, the bliss of being totally aware or conscious of being/pure existence. Saccidananda is the mystical awareness of the person who enters into advaitic or transcendent experience. So that is the background of it. But personal relationships do not come in, are not part of it. The sages were trying to get beyond the multiplicity, and beyond individual persons, beyond the *jivatman* or the individual, to the Ultimate state. But this state, this Ultimate, can also be explored in the light of the Trinity.

In doing so we can think of the Father as *sat*, as Being, the reality behind all things, the Source from which everything comes into existence. Then we can think of the Son as the consciousness of the Father, the Father reflecting Himself, knowing Himself and expressing Himself in His Word. And this corresponds with that *cit*. Then the *ananda* can be seen as the Holy Spirit, the bliss of Love. Of course we are reading a new doctrine into the old. The other is simply a metaphysical doctrine based on a mystical perception, and we are reading a much deeper meaning into it. But then Hinduism itself went through a development where the personal God became much more manifest, and the whole question of human relationship to God became prominent. At the early stage of the *Upanishads* this personalist thrust or emphasis was not present.

And this is perhaps the natural development in religious insight of a contemplative depth. I think behind all these religious experiences is this recognition of one ultimate, infinite, transcendent, incomprehensible mystery which is called brahman, Tao, nirvana, etc. That is the beginning, and I think that every authentic religion reaches out and sometimes touches that infinite mystery. The next stage is to ask: how is human nature, the human being, or human consciousness related to that? We discover that the human being can go beyond its limited mental consciousness; open itself to the Transcendent, and participate in that Divine Reality, actually becoming identified in consciousness with the Divine reality. Now that is, I think, very near to the experience of Jesus in relation to the Father; it is not the same, but it is very close to it. It is very close also to the doctrine of the *Tathagata*, and the *Dharmakaya*. And this is not a theory or a doctrine, but an experience of mystical consciousness.

As we enter into the mystery of the Godhead manifesting itself, expressing itself, we experience this extraordinary bliss, the ananda. Moreover it is really a bliss of love. When we open ourselves to the

Divine we experience this overpowering ananda, this joy, this fulfill-ment, and we realize that it can be taken a step further, because we realize that this bliss is love. Now love is personal relationship. When this is recognized a new dimension is discovered. The nucleus is there from the beginning, and we are gradually developing it, realizing all that is implicit in it, implicit from the beginning. In the original expe-rience of the mystery, the doctrine of Trinity and all these doctrines of the other traditions are implicit, and they are gradually brought out through human experience, the experience of Hindus, Buddhists, and finally the experience of Christ and the church. They are all exploring the mystery and drawing out new aspects of it, but all are congruent, for they are all concerned with the one same Sacred Mystery.

It is crucial to recognize that even in the church's understanding of the Trinity the intuition came only gradually. In the New Testament it is still not developed. God is seen first of all as Father, and then slowly Jesus reveals Himself as the Son in an absolutely unique sense. This is only fully expressed in St John's Gospel. It has been said that the Father was revealed in the Old Testament; the Son was revealed in the New, and the divinity of the Holy Spirit was only gradually realized in the history of the church. So there is a gradual unfolding of the same mystery from the original Hebrew concept of the Elohim, which is the primordial word for that mystery. This is developed further in the revelation of the name of Yahweh where the personal aspect of the Godhead is discovered. Finally Jesus came to reveal the Messiah as the Son, as the Word of God, who is equal to the Father. And then the Holy Spirit is revealed as God in the early church. In all this first comes the experience then the theology, as the church begins to reflect on her experience. Then she discovers the insight that the Holy Spirit must be one with the Father and the Son. In this way the doctrine of the Trinity has evolved. The word "triad" was first used by the Apologists of the second century. It is not found in the New Testament. The formal doctrine then begins to develop from there, from this insight of the second century church. Theological reflection comes out of the experience, just as the whole Christian revelation comes out of the experience of Christ. This experience of God through the Son, in the Spirit which was given to the early church was then gradually explicated theologically.

The church is always conditioned by the culture of the times, and this has an impact on her attempts at theological expression of her experience. The mystery of the Trinity is the subject of the church's deepest mystical experience of the Godhead from the earliest times, but since the seventeenth century the mystical dimension of the church receded into the background. Until that time right up to the time of St John of the Cross mysticism was seen as the very culmination of the Christian life. Then in the seventeenth century with Madame Guyon, the Quietists and others mysticism became suspect by church authorities and was considered dangerous; only very rare individuals could have such experiences, and the ordinary Christian, including priests and religious must keep to the ordinary way of prayer. That attitude prevailed for three centuries, and the Jesuits, in particular, as spiritual directors took this view, but it was really the result of a pastoral concern. Many people were confused by mystical theories and ideas, so it was thought necessary to emphasize the fundamentals: the Incarnation, the eucharist and the other sacraments, the mediatory role of the church. The church thus kept things on that level of theology and practice for three centuries. But I think now that the church is recovering her mystical life she is also rediscovering its very heart, the Trinity.

This rediscovery will have an important influence on the other world religions as we enter into dialogue with them. We cannot really tell what shape an inter-religious Trinitarian theology will take. The problem is that once we begin to discuss this within a dialogical situation we have to use words and terms which are an inevitable source of disagreement and conflict. I remember, for example, that we had a dialogue in Trivandrum, South India, with Christian and Hindu experts, and we came around to discussing the subject of a personal God. One of the Hindus, a Sanskrit professor, said that to him the term "person" implied limitation. So immediately the language of persons in the Trinity was a serious problem and had no meaning for them. And so to develop a terminology we can all share is something we have to give much attention to and on which much effort will have to be expended. In the long run, however, I feel that the various tra-

387

ditions will discover the mystery of the Trinity, as we grow in trust with one another, open in depth, and share the rich fruit of our contemplation and mystical life. Thus I think Panikkar rightly sums it up when he speaks of the Trinity as the "junction where the authentic spiritual dimensions of all religions meet."[34]

87. Self-realization and Trinity[35]

As Bede comments verse 6.20 of the Bhagavad Gita *in* River of Compassion, *he suggests an interpretation in terms of Father, Word and Spirit. This would be a totally interior realization of the Christian Trinity, recalling St. Augustine's theology of the trinitarian image within the human person conceived in terms of memory, intellect and will. Characteristically, however, this 'Indian' conception of the inner trinitarian experience is unitive rather than analytic. There is, finally, only the Self knowing the Self.*

The one Self is manifesting, expressing himself, in each one of us and the aim of yoga is to restrain the senses and the mind so that one enters into the inner Self and becomes aware of the supreme Self dwelling within. A more literal translation is, "Seeing Self by Self in Self" (Besant & Das). This is a beautiful expression of the goal of yoga, "to see the Self in the Self by the Self." It is to discover the Self, the *aramatman*, the ultimate Ground of Being, as dwelling, as manifesting himself 'in' one's own Self, and this can only be done 'by' the Self. It is only God acting in us who can reveal the indwelling Presence and enable us to realize the ultimate unity of being. This can be interpreted in terms of the Christian doctrine of the Trinity. The Father is the *Paramatman, Parabrahman*, the ultimate Ground of Being beyond word and thought. The Father reveals himself in the Son, the Word, the Self-expression, Self-manifestation, of the One. And this Self-revelation of the Father in the Son is made known by the Holy Spirit, the Self-communication of God, the power or energy of the Spirit, acting in the depths of the human being, in the spirit of man, and enabling him to recognize the indwelling presence of the Spirit within. It is this ultimate mystery of being which is being revealed in different ways in the different religious traditions.

88. The Universal Wisdom[36]

Bede Griffiths' most passionate and persistent conviction is the unitive idea, which originates in an interior experience and corresponds, he is certain, to ultimate reality. He finds this reality reflected everywhere in the universe, in human culture and in the world's religious traditions. We have already encountered the unitive reality in various forms, particularly in reviewing Bede's writings on the Vedanta. In the texts which follow, we shall find Bede presenting the central unitive reality both as the 'perennial philosophy' or universal wisdom, and as the common core of all the religious traditions.

The perennial philosophy itself, in Bede's writings, is presented from two perspectives, at different moments. Frequently he will speak of it as being — or being centered in — the unitive experience, or experience of the Self: advaita, atman. At other times he will describe the perennial philosophy or universal wisdom as a vision of reality as consisting of the three interrelated worlds of matter, consciousness and pure spirit or body, psyche and spirit. These two perspectives are related as the interior and exterior, or the center and the whole. If Bede will speak of the central Mystery as the realization of the Self — most clearly revealed in the Upanishads *— he will also see it as the evolutionary process in which all reality is gathered into one body. We can feel both of these movements — inward and outward, backward and forward, eastward and westward — as Bede writes of the one Mystery at the heart of all the religions which is to be experienced in the depths of the soul, and of the convergent movement of all the religions toward the realization of this Mystery.*

The unity of religions is based upon a single sovereign truth which Bede finds most explicitly articulated in the Hindu Vedanta. This is the 'advaitan' principle of a nondual absolute Being and of a nondual knowledge which is a participation in this ultimate reality. Bede finds this truth not only at the heart of the great Asian traditions of Hinduism, Buddhism and Taoism but in the West as well, particularly in the Platonist and Neoplatonist traditions. Through Plato and Plotinus it has come into the western philosophical tradition; through Augustine and Aquinas[37] it has been integrated into the core of the Catholic theological tradition. Bede will call this 'the universal tradition,' 'the eternal philosophy,' 'the traditional order,' 'the universal metaphysical tradition,' 'the perennial philosophy,' 'the universal wisdom.' Convinced of this central truth already before his move to India, Bede would later speak of it as the basis of all his thinking.

What is the nature of the spiritual tradition which is found in its purest form in India and constitutes the supreme heritage of mankind? It is simply this. There is one absolute, eternal, infinite, unchanging Being, which is the unique source of all existence, of all knowledge and of all life; which is above all things and in all things and for which all things exist. This absolute Being may be conceived in different terms, but in one form or another it is the basis of all religion, not only in India but in China and throughout the East. This is the basis of what we have called the spiritual tradition of mankind and the ground of all religion.

What, then, is the relation of man and the universe to this absolute Being? Man is an image of God; the universe is a finite reflection of this infinite Being, a reflection of the One in the many, of the eternal in time, of the infinite in space. Here again this relationship may be differently conceived, but fundamentally it will be found that this is its nature. The universe is not an 'illusion' as it is sometimes said; it has a certain reality, but it is the reality of a reflection in a mirror. Apart from its source it has no reality at all. The real illusion is to mistake the material universe for an independent reality. This is the great illusion of the West, which constitutes materialism. It is against this illusion that the whole of eastern doctrine stands, by affirming the absolute reality of God alone and the wholly dependent and relative reality of the physical universe.

How does man enter into relation with this infinite and eternal Being? Here again there is a deep cleavage between East and West. We in the West have grown up under the influence of Aristotle and the Greeks. We think of reason acting upon the evidence of the senses as the normal mode of human knowledge. But in the East it has always been understood that there is a higher mode of knowledge than sense or reason — the knowledge of spiritual intuition, a knowledge not dependent on the senses or on any logical process, but on the soul's direct, intuitive awareness of itself. It is this which has been sought in the East from time immemorial and which gives the true knowledge of God. It is a knowledge derived from contemplation, a wisdom which descends from above and directly enlightens the soul. To this knowledge all images and concepts can only act as 'supports'; it transcends the finite order and unites man directly with God.

This, we would say, is the basis of all oriental doctrine, of that spiritual tradition which underlies all ancient religion and which survives today in India and the East. But granting this, there are two questions which have to be asked. First, what is the validity of this claim to a higher mode of knowledge? And, secondly, what relation does the whole of this tradition bear to Christianity, and particularly to Catholicism?

We have to recognize that this tradition is not found only in the East. It entered into the current of western thought with Pythagoras and Plato and finds its most eminent exponent in the West in Plotinus. Such a concourse of the greatest minds of East and West, covering thousands of years of human history and permeating the religion of millions of people, is surely in itself an impressive witness to its truth. In a sense, of course, it cannot be proved. One can only prove it by experience, just as if someone claims that a play of Shakespeare or a symphony of Beethoven gives him a unique kind of experience, one cannot either prove or disprove the validity of the claim. It is a matter of experience.

But for a Catholic there is evidence of another kind. The influence of Aristotle, with his logical and analytical method, on our philosophy and theology has been so great that we sometimes forget that our theology was originally formed in the school of Plato. The Greek Fathers were almost all Platonists, and the founder of Latin theology in the West, Augustine, has left on record the fact that he owed the first illumination of his mind to Plato. It is, in fact, precisely this spiritual tradition of the East, coming to us through Plato and Plotinus, which lies at the heart of our Catholic theology. When Aquinas introduced the exact method of Aristotle into theology, he did not discard this Platonic tradition; on the contrary, he incorporated it. His theology is a synthesis of Plato and Aristotle based on the original Hebrew-Christian revelation.

St Thomas' conception of God is identical with that of eastern tradition, as we have described it. In the question of the relation between the universe and God, St Thomas introduced an exact conception of creation which clarifies the eastern tradition, but leaves it essentially unchanged. And in the matter of the knowledge of God by contemplation, St Thomas clearly recognizes a mode of knowledge above both reason and faith, admitting man to knowledge of God by experience, an infused wisdom in which the soul becomes passive to the divine action, *patiens divina.*

We have, then, the right to say that this spiritual tradition is an integral part of Catholicism. It is, in fact, nothing but that perennial philosophy, that universal metaphysical tradition, which is the basis of all religion, both eastern and western. To this tradition Catholicism gives a precision which is generally lacking in the East. It firmly upholds the absolute transcendence of God, while admitting his immanence in all creation. It asserts the reality of the material creation while allowing that this reality is wholly relative and dependent on the absolute being of God. Above all, it brings the whole of this tradition into relation with the doctrine of the incarnation, of man's salvation through the redeeming death of Christ and his need of God's grace if he is to enter into a living relation with him.

89. *The One Spirit in All Religion*[38]

With the bold and vigorous thought that characterizes Return to the Center, *Bede Griffiths develops his assertion of the interior unity of all religions as different expressions and embodiments of the one divine Mystery. He distills each of the great religious traditions into a single word or phrase; each tradition consistently manifests the one divine Mystery in its own, distinct way. It is this Mystery which, at the core of the human person, ever attracts the intellect and the will. It lies also at the heart of the philosophical quest and of the poetic intuition; finally, it is experienced in its purity by the mystic. In Bede's view here in* Return to the Center, *the Truth is at the beginning, closest to the common 'Center,' and subsequent development must remain faithful to the original revelation. The unitive principle predominates and is continually underlined.*

The function of comparative religion is to discern this essential Truth, this divine Mystery beyond speech and thought, in the language-forms and thought-forms of each religious tradition, from the most primitive tribal traditions to the most advanced world religions. In each tradition the one divine Reality, the one eternal Truth, is present, but it is hidden under symbols, symbols of word and gesture, of ritual and dance and song, of poetry and music, art and architecture, of custom and convention, of law and morality, of philosophy and theology. Always the divine Mystery is hidden under a veil, but each revelation (or 'unveiling') unveils some aspect of the one Truth, or, if you like, the veil becomes thinner at a certain point. The Semitic religions, Judaism and Islam, reveal the transcendent aspect of the divine Mystery with incomparable power. The oriental religions reveal the divine Immanence with immeasurable depth. Yet in each the opposite aspect is contained, though in a more hidden way. We have to try to discover the inner relationship between these different aspects of Truth and unite them in ourselves. I have to be a Hindu, a Buddhist, a Jain, a Parsee, a Sikh, a Muslim, and a Jew, as well as a Christian, if I am to know the Truth and to find the point of reconciliation in all religion.

Every religion as long as it continues to live is in a state of evolution. We can watch the process in the development of Hinduism from the original Aryan religion of the Rig-Veda, through the Brahmanas and *Upanishads* and the *Bhagavad Gita*, gradually absorbing elements from the ancient Dravidian religion, learning from Buddhism, later from Islam, and finally from Christianity. We can see Buddhism evolving from the simple, primitive cult of the Hinayana to the vast complexity of the Mahayana, absorbing innumerable elements from Hinduism, yet always giving them a new and distinctive character, and adopting ever new forms as it spreads through China, Tibet and Japan. We can see the primitive Arabian religion of the Koran evolving through its contact with the Syrian and Persian cultures and developing a mystical doctrine through direct contact with Hinduism. As of Judaism, we can watch its evolution in the Old Testament itself from a primitive tribal religion to the universalism of the prophets, learning from Egypt and Babylonia and Persia and Greece and developing new characteristics through its dispersion in the gentile world, yet always conditioned by its past and remaining true to its original revelation. In each tradition the one divine Truth receives a particular mould to which it remains true throughout its evolution.

The need is to discern in each religion the character of this primitive mould. Often it can be summed up in a single word. For Hinduism it is brahman, the 'one without a second', the Infinite, the

Eternal, Saccidananda — Being, Knowledge, Bliss. In Hinduism everything refers back to this one, unspeakable Mystery. In Buddhism it is nirvana, the cessation of being, the blowing out of the fire of life, the state beyond consciousness, the emptiness in which all fullness is contained. It is the negative aspect of the divine Mystery. In Islam, it is Islam itself, the 'surrender' to Allah, the beneficent, the merciful, the one Truth and Reality in its absolute transcendence. In Judaism it is Yahweh, the Holy One of Israel, the Eternal in his self-manifestation in history, the divine Mystery hidden in clouds and darkness, yet ever close to the heart of man.

What of Christianity? It is the revelation of the divine Mystery in the person of Christ. The one, eternal Truth, which cannot be uttered, which cannot be known, is 'symbolized' in the life and death and resurrection of Jesus of Nazareth. At this point in history the veil is pierced, the Mystery shines through. At the resurrection of Jesus, human nature was taken up into the divine, time was taken up into eternity. Yet these are only phrases we use to express the inexpressible. It is not by word or thought but by meditation on the Mystery that we can pierce the veil. This is where all human reason fails. All these words, Brahman, Nirvana, Allah, Yahweh, Christ, are meaningless to those who cannot get beyond their reason and allow the divine Mystery to shine through its symbol. This is done by faith. Faith is the opening of the mind to the transcendent Reality, the awakening to the eternal Truth.

Christianity has its evolution no less than every other religion. It begins as a sect of Judaism, speaking Aramaic and enclosed in the thought-forms of the Semitic world. Then it breaks out into the Graeco-Roman world and begins to speak the language and to adopt the thought-forms of the Greeks. This process begins at its very inception. The first Gospels themselves are translations into Greek of the original Aramaic, interpreting the original message in the light of a new situation, yet always remaining faithful to the original mystery. It is this 'mystery of Christ' which lies at the heart of the Gospels and of all the evolution of Christianity. It cannot be properly expressed. The language of the New Testament is the earliest form of its expression which we possess and comes closest to the original, but the Truth is ever beyond what words can express. It is the Word of God, the eternal Truth made manifest, the mystery of salvation, of man's encounter with God. It is the mystery which was 'hidden for ages in God.'[39] This is the object of faith, expressed in words but always going beyond words, speaking to the heart, awakening the depths of the soul, bringing illumination, peace, joy. And this Mystery when known in its ultimate ground is one with the mystery of Brahman, Nirvana, Tao, Yahweh, Allah. It is the one Truth, the one Word, the eternal Saccidananda.

The goal of each religion is the same. It is the absolute, transcendent state, the one Reality, the eternal Truth, which cannot be expressed, cannot be conceived. This is the goal not only of all religion, but of all human existence   whether they like it or not, all men are continually attracted by this transcendent Truth. The intellect, in and beyond every formulation by which it seeks to express its thought, is in search of the Absolute. It is made for Being itself, for Truth, for Reality, and it cannot rest satisfied in any partial truth, in any construction of the human mind. It is always being carried beyond itself to the ultimate Truth. The will also is always moved by love of the Infinite. In every human love there is a reaching out towards the Infinite, a desire to transcend itself, to make the total surrender of self. This tendency is present in the atheist and the agnostic, in the ignorant and foolish as well as the wise. It is what gives an infinite value to the human person. Every attempt to deny this tendency, to confine human life to the finite and the temporal, is doomed to failure, because it is fighting against nature. It breaks out of all careful formulations and limited objectives. Perhaps Wittgenstein is the best evidence of this, but Marxism also bears witness to it. It is the redeeming element in all philosophy, which prevents it from ever settling down to a partial vision of the Truth.

This of course is the grace of poetry. The poet, the painter, the artist, is always in touch with this transcendent Mystery — in so far as he is an authentic poet — however much he may be enclosed in the world of the senses and the imagination. He may write of nature or war or human love and passion; he may paint a landscape or a portrait without any 'sacred' character: but it is the presence of the sacred

Mystery in his work which makes it poetry. Raïssa Maritain has written well of this when she says that poetry is conceived in "those depths of the soul where intelligence and desire, intuition and sensibility, imagination and love, have their common source." Poetry and mysticism both derive from a common source, the ground or depth of the soul, where the Mystery of Being is experienced. But the poet is always driven to 'symbolize' his experience, to express it in words or in paint or in music. The mystic seeks the experience in itself, beyond words or sounds or images.

90. The Eternal Religion[40]

Once again in Return to the Center, *Bede focuses upon the one Mystery which is the Center: here as the 'eternal religon' or 'sanatana dharma.' In this long sustained treatment of the universal wisdom at the core of all the religious traditions, his emphasis is on the interior realization of the Mystery as the Self or atman, the center of the person. Often in later writings he will speak of a union with God through knowledge and love. Here, under the strong interior gravitational force of the East, the person is conceived as a centered totality.*

Not only is the Mystery present in a different way in each tradition, but we are to learn it from all of them: from the primal, tribal religions as well as the highly developed traditions of Hinduism and Christianity. The way to the realization of the Self, however, is simple: it is the way of surrender: a surrender which proceeds through ever more interior stages. The personal way must also correspond to the traditional wisdom, according to one of the great traditions of faith. The great religious traditions begin with mystical experience and then develop into complex systems of thought. It is necessary, if we would know the Mystery, that we penetrate through the exterior shell of the rationalized system to realize within ourself the original experience: that is, to participate in the divine life which has been shared among human beings. This is the kingdom of God and the essential message of all religion. External religion, with its rites, dogmas and institutional structures, exists only to bring people to the personal experience of this mystery. External forms, the 'language' of religion, must be continually revised to enable them to communicate the mystery to the people of a new age. The mystery, however, already dwells in the heart of every human being, and the church must awaken to this 'universal revelation.'

Here history itself finds its meaning only in a return to the one Mystery which is at the source of each of the traditions. Bede's prophetic radicality resounds as he calls for the demolition of every mediating structure which has obscured this single Mystery and made it inaccessible. At this moment in Bede's life, totally captivated by the gravitation of the Center, he does not point out to us the evolutionary work of the divine Spirit. The movement is almost entirely inward and back, rather than outward and forward.

Where, then, is this eternal religion — the *sanatana dharma*, as the Hindus call it — to be found? It is to be found in every religion as its ground or source, but it is beyond all formulation. It is the reality behind all rites, the truth behind all dogmas, the justice behind all laws. But it is also to be found in the heart of every man. It is the law "written on their hearts."[41] It is not known by sense or reason but by the experience of the soul in its depths. Of this it has been said: "Thy natural senses cannot possess God or unite thee to him; nay, thy inward faculties of understanding, will, and memory, can only reach after God, but cannot be the place of his habitation in thee. But there is a root or depth in thee from whence all these faculties come forth, as lines from a center or as branches from the body of the tree. This depth is called the Center, the Fund or Bottom of the soul. This depth is the unity, the eternity, I had almost said the infinity of thy soul; for it is so infinite that nothing can satisfy it or give it any rest but the infinity of God."[42] It is in this depth that all true religion is to be found. It is the source from which all religion springs, the goal to which it aspires, and it is present in the heart of every man. It was from this Center that man fell and it is to this Center that he must return. Every religion seeks to make this known and to map out the path of return.

Each man must therefore discover this Center in himself, this Ground of his being, this Law of his life. It is hidden in the depths of every soul, waiting to be discovered. It is the treasure hidden in a field, the pearl of great price.[43] It is the one thing which is necessary,[44] which can satisfy all our desires and answer all our needs. But it is hidden now under deep layers of habit and convention. The world builds up a great protective barrier round it. It is the original paradise from which we have all come — as Wordsworth said, "Heaven lies about us in our infancy." We were all once innocent and pure and holy, as we came from God, but we have fallen into this world, and an angel with a flaming sword prevents our return. All these mysteries are hidden in the unconscious. There still stands the original paradise, there the Fall takes place in each one of us, the trauma of birth into this world. There the layers of habit and convention are formed, binding us to this world, beginning their work while we are yet in the womb, weaving the great web of *maya*, which hides us from our true Self and makes us aliens from our home. But everywhere the path of return is to be found. Every myth and ritual of primitive religion is a revelation of the hidden mysteries of the unconscious and a pathway to the discovery of the Self.

If we would find the path of return we must be willing to learn from every ancient tradition, from African and Asian tribal religion, from that of the Australian aborigines and the American Indian. All these people who have been suppressed and almost eliminated by the white races bear within themselves the treasures of the ancient wisdom. By returning to them we are returning to our own past, to the wisdom of the unconscious which has been suppressed in us, to the heart of the child which is hidden in every man. Our civilization will remain for ever psychologically unbalanced until it has done justice to these people. The Negro will remain a perpetual challenge to white civilization until the wisdom which he possesses, the intuitive wisdom of primeval man, has been recognized. In all these people the sense of man's solidarity with nature has been preserved. Nature is for them not what it is to the scientific mind, an external object to be studied by cold reason, but a living part of his own being. He knows himself as part of nature, as having kinship with the earth and the sky, with the plants and animals and birds. He knows himself in the deep ground of the unconscious as a child in the womb of Mother Nature, where the world, as Thales said, is "full of gods." The gods are not fictions of the imagination; they are the living powers of nature, present in earth and sea and sky. They belong to the 'psychic' world, the world which we only know in dream, but which is no less real than the physical world. In this world there are also the spirits of the ancestors. Man knows himself not as isolated in this outer world of time and space, but as in communion with the spirits of the dead. In the depths of the unconscious we are one with all nature and all humanity, open to the divine Spirit which is in all, not enclosed in the prison of a separate individuality in an alien world.

The ancient wisdom is enshrined in a Hindu temple. The temple is the image both of the cosmos and of the soul. To go round a temple visiting the shrines of the different gods is to bring the soul into harmony with the powers of the cosmos and to discover the 'center' both of the cosmos and the soul. The center of the temple is the *garbha-griha* — the 'womb' in which the lingam and yoni are to be found, symbols of the marriage of the male and the female which takes place in this depth or centre of the soul. The ritual of the temple is likewise an external sign of the inner transformation of the soul, the discovery of the divine life hidden in the soul. The breaking of the coconut is a symbol of the breaking of the hard outer shell of the soul to discover the pure white substance and the sweet milk of the divine life within. The ashes put on the forehead are a symbol of the burning up of the lower self, the sinful ego, and manifestation of the true Self from which all impurities have been burnt away. The red spot placed between the eyes is a symbol of the 'third eye,' the eye of wisdom which is 'single,' as opposed to the two eyes which see the world of duality. Thus everything is intended to enable the soul to discover its 'Center,' to free it from the separated ego and integrate it in the cosmic unity. It is a concrete symbol of the path of return to the Self, to the knowledge of God.

All these religions derive from the cosmic covenant,[45] the universal revelation given to all mankind. It is a revelation of God through nature and the soul. The whole cosmos is a revelation of God. To an unsophisticated mind the order and beauty of the universe is a revelation of the wisdom and goodness of the Creator. The sky stretching immeasurably above him is a sign of his transcendence, its boundless space of his infinity, its abiding for ever unchanged, while all things beneath it change, of his eternity. The sky embraces the whole world and all the worlds of the gods above, therefore it is a symbol of eternity,[46] the Supreme Being. Its gaze penetrates everywhere, therefore it is all-knowing. It sends down the warm rays of the sun and the rain from the clouds to nourish the earth, therefore it is benevolent. But it is also the sphere of thunder and lightning, therefore it is to be feared. Fear and terror, awe and wonder, worship and adoration, hope and expectation, praise and thanksgiving are all evoked by the sky. The Chinese call it *tien*, 'heaven', and for them it is the symbol of the Godhead and the 'way of heaven' is the universal law. The ancient Indians spoke of Dyaus-pita, the Sky-Father, the Greeks called him Zeus Pater, the Latins Jupiter. The most primitive tribes in all parts of the world pray to the Sky-Father, and when Jesus taught his disciples to pray he could find no other words to address God but 'Father in heaven.' Such is the continuity of religion.

For modern man, of course, all this is meaningless. The sky, like the earth, has been profaned. It is merely a space through which he travels for his business or pleasure. The moon is no longer a divine power influencing the life of man, but mere matter of which specimens may be taken for chemical analysis. There are no gods in outer space. And yet how true is this 'scientific' view of the universe? It is the universe seen from one point of view in its measurable, quantitative aspect, just as the human body can be observed simply as a biological specimen and medicine can treat it very effectively in that way. But is a man only the body which is laid out on the operating table? Has he not a mind and a will, thoughts and feelings, hopes and desires? How do we know that the stars are not 'intelligences', as Aristotle and the Arabian philosophers believed? How do we know that there are not gods or angels in outer space? What, after all, is outer space? Both space and time are categories of the mind: there is no time or space without a mind to measure them. As the Upanishad says, "There is a space within the heart in which all space is contained. Both heaven and earth are contained within it, both fire and air, both sun and moon, both lightning and stars. Everything that exists is contained in that 'City of Brahman', all beings and all desires."[47] When we pass beyond the mind, with its measuring faculties, its categories of time and space, we discover the true Self, the Ground of the universe, the City of Brahman, in which all is contained. And there, all things are not dead matter but life and intelligence. There all things are found as they exist eternally in the Word, of which it is said, "That which has been made was life in him."[48]

The gods are not to be known by the senses or by scientific

instruments or by mathematical calculations. No amount of exploration of outer space will discover them. They are hidden within, beyond the mind, beyond the senses. As the *Katha* Upanishad says: "The self-existent pierced the opening of the senses so that they turn outwards: therefore man looks outwards not inwards into himself. But one wise man, desiring immortality, looked inwards and saw the Self."[49] This is the revolution which has to take place in the mind of Western man. He has been turning outwards to the world of the senses for centuries and losing himself in outer space. He has to learn again to turn inwards and find his Self. He has to learn to explore not outer space but the inner space within the heart, to make that long and difficult journey to the Center, to the inner depth and height of being, which Dante described in *The Divine Comedy*, compared with which the exploration of the moon and the other planets is the play of children.

But how to find the path to the Center, the way of return? Again the Upanishad answers: "That Self cannot be attained by the study of the scriptures, nor by the intellect nor by much learning. He whom the Self chooses, by him the Self can be attained."[50] The Self, the Truth, the inner Center of being, is not to be reached by any human effort, not by science, not by philosophy, not by theology, nor by any technique, still less by any technology or social engineering. It is not within the grasp of the mind. It is not the mind which grasps the Self, it is the Self which grasps the mind. It is the mind itself which must capitulate, the rational, scientific mind, which wants to dominate the world. As the Upanishad again says: "The wise should surrender speech in mind, mind in the knowing Self, the knowing Self in the great Self, the great Self in the Self of peace."[51] This is the path of wisdom, the path of return to the Self. Speech, by which the mind goes out of itself and communicates with the external world, has to be surrendered to the mind, the mind to the knowing Self, the true Self, the inner person, who knows not by reflection on the senses but by its own inherent powers. Then this inner, individual Self must be surrendered to the great Self, the universal, cosmic consciousness, of which each individual is a reflection, and this cosmic consciousness to the Self of peace, the peace which passes understanding, the One

401

beyond thought, who reveals himself only to those who are totally surrendered to him.

It must not be thought that when reason surrenders to the Self it loses any of its powers. On the contrary, it is only then that it rises to the height of its power. The mind of a Sankara or an Aquinas is equal to that of any modern scientist or philosopher, but it draws on sources of wisdom which raise it to a higher power and carry it beyond their reach. Bertrand Russell was a baby compared with Sankara or Aquinas. His mind, in spite of its excellence, could never get beyond the world of the senses and its extension in logic and mathematics. But Sankara and Aquinas, though no less logical and rational, were both mystics who had experienced the reality of a world which transcends the senses and could bring their intelligence to bear on that. Indeed the trouble with both of them has been that they built up a system which was so logically perfect that it has obscured their mystical vision. Their followers have accepted the system and ignored the vision. The *advaitic* vision of Sankara was a unique insight into the eternal Truth, but his philosophical system when this is ignored is open to grave objections. Aquinas at the end of his life declared that all that he had written seemed to him like straw in comparison with what he had seen, but his followers erected his theological system deprived of its mystic vision into a rigid framework of dogma to be imposed on the human mind. Al-Ghazzali[52] did for the mystical vision of Islam what Sankara and Aquinas did for that of Hinduism and Christianity, and what Nagarjuna[53] and Vasubandhu,[54] the doctors of the Mahayana, did for Buddhism. They gave a rational and logical form to the mystical insight into the transcendent Truth.

But in all these systems the danger is that the logical structure and rational doctrine will obscure the mystical vision, so inherent is the tendency of the rational mind to seek to dominate the truth which it should serve. This is the danger of all religion. It begins with a mystical experience, the experience of the seers of the Upanishads, of the Buddha under the Bo tree, of the Hebrew prophets and the apostles at Pentecost, of Mahomet receiving the message of the Koran. But this experience has to be put into words; it has to descend into the outer world and take the forms of human speech. Already at this stage it is open to misinterpretation; the conflict between the letter and the spirit begins. Then the logical and rational mind comes and creates systems of thought: heresies and sects spring up, and the one Truth is divided. This is due to the defect of the rational mind, imposing its narrow concepts and categories on the universal truth. Yet it cannot be avoided, because the Truth must be proclaimed; it has to be communicated and this cannot be done without words, which both express and veil the Truth. All sacred scriptures, the Vedas, the Buddhist Sutras, the Bible, the Koran, are subject to this law. They betray the Truth which they proclaim.

In each religion it is necessary to go back beyond its formulations, whether in scripture or tradition, to the original inspiration. All scriptures and traditions are historically conditioned; they belong to a particular age and culture and are expressed in a particular language and mode of thought. But behind these historic forms of expression lies the original Mystery, the revealed Truth. To discover this Mystery, to enter into this Truth, it is necessary to participate in the original revelation. No amount of profane scholarship will discover the truth of the Bible, the Vedas or the Koran. One must receive the Spirit by which the scriptures were inspired; one must be initiated into the Truth. This is why in ancient times only Brahmins were allowed to study the Vedas; they alone were held to possess the secret of their interpretation. In the same way, the Catholic Church claimed to have authority to interpret the Bible, because the Spirit by which the Bible was inspired dwelt in her. Protestantism opened the Bible to the private interpretation of every man, and now every Tom, Dick and Harry is free to interpret it for himself. But the Bible, like other scriptures, will only open its meaning to those who have received the gift of the Spirit and are initiated into the Truth. But it is not possible to confine the spirit to one scripture alone. We have to learn to recognize the voice of the Spirit in every scripture and discover the hidden Source from which all scriptures come.

The hidden Source can only be found by those who follow the path of the traditional wisdom. In every religion there is a tradition of faith, in which the truth of the revelation is preserved. The formulation of this tradition it subject to continuous development and may give rise to many different sects and schools, but one can always find the mystery of faith behind its formulations. Saivism, Vaishnavism and Shaktism, and the different schools of Vedanta in Hinduism; Hinayana and Mahayana Buddhism, with their different schools; the Sunni and the Shia sects in Islam, and their different schools of philosophy; Catholicism, Orthodoxy and Protestantism within Christianity, with their different theologies, all are different expressions of the one Truth of revelation, each with its particular insight. But one must learn to discern among these conflicting and partial views the principle which unites them, with transcends their differences and reconciles their conflicts. This Truth is to be found beyond all the formulations of the schools and beyond all the revelations of the scriptures, in the inner depths of the heart, beyond words and thoughts, where the divine Word is spoken and the mystery of Being is made known.

What is this essential Truth of all religion, in the light of which every scripture has to be understood? Of course, it cannot properly be put into words, yet there are words and phrases which symbolize it, which point towards it for those who have eyes to see. Jesus spoke of it as the 'kingdom of God' or the 'kingdom of heaven." This was the essential content of his message: "The kingdom of God is at hand."[55] But what is this kingdom of God? Let us say that it means the divine life among men. This is the essential message of all religion. The infinite, transcendent, holy Mystery, which is what is signified by 'God' or 'Heaven,' is present in the world, has its kingdom, its reign, its dwelling among men. Is not this the message of all the scriptures? "This brahman, this Self, smaller than the small, greater than the great, is hidden in the heart of every creature."[56] "The sun radiates its splendour on all alike:[57] in like manner do the Tathagatas [Buddhas] radiate the truth of noble Wisdom without recourse to words and on all alike." "I will walk among you, and will be your God, and you shall be my people,"[58] says Yahweh. "I am closer to you than your jugular vein"[59] says the Koran. Yet these are only words which point to the Truth. We cannot properly say what 'God' is , what is this brahman, what is this Truth, this noble Wisdom, what is the kingdom of heaven. We have to meditate on these words in the heart, until the Truth shines out and enlightens us, until we experience the presence of God, the kingdom of heaven, within.

All external religion, with its rites and dogmas and organization, exists for no other reason but to lead men to the knowledge which is also the experience of this inner mystery. The church exists for the sake of the kingdom of God. This kingdom is universal, it is the presence of God among men. It has existed from the beginning, in all times and in all places. Every religion bears witness to it: each represents it according to its own particular mode of thought and experience. Each religion has its own particular insight and its own particular limitations. We have to learn to detect the insight and to recognize the limitations. The limitations come from time and place and circumstance, from economic, social and political conditions; the insight comes from the eternal Wisdom reflected in them. The eternal Truth has to be expressed in the forms of space and time, under social and historical conditions, yet these very forms will always tend to betray it. This was the basis of St Paul's attitude to the law. The Law of Moses was given by God. It was the expression of eternal Wisdom in the economic and social and political conditions of a particular people in a particular period of history. As such it was a divine revelation; it established that people in a unique relation with God, that is, with the eternal Ground of being. But the historical conditions, social and political and religious, of Israel were continually changing, like those of every other people, and by the time of Christ the Law of Moses was no longer an adequate expression of the divine Truth. Its doctrine, its ritual and its social organization had all to be transformed in accordance with the very principles which had given them birth. It was the tragedy of Israel that it refused to grow with history, to allow itself to be transfigured according to the divine plan.

The church today is in the same position as Israel in the time of Christ. The church was founded by Christ. He gave it the basis of an organization — Peter and the other apostles; a ritual — baptism and eucharist; and a doctrine — concerning the kingdom of God. This church was intended to be the nucleus of a people, in whom God was to be present by his Spirit, leading them into all truth. In the course of time this church inevitably developed according to the historical conditions in which it was placed. It left its Jewish matrix and grew up in the Graeco-Roman world, developing its theology through contact with Greek philosophy, its organization according to the pattern of the Roman Empire, and its ritual according to the customs of the time. Finally, in the Middle Ages, it achieved a perfect synthesis of organization, ritual and doctrine which embodied the divine truth committed to it in a concrete historical form. This synthesis, as Newman was to show, was a genuine development of the original apostolic tradition. In medieval Christendom the eternal wisdom was manifested in a marvellous creative synthesis, economic, social, political, cultural, philosophical and theological; in every sphere the human soul rose to the summit of its capacity within the limits of its historical situation, reaching to the height and the depth of mystical experience. But this synthesis was historically conditioned; at the very moment of its consummate achievement the seeds of disintegration were already present in it. The Renaissance itself began in the Middle Ages. New languages, new nations, new economic and social conditions and patterns of thought were emerging, and the medieval church was unable to adapt itself to this changing world. Like Judaism after the return from captivity, it closed in on itself. It preserved its structure of organization and ritual and doctrine unchanged, but lost its capacity for creative growth.

This is the challenge to the church today. The structure of doctrine and ritual and organization which it has inherited are no longer adequate to express the divine Mystery, like those of Israel in the time of Christ. The very principle of divine life which originally created those structures is pressing for their transformation. For the eternal Wisdom which remains ever the same has to be manifested in the ever-changing forms of history and society, of language, thought, culture and social organization. The church has a basic structure which derives from the New Testament, alike of doctrine, of ritual and of organization, but the historical development of this structure is subject to continual change. It is the Graeco-Roman structure which was built on the original Jewish basis that is now breaking down. There is nothing in this, whether it is its dogmatic formulas, or its sacramental system or its hierarchical organization, which is not subject to change.

We have to recover the original inspiration which created the church from the ruins of Judaism. The struggle between the letter and the spirit, the law and grace, has to be renewed, as it has continually in all religion. There is nothing which remains unchallenged, no doctrine, no discipline, no law, no custom. What is demanded, as was demanded of Israel, is nothing less than a death and resurrection. "Destroy this temple, and in three days I will raise it up"...But he spoke of the temple of his body."[60]

It is this Body of Christ which has to undergo this transformation, this temple of the eternal Wisdom. From the beginning of the world this temple has been building the whole creation is the temple of God. From the beginning of history this Body of Christ, which is the body of humanity, in which the divine Spirit dwells, has been growing, age by age. Every religion has contributed to the building of this temple, every human being is a member of this Body. Christ is the cornerstone of this temple, the head of this Body, which is the 'pleroma,' the "fullness' of him who fills all in all."[61] Now the church is this Body of Christ. It is the visible structure in which this mystery of the divine life among men is being manifested. But it is not possible to conceive this church in isolation from the rest of the world. This divine Mystery is present everywhere in the hearts of all men. It is present in every religion. The mystery of the church, which is the mystery of the divine life among men, has to be seen in the light of this universal revelation. It is not sufficient to return to the Bible to discover the original source of Christianity. The biblical revelation has to be seen in the context of history as a stage in the manifestation of the Word of God, of the eternal Wisdom, which has been present to the world from the beginning.

This same process of critical evaluation has to take place in each religion. No religion can now remain in isolation. The revelations of the Vedas, of the Buddhist Sutras and of the Koran have to be evaluated in the light of the biblical revelation and of one another. Each has to be seen as a unique revelation of the eternal Truth, the one word, manifested under particular historical conditions. In each religion the limitations of these historical conditions have to be discerned, and the essential Truth, which is ultimately One, to be discovered. But this essential Truth cannot be put into words. It is not to be discovered by any process of dialectic. It is known in the silence, in the stillness of all the faculties, in the depths of the soul, beyond word and thought. Every religion, by means of its doctrine and ritual and organization, is intended to lead to this transcendent Knowledge, this experience of ultimate Reality, this participation in the divine life. In Hindu terms it is the knowledge of the Self, the divine Saccidananda. In Buddhist terms it is the experience of nirvana. In Muslim terms it is *fana* and *baqa* — the passing away and the life in God. For the Jew it is the knowledge of Yahweh, for a Christian it is the knowledge of 'the love of Christ which surpasses knowledge'.[62]

91. The Perennial Philosophy and the Unity of Religions[63]

In the introduction to Universal Wisdom, *Bede's late collection of sacred texts from the world religions, the 'perennial philosophy' naturally occupies a central place. Here he will make one of his boldest assertions of the essential unity within all of the great religions: Brahman, Atman, Nirvana, Sunyata, Tao, Being (to ōn in Greek) and Yahweh all denote the same ultimate reality, a mystery which exceeds the reach of human thought and language. Bede does not offer a conceptual definition of the 'philosophy' here (e.g., as equivalent to nonduality), but leaves it undetermined except by the great traditions which express it. Once again he sees the perennial philosophy arising in the 'Axial' period of the first millennium before Christ, and prevailing almost everywhere in the world through the fifteenth century. In its recovery, he believes, is the only hope for humanity's future.*

One of the greatest needs of humanity today is to transcend the cultural limitations of the great religions and to find a wisdom, a philosophy, which can reconcile their differences and reveal the unity which underlies all their diversities. This has been called the 'perennial philosophy,' the eternal wisdom, which has been revealed in a different way in each religion.

The perennial philosophy stems from a crucial period in human history in the middle of the first millennium before Christ. It was then that a breakthrough was made beyond the cultural limitations of ancient religion to the experience of ultimate reality. This reality which has no proper name, since it transcends the mind and cannot be expressed in words, was called Brahman and Atman (the Spirit) in

Hinduism, Nirvana and Sunyata (the Void) in Buddhism, Tao (the Way) in China, Being (*to ōn*) in Greece and Yahweh ('I am') in Israel, but all these are but words which point to an inexpressible mystery, in which the ultimate meaning of the universe is to be found, but which no human word or thought can express. It is this which is the goal of all human striving, the truth which all science and philosophy seeks to fathom, the bliss in which all human love is fulfilled.

It was in Hinduism, or rather in the complex religion which later became known as Hinduism, that the first great breakthrough occurred. In the *Upanishads* in about 600 BC the ancient religion based on the fire-sacrifice (*yajna*) was transformed by the *rishis* (seers), who retired to the forest to meditate, and who were concerned in this way not with the ritualistic fire outside but with the inner fire of the spirit (*atman*). The ancient brahman, the hidden power in the sacrifice, was discovered to be the hidden power in the universe, and the spirit of man, the atman, the inner self, was seen to be one with brahman, the spirit of the universe. A little later Gautama Buddha, discarding alike the mythology and the ritual of the Vedas, pierced through with his mind beyond all phenomena, which he described as transient (*anitta*), sorrowful (*dukka*) in the sense of giving no lasting satisfaction, and insubstantial (*anatta*), having no basis in reality, to the infinite, eternal, unchanging reality which he called nirvana. In China the author of the Tao Te Ching (*The Book of the Power of the Way*), whatever its origin may be, was able to go beyond the conventional moral philosophy of Confucius and discover the nameless mystery which he called the Tao, as the subtle source of all wisdom and morality. In Greece Socrates and Plato, going beyond all previous philosophers, who had tried to find the origin of the world in a material form, whether water, air or fire or the four elements together, awoke to the reality of the mind as the source alike of the material universe and of the human person. Finally the Hebrew prophets, rejecting the God of the ancient world, revealed the presence of a transcendent Being whose only name was 'I am' as the supreme person, the Lord of the universe. Thus in India, China, Greece and Palestine at almost the same time the discovery of the ultimate reality, beyond all the changes of the temporal world, dawned on the human race.

In the course of time these unique insights were developed by philosophers and theologians over a period of more than a thousand years into great doctrinal systems. In India Sankara in the eight century AD unified the system of Vedanta and set it on the course of further development in the different systems of philosophy which have gone on growing to the present day. In Buddhism, Nagarjuna, the Brahmin philosopher from South India, devised a logical system which was to provide a basis for the Mahayana doctrine of China and Tibet. In China, Taoism and Confucianism, interacting over the centuries, developed the Neo-Confucian system which dominated China until the coming of Marxism. In Greece the new vision of Socrates and Plato led to the growth of the Neoplatonism of Plotinus and became of decisive importance in the growth both of Christianity and of Islam. The Greek fathers, Clement, Origen and Gregory of Nyssa, building on the mystical insights of St Paul and St John, developed a profound mystical theology under the influence of Neoplatonism, which was to flower in the great mystical tradition of the Middle Ages. Finally in Israel and in Islam the religion of the patriarchs and the prophets underwent a vital transformation, as it encountered the cultural tradition of Greece and the oriental world.

In each religion therefore we can trace the development of a comparatively simple and unsophisticated religion into a subtle and complex system of philosophy, which shows a remarkable unity underlying all the differences. This philosophy, which prevailed in almost all parts of the world until the fifteenth century, was rejected in Europe in the sixteenth century and a new system of philosophy based on the findings of western science has taken its place. But the philosophy of western science itself has now begun to disintegrate, as a result of the new scientific developments in relativity and quantum physics. As a result the world today is left with no basic philosophy which can give meaning to life, and we are in danger of losing all sense of meaning and purpose in human existence. When to this is added the devastating effect of western technology on the ecology of the planet, which threatens to destroy the world, on which we depend for our very existence, it can be seen that the need of a philosophy, a universal wisdom, which can unify humanity and enable us to face the problems

410

created by western science and technology, has become the greatest need of humanity today. The religions of the world cannot by themselves answer this need. They are themselves today part of the problem of a divided world. The different world religions — Hinduism, Buddhism, Judaism, Christianity and Islam — have themselves to recover the ancient wisdom, which they have inherited, and this has now to be interpreted in the light of the knowledge of the world, which western science has given us.

92. One Hand[64]

In the course of an interview filmed for 'A Human Search'[65] a few months before Bede's death, he recalls his kindergarten model for the relationship of the great religions. It is not hard to understand why theologians were not pleased with it.[66] Christianity as a world-thumb does not stand out as uniquely supernatural. Despite the obvious limitations of this model, it would be interesting to hear Bede further develop his allegory of the four fingers. He has been speaking of a common understanding of the relation of the world to God in the Vedantic doctrine of Hinduism, in Mahayana Buddhism, in Thomas Aquinas and in Sufism.

So we can safely say that this is the universal wisdom. I think this is what we are coming to today; and it is so important, because behind all the differences of religion which are infinite on the scale of multiplicity and when we get beyond all the multiplicity to unity, we find a common tradition, a common wisdom that we all share. That is the hope for the future: that religions will discover their own depth. As long as they remain on their surface, they will always be divided in conflict. When they discover their depth, then we converge on the unity.

As an illustration, I sometimes use the fingers and the palm of the hand. Each finger represents a religion. The baby finger is Buddhism, the next is Hinduism, the middle one is Islam, the forefinger in Judaism, and the thumb is Christianity. Buddhism is miles from Christianity. And they are all divided separately, but as you go deep into any religion, you converge on the center, and everything springs from that center and converges at that center, which is how we are today.

411

93. At the End, Distinctions Remain[67]

We repeat here part of an earlier text from River of Compassion[68] *in which it is clear that the unity of religions which Bede Griffiths envisions does not eliminate the intrinsic differences between religious experiences in the various traditions — even at the ultimate stage of realization.*

. . . The Buddhist nirvana and the Hindu moksha are not the same, nor are they the same as the Christian vision of God. So the Buddhist, the Hindu, the Muslim and the Christian are all experiencing the ultimate Reality but experiencing it in different ways through their own love and through their own traditions of faith and knowledge. There are obviously various degrees as well. There is a tendency to say that when one reaches the supreme state everything is the same and that there are no differences any more, but I do not think that is true. In a sense, the experience of the ultimate truth is different for each person, since each person is a unique image of God, a unique reflection of the one eternal light and love.

VII

TOWARD THE NEW CREATION

These final texts will serve both as synthesis and as conclusion. Bede Griffiths' thought had always moved toward synthesis, and the conclusive expression of this movement was *A New Vision of Reality*. We shall include several texts from that book. In his later years Bede continued his successive sketches of that integration of the wisdom of East and West which had been his central intellectual project since his move to India. The final synthesis integrated elements which had been excluded by his earlier choices, particularly western science. Now, having encountered a development of this science which is acceptable to him (roughly that scientific perspective known as 'the new paradigm'), Bede recasts his synthetic vision in a new form.

The evolutionary thrust of this contemporary thought brings out once again in Bede's own vision a forward–moving dynamism which had sometimes — as in *Return to the Center* — been almost completely suppressed by the 'perennial philosophy' which he had found in the *Upanishads*. A third element, the 'Cosmic Person,' which Bede finds to be universal in the great religious traditions, joins the timeless universal wisdom and the evolutionary principle in the role of emergent center in Bede's synthesis. The figure of the Cosmic Person — whom Bede recognizes in Jesus Christ — brings together for him Eastern and Christian traditions, perennial philosophy and evolution, nonduality and salvation history.

While Bede's synthesis begins and ends in a cosmic perspective, the evolution which concerns him most intimately is, as always, the development of human consciousness. The quest for transcendent consciousness has been at the center of Bede's life and he has written about this journey again and again, usually from the viewpoint of Vedanta. This time he follows a contemporary western writer, Ken Wilber, in outlining a progressive ascent of the 'spectrum of consciousness.' Recovery of 'the feminine,' we have seen, was a pressing and recurrent theological issue for Bede. Toward the end of his life, at a time of physical crisis, he experienced 'the feminine' in a way that brought him to a new level of consciousness, but not in the direction that his theoretical scheme would have predicted.

Bede Griffiths was always the prophet of an open and expansive Christianity. We have seen this both in his proposals for the renewal of the church and in his view of the relationship between Christianity and the other world religions. During his later years, as he travelled more outside his ashram, Bede began to envision a liberation of contemplation and contemplative life from a virtual confinement within monastic institutions to become available to all of the 'people of God.' If contemplation is truly the manifestation of a transcendent Self within the human person, it can be limited neither by the boundaries of a particular religion nor by those of a particular religious order.

Bede's syntheses were sketches, working models, essentially dynamic and forward-moving, tentative and heuristic. The new 'Christian wisdom' offered by Bede Griffiths is not a final synthesis but a new beginning, in a time of new encounters and new beginnings.

94. Science Today and the New Creation[1]

The 'golden string' which the young Alan Griffiths discovered was not science but wisdom. As he would write again and again, it was the scientific mind which had eclipsed and banished the tradition of Christian wisdom from the western world at the beginning of the modern era. Griffiths and his two Oxford friends inclined toward the simplicity, wholeness and transparency of life which had been largely terminated in England by the industrial revolution and which resonated with the poetic rather than the scientific mind.

We thought that the source of all the evil to which we were opposed was to be found in the scientific mind. I do not think that we should ever have condemned either science or reason in themselves. It was the divorce of the scientific and rational mind from nature, from the world of instinct and feeling and imagination which seemed to us to be the root of all evil. It was when the human mind became separated from its roots in feeling and instinct that it became diseased, and the infallible mark of the disease was the ugliness of its productions.[2]

At this time he could hardly see any hope for the redemption of scientific reason, or conceive that the human desert that it had created might be but one stage of a longer historical journey, a humanization of the world.

When, fifty years later, Bede Griffiths embraced western science, it was a new science that he had encountered. Alongside the monolithic establishment of Cartesian-Newtonian scientific thought was emerging a 'new paradigm' in which reality was seen as an organic whole rather than a mechanical arrangement of individual parts. A shining bridge had been glimpsed between this new scientific vision and the ancient wisdom of the East, between the physical universe and the interior universe of the spirit. A 'transpersonal' psychology had appeared which, with a similar affinity to Asian thought, brought together the rediscovered world of psyche and the world of unitive spirit. In this new scientific thought the three levels of reality which Bede had long seen as one, were once again joined. The way was now ready for Bede to extend his own thinking more boldly into the worlds of cosmology and psychology. He began to work toward a synthesis in which the evolution of the universe, of life and of human consciousness and culture would appear together in the light both of the Gospel and of unitive Asian wisdom. This synthesis would finally appear in A New Vision of Reality *(1989).*

When Bede was invited to address the 1982 meeting of the International Transpersonal Association in Bombay,[3] he had already been reading the work of Rupert Sheldrake and David Bohm for years. Sheldrake had become a close friend, living at Shantivanam for many months and discussing his manuscript with Bede. The ITA conference, entitled 'East and West: Ancient Wisdom and Modern Science,' made Bede aware of a deep and lively interaction at the boundary of these two realms. In his own talk, which was enthusiastically received, Bede boldly integrated the two worlds within a third, Christian perspective. The dynamism of cosmic and human evolution is taken up, together with the unitive 'perennial philosophy,' into the new creation, where all things are brought together into the cosmic Person who is Christ.

Bede seems to accomplish, before this new audience, the magical feat of joining modern science with Christian eschatology. He accepts the challenge of enlisting science to show how matter can be transformed by the Spirit, as in the Pauline 'new creation.' Not only the weight of matter but the weight of a materialist western science have so far defied this aspiration. To fulfill it, the 'power of God' which is the Holy Spirit must be brought into this secular kingdom. Bede enlists two intermediaries. First he calls upon that current of the new science (with which his listeners are comfortable) that sees the world of matter opening to a world of consciousness and, potentially, to the world of spirit. Thus is revealed a 'participatory universe' resembling a single living organism. Secondly, Sri Aurobindo contributes an evolutionary model in which matter is transformed by a descent of Supermind (or spirit). The seams between the different worlds here may not strike the eye immediately, as Bede's intuitive brilliance, his enthusiasm and his eloquence carry us along. But the junctures must, sooner or later, be tested.

What light can modern physics and evolutionary theory throw on the doctrine of the New Creation? St Paul derived his doctrine from the Jewish tradition. The Bible begins with the words, "In the beginning God created the heaven and the earth," and ends with the words of the Apocalypse, "I saw a new heaven and a new earth." Thus the whole Christian revelation is set between these two poles of the first and second creation. In Jewish tradition, this new creation was conceived in terms of a new age, the Messianic age, which would be inaugurated by an intervention of God in history, described in symbolic language in the Apocalypse. St Paul inherits this tradition, but gives it a new interpretation by affirming that in the death and resurrection of Jesus, this new age has begun, and the new creation has actually come into being. So he is able to say, "If anyone is in Christ, there is a new creation," a *kaine ktisis*.

To be "in Christ" for St Paul is to participate in this new creation, to enter into a new mode of existence in which the old world of this creation has passed away, and a new world has come into being. St Paul expresses this dramatically in the letter to the Romans in which he says that "the whole creation has been groaning in travail until now." This introduces a new note of dynamic movement: the creation is seen not merely as waiting for an intervention of God, but as actually "groaning in travail"   undergoing a kind of gestation by which it is being prepared for this great event. St Paul then describes what this preparation is for, saying that "the creation waits with eager longing for the revealing of the sons of God." We can now see the purpose of this travail; it is to bring to birth a new humanity, a New Man, which will be revealed when man becomes a "son of God"; that is, when the human nature is united with the divine. This event, St Paul believes, has already taken place in Christ, when Jesus was raised from the dead and his human nature was finally transfigured

416

by the divine.

The new creation, we can therefore say, is a further stage in evolution, when our present mode of human existence is transcended. Man begins to "partake of the divine nature," to transcend the limits of the present space-time universe, and to experience a new mode of existence and consciousness as far beyond our present mode of existence as ours is beyond that of an animal. This event, St Paul believes, has already taken place in Christ, but it is destined to extend to all mankind and to the whole creation. So it was the plan of God to "bring all things to a head in him, everything in heaven and on earth." We can now see the full scope of St Paul's thought. The whole creation, from the beginning, is moving towards a fulfillment when man will be raised to a higher level of existence and consciousness. With him the whole universe will be transfigured, passing beyond its present level of existence in space and time and participating in an external and infinite mode of existence, understood as the divine.

Let us now see what light modern physics can throw on this. According to Fritjof Capra in *The Tao of Physics*, the division between matter and mind, between existence and consciousness, which has prevailed from the time of Descartes and Newton, has now been overcome. The universe is now conceived as a "web of relations between various parts in a unified whole" of which the human mind is an essential part. We live in what has been called a "participatory universe." Nature is not an "extended substance," outside the human mind, but an integrated whole. "What we observe," as Heisenberg said, "is not nature itself, but nature exposed to our method of questioning." In other words, the object of all scientific knowledge is not nature itself or the "thing as such," as Kant called it but nature mirrored in the human mind and senses, with the instruments we use to extend the range of the senses. We can, therefore, no longer maintain a separation between mind and matter. Just as we ourselves are a psychosomatic unity, so the universe as a whole, as far as we can know it, is a psychosomatic unity.

This means we must consider that consciousness is present in the universe in some way from the beginning. The mathematical order in the structure of the atom, for instance, is a sign of an intelligence at work in matter. In the ancient world, Aristotle and the Arabian philosophers considered that the stars were intelligences, an idea with which the teaching of Sri Aurobindo is related. I consider Sri Aurobindo the greatest philosopher of modern India. Responsible for introducing the theory of evolution into Vedantic philosophy, Sri Aurobindo maintained with all Vedantic philosophers that Ultimate Reality is also pure consciousness. It is *saccidananda*, or absolute Being (*sat*) in pure consciousness (*cit*) which is experienced as perfect bliss (*ananda*). This is the ideal state of being according to all Vedantic philosophy, the state of being in pure consciousness. But according to Aurobindo, the Absolute Being, *Saccidananda*, becomes "involved" in matter. It withdraws its consciousness and allows matter to appear as being, without consciousness. As matter evolves through the *shakti*, the energy inherent in it, and develops more complex organisms, the divine consciousness manifests itself as life. There is evidence today of a kind of consciousness in plants, and in animals consciousness is beginning to manifest itself in sensations, feelings and instinctive intelligence. Finally, in man, we emerge into rational, or what Sri Aurobindo calls "mental," consciousness. The distinctive theory of Aurobindo is that mankind today is in a state of evolution from mental consciousness to supramental consciousness.

The western world has for centuries developed the rational, analytical consciousness, and this has now reached the limits of its development. We are beginning to discover the need to develop the other form of consciousness, the intuitive consciousness that has been developed in the East from the time of Buddha and the Upanishads through the present day. The intuitive consciousness has been developed by Muslim and Christian as well as Hindu and Buddhist mystics, but the western world has concentrated for two centuries almost exclusively on the rational activity of the mind, and it now has to learn the opposite process by contact with the thought and the meditative techniques of the East. In Sri Aurobindo's thought, various stages lead from the first awakening of the intuitive mind, to the development of what he calls the "overmind," to the attainment of the supreme consciousness with the "descent of the Supermind."

Sri Aurobindo's conception of the Supermind as a "descent" is particularly interesting. In Hindu thought the growth of consciousness is normally seen in terms of an ascent from man to God. But Sri Aurobindo introduced two extremely interesting and original ideas. He conceived that as the mind ascends towards God or the Divine, it is met with a corresponding movement of descent from above, and, further, the Supermind descends not only into the soul or psychic consciousness, but also into the body or physical consciousness. Both Aurobindo and the Mother, who accompanied him in all his work, were attempting to transform the body so that it would not be subject to death. Their attempt was not successful, but it corresponds to a deep human instinct which urges us to seek for an immortal body, a diamond body, as it has been called in Buddhist tradition.

I want to suggest that these two ideas of Sri Aurobindo, though unusual in the Hindu tradition, correspond very closely with what I have described of the Christian tradition in St Paul. In the Christian belief, the body of Jesus in the resurrection underwent precisely this transformation, which was followed by a descent of the Spirit at Pentecost when the divine Spirit released by the resurrection of Jesus was communicated to his disciples. The doctrine of the resurrection of the body and the descent of the Spirit are, of course, traditional Christian doctrines, but we can now see how these doctrines can be illuminated in the light of modern physics. Once we conceive of the human body not simply as an extended substance but as a "field of energies," it becomes much less difficult to understand how a dead body could be transformed in such a way that the energies which had been structured in a particular way to form that human body could be so penetrated by consciousness that they would begin to obey a different law. Here I would like to introduce a quotation from Whitehead that seems to throw light on this subject.

> The doctrine which I am maintaining is that the whole concept of materialism applies only to very abstract entities, the product of logical discernment. The concrete enduring entities are organisms so that the plan of the whole influences the various subordinate organisms, which enter into it. In the case of an animal the mental states enter into the plan of the total organism and thus modify the plan of those successive organisms such as electrons. Thus an electron within a living body

is different from an electron outside it by reason of the plan of the body, that is, the general plan of the body including its mental states.

I am suggesting that as consciousness enters into matter, it gradually transforms the structure of the field of energies which makes up that material form. In the resurrection we can conceive of the divine consciousness the saccidananda taking possession of a human body and transforming it from within so that the very electrons and other particles begin to obey a new law. This idea links up with Rupert Sheldrake's theory in *A New Science of Life* that there must be formative causes as well as energetic causes in nature. Energy of itself is indeterminate; it has no specific structure. Sheldrake suggests, therefore, that just as there are fields of energy, whether gravitational or magnetic, so there must be what he calls "morphogenetic fields," which are responsible for the organization of matter. The complex organization of atoms and molecules and cells cannot be due to chance; there must be powers of organization in the universe — what Aristotle called formal causes — that are distinct from material causes. We can conceive of a hierarchy of causes which is responsible for the organization of atoms, molecules, cells and organisms in ever greater complexity. In human beings these formative causes become conscious, so that to some degree we can take responsibility for the organization of our bodies. I suggest that as consciousness develops in man, this power of organization increases until conscious organization can take control of the body, and the atoms, molecules, cells and other organs begin to obey a new law.

It is conceivable, then, that the Spirit, or the divine power, took possession of the body of Christ at the resurrection, so that it was no longer subject to the normal laws of space and time. His body in the resurrection could appear and disappear, no longer conditioned by space and time. Finally, the bodily appearance ceased altogether and it became a "spiritual body," as St Paul calls it, a body in which the elements have been brought totally under the control of consciousness, and matter and mind are integrated.

In this view, the resurrection of the body is the destiny of all mankind. From the beginning of history, the human body has been undergoing a gradual evolution as it comes more and more under the control of consciousness that is not the merely rational, scientific consciousness, but the deep intuitive consciousness that transforms the whole person. In the body of Jesus this final transformation took place, but it was not confined in its effects to Christ alone. No breakthrough in the spiritual sphere occurs in isolation. We are members of a "participatory universe," where every action in space and time, both physical and mental, affects every other organism. Every mystic who rises to a higher level of consciousness affects all human consciousness. The Enlightenment of the Buddha, for instance, released a power of consciousness that transformed a large part of the world and continues to do so in our own time. In the same way, the resurrection of Jesus released a power of transformation in the universe, the effects of which continue to be felt today. Considered the "mystical body of Christ," the church is a kind of social organism in which this power of transforming consciousness, or supermental consciousness, as Sri Aurobindo calls it, is always present. This new consciousness is destined in the course of time to extend to all mankind.

Here we come to another important Pauline concept; that human society is an organism, modelled on the organization of the human body. In this view, all mankind forms one organic whole. As the great medieval Christian philosopher St Thomas Aquinas said, "Omnes homines unus homo"; that is, all men are one man. This finds an echo in many ancient traditions. In the Hebrew tradition, Adam is Man, not just an individual man, but collective man, Man in his integral wholeness. We are all members of one another. No action throughout time and space is without effect on all men. Just as sin disintegrates this body of mankind and causes conflict and destruction like a cancer in the body, so every movement towards truth and love, and every advance in human consciousness affects this total body of mankind. This concept of a Universal or Archetypal Man is found in the Muslim tradition of Ibn al Arabi, and in the Rig Veda it appears as purusha, the Cosmic Man, of whom it is said, "one quarter is here on earth, three quarters are above in heaven." In other words, one quarter belongs to the physical world of matter, and three quarters to the transcendent world of consciousness. We have to conceive, therefore, that man is united not only by physical heredity, but also by a psychic heredity. There is a universal consciousness of which we all partake in varying measures. This is known as the *Mahat* in the Hindu tradition. It is a cosmic consciousness into which we enter as our normal consciousness expands, and we become aware of the transcendent dimension of humanity beyond space and time.

This transcendence of space and time is a key concept in all mystical experience. In our present mode of mental consciousness, we experience the world in terms of space and time; we experience everything separated in space and going from point to point in time. It is well known that modern physics calls this whole space-time system into question, and the transcendence of the space-time dimension is central in mystical experience. I suggest that this transcendence is the nature of the new creation; that is, the world of the resurrection. Bodies will no longer be limited by space and time. Universal divine consciousness will so penetrate the human organism that the body will become as if transparent. All bodies in the universe will be seen as one Body, all the separate centers of consciousness will coalesce in the supreme consciousness, and in the end, as St Augustine said of the Mystical Body of Christ in its final state, there will be "Unus Christus amans seipsum" One Christ loving himself. That is, Christ will be loving himself in all his members, as though all humanity formed one Body, one organic whole, made up of innumerable cells, each distinct in itself yet all sharing in the one Consciousness of the whole Body.

If we conceive, then, of humanity converging on a new mode of consciousness in which the barriers of space and time are overcome, we also have to conceive of the whole universe as transcending space and time in the same way. This is what is implied in St Paul's conception of the new creation. It is to "bring everything to a head," everything in heaven and on earth, both matter and consciousness. Just as the material elements of the human body are transformed by the new consciousness, so also will the elements of the universe be transformed. This is what is meant by the "new heaven and the new earth" of the Apocalypse. If we want to form some idea of this final state of the universe, we have to appeal to the experience of the mystics.

Many people have had the experience of a unifying vision in which the whole creation seems to come together in unity. It is recorded in the life of St Benedict that, one day when he was meditating, he saw the whole creation gathered together in a single ray of light. Plotinus gives perhaps the most profound description of this ultimate state in his description of the archetypal world. Soul, he says — that is, the ordinary mental consciousness — "deals with one thing after another — now Socrates, now a horse, always some one entity among beings but the Intellectual Principle," the *Nous* or pure consciousness, "is all, and therefore its entire content is simultaneously present in that identity. This is pure being in eternal actuality" — the *saccidananda* of Hindu tradition. "Nowhere is there any future, for every then is a now; nor is there any past, for nothing there has ceased to be, everything has taken its stand forever." This intuition of absolute reality is identical in Hindu, Buddhist, Muslim, and Christian tradition.

A conception of the ultimate unity in being and consciousness of man and the universe, therefore, is common to all the main religious traditions and is based on the experience of the mystics in each tradition. What is novel today is that western science, which for centuries has been confined to a materialist conception of the universe, has now begun to discover in the light of relativity and quantum physics that time, space and matter are not absolutes, having an existence independent of the human mind. Matter and mind are interrelated and interdependent, and it is therefore not difficult to conceive how an eventual transformation of matter in consciousness could take place, verifying the experience of the mystics in both East and West. This, I have suggested, has its bearing on the Christian doctrine of the resurrection and the new creation. What the Christian doctrine would perhaps bring to the understanding of the final destiny of man and the universe is that in the final state, the world does not just pass away, and the human individuality is not lost. In the new creation the whole universe is realized in the fullness of being, in the "pleroma," as St Paul calls it, and every human being realizes his full stature as a member of the Mystical Body of Christ. Each person is united with every other person in the communion of the Spirit which is the Spirit of Love, and all persons together form one Person in the Supreme Person, the purusha or Cosmic Person, or the Word of God, who draws all men and all things into unity of the one supreme consciousness, indivisible Being, Knowledge and Bliss — the divine Saccidananda.

95. The Christian Vision of New Creation[4]

'New Creation,' Paul's expression for the renewal of humanity and of the universe in Christ, had long been a central concept for Bede. He used the phrase as title for two journal articles in 1960 and 1967, and new creation was central in his 1982 ITA talk (text n. 94). By this time the words had taken on new meaning for him: he had begun to associate science, and particularly evolution, with the new creation. In the third chapter of A New Vision of Reality, *Bede develops a Christian vision of the universe corresponding to the eastern cosmology which he has just outlined. Here the essentially non-historical 'perennial philosophy,' to which Bede will continue to be devoted, nevertheless begins to give way to a dynamic perspective. Drawing upon the thought of Aurobindo (once again) and Teilhard de Chardin — contemporary evolutionary thinkers of East and West — Bede brings an evolutionary interpretation to the apocalyptic New Testament revelation. This synthetic sketch rushes to its conclusion in a vision of differentiation-in-union, of an ultimate state of the universe which is a communion of interpersonal love.*

The reconciliation of humanity with nature and with God is represented in a later chapter of Isaiah in terms of a marriage, where it is said, "You shall no longer be forsaken nor shall your land to be called Desolate; but you shall be called My Delight and your land Married, for the Lord delights in you and your land shall be married."[5] This brings out again the sense of the solidarity of the people and the land, of humanity with the earth to which it belongs. But the climax of this theme of the reconciliation of heaven and earth is found in the last chapters of Isaiah where it is said, "Behold, I create new heavens and a new earth; and the former things shall not be remembered or come into mind." This reveals the final destiny of humanity and creation. The heaven and the earth which we experience through our limited mental consciousness is only a passing phenomenon. We are destined to pass beyond our present level of consciousness, where we see everything in terms of dualities, of subject and object, time and space, heaven and earth, and to enter into the unifying consciousness beyond the dualities of the mind. Then alone will humanity find its fulfilment. As the text goes on to say, "I create Jerusalem a rejoicing, and her people a joy."[6] With the coming of the new consciousness humanity, typified by Jerusalem, the city of God, enters into the joy, the ananda of Hindu tradition, the blissful state of pure consciousness where all the dualities of sin and evil have been transcended and humanity is at peace with God and creation.

When we turn to the New Testament, we can see how this concept of the relationship of the people to the land, of humanity to this world, undergoes a profound transformation. The key text is that of the letter to the Hebrews, where it is said, "People who speak thus make it clear that they are seeking a homeland. If they had been thinking of the land from which they had gone out, they would have had the opportunity to return. But as it is they desire a better country, that is, a heavenly one."[7] The land of Palestine to which Israel was so attached — and remains so to this day — here undergoes a radical transformation. It becomes a symbol of something much more profound. Human beings desire fulfillment in a concrete manner and seek for fulfillment in this world by the possession of a land, by contact with the earth. But they have to learn that there is no fulfillment in this world of space and time. The real object of human search is not for a dwelling in this world; it is not for an earthly city but for the city of God, the state of transformed humanity. This is what is meant by a "heavenly country." This earth and all that is in it, and the whole cosmic order to which it belongs, has to undergo a transformation; it has to become a "new heaven and a new earth." Modern physics help us to realise that this whole material universe is a vast "field of energies" which is in a continuous process of transformation. Matter is passing into life and life into consciousness, and we are waiting for the time when our present mode of consciousness will be transformed and we shall transcend the limits of space and time, and enter "the new creation."

There is a remarkable anticipation of this view in the Letter to the Romans, where St Paul speaks of the whole creation "groaning in travail." For the creation, he says "waits with eager longing for the revealing of the sons of God." The "revealing of the sons of God" is of course, the passage of humanity into the new state of consciousness. For "we ourselves," he says "groan inwardly as we wait for the adoption of sons, the redemption of our bodies."[8] Our adoption as sons is our passing from human to divine consciousness, which is the destiny of all humanity. And this will come through "the redemption of our bodies." The new consciousness is not a bodiless state; it is the transformation of our present body consciousness, which is limited by time and space, into a state of transformed body consciousness which is that of resurrection. In the resurrection Jesus passed from our present state of material being and consciousness into the final state when matter itself, and with it the human body, passes into the state of the divine being and consciousness, which is the destiny of all humanity.

This is the "new creation" of which St Paul speaks and which is revealed more explicitly in the second Letter of Peter, where it is said, "According to his promise we await a new heavens and a new earth in which righteousness dwells."[9] This is the ultimate goal of human history and of the created universe. Many people today imagine some kind of Utopia, in which humanity will be set free and enjoy peace and prosperity in this world. But this is a pure illusion, as can be seen as each revolution which is to usher in the new age ends in frustration and disillusionment. It is not only that humanity has within itself so much violence and division that in its present state it can never reach a state of equilibrium. The problem is that the very universe to which we belong is threatened with entropy in which all stable order and harmony will be lost. The vision of the New Testament is much more profound. It was recognized that this whole universe has to undergo a radical transformation, in which the present time-space will pass away and a "new heaven and a new earth" will be revealed. It is then only that humanity will find the state of "righteousness" for which it longs. There is no final liberation in this world. Every serious religious tradition has recognized the need to transcend the present condition of this world, if humanity is to attain fulfillment. This goal was commonly expressed in mythological terms, but we recognize today that myth is the most adequate way of expressing what cannot be properly expressed in human language. The ultimate state of humanity and the universe cannot be properly conceived, since it must transcend our present mode of consciousness. Myth or symbolic language is the only way in which the ultimate truth can be presented. Even the language of science is essentially symbolic. Modern science in particular, is ultimately based on mathematical symbolism which expresses one aspect of reality, that is, its quantitative aspect, but ignores all other aspects.

The final statement of the myth of the new creation is to be found in the last book of the Bible, the Revelation of St John, where it is said, "I saw a new heaven and a new earth; for the first heaven and the first earth had passed away, and the sea was no more." Thus the biblical revelation which began with the creation of heaven and earth is brought to a climax with the coming of new heaven and a new earth. Then it is said, "I saw the holy city, the new Jerusalem, coming down out of heaven from God, prepared as a bride adorned for her husband."[10] The "new Jerusalem" is a symbol of redeemed humanity, which "comes down out of heaven" because it emerges out of a new consciousness. Our present world is conditioned by our present mode of consciousness; only when that consciousness passes from its present dualistic mode conditioned by time and space will the new creation appear, which is the eternal reality of which our world is a mirror.

The myth of the new creation has been given a new expression in recent times by Teilhard de Chardin who, writing from a scientific point of view, was able to give it a meaning for modern man. Teilhard presented an evolutionary view of matter evolving into life and into consciousness, as matter developed ever greater complexity and concentration. The point at which all matter and life and consciousness finds its ultimate meaning and purpose he called the "Omega point." He saw the whole universe converging on this ultimate point, where it is totally unified and centered. It is towards that supreme point of unity that the whole creation is moving.

The other person in modern times who had the deepest insight into this mystery is Sri Aurobindo, the sage of Pondicherry in India. What Teilhard de Chardin did for Christianity, Aurobindo did for

427

Hinduism. He developed a system of Vedanta which incorporates the concept of evolution into the Hindu vision of the universe. He starts from the concept of the supreme Reality as *saccidananda*, pure being in perfect consciousness of absolute bliss. This is the one absolute Reality. This supreme reality proceeds to "involve" itself in matter, where it appears as unconscious being, but always behind the unconscious state of matter is the full consciousness of the eternal Spirit, which is manifesting itself in it. This is similar to David Bohm's concept of the implicate order, which is always present behind the explicate order of the world as we know it. In the same way *saccidananda*, the plenitude of consciousness and bliss, is involved in matter from the beginning, and as matter becomes more organized into ever greater complexity, it evolves into life, that is, into the living cell. As life becomes organised into increasingly complex forms in plant and animal, it evolves into consciousness in humanity. In all this it is the *Saccidananda*, the supreme consciousness, which is gradually manifesting its hidden power. In Aurobindo's view we are now in the stage of evolution from mental consciousness, that is, our present state of dualistic, rational consciousness, into "supermental" consciousness, which corresponds with what Teilhard de Chardin calls the "Omega point." The Supermind is the supreme manifestation of the ultimate Reality, which acts upon the whole creation, bringing it to fulfilment.

An important aspect of Sri Aurobindo's thought is that in the final state the differences which exist here on earth are not simply dissolved but are transcended. There is a view, which is very common in India, that when the ultimate state is reached all differences of God and man and creation disappear. But in Aurobindo's view, as in that of Teilhard de Chardin, the divine consciousness penetrates the whole creation and integrates the whole in the final state of transcendence. This is the law of evolution, that at every stage when a lower level of being is transcended, it is integrated in the higher level. As the atom develops it integrates the electrons and the protons and other particles which were originally floating freely. As the molecule develops it integrates the atoms; it does not destroy them. In the same way, as the living cell develops it integrates the atoms and molecules, and as each organism develops it integrates all the different elements in itself. So also as consciousness develops the whole bodily structure is integrated with the mind and form as psycho-physical organism. As we go beyond our rational consciousness, we have to learn to integrate the rational mind and the ego consciousness into our personal being. The human person does not disintegrate as we pass into the unifying consciousness of the transcendent, but on the contrary becomes more fully personal. The human person is a center of consciousness which is capable of infinite extension and as it grows it becomes more and more integrated with the whole complex of persons who make up humanity. We do not cease to be persons but grow into full personal being, which is always a form of relationship. The ultimate reality is the fullness of interpersonal being, which is also interpersonal consciousness.

Teilhard de Chardin always emphasized the principle that union differentiates. We become more ourselves as we enter more deeply into relationship with others. In our ordinary consciousness we are all separated in time and space, but as we go beyond the limitations of time and space we experience our oneness with others. We do not lose ourselves, but we lose our sense of separation and division and discover our integral oneness in the One Reality. This is essentially a mystery of love. When two people love one another, they do not lose their distinction of person; they become more fully personal. The whole process of evolution, as Teilhard de Chardin saw it, is a process of personalization. The ultimate goal of humanity is a communion of persons in love. This is what was revealed in St John's Gospel, when Jesus prayed for his disciples "that they may be one, as you, Father, are, in me and I in you, that they may be one in us."[11] This is the meaning of Christian doctrine of the Trinity, that the ultimate Reality, the Godhead, or whatever name we give to the ultimate Truth, is a communion of love. In the beginning the universe was undifferentiated. The original cosmos was an undifferentiated unity; the earliest human consciousness was an undifferentiated consciousness. We emerge through all the levels of consciousness, the physical, the vital, the emotional, the imaginative, the rational and the transrational until we reach a fully differentiated unity. The ultimate reality is a differentiated unity which transcends all categories of human thought, but in which all forms of being are integrated in a transcendent unity, which as far as it can be described in human terms is a communion of love, that is, of inter-personal relationship, which recalls the description of the universe in modern physics as a "complicated web of interdependent relationships."

96. *The Evolution of Consciousness*[12]

A New Vision of Reality is the product of an impressive work of assimilation. At well over 70, Bede Griffiths has turned his mind in a new direction to absorb in a few years the thought of a number of contemporary scientists and philosophers of science, writing in the diverse fields of physics, psychology and biology. Here in A New Vision of Reality *he traces the horizon of this new thought and attempts to integrate it both with the Asian wisdom in which he has immersed himself for many years, and with his Christian vision of reality. We might expect, given Bede's preoccupation with the ways of knowing, that he would engage himself with studies of consciousness and its evolution. Bede begins this chapter of* A New Vision of Reality *with the problem of the relation of human consciousness to the external world. He is very interested in revindicating the intimate relationship between mind and matter. From Aristotle's theory of knowledge through forms he moves to Karl Pribram's holographic theory of reality, which suggests that we project outside ourselves — onto the forms and energy of the universe — the world which we experience. The whole world is contained within us, as within a hologram, and we then construct it around ourselves. Bede then discusses the progressive opening up of the constricted western concept of mind or psyche in the work of Freud, bringing to light the personal unconscious, and then in that of Jung, revealing the collective unconscious.*

Finally he turns to the still larger world of consciousness which is offered by Ken Wilber:

> . . . there is the level of mental consciousness which is our normal rational consciousness, but below that is a series of subconscious levels, while above it is another whole range of levels of consciousness up to the supreme consciousness to which we are aspiring. The mental consciousness with which we normally identify is in the mid-range of the development of consciousness.[13]

It is not surprising that Bede is powerfully attracted to the thought of Wilber, who has envisioned the entire world of consciousness (or psyche) as a 'spectrum' or hierarchical order which ascends to unitive consciousness — a nondual mind

430

which has been present from the beginning. Wilber then transposes this spectrum of consciousness 'horizontally' into a developmental sequence. Bede adopts both Wilber's hierarchial ordering of the levels of consciousness and his corresponding evolutionary scheme. Bede traces Wilber's developmental scheme[14] through its six levels of consciousness. Beginning with the uroboric or oceanic stage, the development ascends through the four intermediate levels — the typhonic, verbal membership, mental and psychic/subtle — to the supreme level of nondual (transmental and transegoic) consciousness. The ascent often slows, as Bede lingers for awhile on one level or another to sketch a view of human culture and experience at that particular stage. He hardly questions Wilber's hierarchy of levels of consciousness, nor its conversion into an evolutionary progression. As Bede nears the top of the ladder he pauses briefly to stress that as one differentiates from a previous stage of consciousness, one must always integrate it. Finally, moving onward from the level of mental consciousness, Bede writes (using Wilber's Buddhist terminology) of the two final stages: the sambhogakaya (subtle or psychic consciousness) and the dharmakaya (nondual consciousness). Here, lofty as this country is, we recognize it. Bede has often described this ultimate stage of consciousness in his presentations of the Vedanta.

It is the view of Wilber and others that there is, as it were, a spectrum of levels of consciousness, from the basic oceanic consciousness, through all the levels right up to the supreme consciousness. The levels are hierarchically structured in such a way that the lower levels are integrated with the higher. At every point of transcendence there has to be differentiation from the previous level and integration of it. So at the level of mental consciousness one differentiates from the level of the imagination and one opens oneself to the world of concepts, logic, reason, science and philosophy, then one has to integrate the previous level of the imagination, and the senses. There should be no rejection of the other levels nor should they be left behind. Particularly, in going beyond the mental consciousness into the *sambhogakaya*, there must be integration of the mental consciousness. If the mental consciousness is not integrated, the result can be madness. Exploration of this psychic world of angels, spirits, demons and other entities, without retaining and integrating mental consciousness, can result literally in losing one's reason. Because of this it is very dangerous to enter into the sambhogakaya without proper guidance.

That is why in meditation when one goes into that subtle world it is important to have a teacher, a guru who will guide and direct progress. But in meditation the aim is always to go beyond this subtle psychic world, the world of ideas, of gods and angels, and to enter the *dharmakaya*, the realm of ultimate reality, which is beyond duality. In the ultimate reality all levels of previous experience are integrated. This means that, just as mental consciousness has to be transcended and integrated in experience of the sambhogakaya, so when one goes beyond the sambhogakaya, that level also has to be integrated into the experience of the transcendent. The importance of integration is often misunderstood, and it is frequently thought that on reaching the level of nondual awareness everything disappears and there is simply pure identity of being, *saccidananda*, being, knowledge and bliss, without any differentiation. But the truth is that all the lower levels of consciousness have to be taken up into the Supreme and that is what constitutes total realization, that is, realization of the total reality. Boethius, the great sixth-century Christian philosopher, said that eternity is *tota et simul possessio interminabilis vitae*, the total simultaneous possession of unending life. The total reality is present simultaneously. On reaching that final state a person "realizes" the whole creation. At the lower stages we know the forms of things but our knowledge through science, philosophy and ordinary experience is always of objects and persons separated in space and time. When we enter into the sambhogakaya, to a higher, more subtle level of consciousness, we get a deeper awareness of the reality of these forms and their ideas; we discover the eternal realities behind the forms. But now we can go beyond the ideas into the Godhead itself, the Ultimate, and there all is gathered together in the One. The Godhead is the Supreme Reality in which the whole creation and every human being in the creation and every experience in the whole universe is gathered into total unity. This is what Nicholas of Cusa called the *coincidentia oppositorium*, the "co-incidence of opposites" in ultimate truth. And that is the ultimate goal of life, to reach that total unity where we experience the whole creation and the whole of humanity reintegrated in the supreme consciousness, in the One, which is pure being, pure knowledge and pure bliss, saccidananda.

97. The Coming Emergence of the Feminine[15]

The influence of ' the feminine' can be seen in Bede Griffiths' life from the time of his spiritual awakening, which developed in a context of the love of nature and of poetry. At Oxford's Magdalen College, he joined the 'aesthetes' rather than the 'athletes.'[16] After his conversion to Christianity, the attraction manifested itself on the level of spirituality. He began to see his journey of integration in terms of a discovery of the feminine, which he associated with the East. While the average young man is likely to discover the other half of his soul (and thus be drawn to realize the totality of himself) in the form of a young woman, Bede was drawn to India.

> I wanted to experience in my life the marriage of these two dimensions of human existence, the rational and intuitive, the conscious and unconscious, the masculine and feminine. I wanted to find the way to the marriage of East and West.[17]

We cannot suppose that he was not already deeply in touch with that 'feminine,' though he found it largely repressed in the world of modern Europe that surrounded him. We shall observe the emergence of the feminine first with Bede as he sees the pendulum of western culture swinging back from its extreme masculine expression, and then in Bede's own experience at the time of his first great physical crisis.

We have seen Bede Griffiths' vision of the church as 'woman,'[18] and his identification of the Holy Spirit as the 'feminine' expression of God,[19] corresponding to the 'masculine' divine Word. At the end of A New Vision of Reality, Bede contemplates the impending disintegration of the present order of western civilization with little distress. Beyond this, he looks forward toward an optimal 'New Age.' A re-emergence of the feminine within the culture and the religion of the West will be essential to this renaissance. Perhaps there is some caricature in his description of the masculine culture simply as 'aggressive, competitive, rational, analytic,' and some selectivity also in his enumeration of the characteristics of the feminine as 'intuition, empathy and cooperation' and a 'holistic approach.' There is no doubt, however, that Bede has seen deeply into the illness of western culture. It is not immediately evident how the movement toward the feminine which he foresees here relates to the scheme of the evolution of consciousness which he had adopted from Ken Wilber earlier in A New Vision of Reality.

In this way we can envision the emergence of a new world culture as the present materialist and mechanistic system breaks down under the continued crisis of economic, social and political conflict. One of the characteristics of this new culture would be its feminine aspects. For three thousand years the world has been dominated by patriarchal cultures which overcame the ancient matriarchal cultures of the earlier ages. We have now reached the limit of this masculine culture with its aggressive, competitive, rational, analytic character. We are moving now into an age where the feminine principle will be valued, the yin in contrast to the yang. In the Chinese understanding yang is the masculine principle, yin is the feminine and as the yang reaches its limit it begins to move back again to the yin. We have now reached the limit of the yang, the masculine culture, and we are moving inevitably back to the feminine. The feminine will sooner or later begin to take its proper place with its characteristics of intuition, empathy and co-operation, and with its holistic approach. This will necessarily affect not only the economic, social and political orders but also spirituality and religion. The Christian religion has developed an entirely masculine concept of God. We always speak of God as Father, and of the incarnation of the Son. Even the Holy Spirit, which is neuter in Greek but masculine in Latin, we have conceived normally in masculine terms. In the Old Testament, however, the Spirit, the ruach, is feminine and in the Syrian church this same word was used of the Holy Spirit when they spoke of "our Mother, the Holy Spirit." That is found in the second and third centuries but it does not seem to have survived after that. The masculine character of the Godhead has always prevailed since then. There was however a feminine aspect in God in the Old Testament and to some extent in the New, and in the Christian tradition we have particularly Julian of Norwich, who speaks of Jesus as our Mother. St Anselm of Canterbury does the same. So apart from a few exceptions the masculine character of God has strongly prevailed in the West. By contrast, in India God is conceived both as Father and Mother. Obviously theologically God may be conceived as both Father and Mother. Being neither masculine nor feminine he can be represented as either Father or Mother, or both, in masculine and feminine terms. In the Tantric tradition, which derives from the ancient matriarchal culture, the mother aspect of God is dominant. In that tradition the whole universe is seen to derive from the Mother and all worship is offered to the Mother. That is precisely the opposite of the Judaeo-Christian tradition. We may expect therefore a corresponding development in Christian theology recognizing the feminine aspect of God and the place of women in the ministry of the church. There is of course no question of a return to a matriarchal society. It is a matter of the recovery of feminine values and the reconciliation of the masculine and the feminine.

It should be added that in Catholicism the feminine aspect is entirely centered on the Virgin Mary. It is the only way a Catholic, or indeed a Christian, can find a feminine figure in relation to God. So devotion to the feminine archetype centers on the Virgin Mary, but we should recognise that there is a feminine aspect of God himself and that the Virgin Mother is a manifestation of this. This means, in other words, that devotion to the Mother has its origin in God.

98. A Further Awakening to the Feminine[20]

Masculine and feminine were basic categories in Bede's thinking. He had been reflecting theologically about 'the feminine,' in the history of western church and culture and in the relationship between East and West, for many years. The ratio between reflection and experience changed dramatically for him at the time of his first stroke, when he was eighty-three years old. Now the feminine broke through on every level of his person: spirit, mind, psyche and body. Very soon Bede the theologian would return, however, and begin to reflect on this experience which had been characterized above all by its totality. In his account of those weeks during these interviews[21] with Andrew Harvey, therefore, it is difficult to know when experience ends and interpretation begins. Nor can we clearly distinguish a psychological from a spiritual or theological dimension. It is striking that Bede's deepest realization of advaita, nonduality, took place in close relationship both to this emergence of the maternal feminine and to a catastrophic physical event.

On January 25, 1990, I was sitting meditating, as I usually do at six o'clock, on the verandah of my hut; and suddenly, without any warning, a terrific force came and hit me on the head. It seemed like a sort of sledgehammer. Everything seemed like a television screen before the picture is focused. Just everything was like this. Then this force seemed to be dragging me out of the chair. It was coming from the left and pulling me out of my chair. It came suddenly, absolutely unexpected, without any warning. It was very scary, really. I managed to crawl onto the bed. I think I was breathing very heavily. Christudas came about an hour afterward. I lost count of time. He found me there, and then the news went around.

For the next week, I'm told, I didn't speak at all. I can't recall anything in detail. I don't know what happened during that week. There was a period of blankness. Then I began to come around. I woke up one night at about one o'clock, and I thought I was going to die. I decided to prepare for death, so I said the prayers, the normal prayers, and invoked the angels and so on, and waited for death. Nothing happened. Then, after an hour or two, Christudas came along and massaged me, and I began to get back to normal.

I had some breakfast, and then I felt sort of restless, disturbed, not knowing quite what was happening. The inspiration came suddenly again to surrender to the Mother. It was quite unexpected: "Surrender to the Mother." And so somehow I made a surrender to the Mother. Then I had an experience of overwhelming love. Waves of love sort of flowed into me. Judy Walter, my great friend, was watching. Friends were watching beside me all the time. I called out to her, "I'm being overwhelmed by love."

It was an extraordinary experience. Psychologically, I think, it was the breakthrough to the feminine. I was very masculine and patriarchal and had been developing the animus, the left brain, all this time. Now the right brain — the feminine, the chthonic power, the earth power — came and hit me. It opened up the whole dimension of the feminine, of the earth, and so on. When I thought of surrendering to the Mother, it was certainly Mary, because I often say the "Hail Mary," but also it was more the Black Madonna that came into my mind. The mother who is mother of the earth as well as the heavens — Mother Nature, as a whole. I also thought of my own mother, and motherhood in general.

This was really the opening of a totally new dimension to me. I can see how growing up in a patriarchal society, and living all this time so much from the intellect, this [other] side had been suppressed. Now it simply came up like this. It was very violent at first, like something that hits you on the head; but then it is extremely loving. It comes and embraces you. So this was a wonderful experience, and it's gone on ever since.

What I understood this to mean, after a time, was that the left brain and the whole rational system had been knocked down, and the right brain and the intuitive understanding, the sympathetic mind, had been opened up. The left brain keeps going all the time, but the right brain is always in control. I got this sense of *advaita*, nonduality. The divisions between things broke away, and everything was flowing into everything else.

Today I still see the divisions, but I feel differently about people and things: It's all one, in a sense. And I have never lost the sense that all the diversities are contained in the one. This has become more and more my understanding.

99. A Descent into the Body[22]

Later during the same interview of December 1992,[23] Bede looks back over the process which was initiated by his stroke of January 1990. Again we seem to see a reversal of the ascending scheme of the development of consciousness. "What I feel right now is that the spirit is coming down." He imagines the shakti , descending from the highest chakra, traditionally associated with non-dual spiritual realization, "right down to the root chakra," which corresponds to earth and to physical sexuality. When we recall that Bede has understood the stroke as the occasion of his initiation into nondual consciousness, it seems that the emergence of the feminine has been accompanied by an opening of his consciousness to every level of his being. The feminine and masculine images that are emerging in Bede's consciousness here toward the end, however, those of 'Mother' and 'Father,' still reflect the primal Source to which he has always been drawn.

This process of change since my stroke has been very gradual. It is going on all the time. It is not easy to put into words, but something is happening all the time. It is partly a physical transformation. The body itself is undergoing great changes. My problem before was that I was living largely from the head; and then after the stroke, I got down into the heart. But now it goes right from the heart to all the *chakras*,[24] right to the root chakra. The root chakra is the body's connection to the earth. What I feel now is that the spirit is coming down. I always think the *sahasrara*[25] is above the body, and it descends to the head. Then it goes down from the head through the throat to the heart. And now it is descending to the belly, which is very important. The *hara*[26] — that is where all the blood is — is in the belly. It is your flesh and your blood that this has to penetrate. It then moves down through the sex region. That is very important, too, because that tends to be suppressed. In my own experience it was very much repressed. I am rediscovering the whole sexual dimension of life at the age of eighty-six, really. And that also means discovering the feminine. So the whole of this dimension, which I had been seeking for a very long time, is now sort of opening itself up to me.

I think the Mother is gradually revealing itself to me and taking over. But it is not the Mother alone. It is the Mother and the Father, the male and the female, sort of gradually having their marriage. The whole thing is becoming integrated, but it's a continual process. I can't say that it is fully realized. In fact, it is certainly not fully realized. This integration is taking place all the time, and it is quite bewildering at times. There are always the opposite forces working, but something is happening all the time — a sort of inner transformation.

100. Contemplative Life in the World

During Bede Griffiths' final years, he travelled from his ashram to different parts of the world. As he experienced more and more the spiritual hunger and thirst of those with whom he talked, he became convinced that the future of contemplative life lay principally outside the monasteries, among people living an ordinary life in the world. The monasteries too, focused upon external works and liturgical prayer, needed a renewal of contemplative life. Teaching at the John Main Seminar in Indiana in 1991, Bede recalls some of the historical background of the lack of contemplative prayer which he had found in the Benedictine tradition which he had entered.

Bede had great admiration for John Main, the Benedictine monk who had begun to teach a method of contemplative meditation ('Christian Meditation') widely to lay people. John Main's key practical teaching was the continual use of a brief mantric prayer (e.g., 'maranatha') as a way toward contemplative prayer. Bede traces the history of this kind of prayer in Christianity. Unlike the Divine Office, with its length and complexity, the brief mantric prayer is well suited to people living in the world. John Main's two insights, therefore, complement one another: this simplifying and interiorizing of prayer opens the contemplative tradition to people outside the monasteries, everywhere in the world.

There are problems with the classical Divine Office of the monks, and especially with the psalms which make it up. Bede proposes a severe revision of the Psalter, with the elimination of the many psalm verses which, with their violence and vindictiveness and their primitive image of God, cannot be reconciled with the New Testament principle of unconditional love.[27] He reviews the history of the meditation movement and reflects on its significance as connecting the Christian meditator not only with the prayer of Jesus in the gospels but with meditators in the other great traditions of the world — and with the axial breakthrough into unitive consciousness, five centuries before Christ, that is the common root of the great world religions of today.

Bede discusses the integration of meditation into a life in the world, and the various services toward the disadvantaged that a community of meditators may undertake. Meditation has been found especially effective in the context of prison life. He sees it as the key to a renewal of the church: the emergence of a new kind of church, 'focused on contemplative prayer.' Bede shares John Main's vision of a stream of contemplative spirituality flowing deeply and broadly, from a recovered tradition of meditation, out into the world and forward into a new age. Here we include two brief extracts from these conferences.

I[28]

The person responsible for bringing Christian contemplative life to lay people was Father John Main. It was a wonderful achievement, a great gift of God for the church. He found a method of meditation in the *Conferences* of Cassian, a monk of the fifth century, who visited the Fathers of the Desert in their solitude and described their way of life and prayer. Cassian spoke of 'pure prayer' as a way of meditation, using a short word or verse repeated continually in order to avoid distractions and to attain 'purity of heart.' He gives the example, "God, come to my aid. Lord, make haste to help me." That was the earliest Christian mantra. Whatever the situation, whenever anything unexpected happened or any danger arose, "God, come to my aid. Lord, make haste to help me," was the guide in life. Different verses from the Psalms or other parts of the Bible were also used. In the 'Jesus prayer,' which became the norm of this kind of prayer in the eastern church, one repeated constantly, 'Lord Jesus Christ, Son of God, have mercy on me a sinner.' That is another ancient and characteristic

Christian mantra.

In reintroducing 'pure prayer', Father John chose the mantra 'Maranatha' (Aramaic for 'Lord, come'). This is important because Jesus spoke Aramaic. Since our Gospels are written in Greek, no words that Jesus actually spoke in his own language are recorded. To be precise there are just six words. In Mark 5:41 when Jesus raises a little girl, he is quoted as saying, "Talitha cumi" ('Little girl, I say to you, arise.') And on the cross, as reported in the gospels of Mark[29] and of Matthew,[30] Jesus is heard to say, "Eloi, Eloi, lama sabachthani" ("My God, My God, why have you forsaken me?"). Other than these words, everything that Jesus said is translated into Greek. 'Maranatha' occurs in the First Letter of Paul to the Corinthians[31] and was used in the early church as one of the relics of Aramaic, Jesus' own speech. That is why it is a very sacred word. When for ten years I was a member of the Syrian church in Kerala, we learned Syriac which is virtually the same language as the Aramaic spoken by Jesus and the apostles. When we use 'Maranatha,' it takes us back to the time of Jesus himself.

The idea of 'prayer without ceasing' was again taken up in the West, in the fourteenth century, in a book called *The Cloud of Unknowing*, which has had a tremendous influence on so many people today. It is a medieval classic written by an unknown author, probably a priest, in beautiful, simple and direct English. The author suggests taking one word, 'God' or 'Love,' and repeating it silently. As a whole, the book is a beautiful presentation of contemplative prayer. This, like the work of Cassian and the 'Jesus prayer,' is part of the tradition that Father John rediscovered and reclaimed for the ordinary Christian. He devoted his life to spreading the availability of 'pure prayer' throughout the modern church, thus opening the way of contemplation to lay people as well as to monks and nuns. This is really a breakthrough, a new movement in the church. As is clear, the church today is moving towards the recognition of the laity, and this rediscovery and reclamation of an ancient tradition is part of the larger movement of the church of the Laity. You probably know that the word 'laity' comes from the Greek laos, which means 'people,' the people of God. Father John has made it possible for the people of God to share in the deep life of prayer, the inner prayer of the Spirit.

We should remind ourselves that Father John originally learned this way of prayer with a mantra from a Hindu swami whom he met in Malaya before he became a Benedictine monk. This is important. As we have seen, we have our own Christian tradition of prayer with a mantra that can be traced back to the Fathers of the Desert, but we must also remember that it links us with a tradition of prayer from the earliest times in the East, particularly in India. It is important that we see our Christian meditation as part of a whole movement of meditation Hindu and Buddhist, Jain and Sikh, Moslem and Sufi spreading throughout the world. We place ourselves within that movement. Father John made the link when he learned prayer with a mantra from a Hindu swami.

The value of this method is that it simplifies prayer and reduces it to its fundamental ground in the depths of the soul. . .

II[32]

Father John's great insight was that the Divine Office could be a preparation for contemplative prayer and also an overflow from our contemplation, *but that it needed to lead to pure prayer.* This is to change the focus of Christian prayer from the Divine office, the prayer of monks and religious, to the pure prayer of self-surrender in love. That is the essence of this way which is open to every Christian. I think it is a message for monks as well. In our ashram we have spontaneously moved to placing the two hours of meditation, morning and evening, at the center of our lives. In India, the early hours are considered the best time for meditation, and the time of sundown: they call it 'the meeting of the light and the darkness.' In all Hindu ashrams you meditate morning and evening at those times. In our ashram we normally meet between half past five and half past six in the morning, and six and seven in the evening. Many come to sit by the river. We all take our time then to meditate. That is the focus of the day. Then we go to church, we have our communal prayer, we have our Mass, and we share together. It is a kind of overflow from meditation and also a nourishment you take in at that time from the readings and prayers. You open your heart. For me, the focus has changed; it is now on pure prayer, contemplative prayer, and the Divine Office is an overflow from it.

I think this is where Father John is leading us: to introducing monastic prayer to lay people, but also to deepening the prayer of the monks and nuns so that they can enter into the silence and solitude of being 'alone with God' while they keep open to the church and humanity through participation in the Divine Office. So it works both ways. The monk opens to the lay people and shares with them and lay people discover a deeper way of prayer. The fundamental insight of Father John was that this pure prayer of meditation could be shared with people outside the monastery.

101. The New Civilization[33]

In the final chapter of A New Vision of Reality, *Bede Griffiths sets out to imagine a new era of the history of world and church in which the 'marriage of East and West' — of wisdom and science, intuition and rationality, feminine and masculine — will be consummated. We have already seen the first part of this chapter,[34] in which Bede recalled the eclipse of the perennial philosophy in the West at the time of the Renaissance and scientific revolution. As western thought declined into a reductive materialism and a mechanical conception of the universe, the three interrelated worlds of spirit, consciousness and matter were collapsed into a flat, material universe. He discerned a turning point, however, in the emergence of a new conception of reality which was organic rather than mechanistic: in the 'new science' which he had embraced.*

From this perspective it is possible to imagine a new human life in this world and a new society, based upon participation rather than domination. Bede follows the implications of this revolution in consciousness through the three levels of physical, psychological-social and, finally, spiritual or religious reality. First, with Schumacher, he imagines a new technology, returning to the dimensions of human life, a new decentralized society and a rebirth of village life. Following Rudolf Steiner, he envisions a program of education in which first the child's emotional life, then imaginative life, and finally rational powers will be developed. Each of the world religions will have to undergo a death and rebirth in which it opens to the others, in the light of the primordial unitive wisdom. We have already read the sections of this chapter which follow: Bede's projections regarding the future of the church[35] and the emergence of the feminine principle in human life and culture.[36]

We return to Bede's text at its conclusion, where he places the historical drama in a context which is not only theological but apocalyptic. Our society will probably not be able to navigate the radical transition from a mechanistic order to an organic and human order without catastrophe. The West's abandonment of God and of the spiritual world has placed it in the hands of "the hostile forces of the subtle world" which work in the unconscious to destroy humanity. The only way out of this captivity is a return to the perennial philosophy. This must be a move forward, however, insofar as the world religions, separated until now, must join together to provide the spiritual core of a new world order.

Here at the end, as Bede surveys the contemporary world and its prospects, we do not sense the radical optimism with which he has looked forward to a 'new creation.'[37] *With few exceptions, his models for the future are models of the past. Despairing of the conflict and fragmentation of the present, he looks back to a time of unbroken harmony in the past and forward to a time of human and social integration and of global convergence in the future. We may be reminded of Bede's selective reading of the Bible.*[38] *Something is missing in this vision which is so ready to conclude that the only way forward is the way back. What is it that has been coming to birth through the long travail of biblical history and through the agonies of the last few centuries? Can it be — for one thing — the free, differentiated human person that is glimpsed in the Gospels and in Paul's letter to the Galatians, the individual 'microcosm' that corresponds to Bede's all-integrating Cosmic Person?*

We go on now to ask, what will the pattern of the new age be like? What can we discern in the light of our present understanding of the universe and of the knowledge which we have of eastern mysticism and spiritual experience? How in our time can we look forward in the light of our present knowledge of what science has done both for good and for evil, and what are we to make of the past, its art and philosophy, its religion and its mythical experience?

The first thing is that human society will be based on a new relationship to the world of nature, arising from an organic understanding of nature in place of a mechanistic view of the universe. This is a major change which is taking place. We have to learn to see ourselves as part of the physical organism of the universe. We need to develop the sense of the cosmic whole and of a way of relating to the world around us as a living being which sustains and nourishes us and for which we have responsibility. This will give rise to a new understanding of our environment and will put an end to this age of the exploitation of nature. At the present moment the whole movement of economics and politics is characterized and marred by the exploitation of nature at every level. The material resources of the universe are being grossly exploited in order to create more material prosperity for relatively few human beings, no matter at what cost that is done. That trend would be reversed by the new understanding that we are all parts of this universe, of this natural world, that we are integral elements in it and that we have to respect it. This would involve a new attitude to the earth and to the natural resources of the earth, to the sea and all the creatures in it, to the animal world as a whole, to the question of vivisection and the treatment of animals in general, and to our attitude to outer space, whether we try to exploit it for human gain or whether we look on it in another way.

Secondly, the sense of communion with an encompassing reality will replace the attempt to dominate the world. The different understanding of ecology and a greater sensitivity to its realities would revolutionize our understanding of nature and of the world in which we live. This would lead to a new kind of technology based on the new understanding of science, and an appropriate or intermediate technology as Schumacher conceived it, answering the needs of the vast majority of people in Asia, Africa and South America who live in rural communities. The present system of technology has been built up on the basis of mechanistic science and it savagely and indiscriminately exploits the world of nature. This has produced the terrible situation in which we find ourselves with its material conveniences for a minority but with its disastrous consequences of global injustice and destruction. We are looking for a new technology which Schumacher speaks of as appropriate or intermediate technology which builds up from the villages. It would build upon the economy of the village instead of destroying it. There would be respect for the basic crafts of spinning, weaving, pottery, carpentry, metal work and of course all forms of gardening and agriculture. This is very important. All these crafts were evolved in the millennia before Christ, from roughly the fourth millennium onwards, and they represent a summit of human achievement in this sphere. When we look back on the past and see the weaving, the clothing, pottery, woodwork and metalwork of the past ages, we put them in museums as something to marvel at because of their beauty. And that was the ordinary work of the people of those times. To discard those abilities in favour of the progress of the mechanistic system is to degrade civilization and human life.

Respect for the basic crafts enables human persons to live in harmony with nature and with the world around them. Their art and their work express this harmony and therefore it is beautiful. Beauty is always due to this harmony with nature. When we have that harmony the products of our hands are beautiful, and when we do not have harmony the products may be useful and very helpful in other ways but they lose their beauty.

Thirdly, these new values would give rise to a new type of human community. This would be a decentralized society drawing people from large cities to smaller towns and villages where a much more total and integrated human life would be possible. I do not see any future for the huge cities of the present world, London, New York, Tokyo, Bombay and Calcutta. In such cities all over the world in every continent the population may be over ten million. Cities of millions of people do not provide a human mode of existence and depend on a whole economic system which will eventually collapse, for such societies cannot sustain their economies. So we have to look back beyond these industrialized cities to find some kind of norm of human existence. Here I would like to quote from Lewis Mumford, where in his book *The Myth of the Machine* he describes the neolithic village. This is a village the like of which lasted for thousands of years, all over the world, and still exists to some extent to the present day. This is how he describes it. "Where the seasons are marked by holiday festivals and ceremonies; where the stages of life are punctuated by family and communal rituals; where eating and drinking and sexual play constitute the central core of life, where work, even hard work, is rarely divorced from rhythm, song, human companionship and aesthetic delight; where vital activity is considered as great a reward of labour as the product; where neither power nor profit has precedence over life; where the family, the neighbour and the friend are all parts of a visible, tangible, face-to-face community. There the neolithic culture in its essential elements is still in existence." That is to my mind a model of wholesome human existence. All these elements were present in the villages of India until recently and are still basically there although they are being undermined daily. That Indian village life and culture which existed for millennia is being systematically destroyed, year by year.

Mumford's description of the neolithic village remains a model for a human community. Science and appropriate technology, building on that, may introduce improvements, especially forms of transport and communication which may link up the different human centres, but these will be based on natural sources of energy, particularly the sun. Fritjof Capra considers that the new age will be the solar age. The sun provides all the energy that is conceivably necessary for human existence. Such a society would be decentralized. It does not require huge conglomerations of people in cities. The sun is available everywhere and the energy can be made available. Also, of course, water and the wind are appropriate sources of energy. The new society would certainly exclude all forms of nuclear energy which is perhaps the supreme example of this mechanistic system and the most destructive form of it.

Education in the new society would be basic education, as understood for instance by Mahatma Gandhi. It would be an integral education of body, soul and spirit, relating each person to the world in an organic way and developing their personal capacities. Perhaps, following Rudolf Steiner's understanding, such education would center first on emotional growth. Steiner held that during the first seven years the child has primarily to grow at the level of the emotions and the education given should foster this emotional development. During the next seven years the growth of the imagination predominates and education centres on music, art, dance and poetry. Only in the third seven years, from fourteen onwards, should the rational, logical mind be trained to develop seriously. To some extent obviously it is functioning before this but in the Steiner system the emphasis on it only begins there. The result of acting on these principles is an integrated education of the whole person, emotional, imaginative and rational, where each level, emotions, imaginations and rationality, is properly

446

developed, consolidated and stabilized. This is in marked contrast to our usual method of education, which concentrates on developing the rational, logical mind as early as five and so often loses out on these other aspects of human personality.

In medicine, rather than making use almost entirely of modern allopathic methods, there will be a turn to alternative methods such as homeopathy, acupuncture, Ayurvedic and Tibetan medicine, and herbal medicine in general, all of which are concerned with the health of the whole person. These forms of treatment always relate the body to the soul and the spirit and never regard it as something that can be treated in isolation. The human person is conceived as an integral whole, and it is seen that health, wholeness and holiness, being derived from the same root, are totally interrelated. The health of the body, the wholeness of the person and holiness itself are all aspects of the same reality and they cannot be separated.

This leads to the third aspect. We have considered first the physical, material growth of the world and secondly its psychological and social growth. Now we turn to the spiritual order and the place of religion. This involves a return to the perennial philosophy, the ancient wisdom which underlies all religion from the earliest times. It will involve a respect for the traditional wisdom of primitive people, the Australian Aborigines, the American Indians and the tribal peoples of Asia and Africa. More and more today we are discovering the wisdom of these people, the harmony they have achieved in their lives and the very profound understanding they have of how human life is related to the natural world about them and to the world of spirits beyond them. Generally such people evidence an integrated, holistic view of life.

Then we turn to the great religious traditions, Hindu, Buddhist, Jain, Sikh, Taoist, Confucian, Shinto, Zoroastrian, Judaic, Muslim and Christian. These are systems of religion which had their origin during the first millennium before Christ. All are based on the perennial philosophy, developed under different situations and in different circumstances, and all embody in their different ways the ancient wisdom and the wholeness of life. These different traditions will all be seen as interrelated and interdependent, each giving a particular and unique

447

insight into ultimate truth and reality. In fact, of course, they all grew up apart and mostly without contact with each other for many centuries. When they did make contact there was often rivalry, acrimony and conflict, and as a result we have the disastrous divisions of religion today. But we are learning, and we shall continue to learn, that all the different religious traditions, from the most primitive to the most advanced, are interrelated and interdependent, and that each has its own particular insights. For the Semitic religions in particular, Judaism, Christianity and Islam, it is important that they give up the exclusive claims which characterize them. This would free them to recognize the action of God in all humanity from the beginnings of history. For the Semitic religions this is a particularly difficult problem. All three tend to extreme exclusivism and on that account have brought so much conflict into the world. . .

The continuation of this chapter 13 of A New Vision of Reality *will be found in earlier parts of this book: 1) pp. 287-294 on the future church, as text n.29; 2) pp.294-295 on the future emergence of the Feminine, as text n. 97. We resume Bede's text on p. 295, at the conclusion of this final chapter of* A New Vision.

It is possible that the transition from a mechanistic to an organic society will come about gradually, without too much conflict. But it is more likely that there will be a general catastrophe as the economic, social and political structures of the present civilization break down. We must remember, and this is important, that the conflicts of the present world do not derive merely from human failings and miscalculations. There has been a reversal of human values, a spiritual breakdown, which has brought into play forces beyond the material and the human. The present crisis has been prepared by the whole system of science and philosophy, affecting religion and leading to atheism. This is a systematic development where the previous spiritual values have been broken down and the materialistic system discussed earlier has prevailed. This has released forces beyond the material and the human. If a nuclear war takes place it will not be because anyone desires it but because people are being driven by forces of the unconscious which they cannot control. As St Paul says, "We are not contending with flesh and blood but against the principalities, against the powers, against the world rulers of this present darkness."[39] When the truth of the transcendent order of reality is rejected we do not remain neutral. We become exposed to the hostile forces of the subtle world of which we have been speaking, forces which work in the unconscious and bring destruction upon humankind. Western Europe rejected the perennial philosophy at the Renaissance and has been led step by step to the materialistic philosophy which rejects fundamental human values and exposes humankind to the contrary forces at work in the universe. The only way of recovery is to rediscover the perennial philosophy, the traditional wisdom, which is found in all ancient religions and especially in the great religions of the world. But those religions have in turn become fossilised and have each to be renewed, not only in themselves but also in relation to one another, so that a cosmic, universal religion can emerge, in which the essential values of Christian religion will be preserved in living relationship with the other religious traditions of the world. This is a task for the coming centuries as the present world order breaks down and a new world order emerges from the ashes of the old.

102. Bede's Synthesis[40]

The twelfth chapter of A New Vision of Reality *is Bede's final synthetic essay. This little Summa is a most ambitious project. He sets out to integrate all that he has brought before us: not only the three worlds of matter, consciousness and spirit, but East and West, past, present and the end. Having directed our attention so often, in his earlier writings, beyond time and history to the 'nondual' country of eternity, Bede brings us back into this world and sets out to give an account of it, from beginning to end. The development of human consciousness will be seen in this context of the evolution of the universe. This final vision must integrate the perennial philosophy with evolution and the history of salvation: unitive wisdom with modern science and Christian theology. He must find a place in the 'plan' for each of the great religious traditions. Bede has made numerous sketches for this grand synthesis, and in the subtitle of* A New Vision of Reality *he had already marked out the dimensions of the challenge: Western science, Eastern Mysticism and Christian Faith.*

Bede begins, as in the first chapter of A New Vision of Reality, *with* the world of matter, as it originated in the 'Big Bang' and developed in the continual interaction between the two 'forces' of form and matter/energy (matter, for Bede, is a mode of energy). Matter continually expands, moves by chance, becomes more disorganized, dissipates itself. Form organizes and structures matter, centers and concentrates it into larger and more complex wholes. "At each stage the organism becomes more complex and the organizing principle more powerful and more structured....Matter is without, form, the organising force, is within."

The same two principles of form and matter continue to interact as the process of evolution continues through plants and animals to human beings. A new stage is reached with the emergence of human consciousness; in the human person matter becomes conscious and form becomes intelligence. "We are at that stage of evolution at which the material universe is emerging into consciousness in each one of us." Bede follows the development of consciousness to the point of true subjective consciousness or reflexivity: "and that is where real growth begins to take place." As humans become reflexively conscious, the universe begins to emerge, from within itself, into a new mode of existence.

Now the human person experiences itself as an integrated whole, and as participating in the three larger wholes or worlds of the physical universe, the collective psyche with its subtle realms and, finally, the world of transcendent consciousness. Here we rejoin the world's great religious traditions, and Bede recalls once again the Axial breakthrough into unitive consciousness. Here is both the source and the final point of convergence of all reality. From the One, or Spirit, everything flows forth and into the One everything returns.

At this point Bede's discourse becomes properly theological; he begins to speak in the Christian language of Father (the One, Source), Son (creative Word and cosmic Person) and Holy Spirit (divine Energy, source of all natural energies). "As the Word or Son is the source of all form in nature, so the Spirit is the source of all energy..." The Holy Spirit brings human persons into the one cosmic Person, and in this way the whole creation is brought back into a unitive participation in God. Israel had been prepared as the "cell," the "new center of organization," around which the cosmic integration should take place. From this center emerges Jesus, the 'archetypal man,' in whom we all become 'persons in the Person.' As everything is brought together into this new creation in Christ, Bede insists with Teilhard that individual differences are preserved.

In his final synthesis, Bede has outlined a synthetic process of evolution in which the three worlds are united in the divine-human-bodily person who is Christ. The creation is divinized in the humanity of Christ. Through the *archetypal figure of the purusha or 'cosmic person,' the nondual Absolute which is the heart of the perennial philosophy and the wisdom of the East has become manifest as personal, embodied and dynamic: the center of a continuing incarnation.*

The intention of this chapter is to put together the ideas we have been considering, particularly the evolution of the world and the evolution of human consciousness, and to see how the whole process converges on an Ultimate Reality, a Supreme Being. It is important to have some kind of plan in terms of which to identify and unify our experience. It is also important that this unifying plan has a place for all the great religious traditions. Many Christians today feel the need to relate their experience to that of the Hindu, the Buddhist and the Muslim, as well as to the traditional religions, of, for instance, the American Indians and the tribal peoples of Asia and Africa. What follows is an attempt to articulate some kind of framework in which all these modes of experience can be related and seen in their inner unity.

We start with the explosion of matter at the beginning of time, around fifteen billion years ago. It is understood that in the original explosion of matter the forms which were to come into being in the course of the ages were already implicated, enfolded together, and that these forms have gradually unfolded or become explicated in the course of the evolutionary process. We have to go a step further and say that not only was the matter of the universe implicated with all its forms but that consciousness was also already implicated in the original explosion of the universe because consciousness itself emerged from matter as the process advanced. This means that we have to conceive of a universe coming into being in which matter and consciousness are interwoven, and to speak about this I have chosen to use the Aristotelian terms, matter and form. Matter is the energy of the universe, an unformed, unstructured energy, which is behind the whole universe, while form is the principle of order. Form and matter are the two basic principles in the universe. Matter is indeterminate, unpredictable, unintelligible, a pure flux of energy without form. It is the principle of change, of becoming, of chance, of the absurd. All that element in life comes from matter. Form on the other hand is the principle of order, of structure, of intelligibility, of being in actuality. Matter has no being in itself. It is pure potentiality which is organized into being and becomes actual through the action of form upon it.

Matter and form are the two basic principles then and the whole universe evolves through the interplay between them. Part of the dynamic is that matter always tends to dissipate itself, to disintegrate, to become disorganized. Consequently at the very beginning of the universe there was an explosion of matter such that matter was thrown outwards in primordial expansion. It is believed that this principle of expansion is still operating and that the galaxies are expanding all the time as matter pushes itself out in that way. But at the very time that matter expands and tends to disintegrate, another force, the force of form, comes into play and begins to structure matter, organizing and controlling it. The understanding is then that there were originally photons, electrons and other basic particles coming into being and dissolving, and then gradually forms began to be structured and the simplest atoms, those of hydrogen and helium, came into being. From that origin of organization matter became increasingly more organized as the two forces were continuously operative, matter disintegrating and moving outwards and form drawing within, concentrating and centering the matter. So with the galaxies the matter expanded enormously while the forms began to structure it, forming the stars, the galaxies and eventually suns, moons, and planets, including earth. We can understand then that the whole cosmos comes into being by the interaction of these two forces, one working on the other.

It is important to realize that matter is always in a state of disequilibrium. If it were to come into equilibrium it would become simply passive. It is always in disequilibrium as it moves out into a new phase, and from that a new form emerges. It is thought that this is how evolution takes place. There would be a particular form, a chemical, a plant or animal or whatever, and then something in the environment disorganizes that structure and it has to reconstruct itself. In so doing a new form comes into being. In this process certain structures have been identified which Ilya Prigogine calls dissipative structures. Dissipative structures are found even in chemicals and still more conspicuously in plants and animals. These are structures which tend to dissipate their energy, destructuring themselves and then restructuring again somewhat differently. This, it is thought, is how development takes place, always a disequilibrium tending towards the organization of a new structure. Rupert Sheldrake has suggested that what, following Aristotle, we are calling forms, or formal causes, act as morphogenetic fields. These are fields in which matter is moulded into particular forms. Evolution proceeds in stages as a new burst of formative energy is released and this takes place on a large scale. Recent research has suggested that new species come into being not simply by gradual stages but rather by a kind of explosion. This indicates that the matter has been prepared for it by changes having been introduced which make it ready for this explosion of new species. This is at the moment by no means proved but it does seem to be the pattern which is emerging.

There is then a gradual development. Atoms develop into molecules, these develop into cells, cells develop into organisms, then to simple plants and animals, as organs are produced leading to the development of increasingly complex animal forms. All this is a continuous process. What is particularly interesting is that the elements of each stage, atoms, molecules, cells and so on, are each a whole in their own right and as they develop they integrate the other wholes within themselves so that the universe is composed of wholes within wholes. For instance, an atom itself is a complete whole, with its electrons, protons and neutrons and other elements. When that atom enters into a molecule it enters a new whole, and yet it retains its identity as, say, a carbon atom within the molecule, a smaller whole within the greater whole. Similarly, within a cell the molecules still retain their structure within the wider structure of the cell. And again the cells in the body multiply and grow and each is a whole within the greater whole of the tissue, the organ and finally the whole organism. So the whole of nature is composed of all these structures or processes built up one after another, one into the other, in such a way that nothing is lost.

In the course of evolution most processes simply follow mechanical laws. Rupert Sheldrake puts this down to a kind of force of habit, in that once a certain pattern of organization has occurred it tends to repeat itself and so it gets fixed to a certain extent. This pattern appears as a kind of mechanical law. But at the same time there are also continual chance variations and the new form that emerges from these apparently chance changes integrates the chance elements, creating a new structure. So form and matter, order and chance, are working one on the other the whole time. At each stage the organism becomes more complex and the organizing principle more powerful and more structured. This is what Teilhard de Chardin calls the principle of complexification. An atom of hydrogen is extremely simple, consisting of one proton and one electron. But then as there arise more and more complex atoms, and increasingly complex molecules and cells, at each level there has to be a more complex deep structure to hold it together and the energy within has to be stronger. This is Teilhard's point of the within and the without of things. Atoms, molecules, cells, attain their structure from the outside, as it were, with regard to their matter but at the same time a force is appearing within each one which organizes and maintains the structure. Matter is without; form, the organising force, is within. And so the form organizes each thing in a more complex way and becomes more manifest as it develops, leading to increasingly greater and more complex formal order.

This process goes on continuously, through plants and animals to human beings. It appears that the same forces which are at work in matter and sub-human life operate also in the human person and in human consciousness. The same principle of matter and form working together can account for the whole evolution of humanity. But what happens in human beings is that this organizing power, this form, begins to emerge into consciousness. We have seen that there is an organizing power at every level and this organizing power has the character of a mind. Mind, it has been said, reveals itself as "a pattern of self-organization and a set of dynamic relationships". In this sense it can be said that mind is present in matter from the beginning. Form in Aristotle's sense of the word is a power of intelligence. It creates order. It causes the self-organization of all organic structures and creates a set of dynamic relationships. So mind is present in matter, and in plants and animals, and that mind becomes conscious in us. And so, in a very exact sense, it can be said that matter becomes conscious in human beings. This process which has been going on from the beginning of time becomes conscious in us. It evolves into consciousness. We are that stage of evolution at which the material universe is emerging into consciousness in each one of us.

At first this consciousness in us is, as we saw, a global consciousness. The child and the early man is each aware of himself simply as part of the physical universe. This is a beginning of a conscious awareness of oneself as part of this whole physical organism. Later there is awareness of oneself as part of a human organisation, of a human family, of human relationships. So the human person gradually emerges into consciousness. It is a fact, however, that all of us live in a state of half-consciousness for most of our lives. Most of our living goes on without our being conscious of it. All the activity of the atoms, the molecules, the cells in our bodies, for instance, functions of itself without our being conscious of it. And most of the physical functions of the body go on without our awareness. Only certain parts of all of this come into consciousness. We are emerging into consciousness all the time from the unconscious. Every night we go back into the unconscious. It is thought that in deep sleep we go right back to the original unconscious state, before anything emerged. In dreams we begin to come out into consciousness to some extent, and when we wake up we wake into a waking consciousness which is growing from the unconscious.

All this of course is a continual process. From childhood we are growing and our consciousness develops. Certain people develop their consciousness far more than others. Some remain at a very limited level of consciousness all their lives, while others gradually explore the further ranges of consciousness. This is what interests us now, that it is possible for consciousness to develop or expand beyond the present state. We at this stage have emerged into a certain level of consciousness. We can control our bodies to some extent and of course with modern medicine we have another dimension of physical control. We can also control our environment to some extent, but we are still exposed to the tremendous forces of the unconscious. In the same way, at the psychological level we have our emotional life and although to some extent we can control our emotions, they are very largely beyond our control most of the time. Emotions arise from infancy and from childhood habit and these are extremely difficult to control. Only as they gradually emerge into consciousness do we gain a measure of control over them.

In the evolutionary and developmental process, once we reach the level of language we have already crossed a barrier because with language it becomes possible to form symbols and an inner world comes into being. There is the outer world around us consisting of all the energies of matter and nature, and now with language and symbol we create an inner world where we represent, through the imagination, what we take to be the structure of the universe around us. Outside us are all these energies at work, but through our senses, feelings, imagination, reason and will, through all the faculties of our being, we structure a universe around us. It is a very limited universe and a very limited understanding that we have. It is always that we are structuring this appearance of the world around us. It is not as it really is. The world is infinitely greater than we perceive it. We only perceive those aspects of nature, matter and the energies of existence which are reflected through our senses, our feelings, our imagination, our mind and our will, through the whole of our human organism, and this is our particular way of perceiving the universe. So matter emerges into the consciousness in us and we create this inner world by which we can represent the world around us and that can gradually be extended. The whole aim of pure science and of philosophy is to get a more and more accurate knowledge of the world around, but we know now that understanding is always conditioned by the limitations of our minds.

As consciousness develops we become more and more self-conscious. First of all we are conscious of the world around us. Many people live in that world of external consciousness, being aware of the world around, of people, of events happening, of things to do and so on, but they seldom if ever reflect on themselves. On the other hand certain people, particularly at certain stages, develop the power of self-reflection to an extraordinary extent. Self-consciousness begins to grow and it becomes increasingly possible to be more and more aware of the universe around one in its relation to oneself, and of one's own human organism. This is self-reflection on oneself, and as far as we know it is a power unique to the human being. It appears that so far nothing else in the universe can reflect on itself as we do. The mind reflects on itself in such a way that we become conscious of consciousness. It is an inner reflection and that is where real growth begins to take place. That is where the universe now begins to emerge into a new mode of existence. When we begin to reflect on ourselves we can go back in consciousness, right to the beginning, to primeval, primordial consciousness. It is possible now by various methods to go back to the state of consciousness we have in the womb where each of us was one with the whole of nature. We can also go back in consciousness to our early childhood, to discover the emotions which we experienced then. Or we can go back to the stage where the imagination began to awaken, when our personal life began to come into being with the growth of language and all the developments which that brings. And then we can reflect on the functioning of the mind. Not only does the mind function, organizing our experience, but we can reflect on the functioning of the mind. We come to know our minds and how they work, and from that we get the science of logic and epistemology.

In this way the whole realm of consciousness and the degree to which that can grow is infinite. The important thing is that we now begin to experience ourselves as an integrated whole. This is the principle that we have taken from the beginning. We have seen that contemporary physics understands the universe to be an integrated whole, such that every part is related with every other part and no part can be explained except in relation to the whole. So the physical universe is an integrated, interrelated, interdependent whole and we can experience our physical being as part of the universe. The whole universe is in every part. That is the principle. Just as the structure of the whole human organism is present in every cell, so the whole universe is present in each one of us and we become conscious of the physical structure of the universe of which we are a part.

Secondly, as we become conscious of our feelings, our sensations, imagination and thought, we become conscious of ourselves as part of a psychological organism. None of us is an independent reality. We are all parts of a whole, experiencing ourselves through our heredity, our families, our language, our race, our traditions, our customs. In this way we come to be aware of ourselves as part of a psychological organism which eventually we realize stretches right back in time to the beginning of humanity and looks forward to the future. So each of us is part of this integrated whole which is both physical and psychological. And, just as the physical organism is an organic part of the physical universe, so this psychological organism is related to the psychic organism of the universe. We are all members of a whole, interrelated and interdependent. So far this is on a fairly ordinary level of consciousness but we can now go to a higher level of consciousness such that we go beyond our physical consciousness and beyond our normal psychological consciousness, and then we become aware of a transcendent or transpersonal consciousness. Different terms are used for this level of consciousness: transpersonal, suprapersonal, transcendent, spiritual, mystical, and so on. At this point we begin to discover a deeper dimension of being. So far we have seen ourselves as part of the physical universe, part of the whole psychological world, part of our family and people and the human race, but now we begin to discover that we ourselves are related to, and dependent on, powers and energies which are beyond us and above us.

It is at this point that meditation enters the scene, because in meditation we try to become aware of this physical organism and of the psychological level and then, as the mind becomes quiet and settled, we become aware of our transcendent consciousness. This was the great breakthrough in India in the fifth century, with the *Upanishads* and the Buddha: a breakthrough beyond the level of ordinary consciousness into transcendent consciousness. This has been explored in the East particularly but in many other parts of the world as well, through many ages. It is a part of human experience, as we now realize. We have our sense experience, our emotional and imaginative experience and the intellectual and moral experience of human life, but beyond all these there is transcendent experience which is just as real and well-established as any other. In the East particularly the exploration of the psychic universe has been particularly well developed, with Tibetan Buddhism probably going further than any other tradition. In Hinduism much of the psychic world has been charted and it has also been explored deeply in Christian and Islamic mysticism. It is significant that today scientists are recognizing that what comes out of this experience is a valid sphere of knowledge.

At this point an important distinction must be made. As long as we are in the realm of physical being our usual methods of measurement and quantification, of mathematical and logical thought, are all appropriate and ordinary scientific knowledge results. But once we go beyond that order into the psychological, emotional or imaginative world those methods become increasingly less appropriate, and when we come to transcendent, mystical experience they are no longer valid at all. What is important is that we learn to interpret these transpersonal experiences. We have to evolve a consistent conceptual system by which we can interpret and integrate our experience of the transcendent. That is exactly what was done in Tibet and also in other eastern traditions. Tibetan Buddhism is a completely consistent method worked out over hundreds of years, exploring how to interpret and integrate these phenomena of higher consciousness. This is in many respects a scientific method, just as valid in its own sphere as the methods of the physical sciences, but it does not come within the same frame of reference because the kinds of experience which are its data cannot be measured or quantified.

This higher consciousness has been present in humanity from the earliest times. A well-established example is shamanism, which has been investigated extensively by Mircea Eliade, Joan Halifax and others, and is found to occur all over the world. Shamans develop psychic powers and attain psychic knowledge, going beyond the physical and the ordinary psychological domains, to experience the early or lower levels of the transcendent. With such experience are associated what we call psychic phenomena, like visions and revelations, knowledge of the future and the past, and the ability to heal. These and many other parapsychological powers have been developed by shamans over the ages and continue to the present day. Such experiences are all part of what is called the subtle world and they were, of course, developed further in the great religious traditions. There is the gross world which is the world of the senses and of ordinary under-standing. Normal western science belongs simply to the gross world. But beyond the gross is the subtle world, the sphere of the subtle senses, the subtle feelings, the subtle imagination, the subtle mind and the whole subtle organism, and all the forces of that world which are present and can be experienced. Many people today are more and more commonly having these experiences, and we know that in the past this was quite normal. The forces which are encountered in the subtle realm are depicted as both good and evil. Some assist the growth of the universe, of human evolution and of human persons while others prevent and counteract such growth. So when we enter the subtle, psychic world we are exposed, as we are in the ordinary human physical world, to both good and evil forces. These are cosmic and psychological forces working in the universe and in the human consciousness and we have to learn how to understand and how to relate to them. Again in Tibetan Buddhism this complete grasp of both positive and negative forces, and how to relate to and deal with them, has been worked out in great detail.

Not only shamans but all the prophets, seers and visionaries of the past were people who had these psychic powers and psychic vision. Today this whole area is being studied more systematically and the whole sphere of parapsychological phenomena is generally recog-nised. As we have more knowledge of this area we begin to see how it is structured. The experience of the subtle world depends on an intuitive insight. It cannot be attained by rational means. The ordinary, rational, mental level of mind has no access to this realm and ordinary scientific methods are useless to map it. It is important to remember, however, that in these investigations we do not discard our reason. The method is to open ourselves through intuition to these deeper insights and then to try to understand them, to relate them and appro-priately to systematize them through the reason. Reason and intuition always have to be used together. Intuition by itself can be misleading. All sorts of weird fantasies can come up in flashes of intuition and these have to be corrected by reason. It is a matter of the right and the left brain, the right being the intuitive and the left the rational, and for a balanced understanding the two sides have to work in co-operation rather than one to the exclusion of the other. Even in the physical sciences intuition is recognized to be essential and it is well known that some of the greatest discoveries, for instance some of those by Newton and Einstein, have been made by pure intuition. It was by intuition that they caught glimpses of aspects of the inner structure of reality and then with the rational mind they were able to express this mathematically to show how it actually worked. So intuition has always been present but its use is limited in both science and ordinary philosophy. When it comes to the realm of the psychic, however, intuition is fundamental but, and this needs to be repeated, whatever is experienced in this realm always has to be studied in the light of reason. The attempt to understand with the reason is part of the process of gaining knowledge and it can never be dispensed with.

We have, then, the world of psychic experience, but beyond the psychic world there is a deeper dimension, the world of the transcendent. This we find in the great revelations. There what is revealed is not merely the physical or the psychological or psychic world but rather there takes place and intuitive insight into the ultimate, the transcendent. All the great revelations are, as it were, messages from that transcendent world. They are given in the scriptures of the various great traditions, the Vedas and Upanishads, the Quran, the Buddhist scriptures, and the Bible. These are all revelations of transcendent reality. Then again the process is that the revelations are interpreted by the rational mind and so there are the great theologians and philosophers, for example Sankara and Ramanuja for Hinduism, Nagarjuna, Asanga and Vasubandhu for Buddhism, Ibn al Arabi and Al-Ghazzali for Islam, and St Thomas Aquinas, St Bonaventure and others for Christianity. These great thinkers bring the rational mind to bear on the transcendent mysteries which are realities of experience. It is important to realize this because so often the impression is given that these revelations are, as it were, dropped from heaven, and people tend to accept them uncritically and therefore to misunderstand them. The reality is that all religious truth comes from an original experience, that of the seer, the prophet, the saint. But the experience always has to be interpreted in the light of rational, conceptual thought.

In this way then we go beyond the physical, beyond the psychological, and beyond the subtle world of psychic experience to the infinite transcendent reality beyond. As long as we are in the psychic world it is a world of multiplicity. There are many gods, many angels, many spirits, many powers of various sorts and this is why the psychic world is always somewhat ambiguous. One can somehow come under the power of these different spirits and gods, and as long as they are diversified they can be dangerous, because they, like other entities, are only properly themselves when they are part of this integrated whole of which we have been speaking. Idolatry and superstition arise when some psychic or cosmic power is isolated and worshipped in such a way that one comes under that power. All the evils of religion come from that, when some aspect of the whole world, particularly the psychic world, is isolated and worshipped as if it were the ultimate. That is what we know as the worship of false gods.

On the other hand, just as the physical universe is an integrated whole and the whole psychological universe is an integrated whole, so the subtle world is an integrated whole. In the great religions it is always seen that all these powers, these gods and angels, are under the control of one supreme power. This leads to the sense of the cosmic Lord, the cosmic Person, who rules over all. In each religion, as we have seen, the point is reached when the cosmic Lord is acknowledged. But now the next stage is to go beyond that and to realize that in and through the cosmic Person the whole of this universe, physical and psychological, is being reintegrated into its source. When we come to the Supreme, everything returns to unity. Everything comes out of that original unity, exploding into a universe and evolving through all these forms that we see. That outward movement is called *pravritti*, the whole universe coming out from the Supreme, manifesting in all these worlds and in all these forms. But at the same time there is another opposite movement, the movement of return or *nivritti*. These two movements act together, sending forth the universe and drawing it back to its source. And so everything in the universe is all being drawn back to its source, back into its original unity. Or, using a different image, just as everything came forth from an implicated whole into explication, so now it goes back from explication to the implicate and everything is fulfilled in that One. The whole universe is implicated in this unity and exists eternally in a state of absolute oneness in this being. The whole universe, and everything and everybody in it, exists eternally in that one infinite being without any differences, in a total oneness.

In Christian understanding this absolute ground of being from which the whole universe comes is known as the Father, the One, the Source, the Godhead. These terms and others are used to signify the Absolute from which everything originates. The understanding is that from this ground, from this source, there springs a Word, a wisdom, an image of the Godhead, and that is this cosmic Person, who reveals the Father, the Source. In that cosmic Person, in the Word or Son, all the archetypes of all created beings are contained. The archetype of every being in the universe is contained eternally in the Word, in the Godhead; it is, as it were, implicated or enfolded there. These exist eternally in him and are implicated in his being, and of all these archetypes, which are in an integrated order, the supreme is the archetypal man, whom we have seen in Hinduism, in Buddhism, in Islam and in Christianity. The archetypal man contains within himself the whole universe and all humanity. He is the cosmic Person, who is recognised as the Lord of creation, the *tathagatha* of Buddhism, the supreme *dharmakaya* of the Buddha, the *purushottaman* or the *paramatman* in Hinduism and the "universal Man" in Islam. According to the Christian understanding he is that archetypal Son of Man, the supreme Person, who took flesh and was manifested in Jesus Christ. The understanding is then that from the original ground springs this eternal Word, this Wisdom, this image of the Godhead, containing the archetypes of all creation in himself and uniting the whole creation in one.

In Christianity we also speak of the Spirit, understanding that from the original ground there springs the Spirit which is uncreated energy. As the Word or Son is the source of all form in nature, so the Spirit is the source of all energy. It is the uncreated energy which flows forth eternally from the Godhead and which then brings into being the energies of matter and nature. So nature and matter arise as created energies springing from the uncreated energy of the Spirit.

463

The universe can be seen as coming into being as an overflow of this energy, which is love. The love-energy of God is precisely what the Spirit is, and that love-energy flows out to express itself in the universe. God calls into being all the creatures of the universe to express himself, to manifest himself, to manifest his love and to bring forth that love in them. And so the Spirit flows out in this love to cause the whole creation and the Word organises all those energies of matter and the creation, gradually building up the universe as we know it and bringing it back to its source in the cosmic Person.

In the Christian understanding there are contrary forces both in the cosmos and in the human psyche which cause disorder in nature and disease in man. The question is often asked as to how there can be all this evil in the world if everything flows from the love of God and is organized by the wisdom of God. The answer is that there are forces of evil, cosmic forces and psychic forces, which are due to freedom. The Christian view is that God creates a world of free beings, because freedom is the greatest blessing one can have. Freedom is a condition of love and the world was created by love and for love. Without freedom there can be no love.

So the world is created with free beings, both angelic and human, but freedom means capacity also to fail, to fall away from love, to center on the self and to cause disintegration. One way of talking about this is to speak of the fall of the angels resulting in negative, hostile cosmic powers which work against the order of the universe. These are the powers of darkness. In contrast to these are the powers of light, the angelic powers, which are responsible for organizing the matter of the universe. As a result of these cosmic and psychological forces human beings fall away from the life of the Spirit and center on themselves, forming cells of disintegration like a cancer in the body, in this body of mankind. It must never be forgotten that mankind is one. The archetypal man contains in himself all humankind and all the universe. We fall from this order of the one-ness of man into a state of disintegration. Through sin we fall away from the Spirit, from the Word, from the Truth, and we fall into ourselves, into separation, becoming isolated individuals in conflict with one another. That is like a cancer in the body; it is the disease of mankind. It is into this fallen world that we are all born. On the other hand, as the human race falls into disunity and disintegration the redemptive power of the Spirit is also at work. The one goes with the other. At the moment of fall the redemptive process already begins, to restore this unity. So the Spirit is also at work from the beginning. In every human being there is a presence of the Spirit which is drawing us back from our disintegration, from our self-centeredness, into the life of the Spirit, the life of God. And the Spirit is gradually rebuilding human nature in the likeness of the archetypal man, the Supreme Person. We are all part of this process in which, even while we fall away from the truth, from the perfect man, into our disintegrated state, we are all being drawn back by the Spirit, by love, to the likeness of the perfect man, the likeness of Christ.

This process works throughout history. The Spirit is at work in all humankind, in all the different tribal peoples of the world and all the great religions of the world. It is part of the whole cosmic process that certain centers are formed, as for instance when a new species comes into being and there is a new center of organization. In this way Israel was chosen as a new center of organization in and around which the cosmic process of redemption should be consummated.

Through the history of Israel this cell is formed, as it were, in which the organizing power of the universe, the archetypal man, can manifest himself and overcome the powers of sin and death. In our understanding, Jesus is this archetypal man, the eternal man, manifesting in time and undergoing suffering and death so as to free the world from these powers of evil, sin, disintegration, disease and death, thereby releasing redemptive power, this power of the Spirit. So through the resurrection this power of death, of disintegration, in matter is overcome and matter is renewed. The matter of the body of Jesus is totally renewed and becomes spiritual matter, a universal spiritual body. Through that resurrection, which can also be seen as a new creation, the redemptive power of the Spirit is released in the world. The Holy Spirit coming on the church is the descent of that power of redemption at work now in the whole world. This does not mean, of course, that the Spirit is confined to the church. The redemptive presence of the Spirit is everywhere and the redeeming power is present everywhere, but it is focussed, as it were, at this point, coming to a head in Jesus and in the community he establishes. He, in and with his community, is the center for the regeneration of humankind. In this process the Holy Spirit is released as the energizing power overcoming the contrary forces in nature, rebuilding human beings into the likeness of Christ, the archetypal person, and uniting all beings in the love of the Father from which everything comes. In love the whole universe is pouring out and that love is drawing it all back to itself.

So, then, the universe and humanity return to the divine unity and each element and each person discovers its original archetype. We all have our archetype in God, our ideal form. As we grow out of sin, evil, limitation and all the infirmities of this world, we return to that archetypal form and we are reintegrated into the one. We are held together then in Christ, in the supreme Person, and we become persons in the Person. It is important to emphasize what Teilhard de Chardin says so frequently, that it is not a matter of simply dissolving into the one. It is very common in Hinduism to think that all individuality disappears and all differences in the creation disappear and dissolve into the oneness of the Absolute. This is a mistake, for in reality nothing is lost in the process. Every person and every thing is reintegrated into the One in a total unity transcending our present understanding. This is not, of course, something in time and space. It is an eternal and infinite reality and all of us even now are interwoven and interpenetrating in that one reality.

In this way the whole creation is restored and renewed. In the Christian tradition this restoration is understood as the new creation in Christ and the new humanity in Christ. We saw that in Buddhism and in Islam, and in many Hindu doctrines also, there is a clear understanding that it is never simply a fusing into one. There is always a reintegration of the whole into the one. That is the final goal. How the many are in the one and the one in the many can never be explained or fully expressed, but we can get a glimpse of how it is possible.

Thus in meditation we seek to go beyond our personal consciousness into the sphere of the transcendent consciousness. Normally, though not always, that means going through the psychic world and problems can arise because of the presence of evil forces as well as good. On account of this one needs a guide, and a Christian needs the guidance of Christ, to take him through that psychic world. It is important not to stop in the psychic world but to pass on through it. It is good to remember that in that psychic world there are not only evil spirits and demons of all kinds, but there are also all the saints and angels. As we go beyond our limited human consciousness we become aware of the whole world of the saints and angels and other holy beings. Today we are generally much less aware of this than people were in the past. In the eucharist we say, "Now with all the angels and archangels and with all the company of heaven we praise and magnify your holy name." This is a conscious relating for ourselves to the whole world of the saints and angels, which is always present although hidden from our normal mental consciousness. We need always to try to keep in mind that not only is the physical world around us, and the ordinary psychological world of our human experience, but also the psychic world of the saints and angels and the cosmic powers. This subtle world is more real than either the physical or the psychological world and enfolds both in itself. When the New Testament speaks of casting out demons or evil spirits it is speaking of realities.

In meditation then we go into that mahat, the cosmic order or cosmic consciousness, and then we go beyond that to where everything is gathered into the unity of the one Person, the cosmic Lord. Then in and through the cosmic Lord everything returns to the transcendent unity beyond conception. The ultimate is beyond conception altogether. It is totally ineffable. That is why we constantly have to remember that all the words we use to speak of this are only pointers to that which is totally beyond. The Absolute itself is beyond all human comprehension and we use words, images and concepts taken from everyday finite experience in order to direct our mind, our will and our heart towards the Infinite and to allow that Infinite to enter into our lives and transform them.

Notes

Introduction

1. See Shirley DuBoulay, *Beyond the Darkness: A Biography of Bede Griffiths*, New York, Doubleday, 1998.
2. *The Golden String*, 9-10, see text n.1.
3. *Ibid*, 102-132, see texts n. 9, 18.
4. *Kurisumala*: lit. 'hill of the cross.' This was already the name of the place when the two monks arrived. DuB 122-3.
5. *Beyond the Darkness*, ch. 17, "Friendship," 217-226.
6. See the Bibliography by Jesu Rajan and Judson Trapnell in *The Other Half of My Soul*, ed. Beatrice Bruteau, 381-391.
7. *A Human Search: Bede Griffiths Reflects on His Life*, An Oral History Edited by John Swindells, 127.
8. See the Bibliography in note 6 above.
9. See Bede Griffiths, *Pathways to the Supreme*, 1-19.
10 See, for example, *The Golden String*, 170.
11. See, for example, text n. 86, p384-385.
12.See, e.g., texts 43, 44.
13. *hylomorphism*: the Aristotolian and Thomistic view of the universe as composed of the two principles of 'form' and 'matter.'
14. See *Beyond the Darkness*, ch. 18, 227-235.
15. See *A Human Search*, 100-101.
16. *River of Compassion*, 111.
17. See texts 64 and 65, and Wayne Teasdale, *Toward a Christian Vedanata*, 63-64.
18. The positive sense in which Bede himself understood myth is abundantly evident in *The Marriage of East nad West*. See especially 170-171 (text n. 5).
19. See text n. 7.
20. *The Golden String*, 11.
21. *The Golden String*, 33.
22. *The Golden String*, 14; see text n. 21, 'The Myth of the Church.'
23. See *The Golden String*, 171-174.
24. *The Marriage of East and West*, 172.
25. *The Marriage of East and West*, 174-175.
26. See, e.g., *The Marriage of East and West*, 8.
27. Bede Griffiths, *Return to the Center*, 129-130.
28. See Bruno Barnhart, *Second Simplicity*, New York, Paulist, 1999, 4, 229-232.
29. See Judson B. Trapnell, "Two Models of Christian Dialogue with Hinduism: Bede Griffiths and Abhishiktananda," *Vidyajyoti*, 60 (1996), (I) 101-110, (II) 183-191, (III) 243-254.
30. Ephesians 4:9.
31. See note 29 above: Trapnell, Part III, p. 246, note 65.

I Mind, World and Spirit

1. For the sapiential, or wisdom tradition of western Christianity see Jean Leclerq O.S.B., *The Love of Learning and the Desire for God*, New York, Fordham University Press, 1961. On wisdom traditions more generally, see Seyed Hossein Nasr, *Knowledge and the Sacred*, New York, Crossroad, 1981.
2. *The Golden String*, 9-13.
3. *The Marriage of East and West*, 151-159.
4. *Return to the Center*, 75.
5. *Epistemology* is the philosophical inquiry into the nature and origins of knowledge.
6. *The Marriage of East and West*, 46-47.
7. See Genesis 1:26-27, 2:18-25; John 2:1-11; Ephesians 5:25-32.
8. *Tao Te Ching* 6, 10 and 16. From *The Wisdom of China* by Lin Yutang (Michael Joseph, London).
9. D.H. Lawrence, *Apocalypse*.
10. *The Marriage of East and West*, 159-162.
11. Genesis 4:1.
12. The most profound study of sexual love that I know is that of Mary and Robert Joyce in *New Dynamics in Sexual Love* (St Johns, Collegeville, USA, 1970).

13. *The Marriage of East and West*, 162-169.
14. In *Creative Intuition in Art and Poetry* by J. Maritain (Meridian Books, New York, 1954), especially chapter 3, 'The Pre-conscious life of the Intellect', and chapter 4, 'Creative Intuition and Poetic Knowledge', to which I owe much of my understanding of the nature of intuitive knowledge.
15. *Paradiso*, 33, translated by Barbara Reynolds (Penguin Classics).
16. Eckhart, *Sermons*, 90.
17. Katha Upanishad 2:23.
18. *The Marriage of East and West*, 169-171.
19. *The Marriage of East and West*, 51-55.
20. William of St. Thierry, *Golden Epistle*, 62, 35. Quoted by Cyprian Consiglio, *The Space in the Heart of the Lotus*, p. 79.
21. See texts 11, 12, 16, 94, 95, 102.
22. Quoted in Fritjof Capra, *The Tao of Physics*, 144.
23. Bernard D'Espagnat in *Conceptual Foundations of Quantum Mechanics*.
24. *"An appearance of being, without origin, inexpressible in terms of being or of not-being."*: Sankara's commentary on the Brahma Sutras.
25. *The Marriage of East and West*, 57-59.
26. See 1 Thessalonians 5:23 and the contrast between the *'anthropos psychikos'*, the 'psychic man', and the *'antropos pneumatikos'*, the 'spiritual man', in I Corinthians 2:14.
27. Romans 8:16

II West, Part One – Mystery and Drama of the Church

1. *A New Vision of Reality*, 276-281.
2. *The Golden String*, 38.
3. *The Golden String*, 170, 178.
4. *The Marriage of East and West*, 151.
5. Fritjof Capra, *The Turning Point: Science, Society and the Rising Culture*. New York: Simon and Schuster, 1982.
6. *The Golden String*, 83-87.
7. *The Golden String*, 102-109.
8. *Vedanta and Christian Faith*, 54-57.
9. See Wayne Teasdale, *Toward a Christian Vedanta*, 134-146.
10. From a talk at Melbourne, Australia, May 17, 1992, quoted in *Beyond the Darkness*, 253.
11. *A Human Search*, 115f.
12. John 10:30
13. John 14:10
14. John 14:9
15. John 1:12
16. Colossians 1:16
17. John 1:14
18. *A New Vision of Reality*, 119-127.
19. John 8:58
20. John 3:13
21 Philippians 2:6
22. 1 Corinthians 15:47
23. Romans 5:14
24. Ephesians 4:22, 24
25. Ephesians 2:14, 15
26. Colossians 1:15
27. Colossians 1:16
28. Colossians 1:17
29. Colossians 2:9
30. Matthew 11:27; Luke 10:22
31. Hebrews 1:2
32. Hebrews 5:7-8
33. Hebrews 1:3
34. John 1:3
35. Ephesians 1:10
36. *A New Vision of Reality*, 165-171.
37. Ephesians 1:10
38. John 14:11

39. John 17:21
40. *A New Vision of Reality*, 218-226.
41. Matthew 11:27; cf. Luke 10:12
42. John 17:21
43. John 10:30
44. John 15:1-4
45. 1 John 1:3
46. Acts 2:45
47. 1 John 4:20
48. 1 Corinthians 2:10-11
49. Galatians 4:6
50. Romans 8:15-16
51. Colossians 3:3
52. Bhagavad Gita 18:65
53. 1 Corinthians 6:19; 6:13
54. *Return to the Center*, 129-135.
55. See Proverbs ch. 8-9; Sirach ch. 24; The Wisdom of Solomon, ch. 7-9, *The Golden String* 81-82, and text n. 15.
56. Wisdom 7:27
57. Genesis 1:2
58. Genesis 2:7
59. Katha Upanishad, 2.18-22
60. Isa Upanishad, 5
61. Wisdom 7:24
62. See 1 Corinthians 2:14
63. Romans 8:4
64. Romans 8:4
65. Svetasvatara Upanishad, IV.6
66. 1 Corinthians 6:17
67. Sankara (8th century AD), author of the doctrine of advaita, or non-duality, taught that reality is one, absolute, undifferentiated being 'without duality' (a-dvaita), and that all differences are an appearance – maya – superimposed on this one being.
68. Ramanuja (11th century AD) was the author of the doctrine of *visishtadvaita*, 'qualified non-duality,' which maintains that God stands to the world in relation of soul to body.
69. Madhva (13th century AD), author of the doctrine of *dvaita*, or 'duality,' taught that God, the soul and the world are all really different from one another.
70. Saiva Siddhanta is the doctrine of the Southern school of Saivism (13th century AD), which claims to be the perfection of all schools of Vedanta.
71. See Eckhart: "If we say that all things are in God, we understand by this that, just as he is without distinction in his nature, yet absolutely distinct from all things, so all things are in him in the greatest distinction and yet not distinct, and first of all because man in God is God..." (Latin Sermon IV.1). See also Ruysbroeck, *The Adornment of the Spiritual Marriage*, Bk III, ch. 3: "In eternity all creatures are God in God."
72. *Summa Theologica*, I, Q. 15 ad 3.
73. 2 Peter 1:4
74. 1 Corinthians 15:51-53
75. See Patanjali, *Yoga-sutras*, bk. III.
76. *The Tablet*, June 9, 1979 (Bede's Title).
77. See *The Golden String*, 81-82.
78. 1 Corinthians 11:7-9
79. Isaiah 49:15
80. Matthew 23:37
81. Proverbs 8:22-23, 30
82. Sirach 24:1-3
83. Wisdom 7:24-26
84. *Return to the Center*, 113-118.
85. See Matthew 11:27; Luke 10:22.
86. John 17:5, 24
87. John 14:10
88. See John 15:26
89. See John 17, 11

90. See Hebrews 4:15
91. See John 14:9
92. See 1 Corinthians 11:23-26.
93. Matthew 5:8
94. *A New Vision of Reality*, 104-112.
95. See text n. 16.
96. See Ephesians 3:14-21.
97. See text n. 102.
98. Acts 22:3.
99. Galatians 6:15
100. Galatians 3:28
101. 2 Corinthians 5:17
102. 1 Corinthians 13:12
103. 1 Corinthians 15:45
104. Ephesians 2:22
105. Ephesians 1:19-20
106. Ephesians 1:20-21
107. Ephesians 2:2
108. Ephesians 1:22-23
109. Colossians 2:9
110. See Colossians 1:16-18.
111. John 1:9
112. Colossians 1:16-17
113. Ephesians 4:13

III West, Part Two – Mystery and Drama of the Church

1. *The Golden String*, 119-128.
2. See texts 8 and 9 in Part I.
3. *The Golden String*, 119.
4. *The Golden String*, 131-133.
5. *The Golden String*, 184-187.
6. *The Marriage of East and West*, 192-204.
7. *The Shepherd of Hermas*, 2:24.
8. Ephesians 1:22-23
9. 1 Corinthians 15:45
10. John 1:14
11. Mark 1:15
12. Colossians 3:3
13. 1 Corinthians 13:12
14. Galatians 6:15
15. *The Golden String*, 176-179.
16. "The Seekers," *The Tablet*, April 28, 1984.
17. Letter in *The Tablet*, July 27, 1985.
18. English translation: *The Ratzinger Report: An Exclusive Interview on the State of the Church*, San Francisco, Ignatius Press, 1985.
19. *New Blackfriars*, Special Issue, June 1985.
20. "The Claims of the Papacy," letter in *The Tablet*, December 12, 1987.
21. *The Tablet*, November 21, 1987.
22. *The Tablet,* October 31, 1987.
23. *The Tablet*, August 11, 1990.
24. Matthew 23:8-10
25. "The Church of the Future," *Christ in India*, 243-249.
26. *Summa Theologica* II-II, Q. 1 art. 7.
27. "The Church of the Future," The Tablet, April 10/17, 1982.
28. *A New Vision of Reality*, 287-294.

IV East, Part One – The Wisdom of India

1. *The Marriage of East and West*, 7-15.
2. *The Golden String* was published by the Harvill Press in 1954.
3. Dr Panikkar has published *The Vedic Experience*, a translation of the principal texts of the Vedas with notes and commentary, showing the relevance of the Vedas for modern man. It was published by

Darton, Longman and Todd in 1978.

4. *Beyond the Darkness*, 39-40.
5. *Beyond the Darnkess*, 101-102.
6. See text n. 30 above, p. 183
7. *The Cosmic Revelation*, 10, see text n. 31-II below.
8. *The Cosmic Revelation*, 17-19.
9. *The Cosmic Revelation*, 7-11.
10. *The Cosmic Revelation*, 17-19.
11. *The Marriage of East and West*, 59-61.
12. *Return to the Center*, 120-128.
13. See text n. 41.
14. Thomas Aquinas' breakthrough into a transconceptual sense of Being, Meister Eckhart's apophatic mysticism and the mystical theology of St. John of the Cross and his followers are notable exceptions in the West.
15. Brihadaranyaka Upanishad, 2.3.6.
16. Mandukya Upanishad, 7.
17. See Brihadaranyaka Upanishad, 1.4.10.
18. See Chandogya Upanishad, 6.8.7.
19. See Cahndogya Upanishad, 3.14.1.
20. See Brihadaranyaka Upanishad, 3.9.28.
21. Bhagavad Gita, 5.24.
22. See Bhagavad Gita, 6.29.
23. Bhagavad Gita, 6.30.
24. Bhagavad Gita, 18. 61-62.
25. Chandogya Upanishad, 3.14.1.
26. Rig-Veda, 10.90.
27. Katha Upanishad, 5.9.
28. Katha Upanishad, 5.10.
29. Katha Upanishad, 5.11.
30. Katha Upanishad, 5.12.
31. Svetasvatara Upanishad, 4. 6.
32. See Ruysbroeck, *The Adornment of the Spiritual Marriage*, bk. II, ch. 64.
33. See Eckhart: 'If we say that all things are in God, we understand by this that, just as he is without distinction in his nature yet absolutely distinct from all things, so all things are in him in the greatest distinction and yet not distinct, and first of all because man is God in God...' (Latin Sermon IV.I.). See also Ruysbroeck, *The Adornment of the Spiritual Marriage*, bk. III, ch. 3: 'In eternity all creatures are God in God.'
34. *Christ in India*, 171-172.
35. See Judson B. Trapnell, "Two Models of Christian Dialogue with Hinduism: Bede Griffiths and Abhishiktananda," *Vidyajyoti*, 60 (1996), (I) 101-110, (II) 183-191, (III) 243-254.
36. See texts 61, 62, 63. 64.
37. *River of Compassion*, 110.
38. "Eastern Religious Experience," *Monastic Studies* 9 (1972), 153-154.
39. "Eastern Religious Experience," *Monastic Studies* 9 (1972), 159-160.
40. "The Mystical Tradition in Indian Theology," *Monastic Studies* 13 (1982), 162-165.
41. Brihadaranyaka Upanishad 4.3.7 and 3.8.11.
42. Mandukya Upanishad 7.
43. Katha Upanishad 2.12.
44. Katha Upanishad 2.23.
45. Katha Upanishad 3.1.
46. Svetasvatara Upanishad 4.16 and 4.17.
47. Svetasvatara Upanishad 4.10.
48. See. Brihadaranyaka Upanishad 2.4.13.
49. Katha Upanishad 2.24.
50. *River of Compassion*, 123-124
51. See Part V, n. 67, 68, 69, 70.
52. The Marriage of East and West, 89-94.
53. See n. 31, 32, 33, 34, 36, 37, 38, 40, 41, 54, 61, 62, 63, 64, 65.
54. See *Ascent to the Depth of the Heart: The Spiritual Diary of Swami Abhishiktananda* selected and introduced by Raimon Panikkar, translated by David Fleming and James Stuart, Delhi, ISPCK, 1998, and the Trapnell articles in note 35 above.
55. Brihadaranyaka Upanishad 3.7.23.

56. Brihadaranyaka Upanishad 2.4.13.
57. Commentary on the Taittiriya Upanishad 2.1.
58. *Unus Christus amans seipsum.*
59. This theory has been developed at Length by Karl Rahner. See especially *Foundations of Christian Faith*, 1, 3, 'Man as Transcendent Being' (Darton, Longman and Todd, 1978).
60. Katha Upanishad 2.23.
61. cf. also Taittiriya Upanishad 3:2-6 on the five 'sheaths' (*kosas*) of consciousness.
62. *A Human Search*, 90-94.
63. See *Beyond the Darkness*, 227-236.
64. "diversity in unity," as Bede often described it.
65. *Return to the Center*, 119-120.
66. Udana, 80-1, from the Pali Canon of Hinayana Buddhism.
67. *Universal Wisdom*, 23-25.
68. Lankavatara Sutra.
69. *River of Compassion* 117, commenting Gita 6.19.
70. *River of Compassion* 125, commenting Gita 6:30.
71. *The Marriage of East and West*, 78-87.
72. See 'Bede's Synthesis,' text n. 102, p. 463-466.
73. Brihadaranyaka Upanishad 4.4.15.
74. Isa Upanishad 1.
75. Svetasvatara Upanishad 1.7-9.
76. Non-duality, qualified non-duality, and duality.
77. Svetasvatara Upanishad 3.7.
78. Svetasvatara Upanishad 3.9.11.
79. See *The Love of God in Saiva Siddhanta* by M. Dhavamony, Oxford University Press, 1971, Part 3.1b.
80. Svetasvatara Upanishad 3.19.
81. Svetasvatara Upanishad 3.12.
82. Svetasvatara Upanishad 3.13.
83. Svetasvatara Upanishad 6.7.
84. Svetasvatara Upanishad 5.11-12.
85. *Summa Theologica* I.8.3.
86. Acts of the Apostles 17:28
87. *Summa Theologica* I.1.1 ad 3.
88. Bhagavad Gita 9.4-5.
89. Bhagavad Gita 5.20.
90. Bhagavad Gita 5.21.
91. Bhagavad Gita 5.29. cf. also 6.29. 'He sees the Self abiding in all beings and all beings in the Self', followed by 6.30: 'He sees me in all things and all things in me.'
92. Bhagavad Gita 15.16-17.
93. *River of Compassion*, 271-273.
94. *River of Compassion*, 152-153.
95. *A New Vision of Reality*, 67-77.
96. *A New Vision of Reality*, ch. 12, 'Synthesis: Towards a Unifying Plan,' text n. 102.
97. Brihadaranyaka Upanishad 2.1.20.
98. Brihadaranyaka Upanishad 2.4.1-5.
99. Chandogya Upanishad 8.1
100. Katha Upanishad 3.10-11.
101. Svetasvatara Upanishad 1.7.
102. Svetasvatara Upanishad 4.14.
103. Bhagavad Gita 9.4.
104. Bhagavad Gita 9.5.
105. Bhagavad Gita 10.19-20.
106. Bhagavad Gita 11.9, 13.
107. Bhagavad Gita 11.4-5.

V East, Part Two – The Way (Life and Spiritual Practice)

1. *Return to the Center*, 9-12.
2. See John 3:8.
3. Matthew 10:9-10; 8:20.
4. *The Marriage of East and West*, 42-44.
5. Acts I:3

6. John 16:7
7. John 12:24
8. *River of Compassion*, 105-107.
9. *River of Compassion*, 303.
10. See texts 68 and 69.
11. *River of Compassion*, 272
12. Mark 2:27
13. "The Monastic Order and the Ashram," *American Benedictine Review*, vol. 30 n.2, June 1979, 137-140.
14. See, in the West, the *Rule of Benedict*.
15. See Sister Vandana, *Gurus, Ashrams and Christians*, London, Darton, Longman and Todd, 1978.
16. J. Monchanin, S.A.N. and Dom Henri Le Saux, O.S.B., *A Benedictine Ashram* (Athol Street, Douglas, Isle of Man: Times Press, 1964). Originally published as *An Indian Benedictine Ashram* (Tiruchirapalli, 1951).
17. See *In Quest of the Absolute: the Life and Work of Jules Monchanin*, edited and translated by S.G. Weber, Kalamazoo, Cistercian Publications, 1977.
18. Henri Le Saux, *Prayer*, Philadelphia, Westminster, 1973.
19. *The New Creation in Christ*, 47-48.
20. *The New Creation in Christ*, 49-51.
21. *The New Creation in Christ*, 63-65.
22. Romans 8:16
23. *The New Creation in Christ*, 68-69.
24. *A New Vision of Reality*, 274-275.
25. See text n. 24.
26. Congregation for the Doctrine of the Faith, *Letter to the Bishops of the Catholic Church on Some Aspects of Christian Meditation*, October 15, 1989, released Dec 14, 1989. The English text of the letter was published in *Origins*, vol. 19 no. 30, December 28, 1989, pp. 492-498.
27. The *National Catholic Reporter*, May 11, 1990. See *Beyond the Darkness*, p. 233f.
28. "In Jesus' Name," *The Tablet*, April 18/25, 1992.
29. *Return to the Center*, 136-143.
30. See esp. *The Life Divine* (2nd ed., Arya Publishing House, Calcutta, 1944, and Sri Aurobindo Library, New York, 1951) and *The Synthesis of Yoga* (Sri Aurobindo Library, Madras, 1948).
31. Romans 8:23
32. Romans 8:21
33. See Bhagavad Gita, esp. bks. 2-6.
34. See Brihadaranyaka Upanishad, 4.4.15.
35. John 14:23
36. See Katha Upanishad, 2.23; and Mundaka Upanishad, 3.2.3.
37. John 12:24
38. Matthew 16:25
39. Svetasvatara Upanishad, 6:14.
40. See Mundaka Upanishad, 1.1.3.
41. *River of Compassion*, 121.
42. The Bhagavad Gita, translated by Annie Besant and Bhagavan.Das.
43. The Bhagavad Gita, translated by R.C. Zaehner.
44. *River of Compassion*, 130-131.
45. *River of Compassion*, 170.
46. *River of Compassion*, 224.
47. *Return to the Center*, 16-17.
48. See Katha Upanishad, 4.1.
49. John 8:32
50. *The Marriage of East and West*, 64-78.
51. A familiar example in modern western spirituality is St. Teresa of Avila's description of the seven successive 'mansions' of the soul in *The Interior Castle*.
52. Chandogya Upanishad 8.7-12.
53. See Rig Veda 1.164.46: "The one being (ekam sat) the wise call by many names."
54. Katha Upanishad 2.23.
55. Romans 6:3
56. Katha Upanishad 2.9.
57. Katha Upanishad 2.12.
58. Rig Veda 10.90.
59. Chandogya Upanishad 8.3.

60. Katha Upanishad 3.10-11.
61. Brihadaranyaka Upanishad 4.3.7.
62. Katha Upanishad 3.13.
63. Brihadaranyaka Upanishad 3.8.11.
64. Katha Upanishad 2.23.
65. Katha Upanishad 3.1.
66. Svetasvatara Upanishad 4.6-7.
67. 1 Corinthians 2:12
68. 1 Corinthians 2:14-15.
69. Svetasvatara Upanishad 2.14-15.
70. *A New Vision of Reality*, 176-182.
71. Isa Upanishad 6.
72. Katha Upanishad 3.10.11.
73. Katha Upanishad 3.10.13.
74. Katha Upanishad 3.10.13.
75. Katha Upanishad 6.10.
76. Mandukya Upanishad 7.
77. *A New Vision of Reality*, 201-203.
78. Kena Upanishad 29-30.
79. See Part I, texts 2, 3,4, 5.
80. *River of Compassion*, 237.
81. *River of Compassion*, 245.
82. *River of Compassion*, 318.
83. Ephesians 3:19
84. John 14:23
85. John 15:5
86. *River of Compassion*, 74.
87. Besant and Das translation.
88. *River of Compassion*, 101-103.
89. See texts 50, 51, 60.
90. *River of Compassion*, 271-273. This passage has already appeared as part of text n. 45,p. 236-237
91. *River of Compassion*, 301-302.
92. *River of Compassion*, 86-88.
93. *River of Compassion*, 89-90.
94. See also texts 67, 68, 69, 70.
95. See texts 48 and 49.
96. See texts 34, 36, 37, 62, 63.
97. *River of Compassion*, 225.
98. *River of Compassion*, 229.
99. *River of Compassion*, 289-291.
100. "The Ideal of Non-violence," *Christ in India*, pp. 134-142.
101. *The Golden String*, 23.
102. *The Golden String*, 30.
103. *The Golden String*, 31.
104. See *Christ in India*, ch. 10, "Walking with Vinoba," pp. 126-133.
105. *Beyond the Darkness*, 210.

VI *Christianity and the Eastern Religions*

1. See Introduction, pp. 17-18.
2. "The Incarnation and the East," *Christ in India*, 69-76.
3. *Christ in India*, 81-82.
4. *Christ in India*, 110-111.
5. *Christ in India*, 172-174.
6. *Christ in India*, 172. See text 34, p. 204
7. *Christ in India*, 186-188.
8. *The Cosmic Revelation*, 128-131.
9. *A New Vision of Reality*, 251-254.
10. Colossians 2:9
11. Matthew 10:39
12. The 1989 Hibbert Lecture, AIM Monastic Bulletin no. 49 (1991), English edition, 51-58.
13. "Monastic Life in India Today," *Monastic Studies* n. 4 (1966) 117-119.

14. See G. Ghurye, *Indian Sadhus*, Bombay 1953, for a history of asceticism in India.
15. "The Future of Christian Monasticism in India," *Kurisumala: A Symposium on Ashram Life*, edited by M.F. Acharya, Bangalore, Asian Trading Corporation, 1974, pp. 110-113.
16. See *The Golden String*, 165.
17. *River of Compassion*, 182.
18. *River of Compassion*, 221.
19. *River of Compassion*, 230.
20. *River of Compassion*, 226-227.
21. *River of Compassion*, 317.
22. *River of Compassion*, 319.
23. *Return to the Center*, 86-87.
24. "A Meditation on the Mystery of the Trinity," *Monastic Studies* n. 17 (1986), 69-79.
25. This is Ewert Cousins' summary of Panikkar's understanding of the Trinity, as cited by Francis X. D'Sa, S.J., "The Notion of God" in *The Intercultural Challenge of Raimon Panikkar*, Joseph Prabhu ed., Maryknoll, Orbis, 1996, p. 41. See Ewert Cousins, "Raimondo Panikkar and the Christian Systematic Theology of the Future," *Cross Currents* 29 (Summer 1979), 141-155, esp. p. 147.
26. See text n. 14.
27. Raimondo Panikkar, *The Trinity and the Religious Experience of Man*, New York, Orbis Books, 1973, p. 42.
28. Ephesians 1:4
29. John Tauler, "Second Sermon on the Nativity of John the Baptist" (Sermon 44).
30. The doctrine of non-duality which originated with Sankara in the seventh century A.D. See text n. 39.
31. Acts 17:28
32. *Tathagata* is the name for the Buddha in his *Dharmakaya*. It comes from the Mahayana text of the longer *Prajnaparamita hridaya Sutra* or the *Sutra of the Perfect Wisdom of the Heart*. In this sutra we read: "*Gate, gate, paragate, parasamgate, bodhi, svaha,*" which means "Gone, gone, gone beyond, gone altogether beyond. O what an awakening. All hail!"
33. Chandoga Upanishad, VI:8.7; 9.4; 10.3.
34. See the longer citation on p. 378, and note 27 above for the source.
35. *River of Compassion*, 118.
36. *Christ in India*, 79-82.
37. Bede goes on to show how Aquinas brought the precision of Aristotelian thought to this Platonic tradition, offering a distinction which is lacking in the Indian conceptions. See *Christ in India*, 81-82.
38. "The One Spirit in All Religion," *Return to the Center*, ch 10, 71-75.
39. Ephesians 3:9; see Romans 16:25.
40. "The Eternal Religion," *Return to the Center*, ch 15, 98-112.
41. Romans 2:15
42. William Law, *The Spirit of Prayer*, ch. 11.
43. Matthew 13:44-46.
44. Luke 10:42
45. See Jean Danielou, *Holy Pagans of the Old Testament*, London, Longmans, Green, 1957.
46. See Mircea Eliade, *Patterns in Comparative Religion*, ch. 2.
47. See Chandogya Upanishad, 8.1.3.
48. John 1:4; according to one reading.
49. Katha Upanishad, 4.1.
50. Katha Upanishad, 2.23; see Mundaka Upanishad, 3.2.3.
51. Katha Upanishad, 3.13. The 'knowing Self' is the intellect, the *buddhi*, the *Nous* of Aristotle. The 'great Self' is the *mahat*, the cosmic consciousness, the 'divine soul' of Plotinus. The 'Self of peace' is the supreme Self, the *Paramatman*, the Word of God.
52. Al-Ghazzali (d. AD 1111): see A.J. Arberry's *Sufism*, Allen & Unwin, London, 1950, and Harper and Row, New York, 1970.
53. Nagarjuna (c. AD 150): founder of the Madhyamika school of Mahayana Buddhism, with its doctrine of the Void (*sunyata*).
54. Vasubandhu (c. AD 400): founder of the Yogacara school of Mahayana Buddhism, with its doctrine of 'mind only': cf. E. Conze's *Buddhism*, Cassirer, Oxford, 1951.
55. Mark 1:15
56. Svetasvatara Upanishad, 3.20.
57. From the Lankavatara Sutra.
58. Leviticus 26:12
59. Koran, L. 16.
60. John 2:19, 21

61. See Ephesians 1:22, 2:20, 4:15-16.
62. Ephesians 3:19
63. *Universal Wisdom*, 8-10.
64. *A Human Search*, 94.
65. For information on the film, *A Human Search*, see the Bibliography, p. 479.
66. See *Beyond the Darkness*, 208.
67. *River of Compassion*, 130.
68. See text n. 59, p. 282-283.

VII Toward the New Creation

1. "Science Today and the New Creation," in *Ancient Wisdom and Modern Science*, ed. Sanislav Grof, Albany, State University of New York Press, 1984, 50-58.
2. *The Golden String*, 38.
3. *Beyond the Darkness*, 198.
4. *A New Vision of Reality*, 88-95.
5. Isaiah 62:4
6. Isaiah 65:17-18
7. Hebrews 11:14-16
8. Romans 8:22-23
9. 2 Peter 3:13
10. Revelation 21:1-2
11. John 17:21
12. *A New Vision of Reality*, 54-56.
13. *A New Vision of Reality*, 33.
14. Bede's reference is to Ken Wilber's *Up from Eden: A Transpersonal View of Human Evolution*, Boulder, CO., Shambhala, 1983.
15. *A New Vision of Reality*, 294-295.
16. *Beyond the Darkness*, 18.
17. *The Marriage of East and West*, 8. See text n. 30.
18. See text n. 21.
19. See texts n. 14, 15.
20. *A Human Search*, 88-90.
21. Interviews by Andrew Harvey, along with the Australian film crew. See *Beyond the Darkness*, 255.
22. *A Human Search*, 97-98.
23. *Beyond the Darkness*, 255.
24. *chakras*: "Energy wheels," a series of energy centers that run along the spinal column of the body, as defined in Kundalini Yoga, which is a division of Tantric Yoga.
25. *sahasrara*: The crown or coronal *chakra*. It is located on the top of the head and is related to the experience of self-realization or enlightenment.
26. *hara*: In some yogic systems, the power center or third *chakra* is referred to as the hara, and it relates to raw emotions, power drives and social identification.
27. See Bede's abridged edition of the biblical Book of Psalms: *Psalms for Christian Prayer* (see Introduction above, p. 9 and Bibliography p. 478.
28. *The New Creation in Christ*. 16-19.
29. Mark 15:34
30. Matthew 27:46
31. 1 Corinthians 16:22.
32. *The New Creation in Christ*, 20.
33. *A New Vision of Reality*, 281-287; 295-296.
34. See text n. 7.
35. See text n. 29.
36. See text n. 97.
37. See texts n. 94, 95.
38. Bede's limited tolerance for the Old Testament is evident in the exclusiveness of his selections for *Universal Wisdom* and for *Psalms for Christian Prayer*.
39. Ephesians 6:12
40. *A New Vision of Reality*, 255-275.

Select Bibliography

Books by Bede Griffiths

The Golden String: An Autobiography, Springfield, Illinois, Templegate Publishers, 1954, 1980.

Christ in India: Essays Towards a Hindu-Christian Dialogue, Templegate, 1966, 1984.

Vedanta and Christian Faith, Clearlake, California, Dawn Horse Press, 1973, 1991.

Return to the Center, Templegate, 1976.

The Marriage of East and West: A Sequel to The Golden String, Templegate, 1982.

The Cosmic Revelation: The Hindu Way to God, Templegate, 1983.

River of Compassion: A Christian Commentary on the Bhagavad Gita, Templegate, 1987, 2001.

A New Vision of Reality: Western Science, Eastern Mysticism and Christian Faith, Edited by Felicity Edwards, Templegate, 1990.

Modern Spirituality Series:: Bede Griffiths Templegate 1990

The New Creation in Christ: Christian Meditation and Community, Edited by Robert Kiely and Laurence Freeman, Templegate, 1995.

Universal Wisdom: A Journey through the Sacred Wisdom of the World, Edited by Roland Ropers, San Francisco, HarperCollins, 1994.

Pathways to the Supreme: The Personal Notebook of Bede Griffiths, Edited by Roland Ropers, London, HarperCollins, 1995.

Psalms for Christian Prayer, Edited by Roland Ropers, London, HarperCollins, 1995.

Audiotaped Lectures

Riches from the East: East-West Monastic Conference on Formation, Kansas City, Kansas, 1983, NCR Credence Cassettes, 1983. Five lectures.

Christian Meditation: The Evolving Tradition, The John Main Seminar, New Harmony, Indiana, 1991. Chevy Chase, Maryland, The John Main Institute, 1991. Five lectures, followed by discussions. Lectures and discussions have been edited and published as a book, *The New Creation in Christ*.

Interviews

On Poverty and Simplicity: Views of a Post-Industrial Christian Sage," Interview by Renee Weber, ReVision 6, no.2 (Fall 1983), 16-30, Reprinted in Renee Weber, *Dialogues with Scientists and Sages: The Search for Unity*, Arkana, 1990, 157-180.

"Interview: Father Bede Griffiths, O.S.B.," interview by Johannes Agaard and Neil Duddy, Europe, Summer 1984, *Update* 9 (1985), 22-36.

"Interview with a Spiritual Master: The Trinity," interview by Wayne Teasdale, Shantivanam, India, December 1986, *Living Prayer* 21, no.3 (May-June 1988), 24-31.

"Reincarnation: A Christian View," interview by Wayne Teasdale, Shantivanam, India, December 1986, *Living Prayer* 21, no. 5 (Sept-Oct 1988), 22-28.

"Contemplative Community and the Transformation of the World," interview by Wayne Teasdale, Shantivanam, India, December, 1986, *Living Prayer* 22, no.1 (Jan-Feb 1989), 11-15.

"Father Bede Griffiths," interview by Malcolm Tillis, January 27, 1981, Shantivanam, India, in *Turning East: New Lives in India: Twenty Westerners and their Spiritual Quests*, Edited by Malcolm Tillis and Cynthia Giles, New York, Paragon House, 1989, 119-126.

A Human Search: Bede Griffiths Reflects on His Life, An Oral History, interview by Andrew Harvey and John Swindells, Edited by John Swindells, Liguori, Missouri, Triumph Books, 1996.

Collections of Letters

Catholic Ashrams: Adopting and Adapting Hindu Dharma, ed. Sita Ram Goel, New Delhi, Voice of India Publications, 1988.

A Follower of Christ and a Disciple of Sri Aurobindo, Correspondence between Bede Griffiths and K.D. Sethna (Amil Kiran), U.S.A., Integral Life Foundation, 1996.

Video Recordings

Christ in the Lotus: An Interview with Bede Griffiths, interview by Laurence Freeman, Shantivanam, India, Produced by Mark Schofield, Christian Meditation Media, 40 min., videocassette.

The Space in the Heart of the Lotus, series of talks at Shantivanam, BBC TV.

Christian Meditation: The Evolving Tradition, The John Main Seminar, New Harmony, Indiana, 1991. Chevy Chase, Maryland, The John Main Institute, 1991.

Exploring the Christian-Hindu Dialogue: A Visit with Bede Griffiths and Russill Paul, interview by Tyra Arraj, Chiloquin, Oregon, Inner Growth Videos, 1992.

The Wisdom of a Prophet: The New Vision of Reality, talks and questions in Perth, Western Australia, May, 1992, Sydney, Australia, More Than Illusion Films, 1993, videocassette.

The History and Interpretation of the Bible, talk at Shantivanam, Sydney, Australia, More Than Illusion Films, 1993, 40 min. videocassette.

Discovering the Feminine, talk at Shantivanam, Sydney, Australian, More Than Illusion Films, 1993, 32 min. videocassette.

A Human Search: The Life of Father Bede Griffiths, documentary and interview by Andrew Harvey and John Swindells, Produced by John Swindells, Sydney, Australia, More Than Illusion Films, 1993, 59 min. videocassette.

Books About Bede Griffiths

Bruteau, Beatrice, ed., *The Other Half of My Soul: Bede Griffiths and the Hindu-Christian Dialogue*, Wheaton Illinois, Quest Books, 1996 (expanded edition of Beatrice Bruteau, ed., *As We Are One: Essays and Poems in Honor of Bede Griffiths*, Pfafftown, North Carolina, Philosophers' Exchange, 1991).

Consiglio, Cyprian, *The Space in the Heart of the Lotus: Spirit as an anthropological element based on the writings of Bede Griffiths*, unpub. Masters' thesis for M.A. in Theology, St. John's Seminary, Camarillo, California, Spring 1997.

Du Boulay, Shirley, *Beyond the Darkness: A Biography of Bede Griffiths*, New York, Doubleday, 1998.

Fernandes, Albano, "The Hindu Mystical Experience according to R.C. Zaehner and Bede Griffiths: A Philosophical Study," Ph.D. dissertation, Rome, Gregorian Pontifical University, 1993.

Kalliath, Antony, *Inward Transcendence: A Study on the Encounter of Western Consciousness with Indian Interiority Based on the Works of Fr. Bede Griffiths*, Masters dissertation, Dharmaram Pontifical Institute, 1986.

Rajan, Jesu, *Bede Griffiths and Sannyasa*, Bangalore, India, Asian Trading Corp., 1989 (Originally a doctoral dissertation submitted to the Pontifical University of St. Thomas Aquinas in Rome, 1988).

Savio, Samuel, *The Principle of Relatedness in the Ecological Ethic of Bede Griffiths*, a doctoral dissertation in theology, School of Religious Studies, Catholic University of America, Washington D.C., May 2000.

Spink, Kathryn, *A Sense of the Sacred: A Biography of Bede Griffiths*, Maryknoll, New York, Orbis Books, 1989.

Teasdale, Wayne Robert, *Toward a Christian Vedanta: The Encounter of Hinduism and Christianity According to Bede Griffiths*, Bangalore, India, Asian Trading Corp., 1987 (Originally a doctoral dissertation submitted to Fordham University, Bronx, New York, 1986).

Trapnell, Judson B., *Bede Griffiths' Theory of Religious Symbol and Practice of Dialogue: Towards Interreligious Understanding*, Ph.D. dissertation, The Catholic University of America, 1992.

Trapnell, Judson B., *Bede Griffiths: A Life in Dialogue*, Albany, State University of New York Press, 2001.

Swami Bede Dayananda: Testimonies and Tributes, India, Shantivanam Publications, 1994.

Articles About Bede Griffiths

Fastiggi, Robert, and Pereira, Jose, "The Swami from Oxford," *Crisis*, March 1991, 22-25

Freeman, Laurence, Sheldrake, Rupert, and Ropers, Roland, "Obituary." *The Tablet* 247, no. 7971 (22 May 1993), 667-668.

Hoblitzelle, Harrison, "India's Christian Guru: A Visit with Father Bede Griffiths," *New Age* 9 (1983), 37-43.

Panikkar, Raimon, "The Wider Ecumenism: An Explorer Crosses the Borders," Review of *River of Compassion*, by Bede Griffiths, in *The Tablet* 246, no.7938 (26 Sept 1992), 1192-1193.

Rice, Ed., "Christian Monks on an Inner Journey to the Hindu Experience of God," *The Sign*, April 1968, 36-43.

Rodhe, Sten, "Christianity and Hinduism: A Comparison of the Views Held by Jules Monchanin and Bede Griffiths," *Vidyajyoti* 59, no.10 (Oct 1995), 663-677.

Smith, R., "Religious Diversity, Hindu-Christian Dialogue and Bede Griffiths," in *Proceedings of the Eighth International Symposium on Asian Studies*, Hong Kong, Asian Research Service, 1986, 1413-1429.

Teasdale, Wayne R., "Bede Griffiths and the Uniqueness of Christianity," *Communio* 9, (Spring 1984), 177-186.

Teasdale, Wayne R., "Bede Griffiths as Mystic and Icon of Reversal," *America* 173, no.9 (Sept 30, 1995), 22-23.

Teasdale, Wayne R., "The Other Half of the Soul: Bede Griffiths in India," *The Canadian Catholic Review* 3 1985).

Teasdale, Wayne R.,"Forest of Peace: Shantivanam at the Heart of the World," *The Canadian Catholic Review* 7 (June 1989).

Trapnell, Judson B., "Bede Griffiths, Mystical Knowing and the Unity of Religions," Philosophy & Theology 7, no.4 (Summer 1993), 355-379.

Trapnell, Judson B., "Bede Griffiths as a Culture Bearer: An Exploration of the Relationship Between Spiritual Transformation and Cultural Change," *American Benedictine Review,* 47 no. 3 (September 1996), 260-283.

Trapnell, Judson B., "Two Models of Christian Dialogue with Hinduism: Bede Griffiths and Abhishiktananda," *Vidyajyoti* 60 (1996), (I) 101-110, (II) 183-191, (III) 243-254.

Trapnell, Judson B., "The Mutual Transformation of Self and Symbol: Bede Griffiths and the Jesus Prayer," *Horizons*, 23 no. 2 (Fall 1996), 215-241.

Valiaveetil, Chacko, "An Indian Christology: The Shantivanam School," *The Golden String, Bulletin of the Bede Griffiths Trust*, Big Sur, California, Winter 1997-98 p.9-10; Summer 1998, p.8-10; Winter 1998-99, p.8-9.

Wong, Joseph, "Jesus Christ in Bede Griffiths' Hindu-Christian Dialogue," *The Golden String, Bulletin of the Bede Griffiths Trust*, Winter 1996-97, p.1-3; Summer 1997, p.4-6.

1. This Bibliography is based on the Bibliography compiled by Jesu Rajana nd Judson Trapnell for *The Other Half of my Soul*, edited by Beatrice Bruteau, pp. 381-393. An extensive listing of Bede's published articles and lectures will be found there, pp. 318-391. See also Trapnell, *Bede Griffiths: A Life in Dialogue* 262-265.

Glossary

Anglicised Sanskrit is not consistent in its spelling. Where there are variations I have adopted the spelling used by Bede Griffiths.

advaita — non-duality

ananda — bliss, considered as a divine attribute

arhat — a fully realized, liberated spiritual practitioner (Buddhism)

ashram — place of retreat for spiritual practice and the study of sacred teachings.

atman — soul, true and immortal self (from the Sanskrit 'to breathe.')

avatara — an incarnation of divine consciousness in this world

avidya — ignorance

bhakti — devotion, love

bhakti yoga — the way of devotion

bodhisattv — a realized being who renounces entry into nirvana until all beings have been saved (Buddhism)

Brahma — the name of God, the creator

brahman — the non-dual absolute Reality without properties, the ground of being

Brahmana — instructional section of a Veda

chakra — one of the seven centers of psychic energy in the body

cit — consciousness, divine consciousness

dharma — order of the universe and of human life; righteousness, foundation of religion

dharmakaya — lit "body of the great order," the true being of the Buddha, one with all reality

dhyana — meditation, concentration, stilling of the mind

indriyas — organs of sensing, thinking, acting, speaking, procreation, excretion

jivatman — the individual, embodied self

jnana — wisdom, spiritual knowledge, illumination

jnana yoga — the way of knowledge, of the discriminating intellect

kaivalya — release, liberation from matter and from further rebirth

karma — work, ritual action, the law of causation of actions

karma yoga — the way of active service

kundalini — "serpent-power" or earth-power, cosmic and psychic energy, one with *Shakti*

lila — divine play in the world, or world as divine play; the relative mode

482

of being

mahat — "great world," the world of the gods and cosmic powers

mantra — a sacred word or phrase of spiritual significance and power

maya — basis of mind and matter, yet a veil of illusion concealing absolute nondual being

moksha — final liberation: from karma, from the cycle of death and rebirth

nama rupa — lit "name-form," the external world of particulars, equivalent to *maya*

nirvana — final liberation, realization of oneness of self with *brahman*

nirguna brahman — brahman (the Absolute) without qualities

nirmanakaya — lit "body of transformation," earthly body in which buddhas appear

Om — the sacred syllable, the sound symbolizing the ultimate reality and manifesting its power

Paramatman — supreme Self, absolute consciousness, one with brahman

paravidya — direct, absolute knowledge of *brahman*

prajna — consciousness as the true nature of the self (*atman*); intuitive wisdom

prakriti — nature or matter as cosmic principle

pravritti — evolution, the unfolding of that which had been unmanifest

purnam — fullness, corresponding to the Greek *pleroma*

purusha — primal person, archetypal man, identical with *atman* and *brahman*

Purushottaman — the highest Self, comprehending all being in itself

raja yoga — lit "the royal yoga," classical yogic way of Patanjali, culminating in meditation

Saccidananda — the Godhead, from *sat* 'being,' *cit* 'consciousness,' and *ananda* 'bliss.'

saguna brahman — the lower aspect of brahman, brahman with qualities

sahaja samadhi — unified consciousness, true self in the state of samadhi

sahasrara — the seventh *chakra*, in the crown of the head

sangha — community of spiritual practitioners

samadhi — state of consciousness with cessation of mental activity; non-dual consciousness

sambhogakaya — lit "body of delight," paradisical body of the realized buddhas

sannyasa — renunciation of the world in order to seek God

sannyasi — one who renounces the world and earthly possessions

Sarvodaya — lit. "service of all," social movement of Gandhi, continued by Vinoba Bhave

sat — absolute Being, identical with brahman.

Shakti — the divine energy personified as a feminine principle, spouse of Siva,

siddhis — psychic powers developed through spiritual practice

Siva — the supreme Godhead, God as the destroyer and regenerator

sruti — lit "what has been heard," an expression for the Vedas

sunyata — emptiness, the Void (Buddhism)

svabhavikakaya — the ultimate state of consciousness (Buddhism)

Tantra — development of the divine energy, creative power (Shakti) with in the person

tapas — intensive spiritual exercises undertaken toward the goal of realization

tathagata — lit "the thus-gone one," one who has attained supreme enlightenment (Buddhism)

turiya — the fourth, ultimate state of consciousness beyond waking, dreaming, deep sleep.

Vedas — the oldest sacred books of Hinduism, regarded as divinely inspired

Vedanta — a school of philosophy founded on the *Upanishads*

yantra — symbolic diagram representing the divine, its aspects and powers

yoga — lit "yoke": union, harmony, spiritual practice, a way toward divine union

In addition to the works of Bede Griffiths, the following sources were consulted in the preparation of this glossary: 1) F-K. Ehrhard I. Fischer-Schreiber, Kurt Friedrichs, Michael S. Diener, *The Encyclopedia of Eastern Philosophy and Religion* (Boston: Shambhala, 1994)., 2) S. DuBoulay, *Beyond the Darkness*, pp. 291-292.

Index

486

487

488

Krishna 90-91, 101, 195, 197, 233-234, 244-245, 255, 317, 323, 342, 358, 372, 375-376, 379
kshara 235
kundalini yoga 247-248, 277
Kurisumala ashram 3-4, 259, 363-366, 468n.4
kutastho 236

laity 9, 155, 157-158, 175, 438-442
language 124
       stage of consciousness 456
Lao-Tzu 336, 379
law of evolution (integration of lower stages) 428
law 38, 105
      of the flesh 105
      of karma 105
      of the Spirit 105
laws, mechanical 453-454
Lawrence, D.H. 43-44, 468n.9
lay Christian communities 175
Le Saux, Henri 1, 4, 22, 23, 95, 208, 212, 221, 253, 262, 286, 309, 468n.29, 72nn.35,54,474nn.16,18
lectio 273
Leo the Great, Pope 131
Lewis, C.S. 2,5
light, uncreated 232
lila (divine play) 315
literalism 117
liturgy, reform of 163
      Vatican II Constitution on 159
Logos, Divine (and see *Word, Divine*) 81, 88, 93, 377, 380, 384
logos (reason, word) 123
lotus 292
Lou, Abbot 337
love 12, 97-101, 282-285
      of God 99
      of God for the soul 374
      of neighbor 99, 309-314
love-knowledge 307

madhbhaktim 374-375
Madhva 106, 276, 470n.69
magisterium (of the church) 156-158
      four organs of 157
Mahabharata 154
Mahanjadaro sculpture 230
maharishi 243
mahat 235, 242, 267-268, 292-295, 298, 300-302, 422, 467, 476n.51
Mahayana Buddhism 60, 221, 223, 299, 404
Mahesvara 234
Maheu, Francis OCSO 3-4
Mahomet , see *Mohammed*
Main, John, OSB 438-442
manas 235, 241, 281-282, 292, 298, 300-302
mantra, mantric prayer 9, 438-442
maranatha 438
Marcus Aurelius 69
Maritain, Jacques 39, 48, 469n.14
Maritain, Raissa 396
marriage of reason and intuition 44
The Marriage of East and West 8, 10, 13, 19-20, 36, 44

marriage of East and West 19-21, 331-412
Marxism 64
Mary, Virgin 110, 278
masculine culture 179, 433-434
masculine dimension of person 37, 179
materialism 60
      reductive 17, 64-68, 442
      philosophy of 64-65
maths (Hindu monasteries) 364
matriarchal cultures 434
      religion 245
matter/energy 450
Maximus the Confessor 379
maya 58, 200-201, 209, 293
mechanical model of universe 64
medicine
      in the new society 447
      western 57
meditatio 273
meditation
      eastern 9, 295, 438-442
      movement 439
      and psychic universe 458-460
mental stage of consciousness 431
Merton, Thomas 122, 125, 220
Messianic Age 416
metanoia (change of heart, conversion) 148
Methodius, St. 337
miracles 70
mirror 227, 232-233
Mohammed 359, 402
moksha 106-107, 282, 285, 360, 364, 369, 412
monastery 135, 259-263, 363-372
monastery
      as center of ecumenism 371
      as spiritual center 369
      open to the world 366-372
monastic life characterized by freedom 369-370
monastic communities as sources of
      new civilization 175-176
Monastic Studies 204
Monastic order, the 191
monasticism
      Benedictine 365
      Christian, development 366-368
      Indian, development 366-367
      Indian Christian 363-372
      temporary 369
Monchanin, Jules 4, 219, 261-262, 368, 474nn.16, 17
monism 345
monk, monks 134-135
      charismatic and prophetic character 369
morphogenetic fields 420, 453
Mother
      The 15
      God as 109
      Goddess 199
      Griffiths' experience of 15, 435-438
      Holy Spirit as 103-112
      Nature 436
Muhammad, see *Mohammed*
Muktananda, Swami 246

Plato 69, 301, 340, 391
Platonism 270
    Christian 285, 391
pleroma, cosmic 79, 423
pluralism in the church 160-170
    liturgical 160, 163-164, 169
    theologica 160, 169
Pluscarden 3
pneuma (Spirit) (and see *anthropos pneumatikos*) 55, 61 92, 297, 357, 361
Poet, Divine 237
poetic imagination 48
poetry 10, 36, 395
    as language of the Spirit 103
polarities, in Griffiths: see *contrasts*
Porphyry 270
positive way: see *kataphatic way*
potentiality, matter as 58, 451-452
poverty 182-183, 365
powers, parapsychological (and see *siddhis*) 459-460
pradhana 227, 243
Prajapati 287
prajna 224
prakriti 44, 59, 105, 141, 228, 275, 295, 300-301, 314-315
pratyeka Buddha 236
pravritti 94, 462
prayer, four stages of 273
pre-rational stage of human culture 123
Pribram, Karl 430
priesthood 90, 161, 256
    and marriage 161
    and monastic life 256
Prigogine, Ilya 452
'Primordial Wisdom' 17, 21
principle
    of complexification (Teilhard) 454
    of differentiation (Word as) 93-94
    of expansion in universe 452
    of organization in universe 452
    of potentiality (*prakriti*) 295
principles for development of 131
    doctrine, seven (Newman)
Priknash 3
Prophets, Hebrew 67
Psalms for Christian Prayer 9
Psalms, biblical 9, 439
psyche 15, 21, 40, 65, 92, 357, 361, 389
psychic
    body 91
    man 105
    organism of the universe 458
    realm 121
    (subtle) stage 431-432
    world 467
psychoanalysis 40, 65
psychology 9, 65
    transpersonal 9, 415
psychosomatic disease 57
pure thought 194
purity of heart (Cassian) 439
purnam 122

purusha (and see *Person, Supreme*) 13, 44, 196, 227-234, 292, 298, 300-301, 463
Purushottaman (and see *Person, Supreme*) 213, 216, 234-235, 463
Pythagoras 391

Q'uran   see *Koran*
Quakers 126, 327
Quietists 387

Rahner, Karl 379, 473n.59
raja yoga 275-278
Rama 90
Ramakrishna 43, 81, 284
    Order 367
Ramana Maharshi 81, 303, 313
Ramanuja 106, 276, 470n.68
Ramayana 195
ratio 241
rational understanding, emergence of 193-194
rationalism 117
rationality, scientific 36
Ratzinger, Joseph (Cardinal) 153-154, 268
reconciliation:humanity,nature, God 424
reductionism (and see *materialism*) 17, 64-68
reflection, reflexivity (subjective consciousness) 37-44, 450, 456-457
reflexivity (subjective consciousness) 287
Reformation 12,127, 144, 149, 151, 165, 172, 354
relationship 23, 81, 97-99, 218, 344, 363
    of knowledge and love 362
    of love 97-99
    personal 81, 344
    subsistent 218
relativity 56-57
religion
    the eternal 396-397
    exterior/formal and interior 152-153, 396-408
    of nature 8, 11
    primitive religions 11, 54, 339
    evolution of 393
religious orders 326
Renaissance 12, 37, 335
renunciation 250-258, 309-314
    interior 255-258
repentance (Griffiths') 72-78
Representative Man 120
Resurrection 70, 119-121, 419, 426
Return to the Center 4, 7-8, 13, 14
return to nature 35
revelation
    biblical 11, 36
    Christian 36
    cosmic 186-192, 339, 392ff, 396-410
    Hindu 185-192, 349
    historical 11, 341, 343-344
    Judaic 36, 334
    universal 334
    Vedic 12, 13, 36, 185-192
rishis 188, 237
ritual 5, 43, 53, 95, 113-117, 119, 123, 127, 140, 186,

492

493

494

Bruno Barnhart is a Camaldolese Benedictine monk of New Camaldoli Hermitage, Big Sur, California. Since concluding his service as prior of the Big Sur community, Fr. Bruno has been largely occupied with the Christian sapiential (wisdom) tradition and its rebirth in our time. He has studied the work of Bede Griffiths for many years and has edited *The Golden String*, bulletin of the Bede Griffiths Trust, since its beginning in 1994. Fr. Bruno is author of *The Good Wine: Reading John from the Center* (Paulist Press, 1993) and *Second Simplicity: The Inner Shape of Christianity* (Paulist, 1999).